THE BUILDINGS OF SCOTLAND

FOUNDING EDITORS:
NIKOLAUS PEVSNER
COLIN MCWILLIAM
CONSULTANT EDITOR: JOHN NEWMAN

HIGHLAND AND ISLANDS

JOHN GIFFORD

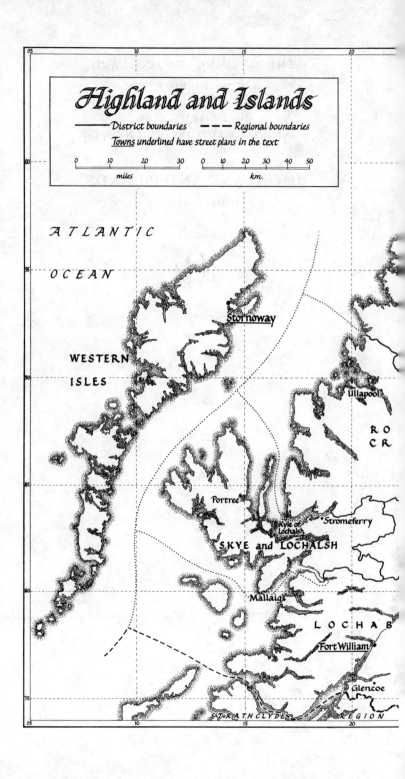

Highland and Islands

BY

JOHN GIFFORD

THE BUILDINGS OF SCOTLAND

PENGUIN BOOKS

THE BUILDINGS OF SCOTLAND TRUST

PENGUIN BOOKS
Published by the Penguin Group
Penguin Books Ltd, 27 Wrights Lane, London w8 5tz, England

Viking Penguin, a division of Penguin Books USA Inc.,
375 Hudson Street, New York, New York 10014, USA
Penguin Books Australia Ltd, Ringwood, Victoria, Australia
Penguin Books Canada Ltd, 10 Alcorn Avenue, Toronto, Ontario, Canada m4v 3b2
Penguin Books (NZ) Ltd, 182–190 Wairau Road, Auckland 10, New Zealand

Penguin Books Ltd, Registered Offices: Harmondsworth, Middlesex, England

First published 1992

ISBN 0 14 071071 X

Made and printed in Great Britain by
Butler & Tanner Ltd, Frome and London
Set in Monotype Plantin

TO
THE MEMORY
OF MY GODMOTHER
MADELEINE, COUNTESS OF MIDLETON
OF THE LINE OF KINTAIL

The numbers printed in italic type in the margin against the place-names in the gazetteer indicate the position of the place in question on the index maps at the beginning of each section, which are divided into sections by the 10-kilometre reference lines of the National Grid. The reference given here omits the two initial letters (formerly numbers) which in a full grid reference refer to the 100-kilometre squares into which the country is divided. The first two numbers indicate the *western* boundary, and the last two the *southern* boundary, of the 10-kilometre square in which the place in question is situated. For example, North Ronaldsay (Orkney), reference 7050, will be found in the 10-kilometre square bounded by grid lines 70 and 80 on the *west* and 50 and 60 on the *south*; Arisaig (Lochaber), reference 6080, in the square bounded by grid lines 60 and 70 on the *west* and 80 and 90 on the *south*.

CONTENTS

Many of the buildings described in this book are in public places, and in some obvious cases their interiors (at least the public sections of them) can be seen without formality. But it must be emphasized that the mention of buildings or lands does not imply any right of public access to them, or the existence of any arrangements for visiting them.

Some churches are open within regular hours, and it is usually possible to see the interiors of others by arrangement with the minister or church officer. Particulars of admission to Ancient Monuments and other buildings in the care of the Secretary of State for Scotland (free to the Friends of Historic Scotland) are available from Historic Scotland, 20 Brandon Street, Edinburgh EH3 5RA. Details of access to properties of the National Trust for Scotland are available from the Trust's head office at 5 Charlotte Square, Edinburgh EH2 4DU. Admission is free to members, on whose subscriptions and donations the Trust's work depends.

Two useful current directories (1992) are *Historic Houses, Castles and Gardens Open to the Public* (British Leisure Publications), which includes many private houses, and the annual booklet listing gardens and houses open to visitors under Scotland's Gardens Scheme, available from 31 Castle Terrace, Edinburgh EH1 2EL.

Local Tourist Offices, run by the District or Islands Councils, can advise the visitor on what properties in each area are open to the public and will usually give helpful directions as to how to get to them.

FOREWORD

The first volume of Sir Nikolaus Pevsner's The Buildings of England
*was published in 1951, the last in 1974, when several of the earlier
volumes had already been republished in revised editions. Not long
before his completion of the English series Pevsner set out to launch
equivalent series for Ireland, Scotland and Wales, entrusting the edi-
torship of the Scottish series to Colin McWilliam, who himself wrote*
Lothian, *the first volume to appear in 1978, was co-author of the next
volume,* Edinburgh, *and had begun work on* Dumfries and Galloway
before his sudden death in 1989, a year after the publication of Fife
and a few months before that of Glasgow.

    *At the start of the Scottish series Colin McWilliam stated its objectives
as being 'to present all the buildings that merit attention on architectural
grounds, to do it for the whole country, and to do it with all possible
speed.' To those objectives must be added the aim that the volumes
be thoroughly researched and their authors sceptical of secondhand
information unsupported by documentation, even though this might
mean upsetting some buildings' owners, who are endearingly eager to
pass on family or local tradition. This desire for thorough research has
meant some sacrifice of speed, although increasing familiarity with the
available sources has seen progressively less time wasted in searching
for information.*

    *Starting points for research have been provided by David Mac-
Gibbon and Thomas Ross's two works,* The Castellated and Dom-
estic Architecture of Scotland *(5 vols., 1887–92) and* The
Ecclesiastical Architecture of Scotland *(3 vols., 1896–7), and by
the Royal Commission on the Ancient and Historical Monuments of
Scotland's Inventories of* Caithness *(1911),* Sutherland *(1911),* Outer
Hebrides, Skye and the Small Isles *(1928),* Orkney and Shetland
(3 vols., 1946), and Argyll, iii: Mull, Tiree, Coll and Northern
Argyll *(1980); but only the last of these provides information on
buildings constructed after 1707 and none covers Victorian or C20
buildings. For buildings of the C18 and later, quite a lot of information
is provided by the Scottish Development Department's List of Buildings
of Special Architectural or Historic Interest, whose compilers have been
under at least as much pressure as any author of* The Buildings of
Scotland *to produce lists quickly, with some unavoidable skimping on
research and analysis. Moreover, the lists omit a goodly proportion of
buildings mentioned in the volumes of this series. For the series as a
whole, I extracted some years ago all Scottish references from C19
and C20 architectural and building periodicals (* The Builder, The
Building News, The Architect *etc.). For the* Highland and Islands
volume, this has been supplemented by a trawl through the Inverness

newspapers, principally the Inverness Advertiser *and* Inverness Courier, *to find information about architects and dates from the very large number of advertisements for tenders for building work in Highland between 1808 and 1914, and I must thank the late Miss Eveline Barron, the formidable proprietor of the* Inverness Courier, *and the staff of Inverness Public Library for enabling me to carry out this task. Such sources as the various* Statistical Accounts of Scotland, *c19 gazetteers (* The Ordnance Gazetteer of Scotland, *ed. Francis H. Groome, 5 vols., 1882–5, being the fullest), the publications of such learned bodies as the Scottish Record Society and the Spalding Club, family histories and a mass of local histories and guidebooks have provided much. So too have studies of particular building types, e.g. John R. Hume,* The Industrial Archaeology of Scotland *(2 vols., 1976–7), Elizabeth Beaton,* The Doocots of Caithness *(1980), Allan MacLean,* Telford's Highland Churches *(1989), and K. A. Steer and J. W. M. Bannerman,* Late Medieval Monumental Sculpture in the West Highlands *(1977). Manuscript sources, especially ecclesiastical and estate papers now housed in the Scottish Record Office and the National Library of Scotland, have given even more, and I have become so accustomed to the help and long-suffering patience of the staffs of those institutions that I speculate only occasionally as to whether these result from genetic inheritance or environmental conditioning. Just as helpful have been the staff of the Edinburgh Central Public Library (especially the Scottish and Fine Art Departments). Above all I must thank the staff of the National Monuments Record of Scotland (an integral part of the Royal Commission on the Ancient and Historical Monuments of Scotland), whose familiarity with my disorganized rummaging through their collections of drawings, photographs and pamphlets must surely one day breed contempt. On my frequent visits there Catherine Cruft, Ian Gow and Simon Green have proved all too willing to be diverted from their work to discuss my tentative analyses of individual buildings and to pass on information which they think might aid me.*

Other architectural historians have been generous in sharing their own discoveries and I must particularly thank Anna and Graham Ritchie, who read the Prehistoric, Pictish and Viking section of the Introduction in typescript and whose suggestions much improved it, Elizabeth Beaton, Howard Colvin, Deborah Mays and Anne Riches. Even greater is my gratitude to the many priests, ministers, church officers, and the owners of country houses and other private buildings who have put themselves to considerable trouble to let me see over the buildings in their care and have often provided valuable information and generous hospitality. Planning, architects' and building control departments of regional, district and islands' authorities have supplied the names of architects and the dates for several recent buildings.

The maps and town plans for this volume were specially drawn by Reg Piggott, and the plans of buildings by Richard Andrews. Photographs were especially taken by Eddie Ryle-Hodges; Susan Rose-Smith organized the commissioning and production of all this material with her usual efficiency and not showing too open irritation at my delays in deciding what was needed. Judith Wardman prepared the typescript for the printer and compiled the Index of Places. Her unflappability

*when confronted with inconsistencies, omissions and authorial inde-
cision still amazes me.*

In Highland and Islands, *as in the preceding volumes of* The
Buildings of Scotland, *certain general policies have been adopted.
The format remains that established by Sir Nikolaus Pevsner in* The
Buildings of England, *but with some Scottish quirks. Almost all
churches and public buildings are included as a matter of course, as are
buildings, especially in towns and villages, which are too conspicuous,
whatever their architectural quality, to be entirely ignored. With some
minor buildings, such as late Georgian farmhouses, those which are in
or immediately next to a village or town have been mentioned but
isolated identical examples left out. The more important rural buildings
such as castles and country houses have individual entries in the
gazetteer. An entry in brackets shows that the building has not, for
whatever reason, been personally visited. This volume is much more
selective than its predecessors in the choice of archaeological monuments
for mention. The huge quantity of these in the area meant that to include
more than a small percentage of the total would have transformed the
volume from a* Buildings of ... *to an* Archaeology of ... *The area
is so large and its architecture so little studied that there are bound to
be many mistakes and omissions in this volume. I shall be grateful to
anyone who takes the trouble to tell me about them.*

*The research and travelling costs for this series are necessarily high
and for many years were underwritten by the National Trust for
Scotland. The task has now been taken over by The Buildings of
Scotland Trust, which is raising from public and private sources the
funds necessary to see the series through to completion.*

ACKNOWLEDGEMENTS FOR THE PLATES

We are grateful to the following for permission to reproduce photographs:

Aberdeen Archaeological Surveys: 76
Arup Associates: 120
Tom Baker: 23, 32, 44, 54, 107, 109, 116, 118
Martin Charles: 94
Historic Scotland: 2, 5, 6, 69, 71, 72
Grampian Regional Council: 65
Courtesy Mrs Hughes: 82
A. F. Kersting: 46, 60, 63, 101, 108, 110
Royal Commission on the Ancient and Historical Monuments of
    Scotland: 7, 10, 11, 12, 13, 14, 17, 18, 22, 25, 28, 30, 33, 34, 36,
    38, 49, 50, 61, 66, 70, 77, 78, 79, 80, 84, 88, 90, 92, 95
Eddie Ryle-Hodges: 3, 4, 9, 15, 16, 19, 20, 21, 24, 27, 29, 31, 35,
    37, 39, 40, 41, 42, 43, 45, 47, 48, 51, 52, 53, 55, 56, 57, 58, 59,
    62, 64, 67, 68, 73, 74, 75, 81, 83, 85, 86, 87, 89, 91, 93, 96, 97,
    98, 99, 100, 102, 103, 104, 105, 106, 111, 112, 113, 114, 115,
    117, 119, 121, 122, 123, 124, 125
Edwin Smith: 1, 8, 26

The plates are indexed in the indexes of artists and places, and references to them are given by numbers in the margin of the text.

ARRANGEMENT OF THE GAZETTEER

The parts of Scotland covered in this volume are those which fall under the administration of the Highland Regional Council, the Western Isles Islands Council (Comhairle nan Eilean), the Orkney Islands Council and the Shetland Islands Council. Because of the huge size of the area and the diversity of its parts, the Gazetteer entries have been grouped by the present District Council or Islands Council areas, i.e. Badenoch and Strathspey, Caithness, Inverness, Lochaber, Nairn, Orkney, Ross and Cromarty, Shetland, Skye and Lochalsh, Sutherland, and Western Isles, and the groups have been arranged alphabetically, e.g. Shetland is to be found between Ross and Cromarty and Skye and Lochalsh. The map at the front (pp. 2–3) shows the boundaries of the District Council and Islands Council areas, and a map for each area is placed at the beginning of its section of the Gazetteer.

I am all too aware that many readers will be displeased by such an arrangement, thinking it a weak-kneed deference to bureaucracy to allow small parts of the old county of Ross and Cromarty to be placed under Skye and Lochalsh or Sutherland and a quite geographically large stretch of the old Sutherland county to appear as part of Caithness. However, to have attempted to retain the old county divisions within the present Highland Region boundary would have forced sizeable parts of the old counties of Argyll and Moray either into little sections of their own entitled 'Argyll' and 'Moray' (divorced from the rest of the present Argyll and Moray districts) or into a county or counties to which they had never belonged.

INTRODUCTION

TOPOGRAPHY AND BUILDING MATERIALS

The broad central core of Highland stretching s from Caithness to Badenoch and Strathspey is composed of metamorphic rock, formed from deposits of sediment rendered crystalline by heat and pressure from the earth, then folded in mountains and hills during the Caledonian period *c.* 601–1200 million years ago, and finally carved and sculpted by glacial action. Pushing up through this are patches of granite, e.g. the Monadhliath Mountains E of the Great Glen. At the NW a belt of Torridonian sandstone, built up of stratified layers of sediment laid down *c.* 801–1100 million years ago, runs from Durness (Sutherland) s to Applecross (Ross and Cromarty) as a line of hills. This sandstone overlies the earlier metamorphic Lewisian rock which outcrops on or near the w coast, e.g. in the lower ground around Kylesku (Sutherland) and Loch Maree (Ross and Cromarty), and which is the predominant stone of the Western Isles, where low and bare rocky knolls stick up from peat bogs. Volcanic rock is prevalent in Ardnamurchan and Morvern (Lochaber) and on Skye (the Cuillins are the craters of volcanoes), where petrified lava flows have formed basalts. Gentler in its geological formation is the Old Red Sandstone, created *c.* 350–400 million years ago from water-laid deposits of sediment, which forms the low-lying and fertile coastal strip extending from Nairn to Thurso (Caithness) and reappearing in Orkney N of the Pentland Firth. Further pockets of this sandstone are found again in Shetland, but there granite and schists predominate.

The landscape is generally mountainous and difficult to traverse except through a few straths, e.g. by Loch Laggan and Glen Spean, the Great Glen, Strathglass, Strathconon, Strath Bran, Strath Oykel, Loch Shin, Strath Vagastie and Strath Naver, or the Strath of Kildonan. The w coast is deeply indented by sea lochs or fïords, the E coast relatively unbroken except for the big sheltered anchorages provided by the Firths of Moray, Beauly, Cromarty and Dornoch. It is along this E coast and in Orkney that is found the gentle and fertile land where towns developed from the early Middle Ages, where tower houses were built on small estates in the C16 and early C17, and where prosperous farms were established in the C18 and C19.

The underlying geology has provided plenty of stone, but much

of it, like the gneiss, quartzite and schists, or the basalts and
granites of the prevalent metamorphic and igneous rocks, is hard
to work except as laboriously coursed rubble. Much better for
building is the sandstone of the E coast, Orkney and parts of
Shetland. In Caithness and Orkney it often appears as flagstones,
thin strata which, when exposed to the action of the sea, seem
sometimes to have been naturally quarried and dressed for building, a phenomenon exploited by the builders of chambered cairns
and brochs. Further S, in Easter Ross, NE Inverness and Nairn, a
pinky-coloured sandstone provided good-quality ashlar used for
the more important buildings since the Middle Ages.

Woodland once covered much of the area below the hilltops,
and it was not until the end of the C18 that the Great Caledonian
Forest in Speyside was finally almost extinguished in the pursuit
of quick commercial return. There is some evidence at Muckrach
Castle (Badenoch and Strathspey) for the continuation of a
timber-building tradition into the C16, and at The Doune, Rothiemurchus (Badenoch and Strathspey) the main cornice (doubling
as a rhone) was made of pine-trunks in the early C19. Elsewhere
timber was scarce by the late C17 and perhaps earlier and often
had to be imported. The most startling evidence of the use of
imported timber comes from Shetland, where in the Neolithic
'temple' at Stanydale, near Gruting (Shetland), one of the main
uprights supporting the ridge-pole was of spruce, presumably a
lucky find of driftwood from North America. By the C17 large
quantities of timber were imported to Scotland from the pine
forests of the Baltic.

Until the late C17, lime for mortar and harling was often made
from shells burnt over peat fires. Pockets of limestone exist in
Highland and some was quarried for building and agriculture by
the later C18, but the late C19 limekilns at Eriboll (Sutherland)
are exceptional in Highland and most lime was brought in from
outside the area.

Before the C19 most houses were roofed with turf or thatch.
Grander buildings might be covered with wooden shingles (e.g.
the Parish Church at Inverness in 1558) or with 'grey' slates (i.e.
sandstone slabs). Flagstones could provide a durable cover but
their weight meant that a roof of sizeable span required so much
timber for their support that it was often cheaper to import 'blue'
slates, as did the Earl of Caithness in 1726 when he shipped 20,000
slates to Scrabster (Caithness) from Easdale (North Strathclyde),
whose quarries had been opened in the C17. Another source of
'blue' slates was Ballachulish (Lochaber), but its quarries were
not worked on an extensive basis before the C19. Brick was made
on the Kilcoy estate (Ross and Cromarty) in the 1790s, and a
brickworks at Brora (Sutherland) operated from 1813 to 1828 and
then reopened in 1872; but most brick was shipped in from
Grampian.

The commonly held assumption that buildings before the C20
were generally constructed of local materials did not hold true of
Highland once houses more substantial than those built largely
of turf were thought desirable. James Loch, the Commissioner of

the Sutherland estates, made clear the difficulties he had experienced in finding building materials in Sutherland at the beginning
of the C 19:

> ... it must be recollected ... that the lime, whether used in building or in
> agriculture, was to be imported from Sunderland – that Newcastle sup-
> plied coals – the interior of Aberdeenshire and the west coast of Scotland,
> slates – Speyside, timber – Peterhead, bricks and tiles. With the single
> exception of stones, none of the materials were found in the country. Even
> these were, with the exception of two quarries, almost unfit for building.
> Such as they were, they had to be sought for within high-water mark, or
> the tops of the mountains, so that the labour of procuring them, and the
> expence of forming them into shape, opposed obstacles to which few
> districts of the country are subject.

It is not, perhaps, surprising that in Highland and the Islands
most building materials are imported today, nor is this practice
without the support of tradition.

PREHISTORIC, PICTISH AND VIKING
HIGHLAND AND ISLANDS

The first human immigrants to reach Highland and the Northern
and Western Isles probably arrived *c.* 6000–7000 B.C. after the
end of the last ice age. These MESOLITHIC hunter-gatherers
were few in number and lived in small groups. Some of their chert
or flint tools have been found in Orkney and on west-coast sites
at Red Point in Loch Torridon (Ross and Cromarty) and at
Morvern (Lochaber). On the island of Rum (Lochaber) they
made tools from bloodstone. Another tool-making settlement of
the early fourth millennium B.C., perhaps inhabited seasonally,
was the small island of Risga in Loch Sunart, Ardnamurchan
(Lochaber), where excavation of a kitchen-midden has revealed
thousands of worked and waste flakes, together with an extensive
collection of tools, including mattocks, harpoons and limpet
hammers, made of bone, flint and quartz. The Risga inhabitants
seem to have enjoyed a diet of fish, shellfish, sea-fowl and
mammals.

From *c.* 4000 B.C. new immigrants or, at least, new skills spread
throughout northern Scotland. The basis of the economy was
now agricultural, grain crops (wheat as well as barley) being
grown, and cattle, sheep and pigs raised, whilst fishing remained
important. The earliest surviving NEOLITHIC settlement is at
Knap of Howar on Papa Westray (Orkney), a site occupied,
according to radiocarbon dating, from *c.* 3700 B.C. to *c.* 2800 B.C.
The existing house there, apparently replacing an earlier one,* is
a substantial drystone-walled oblong with rounded corners, its
interior of *c.* 10m. by 5m. divided by a partition of upright stone
slabs and wooden posts into two rooms, both provided with

---

*The present house is built on top of a layer of midden.

wooden or stone benches and the inner room having a hearth. Probably built slightly later and tenuously attached to one wall of this house is a rather smaller workshop building well equipped with a large hearth, cupboards and aumbries. Broadly similar houses of the second and third millennia B.C. have been found at Gruting School, Pettigarths Field on Whalsay and Scord of Brouster, near Walls (Shetland), substantial oval-shaped dwellings, each standing at the end of an oval enclosure, perhaps a cattle pen. The relationship of these houses to each other is much like that of present-day crofts, and it is likely that each housed a family of independent farmers which co-operated with its neighbours on an occasional rather than daily basis.

A settlement of a rather different character is suggested by the remains at Stanydale, near Gruting (Shetland), where four oval houses accompany a fifth which is much larger, with a floor area of c. 12m. by 6.7m., and whose roof's central ridge has been supported by wooden posts. At the house's inner end was a symmetrical arrangement of alcoves separated by stone piers, and there were hearths round the periphery, but not in the centre. Perhaps the building had a religious or communal function, but it must be as likely that it was the home of some chieftain.

Even more strongly different in character from the settlements of the third and fourth millennia B.C. at Knap of Howar (Orkney) and on Shetland have been those discovered by excavation at Rinyo on Rousay and Links of Noltland on Westray, and the still clearly visible settlement at Skara Brae (Orkney), all dating from the third millennium and inhabited at the same time as Knap of Howar. Skara Brae, the best-preserved, can serve as an exemplar. The houses were clustered together, all entered from a main passage (except one, entered from a branch passage). This tight-knit cosiness was reinforced by their semi-subterranean construction, for they were dug into and surrounded by midden material. The one-room interiors varied in size from c. 4.5m. to c. 6m. square and were comfortably finished. In the centre of each was a stone-lined hearth. On the wall opposite the entrance stood a stone dresser, perhaps for the display of pottery. At the side walls were box-beds, perhaps canopied, again constructed of stone slabs and probably filled with heather, with cupboards above. More cupboards were placed elsewhere in the walls. These also contained cells, probably mostly for storage, but one in each house had a drain running under the house floor to the village's main drain, suggesting that the cell may have been a lavatory. The cultural differences suggested by the settlement patterns and house types of e.g. Knap of Howar and Skara Brae seem to be confirmed by the different pottery types found at these sites – Unstan ware at Knap of Howar, grooved ware at Skara Brae.

That different cultures co-existed or overlapped in Highland and the Islands during the third millennium B.C. seems evident from the CHAMBERED CAIRNS built for the burial of bodies or bones and used over many generations. All chambered cairns contain a stone-built cell (the chamber), usually entered from a stone passage at one end or, less frequently, one side. Both chamber and passage were covered by a cairn or mound of stones or earth, usually circular and domed, unless the chamber were so long that the cairn would have had to cover a huge amount of land; then the cairn might be oblong or oval. At most cairns the entrance faced SE, presumably to be lit up by the rising sun, but at the cairns of the Clava Group around and S of the Moray Firth it faced SW for illumination by the setting sun or moon.

Most of the cairns in Highland belong to the type classified as the Orkney-Cromarty group found on the mainland N of a line between Inverness and Ullapool (Ross and Cromarty) and extending N into Orkney. Generally, each seems to have been erected for a single family of farmers, and the cairn is often prominently sited on a hillside overlooking arable land with pasture behind. All cairns of this group have a passage leading to a round, oval, polygonal or rectangular chamber. Often this chamber was divided, in the same manner as was the house at Knap of Howar, by upright stone slabs into two or three compartments or rooms. At some cairns the chamber was extended to contain more compartments, the cairns of Black-hammer, Knowe of Rowiegar, Midhowe and Knowe of Ramsay, all on Rousay (Orkney), containing from seven to fourteen compartments within chambers ranging from 13m. to 26m. in length. One of the best-preserved of these 'stalled cairns' is that of Midhowe, its 22m.-long chamber divided into twelve pairs of stalls containing the shelves upon or under which were placed the skeletons or bones. The chambers of the Orkney-Cromarty group of cairns, like those of most chambered cairns, had drystone walls corbelled progressively inwards as a 'false vault' or stepped coomb to narrow the centre space of the ceiling, which was capped by slab stones.

Another and much grander type of cairn, found now only at ten sites on Orkney, makes up the Maes Howe Group. The passages of these cairns give access to rectangular chambers (*c.* 4m. by 2m. at Quoyness (Sanday) and 6.5m. by 1.9m. at Quanterness (Wideford Hill), but 20.5m. by 1.5m. on Holm of Papa), whose ceilings are exceptionally high (*c.* 3.5m. at Quanterness and 4m. at Quoyness). Off the chambers are inconspicuous doorways, fairly symmetrically disposed at waist height, to short passages into wall cells. The most sophisticated of these, the cairn at Maes Howe (Stenness) itself, which was built *c.* 2700 B.C., is externally a domed round mound 7m. high and 35m. in diameter, enclosed by a low bank and ditch. Inside, the plan is symmetrical, the passage entering at one side of the *c.* 4.5m.-square chamber, whose other three sides have central doors into the wall cells. At each of the chamber's corners is a buttress faced with a tapering orthostat or upright monolith to help support the weight of the corbelled roof, built like the rest of the walls of beautifully laid huge slabs. The organization required to construct Maes Howe, estimated to have taken 100,000 manhours, was quite exceptional for Neolithic times.

The embellishment of what seem often, or perhaps always, to have begun as quite ordinary chambered cairns with circular mounds produced 'long cairns', e.g. at Knowe of Lairo on Rousay and Point of Cott (near Kirkbrae) on Westray (Orkney), Barpa nan Feannag (near Trumisgarry) and Caravat Barp (near Carinish) on North Uist (Western Isles) or Camster (Caithness), hugely elongated mounds up to 70m. long, covering one or more chambers (probably of originally separate cairns), usually with a concave forecourt at the broader end and sometimes with another forecourt at the other end, their façades generally faced with drystone walling. Often the forecourts were extended outwards with long drystone 'horns'. The same idea was behind the much more modest embellishment of round cairns with one or two pairs of horns to produce respectively 'heel cairns', e.g. at Punds Water (near Brae) or Vementry (Shetland), and 'short horned' cairns, e.g. at Cairn of Get, near Bruan (Caithness).

The forecourts and edges of cairns might be marked by kerbs of stones. In the Western Isles these were formed of split rectangular stones placed on edge or on their side at regular intervals parallel to the line of the cairn and joined by stretches of drystone walling. Similar kerbs occur at the cairns of the Clava Group around and s of the Moray Firth, but their kerbs are composed of a continuous walling of boulders or slabs, whose height is graded from the taller stones flanking the entrance at the SW down to the smallest at the NE, except for the cairns at Carn Urnan (Ross and Cromarty) and Clava (Inverness), whose smallest stones are at the SW and tallest at the NE. Among the cairns of the Clava Group are both those with conventional passages leading to quite small round chambers, e.g. at Corrimony (Inverness), and also ring cairns without passages, their mounds surrounding much larger chambers which were probably left unroofed and then later filled with earth and stone over the burials.

Chambered cairns seem certain to have been connected with religious and ritual observances. So too, and presumably for ceremonies of less localized importance and probably associated with astronomical observations, must have been the few third millennium B.C. CEREMONIAL CIRCLES of standing stones erected in Highland, Orkney and the Western Isles. The nearby circles at Stenness and Brodgar (Orkney) are both surrounded by ditches. At Callanish (Western Isles) one circle is a double ring of stones, another seems to have been a double ring, and a third is a single ring round a central monolith, the ring approached by an avenue of stones and with single rows radiating from it. The erection of large stones, not in a ring but in a U-shape, is found in Caithness at Achavanich (near Lybster) and, in ruinous form, at Broubster (near Shebster). Also found in Caithness and Sutherland are settings of small upright stones placed in rows forming a fan-shape, most memorably at Mid Clyth, near Bruan (Caithness), where about two hundred stones fan out down the hillside. Individual STANDING STONES or pairs of them, some probably marking Bronze Age burials and others perhaps boundary markers or denoting meeting places, are common (almost ubiquitous in Orkney), one of the tallest the almost 6m.-high stone at Clach an Trushal, near Shader, on Lewis (Western Isles).

From the later third millennium B.C. a new element in the population or a change in its culture appears with the introduction of bronze-working and the pottery known as Beaker ware. With the BRONZE AGE a change took place in burial customs, with interment in the communal mausolea or ossuaries provided by chambered cairns being replaced by the burial of individual bodies, usually in a crouched position, inside a stone slabbed cist which was covered by a small round cairn or mound, sometimes surrounded by a drystone kerb, e.g. at Nesbister Hill, near Whiteness (Shetland). In the second millennium B.C., cremation became common, the ashes being buried in a pottery vessel, the site sometimes marked by a cairn.

Settlement patterns of the second and early first millennia B.C. have become clearer through the identification of groups of hut-circles, often with associated field systems or groups of small clearance cairns, as well as the realization that 'burnt mounds', e.g. at Liddel, near Burwick (Orkney), are an almost ubiquitous feature of the landscape of Highland and the Islands. These mounds of fire-shattered stones are the debris of a cooking method that involved placing heated stones in a trough of water containing a joint of meat. One quite well-preserved Bronze Age house can still be seen at Jarlshof (Shetland), its paved central area surrounded by cells with thick piers between them. The discovery of fragments of clay moulds for casting axes, swords and pins of C7–8 B.C. date provided evidence of bronze working here.

A worsening of climatic conditions towards the end of the second millennium may have halted a growth of prosperity, but an economic revival seems to have begun c. 600 B.C. with the beginning of the IRON AGE, the working of iron, especially for ploughs, making possible a much improved agriculture. The great majority of Iron Age settlements now visible have been protected by defences. Some, whose defences enclosed an area of up to 375 sq. m., are classified as duns, others, generally similar but larger, as forts. These usually occupied a promontory, e.g. Brough of Stoal on Yell (Shetland), a hilltop, e.g. Craig Phadrig, Inverness, or sometimes a knoll, e.g. Dun-da-Lamh, near Laggan (Badenoch and Strathspey), or an island, e.g. Dun an t-Siamain, near Carinish, on North Uist (Western Isles). Their common feature is the supplementing of the site's natural defence by a stone rampart that has sometimes incorporated a timber framework, which, if set on fire by accident or an attacker, could burn with such intensity as to fuse the stone into a vitrified mass, as at Craig Phadrig or Dun Lagaidh, near Ullapool (Ross and Cromarty). Several forts have more than one rampart, usually with intervening ditches, as at Castle of Burwick (Orkney) or Broch of Burland (near Quarff), Brough of Stoal (near Mid Yell) or Ness of Garth (near Melby; all in Shetland). Inside the enclosure of some Shetland forts (e.g. Clickhimin; Ness of Burgi and Scatness East, near Sumburgh; Burgi Geos, near Gloup, on Yell; or Huxter on Whalsay) is a blockhouse, i.e. a gateway either associated with the ringwall or free-standing, its walls containing rooms either side of the entrance. The foundations of oval houses inside some forts, e.g. Ness of Garth, suggest that they were fortified villages rather than occasional refuges.

A distinctive type of fortification is provided by the brochs. These are common in Shetland, Orkney, Skye and Lochalsh and Caithness and appear occasionally elsewhere. Radiocarbon testing dates some from as early as c. 600 B.C. (the date of a demolished Orkney broch at Bu, near Stromness), but most were built between 100 B.C. and A.D. 100. Like forts and duns, their sites are usually naturally defensible (promontories, knolls, islets) and often fortified with one or more ramparts and ditches. Inside the enclosure stood the broch itself, a circular court, generally of 9m.– 12m. diameter, enclosed by a drystone wall c. 4.5m. thick, its outer face battered and with no opening other than the entrance.* Usually the wall's bottom or ground-floor storey was of solid construction, with the entrance passage and one or more cells hollowed out of the masonry. Above, the wall was always composed of two thicknesses of drystone with a hollow centre, the two masonry skins being tied together by slabs bonded into both and laid horizontally to form the floors and roofs of mural galleries. The lowest of these galleries may well have been used for storage; the upper, narrower because of the batter of the outside wall, were probably of little or no practical use. Usually the wall's hollow centre contained also a stair to the wallhead of the broch. In a few cases, e.g. Midhowe Broch on Rousay (Orkney), the wall construction was hollow from bottom to top. All surviving brochs have been robbed of some or most of their upper stonework and it is now impossible to do more than guess as to whether the general standardization of plan-size was accompanied by a standardization of height. There is no necessary reason to suppose so. A height of c. 4m. would have been sufficient for defence and for supporting the wooden domestic structures built against the inner wall-face. Where practical considerations were uppermost the brochs may have been quite low, but if display of status were thought important, height may have seemed desirable. Two of 5 the most complete surviving brochs, Mousa (Shetland) and Dun Telve, near Glenelg (Skye and Lochalsh), stand to heights of c. 13m. and 10m. respectively, but at Mousa the wall is exceptionally thick and the internal courtyard correspondingly small, and its height may have been quite out of the ordinary.‡ The wall thickness at Mousa was intended to give the structure stability. At Dun Telve there are apertures in the inner wall above doorways, their primary purpose apparently to reduce the weight of the wall over the lintels. An attempt to spread the weight of the wall over a lintel was made by the use of a massive triangular-shaped lintel over the doorway into the entrance passage at such brochs as Caisteal Grugaig, near Shiel Bridge (Skye and Lochalsh), Clachtoll, near Stoer (Sutherland), Dun Dornaigil, near Altnaharra

---

*Clickhimin Broch at Lerwick (Shetland) is quite exceptional in having two subsidiary entrances.

‡That Mousa was regarded as exceptional in the early Middle Ages, when brochs were probably less ruined than they are today, is clear from the references to it in the sagas.

(Caithness), and Culswick, near Easter Skeld (Shetland), although there is no reason to suppose that these brochs were of exceptional height.

The main living accommodation of a broch was in the inner court, at whose centre was a stone hearth, well preserved at Dun Troddan, near Glenelg (Skye and Lochalsh). A scarcement, provided by either an intake in the wall or a corbelled projection, usually at a height of 2m.–3m. above the ground, supported one end of the beams of a roof or floor; the other end was carried on wooden posts, whose socket-holes have been found in excavations at Dun Troddan, Clickhimin Broch at Lerwick (Shetland) and Howe near Stromness (Orkney, now destroyed). That some at least of these wooden structures inside the court had an upper floor is indicated by the first-floor doors from the wall galleries at Caisteal Grugaig, near Shiel Bridge (Skye and Lochalsh), and Rhiroy (Ross and Cromarty) and by the scarcements at two levels, the upper probably for a roof, at Dun Telve and Mousa.

Standing between the broch and the fort in design are the semi-brochs, D-plan fortifications with a thick curved wall projecting landwards from a cliff-edge. The semi-broch at Dun Ardtreck, near Portnalong (Skye and Lochalsh), has a wall which, like that of a broch, is of hollow-wall construction, with galleries between the drystone masonry skins. Another feature it shares with many brochs is the guardchamber contained in the wall and entered from the entrance passage. Excavation of a couple of semibrochs has produced evidence to suggest they were built in the first or second centuries B.C., i.e. at the same time as, or a little earlier than, most brochs, of which the semibrochs should perhaps be seen rather as variants than as prototypes.

At several brochs, e.g. Broch of Gurness (Orkney) or Carn Liath, near Golspie (Sutherland), there is evidence of houses built between the outer rampart and the broch itself. These seem to have been put up after construction of the broch but before its abandonment and suggest a society of village farmers dependent on a chieftain living in the broch. It is possible that the erection of such houses may have been connected with the conversion of several brochs, e.g. Clickhimin Broch at Lerwick or Jarlshof (Shetland), into wheel houses in the third or fourth centuries A.D. The conversion was made by dividing the broch's court with stone slab piers to form a ring of radiating compartments round the central hearth and to carry the roof. More unusual was the division of the court of Midhowe Broch (Orkney) into two semicircular segments, each with its own hearth and an upper storey. At Midhowe the N segment also contained an underground chamber which may have been a spring-fed well or a foodstore. Earlier SOUTERRAINS or EARTH-HOUSES below wooden farmsteads were quite common from the first millennium B.C. Two impressive surviving examples are in Orkney, at Grain, Kirkwall, and Rennibister, Finstown; each entered through a stone-lined passage leading down to an oval drystone-walled chamber with a stone roof supported on chunky stone piers. Simpler are the souterrains of north Highland, their chambers usually oblongs, as at Laid (Sutherland).

The PICTS ('Picti' or painted people) are first mentioned in A.D. 297, but their history is traceable only from the reign of Bridei, son of Maelchon, in the mid-C 6, one of whose forts was near Inverness, and their archaeological record from the C 7. Their culture was agricultural, based on the rearing of livestock, fishing and the growing of cereal crops on individual farmsteads. Some Pictish houses have been excavated. At Buckquoy and Gurness (Orkney) have been found houses composed of cells round a central area containing the hearth. Other houses, found at Buckquoy and Red Craig (Orkney), Udal in North Uist (Western Isles) and Yarrows (Caithness), have a figure-of-eight plan made up of two round or oval chambers, one, usually the larger, containing the hearth. The most striking reminders of Pictish civilization are now provided by the symbol stones which they erected, in some cases to mark graves and probably sometimes boundaries. The earliest are rough boulders or slabs incised with animals, e.g. the Eagle Stone at Strathpeffer (Ross and Cromarty) or the Boar Stone at Inverness, and objects, predominantly combs and mirrors, but also with curvilinear and geometrical designs (the 'crescent and V-rod', the 'double disc and Z-rod', the 'serpent and Z-rod') of enigmatic significance, e.g. on the worn stone at the entrance to St Clement Churchyard, Dingwall (Ross and Cromarty), or on the better-preserved Clach Ard at Tote, near Kensaleyre (Skye and Lochalsh), both probably dating from about the C 7. The spread of Christianity was accompanied by the erection of dressed slabs, carved on one or sometimes both faces with a cross, always accompanied by animal and human figures and symbols, the carving often in quite high relief. Most of these stones are now housed in museums, but one of the most elaborate is in Nigg Parish Church (Ross and Cromarty) and one of the largest and grandest stands in a glass shelter at Shandwick, near Balintore (Ross and Cromarty). In the design of these stones the panels formed by the cross are boldly enriched with figures and symbols, but in other stones of the C 8 and C 9 the cross clearly dominates, e.g. at Edderton Free Church (Ross and Cromarty), where it is carved in high relief but two of the accompanying figures of horsemen are only incised, or at the former Farr Parish Church at Bettyhill (Caithness), where the high-relief cross's arms are carved with key pattern and the pair of necking birds at the base firmly subordinate.

VIKING colonization of Shetland, Orkney, Caithness and the Western Isles began c. 800, and the rapid success of the Norse earldom established in the Northern Isles and Caithness is evident from the density of Scandinavian place-names, e.g. Wick (bay), ness (headland) or setr (dwelling). The economy of these new settlers was based on scattered farmsteads, their buildings often erected on top of Iron Age or Pictish sites, as at Broch of Birsay (Orkney) or Jarlshof (Shetland). At first, the typical farmstead had an oblong dwelling house or hall house, with the byre, barn, stables and storehouses in detached outbuildings, but by the end of the C 11 the byre was often added to one end of the dwelling. *The Orkneyinga Saga* also mentions the drinking halls of leading Viking farmer-raiders, the largest in the mid-C 12 reputedly that of Svein Asleifarson on Gairsay (Orkney), said to be capable of holding eighty men; and the foundations of another C 12 drinking hall probably survive at the Earl's Bu at Orphir (Orkney). Viking monuments earlier than their C 12 churches (*see* Medieval Churches, below) are few, the most notable their graffiti on the Neolithic cairn at Maes Howe, near Stenness (Orkney).

The wealth of some of these Norse settlers in the C 9 and C 10 has been shown by the discovery of goods (now mostly in the Royal Museum of Scotland) buried in the graves of pagan Vikings. One on Eigg (Lochaber) contained an elaborately decorated bronze sword hilt. Another, in a cemetery at Westness on Rousay (Orkney) which contained two boat burials, was of a woman whose progress into the afterlife was accompanied by Celtic brooches, a bead necklace, comb and cloth-making tools, indications of settled prosperity doubtless associated with the nearby site of a farmstead. Even more spectacular was the C 19 discovery at Skaill (Orkney) of a silver hoard, probably buried in the C 10, its hundred-odd pieces (now in the Royal Museum of Scotland) weighing about 8kg. and including no fewer than sixteen 'ball-type' brooches, as well as arm-rings, necklets and coins.

MEDIEVAL CHURCHES

Christianity was brought to Highland and the Islands from the C 6 by missionaries from both the Picts of SW Scotland and the Celtic communities of Argyll (North Strathclyde). Place-names beginning with 'Kil' (church) commemorate some of these early missionary saints, e.g. St Donan at Kildonan (Skye and Lochalsh), St Finan at Kilfinnan (Lochaber), St Ernan at Killearnan and perhaps Kiltearn (Ross and Cromarty), St Moluag at Kilmaluag (Skye and Lochalsh) and Kilmonivaig (Lochaber), and the Pictish St Talarican at Kiltarlity (Inverness). Evidence for early monastic establishments of eremitic type is provided by place-names derived from 'papar' (the Norse nickname given to Celtic hermits in Iceland), such as the islands of Pabay or Pabbay (Western Isles and Skye and Lochalsh), Papa and Papa Stour (Shetland), and Papa Stronsay and Papa Westray (Orkney), as well as by the foundations of the monks' beehive cells surviving at Burgar on Unst (Shetland). There may have been beehive cells also at Brough of Deerness (Orkney), where excavation has revealed the foundations of a chapel, probably of the C 10, built with a timber frame and stone cladding.

The conversion of the Norse Earls of Orkney to Christianity in 995, probably some time after many of their compatriots in the Northern Isles and Caithness had espoused the Faith, was followed by the creation of a diocese of Orkney in the mid-C 11, its

bishop's first residence and cathedral church being built at Birsay. Possibly an accompaniment to the establishment of this diocese was the foundation in the C12 of what may have been small Benedictine monasteries at Brough of Birsay and Eynhallow (Orkney), each having a church consisting of a nave, choir and, apparently, a square W tower, with the associated domestic build-ings of the putative monastery to one side. Better-preserved and
7 more impressive is St Magnus Church on Egilsay (Orkney), prob-ably built c. 1130 on the site of the chapel where the saint had prayed before his death in 1116. It is a startling apparition, its round W tower a conspicuous landmark from the sea and nearby islands. Perhaps the tower is of Irish inspiration, but the church's other details, notably the doors' and windows' round arches, set well back on the jambs to allow support for the wooden framework used in their construction, suggest a half-apprehended recognition of the Romanesque.

Fully developed Romanesque followed very quickly with the
8 first stage of construction of St Magnus Cathedral at Kirkwall (Orkney), begun c. 1140. The cathedral's masons were of the Durham school and, although St Magnus is little more than half the size of Durham Cathedral, its plan (an aisled nave, transepts with E chapels, and a three-bay aisled choir with projecting presbytery) is very close to that of Durham as first completed. Another quotation from Durham, although less direct, is the mid-C12 blind arcading of the interior at St Magnus. Changes were made to the cathedral's design in the second phase of building work during the late C12 and early C13, the choir being lengthened and detail altered to Transitional.

Around 1230, before this second phase of work at St Magnus had been completed, the construction of two new mainland cathedrals had been begun, those of the diocese of Caithness at
9 Dornoch (Sutherland) and of the diocese of Ross at Fortrose (Ross and Cromarty). Of the C13 work at Fortrose there now survives only the much altered groin-vaulted sacristy. Dornoch, despite the demolition of the nave aisles, has fared better. It is a straightforward cruciform but with the lancet windows in its
10 transepts and unaisled choir smartly framed in arcading, the arches alternately broad and narrow. Arcading of the same type was used to frame the choir windows at Beauly Priory (Inverness),
13 a Valliscaulian monastery also founded c. 1230, but its church's transepts and nave were not completed until the C14. Another monastic house (for Premonstratensian canons) was founded at Fearn c. 1225 and moved to Hill of Fearn (Ross and Cromarty) c. 1238. There, Fearn Abbey's church (much altered after the Reformation) seems to be C14, a very simple buttressed rectangle with lancet windows. One pillar, perhaps mid-C15, survives of the church of the Dominican convent founded at Inverness by Alexander II in the early C13.

The late medieval fashion for votive masses and the endowment of chaplains to say them may have lain behind the addition of chapels to Fearn Abbey in the C15 and C16. Architecturally grander were the two large chapels built c. 1400–30 on the S side

of Fortrose Cathedral (Ross and Cromarty), their join marked by 11
a tower. Both opened into the cathedral's nave through pairs of
broad arches springing from clustered shafts. Another means of
providing votive masses was through the foundation of a collegiate
church staffed by a 'college' of chaplains. Highland acquired one
in 1487 when St Duthus Memorial Church was founded at Tain 12
(Ross and Cromarty), an elegant box with large Y-traceried s and
w windows and Geometrical tracery in the E.

A parochial system had been established in Scotland and the
Northern Isles by the early C12. Few of these parish churches
seem to have been more than stone-built rectangles with a rood-
beam to mark off the sanctuary, but some were built with or
acquired a chancel. The most peculiar, although now very fragmentary, is St Nicholas, Orphir (Orkney), with a round nave and
apsed chancel. The circular shape, unique in Scotland, suggests
that its plan was based on that of the Church of the Holy Sepulchre
at Jerusalem and its construction associated with a crusading
expedition, probably that of Earl Haakon c. 1116–18. At St Peter,
Thurso (Caithness), the chancel of c. 1200 is rectangular outside
but apsed internally, the only directly comparable example of this
arrangement on such a small scale being at St Margaret's Chapel
in Edinburgh Castle. Starkly impressive is the early C16 St
Clement, Rodel (Western Isles), perhaps built to celebrate the 14
new importance of the MacLeods after the collapse of the Lordship of the Isles, a cruciform with a w tower visible from their
other lands in Skye and Uist. w towers seem also to have been a
feature of the medieval burgh churches at Inverness and Dingwall
(Ross and Cromarty).

Some fragments of medieval parish churches have been incorporated in post-Reformation churches, e.g. at the Old Parish
Church of Alness (Ross and Cromarty) or St Magnus Church,
Birsay (Orkney). Plain late medieval SACRAMENT HOUSES
survive in the present parish churches at Avoch and Contin (Ross
and Cromarty). Otherwise, medieval church furnishings were
destroyed after the Reformation, perhaps as much through neglect
as iconoclastic fervour.

MONUMENTS have survived much better. Probably the earliest
medieval effigy is at Dornoch Cathedral (Sutherland), the figure
of a recumbent knight, said to be Richard de Moravia † c. 1245,
with a lion at his feet. At Fortrose Cathedral (Ross and Cromarty)
are the canopied recesses of Euphemia, Countess of Ross, † 1394,
and Bishop Robert Cairncross † 1545, both now covering fragments of effigies, and a third early C16 canopy bereft of its effigy.
The canopied wall-tomb of Abbot Finlay McFaed † 1485 is complete with weathered effigy at Fearn Abbey, Hill of Fearn (Ross
and Cromarty). Very similar and again with its effigy is the monument to Kenneth Mackenzie of Kintail † 1492 at Beauly Priory
(Inverness). The most sumptuous of these monuments are the
early C16 canopied effigies commemorating the MacLeods in St 17–18
Clement, Rodel (Western Isles), the canopy and back of Alasdair
Crotach MacLeod's monument of 1528 covered with lavishly
carved religious emblems, figures of Apostles and saints, and

Scriptural scenes, together with the apparently quite secular relief of a hunting party.

Late medieval GRAVESLABS of the C14 and C15 are common in the coastal churches of Lochaber and on Skye, and a few appear elsewhere. One motif is the floriated cross, e.g. on slabs at Ardnamurchan Parish Church (St Congan) at Kilchoan, and Keil Church at Lochaline (Lochaber). Another is the claymore, found on stones in the churchyards of Kilmuir and Trumpan (Skye and Lochalsh). Sometimes cross and claymore are combined, as at St Maelrubha, Arisaig, and Keil Church, Lochaline (Lochaber), and in the churchyard at Bracadale (Skye and Lochalsh). Sometimes the sword was placed in a surround of foliage, which at Arisaig issues from a dog's tail and at Lochaline is crossed by the figure of a horseman. Hunting scenes appear at Kilchoan and Arisaig. Some stones are carved with full-length portraits. There are knights in the churchyards at Bracadale and Kilmuir and in St Columba, Eye (Western Isles), a naked man holding a sword and staff in St Clement's Churchyard, Dingwall (Ross and Cromarty), and a priest, accompanied by a cross and chalice, at Trumpan. Bishops are carved on the cross-slabs at Eynort (Skye and Lochalsh) and Lochaline. The most ambitious gravestones are decorated with several figures and objects. In Glendale Church-yard (Skye and Lochalsh) is a slab bearing a harper, a bishop, a chalice, claymore and foliage. In St Maelrubha, Arisaig, one slab is
16 carved with a claymore flanked by panels depicting the Crucifixion and a bishop. At Lochaline, a stone shows a galley under tabernacle niches containing the figures of a knight and a swordsman.

POST-REFORMATION CHURCHES

The Scottish Reformation of 1560 deprived monastic churches of their function as a setting for conventual worship and removed from cathedrals their chapters of canons enjoying their own services in the choirs. Beauly Priory (Inverness) and Fortrose Cathedral (Ross and Cromarty) were consequently abandoned. Fearn Abbey (Ross and Cromarty), the collegiate church at Tain (Ross and Cromarty), and the cathedrals of Kirkwall (Orkney) and Dornoch (Sutherland) continued in use as parish churches, but at both these cathedrals only the choir was used for worship, the nave at Kirkwall becoming a burial ground and that at Dornoch left roofless after it was burned in 1570.

The new forms of worship placed as much emphasis on prayer and preaching as on the sacraments and required that the minister be heard and seen by his congregation. The naves of most medieval parish churches were simple unaisled rectangles and fairly easily adapted to these requirements by positioning a pulpit at the centre of one of the long walls, usually the S, or, less commonly, at one end, and arranging seats to face it. If the congregation were large, galleries might be erected. One sizeable medieval church,

Old St Peter at Thurso (Caithness), exemplifies the response to 20
theological and liturgical change. At the Reformation it comprised
a nave and narrow chancel. Soon after 1560 a pulpit seems to
have been erected against the s wall of the nave and galleries at
its E and W ends. The chancel, now redundant, was taken over by
the Sinclairs of Forss as a family burial place. In 1664 further
accommodation for worshippers was provided by the addition of
a transeptal N 'aisle' or jamb opposite the pulpit. Unusually, a
second transeptal 'aisle' had been built earlier in the C17 on
the church's s side to serve as a communion aisle into which
communicants moved for the celebration of the Sacrament. The
provision of a communion aisle was not thought generally necessary, although the s aisles added to Canisbay Church, Kirkstyle
(Caithness), in 1724 and St Andrew, Golspie (Sutherland), in
1750 may possibly have served as such.*

   New parish churches built in the C16, C17 and C18 were
conservative. Many, often perhaps because they stood on med-
ieval foundations, were narrow rectangles, like the C16 East Parish 30
Church at Cromarty (Ross and Cromarty), the probably C16
Dunnet Church (Caithness), Old Durness Church at Balnakeil 19
(Sutherland) of 1619, Nigg Parish Church (Ross and Cromarty) of
1626, St Peter, Kirkhouse (Orkney), of 1642, the former Duirinish
Parish Church at Dunvegan (Skye and Lochalsh) of 1689,
Latheron Church (Caithness) of 1725–38, or Croy Church 21
(Inverness) of 1764. Less often they were built on a T-plan, the
earliest being Cawdor Church (Nairn) of 1619, followed in the
C18 by the churches at Golspie (Sutherland) of 1736–7 and Reay
(Caithness) of 1738–9. Others began as simple rectangles but were
later made T-plan by the addition of an 'aisle', as happened at
Old Durness Church at Balnakeil (Sutherland) in 1692, at Nigg
(Ross and Cromarty) in 1730, and at the East Parish Church
at Cromarty in 1739. Tongue Church (Caithness) of 1728–9 is
unusual in that, although it is T-plan, the cross-bar is composed
of two 'aisles'. All were stone-built, but roofs might well be
thatched with heather, as at the churches (some since replaced)
built at Eddrachillis (Sutherland) in 1728–31, Assynt (Sutherland)
in 1741–3, Edderton (Ross and Cromarty) in 1743, Killearnan
(Ross and Cromarty) in 1745, and Kincardine (Sutherland) in
1745–50. Other churches, in parishes which were no more prosperous, had slated roofs from the start, e.g. the now roofless
Durness Parish Church at Balnakiel (Sutherland) of 1727–8 and
the demolished Alvie Church (Badenoch and Strathspey) of 1729.

   Architectural decoration was rare. Most churches were utilitarian preaching boxes, with even the occasional provision of
roundheaded windows appearing an extravagance, the hint of
open pediments at the gables of Urray Church (Ross and
Cromarty) of 1775 quite unexpectedly sophisticated, and the
Venetian windows given to Fearn Abbey, Hill of Fearn (Ross and
Cromarty), in 1772 almost sinful in their ostentation.

---

*The main reason for building the s 'aisle' at Golspie seems to have been the need
to rebuild part of the then T-plan church's s wall.

Often the chief external ornament was a bellcote. The provision of a bell for each parish church was a legal requirement by 1642 and some housing for it a sensible precaution. Most bellcotes were of simple birdcage type, that at Alness (Ross and Cromarty) of 1625 probably the oldest surviving. The bellcote of *c.* 1700 at
22 Tarbat Old Parish Church, Portmahomack (Ross and Cromarty), is memorably ambitious, with a lucarned dome supporting four balls and a finial, the resulting ogee profile reproduced more conventionally at Golspie (Sutherland) in 1774. At Contin (Ross and Cromarty) the bellcote of 1760 has an octagonal spire, at Kilmallie Church, Corpach (Lochaber), a crown spire of 1781–3. At Latheron (Caithness) and Ardclach (Nairn) the bell in the C 17 was housed in a detached tower some way from the church,
49 Latheron's bell tower so crude as to appear almost prehistoric,
50 Ardclach's of 1655 hardly sophisticated.

Towers attached to churches are few. The massive W tower at
23 the Old High Church at Inverness may be mid-C 16, its balustered parapet and lead-spired belfry probably of 1649. Hardly less
19 massive are the saddlebacked tower of *c.* 1700 at Dunnet (Caithness) and the W tower of 1704 at Canisbay Church, Kirkstyle (Caithness). Almost delicate by comparison are the pyramid-roofed towers at Reay Church (Caithness) of 1738–9 and the Gaelic Chapel, Cromarty (Ross and Cromarty), of 1783.

Standing quite apart from the generality of C 18 parish churches is the military Chapel at Fort George (Inverness), built in 1763–7 with a battlemented W tower, bowed transeptal stairtowers,
28 pedimented E gable and apse. The interior is just as unusual, divided into a nave and aisles by roundheaded arcades on Roman Doric columns, and with a groin-vault over the apse. Even more startling would have been the unexecuted parish church designed by *R. & J. Adam, c.* 1775, for Cromarty, an elongated piend-roofed octagon with temple-fronted rectangles projecting at the ends, one topped by a cupola bellcote.

27   The C 19 began in style with the completion of *George Burn*'s St Clement, Dingwall (Ross and Cromarty), in 1803, its pedimented centrepiece surmounted by an octagonal steeple. Over the next forty years expensive churches were provided in other burghs, their architecture illustrating the competing fashions of the early C 19. In 1811–14 *James Smith* gave Tain (Ross and Cromarty) a new parish church (now the Duthac Centre), its ends dressed up as battlemented towers, its pulpit flanked by large Gothick windows. *James Milne* designed St Columba, Lerwick (Shetland), in 1826 as a slice of astylar ashlar urbanity. Much grander in their
24 architecture and siting are the Tudor Old Parish Church at Wick (Caithness) by *John Henry*, 1820–30, and the Perp St Peter and
29 St Andrew, Thurso (Caithness), by *William Burn*, 1830–2, both with end towers, that at Wick with a spire rising inside its parapet. In Inverness, *Robert Caldwell*'s West Parish Church of 1837–40 has an Ionic temple front to the street and a cupola-topped tower at the back.

Episcopalians and Roman Catholics, freed from the restraint of the penal laws in 1792, also commissioned urban churches of some pretension. The first of these, built in 1828, was St Andrew (Episcopal), Fortrose (Ross and Cromarty), a buttressed and pinnacled Gothic box. In 1836 *William Robertson* designed Roman Catholic churches at Wick (Caithness) and Inverness, the first with an unassertive pedimented front, the second a joyous display of carpenter's Gothic as gift wrapping for the Tudor interior. 32 Three years later Robertson provided the Episcopalians of Inverness with the now demolished St John, its entrance front's Tudor tower decorated with ogee hoodmoulds over the door and windows. The interior had a clearstoreyed nave and aisles, the arcades' slender columns carrying plaster fan vaults with pendant bosses. Rather simpler but with a tower and plaster-vaulted interior is St Peter (Episcopal), Stornoway (Western Isles), of 1837–9.

Rural parish churches of the early c 19 were still often very simple, but a minimum standard was set by the designs for the 'Parliamentary' churches erected between 1825 and 1835 and financed by the Government under An Act for building additional Places of Worship in the Highlands and Islands of Scotland (1823). The engineer *Thomas Telford* was appointed general superintendent, but the churches' design seems to have been principally the work of one of his surveyors, *William Thomson*. In 1825 the Commissioners for Highland Churches adopted Thomson's design for a 'Standard Church', a T-plan building large enough 31 to seat 312 without galleries but capable of containing up to three galleries, each with a seating capacity of sixty places. Where the 'Standard Church' would be too large, the 'aisle' could be omitted and 0.91m. deducted from the height of the walls (galleries not being required) to give a church to seat 250. It was estimated that a simple rectangular church without galleries would cost £600, a T-plan church with the full complement of galleries at the ends and in the 'aisle' £948. The design was economical but decently sturdy, the walling of rubble (usually harled), the roofs covered with Easdale or Ballachulish slates, the windows and doors Tudor-arched, and one gable surmounted by a spikily pinnacled birdcage bellcote. One 'Parliamentary' church was built in Shetland, three in Caithness, five in Ross and Cromarty, three in Skye and Lochalsh, five in Lochaber, and four in the Western Isles.

The standard set by the 'Parliamentary' churches, intended as they were for the poorer areas, was more than met by contemporary parish churches. Those in the more prosperous locations could be quite smart. In 1821–2 the plain early c 18 rectangle of Latheron Church (Caithness) acquired an 'aisle' (by 21 *William Davidson*) ending in a small domed belfry. Tall battlemented towers were provided at the new churches of Logie Easter (Ross and Cromarty) by *James Gillespie Graham*, 1818–19, Rosemarkie (Ross and Cromarty) of 1818–21, and Duirinish Church at Dunvegan (Skye and Lochalsh) of 1832, Logie Easter's tower having crosslet belfry openings, Rosemarkie's crocketed pinnacles. At Daviot Church (Inverness) of 1826 a dottily tall tower 26 conspires with Venetian windows to produce an innocent image of rustic high fashion. More conventionally accomplished is the

33 former Rosskeen Parish Church (Ross and Cromarty) by *James
   Smith* of Edinburgh, 1830–2, with its squat domed tower flanked
   by tripartite windows under overall fanlights. A stolid Gothick
   version of this design was produced ten years later by *Donald
34 Munro* for the new Edderton Parish Church (Ross and Cromarty).
   Even churches which kept to the C18 formula of a preaching box
   with a bellcote could look decidedly expensive, such as Loth
   Church at Lothmore (Sutherland), whose spired bellcote sits
   astride a full-height porch, both porch and bellcote decorated
   with crocketed pinnacles. *William Robertson* displayed a wide-
   ranging repertoire of motifs at Urquhart Church, Drumnadrochit
   (Inverness), in 1836–8, mixing crowsteps, Y-tracery, blind 'Saxon'
   windows, a Tudor door and a classically foliaged finial on the
   bellcote.

   Rural Roman Catholic churches varied from the determinedly
   economical to the decidedly expensive. The first and humblest
   was *James Gillespie Graham*'s church (now the Parish Church) at
   Arisaig (Lochaber) of 1810–11. Not much more ambitious except
   for its pinnacled buttresses was St Mun, Ballachulish (Lochaber),
   of 1836. The two churches on South Uist (Western Isles) at
   Ardkenneth of 1829 and Bornish of 1837 both combined the
   church and priest's house under a single roof. St Mary, Eskadale
   (Inverness), of 1825–6 is much more ambitious, its independently
   roofed nave and aisles lit from 'Saxon' windows and separated
   internally by roundheaded arcades on chunky columns. More
   forceful, even martial, is the crowstepped and battlemented St
   Columba, near Bonnavoulin (Lochaber), designed by *James
   Anderson* in 1838, its E tower visible from the Sound of Mull.

   At the Disruption of 1843 about one-third of its ministers left
   the established Church of Scotland to form the Free Church of
   Scotland. In Orkney and Shetland the effects of the Disruption
   were no greater than in southern Scotland, but in the Western
   Isles and Highland they were marked. More than half of Highland
   ministers joined the Free Church, the exodus greatest in Caithness, where ten out of thirteen 'came out', and in Ross and
   Cromarty, where twenty-two of the twenty-nine ministers in the
   presbyteries of Chanonry, Dingwall and Tain acceded to the
   Free Church. In almost every parish, whatever the attitude of its
   minister, there were some adherents to the Free Church; in many
   they made up a large majority. Even before the Disruption the
   leaders of the Free Church party had appealed for money for the
   building of new churches and manses, and by 1845 they had raised
   a total of £359,573, as well as gifts of sites and materials. Designs
   for cheap churches, built of wood and brick and roofed with felt,
   had been produced before the Disruption, but in the event most
   early Free churches were plain versions of the 'Parliamentary'
   churches, rectangular or T-plan, with a birdcage bellcote, stone-
   built with slated roofs. The cottagey Gothic design of 1850 by *John
   Hay* of Liverpool for the church at Portree (Skye and Lochalsh) is
   a welcome and rather more expensive variant; more expensive
   again was the Gothick church with a tower at Stornoway (Western
   Isles) by *Alexander Mackenzie*, 1851. Exceptional for its size was

the Perp Free High Church (now St Columba High) at Inverness, designed by *Mackenzie & Matthews* in 1851, its diagonally buttressed tower topped by a spire rising from between flying buttresses.

Rebuilding or extension of many of the first Free churches and the provision of others on new sites got underway *c.* 1860. The churches of this second wave could be large, often dwarfing the parish church, and architecturally ambitious. *Ross & Joass* cribbed from the work of the Hays of Liverpool for their Dec design of 1859 for Invergordon Free (now Parish) Church (Ross and Cromarty). Its square tower, broached to a needle spire studded with lucarnes, bisected the gable to suggest a nave and aisles behind, a device used in 1865 by *John Rhind* at Cromarty Free (now West Parish) Church (Ross and Cromarty). Two years later, at Dingwall Free Church (Ross and Cromarty), Rhind disguised 40 the gable's width by placing a stairtower on one side and a domed steeple on the other. A similar solution was adopted in 1868 for the First Free Church at Thurso (Caithness) by *J. Russell Mackenzie*, but he also dressed up the front gable as a semioctagonal centrepiece. The same formula again, but with starker detailing and a huge steeple, was used in 1890 by *Ross & Macbeth* for the Free North Church at Inverness. All these were Gothic, 42 but the Free Church felt no ideological loyalty to that style. At Avoch (Ross and Cromarty) *Alexander Ross*'s Free Church of 1872–3 was Romanesque, perhaps to avoid confusion with his Gothic parish church begun two years earlier. Ross's Free Church at Halkirk (Caithness), 1884–6, is Italianate. So too are the flabby Palladian Queen Street Free Church, Inverness, by *J. Pond Macdonald*, 1893–6, and the Mannerist Free (now Parish) Church at Tain (Ross and Cromarty) by *Andrew Maitland & Sons*, 1891–2, its campanile poking up above the town.

The United Presbyterian Church, formed in 1847 by the union of sects which traced their secessions from the Church of Scotland and from each other back to the early c 18, was weak in Highland and the Western Isles but built a couple of sizeable churches in Orkney, at Kirkwall in 1847–9 and at Stromness (designed by *Richard Spence*) in 1862–3, both still distinctly Gothick in feeling.

The established Church of Scotland, although weakened numerically by the Disruption, was not quite moribund. Inverallan Parish Church at Grantown-on-Spey (Badenoch and Strathspey) by *Alexander Smith*, 1884–6, is a hugely inflated kirk of late Georgian type but with baroque tracery in the main windows. Triumphalism is evident at *John Starforth*'s Old Parish Church, 43 Nairn, of 1893–7, a Transitional D-plan edifice with a battlemented tower. Smaller and friendlier is St Stephen, Inverness, 44 designed in 1895 by *W. L. Carruthers* in a Gothic Arts and Crafts manner, its crenellations quite pacific and with a tiny needle spire for emphasis.

During the second half of the c 19 the Episcopalians set up their own parochial system in Highland, and by 1914 they had a church to serve every significant centre of population. *J. L. Pearson* provided an austere church at Dingwall (Ross and Cromarty) in 1851,

Alexander Ellis one of character at Lerwick (Shetland) in 1863–4. The dominant architect favoured by the Episcopalians was *Alexander Ross*, who designed a string of villagey Gothic churches, the earliest, St Ninian, Kilmartin (Inverness), of 1853 and originally thatched. His largest was St Andrew's Cathedral, Inverness, of 1866–9, a huge stodgy box brooding beside the River Ness, perhaps lamenting the lack of its intended w spires, but with an
39 interior arranged along the best Tractarian lines. More inventive
41 and lavishly finished is St Andrew, Fort William (Lochaber), of 1879–84. The Roman Catholics provided large and austere churches to serve their pockets of strength, most notably *William Burn*'s lanceted St Mary, Arisaig (Lochaber), of 1849, *Joseph Hansom*'s churches of 1866 at Cannich (Inverness) and of 1871 at Dornie (Skye and Lochalsh), and *E. W. Pugin*'s Our Lady and St Finnan, Glenfinnan (Lochaber), of 1873. Their biggest late C19 enterprise was the construction of St Benedict's Abbey, Fort Augustus (Inverness), begun by *Hansom* in 1876 with the reconstruction and extension of the Hanoverian fort in a stern institutional Gothic dress. In 1890 *P. P. Pugin* laid out the Abbey Church, but only two chapels of his Dec scheme were built before work halted in 1893.

The Roman Catholics have produced the most impressive C20 church buildings in Highland, beginning with *Reginald Fairlie*'s simplified Romanesque choir at the Abbey Church of Fort Augustus in 1914–17. Fairlie's Romanesque was further simplified and acquired massive strength at his churches at Roy Bridge
45–6 (Lochaber) of 1929 and Fort William (Lochaber) of 1933–4. A blockier Romanesque but without Fairlie's starkness was employed by *John Burnet, Son & Dick* at Kingussie (Badenoch and Strathspey) in 1930. *Ian G. Lindsay* produced an idealized image of the couthy crowstepped Scots kirk in 1938 at St Finnan, Invergarry (Lochaber), but its simplicity looks artificial when compared with that of *J. Ninian Comper*'s St John the Baptist (Episcopal) at Rothiemurchus (Badenoch and Strathspey) of 1928–9. The Second World War produced a kitsch curiosity with *Domenico Chiochetti*'s conversion of two Nissen huts into the Italian Chapel on Lamb Holm (Orkney). In 1949 *Fairlie* resumed work on the Abbey Church at Fort Augustus, providing a nave of impressive height but so stripped of detail that it has lost the strength of its Romanesque origin without gaining the conviction of the Modern Movement. For unaffected simplicity on a tiny scale it is hard to fault *William Glashan*'s St Maelrubha (Episcopal) at Poolewe (Ross and Cromarty) of 1965.

The FURNISHINGS of a well-equipped church before *c.* 1850 are displayed at *A. & W. Reid*'s Lochbroom Parish Church (Ross and Cromarty) of 1844–5, the area filled with box pews and two long communion tables, the pulpit with a pilastered back and sounding board, the gallery with a panelled front. Pulpits were regarded as necessary to the furniture of a post-Reformation church by 1649, when a presbytery visitation ordered their provision at three west-coast churches where they were lacking. The earliest surviving in Highland, at St Duthus Memorial Church,

Tain (Ross and Cromarty), is of *c.* 1575, with quite elaborately
carved panelling at the base and back and with a pinnacled
sounding board. The smarter C18 examples, e.g. at St Andrew,
Golspie (Sutherland), of 1738, at Kildonan (Sutherland), probably of 1768, and at Farr Church, Bettyhill (Caithness), of 1774,
have fluted pilasters and sounding boards, the sounding board's
frieze at Golspie carved with gryphons and flowers. A three-decker
pulpit was provided for the Chapel at Fort George (Inverness) in
1767, and the pulpit at the old Applecross Parish Church (Ross
and Cromarty) of 1818 has a precentor's seat. At Loth Church,
Lothmore (Sutherland), the pulpit is of 1822, with concave sides
and an Adamish plaster frieze and urn finial. Another urn finial,
together with corner pinnacles, is at Duirinish Parish Church,
Dunvegan (Skye and Lochalsh), of 1832. Long communion tables
around which the congregation sat have mostly fallen victim to
ecclesiological fashion, but early C19 examples survive at St
Callan, Rogart (Sutherland), Loth Church, Lothmore
(Sutherland), and St Peter, Kirkhouse (Orkney). Galleries are
common, usually with simply panelled fronts. In St Olaf
(Episcopal), Kirkwall (Orkney), are bits of the carved early C17
gallery erected by Bishop Graham in St Magnus Cathedral. At St
Duthus Memorial Church, Tain (Ross and Cromarty), survives
the front of the old Trades Loft painted with craft emblems and 37
the dates 1680 and 1776. Some lairds' lofts remain. The Reay
Loft in St Andrew, Tongue (Caithness), perhaps of 1728–9, has
lost its Corinthian-columned and canopied superstructure to the
Royal Museum of Scotland (Edinburgh), but the Sutherland Loft 36
of 1738, again with Corinthian columns and with its entablature
carved with coronets placed among branches, survives in St
Andrew, Golspie (Sutherland). So too does the Cromartie Loft 38
in the East Parish Church, Cromarty (Ross and Cromarty), of
1756, with a screen of Ionic columns set in front of a screen of
Tuscan piers. On this gallery's ceiling is a late C18 hatchment,
and fragments of C18 funeral escutcheons are incorporated in the
church's pews.

Victorian church building produced little change in the general
furnishings of Presbyterian churches except for the introduction
of pitch-pine and dark varnish, but some acquired organs. At St
Columba, Lerwick (Shetland), a chancel was built in 1895 to
house the instrument. At Tain Parish Church (Ross and
Cromarty) in 1931 the organ displaced the pulpit from the focal
pilastered recess at the s end.

Episcopalian and Roman Catholic churches could have quite
lavish decoration. At St Magnus (Episcopal), Lerwick (Shetland),
the chancel walls were stencilled in red and gold in the 1860s. At
the same time the roof of St Andrew's Cathedral, Inverness, was
marked out for stencilling, and the chancel roof of St Andrew
(Episcopal), Fort William (Lochaber), was decorated with gold
stars and foliage on a red ground. Consciously archaic figures of
saints were painted in the C20 on the walls and ceiling of the
Relics Chapel of St Benedict's Abbey, Fort Augustus (Inverness),
by *Father Luke Cary-Elwes* and *Father Lawrence Mann*. Encaustic

tiles appeared in chancels in the later C 19. At St Andrew's Cathedral, Inverness, and St Andrew (Episcopal), Fort William (Lochaber), they are by *Minton & Co.*, 1869 and 1880, depicting Old Testament types of the Eucharist. The Episcopalian and Roman Catholic emphasis on the Eucharist produced large and heavily carved altars of both wood and stone. At St Andrew's Cathedral, Inverness, the stone altar of 1869 is set with alabaster panels and surmounted by a reredos executed by *Earp*. The reredos of 1880 in St Andrew (Episcopal), Fort William, has carved and painted reliefs by *D. & A. Davidson* and a central mosaic by *Salviati*. More carved reliefs are to be found on the altar and reredos designed by *P. P. Pugin* and executed by *Boulton* at St Mary (R.C.), Eskadale (Inverness), in 1881. Statues make an appearance on the reredos erected in 1893–4 at St Mary (R.C.), Inverness.

In 1914–17 *Reginald Fairlie* gave the Chapel of the Blessed Sacrament at St Benedict's Abbey, Fort Augustus (Inverness), a baldacchino of deerskin decorated with embossed harts and painted ravens, its posts topped by carved pelicans. A simpler baldacchino of red damask was provided by *Comper* at St John the Baptist (Episcopal), Rothiemurchus (Badenoch and Strathspey), in 1929, the year after he had designed a gilded tester carved with a dove for St Michael and All Angels (Episcopal) at Inverness. Less conventional is the tester of metal lampshades placed above the high altar of the Abbey Church at Fort Augustus by *W. W. Allan* in 1980.

Fonts are often of stone, frequently enriched with marble. At St Andrew's Cathedral, Inverness, the font is a copy of 1871 of Thorwaldsen's Kneeling Angel font but with the angel's face replaced by a portrait of the donor's wife. At St Andrew (Episcopal), Fort William (Lochaber), *Harry Hems* carved the steepled oak font cover with figures of saints in 1884, and *Comper* 47 provided another steepled cover at St Michael and All Angels (Episcopal), Inverness, *c.* 1910.

Pulpits, often large and expensive, are generally unexciting. 48 One exception is the baroque pulpit of 1886 in Inverallan Parish Church, Grantown-on-Spey (Badenoch and Strathspey), made up from Italian carving of 1639 and including a pedimented back and term figures.

STAINED GLASS did not appear in Highland churches before the mid-C 19, the Episcopalians giving the lead. Among the earliest windows are ones by *Jemima Blackburn* at St Finan (Episcopal), Kinlochmoidart (Lochaber), *c.* 1859, and by *O'Connor* at St Paul (Episcopal), Croachy (Inverness), of 1869, their scenes looking like plates from a children's Bible. Quite different in quality and a wonderful complement to the architecture is the complete scheme executed at St Andrew's Cathedral, Inverness, by *John Hardman & Co.* in 1869–87. Another complete scheme, but with instructive narrative scenes less complementary to the building, was provided from 1879 by *James Ballantine & Son* at St Duthus Memorial Church, Tain (Ross and Cromarty). The Ballantine firm's dull competence appeared again in the Old Parish Church,

Nairn, from *c.* 1900 and, more extensively, in 1906 in the small mission church at Kingairloch (Lochaber). Far better drawn and joyfully coloured are *J. Ninian Comper*'s windows made in 1904–6 for the House of Charity and now in St Magnus (Episcopal), Lerwick (Shetland). Other Comper glass was placed in Highland churches during the next half-century, in St Columba (Episcopal), Nairn, in 1914, St Michael and All Angels (Episcopal), Inverness, in 1928, and in St Regulus (Episcopal), Cromarty (Ross and Cromarty), in 1932 and 1951.

Complete or nearly complete schemes of c 20 glass can be found at St Magnus Cathedral, Kirkwall (Orkney), mostly by *Oscar Paterson*, with well-coloured figures of saints, and at Dornoch Cathedral (Sutherland), which includes examples of *Percy Bacon*'s lush post-Raphaelite manner, *Christopher Whall*'s accomplished style, and *William Wilson*'s and *Gordon Webster*'s colourful productions, as well as some windows of routine and others of excruciating quality. More consistent is the collection of c 20 glass at Ness Bank Church, Inverness, with examples of the work of *Isobel Goudie*, the *St Enoch Studios*, *William Wilson* and *Gordon Webster*.

Individual windows are worth seeking out. *Shrigley & Hunt* produced a rich and painterly window at St Bride (Episcopal), North Ballachulish (Lochaber), in 1896. There are windows by *Percy Bacon* at St Finnbarr (Episcopal), Dornoch (Sutherland), of *c.* 1920, and at Creich Parish Church, Bonar Bridge (Sutherland), of 1923. Characteristically colourful late c 20 windows by *William Wilson* are in Auldearn Parish Church (Nairn) and in the Parish Church and St Andrew (Episcopal) at Tain (Ross and Cromarty), and by *Gordon Webster* in Kilmallie Parish Church, Corpach (Lochaber), and Kilmonivaig Parish Church, Spean Bridge (Lochaber). *Douglas Strachan*'s Expressionist glass can be found at St Magnus Cathedral, Kirkwall (Orkney, of 1912), and in the Old High Church at Inverness (of 1925).

MAUSOLEA AND MONUMENTS

In 1581 the reformed Church of Scotland forbade burial inside churches. The spirit of this decree might be circumvented by the conversion of a redundant chancel into a family burial vault as at Old St Peter, Thurso (Caithness), or, as at St Andrew, Tongue (Caithness), in 1728–9, by the provision of a vault under a laird's loft; but some of the more ostentatious lairds built mausolea. These could be attached to a church. At Kilmuir Easter (Ross and Cromarty) the Munro burial aisle of 1616 was added to the 25 church's E end, its round tower surmounted by a decoratively corbelled belfry. The same combination of mausoleum and belfry at the E end of a church was produced in two stages at Kirkhill (Inverness), where the Lovat Mausoleum was built by *William* 51 *Ross* in 1633–4, with fashionable buckle quoins at the corners, and

a dumpy belfry added in 1722. Less demonstrative is the Coul
Mausoleum added to Fortrose Cathedral (Ross and Cromarty) *c.*
1635, its cornice and round-arched door with projecting imposts
hinting at a classicism which is belied by the Gothic s window.
Later and grander Gothic-survival is found at the Mackintosh
Mausoleum added to the E end of the former Petty Parish Church
(Inverness) *c.* 1686 but enlarged by a classical wing with a blind
Venetian window in 1742.

Detached burial enclosures marking off the portion of a graveyard reserved for a particular family first appear in the C 17. The
52 Robertson Enclosure in the Old High Churchyard at Inverness
of 1664–5 is a vigorously inept stab at classicism coupled with
naturalistic carving. More restrained but not more correctly classical is the Grant Enclosure at Kirkmichael Churchyard near Jemimaville (Ross and Cromarty) of 1680. C 18 burial enclosures
were less flamboyant. One of 1746 at Kilmore (Skye and Lochalsh)
is merely four balustraded walls with ball finials at the corners. In
the same churchyard is an early C 19 mausoleum masquerading
as a toy fort. Much more starkly purposeful is the buttressed and
53 crenellated Seafield Mausoleum, by *William H. Playfair*, 1837, at
Duthil (Badenoch and Strathspey). For sheer wackiness it is hard
54 to beat the late Victorian Christie Mausoleum in Tomnahurich
Cemetery, Inverness, its marble door guarded by an angel, the
top surmounted by the half-naked figure of a youth (the soul).

Monuments were erected on the walls of both mausolea and
churches. One of the earliest, in the old Durness Parish Church
at Balnakeil (Sutherland), is of *c.* 1625, an arched tomb recess,
the sarcophagus's top carved with a panel showing an archer
shooting at an up-ended stag. This is still essentially medieval,
but classicism appeared in 1642 with *John Diren*'s Corinthian
aedicule to Christian Mowat in the Sinclair Enclosure at Latheron
(Caithness). Instead of a jolly depiction of the joys of life, grim
reminders of death are carved on its frieze. Classicism of a sort
was also attempted in the late C 17 at St Magnus Cathedral,
Kirkwall (Orkney), where several monuments are small aedicules
with etiolated Ionic columns and vigorous naturalistic carving.
On a much bigger scale is the monument to Thomas Watson
erected in the Chapel Yard, Inverness, in 1674, the panels divided
by atlantes and caryatids, and with symbols of death at the sides
and on the frieze. Correct and very grand classicism appears with
the early C 18 pedimented aedicule in the Dunbar Aisle at the
Old Parish Churchyard, Wick (Caithness), with its Composite
columns and trumpeting angels. A mid-C 18 version of this was
produced at Ollaberry (Shetland) by *John Forbes*. Continental
classicism of a chaster variety is found in the huge Doric aedicule
designed by *James Byres* in 1768 to commemorate Sir James
Macdonald at Kilmore (Skye and Lochalsh); so as to save money
it was executed in Rome. Smaller and suaver is the monument of
1769 by *John Veitch* to the Earl and Countess of Sutherland
in Dornoch Cathedral (Sutherland), its pair of Doric columns
supporting coroneted urns. This monument's use of contrasting
grey and white marbles was followed in a monument of *c.* 1800

in the Mackay Mausoleum at Reay Old Churchyard (Caithness), with its mourning riflemen flanking an heraldic plaque. This is restrained when compared to a couple of monuments of the 1790s. At Fearn Abbey, Hill of Fearn (Ross and Cromarty), *John Baxter Jun.* designed and *A. Farquhar* executed the huge memorial to 56 Admiral Sir John Lockhart Ross, carved with heraldry, trophies and an obelisk bearing a sarcophagus decorated with the relief of a man-of-war. Even larger is the Ionic screen erected at Fortrose Cathedral (Ross and Cromarty) to Sir Alexander Mackenzie of 57 Coul, with a figure of Father Time sitting among ruins over the door. A curiosity is the early C19 stone sentry box sheltering an urn which commemorates Patrick McDonell at Invermoriston (Inverness). The Gothic revival produced an accomplished piece of neo-medievalism with the tomb recess and heraldically decorated sarcophagus of the Lovat monument, probably of 1881, in St Mary (R.C.), Eskadale (Inverness).

The best collection of graveslabs from the C16 to the C18 is in St Magnus Cathedral, Kirkwall (Orkney), well preserved because the nave retained its roof despite its conversion to a graveyard after the Reformation. One of the earliest, commemorating T. Murray † 1577, is carved with a cross and coat of arms. Coats of arms recur on most of the others, but the cross, considered popish, was omitted, whilst grisly reminders of death became common from the beginning of the C17. This combination of heraldry and intimations of mortality was the standard repertoire for graveslabs and wall monuments throughout Scotland in the C17 and C18 but was abandoned in the C19, despite its literary relish for improving death-bed scenes.

Obelisks belonged to the routine repertoire of Victorian monumental masons, but some earlier examples have more elegance. The early C18 obelisk to the first Earl of Cromartie at St Clement, Dingwall (Ross and Cromarty), has been replaced by a smaller version marooned in a car-park, and the obelisk of *c.* 1800 carved with the head of Ossian erected in memory of James Macpherson at Balavil (Badenoch and Strathspey) is now almost lost beside the A9; but the Well of the Heads near Invergarry (Lochaber) of 1812 is an elegant reminder of a gory event, and the tall early C19 obelisk to Colonel John Cameron outside Kilmallie Parish Church, Corpach (Lochaber), still makes an impact.

Commemorative statues are few, and *Francis Chantrey*'s depiction of Sir John Sinclair at Thurso (Caithness), 1835, is now badly weathered. Better-preserved is *John Greenshields'* statue of 1834 on top of the tower at Glenfinnan (Lochaber). The largest and most grandly sited is the colossal statue of the first Duke of 58 Sutherland carved by *Joseph Theakston* from a maquette by *Chantrey* and erected on Ben Bhragaidh outside Golspie (Sutherland) in 1836–8. One of the Duke's more vociferous critics, Hugh Miller, has a rather smaller statue by *A. Handyside Ritchie*, erected in 1858–9 on a Doric column at the Gaelic Chapel, Cromarty (Ross and Cromarty). The later C20 has contributed *Hew Lorimer*'s stylized statue of Our Lady of the Isles on Rueval Hill (Western Isles) of 1955–7.

Towers have been considered appropriate reminders of martial events. In 1815 a battlemented round tower was built to commemorate the beginning of the 1745 Jacobite rising at Glenfinnan (Lochaber). Much fiercer in appearance are the aggressively Baronial towers commemorating General Sir Hector Macdonald at Dingwall (Ross and Cromarty) by *James Sandford Kay*, 1904–7, and Lord Kitchener near Birsay (Orkney), 1926, and the Lewis War Memorial by *J. Hinton Gall*, 1922–4, overlooking Stornoway (Western Isles). Less aggressive are the clocktowers built as war memorials at Brora (Sutherland) *c.* 1920 and Helmsdale (Sutherland) in 1924, and the miniature castellated towers which form the Lovat Scouts Memorial, by *Edward Stourton*, 1905, at Beauly (Inverness) and the war memorial, by *John G. Chisholm*, 1922, at Tarbert (Western Isles). Less obviously martial war memorials are provided by the Ionic and Doric columns designed by *A. Marshall Mackenzie* for Nairn *c.* 1920 and Grantown-on-Spey (Badenoch and Strathspey) in 1921. *Percy Portsmouth* produced allegorical figures of Repentance for the memorial at Castletown (Caithness) in 1925 and of Victory and Peace at Thurso (Caithness) in 1920–2. Statues of Highland soldiers had a steady popularity, one of the more competent being *Alexander Carrick*'s bronze Seaforth Highlander of 1922 at Dornoch (Sutherland). The combination of a whiskery Cameron Highlander and scantily clad allegorical females at *Louis Deuchars*'s War Memorial at Glenelg (Skye and Lochalsh) of 1920 suggests a tour of the West Highlands by the Folies Bergères.

CASTLES, TOWER HOUSES AND PALACES

The earliest surviving stone castles in the Islands and Highland seem to have been built for Norse aristocrats. Cubbie Roo's Castle on the island of Wyre (Orkney) was constructed *c.* 1145 by Kolbein Hruga, a substantial landowner in both Orkney and western Norway, and is mentioned, perhaps because it was exceptional, in *The Orkneyinga Saga* as 'a fine stone castle' and 'a safe stronghold'. The site is the summit of a low hill which has been fortified by two ditches, an earth rampart and a stone wall. Inside the enclosure stood an almost square keep of coursed rubble, its entrance apparently at the first floor, reached by a ladder. Perhaps also C 12 are two Norse castles in Caithness, those of Old Wick and Forse, both standing on promontories jutting into the sea, the landward approach to Old Wick defended by a rampart and ditch, that to Forse by a ditch. Each has had a rectangular rubble-built keep with an unvaulted interior, the entrance to Forse Castle, like that to Cubbie Roo's Castle, placed at the first floor. All three were intended to house men whose usual means of travel was by sea, and at Old Wick there is still a steep path leading from the beach of the narrow inlet on the W up to the entrance.

The combination of a naturally defensive site and proximity to a sheltered anchorage is common to most early medieval castles in Highland and the Islands. Many of their sites had probably been fortified long before, and some whose names are prefixed by the Celtic 'Dun' (fortress), such as Dunrobin (Sutherland), Dunvegan (Skye and Lochalsh) or the demolished Dunskeath (Ross and Cromarty), had certainly been early strongholds. The remains of a vitrified rampart found at Urquhart Castle (Inverness) show that an Iron Age fort had preceded the medieval castle. Auldearn (Nairn) is unusual in having had a castle erected on an artificial motte or mound, its summit now occupied by a doocot.

By the late C 12 there were royal castles at Nairn astride the coastal plain E of Inverness and guarding the entrance to the River Nairn, at Inverness commanding the N entrance to the Great Glen, and at Redcastle and Dunskeath (Ross and Cromarty) overlooking the Beauly and Cromarty Firths and dominating the fertile lands of Easter Ross. The granting of two Crown charters by Alexander II in 1229 is indicative of the Scottish monarchy's determination in the C 12 and C 13 to establish control over the country through barons of Anglo-Norman descent and familiar with feudalism. Thomas Durward, Sheriff of Inverness and hereditary doorkeeper to the King, obtained the lands of Urquhart (Inverness) on the W side of Loch Ness and Walter Comyn the vast lordship of Badenoch and Lochaber. New castles were quickly erected on these lordships. At Urquhart, a large naturally defen- 65 sive site was enclosed by a palisade or walls and a stone shell-keep built on the highest part. At Castle Roy (Badenoch and Strathspey) the Comyns constructed a simple shell-keep or castle of enclosure on the top of a small hill. Later in the C 13 they put up castles at Lochindorb (Badenoch and Strathspey) and Inverlochy near Fort William (Lochaber), one occupying an island, the other defended by a ditch on three sides and the River Lochy on the fourth. Both are quadrangular castles of enclosure, but, unlike Castle Roy, they have corner towers, the large NW tower at Inverlochy having been the donjon or lord's residence. Another product of C 13 Anglo-Norman penetration into Highland was Skelbo Castle (Sutherland), built by Gilbert de Moravia, Archdeacon (and later Bishop) of Caithness, a member of a Morayshire family said to have been of Flemish descent. Again it is a stone-walled castle of enclosure sitting on top of a steep hill, its strong natural defence supplemented by ditches.

A Celtic-Norse dynasty, descendants of Somerled, Lord of the Isles, was responsible for a remarkable string of C 13 castles along the coast of Lochaber. Knowledge of the new castles put up by the Comyns must be presumed, and one of this dynasty, Alexander MacDougall, was brother-in-law of John Comyn. These castles of Ardtornish, Mingary and Tioram are all on promontories, 61 Castle Tioram's rocky site being cut off from the mainland at 63 high tide. Both Castle Tioram and Mingary Castle are castles of enclosure, but Ardtornish was a large hall house, its defence provided primarily by its steeply rising site. A cousin of these descendants of Somerled, Leod the ruler of Skye, built a C 13 castle at Dunvegan (Skye and Lochalsh) enclosing the summit of a basaltic promontory with a stone curtain wall. Probably also C13 was another castle of enclosure, built on an island at the mouth of Loch Duich, Eilean Donan (Skye and Lochalsh), apparently a western outpost of the earldom of Ross.

Most of the living accommodation of these C13 castles was provided by wooden buildings inside the courtyard, although some might be in corner towers, and Mingary Castle (Lochaber) seems to have had a stone hall from the start. In the C14 several castles were remodelled, with stone buildings being erected inside the courtyard. Plain rectangular keeps appeared at Dunrobin Castle (Sutherland), Dunvegan Castle (Skye and Lochalsh) and

63 Castle Tioram (Lochaber). At Urquhart Castle (Inverness) the
66 original outer bailey became the site of both a new detached tower and also a range which seems to have contained a kitchen, hall, great chamber and solar. A similar desire for comfort is found at

62 Rait Castle (Nairn) of *c.* 1300, which was perhaps intended as a private retreat for the constables of the royal castle at Nairn. Its not obviously defensive site was guarded only by a barmkin wall, and the 'castle' within is a long two-storey-and-attic block with large Gothic windows lighting the first-floor hall, off which is a domical-vaulted private room in the round corner tower. An earlier example, probably of *c.* 1200, of a hall block divorced from a castle of strength may be provided by the Bishop's Palace at Kirkwall (Orkney), which incorporates the undercroft of a huge hall.

Stone tower houses built to accommodate a laird but not the large retinues suggested by castles of enclosure made a first appearance in Highland, probably in the C14, with Braal Castle (Caithness), a small rubble rectangle of three unvaulted storeys, the site defended by wet ditches and a bend of the Thurso River. Even less assuming are the small C15 tower houses at Glensanda and Kinlochaline (Lochaber), of two and three storeys respectively, the interiors originally without vaults. At the larger C15 U-

64 plan tower of Castle Girnigoe (Caithness), the ground floor is vaulted and the stair contained in one jamb. More ambitious
68 is the late C15 tower at Cawdor Castle (Nairn), externally a straightforward but large rectangle with small angle turrets but with an interior composed of two superimposed vaults, the lower a semicircular tunnel over the ground floor, the upper (subdivided by wooden floors) rising to a pointed arch.

Over Scotland in general the C16 was a period when the huge land holdings of secular and ecclesiastical magnates were broken up into smaller estates by the granting of charters to land held in feu-ferme, i.e. in return for a capital sum and a fixed annual payment, its value in the event quickly eroded by inflation. The new lairds built tower houses, often quite small but expressing their status usually with a display of gunloops and often with a corbelled parapet or battlement and angle turrets. At Castle Craig

67 (Ross and Cromarty) of the earlier C16, the E gable's angle turrets are linked by a parapet walk and the interior has superimposed stone vaults. The small but lofty mid-C16 Fairburn Tower (Ross

and Cromarty) was also originally rectangular but only its ground floor was vaulted. By the later c 16, tower houses were often built on an L-plan, the jamb usually containing the main stair to the first-floor hall. Simple small examples are the late c 16 Little Tarrell (Ross and Cromarty) and Brims Castle (Caithness) of *c*. 1600. Taller and rather smarter is Ardvreck Castle (Sutherland) of the 1590s, its round stairtower topped by a square cap-house. A further development was the adoption of a Z-plan, with two towers set at diagonally opposite corners of the main block. One reason for designing a house on the Z-plan may have been that it allowed defenders shooting through gunloops in the towers to enfilade the walls of the main block. Probably a more common reason was a wish for comfort, the plan's provision of two towers enabling one to house the main stair and the other a private room off the dais end of the hall. At the mid-c 16 Ballone Castle (Ross and Cromarty), one tower is square, the other round. At the late c 16 Inshoch Castle (Nairn) and the early c 17 Kilcoy Castle (Ross and Cromarty) both towers are round. At both Ballone and Inshoch there are turrets in the inner angles of the main block and both towers; at Kilcoy only one inner angle contains a turret. Somewhere between the L- and Z-plan is Kinkell Castle (Ross and Cromarty), built in the 1590s, with a fat round stairtower at one corner and a slimmer turret corbelled out above the ground floor at the other. Rarer are houses designed on a U-plan. One such is the asymmetrical Redcastle (Ross and Cromarty) of *c*. 1641, a house whose main decoration is provided by cannon spouts projecting from the stairtower in one inner angle.

Some houses can be put in the general classification of tower house but are much more than lairds' houses. One of the strangest is Noltland Castle (Orkney), built *c*. 1560–72 on a large Z-plan with square corner towers, but its two lowest floors form an artillery casemate of frightening appearance, the lord's living quarters sitting above. Muness Castle (Shetland), begun for Laurence Bruce in 1598, is another large Z-plan but with round corner towers. Like Noltland it has a profusion of gunloops and shot-holes, but whereas at Noltland they are grimly utilitarian, here they appear as a catalogue display of the different varieties available from a skilled master mason – inverted keyholes, jumelles, quatrefoils, circles and saltires. Bruce's nephew, Patrick Stewart, Earl of Orkney, built Scalloway Castle (Shetland) in 1600. It is 72 L-plan but with turrets at all the corners and with circular and quatrefoil gunholes just like those at Muness. Another detail taken from Muness is continuous corbelling topped by chequer-set corbels alternating with dummy gunholes. Even more conscious of architectural delight is Castle Stuart (Inverness) of 1619–25, a 73 U-plan with square towers tenuously attached to the s corners, tall round turrets in their N inner angles, and diagonally set turrets at the main block's N corners. But this symmetrical plan is disturbed by a wilful asymmetry of detail, providing a romantic version of the tower house as villa rather than stronghold.

The largest houses of the c 16 and early c 17 were quadrangular.

Of the Bishop's Palace at Dornoch (Sutherland), now known as
Dornoch Castle, there survives only the L-plan lodging of *c.* 1500
at the vanished courtyard's NW corner, much like a contemporary
tower house with a stairtower in the inner angle. The Earl's Palace
71 at Birsay (Orkney), begun *c.* 1574 for Robert Stewart, Earl of
Orkney, was intended to be a quadrangle from each of whose
corners projected a tower, so that the main walls could be enfi-
laded. Some of this defensive strength was lost *c.* 1600 when
Robert Stewart's son built the N range further N than originally
intended. Externally it is quite plain, but the whole of the W
range's first floor was occupied by a gallery, and the N range
contained a suite of hall, withdrawing room and lord's chamber.
Grandest of all, despite being only a fragment of the intended
69 huge quadrangle, is the Earl's Palace at Kirkwall (Orkney) of
1606, a show-off display of Franco-Scottish architectural ideas,
with oriel windows, decorative gunholes and a lavishly varied
exhibition of corbelling.

COUNTRY HOUSES

The execution in 1612 of Patrick Stewart, Earl of Orkney, brought
the Northern Isles under the effective control of the Crown. Soon
after, lairds' houses were built in Orkney, quite peaceful in their
appearance, without even the baronial symbols of gunloops or
corner turrets. One of these, Carrick House on Eday, built in
1632–3 for Earl Patrick's brother, John, Earl of Carrick, was a
simple rectangle of two storeys and an attic; another, Breckness
House of 1633, built for a younger son of the Bishop of Orkney,
was L-plan but with the door placed in a porch at the centre of
the main block's long wall and not in the defensible inner angle.
Just as pacific is Greenwall, built for another of the Bishop's sons
in 1656, its porch again placed in the centre of the front. Such
houses were not confined to Orkney. In 1641–4 Dunrobin Castle
(Sutherland) was enlarged by the addition to its medieval tower
of two crowstepped ranges forming an L-plan. Their round corner
towers with candle-snuffer roofs may have symbolized noble
status, but the effect is more romantic than martial. C17 additions
to Cawdor Castle (Nairn) seem to have been principally con-
cerned to increase the family's comfort, although the elaborately
carved late C17 chimneypieces inside are not afraid to attempt
display. Classicism was generally confined to details such as pedimented frames for coats of arms (e.g. at Greenwall and Cawdor
Castle). However, at Dunvegan Castle (Skye and Lochalsh) in
1664 a parapet on the hall-range was replaced by a balustrade,
making the entrance front a precursor of that group of houses
associated with John Mylne Jun. and Sir William Bruce which
have a balustraded centre gripped by projecting gables (towers in
the case of Dunvegan). The most ambitious late C17 house in
Highland was the (demolished) New Tarbat House (Ross and

Cromarty), built in 1681 for Sir George Mackenzie (later first Earl of Cromartie), its front very close in design to one of the schemes proposed by Bruce in the 1670s for the remodelling of Brunstane House (Edinburgh), being a U-plan with octagonal stairtowers in the inner angles and round towers at the wings' outer corners. New Tarbat House also had small turrets, a self-consciously archaic touch.

Country houses on the Anglo-Dutch model of the plain piend-roofed box appeared in Highland from c. 1720 with Novar House (Ross and Cromarty) and Balnain House at Inverness, and in Shetland with Gardie House on Bressay of 1724. The largest, latest and most elegantly austere of such houses was the four-storey ashlar-fronted N block of Castle Grant (Badenoch and 80 Strathspey), designed by *John Adam* in 1753. Less severe and more horizontal than Castle Grant were houses of similar derivation but with a pedimented centre. Foulis Castle (Ross and Cromarty) of 79 c. 1740–54 has an eleven-bay front, the three centre bays slightly advanced and pedimented; at the back is a gazebo-topped tower. The near-by Poyntzfield of 1757 is a smaller country cousin, again 82 with a pediment (projected on blocks) and gazebo tower. Humbler lairds' houses might be content with a crowstep-gabled centre, as at Flowerdale House (Ross and Cromarty) of 1738, or with a shaped gable or gablet, as at Old Allangrange (Ross and Cromarty) of 1760 or Sandside (Caithness) of 1751. Others marked the centre, if at all, only by a moulded doorpiece or armorial panel but showed the hierarchy of floors inside by having the windows of the second-floor bedrooms smaller than those below, as at Sand House (Shetland) of 1754, Geanies House (Ross and Cromarty) of c. 1760, and Dundonnell House (Ross and Cromarty) of 1767. Exceptionally smart is Hall of Clestrain (Orkney), a villa of 1769 with a plinth-like basement and slightly set-back ashlar corners. Rather later country houses of the rustic villa type are Belmont (Shetland), with an open-pedimented centrepiece containing a superimposition of corniced door, Venetian window and roundheaded window, and Embo House 81 (Sutherland), with a round-arched window in its skied pediment. Larger and architecturally more ambitious are Cromarty House 83 (Ross and Cromarty) of c. 1775 and Culloden House (Inverness) 85 of 1780, each with a centre block and lower wings and displaying a range of classical motifs whose disposition is varied from the front to the back. Both contain elegant marble chimneypieces and Adamish plasterwork. *Robert Adam*'s own interior at Balavil House (Badenoch and Strathspey) of 1790–6 was lost to a fire in 1903, but its front, despite the subsequent reconstruction, still exhibits his individual neo-classicism. By comparison, *James McLeran*'s Tarbat House (Ross and Cromarty) of 1787 is austere, its droved 84 ashlar front relieved only by a pediment and window cornices. Its interior, with a columned screen between the vestibule and stairhall, showed the same chilly restraint. McLeran was responsible also for the addition of another range to Dunrobin Castle (Sutherland) in 1785, politely following the detail of the outer elevations of the C17 work (except for his use of Gothick windows at his corner tower) but remodelling the courtyard fronts of the earlier building in classical form.

86   Muirtown House, now swallowed up by a suburb of Inverness, shows the stylistic choice available to architectural enthusiasts of the early C 19, although its owner and apparent designer, *Major Hugh Robert Duff*, was unique in combining quite so many styles (Palladian, neo-Greek, castellated and Gothick) in one not very large house. The castellated manner, sometimes with Gothick or Tudor details, was the most popular, beginning in 1802 with
87 *James Gillespie Graham*'s toy fort of Achnacarry Castle (Lochaber), continuing with his more picturesquely composed Sleat Old Manse at Kilmore (Skye and Lochalsh) of 1811–12, and reaching a climax in 1815–19 with his remodelling of the now largely demolished Armadale Castle (Skye and Lochalsh), whose Gothic detail extended from the front's porch and tower into
89 the plaster-vaulted principal rooms. Geanies House (Ross and Cromarty) was dressed up, *c.* 1810, with both a Roman Doric loggia across the front and a little castellated addition to one side. Around 1830 Fetlar (Shetland) acquired the dotty castellated Gothic villa of Brough Lodge. Much stodgier was *Robert Brown*
90 *Jun.*'s castellated remodelling of Dunvegan Castle (Skye and Lochalsh) in 1840–50, but the sculptor *Richard Westmacott* designed a muscular addition to Dunrobin Castle (Sutherland) in 1835 and *Charles Wilson* the large and serious-minded Lews Castle at Stornoway (Western Isles) in 1848.

The unpretentious laird's house with a few classical touches, which had become common by the late C 18, continued to be built, e.g. Geddes House (Nairn) of 1801–5 and North Haa (Shetland) of *c.* 1830; but a more thoroughgoing and smoothly detailed classicism was now generally required. Overarched windows and Roman Doric doorcases or porticoes were provided at Holme Rose (Nairn), Orbost House (Skye and Lochalsh) and Symbister House on Whalsay (Shetland) by *c.* 1835. *William Robertson*'s Reelig House, Kirkhill (Inverness), of 1837–8 had an Ionic portico, as did *Archibald Simpson*'s more strongly neo-Greek
88 Boath House (Nairn) of *c.* 1830. The cottage style provided a less formal alternative, externally unpretentious except for a pedimented portico, at Ness Castle (Inverness) of *c.* 1820 and Coul House (Ross and Cromarty) of 1821, going Italian at *William Robertson*'s Dochgarroch and Dochfour (both Inverness) of 1839 and his now much altered Lochluichart Lodge (Ross and Cromarty) of 1840. A villa of smooth precision, its front relieved by stone window canopies, but with an unexpectedly asymmetrical side elevation was built for Lord Dundas of Aske at Grainbank House, Kirkwall (Orkney), in 1829. Interiors are generally plain classical, but at Drimnin House (Lochaber) of the 1850s the hall and stair are expensively marbled with subtle skill and the drawing rooms decorated with painted panels. Just as complete and even more opulent is the Frenchy decoration of *c.* 1830 in the drawing room at Geddes House (Nairn).

Scottish Baronial appeared first in Highland in 1840, with *William Burn*'s tactful addition of a tower to the C 17 Redcastle

(Ross and Cromarty). Burn's design sixteen years later for Braal
Castle (Caithness) was disappointingly plain, but his former
partner *David Bryce* produced a confidently relaxed Baronial
house at Balfour Castle on Shapinsay (Orkney) in 1846–50 and a
taut harled composition at Keiss Castle (Caithness) in 1859–62.
Bryce's other works were humdrum, the castellated Amhu-
innsuidhe Castle (Western Isles) of 1864, the Jacobean Glengarry
Castle at Invergarry (Lochaber) of 1866, and the thrifty Trumland
House on Rousay (Orkney) of 1872. *Wardrop & Reid* designed
the Baronial Fairburn House (Ross and Cromarty) with routine
competence in 1877. Even less inspired was *Alexander Ross*'s Duncraig Castle (Skye and Lochalsh) of 1866, whilst *J. Macvicar
Anderson*'s work of 1892 at Inverlochy Castle (Lochaber), and
Ross & Macbeth's huge additions to Skibo Castle (Sutherland),
built for Andrew Carnegie in 1899–1903, look as if they were
bought by the yard. More light-heartedly Baronial and enjoyably
over the top are *John Rhind*'s Ardverikie (Badenoch and
Strathspey) of 1874–8 and *Matthews & Lawrie*'s Aigas House 93
(Inverness) of 1877. Baronial of a non-historicist kind was
employed in 1885 by *William Leiper* at Kinlochmoidart House 92
(Lochaber), a large Helensburgh villa dumped in one of Highland's most remote parts, its original internal finishings still largely
intact. At the nearby Glenborrodale Castle (Lochaber) of 1898,
Sydney Mitchell stretched his Scots Renaissance detail too thinly
over the Baronial outline. Much more satisfying has been *R.
Rowand Anderson*'s Scots Renaissance shooting lodge at Glencoe
(Lochaber), 1896, now a hospital. At Vaila Hall (Shetland) in
1895, the Bradford architect *E. P. Peterson* extended a late c 17
laird's house into a bare castellated mansion, its two blocks of
rooms separated by a Baronial great hall. A quite different
approach to the enlargement of a c 17 laird's house was shown by
W. R. Lethaby's additions of 1898 to Melsetter on Hoy (Orkney), 94
the unforced restraint of the exterior matched by the careful
simplicity of the interior, strongly redolent of high thinking and
simple living supported by an ample income. At the same time
Lethaby extended Hoy Lodge and designed Rysa Lodge, near
Lyness, both also on Hoy, giving that island three of the best Arts
and Crafts houses in Britain. A precursor of these Arts and Crafts
houses, but designed without reference to specifically local architecture, was *Philip Webb*'s Arisaig House (Lochaber) of 1863–4,
an essay in the parsonage manner of G. E. Street, sadly emas-
culated in *I. B. M. Hamilton & Orphoot, Whiting & Lindsay*'s
reconstruction of 1936–7 after a fire. Quite different in character
from anything else and from each other were a handful of Highland houses of the c 19 and early c 20. Dunrobin Castle 91
(Sutherland) was massively extended by the second *Duke of Sutherland* in collaboration with *William Leslie* and *Charles Barry* in
1845–51, the exterior treated in a mixed Franco-Scottish manner,
the interior a lavish if heavy display of ducal magnificence. Both
exterior and interior were remodelled by *Robert S. Lorimer* after a
fire in 1915; the Frenchy tower roofs were replaced by ogee caps
and the rooms inside recast in an eclectic style owing much to

C 18 sources. More consistently C 18 but also eclectic was *John Kinross*'s internal remodelling in 1908 of Ardtornish House (Lochaber), providing this gigantic but undistinguished villa with fastidiously detailed and very cold-blooded rooms worthy of a grand hotel. Also eclectic was *William Flockhart*'s reconstruction of the now demolished Rosehaugh (Ross and Cromarty) in 1893–1903 as a French château, the interior containing not only a swimming pool and Turkish bath but also a modelled plaster ceiling incorporating as its centrepiece a late C 17 painting by *Jacob de Witt*. The ceiling is now installed at Novar House (Ross and Cromarty).

The C 20 has produced a smattering of rogue houses. *George Mackie Watson*'s Eilean Donan Castle (Skye and Lochalsh) was built in 1912–32 as a sober Disneyland version of the site's medieval castle, destroyed two centuries before. *Ian Begg*'s Ravens' Craig (Skye and Lochalsh) of 1987–9 is a tower house built of harled breeze blocks. *Martyn Beckett*'s Callernish (Western Isles) of 1962 takes inspiration from the C 18 'round square' at Gordonstoun. *Francis Johnson*'s Strathconon House (Ross and Cromarty) of 1986 is a polite neo-Georgian apparition stranded in a Highland glen.

PARKLAND settings for Highland country houses are comparatively rare, although some exist, e.g. at Castle Grant (Badenoch and Strathspey) or Novar House (Ross and Cromarty). An arboretum was planted at the now demolished Brahan Castle (Ross and Cromarty) in the early C 19. At Inverewe near Poolewe (Ross and Cromarty) the C 19 and C 20 garden is of more significance than the house. Dunrobin Castle (Sutherland) has terraces and parterres formed in the mid-C 19. WALLED GARDENS were common by the later C 18. In Dunrobin Castle's is a summerhouse pavilion (now Museum) of 1732. Another of the mid-C 18 is at Bighouse Lodge (Caithness) and a third, divorced from the walled garden, was built at Geanies House (Ross and Cromarty) in 1760. STABLES were a necessary appendage of any country house and often designed to be seen from the approach. Among the smartest are the late C 18 block, its interior divided into two plaster-vaulted aisles, at Cromarty House (Ross and Cromarty) and the Gothick block of 1820–2 at Armadale Castle (Skye and Lochalsh). LODGES are mostly low-key introductions to the main house, but the mid-C 19 lodges at Castle Grant (Badenoch and Strathspey) are grandly Baronial, the 1870s
98 gateway and lodge by *David Smith* at the entrance to Thurso Castle (Caithness) a nightmare fantasy.

FORTS

The period of Cromwellian government in Scotland between 1650 and 1660 was virtually a military dictatorship, with garrisons placed at key locations where they could command the country's

principal communication routes and ensure that any revolt would
be localized. Four main citadels or forts were built (one being at
Inverness*), a fort of lesser importance was also constructed at
Inverlochy, now Fort William (Lochaber), at the s end of the
Great Glen, and troops were stationed in the medieval stronghold
of Ruthven Castle near Kingussie (Badenoch and Strathspey),
standing at the junction of routes from the w and s to the Spey
valley.

The Inverness citadel, designed in 1652 by the 'German inge-
nire' *Joachim Hane* and based on a plan illustrated in Robert
Norwood's *Fortification or Military Architecture* of 1639, was in
accordance with up-to-date European ideas of military architecture. It was a pentagon with triangular bastions projecting from
the corners to allow defenders to enfilade the stone walls. Further
defence was provided by a moat filled from the River Ness, which
flowed past the citadel's w side and enabled it to be provisioned
from the sea. Inside these defences were placed a central block
housing the magazine and granary with a chapel on the top floor,
two barrack ranges, stables, stores and 'a great long tavern quher
all manner of wines, viands, beer, ale, cider, was sold'.

The fort built at Inverlochy in 1654 was a poor relation of this
citadel. Like it, its position on a promontory at the entry of the
River Nevis into Loch Linnhe allowed provisioning from the sea
and it was cut off from landward attack by a moat. The shape was
again that of a pentagon but very irregular and with a full bastion
at only one corner, the other corners' demi-bastions each enfilading only one wall. The ramparts were not of stone but of turf
and wattles.

After the Restoration of the monarchy in 1660 these Cromwellian forts were abandoned, the Inverness citadel being used as a
quarry for dressed stone. The new ideas of fortification were
quickly revived when, in 1665–6 during the Second Dutch War,
a fort (now Fort Charlotte) was erected at Lerwick (Shetland),
its contractor and probable designer being *John Mylne Jun.*, the
Master Mason to the Crown. Again it was an irregular pentagon
with bastions at the corners. Intended to defend the harbour
against foreign attack rather than to overawe the local inhabitants,
it was occupied only briefly, the garrison being withdrawn after
peace was signed with the Netherlands in 1667, a possibly ill-
considered decision since six years later, after the resumption of
hostilities, both the fort and the town of Lerwick were burnt by
Dutch raiders.

The Glorious Revolution of 1688–9 was followed by a return
to something like the Cromwellian system of military control over
Highland, a sizeable force of soldiers being stationed at each end
of the Great Glen and a body of men being placed at Ruthven
Castle, which was repaired in a makeshift manner, having been
burnt in 1689. Instead of rebuilding the Cromwellian citadel at
Inverness, that town's medieval castle, whose defences had been

---

*The others were at Perth (Tayside), Ayr (South Strathclyde) and Leith
(Edinburgh).

slighted in 1649, was refortified to a plan prepared by *Captain Theodore Dury* in 1690, the hill on which it stood being surrounded by a ditch and palisade. At the same time the Cromwellian fort at Inverlochy was reconstructed in stone and rechristened Fort William in honour of the new King.

In 1717, after the defeat of the Jacobite rising begun two years before, the Government decided to disband the Independent Highland Companies and replace them with regular troops organized in permanent garrisons. At the same time it was decided to supplement the existing forts at Inverness and Fort William with
74 new forts on the site of Ruthven Castle and at Kiliwhimen, now Fort Augustus (Inverness), halfway down the Great Glen, and at Bernera by Glenelg (Skye and Lochalsh), commanding what was then the principal crossing from Skye to the Scottish mainland. Designs for these forts were produced by 1718, the architect almost certainly *James Smith*, who had been appointed Surveyor and Chief Director for Carrying on the Barracks in North Britain. All these forts shared the same general plan of a rectangular enclosure, its stone walls well provided with musket loops and with bastion towers at two diagonally opposed corners. The accommodation in each fort was placed in two barrack blocks facing each other across a parade ground.

The last of the forts was completed in 1723, just before the construction of the military roads from Dunkeld to Inverness and from Inverness to Fort William was begun by General Wade. Wade had expressed the opinion as early as 1724 that the new fort at Kiliwhimen was 'situate at too great a distance from Lake Ness', presumably because it was serviced by a galley on the loch, and in 1729 another new fort, designed by *Captain John Romer*, was begun on a site immediately beside the loch. This fort, known from its completion in 1742 as Fort Augustus, was rectangular like Smith's forts but it had bastions at all four corners and buildings on all sides of the enclosure, the two barrack blocks of the Smith forts being supplemented by a gatehouse and a governor's house flanked by captains' houses. It was also consciously architectural in a ponderous classical manner, the gatehouse having a pedimented centrepiece and both it and the governor's house enjoying Venetian windows and rusticated quoins and doorways.

The Jacobite rising of 1745–6 inflicted considerable damage on the Highland forts. Fort William was badly knocked about in a siege, Ruthven Barracks (the successor to Ruthven Castle) burned, and at Fort Augustus the bastion housing the powder magazine received a direct hit and was destroyed, the other three bastions being wrecked after the fort's subsequent capture by the Jacobites. The worst damage was at Inverness, where the castle, known as Fort George since a remodelling in the 1720s, was largely destroyed by the explosion of its magazine. Fort William and Fort Augustus were repaired in 1746–7 but Ruthven Barracks was abandoned.

It was decided not to attempt to refortify the castle at Inverness
76 but to build a new Fort George. The first site chosen, that of

the Cromwellian citadel at Inverness, was quickly superseded by Ardersier Point, a promontory commanding the entrance to the sheltered waters between Inverness and the Black Isle. The undertaking was massive and massively expensive, the fort designed by *Colonel William Skinner* in 1747 being intended to house more than 1,600 men and equipped with the fullest possible complement of defences provided by a glacis, ditch, ravelin, bastions and demibastions. The buildings are just as expressive of military might, the pedimented gatehouse flaunting the royal arms of the House 77 of Hanover, the barrack blocks symmetrically disposed round a 78 large central square, the occasional use of a Doric order reinforcing rather than lightening the purposeful severity. In practical terms the money was probably wasted. When Fort George was finally completed in 1769, another Jacobite rising had become highly unlikely, and within another fifty years the defences would be regarded as inadequate against new artillery. Much less ambitious and much less expensive were the repair of the C17 defences and the erection of new barrack blocks at Fort Charlotte at Lerwick (Shetland), carried out by *Captain Andrew Frazer* in the 1780s when hostilities with France seemed threatened.

The wars with France in 1793–1815 produced a distinctive new type of fortification in Britain, the Martello tower. These squat round towers were built for coastal defence, their lower floors housing stores and a small number of troops, their flat roofs intended as gun platforms. Two well-preserved examples of *c.* 1812–18 survive in Orkney, at Lyness (Hoy) and on South Walls.

By the early C19 the Hanoverian forts were obsolete, their defences unable to withstand attack from improved artillery and their garrisons no longer needed to suppress a Jacobite rising. Fort William, its rampart partly destroyed by the flood-swollen River Nevis in the late C18, was sold in 1864 and later largely demolished to make way for a railway goods yard. Fort Augustus had its ramparts dismantled and its ordnance removed *c.* 1820, was sold in 1867 and afterwards transfigured as a Roman Catholic abbey and school. Fort Charlotte retained a minor military function as a coastal battery. Coastal batteries were also installed at Fort George but it found a real use only in 1881, when it became the regimental depot of the Seaforth Highlanders, the rival Cameron Highlanders perhaps enjoying greater comfort in the Cameron Barracks at Inverness, a Baronial pile unencumbered by defences, provided for them by the *Royal Engineers' Office* in 1880–6.

ROADS, RAILWAYS, CANALS, HARBOURS AND LIGHTHOUSES

Until the C19, communications in Highland and between the Northern and Western Isles were mostly either by water or by foot tracks. When Samuel Johnson and James Boswell travelled

to the Hebrides in 1773 they found no road N of Inverness capable
of taking wheeled traffic,* and in 1786 John Knox reported a
complete absence of roads in Ross and Cromarty, Sutherland and
Caithness.

Those roads which did exist had been made by the Army. The
first were constructed by *General George Wade* between 1725 and
1733 and comprised those from Dunkeld (Tayside) to Inverness
by way of Drumochter Pass and Ruthven Barracks (Badenoch
and Strathspey), from Inverness down the Great Glen to Fort
Augustus (Inverness) and Fort William (Lochaber), and from
Fort Augustus across the Pass of Corrieyairack to Dalwhinnie
(Badenoch and Strathspey). A road from Spean Bridge
(Lochaber) through Glen Roy to the Fort Augustus–Dalwhinnie
road may also have been the product of this campaign. Wade's
roads were designed less for ease of use than for cheapness of
construction, often running in straight lines between van-
tagepoints or following the ridges of hills; major climbs, as on
the Corrieyairack road, were negotiated by zig-zags, but shorter
ascents could be by gradients as steep as 1 in 6 (17%). At first
they relied on fords rather than bridges, although these were soon
found necessary. The standard width of these roads was 4.88m.
but could be reduced to 3.05m. in difficult terrain and to as little
as 2.59m. between the parapets of bridges. They were constructed
by excavating peat and soil down to a firm foundation, on which
were placed layers of stones, usually covered by gravel.

The building of military roads in Highland resumed in 1750
under the direction of *Major William Caulfield*, who began the
construction of the route from Stirling by Lochearnhead and
Tyndrum (Central) to Fort William (Lochaber) in 1750. About
the same time he started work on the road from Braemar
(Grampian) via Grantown-on-Spey (Badenoch and Strathspey)
to Fort George (Inverness), which seems to have been completed
in 1757. Six years later he rebuilt the stretch of Wade's road
between Crubenmore and Kingussie (Badenoch and Strathspey)
on a new line passing through Newtonmore. Caulfield's roads
were more sophisticated than had been Wade's, adhering less
strictly to straight lines, although still with steep gradients, and
with a greater use of cuttings and embankments, as well as stone
retaining walls and culverts to channel off surface water. Bridges
were provided, their roadways generally of between 3.66m. and
3.81m. width, significantly broader than on the earlier C18
bridges. In the 1770s another military road, presumably laid out
by Caulfield's successor, *Colonel Skene*, was begun, leading from
Fort Augustus (Inverness) through Glen Moriston to Bernera
Barracks at Glenelg (Skye and Lochalsh), but by 1803 there
remained of it 'just the vestiges'.

A major force behind the provision of roads intended primarily
for civilian traffic was the British Fisheries Society, formed in 1786
and funded by public subscription to develop a herring fishing

*A road had been made from Contin through Strath Bran to Poolewe (Ross and
Cromarty) *c*. 1760, but it was unusable by 1799.

industry on the W coast. Among its first projects was the establishment of the village of Ullapool (Ross and Cromarty) beside
Loch Broom in 1788. Two years later a line of road between
Ullapool and Contin (Ross and Cromarty) was surveyed by *George
Brown*, and the road itself was built in 1792–7, the Society acting
as agent for the Treasury. *Thomas Telford* was appointed Surveyor
to the British Fisheries Society in 1796 and was instructed by the
Treasury in 1801 to select sites for fishing stations on the W
coast, to plan safe communications between the mainland and the
islands, and to investigate the possibility of a canal between the
W and E coasts. In 1802 the brief was widened to include con-
sideration of the causes of Highland emigration. In his report of
1803 Telford recommended both the making of the Caledonian
Canal through the Great Glen and the construction of roads to
its N and S. The same year Parliament passed two acts appointing
commissioners to make the Canal and to build roads and bridges
in the Highlands of Scotland, a number of directors of the British
Fisheries Society being appointed to each commission. The
Government undertook to pay half the cost of the new 'Parliamentary' roads, the remainder being found by local landowners.
Work began in 1804 on the completion of a road, already started
by local proprietors, from Fort William to Arisaig (Lochaber) and
on the construction of new roads from Invergarry to Kinloch
Hourn (Lochaber) and from Corran Ferry to Kinlochmoidart
(Lochaber). In 1814 responsibility for the existing military roads
in Highland was transferred to the Commissioners and by 1828
they had built 1,435km. of new roads and improved or maintained
a further 495km. By far the greater part of this network was in
Highland, where they had completed a road from Inverness to
Thurso (Caithness), another from Bonar Bridge (Sutherland) to
Tongue (Caithness), roads from Dingwall (Ross and Cromarty)
and Invermoriston (Inverness) to the W coast, where they were
linked by a road from Kyle of Lochalsh (Skye and Lochalsh) to
Shieldaig (Ross and Cromarty), a network of roads on Skye and
a new road from Spean Bridge (Lochaber) through Glen Spean
and beside Loch Laggan to Laggan (Badenoch and Strathspey)
to replace Wade's road across the Corrieyairack Pass, which was
blocked by snow for several months each winter. These 'Parliamentary' roads were designed specifically for wheeled traffic,
Telford specifying a standard carriageway width of 4.88m. to
allow two wagons or coaches to pass each other, although in
practice the width could be as little as 3.66m. where the road
was cut through rock. Curved lines were common and gradients
gentle, the aim being to restrict them where possible to no more
than 1 in 30. The standard of construction surpassed that of the
late C18 military roads. Most of the bridges were small and plain,
with a breadth of 3.66m. between parapets. One of the bigger of
these standard bridges survives at Sligachan (Skye and Lochalsh),
humpbacked, with three unequal-sized arches and triangular cutwaters. Much showier is the non-standard bridge at Torgyle near
Invermoriston (Inverness) of 1825–6, its battlemented cutwaters
decorated with cross-slits.

Many of these bridges have been replaced in the c 20. In 1925–8 the main A9 road between Blair Atholl (Tayside) and Inverness was reconstructed to make it suitable for the motor-car, with large concrete bridges erected over the Rivers Spey, Dulnain and Findhorn. Further major improvements to this road were begun in 1974, both s of Inverness and between Inverness and Wick (Caithness), the most striking engineering achievement the 1,052m.-long Kessock Bridge, opened in 1982. Far more dramatic is the elegant curved span over a ravine of *Ove Arup & Partners'* bridge at Kylesku (Sutherland) of 1984. Its sense of style is a match for the Victorian suspension bridges, best represented by those at Aberchalder (Lochaber) of 1850 and the Infirmary and Greig Street bridges at Inverness, provided in 1881 to *C. R. Manners'* design.

Maintenance of the 'Parliamentary' roads was funded by the collection of tolls from travellers. Many of the TOLLHOUSES have been sacrificed for road widening. Two of the prettiest to survive are the semi-octagonal-fronted example of *c*. 1815 at Thurso (Caithness) and *Joseph Mitchell*'s of 1828 at Conon Bridge (Ross and Cromarty), octagonal and with a verandah.

The great early c 19 road-building projects in Highland facilitated one form of travel, but both road and sea transport were challenged from the 1850s by the advent of the railways. The first stretch of railway line in Highland was that between Inverness and Nairn, completed in 1855 and intended by its engineer, *Joseph Mitchell*, as part of a direct link to Perth (Tayside). However, in 1858 this line was extended E to Keith (Grampian) to provide a route s via Aberdeen. In 1863 was opened a branch from the Inverness–Keith railway which ran sW from Forres (Grampian) across Dava Moor and down the Spey valley to Aviemore (Badenoch and Strathspey), whence it accompanied the line of the old A9 to join the railway N from Perth at Dunkeld (Tayside). At the same time the railway system was extended N of Inverness, first in 1862 with a line to Dingwall (Ross and Cromarty), carried on over the next twelve years to Wick and Thurso (Caithness). A line to the W coast from Dingwall to Stromeferry (Skye and Lochalsh) was opened in 1870, although it did not reach its eventual terminus at Kyle of Lochalsh (Skye and Lochalsh) until 1897. A line up the W coast from Helensburgh (Strathclyde) to Spean Bridge and Fort William (Lochaber) was constructed in 1889–94 and extended to Arisaig and Mallaig (Lochaber) in 1901. An unsuccessful venture to transport travellers from this W route up the Great Glen to Inverness was begun in 1897, and in 1903 a railway line was opened from Spean Bridge to Fort Augustus (Inverness), whence travellers continued their journey by boat. This line closed in 1911, its failure perhaps partly the result of the Perth–Inverness line having been shortened by *c*. 48km. when a direct line from Aviemore to Inverness via Carrbridge (Badenoch and Strathspey) was opened in 1898. Several branch lines (now closed) were also built, including a line to Strathpeffer (Ross and Cromarty) in 1885, the Black Isle Branch from Muir of Ord to

Fortrose (Ross and Cromarty) and a line to Dornoch (Sutherland) in 1902.

VIADUCTS are the most impressive products of railway engineering. The earliest, such as those at Nairn of 1856–7 and Alness (Ross and Cromarty) of 1861–3, both by *Joseph Mitchell*, have martial decoration, as did one of the latest (of 1897–1903) at Fort Augustus (Inverness) by *William Roberts*. Much more starkly functional are those designed by *John Fowler* and *Murdoch Paterson* in 1893 for the Aviemore–Inverness line, the 400m.-long Findhorn Viaduct at Tomatin (Inverness), with stone piers supporting steel lattice girders, the 549m.-long Clava Viaduct (Inverness) carried 119 on twenty-nine arches across the valley of the Nairn. Mass-concrete was used in 1897–1901 by *Simpson & Wilson* for the viaducts of the Spean Bridge–Mallaig line, that over the Borrodale Burn near Arisaig (Lochaber) with a central arch spanning no less than 38.9m. The most idiosyncratic is the castellated bridge by *Joseph Mitchell*, 1863–4, over the road at Castle Grant (Badenoch and Strathspey), where Lord Seafield could catch a train by stepping out of the first-floor door of his adjoining contemporary Baronial gate lodge.

RAILWAY STATIONS generally were of villa type. In the 1860s *Joseph Mitchell* designed for the line N of Inverness broad-eaved stations at Hill of Fearn (Ross and Cromarty) and Ardgay (Sutherland) and gave a shaped centre gable to the station at Invergordon (Ross and Cromarty). *William Fowler* produced cottage-Tudor at Golspie (Sutherland) in 1868, and in 1902 at Dunrobin (Sutherland) *L. Bisset* designed a station adorned with half-timbering and a tree-trunk verandah. Some of the later stations made much of their platform awnings. At Strathpeffer (Ross and Cromarty) by *Murdoch Paterson*, 1885, it is gableted; at Aviemore (Badenoch and Strathspey) by *William Roberts*, 1898, double-pitched with wheel decoration in the spandrels of the supporting brackets. One feature, decorative as well as functional, common to almost all Highland stations was a lattice-girder footbridge over the track.

For most of the C19 the principal E–W route for freight across Highland was provided by the CALEDONIAN CANAL. It was constructed to *Thomas Telford*'s design in 1804–22 and links the Beauly Firth at the NE to Loch Linnhe at the SW, carrying traffic through canal stretches which join together the natural lochs of Ness, Oich and Lochy. The most impressive ladders of locks are at Inverness, Fort Augustus (Inverness) and Corpach (Lochaber).

Improvements to inland communications in the C19 were intended to aid the development of a fishing industry and complement sea-borne navigation. In Highland and the Islands travel of any distance had been largely by boat before 1800, but there is little evidence that HARBOURS consisted of much more than sheltered anchorages in bays or river mouths. Inverness had some sort of dock or wharf by the early C17, a pier was built at Portmahomack (Ross and Cromarty) in the late C17, and in the later C18 a pier was constructed at Fort George (Inverness) to serve both the fort and the ferry to the Black Isle. Almost certainly there were several more piers or slips, perhaps of fairly rudimentary construction, built before 1800 from which grain was shipped for sale.

A harbour was built at Stornoway (Western Isles) *c.* 1785, but it was the foundation of the British Fisheries Society the next year that signalled the beginning of a concerted attempt to establish a fishing industry. The Society's first harbours (associated with new planned villages) were built at Ullapool (Ross and Cromarty) in 1788 and Stein (Skye and Lochalsh) in 1796, the pier at Stein constructed with advice from *Thomas Telford*, who was appointed Surveyor to the Society the next year. In the first two decades of the C19 the Society was instrumental in the provision of other fishing harbours at Wick, Scrabster and Keiss (Caithness), Avoch, Balintore, Fortrose and Portmahomack (Ross and Cromarty), Nairn, Portree (Skye and Lochalsh), and Kirkwall (Orkney). At the same time the Countess of Sutherland built fishing harbours at Helmsdale and Lochinver and a harbour for her coal works at Brora (Sutherland). A little later James Traill made a harbour at Castletown (Caithness) for the export of flagstones. Fishing harbours continued to be built or improved through the C19 and into the C20. Several were small-scale, such as Sandside Harbour at Reay (Caithness) or Balintore (Ross and Cromarty), some very large, like Scalloway (Shetland), Mallaig (Lochaber) or Kinlochbervie (Sutherland). One of the most complete C19 examples is Lybster (Caithness), begun in 1833 and enlarged in the 1850s and 1880s, with its small lighthouse and early C19 warehouses. Other harbours have developed as ports to serve general trade as well as fishing, the present grimly utilitarian character of Stornoway (Western Isles), Kirkwall (Orkney) and Lerwick (Shetland) a testimony to their success.

LIGHTHOUSES, clearly desirable for safe navigation, appeared in northern Scotland as a result of the 1786 act 'for erecting certain Light-houses in the Northern Parts of Great Britain'. This established a board of commissioners to build four lighthouses, of which one was on Scalpay (Western Isles) and another on North Ronaldsay (Orkney), and to levy duties on all ships passing these lights. The commissioners' powers were enlarged in 1789 to build more lighthouses, among the first being two towers (since replaced) on Pentland Skerries (Orkney), whose construction was supervised by *Robert Stevenson* in 1794. Five years later Stevenson was appointed engineer to the Northern Lighthouse Board, a post held successively by his sons and grandsons until 1938. During the first fifty years of the C19 the Stevenson firm designed eight lighthouses in Highland and the Islands. Fourteen more followed between 1850 and 1875, another eight by 1900 and a further six by 1915. All were round towers, varying a great deal in height, and usually accompanied by flat-roofed keepers' houses and stores, those designed by *Alan Stevenson* in the 1840s at Cromarty, Fortrose (Ross and Cromarty) and Noss Head (Caithness) having neo-Egyptian detail. A square lighthouse tower was designed in 1925 by *D. Alan Stevenson* for Esha Ness (Shetland).

Through the Middle Ages and until the late C17 the right to engage in foreign trade was restricted to royal burghs, but in 1700 Highland contained only seven. Of these, three (Inverness, Dingwall (Ross and Cromarty) and Nairn), all associated with royal castles, were in existence by the C13.* Another three, Wick (Caithness) and Tain and Fortrose (Ross and Cromarty), had gained this status in the late C16 and Dornoch (Sutherland) in 1628. The only royal burgh in the Islands was Kirkwall (Orkney), which had been granted a charter in 1486. Burghs of barony, dependent on a landowner but entitled to hold regular markets for the sale of domestically produced goods, were no more numerous. Rosemarkie (Ross and Cromarty) held this status from the C13, Auldearn (Nairn) acquired it in 1511, and Reay and Thurso (Caithness), Fort William (Lochaber) and Stornoway (Western Isles) in the early C17. Two further burghs of barony were created in 1817 and 1818 at Stromness (Orkney) and Lerwick (Shetland). Municipal self-government was extended to many new industrial centres in Scotland after the reform of local government in 1832, but only two of these 'police' burghs were erected in Highland, Invergordon (Ross and Cromarty) in 1864, and Grantown-on-Spey (Badenoch and Strathspey) in 1898.

The burghs were very small. At the end of the C18 Inverness contained a population of over 5,000, and the next largest was Kirkwall, with about 2,000 inhabitants. Wick, Nairn, Tain, Stromness and (probably) Thurso had over 1,000 and Lerwick about the same number, but Dingwall, Stornoway, Dornoch and Fortrose considerably less. By the end of the C19 only Inverness had a population of over 20,000; the second biggest burgh, Wick, had less than half that; no other burgh had more than 5,000, and the populations of Fortrose and Dornoch were still under 1,000 apiece. The C20 has seen considerable growth, but the only large town is Inverness.

The founding of planned villages was part of the economic improvement of Scotland in the C18 and C19. In Highland the first proposals for such villages were intended to attract craftsmen from the economically and technologically more advanced Lowlands and so to introduce civilization and industry as well as to serve the needs of the local gentry. In 1739 Sir Alexander Macdonald's Edinburgh agent was attempting to find a shoemaker, wright, smith, weaver and bonnet-maker willing to settle on Skye but concluded that the 'first Step is to resolve on a Village at Portree.' Nothing was done then nor in 1763, when Sir James Macdonald wrote enthusiastically:

I have planed [*sic*] a compleat City at this place [Portree] ... The present plan consists only of two & twenty houses, with one acre of ground for a Garden behind each of them; & a large space behind the gardens which

*As was also Cromarty (Ross and Cromarty), which was removed from the roll of royal burghs in 1685.

is divided into inclosures of about eleven acres ... I am so full of the
scheme that I fancy I see the street & the shops & warehouses on every
side ...

Two years later Sir Ludovick Grant of Grant did found a new
village at Grantown-on-Spey (Badenoch and Strathspey), which
proved a success, the parish minister's description of it in the early
1790s showing that that success was to be judged by the number
and quality of craftsmen it had attracted:

It now contains from 300 to 400 inhabitants, some of whom are as good
tradesmen as any in the kingdom. Shoemakers, taylors, weavers of wool,
linen and stockings, blacksmiths, wrights, masons and 12 merchants keep
regular shops in it. There are 2 established schools ... A brewery was
established in this place immediately at the building of it, on purpose to
keep the people from drinking spiritous liquors, and it continues to give
satisfaction. Two bakers carry on the business of their profession with
success ... There are two or three public houses in it, with an elegant
town-house, covering a prison ...

Grantown-on-Spey was laid out around a long square, the centre
of each side pierced by a road. Less grand but still formal was the
gridiron layout of Kingussie (Badenoch and Strathspey), begun
in 1799. A square is again the central feature of the plan of Beauly
(Inverness), c. 1805, of which an observer in 1808 predicted
incorrectly that, since the building plots were offered only on 38-
year leases, 'the spur which the enjoyment of property gives to
human industry is altogether wanting' and that 'the houses will
be mean, and the villagers poor and spiritless.' At Kyleakin (Skye
and Lochalsh) an almost totally unsuccessful attempt was made
to establish a village, c. 1810, its formal crescents designed by
James Gillespie Graham to look like a substantial part of Edinburgh's New Town. By contrast Halkirk (Caithness) was laid out
c. 1800 as a single long street.

   The erection of fishing villages to be populated by Highlanders
cleared from land turned over to sheep-farming was a main objec-
tive of the British Fisheries Society on its foundation in 1786 and
one soon adopted by the more socially conscious or farsighted
landowners. The Society's first village was Ullapool (Ross and
Cromarty), laid out on a grid pattern in 1788. Here the Society
built a pier and the first plots were developed for warehouses.
Much smaller was the Society's village at Stein (Skye and
Lochalsh) of 1796, where no more than a single row of houses
along the shore got built. Two villages, Dornie and Plockton
(Skye and Lochalsh), were laid out in 1794 on the Kintail estate
of the Mackenzies of Seaforth, although almost all their present
housing is c19. At Lybster (Caithness) the Sinclairs laid out a
single street, broadening at its centre, on land above the harbour
in the early c19. The most ambitious of fishing villages planned
by landowners were those at Golspie and Helmsdale (Sutherland)
laid out by the Countess of Sutherland in 1805 and 1818, although
her comparison of Helmsdale with Liverpool was perhaps far-
fetched. The fishing village of Latheronwheel (Caithness) was
laid out as late as 1853. A village to house those employed in the
adjacent coal mines, brickworks and saltpans was begun at Brora

(Sutherland) in 1814. One C19 planned village intended for tourism rather than fishing or industry was Strathpeffer (Ross and Cromarty), designed in 1806 as a spa whose waters' nauseous taste and smell vouched for their medicinal properties. *George Devey* produced a plan for the village's further development in 1860, twenty-five years before the arrival of the railway, after which an enjoyably dotty collection of villas came into being. Architecturally less enjoyable and without a mineral spring is the C20 resort of Aviemore (Badenoch and Strathspey).

The C19 development of burghs involved both redevelopment and extension. Inverness exemplifies both processes with its new commercial streets of Union Street and Queensgate, formed in 1863 and 1884, cutting through the medieval close pattern, and with major development of greenfield sites to the W and on the N side of the River Ness. At Thurso (Caithness) in 1798 Sir John Sinclair laid out a 'New Town' beside the existing burgh, its wide and straight streets centring on a square dominated by a public building (originally intended for the Town House but filled in 1830–2 by a new parish church). Wick (Caithness) acquired the regularly planned suburb of Louisburgh in the late C18. Its second and much larger suburb, Pulteneytown, was developed after 1808 by the British Fisheries Society on a formal layout with a long octagonal 'square' at its centre. C19 villa developments made Nairn a town of considerable extent, although the generosity of layout precluded a large population. Another 'New Town' beside an existing burgh was begun at Lerwick (Shetland) in 1862.

A clear sign of burgh status in the C16, C17 and C18 was provided by the MARKET CROSS, generally a shaft topped by a capital and perhaps a finial. Many survive, e.g. at Inverness, Nairn, Cromarty and Dingwall (Ross and Cromarty), mostly badly weathered. The cross at Kirkwall (Orkney) is exceptional in actually having a (very crude) cross-shaped finial. Much better preserved is the ball-finialled market cross of 1779 at Milton of Kildary (Ross and Cromarty), a village hardly entitled to such a status symbol. Necessary both as a symbol and for use in any royal burgh was the TOLBOOTH, a building to house the town's taxes or tolls, meetings of its council, and prisoners awaiting trial or incarcerated for debt. The Tolbooth at Tain (Ross and 99 Cromarty), built by *Alexander Stronach* in 1706–8, is a massive and very old-fashioned tower. Almost as old-fashioned for its date is the steeple added to Dingwall's Town House (Ross and Cromarty) by *John Boog*, *Donald Morrison* and *Donald McNeil* in the 1770s. More sophisticated was the Court House built at 100 Cromarty (Ross and Cromarty) in 1782, with its roundheaded first-floor windows and cupolaed tower. A taller and martially battlemented tower was provided at Nairn's Court House in 1817–18. Much more urbane were Inverness's Burgh Courthouse of 1787–91 and its Town Steeple, designed by *Alexander Laing* in 101 1789, the elegance of the 47.3m.-high steeple far removed from the determined defensiveness shown at Tain eighty years before.

Acts of 1819 and 1839 established proper financing for the building of PRISONS AND SHERIFF COURTS. The largest and

most prominently sited of these C 19 prison and courthouse groups was built on the site of the medieval castle at Inverness, the
103 courthouse designed by *William Burn* in 1833 as a stolid toy fort, the prison of 1846–8 by *Thomas Brown Jun.* in a much lighter castellated manner, with a slim tower for picturesque emphasis. Brown's other courts and prisons of the 1840s, at Dingwall and Tain (Ross and Cromarty), Dornoch (Sutherland) and Stornoway (Western Isles), are less fun, Tudorish with some Baronial touches. More courthouses and prisons were built in the 1860s and 1870s. The courts by *Matthews & Lawrie* at Kingussie (Badenoch and Strathspey) and Lochmaddy (Western Isles), by *D. & J. Bryce* at Kirkwall (Orkney), and by *David Rhind* at Lerwick (Shetland) are hardly distinguishable from villas. Only Rhind's Sheriff Court of 1862–6 at Wick (Caithness) attempts judicial pomp on a small scale. The new prison of 1903 at Inverness is grimly utilitarian, its chimneys' machicolations hinting at punishment rather than rehabilitation.

TOWN HALLS to accommodate public meetings and perhaps also burgh council meetings were an expression of C 19 civic pride. One of the earliest (of 1826–8) is at Wick (Caithness), quite small but heavily classical and with a small tower. Classical again but less assertive was the combined Museum and Town Hall built at Stromness (Orkney) in 1854–8. In 1876 *Matthews & Lawrie*
105 adopted Flemish-Baronial as a garb for the Town House at Inverness, their design cribbed by *Alexander Ross* in 1881 for Lerwick Town Hall (Shetland). Flemish again but without inspiration was *John Robertson*'s design of 1903 for the Old Town Hall at Stornoway (Western Isles). Tain Town Hall (Ross and Cromarty) by *Andrew Maitland & Sons*, 1874–6, is very free Renaissance, *David Smith*'s Drill Hall (now Masonic Hall) at Thurso (Caithness), 1873, Baronial with a vengeance. Rather quieter is the Kirkwall Town Hall (Orkney) by *T. S. Peace*, 1884–6. VILLAGE HALLS of the late C 19 and earlier C 20 are quite common but few are of much pretension. One which tries hard to make an impression is the Scots Renaissance Perrins Centre of 1903–4 by *Henman & Cooper* at Alness (Ross and Cromarty). More satisfying in its economy of effort is the beautifully simple Astley Hall at Arisaig (Lochaber), designed by *Philip Webb* in 1893.

The provision of SCHOOLS in every burgh and parish, one of the earliest ideals of the C 16 ecclesiastical reformers, was largely accomplished by the C 18. Most were very simple, consisting of no more than a schoolroom and living accommodation for the schoolmaster. Something rather grander was envisaged by the Inverness Burgh Council in 1664, when it gave orders for the erection of a grammar school in the town. Grander still and educationally ambitious was the Royal Inverness Academy (Nos. 40–44 Academy Street), designed in 1788 to look like a plain but elegant town house but containing a library and laboratory as well as a large hall and classrooms. Its building was financed by public subscription. So too, in 1811–13, was the Academy (now Duthac House) at Tain (Ross and Cromarty), for which *James Smith* provided an austere but dignified design. Originally it had an observatory, but its cupola was removed after a few years, having been found 'completely useless'. The domed observatory tower survives at Ardkeen Tower, Culduthel Road, Inverness, built in 1834-6 to house a juvenile and infants' school as well as the Ladies' Female Work Society and looking like a classical villa. A much larger and uncompromisingly Greek public building is *William Robertson*'s Dr Bell's School (now Public Library) of 1839-41 at Inverness. Robertson also provided the design in 1841 for the Infant School (now Jamesmount) at Auldearn (Nairn), low-key but with a pedimented centre. Also small-scale but of considerable presence was *Mackenzie & Matthews*' Free Church School of 1847-8 at Nairn. It is Italianate, but classicism with a Greek inflexion was still thought appropriate for an educational institution in 1859 when *William Smith* designed the Miller Institution (now Public Library) at Thurso (Caithness). The next year, however, Smith adopted Scots Jacobean with Frenchy touches for the Anderson High School at Lerwick (Shetland). In 1863 *Ross & Joass* introduced a mixed Gothic and Baronial style at their Mackenzie Foundation School in Avoch (Ross and Cromarty). Many new schools were built after the Education Act of 1872 established a national system of School Boards. Most are cheap, with little more than a Gothic bellcote for emphasis, but *Andrew Maitland & Sons* produced boldly composed Gothic designs for schools at Cromarty, Kilmuir Easter and Tain (Ross and Cromarty) and *Alexander Ross* a punchily detailed Gothic Episcopalian school (now St Andrews House, Fassifern Road) at Fort William (Lochaber). Ross was the most prolific of the School Boards' architects, producing designs for forty-one schools in the year 1875 alone, but his largest school commission was for a private establishment, the Northern Counties Collegiate School (now Regional Buildings) of 1875-6 at Inverness, a sober edifice in the collegiate Tudor manner. For the new Royal Inverness Academy (now Inverness Technical College) of 1893-5 he turned to a free François I style. The C 20 began well with *J. M. Dick Peddie*'s Scots Jacobean Sutherland Technical School (now High School Technical Annexe) at Golspie (Sutherland) of 1903-4. Thirty years later *Reid & Forbes* produced the Art Deco Inverness High School. The later C 20 has contributed lightweight buildings, first with flat roofs and then with huge tiled pitches.

After 1854 councils were able to finance PUBLIC LIBRARIES from the rates, but few took this as an invitation for grandiose display. Only *Leadbetter & Fairley*'s Queen Anne design of 1896 for the library at Wick (Caithness) is memorable. THEATRES have not been popular in Highland or the Islands, although late C 19 Inverness enjoyed both a theatre and a music hall. These have been demolished, but *Law & Dunbar-Nasmith* provided the town with Eden Court Theatre in 1973-6, its central mass surrounded by airy pavilions. Deliberately self-effacing in its wood is the Landmark Visitor Centre at Carrbridge (Badenoch and Strathspey) by *John L. Paterson*, 1969-70. By contrast the LEISURE CENTRES designed by *Faulkner Browns* in the 1980s for Shetland are unashamedly gaudy.

ALMSHOUSES for orphans or the elderly, popular enough elsewhere in Scotland as recipients of mercantile generosity, are few.
In Inverness, Dunbar's Hospital, Church Street, was built in
1668, its scrolly pediments carved with the figure of a bedesman
and Biblical texts. In 1824 Grantown-on-Spey (Badenoch and
102 Strathspey) acquired the Speyside Orphan Hospital (now Speyside House), its dumpy classicism and belfry tower giving it the
appearance of a tolbooth. Less prominently sited are Anderson's
Homes at Lerwick (Shetland), built in 1865 to accommodate the
widows of sailors and fishermen. HOSPITALS for the sick are first
represented by the Royal Northern Infirmary at Inverness of 1799–
1804, a sizeable but unexciting piece of country-house classicism.
One of the largest is the superbly sited Craig Dunain Hospital,
Inverness, by *James Matthews*, 1860–4, but the architecture,
despite Frenchy towers and a Gothic centrepiece, is thrifty. The
C20's chief contribution has been the *Matheson Gleave Partnership*'s Raigmore Hospital, Inverness, of 1983, a tall brown
landmark easy to find in an emergency.

POST OFFICES were built as public buildings and in the C19
and early C20 bore witness to Government's commitment to
public services. The grandest (now in other use) was built in High
109 Street, Inverness, in 1841–4, brute classical with giant columns at
the recessed centre. By the early C20 something friendlier was
expected, and in 1907–12 *W. T. Oldrieve* of *H.M. Office of Works*
provided a Queen Anne office at Stornoway (Western Isles) and
Scots Jacobean buildings at Lerwick (Shetland) and Wick
(Caithness). By the mid-C20 a jazzier image was sought and
the *Ministry of Public Buildings and Works* duly tried its hand at
commercial flashiness with a block in Queensgate, Inverness.

Of BANKS the earliest is the former Bank of Scotland in Bank
Street, Inverness, built in 1804 and hardly distinguishable from a
substantial but old-fashioned private house. Rapid expansion of
the banking system during the C19 quickly established the rule
that a bank in any prominent town should have the character of
a public building. The earlier ones were mostly classical, like
the Commercial Banks of 1828 and *c.* 1835 at Tain (Ross and
111 Cromarty) and Wick (Caithness) or the National Banks built at
112 Nairn (now Royal Bank) and Dingwall (Ross and Cromarty) in
the 1830s. Around 1840 the British Linen Co. built a palazzo
at Nairn, and then in 1847 *Mackenzie & Matthews* designed a
110 magnificently ornate head office for the newly formed Caledonian
Bank (now Bank of Scotland) in High Street, Inverness, its classicism given a distinctly Italianate twist. Palazzi were favoured until
the late C19, e.g. *William Mackintosh*'s Bank of Scotland at Nairn,
1874, and two banks at Wick (Caithness), the Aberdeen Town &
County (now Clydesdale) by *J. Russell Mackenzie*, 1875, and the
North of Scotland by *A. Marshall Mackenzie*, 1886. But in 1897
J. M. Dick Peddie gave Thurso (Caithness) its British Linen Bank
(now Bank of Scotland) in the Flemish style, and in 1904–6 *John
J. Burnet* produced exuberant English baroque for the Union
Bank (now Bank of Scotland) at Lerwick (Shetland). C20 banks
could almost have been designed by H.M. Office of Works on an

off day: the Bank of Scotland at Wick (Caithness), by *John Keppie & Henderson*, 1933–5, is fag-end Lorimerian Scots, and the Royal Bank at Kirkwall (Orkney), by *Dick Peddie, Todd & Jamieson*, 1938, tired neo-Georgian. Village banks, often housing the agent as well as the banking room, tried to look like villas – Jacobean at the British Linen Bank (now Bank of Scotland) in Golspie (Sutherland) of 1847, Gothic at the Caledonian (now Bank of Scotland) in Portree (Skye and Lochalsh) by *Matthews & Lawrie*, 1873, crowstepped at the same architects' Bank of Scotland in Kingussie (Badenoch and Strathspey) of 1875–6.

COMMERCIAL BUILDINGS are a feature of any town or large village but many in Highland and the Islands have been converted from houses; and of those which were purpose-built in the C19, most are utilitarian tenements with ground-floor shops. But Inverness has a grandly scaled Victorian commercial and office centre, including a Market Arcade, begun by *Matthews & Lawrie* in 1869. The same firm designed a showy palazzo in Academy Street as the Highland Railway Co.'s head office in 1873. Late C20 commercial architecture in Inverness has been less happy, with two of the more boorish intruders facing each other across Bridge Street and *Hugh Martin & Partners'* Eastgate Centre of 1983 making a forbidding fortress on the approach to the town.

HOTELS were erected from the late C18. The Caledonian Hotel in Inverness (replaced in 1965) was built *c.* 1780 and then included stabling for nineteen horses. After enlargement in 1822 at a cost of £2,000 it contained over eighty beds. Subsequent additions followed, the biggest, costing £6,000, in 1881. Before then it had been challenged by the Union Hotel in High Street, designed by *William Robertson* in 1838 with gentle classical detail, and by the muddled Italianate makeshift of the Station Hotel built in the 1850s in Academy Street. Tourism was the chief reason for the building of many Highland hotels. In 1873–5 *A. Marshall Mackenzie* provided Grantown-on-Spey (Badenoch and Strathspey) with the Grant Arms Hotel, a peaceful Baronial monster. Further N, *Thomson Sinclair*, the owner of John o' Groats (Caithness), designed an hotel there in 1875 as a deliberate reminder of the famed octagonal house supposed to have stood on the site in the C16. At Ballachulish (Lochaber) in 1877 *John Honeyman* designed a Gothic edifice for visitors to the W coast. The development of Kingussie (Badenoch and Strathspey) as a Speyside resort was marked in 1906 by the erection of *Alexander Cattanach*'s barge-boarded Duke of Gordon Hotel, whose air of relaxed comfort was repeated on a huge scale by *Cameron & Burnett*'s Highland Hotel at Strathpeffer (Ross and Cromarty) in 1909–11. But businessmen as well as travellers seem to have been expected to enjoy the Baronial splendour of *W. Hamilton Beattie*'s Grand Hotel at Lerwick (Shetland), 1886–7, and it is for businessmen that most of the purpose-built late C20 hotels have been developed. Even those at Aviemore seem designed to give the visitor a taste of the rigours of international business life rather than provide holiday relaxation.

HOUSING in towns and villages before the later C18 varied

from the substantial to the primitive. The poorer houses, often
present in large numbers, had walls and roofs of turf supported
by a cruck frame, like the dwellings of the rural peasantry. More
substantial houses, seldom of more than two storeys and an attic,
were built of stone, usually harled, with roofs sometimes of slate
but often of thatch or shingles. That the houses in Kirkwall
(Orkney) were 'for the most part slaited' was thought worthy of
note in 1726, while it was reported that Inverness had had no
slate-roofed house before the Treaty of Union of 1707. Upper
floors were often reached by an external forestair or, in the case
of the grander houses, by a stair contained in a projecting tower
or jamb. The smartest of these were the town houses built by
local lairds as retreats from the discomfort of rural life and as
places from which to conduct business. Tankerness House at
Kirkwall (Orkney) was begun in 1574 as a three-storey range
forming one side of a courtyard entered by an archway from the
main street; it was enlarged in the C18 and early C19 to a U-plan,
presumably to satisfy the increasing desire for comfort of the
Baikies, a family of merchant-lairds who acquired the property in
113 1641. The Frasers of Lovat built Abertarff House at Inverness in
1593, a crowstepped main block with a projecting stairtower.
Millars' House at Stromness (Orkney) of 1716 was dressed up
with an Artisan classical doorpiece carved with heraldry. A carved
heraldic panel surmounts the entrance to the Old Hall at Scalloway (Shetland) of *c.* 1750. As late as 1812, when most landowners kept or rented town houses in Edinburgh or London,
the Mackintoshes of Aberarder built one in Academy Street,
Inverness.

   The early C19 preference for regularly laid out streets whose
houses formed a unified whole made a limited mark on Highland.
At Thurso (Caithness) elevations were prepared *c.* 1800 for houses
115 in the newly formed Janet Street, all to be joined by colonnaded
links, but in the event deviations were permitted. At Inverness,
the more important of the workers on the Caledonian Canal were
housed in a unified terrace (Nos. 26–38 Telford Street), built *c.*
1806, and a shorter but flashier terrace was built in 1828 at Nos.
1–3 Portland Place. In Pulteneytown at Wick (Caithness) *Thomas
Telford*'s formal planning of 1808 is inexactly matched by the
architecture. Only at the mid-C19 Breadalbane Terrace is there
a unified curve of Georgian-survival houses set behind front
gardens. Unified terraces continued well into the Victorian period,
John Rhind giving Fortrose (Ross and Cromarty) a pretty Gothic
group at Nos. 17–21 High Street in 1869 and *Alexander Ross*
providing Gothic and Baronial houses in Ardross Terrace and
Ardross Street outside the w door of his St Andrew's Cathedral at
Inverness in 1872–81. In many of the new villages and fishertowns
stone cottages were built to standard designs and often with slated
roofs. C20 redevelopment has seen the widening of closes to allow
more light, giving some areas a mildly suburban air. Most startling
is the post-Modern sheltered housing scheme (The Glebe) tacked
onto the N end of Kingussie (Badenoch and Strathspey) by
G. R. M. Kennedy & Partners, 1982–3.

Every town acquired VILLAS in the C19. The best collections are at Inverness and Nairn, which show a varied display of styles, classical, castellated, Italianate and Gothic, sometimes juxtaposed on the same building. At the end of the C19 and the beginning of the C20 *W. L. Carruthers* gave Inverness the best array of Arts and Crafts suburban villas in Scotland. *W. R. Davidson*'s early C20 villas at Nairn are also Arts and Crafts, but without the same relaxed confidence. In the 1930s Inverness again led Scottish taste with the Dudok-inspired assemblages of white rendered box-shaped designs by *Carruthers Ballantyne, Cox & Taylor* in Culduthel Road. Their modernity is still striking, perhaps through lack of later competition.

116

118

RURAL BUILDINGS

The rural economy of Highland and the Islands until the beginning of the C19 was based on peasant agriculture. The fertile land was worked by tenants grouped together in 'townships', generally with the arable land enclosed by a dyke to keep out cattle (the principal form of livestock), which were turned out to graze on the pasture beyond if not taken to hill pasture further away. There was little security of tenure, and rents were paid in kind, often through an intermediary tacksman who held a tack or lease over a substantial part of an estate.

The most substantial building in any parish, besides the church and any laird's or tacksman's house, was usually the minister's manse. After 1663 there was a legal obligation on the heritors (landowners) of each parish to provide a 'competent' manse costing between £27 15s. 6d. and £83 6s. 8d. sterling.* An idea of the accommodation which might be provided by a manse at the end of the C17 is given by the local Presbytery's description of the late C17 manse at Kilmorack (Inverness) in 1713. It was of two storeys, the ground floor containing a hall, one large room, one smaller room, a closet and two store rooms, all in line, and the first floor four rooms. There was a wooden internal stair and a stone forestair. Each of the principal rooms had a fireplace (one a hanging lum) and the windows were either casements or fixed lights, some with shutters below the glass. There were also office houses containing the kitchen, brewhouse, stable and barn. Extensive as this accommodation was, the manse was not necessarily soundly built and was, indeed, replaced in 1750. As late as 1732 a new manse at Edderton (Ross and Cromarty) was built using clay rather than lime mortar, and manses in the early C18 were commonly built with turf roofs, e.g. the manses at Kiltearn (Ross and Cromarty) of 1708, Moy (Inverness) of 1717, Farr (Sutherland) of 1731, Dores (Inverness) of 1740, and Kincardine (Sutherland) of 1745. However, by *c.* 1730 a standard type of

*A legal decision in 1760 held that the upper limit did not apply to the rebuilding of a manse.

manse was coming to be accepted, a two-storey-and-attic rectangle of *c.* 12.2m. by 4.6m. internally, with offices (the kitchen,
stable and byre) contained in single-storey wings, the walls built
of stone with lime mortar and often harled, the roof of the main
block covered with slates. This standard type was the basis for
the design of the new manse built at Kingussie (Badenoch and
Strathspey) by the masons *Adam Brown, Thomas Clerk* and *John
Sanders* in 1726–9, its T-plan main block containing four main
rooms, two cellars and an attic, and projecting wings housing
the kitchen and stable. Similar was the manse built at Tongue
(Caithness) in 1731. It had four main rooms, a cellar, closet and
attic, and also wings containing the kitchen, stable and barn. The
internal partition walls of these two manses were of wood or lath
and plaster, but at Durness Manse (Sutherland) of 1727 the
ground-floor partitions were of stone. When a manse was built at
Glenelg (Skye and Lochalsh) in 1764, its ground-floor partitions
were again of stone but those of the first-floor were brick-built.
The manse at Creich (Sutherland) was given a roof of heather
thatch (much more durable than turf) as late as 1772, but in
general new manses after 1750 were slated, although new office
wings might still be given turf roofs, as at Kincardine (Sutherland)
in 1775 or Kilmuir Easter (Ross and Cromarty) in 1776. Sash
windows also became common in the C18, the earliest recorded
those at Durness Manse (Sutherland) in 1727. The manse at
Kilmonivaig (Lochaber) acquired a water closet in 1804.

Substantial farmhouses were a product of the revolution in
agriculture in the late C18 and early C19, which cleared the
peasantry from the more fertile land and created large farms, often
sheep walks, leased to men with access to capital and pretensions
to gentility. The houses built for these new Highland farmers were
substantial but plain, of two storeys, the walls constructed of stone
and lime mortar and often harled, the roofs slated. Usually they
contained five or six principal rooms, with the kitchen placed in
a back wing. Later in the C19 these farmhouses and parish manses
were often enlarged or rebuilt, sometimes with architectural
embellishments and usually with bay windows. Attics, formerly
barrack rooms lit only from windows in the gables, were divided
into small bedrooms, each with a dormer window.

The dwellings of the peasantry until the mid-C19 excited the
indignation of visitors, who described them as 'hovels'. They were
single-storey buildings, usually with a byre at one end and two
rooms, perhaps divided only by a bed, at the other. Heat was
provided by a peat fire on the floor, some of its smoke escaping
through a hole in the roof but most of it filling the dwelling end,
but largely excluded from the byre by a flattening of the roof pitch
at that end. The peat-impregnated roof covering was stripped in
whole or in part every few years, sometimes annually, and used
as a manure for potatoes.

The materials of these peasant houses varied according to local
availability or, perhaps more important, scarcity. In Orkney, Shetland and the Hebrides the walls were generally of drystone, the
houses on Skye and Barra (Lochaber) having their walls con-

structed of two skins of stone, with the cavity between filled with earth. Over much of the mainland of Highland the walls were built of thick sods of earth shaped as bricks. In the better-wooded parts of Badenoch and Strathspey, Inverness and Lochaber, these might be mounted against a frame of wooden stakes and wattle. In other areas the frame was of birch crucks joined at the top by wooden pins and longitudinally by thin pieces of wood. Some houses had their walls' lower part (*c.* 0.6–0.9m.) constructed of stone and the upper part (*c.* 0.9–1.2m.) built of turf. Roofs were covered generally with turf, often sliced thinly like slates, sometimes topped by straw, fern roots or heather. In Orkney and Shetland, houses were often thatched with straw or heather; but heather thatching, although producing a durable cover, was a skilled process and it was reported from western Sutherland in 1857 that no one there knew the art. The thatch was kept in place by ropes of plaited straw or heather weighted with stones, making the roof look, in James Boswell's phrase, 'like a lady's hair in papers'.

Cottages of more substantial construction, with mortared stone walls and slated roofs, were uncommon before the mid-C 19, even for workers on the large new farms. In 1855 the Tain (Ross and Cromarty) architect Andrew Maitland reported that:

I have done all in my power in this quarter [Easter Ross] to induce Proprietors and their Factors to improve Labourers Cottages but without success, – my proposals having been met with the answers, 'too good for them', 'ridicolous' [*sic*] &c &c.

As late as 1876 the houses of cottars on the estate of Balnagown (Ross and Cromarty) had walls built with clay mortar and turf roofs. But that was by then exceptional, and more than thirty years earlier the minister of Ardclach (Nairn) stated that in that parish:

The old turf hovels are everywhere fast disappearing; the smallest crofter now aims at building his comfortable and substantial cottage of stone and lime . . .

Progress was uneven across the area, but by the end of the C 19 even the still largely traditional houses in the Western Isles had acquired chimneys and windows in the walls instead of holes in the roof. Thatch continued to be used into the C 20 but was not infrequently replaced by corrugated iron, if not by slates or tiles.

The creation of large farms was accompanied by the provision of regularly laid-out steadings of farm offices. In the C 18 most office houses had been built of turf or of stone and turf, but in 1767 the Countess of Sutherland's Tutors were considering whether to rebuild the offices on the Mains Farm of Dunrobin (Sutherland) in turf or to put up a substantial steading designed by *John Adam*. In Orkney in 1808 there were said to be 'many substantial, convenient, and even some expensive, single and detached farm buildings, as barns, cow-houses, &c.' but, as yet, no 'regular court of farm offices'. However, by the same date the larger farms in Badenoch and Strathspey, Caithness, Inverness, Lochaber and Nairn had acquired new steadings laid out as

quadrangles, the ranges containing stables, byres, cartsheds, a
barn and horsemill. One of the grandest courtyard steadings is at
97 the Home Farm of Conan House (Ross and Cromarty), built in
1822, with a domed tower over the entrance pend. The mid-c19
steading at Balmacara (Skye and Lochalsh) has an Italianate
tower, and above the entrance to the steading of 1864 at Waternish, near Stein (Skye and Lochalsh), is an obelisk. Much
smaller but of picturesque presence is *Philip Webb*'s contemporary
steading at Borrodale Farm, near Arisaig (Lochaber). Quite
different is the powerful muscularity of the nine parallel crowstepped ranges of 1853 at Skelbo (Sutherland). One curiosity,
now demolished, was the steading on Raasay (Skye and Lochalsh)
designed by the factor *A. E. Stewart* in 1880 and built, together
with a range of cottages, entirely of corrugated iron. Pioneering
use of another new material, mass-concrete, for farm buildings
and cottages was made by *Samuel Barham* on the estate of Ard
tornish (Lochaber) from the 1870s.

INDUSTRIAL BUILDINGS

The chief industries in Highland and the Islands have traditionally
been agriculture and fishing. Fishing was promoted from the end
of the c18 by the British Fisheries Society and by local landowners. Storage of fish for export to southern markets required
either its refrigeration or smoking. Consequently, large ICE
HOUSES were constructed, often built into natural banks like the
row of early c19 vaulted ice houses along Harbour Quay at Wick
(Caithness), the contemporary salmon house beside Quay Brae
at Portree (Skye and Lochalsh) or the massive ice house at
Helmsdale (Sutherland). At Cromarty and Fortrose (Ross and
Cromarty) the ice houses sit above ground, their tunnel-vaulted
stone roofs originally covered by turf. CURING HOUSES for the
smoking of fish were built in the early c19. One of *c.* 1817 survives
beside the harbour at Helmsdale. A melancholy reminder of an
abandoned branch of the fishing industry is provided by the tall
brick chimney and ramps for hauling carcasses of the WHALING
STATION founded at Bunavoneader (Western Isles) in 1904.
   Agriculture until the c19 was largely for subsistence, but rents
to the landlord were paid, at least partly, in grain, which was
shipped s for sale. The STORE HOUSES built for this grain were
typically of two storeys, often with a forestair to the upper floor,
like the surviving examples from the 1640s at Burray and St
121 Mary's (Orkney). The store house built by *Alexander Stronach* in
1699 at Portmahomack (Ross and Cromarty) is purposefully
squat, its neighbour of 1779 (remodelled in the early c19) austerely elegant. MILLS for threshing grain have been common. In
the Northern and Western Isles several Norse or click mills
survive, e.g. at Dounby (Orkney) or Southvoe near Dunrossness
(Shetland). They were constructed with a horizontally mounted

wheel turned by water carried in a lade from a burn. Much more powerful were the water mills introduced by the later C18 with wooden or metal wheels mounted perpendicularly. Early examples can be found at Boardhouse near Birsay (Orkney) and Glendale (Skye and Lochalsh), both quite small. Of C19 mills Orkney has a plenitude, Tormiston Mill at Stenness of 1884–5 one of the best-preserved. Most are utilitarian, embellished perhaps with crowstepped gables, as at Golspie (Sutherland) of 1814 or Kergord Mill at Weisdale (Shetland) of 1855. The huge late C19 Ayre Mill at Kirkwall (Orkney) is exceptional in having a clearly defined centre and ends.

The late C18 regarded BREWERIES as potential sources of both profit and social improvement, their product a less harmful alternative to whisky. Two ranges survive of the former brewery built at Cromarty (Ross and Cromarty) c. 1785. Slightly later is the crowstepped Old Brewery at Thurso (Caithness). DIS- TILLERIES for the production of malt whisky became common in the late C19, their pagoda ventilators often a picturesque feature in townscape or landscape; but the Highland Park Distillery at Kirkwall (Orkney) is now one of the few whose C19 bonded stores still form a rubble-built procession beside the road.

A variety of other industries have been introduced to Highland, many short-lived. In 1755–6 the Trustees for Encouraging and Improving Linen Manufacture in Highlands of Scotland built a LINEN FACTORY at New Kelso near Lochcarron (Ross and Cromarty), but the experiment was abandoned little more than thirty years later. A large quadrangular ROPEWORKS, three of its four ranges still standing, was built at Cromarty (Ross and Cromarty) in 1773–6. A COTTON MILL built at Spinningdale (Sutherland) in 1792–4, architecturally smart with end towers and Venetian windows, was abandoned after a fire in 1806. At Brora (Sutherland) COAL MINING was undertaken for a short period after 1598, then again in 1813–28 and between 1872 and 1970, the two C19 mining operations accompanied by the manufacture of bricks and the last by the construction of an engineering works (later converted to a woollen mill). Inverness contained FOUN- DRIES in the C19, the Rose Street Foundry's front block (by *Ross & Macbeth*, 1893) decorated with mosaics depicting the activity inside. In 1896 an ALUMINIUM WORKS was founded at Foyers (Inverness), being followed by other works opened at Kinlochleven (Lochaber) in 1909 and Fort William (Lochaber) in 1928 and a smelter built at Invergordon (Ross and Cromarty) in 1969–70. A PAPER MILL was established at Corpach (Lochaber) in 1963–6. The off-shore OIL INDUSTRY has given Shetland the Sullom Voe Terminal, opened in 1982. Much smaller but perhaps a presage of future developments is the HY- DROPONICUM built at Achiltibuie (Ross and Cromarty) in 1984.

DAMS were built to provide hydro-electric power for the early C20 aluminium works, Kinlochleven being served by the Black- water Dam, begun in 1904, and Fort William by dams across the N end of Loch Treig and the W end of Loch Laggan, completed in 1934. In 1943 an Act of Parliament established the North of

Scotland Hydro-Electric Board to bring electricity to the general populace. Of the resulting dams one of the most impressive for uncompromising functionalism is at Mullardoch (Inverness), by *Kennedy & Donkin* and *Sir William Halcrow & Partners*, 1947–52. The accompanying POWER STATIONS, e.g. those by *James Shearer*, 1951–2, at Gruidie near Lochluichart (Ross and Cromarty) and Fasnakyle (Inverness) or by *Robert Hurd & Partners*, 1958–63, at Aigas and Kilmorack (Inverness), are modern-traditional, their crazy-paved rubble walls decorated with carved reliefs. Unequivocally of its time is the nuclear power station at Dounreay (Caithness), begun in 1955, the fast reactor housed in a giant golfball.

BADENOCH AND STRATHSPEY

A district which for most of its length presents a contrast between the fertile and well-wooded valley of the Spey and the surrounding bare heights of the Cairngorm and Monadhliath Mountains. Badenoch was one of Scotland's great medieval lordships, held by the Anglo-Norman family of the Comyns from *c.* 1229 to 1306 and then granted by Robert I to his close ally, Randolph, Earl of Moray, and by Robert II to his illegitimate son, Alexander, Earl of Buchan, famous or infamous as the 'Wolf of Badenoch'. After 1452 the Earls of Huntly (later, Dukes of Gordon) were the most powerful landowners in the area, but other families, notably the Macphersons in the s of the district and the Grants to the N, established themselves as substantial lairds. In the C18, attempts at 'improvement' were begun with the introduction of new agricultural methods and the layout of planned villages at Grantown-on-Spey and Kingussie. 'Improvement' continued in the C19, when the district began to develop as a place for salubrious holidays after the opening of the railway from Perth to Aviemore in 1863. The C20 has seen improvement of the main Edinburgh–Inverness road (the A9) running through the district and, less welcomed by some, the creation of a year-round tourist resort at Aviemore, the unsunny Benidorm of Highland.

ALVIE

8000

Parish Church and manse in isolation beside Loch Alvie.

FREE CHURCH. *See* Kincraig.

PARISH CHURCH. A long rectangle built in 1798, harled except for the w gable, which is of granite ashlar. Round-arched windows in the s wall and gables, the w with a bellcote, the E ball-finialled. Interior altered in 1880 by *John Rhind*, whose varnish was stripped off in 1952. – MONUMENTS on the N wall. Lillian B. Henschel † 1901, a marble relief bust signed by *E. Onslow Ford.* – James Anderson, a bronze relief portrait signed by *Frank Lynn Jenkins*, 1914.

Former MANSE to the NW, built by *John MacCulloch*, carpenter at Kingussie, in 1807–9 and baronialized by *Thomas Mackenzie* 1847–8.

KINRARA. *See* p. 92.

ARDVERIKIE
12.6km. sw of Laggan

Huge villa-like shooting lodge designed by *John Rhind* and built
for Sir John Ramsden in 1874–9, incorporating a wing which
had been added to the previous house on the site for Queen
Victoria's visit in 1847. Mostly of two and three storeys, a
relentlessly asymmetrical display of canted bays, broad-eaved
gables, round and octagonal towers with machicolations under
their witch's-cap slate roofs, and even a turret corbelled out
from a squinch arch. The effect, despite the corbelling, transomed windows, Tudorish hoodmoulds and occasional crosslet
arrowslits, is more *cottage orné* than Baronial. Or would be, were
it not for the E tower which rises above it all. This is Baronial
with a vengeance, rising sheer for four storeys from a strongly
battered base to a powerfully corbelled battlement with bartizans at the E corners, unequal-sized turrets at the W. Inside
the battlement, a tall cap-house, its gables adorned with stepped
crenellations, their merlons extravagantly tall and close-set.
On top of the cap-house's E face, a small battlemented turret
designed to carry a flagstaff.

(Inside, a neo-Jacobean stairhall, its walls decorated with low
reliefs of sporting equipment carved by *William Ramage* for the
Duke of Sussex's dining room in Kensington Palace and bought
by Ramsden in 1875. Panelled library, its chimneypiece's overmantel flanked by caryatids. It is set in an inglenook whose
roundheaded arch springs from Corinthian columns. Barley-
sugar colonnettes on the bookcases.)

LODGE to the E, apparently of the 1870s and by *Rhind*. Broad
eaves, transomed windows and a jettied upper floor. Round NE
tower with machicolated eaves to its witch's-cap roof. Across
the N front, a slated canopy, its wooden brackets decorated with
pendants.

AULTMORE
1.7km. NE of Nethybridge

Very polite neo-Georgian harled mansion designed by *C. H. B.
Quennell* and built for the owner of a Moscow department store
in 1912–14. Two storeys and an attic with prominent segmental-
topped dormer windows and tall chimneys along the piended
roofs. Entrance front of eleven bays, the outer pair recessed at
each end, the W ground-floor window a Venetian. Otherwise
the elevation is symmetrical, with the main block's three-bay
centrepiece given tall and narrow pilasters carrying an urn-
topped parapet into which a small open pediment breaks up.
Over the door, a scrolly pediment broken by an urn. From the
ends of this front low balustraded screen walls step forward to
end in square ogee-roofed garden pavilions, their inspiration
those at Sir William Bruce's Kinross House (Tayside). Discreet
but unbalancing E addition of 1922. The long S front is quiet.
Two-bay piend-roofed projections flanking the centre, across

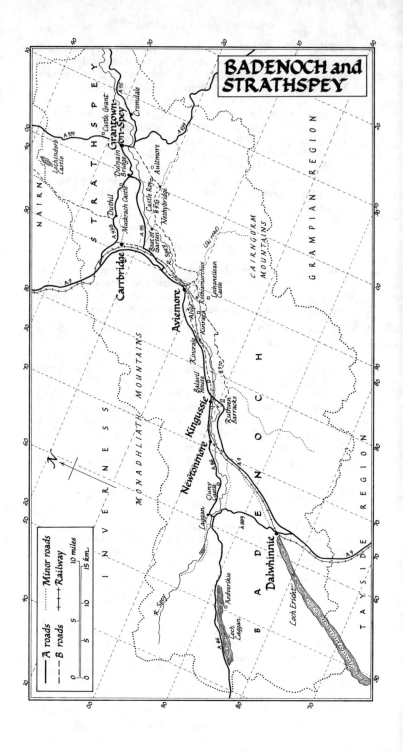

which has been added a pilastered and balustraded glazed loggia, its doorpiece pedimented. W gable dressed up with pilasters and a pediment. Inside, marble chimneypieces of best late C18 type, but are they Georgian or neo-Georgian?

To the NE, a short harled range of buildings of *c.* 1915 stepping uphill. At its lower (W) end, a two-bay ASSEMBLY HALL with straight skews at the gable and tall windows rising into piended dormerheads. Attached to its E end, a projecting piend-roofed cottage (CURLEW). Then a double cottage (KESTREL and OSPREY), again piend-roofed.

At the entrance to the drive from the W, a LODGE by *Quennell* of 1912–14, neo-Georgian but with a bay window; pair of granite GATEPIERS.

8010

AVIEMORE

A late Victorian village which grew up after the opening of the railway to Perth in 1863 and its extension to Inverness in 1898. Expansion to the N came in the 1920s and 1930s; the tourist complex for which it is now known was begun in 1963.

ST ANDREW'S CHURCH. By *James Gilbert*, 1899–1901. Economical Gothic in granite.

RAILWAY STATION. By *William Roberts*, 1898. The biggest (excepting Inverness) of the Highland Railway Company's stations, and the most accomplished. Wooden main offices on the W platform, which is covered by a double-pitched awning; wheel decoration in the spandrels of the brackets springing from cast-iron columns. Shorter free-standing awning of the same type on the island platform to the E. Lattice-girder footbridge. To the N, an engine shed of 1896, also by *Roberts*.

SCHOOL. By *Douglas Calder*, 1968. Self-indulgent grouping of shallow monopitch roofs.

DESCRIPTION

W of the A9 is the tourist development begun in the 1960s, poorly laid out and architecturally undistinguished. Its core is provided by two hotels, the seven-storey FOUR SEASONS with a silly monopitch roof, and the butterfly-plan BADENOCH, the STRATHSPEY THEATRE, and ICE RINK, all by *J. G. L. Poulson*, 1965–6. To the N, barracks-like POST HOUSE HOTEL by *Nelson Foley* in association with *Sir John Burnet, Tait & Partners*, 1970–1.

The older village lines the main road. At its S, the Railway Station (*see* above). Opposite, the CAIRNGORM HOTEL of *c.* 1900, bargeboarded with a conical-roofed tower at one end, is followed by late Victorian shops and a couple of villas. Late C20 shantytown ensues, but then comes the interwar local authority housing begun by *Alexander Cattanach* in 1921, traditional two-storey blocks with steep gablets, admirably unfussy, with the church sitting dourly in the middle. More late

Victorian villas across the road. At the village's N end, bleak housing by *Douglas Calder*, 1968.

BALAVIL HOUSE
3.5km. NE of Kingussie

7000

Badly altered country house designed by *R. & J. Adam* and built in 1790–6 for James Macpherson, the 'translator' and part author of the works of Ossian. Surprisingly, given its Highland setting and Macpherson's part in the romantic movement, it is not in the Adams' castle style but unequivocally classical. All harled with ashlar dressings. Entrance front on the N and originally austere. Main block of three storeys with strip quoins at the corners and bandcourses delineating the floors. Seven bays, the centre three slightly advanced under an ashlar pediment. In the middle of the second floor, the coat of arms of Macpherson with flanking swags. Pompous balustraded porch with urn finials added by *W. L. Carruthers* in 1899. The steep pediments over most of the first-floor windows date from *Mac-Gibbon & Ross*'s reconstruction of the house in 1904–5 after a fire. Low range of offices on the E built by the mason *James Russell* in 1823 and raised to two storeys and an attic by Mac-Gibbon & Ross.

The show front is on the S overlooking the Spey valley, but the main block's symmetry is badly jolted by the pyramid-roofed tower added to the E gable in 1904–5, and much of the delicacy of the Adams' detailing has been smothered by alterations. The 1790s design was swishly sophisticated. Seven bays, the broad ends slightly advanced with giant Ionic pilasters rising from the first floor to support rosetted friezes. In each end, a three-light window at the ground floor. First-floor window, again of three lights but taller and crowned by an overall semicircular fanlight. Under the attic window, a bandcourse carved with guilloche enrichment. At the five-bay centre, another rosetted frieze. Central window of three lights, but its fanlight is segmental-arched. In *Carruthers*' alterations of 1899, the ends' attic windows were heightened, the broad centre was given a heavy balustrade broken by pedimented stone dormers and a large balustraded bay window was added each side of the door. Carruthers' flimsy-looking porch has since been removed and replaced by French windows.*

BALAVIL MAINS on lower ground to the SW. Early C19 farmhouse of two storeys and three bays, with a low courtyard steading behind. – Italianate WEST LODGE just to the SW again but cut off by the new line of the A9. It is of 1864–5, by *Peddie & Kinnear*, single-storey L-plan with a pedimented portico and Venetian window. – On a hillock beside it, a smart classical MONUMENT of *c.* 1800 to James Macpherson. Urn-finialled slate obelisk, its N face bearing a white marble crest.

---

*The Adams' designs show a columned doorpiece.

Plinth of white marble with a grey marble cornice. On the plinth's N front, a relief portrait bust of Macpherson, on its S a mourning lady.

9010　　　　# BOAT OF GARTEN

Small village developed in the late C 19 and early C 20 with a sprinkling of villas among the humbler dwellings.

St Columba's Church. Bargeboarded broad Gothic box of 1900 with a diagonally set slate-spired bellcote.

Public Hall. Dated 1896 and very like the contemporary hall at Dulnain Bridge, with continuous hoodmoulding linking the round-arched openings in the bargeboarded gable front.

Railway Station. By *William Roberts*, 1904. Wooden offices with a stone cottage at one end. Lattice-girder footbridge of standard Highland Railway type.

9020　　　　# CARRBRIDGE

Late C 19 vernacular village reached by the railway in 1898, the large Hotel at the N end being extended in 1892 and 1911.

Church. Originally United Free. By *Alexander Cullen* of Hamilton,* 1909. Like a squat institute, with a flattened ogee-cupolaed ventilator on the roof. Bellcote above the porch to show it is a church.

Hall. By *John Robertson*, 1892. Broad-eaved and broad-gabled, with round-arched door and windows.

Landmark Visitor Centre. By *John L. Paterson*, 1969–70. Large but quite at home in its forest setting. Round brick auditorium contained within an octagonal exhibition space clad in dark-stained wood. Wooden cladding continues along the foyer, which links to the angular funnel-shaped restaurant whose fully glazed bay window looks E over an artificial lochan to the Cairngorms.

Railway Station. 1898 and presumably by *William Roberts*. Wooden buildings, the E with a verandah on the platform side. Lattice-girder footbridge of standard Highland Railway type.

0020　　　　# CASTLE GRANT
2.3km. NE of Grantown-on-Spey

Mansion house with two faces, to the S harled and rugged with just a touch of civility, to the N ashlar austerity. The lands of Freuchie were acquired by Duncan Grant, son of a Sheriff of Inverness, *c.* 1450; but there is no mention of a tower here

---

Alexander Cattanach of Kingussie was executant architect.

before 1536, and it is likely that the earliest part of the present house is of about that date. It formed a substantial L-plan, the square jamb projecting to the s and w. Crowstep-gabled main block, probably originally of three storeys and an attic. In the SE inner angle, a round turret corbelled out above the ground floor. On the jamb, a corbelled battlement within which rose a cap-house. Repairs and alterations were made to this house in 1629 and 1649, and the jamb's cap-house may have been heightened at that time.

In 1694 Ludovick Grant of Freuchie had his lands erected into a regality,* thereafter styling himself 'of Grant' and renaming his house Castle Grant. This may have been the spur for its remodelling and enlargement, the main block being heightened by one floor, the windows of its s front enlarged and regularized and a central entrance provided, probably replacing one in the inner angle. At the same time a four-storey-and-attic addition was built across the E gable, projecting both to the N and to the s, where it roughly balanced the C16 sw jamb, whose turret was also echoed in a turret rising from the ground in the new inner angle. The s court thus formed had low office ranges either side to the edge of a terrace reached by a flight of steps.

By the mid-C18 the roughly symmetrical house fashioned in the late C17 must have appeared old-fashioned; in 1753–6 Sir Ludovick Grant of Grant employed *John Adam* to remodel and enlarge it. Adam turned the house round, adding a new front 80 block right across the N elevation. This is wonderfully severe, a four-storey seven-bay front built of granite ashlar, the hierarchy of rooms behind shown by the large first- and second-floor windows and the square windows at the third floor. Round-arched door in the centre, its rusticated quoins reinforcing rather than relieving the severity. Piended platform roof over both the N addition and the older house. At the same time Adam rebuilt the s court's E range as a piend-roofed kitchen block, its five-bay front provided with round-arched openings at the ground floor, their projecting imposts another muscular note, the door placed in a fanlit overarch; small horizontal windows above. He also thickened the crowstepped gable of the main late C17 addition to take the new kitchen flue. The new interiors were not finished until 1765–6 (and then economically), Adam again acting as architect. More lavish decoration in several rooms was provided, *c.* 1830, a likely date for the addition of an iron first-floor balcony on the E. Perhaps at the same time this side's top-floor windows were given stone dormerheads.

The interior is a mixture of periods. Vaulted ground-floor rooms in the C16 and C17 work. At the centre of Adam's N addition, a restrained entrance hall of 1765–6. To its w, his stairhall. Cantilevered stone stair; balustrade with foliaged iron scrolls. The ceiling's modillion cornice is of the 1760s, as presumably is its umbrella-rose with foliage sprouting from the

---

*An area in which the laird had legal powers over all matters except high treason.

spokes. The whole of the C 16 main block's first floor is filled
by the dining room, a late C 17 remodelling of the original hall
with heavily moulded fielded panelling on the walls. Is the wood
panelled ceiling also C 17 or of *c.* 1830? Late C 19 grotesquely
carved neo-Jacobean chimneypieces at the ends. To the E, the
ante-chamber and drawing room produced in an early C 19
remodelling of the late C 17 state bedchamber and drawing
room, both with blowsy anthemion and palmette friezes and
early C 19 marble chimneypieces, that of the drawing room with
coupled pilasters topped by eagles grasping dead rabbits. N of
the drawing room, the charter room, its iron door and shutters
provided by John Adam in 1766. In the centre of the N front,
the library, its wood panelled walls and coffered segmental vault
probably of *c.* 1830.

WEST LODGE by *G. Fowler Jones* of York, 1845, purposefully
martial, the octagonal base of its candle-snuffer-roofed round
corner tower echoed by a battlemented octagon across the
drive. – EAST LODGE of 1864, built against the railway
embankment and a gift of the Inverness & Perth Railway Co.
Baronial, with a fat round conical-roofed NW tower from whose
upper floor the Earl of Seafield* could 'step out . . . and get into
the train in passing.' Castellated RAILWAY BRIDGE to the W
by *Joseph Mitchell*, 1863. – Over the entrance to the drive to the
castle, a castellated GATEWAY of 1864, looking like part of a
stage-set. – In the park to the NE, a castellated BRIDGE over
the former railway line, probably of 1863, by Mitchell.

0020
CASTLE ROY
1.3km. N of Nethybridge

Very simple castle of enclosure on a small hill overlooking the
Spey. It was built, probably for the Comyns, in the early C 13.
Walls of rubble brought to courses by flat pinnings surround a
courtyard 24m. by 15m. in which were wooden structures built
against the walls. NW corner tower, probably an addition, which
projects only minimally to the N but quite boldly to the W.
There seems to have been a first-floor window in its N face. In
the main enclosure's N wall, a large off-centre gateway, its
pointed rear-arch still surviving. Remains of a postern gate in
the W wall beside the tower. Inside, at the main W wall's S end,
a recess, perhaps for a fireplace.

6090
CLUNY CASTLE
3km. E of Laggan

Lighthearted castellated-classical villa built for the Macphersons
of Cluny in 1805, the S front of grey granite ashlar, the sides
and back of rubble. All round the two-storey-and-basement

---

*Sir Lewis Grant of Grant had inherited that peerage in 1811.

main block, a corbelled battlement with stone-spired bartizans
at the corners. More bartizans at the three-bay s front's centrepiece, which is enclosed in a thin frame, its uprights rising from
red sandstone bases and crossed by Ionic capitals; above these
the frame continues its rise without any hint of an entablature,
a very early post-classical joke. Three-light first-floor windows.
In the outer bays, overarched Venetian windows at the ground
floor; Queen Anne porch added by *W. L. Carruthers* in 1891.
On the sides, broad bows at the front ends. Single-storey wings
enclosing a back court. Plain NW wing with bartizans but no
battlement, by *Alexander Mackenzie*, 1908. (Inside, in the
entrance hall, a coffered-vaulted plaster ceiling with a centre
pendant. Engaged Corinthian columns at the sideboard recess
in the former dining room at the sw.)

CROMDALE   *0020*

Church and manse alone beside the Spey.

PARISH CHURCH. Standard late Georgian kirk built of harl-
pointed granite in 1812. Birdcage bellcote. Rectangular
windows in the gables; in the side walls, round-arched windows,
their wooden tracery inserted in 1892–3 by *Ross & Macbeth*,
who also added the vestry at the E. In the s wall, high above the
door, a reused armorial stone with the initials WG and BG and
the date 1602. Interior recast in 1892–3. – STAINED GLASS. E
window (Christ the Good Shepherd) by *Alexander Strachan*,
1952.
    Harled MANSE to the E, built in 1834, its box dormers added
in the C20.
BRIDGE. Built in 1921 and very utilitarian, the iron superstructure
carried on concrete piers.

DALWHINNIE   *6080*

Late Victorian distillery village in the middle of moorland.

CHURCH. Secularized. By *Alexander Mackenzie*, 1897. Villa-
Gothic with a slate-spired bellcote. – MANSE behind, by *J. D.
Swanston*, 1902.
DISTILLERY. Extensive white-painted late C19 range, with a pair
of pagoda ventilators in the middle.
RAILWAY STATION. By *Joseph Mitchell & Co.*, 1864, with a
lattice-girder footbridge of the usual Highland Railway type.

DULNAIN BRIDGE   *9020*

Scrappy hamlet on both sides of the Spey.

CHURCH. Built for the United Free Church in 1904. Broad
granite ashlar box with a spired bellcote.

CHURCH HALL. Pink and grey corrugated-iron mission church of 1912, with a small bellcote on the gable.

HALL AND INSTITUTE. Dated 1896 and very like the contemporary hall at Boat of Garten. Bargeboarded gable front, the round-arched door and windows linked by a continuous hoodmould.

MUCKRACH CASTLE. *See* p. 95.

DUN-DA-LAMH *see* LAGGAN

9020

DUTHIL

Upland hamlet beside the Parish Church.

PARISH CHURCH. Disused. Tall harled box built in 1826. Chamfered granite margins at the large rectangular windows. On the W gable, a bellcote with cusped openings and a flowery finial. (Interior recast by *P. MacGregor Chalmers*, 1913–14. – STAINED GLASS window by *Gordon Webster*, 1949.)

53   Immediately E, SEAFIELD MAUSOLEUM by *William H. Playfair*, 1837. Very sturdy granite ashlar Greek cross. Round-arched recess in each front, the N and S containing doorways. Angle buttresses and a heavy crenellated parapet, its S face carved with a coat of arms. Just outside the graveyard, a replica Mausoleum built by *R. Dow* in 1884.

To the W, harled former MANSE of 1837–8, with a consoled doorpiece at the porch.

GARVAMORE *see* LAGGAN

0020

GRANTOWN-ON-SPEY

Planned village founded by Sir Ludovick Grant of Grant in 1765, when leases of building plots were offered for sale. The first houses were built the next year, as was a brewery erected 'on purpose to keep the people from drinking spiritous liquors', its success in this perhaps one cause of the village's late C18 prosperity as a centre for shopkeepers and craftsmen. C19 development followed Queen Victoria's 'very amusing and never to be forgotten visit' of 1860 and the railway's arrival three years later. Grantown became a police burgh in 1898 and still serves as a local commercial and holiday centre.

CHURCHES

BAPTIST CHURCH, High Street. Plain lancet-windowed box of 1851 reconstructed and refronted by *John Robertson*, 1900–1.

Robertson's Dec front of dark whinstone and white sandstone dressings is divided by pinnacled buttresses into a 'nave' gable, narrow w 'aisle' and e tower squashed by a thin Germanic slated spire.

FREE CHURCH, Woodside Road. Disused. By *Brown & Watt*, 1898, a lanceted box hiding behind a lumpy Gothic front; needle-spired flèche for a touch of elegance.

INVERALLAN PARISH CHURCH, Mossie Road. Built in 1884–6 as a memorial to the seventh and eighth Earls of Seafield and designed by their estate architect, *Alexander Smith*. Formally sited at the top of Church Avenue, it is a large cruciform on plan but architecturally indecisive. The E transept's birdcage bellcote suggests a late Georgian kirk, but its detail is Victorian Gothic, and a Georgian bellcote would usually have been at one end of the body of the church and not on an 'aisle'. The w transept is inexplicably lower. Even more disconcerting is the mixture of detail. Most of the windows are plain lancets, some with Y-tracery, but those in the ends of the nave, chancel and w transept and the nave's gableted E window are filled with baroque tracery incorporating the initials of the dead earls and of the seventh Earl's widow, Caroline. The effect is at its most jarring at the nave's s gable, whose exuberant window is juxtaposed with a mechanical Gothic doorway.

The interior is a huge ashlar-walled space unbroken by aisles and only just interrupted by the elliptical stone arch into the w transept. Elaborately engineered open wooden roofs across the broad spans. It is sparingly but expensively furnished. – s GALLERY FRONT with restrained baroque cartouches in the end panels. In the long centre panel, the Lord's Prayer. – On the wall below, early C17 PANELLING, formerly in the House 35 of Shillochan. The top row of panels is carved with the arms of prominent families of NE Scotland accompanied by identifying inscriptions. In the two rows below, roses, thistles and decorative patterns. Between the rows, carved verses from the Psalms. – PULPIT made up from Italian carving said to have 48 come from a chest, the pedimented back carrying the date 1639. Terms and deep relief foliage. On the centre panel, a relief of the Presentation of Our Lord in the Temple. – On the w side of the entrance to the chancel, a CLOCK whose carved wood surround is again dated 1639 and probably from the same source as the pulpit's woodwork. – Marble MONUMENTS in the chancel. On the E wall, seventh Earl of Seafield † 1881, with a bust; on the w, eighth Earl of Seafield † 1884, with a relief portrait. – ORGAN by *H. Hilsdon Ltd*, 1925; rebuilt by *A. F. Edmondstone*, 1981.

Humble Gothic late C19 HALL across the road.

ST COLUMBA (Episcopal), High Street. By *Ross & Macbeth*, 1892–3. Small granite rectangle with a flèche. Hammer-beam roof inside. – STAINED GLASS of *c.* 1900. Three-light E window (the Crucifixion). In the s wall, one light (St Cecilia).

PUBLIC BUILDINGS

COURTHOUSE, The Square. Plain Tudor Gothic, by *Matthews &
Lawrie*, 1867.

IAN CHARLES HOSPITAL, Castle Road. Built in 1884 by Caroline Countess of Seafield as a memorial to her son and presumably designed by *Alexander Smith*, the architect for the
Seafield estates. Very plain, of whinstone. Late C20 additions
to the E.

OLD SPEY BRIDGE, 1.5km. SE. Built as a military bridge in
1754. Rough ashlar. Three segmental arches increasing in size
towards the S, the tiny N arch rebuilt after the Spey flood of 1829.
Triangular cutwaters broached to semi-octagonal refuges. It
is now tied together by railway girders.

SCHOOL, South Street. By *A. Marshall Mackenzie*, 1875. Sprawl-
ing, with mild Italianate detail.

SPEY BRIDGE, 0.9km. S. By *Blyth & Blyth*, 1929–31. Huge
reinforced concrete arch of 73.2m. span. Semi-octagonal cutwaters at the ends.

102 SPEYSIDE ORPHAN HOSPITAL, The Square. Now Speyside
House. Built in 1824; its site and appearance are both suitable
for a town house. Five-bay front of granite ashlar, the centre
advanced and carried up as a four-storey tower, its third stage's
corners crowned with urns, the top stage an ogee-domed belfry.
At the tower's first floor, a Venetian window; at the second, a
tripartite.

VICTORIA CHRISTIAN INSTITUTE, High Street. Now
Y.M.C.A. Community Centre. Dated 1897. Gable front with
a conical-roofed turret on the l.

DESCRIPTION

The first incident on the entry from the W is the CRAIGLYNNE
HOTEL, two late C19 villas (the r. with prettily carved
bargeboards) joined by a twin-towered block of *c.* 1900. St
Columba's Episcopal Church (*see* Churches, above) stands
at the beginning of HIGH STREET, whose undemonstrative
granite-built C19 vernacular is interrupted but not challenged
by *McLeod Building Ltd*'s development (SOUTH-WEST HIGH
STREET) of 1986. After the Baptist Church and Victoria Christian Institute (*see* Churches and Public Buildings, above), late
Georgian is the architectural norm, broken by some intrusions.
On the l., the ROYAL BANK OF SCOTLAND, an Italianate villa
dated 1864 and signed with the initials of *Peddie & Kinnear*.
Sub-Baronial BEN MHOR HOTEL of 1902. On the r., Nos.
34–38 of *c.* 1900 with Art Nouveauish oriels. Nearly at the S
side's end, the large but plain late C19 spread of the PALACE
HOTEL. Opposite, a late Victorian POST OFFICE with a
French-roofed turret corbelled out of the centre of its front,
followed by the Georgian-survival BANK OF SCOTLAND (by
Matthews & Lawrie, 1865–7) at the corner with The Square.

THE SQUARE, a long rectangle, is Grantown's civic centre but an architectural jumble. The N side is bisected by Church Avenue, focused on Inverallan Parish Church (*see* above). At the Avenue's base, the WAR MEMORIAL by *A. Marshall Mackenzie & Son*, 1922, a granite Doric column, the pedestal bearing the bronze relief of a kilted soldier. To its E, after a block dated 1884, the Georgian-survival MORLICH HOUSE, built as the National Bank in 1851, is followed by a Tudorish villa of 1866. At the corner, the Edwardian GARTH HOTEL, cottagey in white harl with black trimmings. The Square's S side should have the Speyside Orphan Hospital (*see* above) on the axis of Church Avenue, but it is off-centre. To its E, the GRANT ARMS HOTEL, pacific Baronial by *A. Marshall Mackenzie*, 1873–5, later extended E in a tamer version of the original style. Three late C18 vernacular houses at the E end. CASTLE ROAD is the way out, its Georgian vernacular giving way to 1930s local authority housing. In BURNFIELD AVENUE to the S, BURNFIELD, an early C19 Tudor *cottage orné*.

CASTLE GRANT. *See* p. 82.

KINCRAIG

Informal village well studded with villas built after the railway's arrival in 1863.

ALVIE FREE CHURCH, 1.4km. NE. Now a house (KIRKBEAG). Georgian-survival kirk of 1851 with roundheaded windows and a gableted bellcote.

INSH PARISH CHURCH, 0.5km. E. A long white harled rectangle, perhaps early C18 in origin but given its present form in 1792. Birdcage bellcote on the N gable. The roundheaded windows' intersecting wooden tracery dates from *W. Schomberg Scott*'s restoration of 1963. Very simple interior, the galleries removed and the pulpit shifted from the W wall to the S end in 1912, probably the date of the wooden ceiling, its ribs springing from consoles. Late Victorian varnished PEWS. – ENGRAVED GLASS S window by *Helen Turner*, 1963, depicting St John's Cross, Iona (Strathclyde). – In a recess in the W wall, bronze BELL of *c.* 900, flanked by wrought-iron silhouettes of doves of 1963.

KINCRAIG UNITED FREE CHURCH (now Badenoch Christian Centre). Humble Gothic by *Alexander Cattanach*, 1909.

ST DROSTAN'S CHAPEL, 1.3km. SW. Roofless chapel in a small graveyard. It is probably C16, a rubble-built rectangle with round-arched windows. In the late C18 it became a mausoleum, the W gable dressed up with a large granite ashlar doorway, its imposts bearing tablets, one recording that it was built at the desire and expense of Captain George Mackintosh † 1780, late of the 60th Regiment of Foot, the other (now on the ground) carved with a crossed sword and scabbard.

KINCRAIG HOUSE, 0.5km. NW. Classy laird's house of the late C18. Main block of two storeys and an attic. Slightly advanced centre, with urn finials on its blocking course and a first-floor

Venetian window; Victorian porch. Each side, a barely projecting single-storey wing, a Venetian window in its front gable.

₇₀₀₀   KINGUSSIE

A Speyside village built on land formerly belonging to the Duke
of Gordon, who offered plots for sale in 1799. The layout was a
simple gridiron bounded by High Street on the N and Spey Street
on the S, with cross-streets provided by Ruthven Road, King
Street and Duke Street. Although intended as a centre of woollen
manufacture it failed to prosper, and in 1861 Queen Victoria
found it 'a very straggling place with very few cottages.' The
opening of the railway to Perth in 1863 and its extension to
Inverness in 1898 brought new prosperity and development as a
holiday centre, a role which continues, though Kingussie is now
dwarfed by the brasher Aviemore.

CHURCHES

FREE CHURCH, Ruthven Road. Desperately plain Gothic, by
  Matthews & Lawrie, 1877–9.
OUR LADY AND ST COLUMBA (R.C.), Newtonmore Road. By
  John Burnet, Son & Dick, 1930, in the blocky Romanesque style
  first used by John J. Burnet more than thirty years before. The
  squat nave is largely hidden from the street by the presbytery
  added in the 1950s. Half-timbering in the NW porch's gable. E
  tower (containing the chancel) as wide as the nave. Above
  the chancel, marked off by a semicircular stone arch, a semi-
  octagonal ceiling. – STAINED GLASS. In the nave and chancel,
  figures of saints of *c.* 1970. – In the small N chapel, two-light E
  window of *c.* 1935 containing angels.
PARISH CHURCH, High Street. Harled box built in 1792 with
  roundheaded windows and a birdcage bellcote. The interior,
  gutted by fire in 1924, was restored in 1926 and altered again
  in 1971. – Wooden PULPIT, the panels carved with Celtic
  motifs by *James Angus*, 1926. – STAINED GLASS E window (the
  Crucifixion) by *C. E. Kempe & Co. Ltd*, *c.* 1926. – ORGAN by
  Evans & Barr.
    In the graveyard, to the W of the church, a white marble
  MONUMENT to Lucy McEwen Haslam † 1904; its niche houses
  a small marble statue of the Madonna and Child signed by *E. R.
  Mullins*, 1881. – E of the church, a large classical MONUMENT to
  James Macpherson of Belleville † 1833, of granite with Coade
  stone paterae, their centres modelled as faces, at the ends; big
  urn on top.
ST COLUMBA (Episcopal), Spey Street. Disused. By *Ross &
  Macbeth*, 1903. Lancet Gothic in pink sandstone, a lead-covered
  flèche on the roof.
UNITED FREE CHURCH (now Church House and Chapel of St
  Andrew), King Street. By *Alexander Cattanach*, 1908–9.
  Ambitious but unloveable. A large buttressed box, its broad

bulk disguised by the E front, which is dressed up with pinnacled
corner towers of differing height and width. Mechanical Dec
detail.

PUBLIC BUILDINGS

CLOCKTOWER, East Terrace. Dated 1925. Quite small but
prominently sited tower with machicolated battlements.
DISTRICT COUNCIL CHAMBERS AND COURTHOUSE, High
Street. By *Matthews & Lawrie*, 1864, a Georgian-survival villa
very like their near-contemporary Courthouse at Portree (Skye
and Lochalsh).
DRILL HALL, High Street. Dated 1911. Single-storey, mixing
early and late C17 classical detail.
HIGH SCHOOL, Ruthven Road. By *Allan Ross & Allan*, 1970,
with extension and alterations of 1991 by *Highland Regional
Council*.
PRIMARY SCHOOL, Ruthven Road. By *William Lawrie*, 1874–6.
Gothic front, the gabled ends each containing a stepped
three-lancet window under a trefoil vent. Tall bellcote over
the centre porch. Tactful rear additions of 1893 (by *Alexander
Mackenzie*), 1895, 1900, and by *Alexander Cattanach*, 1907–8
and 1914.
RAILWAY STATION, off Ruthven Road. By *William Roberts*, 1893.
Single-storey L-plan offices, the jamb ending in a two-storey
house, all the gables aggressively crowstepped. The platform
awning's cast-iron columns carry brackets with wheel decoration in the spandrels. Lattice-girder footbridge of the usual
Highland Railway type.
ST VINCENT'S HOSPITAL, Gynack Road. Long two-storey villa
by *Alexander Mackenzie*, 1900–1; big round-arched windows
and a central verandah.
VICTORIA HALL, Spey Street. Free Renaissance of a sort, by
William Mackintosh, 1888.

DESCRIPTION

NEWTONMORE ROAD is the entry from the W. Prosperous late
C19 villas. Among them the single-storey KILDRUMMIE of
c. 1890, with corrugated-iron gables, the front covered with
decoratively patterned wood. More assertive is Our Lady and
St Columba R.C. Church (*see* Churches, above). The start of
the commercial centre is announced by the DUKE OF GORDON
HOTEL by *Alexander Cattanach*, 1906, large and relaxed, with
prettily bargeboarded gables and elaborate iron cresting on the
Frenchy central turret, the effect rather obscured by the broad-
eaved lower block projecting towards the street, its original
gabled porch replaced by a sun lounge.
RUTHVEN ROAD, at right angles to the main street, leads S. On
its l., a public garden with a Celtic cross WAR MEMORIAL of
1921 in the centre. On the r., the Primary School and Free
Church (*see* Public Buildings and Churches, above). Then the

Railway Station (*see* above), its forecourt dominated by the
MACKENZIE FOUNTAIN, two tiers of whinstone and granite,
by *Alexander Mackenzie*, 1910–11. In SPEY STREET to the E,
St Columba's Episcopal Church and the Victoria Hall (*see*
above). Opposite, the broad-gabled POST OFFICE by *Alexander Cattanach*, 1909.

HIGH STREET for the most part is undistinguished late Victorian.
On the N, the large BANK OF SCOTLAND, sturdy and crowstepped, by *Matthews & Lawrie*, 1875–6. On the S, at the corner
with King Street, the STAR HOTEL, dated 1892, its rounded
corner rising to a turret now deprived of cresting. Just E of the
set-back District Council Chambers (*see* above), a close leading
to the OLD CHURCHYARD, its corniced C18 gatepiers' stepped
finials topped with balls. Plain late C18 and C19 headstones
inside. At the bottom of DUKE STREET is PITMAIN LODGE
of *c.* 1800, its W wing an addition of *c.* 1830, its dormer heads
late C19. It is now the Highland Folk Museum. In the garden
behind, late C20 reconstructions of vernacular Highland
buildings, including an earth house, a traditional house of
Lewis type, a click mill and a salmon smoking house. Near the
end of High Street, the Drill Hall beside the entrance to the
Parish Church (*see* above). At the end of MANSE ROAD,
the former MANSE (now COLUMBA HOUSE HOTEL)
by *Peddie & Kinnear*, 1864–6, a broad-eaved villa with
a centre wallhead chimney. The village ends with THE
GLEBE by *G. R. M. Kennedy & Partners*, 1982–3, large-
scale and incongruously colourful post-Modern sheltered
housing.

RUTHVEN BARRACKS. *See* p. 98.

8000   KINRARA
                        1.2km. SE of Alvie

Rambling harled two-storey country house at the base of a well-
wooded hill beside the Spey, its present appearance owing
much to *Reginald Fairlie*'s reconstruction of 1939. It was begun
c. 1800 (possibly to a design of *John Sanders*) by Jane Duchess
of Gordon, 'in the form of a cottage', and was then a single-
storey U-plan. The wings were extended by *John Paterson*
c. 1814, and the house was further enlarged in 1836. On the
bow-ended garden front to the S, an early C19 prettily latticed
and arched verandah.

To the SE, MONUMENT to Jane Duchess of Gordon † 1812.
Granite pyramid, its plinth bearing a marble coat of arms. –
WATERLOO CAIRN on top of the hill behind the house, erected
in 1815, of granite rubble with a basket-arched niche for the
inscription plaque. – To its E, MONUMENT to the fifth Duke
of Gordon, a tall granite column of 1839–40, a marble coat of
arms on the stepped plinth.

LAGGAN

Tiny village N of the bridge carrying the road to Fort William across the Spey.

FREE CHURCH, 0.6km. S. By *John Rhind*, 1867, and now roofless and partly demolished. It has been a lanceted box, all very simple except for the W tower, whose diagonally set buttresses fade into broaching under the stone-spired octagonal belfry. – Beside it, the former MANSE (now MONADHLIATH HOTEL) of 1911, by *Lake Falconer*.

PARISH CHURCH. By *James Ross*, 1842–4. Routine whinstone rectangle, but the centre of each gable is slightly advanced, the W carrying a birdcage bellcote. Round-arched windows in the S wall; the N blind except for a door at each end, the r. sheltered by a later porch.

CATLODGE, 2.3km. SE. Bay-windowed *cottage orné* of *c.* 1840. Gothick window in the gabled centre; gableted dormerheads over the horizontal-paned first-floor outer windows.

CLUNY CASTLE. *See* p. 84.

FORT, Dun-da-Lamh, 3.5km. SW. Fort of the first millennium A.D., its massively broad stone rampart, now much ruined, enclosing the NE end of a long ridge, the area inside the wall rising into two knolls, perhaps explaining the place-name ('fort of two hands').

GARVAMORE, 8.7km. W. Standing in isolation beside General Wade's military road over the Corrieyairack Pass is the rubble-built KING'S HOUSE (GARVAMORE BARRACKS), an inn built to serve travellers, military or civilian, *c.* 1732. Quite plain, of two storeys. – 0.8km. NW, the GARVA BRIDGE of 1731–2, 54.9m. long, of two rubble arches.

LOCHANEILEAN CASTLE

1.9km. SE of Rothiemurchus

Ruin of a small castle sitting on an island in a loch. The earliest part, probably built for the Mackintoshes in the late C15, is at the N, a tower built of well-coursed large stones with few pinnings. The line of its N gable is continued E by a contemporary wall containing the remains of a gate. The tower itself is a simple rectangle, now of only two storeys but originally of at least three. In the W wall, a ground-floor loophole. Quite large first-floor windows to E and W. At the E side's N end, entrance to a stair which has risen inside the wall-thickness to the upper floors. The ground floor has been vaulted. Small aumbries in the N and S walls. In the S gable of the first-floor hall, remains of a fireplace flanked by aumbries. S of the tower, a stretch of curtain wall not bonded with its SW corner and so clearly later, perhaps mid-C16. In this wall is a doorway. Above it, a fireplace with a garderobe to its N, so there must have been a two-storey building, perhaps largely wooden, here, although part of the

area is now filled by a single-storey stone building, perhaps late
C 16 or early C 17, abutting the tower's s gable. To the s, remains
of a two-storey hall block, apparently later than the tower but
earlier than the wall to its N, which butts against the quoins of
its NW corner; it may be early C 16. Unvaulted interior, the
upper floor having been supported on a chase in the walls.
Extending N from the hall block's E end as far as the C 15 N wall,
scanty remains of a lodging block, probably built in the C 17,
its N gable and E wall apparently having incorporated part of
the C 15 curtain wall.

LOCHINDORB CASTLE
10.4km. NW of Grantown-on-Spey

Island stronghold in the loch of the same name. The surrounding
hills, now bare, were well wooded in the Middle Ages, when
the position beside two relatively easy routes from Strathspey
to the Moray Firth was of some strategic significance.

The castle is first recorded during the Wars of Independence
when Sir John ('the Black') Comyn died there in 1300. Three
years later it was occupied for ten days by Edward I. In 1336
the castle, then housing the widow of David, Earl of Atholl, to
whom it had passed by descent from the Comyns, was besieged
by Sir Andrew de Moray, Warden of Scotland, and relieved by
Edward III. After the victory of the pro-Bruce party, Lochindorb was forfeited to the Crown and then, in 1371, granted
by Robert II to his son Alexander, the 'Wolf of Badenoch'. By
1455 the castle was in the hands of Archibald Douglas, Earl of
Moray, whose purportedly treasonable acts included its gar-
risoning and fortification against the King. The next year, after
Douglas's defeat and death at Arkinholm, Lochindorb
was again forfeited to the Crown and this time ordered
to be slighted, the work of dismantling its defences being
entrusted to the Thane of Cawdor. Since then it has been left
as a ruin.

The site, an island c. 320m. from the loch's E shore, seems
substantially natural, but C 18 reports that 'Great rafts, or planks
of oak' were occasionally exposed suggest that it has been
strengthened by piles. The castle's main part seems to be late
C 13, probably built for Sir John Comyn. It consists of a curtain
wall, c. 5.5m. high to the rampart, enclosing an irregular quadrangle of c. 46.3m. by 38.4m., the N side considerably longer
than the s, and the E sharply angled in consequence. The
battlements, presumably removed in the 1450s dismantling,
seem to have risen flush with the wall below. At each corner
has been a two-storey-and-attic tower (the NW and SW partly
and the SE almost wholly demolished), shallow D-plans at the
S, almost round projections at the N, each with a diagonal wall
cutting across one of the enclosure's internal corners. The
towers have been entered from the courtyard; no evidence of

stairs inside them, so the upper floors must have been reached by ladders. In the curtain walls' thickness beside the two N and the SW towers are garderobes, the SW having been two-storeyed, with a wooden projection to the outside. All this is built of random granite and whinstone rubble brought to a level course about every 1.8m. by flat pinnings; bulging battered base all round. The towers have oblong windows; in the NE and SW are also long fish-tailed slits. In the W wall, a (blocked) low postern gate. The principal entrance has been in the middle of the N wall, where it faces a small cove. Outside the C13 castle, both on this N side of the island and also on the E, was a sizeable amount of land, perhaps originally enclosed by a stockade; if enclosed from the start, the gateway in the E wall may be original.

Soon after the completion of this quadrangular castle of enclosure, it was enlarged by the building of an outer curtain wall enclosing land on the N side E of the main entrance and on the E side (i.e. the area perhaps originally fenced by a stockade). This wall's masonry is almost identical to that of the original castle but is not bonded with it and lacks a battered base. In this outer court's NW part has been a hall (mostly demolished), its S side provided by the C13 castle's N wall in which have been cut crude sockets for the joists of the main floor *c.* 1.5m. above the ground; sizeable window (blocked) in the W gable. Near the N end of the outer curtain's E wall, remains of a gateway (said to have had a depressed arch) with grooves for a portcullis.

Inside the C13 quadrangle, remains of a range of buildings against the E wall. They may be early C15. Probably contemporary with their erection has been the rebuilding with smaller stones of the top parts of the NE tower and E curtain.

MUCKRACH CASTLE   *9020*
1.2km. W of Dulnain Bridge

Small harled and crowstep-gabled tower house built for Patrick Grant of Rothiemurchus in 1598; it may have been intended as a jointure house.* Almost square main block of three storeys and an attic, its Victorian stone dormerhead on the E added in *Ian Begg*'s restoration of 1978–85. At the NW corner, a round stairtower, its upper part corbelled out to the square. In the tower's S inner angle, a circular conical-roofed turret carried on a squinch arch. Below it, the entrance. Inside, a tunnel-vaulted ground floor. The house originally stood nearly at the SW corner of an enclosure which had long buildings on its W and E sides, the W range's round SW corner tower still partly surviving.

*i.e. dower house.

NETHYBRIDGE

Scattered village on both sides of the Dorback Burn.

ABERNETHY PARISH CHURCH, 1.2km. N. Simple kirk of 1762 enlarged and remodelled by *A. Marshall Mackenzie* in 1872–3. Originally very simple, the long E wall faced in granite ashlar, the others harled. Roundheaded windows; circular bellcote projecting from the S gable. Mackenzie added crowsteps, a lean-to W aisle and SW vestry, made a new door in the S gable, and inserted wooden mullions in the windows. The interior is all his. Open wooden roof; a row of cast-iron columns between the aisle and the body of the church.

NETHY BRIDGE CHURCH. Built as Abernethy Free Church, *c.* 1850, and originally very simple, with roundheaded windows. Gable front added *c.* 1900, with pinnacled angle buttresses, a big rectangular window filled with wooden tracery, and a small spired bellcote. – Plain MANSE of *c.* 1850 behind.

COMMUNITY CENTRE. Cottagey, by *Alexander Mackenzie*, 1904.

BRIDGE. Two unequal sized arches, by *Thomas Telford*, 1810–11.

DESCRIPTION. The NETHY BRIDGE HOTEL on the N bank dominates by sheer size. It was begun in 1898; bargeboarded gables and a glazed awning across the front. N addition with a tower of 1912. Further E, the white harled ARDAVON, dated 1908, Arts and Crafts, with tall chimneys and touches of half-timbering. On the S bank, the Community Centre and Church (*see* above).

AULTMORE. *See* p. 78.
CASTLE ROY. *See* p. 84.

NEWTONMORE

Long main street of C19 vernacular housing with an hotel at each end (the CRAIGMHOR at the W given its present appearance by *Alexander Cattanach*, 1909, the BALAVIL ARMS at the E by *W. L. Carruthers*, 1900). Late C19 villas to the S, local authority houses to the N.

ST BRIDE'S CHURCH. Built as a Free church, *c.* 1900. Low and cruciform, with a semi-octagonal chancel at the S. Broad eaves; a round bellcote on the nave's S gable. Simple interior. – STAINED GLASS. In the chancel, four lights (scenes from the Life of Our Lord) by *Gordon Webster*, 1964. In the W transept, one light (Charity), Glasgow-style, after 1912.

HALL. By *Alexander Cattanach*, 1912–13. Broad bargeboarded gable front with sparing Wrenaissance detail.

PRIMARY SCHOOL. By *Alexander Cattanach*, 1910.

RAILWAY STATION. Dated 1893. Single-storey U-plan with Tudor touches, the open centre towards the platform filled by a verandah.

ROTHIEMURCHUS

Place-name for the ecclesiastical and economic focus of a largely moorland parish whose good land, together with the former church and the mansion house of The Doune, lies beside the Spey.

PARISH CHURCH. Disused and roofless. By *Thomas Telford* and *Joseph Mitchell*, 1827–30, incorporating bits of a previous church on the site. Surprisingly the design is not that of a 'Parliamentary' church. Rectangular windows. At the W gable, a porch and pedimented birdcage bellcote. – MANSE, 0.8km. NE. Harled single-storey U-plan 'Parliamentary' manse (i.e. probably to *James Smith*'s design) built by *William Thomson* in 1830.

ST JOHN THE BAPTIST (Episcopal). By *J. N. Comper*, 1928–9. Beautifully simple white harled Latin cross. Y-tracery in the pointed windows; conical-roofed round bell turret corbelled out from the W gable. Whitewashed groin-vaulted interior furnished with neo-Jacobean pews, dado and altar rail. Over the altar a baldacchino of dark red damask.

THE DOUNE OF ROTHIEMURCHUS. Laird's house, built, extended and altered over three centuries by the Grants of Rothiemurchus, one of whom, Elizabeth Grant, has left an evocative account of it in the early C19 in her *Memoirs of a Highland Lady*. The earliest part is the rubble-built N wing, probably late C17 but heightened to three storeys in 1877 by *John Lessels*, who added a corner turret (removed in *Benjamin Tindall*'s alterations of the 1980s). Over the door, a reused lintel carved with the initials PG (for Patrick Grant of Rothiemurchus) and the date 1598, said to have been brought here from Muckrach Castle. A S addition was built at right angles to this C17 house by Dr William Grant *c.* 1780. Dr Grant's son *Sir John Peter Grant*, apparently acting as his own architect, carried out more ambitious aggrandizement in 1797–1803, heightening his father's addition and extending it E. This Georgian block's S front has a full-height bow l. of the door; above the door, a Venetian window. Masculine detail with rusticated quoins and a heavily bracketed eaves-course-cum-rhone made of local timber. The erection of a matching wing N of the old house and a linking colonnade was projected but never executed.

THE CROFT, 1.7km. E. Cottage-picturesque of 1812, the design produced by *Jane* and *Elizabeth Grant* (aged twelve and fifteen) with some help from their father, *Sir John Peter Grant*. Latticed panes and broad eaves.

LOCHANEILEAN CASTLE. See p. 93.

THE POLCHAR, 0.7km. E. Built as a gamekeeper's house in 1812 to a design by *Jane* and *Elizabeth Grant*. Single-storey, with lattice glazing and a big central chimneystack; originally, it was heather-thatched. Victorian porch and late C19 rear additions. – To the W, MONUMENT of *c.* 1900 to Dr James Martineau, the

Unitarian divine. Triangular column with carved Celtic designs on the faces and a flat capital.

7090   ## RUTHVEN BARRACKS
1.1km. s of Kingussie

74 Almost complete but roofless remains of an early Georgian fort built on the site of a medieval castle. Ruthven Castle, reputed to have been a stronghold of the Comyn Lords of Badenoch and of Alexander Stewart, Earl of Buchan (the 'Wolf of Badenoch'), was acquired by Alexander Gordon, Earl of Huntly, in 1451 and reconstructed or rebuilt by the sixth Earl of Huntly in 1590. Captured and burned by the Earl of Dundee's Jacobite forces in 1689, the castle's main walls were subsequently patched up to make an enclosure within which were erected wooden shelters to house an independent Highland company* loyal to William III. In 1717 the Government disbanded the independent companies, replacing them with regular troops, and decided to supplement the existing Highland forts at Inverness and Fort William with four more commanding the main routes into and across the Highlands. Ruthven was chosen as the site of one of these.‡ During the next year *James Smith*, the then Surveyor and Chief Director for Carrying on the Barracks in North Britain, inspected the proposed sites and had almost certainly produced designs for all four forts before his dismissal from office in January 1719,§ the year in which *Sir Patrick Strachan* of Glenkindie contracted to build Ruthven Barracks for a price of £1,555 3s. 0d. Completed by 1724 this military stronghold of the new Hanoverian dynasty was burned by the Jacobites in 1746 and thereafter abandoned.

The location near the junction of the principal land route from Perth to Inverness with the branch through Glen Spean to Fort William was of strategic importance. The site is strong, a steep-sided mound (probably a motte) rising up from the Spey valley, almost the whole of its summit occupied by the fort. This is an almost square enclosure (28.35m. by 25.6m. externally); at the NE and SW corners, projecting towers. The walls are all of rubble, formerly harled. The single-storey E and W ranges, originally surmounted by parapets, return for short stretches along the enclosure's longer E and W sides, each of which is mostly filled by a three-storey-and-attic barrack block. To the outside it presents a very defensive gaze. At each of the barrack blocks' main storeys are eight musket loops grouped

---

*After the Restoration, Crown commissions had been granted to certain Highland nobles and lairds to raise companies of part-time soldiers to suppress cattle rustling and blackmail.

‡The others were at Bernera, Glenelg (Skye and Lochalsh), Fort Augustus (Inverness) and Inversnaid (Strathclyde).

§Inversnaid and Fort Augustus were begun in 1718 before Smith's dismissal, and all four forts, though differing in size, were built to a standard plan.

four and four; two more loops in the s block's basement, regular rows of loops in the E and W ranges, and yet more in the corner towers to cover the main walls against direct assault. All these are set in deeply splayed rectangular surrounds. Only the corner towers' windows hint at domesticity.

The elliptical arched entrance in the centre of the E range gives access to the courtyard. Here most of the segmental vaults which carried the parapet walks at the E and W survive. The E walk was reached by stone stairs at the ends of the barrack blocks, the W by a central stair. The space behind that W stair was originally occupied by the officers' latrine, but this was removed in 1734, when a postern gate was inserted and a new latrine made under the parapet walk immediately W of the S barrack, facing the men's latrine on the opposite side of the courtyard. Outside the men's latrine, remains of a draw well.

The barrack blocks lack only their roofs and floors. To the courtyard each shows a symmetrical five-bay elevation, the segment-headed windows grouped 2/1/2. Inside, each floor contained two rooms separated by the central staircase. Of the two-storey corner towers, the NE was occupied by a ground-floor guardhouse with a prison cell below and officers' quarters above. In the SW tower were a brewhouse and bakehouse, the oven still largely intact.

W of the main fort is a STABLE built in 1734 to house thirty dragoons and their horses, apparently as a self-contained unit. It is a straightforward single-storey range with an attic reached by a forestair on the E. On the W side, what appears to have been the guardhouse (now very ruinous) covered by catslide roofs. The ground floor is lighted and ventilated by musket loops. Big attic windows in the gables.

To the S, a low stretch of masonry. Was this built as part of an attempt to strengthen the defences, perhaps in 1734, or is it only a retaining wall?

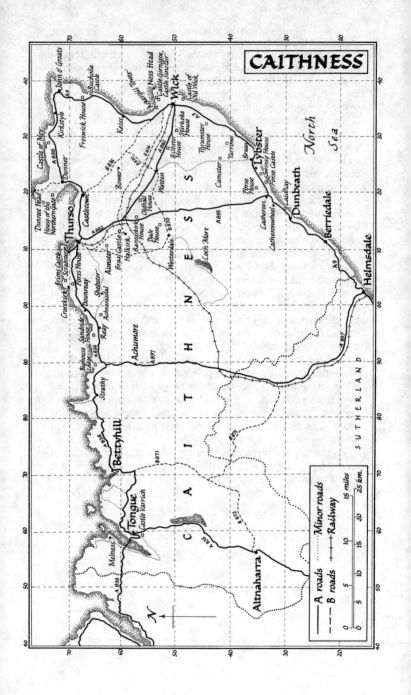

CAITHNESS

The NE corner of the Scottish mainland, with a broad and fertile plain on much of its N and E, to whose S and W lie bogs and moorland. The coastline is largely composed of serrated cliffs, their promontories providing sites for forts or castles, the adjoining geos or inlets sheltered berths for boats. The earliest inhabitants were subdued or replaced by Norse settlement from the C9, and the Norse Earls of Orkney were recognized until the C14 as holding an earldom of Caithness (originally including Sutherland) under the Scottish Crown, whose supremacy had been established by William I (the Lion) in 1196. Soon after, families of Anglo-Norman descent obtained lands in Caithness, one of these, the Sinclairs, eventually obtaining a grant of the earldom in 1470. In the late C18 and early C19 Sir John Sinclair of Ulbster argued persuasively for the introduction of 'improved' farming to Caithness. His own agricultural experiments were not wholly successful, his Merino sheep proving susceptible to foot-rot despite being given bootees, but his ideas were quickly adopted by other landowners. Sinclair also laid out the New Town of Thurso and the British Fisheries Society its equivalent at Wick, which, by the mid-C19, had become the largest herring fishing port in Europe, that fishery's subsequent sharp decline robbing it of vitality. The later C20 has brought the development of a nuclear power industry at Dounreay, its future now uncertain, and increasing afforestation, the long-term vitality of the trees also uncertain.

ACHAVANICH see LYBSTER

ACHUMORE   *8050*

Church and mill in the isolation of Strath Halladale.

HALLADALE FREE CHURCH. Built in 1853. Very simple little harled box with a ball finial on the S gable. Lattice glazing in the rectangular windows.

MILL. Mid-C19 rubble-built mill, its wheel still attached to the gable.

ACHVARASDAL
1.4km. E of Reay

Much gabled and gableted shooting lodge built for Sir Robert
Sinclair of Murkle *c.* 1870.

ACKERGILL TOWER
3.8km. NW of Wick

Late C15 tower house built for the Keiths of Inverugie, now
framed by Victorian Baronial additions, standing beside the
shore of Sinclair's Bay. The tower itself, clearly in existence by
1510, when Gilbert Mowat was Captain or Keeper of the House
of Ackergill, is an austere rubble-built rectangle, *c.* 14.6m. by
10.4m. At the NW corner, a square pyramid-roofed turret, an
upward extension of the walls, built in the alterations of 1851
by *David Bryce.* Also of 1851 are the corbelled rounds at the
other corners and the battlement flush with the walling below;*
cannon spouts under the parapet. Inside the battlement, a
crowstep-gabled cap-house, another addition of 1851. In the W
wall, a roundheaded window, in the E a Y-traceried Gothick
window, both Georgian like all the others. Off-centre round-
arched S door with a cable hoodmould of 1851. Across the
tower's N side, a crowstep-gabled early C18 block made T-
plan in 1851, when Bryce added a N wing with gabled turrets
corbelled out at the corners. On the tower's E side he placed a
discreet block, unaggressive Baronial with a fat turret at the SE
corner, a rectangular oriel canted across the NE. On the W he
provided a low castellated range linked by garden walls to a low
range of stabling and coachhouses.

Bryce's S entrance opens into a vaulted room, perhaps the
C15 kitchen, behind which is a neo-Jacobean stair of 1851. First-
floor dining room (the C15 hall), its tunnel-vaulted ceiling
decorated by Bryce with neo-Jacobean plasterwork pendants
and panels enclosing strapwork motifs and coats of arms. The
Jacobean manner extends to the panelling on the walls and
the segmental-arched E inglenook under a window (its light
borrowed from a wall-passage behind) containing armorial
stained glass. Simple bolection-moulded chimneypieces of late
C17 character, again provided by Bryce. In the E addition of
1851, two first-floor drawing rooms, both with marble chimneypieces.

To the house's SE and SW, a pair of early C18 crowstepped
lectern DOOCOTS, symmetrically placed like outer fortifications to the tower. Each has two ratcourses, the upper
under the eaves and stepping up at the gables. In the E
doocot, two chambers, each with 900 stone nesting boxes.
The W 'doocot' has no nesting boxes but has had an upper

---

*An early C19 engraving by William Daniell shows the tower with ogee-roofed
corner turrets and a corbelled battlement.

floor equipped with a fireplace, so is unlikely to have been intended to house pigeons. Was it a garden room or, possibly, a heated henhouse?

Large STEADING to the SE built in 1878, with tall brick chimneys at both its main ranges. It has been enlarged in the late C20.

AIMSTER 1060
3.9km. N of Halkirk

Harled house built *c.* 1800 by Captain John Henderson, author of the *General View of the Agriculture of the County of Caithness*. At the centre, a chimney gablet; semicircular fanlight over the door. – Behind, a courtyard STEADING with a central gablet on the front; it looks like a mid-C19 rebuilding or remodelling.

ALTNAHARRA 5030

Hamlet at the W end of Loch Naver.

CHURCH. Built as a Free church in 1854–5 by *Hugh Mackay*. Gothic box of hammer-dressed snecked rubble. On the E gable, a Celtic cross on a tall stepped base. Little altered interior. The focus is on the PULPIT, probably made by *Thomas McIver*, who was responsible for the seating. – Victorian OIL LAMPS (now converted to electricity). – STAINED GLASS. One colourful light (St David of Scotland) in the S wall, by *T. S. Halliday*, *c.* 1965.

BRIDGES. At the N end, a rubble-built slightly humpbacked bridge of three segmental arches, by *Thomas Telford*, 1815–18. – Probably contemporary is the single-span rubble bridge at the hamlet's S end.

ALTNAHARRA HOTEL. The crowstep-gabled back range was built in 1832; big front extension of *c.* 1900. All harled.

BROCH (DUN DORNAIGIL), 14.5km. NW. Very fragmentary remains of a circular broch of *c.* 500 B.C.–A.D. 500, but the battered wall above the entrance on the E stands to a height of *c.* 6.7m. Over the entrance, a massive triangular lintel.

BANNISKIRK HOUSE 1050
3.4km. SE of Halkirk

By *W. L. Moffat*, 1857. Big plain Tudorbethan, with strapwork over the door.

2070   BARROCK

Scattered crofting settlement.

DUNNET FREE CHURCH. Disused. Twin-aisled church built in
  1844, the M-roof's shape disguised at the gable front by a
  parapet to make it appear a platform. Projecting centre finished
  with a slated pyramid roof. Was a tower intended?

BEN FREICEANDAIN *see* WESTERDALE

1020   BERRIEDALE

C 19 estate hamlet with simple but picturesque housing.

PARISH CHURCH. Harled T-plan 'Parliamentary' church (i.e. to
  William Thomson's design) built by *William Davidson* in 1826.
  Standard spikily pinnacled bellcote on the W gable and latticed
  glazing in the Tudor-arched windows. Piend-roofed vestry
  addition on the N of the jamb; off-centre S porch, also an
  addition. The interior has been refurnished with a Victorian
  pulpit and pews.
WAR MEMORIAL. By *Ernest George* and *Alfred B. Yeates*, 1919.
  Big gabled granite plinth surmounted by a small bronze of St
  Andrew.
BERRIEDALE CASTLE. Very scanty remains of the castle which
  occupied the promontory at the mouth of the Langwell Water.
  The landward approach has been cut across by a ditch. On the
  promontory have been two ranges of rubble buildings with a
  narrow courtyard between. It was probably built for the Oliphants in the C 16.
BROCH, Ousdale, 6.2km. SW. Remains of a broch, perhaps of the
  first millennium B.C., built on top of a steep bank with sharply
  sloping ground to the S and E and defended by a thick wall on
  the N and W. The broch itself is *c.* 15m. in diameter. Entrance
  at the SW. Inside the court, an opening over the passage
  entrance and another over the doorway to the stair which rises
  in the thickness of the hollow wall. Small wall cell S of the
  entrance. Scarcement round the court's wall-face *c.* 2.4m.
  above the ground.

7060   BETTYHILL

Extensive but architecturally undistinguished village at the mouth
of the Naver.

FARR FREE CHURCH. Simple T-plan kirk of 1845, the roofs now
  tiled. Pointed window in the jamb's gable; above, a birdcage
  bellcote, its top swept up to a ball finial.
FARR PARISH CHURCH. Built as a United Free church in 1909.

Just like a hall except for the front gable's Gothic window and the wooden canopy for a bell above. – Contemporary MANSE next door.

Former FARR PARISH CHURCH (now Strathnaver Museum). Big drydashed (formerly harled) box built in 1774, an elegant ball-finialled birdcage bellcote on the E gable. Rectangular windows, tall where they flank the pulpit, smaller and in two tiers to light the galleries. At the gables, forestairs* to the gallery doors. The interior was recast in 1881–2, when the galleries were removed and the end bays partitioned off as a porch and vestry. – PULPIT bearing the date 1774 and the initials MGM for Mr George Munro, the then minister. Fluted Ionic columns at the back; big octagonal canopy. – The roomy PEW in front looks C 19. – Among the museum exhibits are C 18 GRAVESLABS collected from various local churchyards and carved with heraldry and reminders of death.

In the GRAVEYARD, W of the church is the FARR STONE, probably C 8 or C 9, carved with a Celtic cross decorated with Greek key pattern; a pair of intertwined birds at the base. – S of the church, a big pedimented MONUMENT to Captain Charles Gordon of Pulrossie † 1790.

Plain harled former MANSE of 1818 to the E.

CAIRNS, Coille na Borgie, 2.9km. S. Substantial remains of three cairns, probably of the third or fourth millennium B.C. The best preserved is at the S, a c. 72m.-long cairn with square forecourts formed by horns projecting at the ends. Passage from the N end to a ruinous chamber divided by pairs of upright slabs into three compartments. – The two cairns to the N are in a line. The S is c. 31m. long, tapering to the N. At its S end, horns and a debris-filled concave forecourt. – Almost square (c. 18.3m. by 15.2m.) N cairn with traces of projecting horns enclosing a deep N forecourt.

CAIRNS, Skelpick, 5.3km. S. Several cairns, the most impressive a 59m.-long cairn, probably of the third or fourth millennium B.C. Horns at both ends, more eroded at the S. At the N they enclose a concave forecourt choked with stones. Short passage (blocked) from this end to a chamber divided into two compartments by upright slabs. – To the NE, very ruinous remains of a round cairn, c. 28m. in diameter. – To the SE, a quite small, almost square cairn, rather ruined, with low horns projecting at the corners and concave sides.

BIGHOUSE LODGE
6.7km. W of Reay

8060

Harled house of c. 1800. Two storeys above an exposed basement. Five-bay W front, the centre slightly advanced and pedimented. The bowed porch with a rusticated and corniced doorpiece is a late C 19 addition, as is the N extension with its full-height

*Reinstated in the restoration of the 1970s.

canted bay window. Back wing and office court, both looking mid-C19.

To the s, a big WALLED GARDEN, with buttresses against its N wall. At the centre of its s side, a mid-C18 two-storey GARDEN PAVILION. Harled with rusticated quoins, its first-floor windows taller than those below. Wallhead chimney at the front's centre; at its corners, tall fluted pedestals topped by ball-finialled stalks. – In the garden's N wall, rusticated GATEPIERS, probably mid-C18. – On the opposite side of the house's fore-court, another pair of rusticated GATEPIERS, but of the early C19. – At the forecourt's NW corner, BIGHOUSE BARRACK, a harled two-storey house. Its present U-plan, with piended roofs and chamfered window margins, may date from the alterations made in 1763 by the mason *Alexander Broune*, who perhaps extended and recast an existing L-plan house. In the front's recessed centre, an almost square first-floor window with a moulded surround, its lintel inscribed [?16]58. Buttressed s wall.

BILBSTER HOUSE

2050

4.2km. SE of Watten

Plain harled late C18 laird's house, its r. gable crowstepped, its l. rebuilt and now without a chimney. Late C19 bay window on the r. of the front; contemporary wing projecting from the l. The wood and glass porch looks a little later. – Rather altered early C19 STEADING on the approach.

BOWER

2060

Small settlement with an inn, school and parish church, the old Parish Church 0.7km. SE, the old Free Church 1.7km. SW.

FREE CHURCH. Now a community centre. Plain harled box of *c.* 1845, its walls heightened in 1855. Big Tudor window in the gable.

OLD PARISH CHURCH. Ivy-clad roofless ruin in a graveyard. Whinstone-walled rectangle, possibly medieval in origin but reconstructed in 1718 and the w gable partly rebuilt in 1803. Blocked doors in the E gable and the w end of the N wall. A third door near the w end of the s wall, in which are a large and a small rectangular window.

PARISH CHURCH. Tall rendered box, by *William Davidson*, 1847–8. Diagonally set obelisk finials at the corners; a spiky pinnacled bellcote on the w gable. In the Tudor-arched windows, wooden tracery testifying to *Donald Leed*'s recasting of the interior in 1902.

BRAAL CASTLE
1km. E of Halkirk

1060

Remains of a medieval castle with a Victorian mansion to its S. Traditionally Braal has been associated with Harald, Earl of Caithness, † 1206, and the wet ditch of which traces remain to the N (the River Thurso provides a S and E defence) could point to a C12 or C13 date; but the tower seems more likely to have been built in the C14. It is a small rectangle, *c.* 13m. by 12.3m. externally, the walls *c.* 3m. thick, built of local rubble bonded apparently with clay mortar. Three storeys, the roof and battlement now missing. At the ground floor, a slit window in each of the W and N walls. First-floor door at the SW corner. This opens ahead into the hall. In the wall thickness on the r., a straight stair to the second floor. In the first-floor hall, W and N windows, both with stone seats in their embrasures. The E wall has a fireplace and garderobe. Narrow closet with a slit window at the W wall's S end. More wall chambers at the second floor. No vaults, the floor joists having been carried on heavy stone corbels.

The adjoining tall mansion house was built for Sir George Sinclair of Ulbster in 1856, incorporating a vaulted basement probably of the C17. It is by *William Burn*. Plainest Baronial, with a thrifty sprinkling of turrets.

BRIMS CASTLE
7.7km. NW of Thurso

0070

Roofless small tower attached to a farmhouse. The three-storey-and-attic L-plan tower house, probably built *c.* 1600 for Henry Sinclair of Brabster and Brims, is of harled whinstone with crowstepped gables and chamfered window margins. Corbelled out from the square NE jamb's E face, a round turret. Inside the main block, a tunnel-vaulted ground-floor store, perhaps a wine cellar. It has a hatch in the ceiling. In the wall-thickness of the SE corner, a tight stair to the first-floor hall. Its E door is an insertion, probably of the early C19. The hall was originally entered from outside by a door in the E gable, presumably reached by a forestair. From this level a turnpike stair in the jamb gives access to the second floor and attic. To the N of the house has been a courtyard enclosed by a BARMKIN WALL. On its W side, a roundheaded moulded gateway. In the early C19 a plain crowstepped farmhouse was added on the tower's E side. Lean-to addition against the W gable.

CHAPEL or MAUSOLEUM, 0.5km. NW, probably late C16 or C17. Almost square, the E gable's door with a bead-and-hollow moulding. The W door is a C20 insertion. Tunnel-vaulted interior.

BROUBSTER *see* SHEBSTER

BRUAN

Handful of houses and a couple of churches.

CHURCH OF SCOTLAND. Built as a United Free church in 1910.
Small harled box with a broad five-light window in the bellcoted
gable front.

FREE CHURCH. Disused. Tall and gaunt mid-C19 kirk with
round-arched windows; stone spired birdcage bellcote, rather
too small for the building.

CAIRN OF GET, Garrywhin, 1.6km. N. Short horned cairn of the
third or fourth millennium B.C., the body c. 13m. by 14m., the
longer E and W sides slightly concave. Deeply projecting horns
at the ends enclosing more pronouncedly concave forecourts.
Entrance in centre of the S front. The passage ends in a small
rectangular antechamber. Roughly circular chamber (now
roofless), its walls constructed of upright slabs with drystone
masonry between.

FORT, Garrywhin, 1.9km. N. Ruinous remains of a fort of the first
millennium B.C., its wall enclosing the elongated oval shape of
a steep-sided ridge summit, c. 180m. by 57m. Entrance at the
N end, where the wall-thickness is doubled. There seems to
have been a second entrance at the S.

STONE ROWS, Mid Clyth, 2.1km. SW. Setting of small upright
stones, perhaps erected in the second millennium B.C., placed
on the slope of a low hill. About two hundred stones still stand,[*]
set in at least twenty-two rows, forming a broad fan-shape.

GRAVEYARD, Ulbster, 3.2km. NE. Rubble-walled enclosure with
a pair of smart channel-rusticated gatepiers topped by tall urns.
They are probably contemporary with the SINCLAIR MAUSO-
LEUM inside, a square ogee-roofed box, its flag-weathervane
dated 1700.

BUCHOLIE CASTLE
5.7km. NE of Keiss

Craggy ruin of the castle of the Mowats of Freswick occupying a
small cliff-edged rock peninsula. The peninsula's narrow NW
neck has been cut through by a ditch c. 2.7m. deep, which must
have been spanned by a moveable wooden bridge. On the
ditch's seaward (E) side stand the remains of the W and S walls
of a rectangular rubble-built gatehouse-tower, probably of the
C15. Vaulted passage through the tower, with a vaulted room
to its S. Above has been a tall vault divided by a wooden floor.
The peninsula has had ranges of buildings extending S down
its E and W sides either side of a narrow courtyard.

[*]In 1871 about two hundred and fifty stones were visible, and there may originally
have been as many as six hundred.

CAMSTER

Moorland, a setting for cairns of the third or fourth millennium B.C.

CAIRNS. The much restored LONG CAIRN is a mound of stones, 69.5m. long, with, at each end, short projecting horns defining a forecourt. It contains two chambers, each probably originally covered by a separate round cairn, the two later united under the long cairn. Drystone retaining wall round the sides, rebuilt at the S end. In the N forecourt, a stone platform, now grassed over. Entrances in the long E side to the low passages which lead to the chambers. N chamber a small irregular pentagon, its walls constructed of edge-set slabs with drystone masonry corbelling out above. Larger S chamber divided by upright slabs into three compartments, the two W originally under a single stone roof. The chambers are now covered by fibreglass domes. – c. 183m. S, the almost intact ROUND CAIRN, c. 18m. in diameter and 12m. high. Drystone-walled entrance passage from the E ending in a small antechamber. Main chamber divided by a pair of transverse slabs into two compartments. Walls of drystone masonry corbelled to carry the roof's capstone.

CANISBAY *see* KIRKSTYLE

CASTLE GIRNIGOE AND CASTLE SINCLAIR

4.4km. N of Wick

Dramatic ruins of two tower houses sharing a promontory beside the North Sea, the chief stronghold of the Sinclair Earls of Caithness from the C15 to the C17. 64

In 1455 James II granted the earldom of Caithness* to William Sinclair, Earl of Orkney, who resigned his earldom and lands of Orkney to the Crown fifteen years later. It was probably this earl who built a castle at Girnigoe, which is first documented in 1497, when his son signed a charter there. Alexander Keith, the Keeper of Ackergill Tower, was imprisoned in Girnigoe c. 1545, as was the fourth Earl of Caithness's son in the 1570s. In 1607 the accommodation was enlarged by the building of a second tower house (Castle Sinclair), perhaps as a result of the fifth Earl's having resigned the earldom to his son in 1592 with reservation of a life rent. In 1672 George, sixth Earl of Caithness, heavily in debt and lacking a close heir, sold his estates and earldom to Sir John Campbell of Glenorchy. Glenorchy's assumption of the earldom in 1677 was challenged by George Sinclair of Keiss as heir-male, and in August 1679 Glenorchy sent a garrison to Girnigoe who 'did immediately fortifie the said castle by repairing and strengthening the gates thereof and lifting up the draw bridge

*Which had fallen to the Crown the year before.

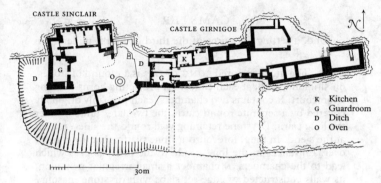

Castle Girnigoe and Castle Sinclair.
(Redrawn by permission of the RCAHMS)

upon the fowsee of the said castle ...' In January 1680 George
Sinclair of Keiss retaliated, captured the castle and thereupon

did throw down and demolish the forts of Castle Sinclare and Girnigo
belonging to the said Earle [of Caithness], and broke down the rooffe
thereof and the doores or windows, drawbridges and iron gates thereof
and pull up the floores and threw down to the ground the hewen stone of
the battlement. Likeas they did cary with them all the beds, furniture and
whole timber work of the saids severall houses ...

Thereafter, the castle was abandoned to decay.

The promontory site is parallel to the mainland, to which its broad
W end is attached. On the N side, cliffs with a sheer drop to the
sea. Narrow E end. On the S, a goe or inlet filled by the sea for
its E quarter to make a small natural harbour from which the
ground rises not too steeply up to the promontory's W end. A
small second inlet on the N makes a notch roughly halfway
along the promontory's length.
    The site's natural strength has been reinforced by the cutting
of a ditch across the W end. On the line of the N inlet has been
made a second ditch, its S end a narrow ledge from which it
slopes steeply down towards the sea. The whole summit of the
promontory was probably surrounded by a wall from the C15;
across the N inlet it is carried on a wide arch. The relatively
easy access from the S goe has been blocked by a wall, its gate
placed at the N end and set at a high level (presumably reached
by a ladder or removeable ramp), the N jamb part of the walling
of Castle Girnigoe's tower house. Within these defences the
promontory, almost severed by the N inlet and its ditch continuation, makes two distinct parts now known as Castle Sinclair (the W) and Castle Girnigoe (the E). In the C15 Castle
Sinclair probably formed an outer courtyard of stores and stabling, Castle Girnigoe an inner court containing the Earl's
tower house and ancillary buildings.

There are two approaches to the castle. From the S goe's beach a path led uphill to the gate beside Castle Girnigoe's tower house; of this gate, only the N jamb survives. Immediately W of the tower is a second gate which opens through the castle's enclosure wall; above it, an empty frame for a heraldic panel, perhaps early C 17. This gate opened onto the ledge above the central ditch and inlet. At the ledge's W end were steps up to another gateway (now demolished) into the courtyard of Castle Sinclair. The W approach was much more straightforward, a drawbridge (now replaced by a narrow causeway) crossing the ditch to the gatehouse of Castle Sinclair.

The main block of Castle Sinclair, probably replacing a C 15 gatehouse, was built across the W end of the courtyard in 1607 (the date noted by John Brand on a window lintel in 1701). Now very ruinous, it has been a four-storey tower house built of local basalt slabs with red sandstone dressings, its two upper floors jettied out on continuous corbelling. Remains of tall corbelled turrets on the N and E fronts. At the apex of the front gable was a panel carved with the royal arms.* The passage from the W doorway to the courtyard behind survives, its segmental tunnel vault pierced by grooves for a portcullis. The room above (housing the portcullis) has had a tunnel-vault. On the N of the passage, a guardroom, its entrance immediately E of the portcullis. In the courtyard behind, remains of lower unvaulted buildings, probably also early C 17, built against the enclosure walls. Near the courtyard's E end has been a round oven.

Immediately E of the central inlet and ditch is Castle Girnigoe's C 15 tower house, occupying the full width of the promontory and formerly reached by a drawbridge. It is of three storeys, attic and basement, built on a U-plan with walls of the same local rubble as used at Castle Sinclair but the sandstone dressings much pinker in colour. The SE wing is a stairtower; slightly angled and much larger NE wing projecting N of the main block's gable. Along the N fronts of both the main block and the wing, stone corbels for a first-floor bretasche; there has been another (second-floor) bretasche on the SE jamb's S wall. At the W front's N end, the moulded entrance doorway; below it, corbels for the drawbridge. Almost directly above has been an oriel window, its sloping roof's top stone carved with the Sinclair crest; only the base now survives.

From the tower's W entrance a dogleg passage leads through the house to the courtyard behind. Here are three doors. On the N, the door to the NE wing's tunnel-vaulted ground-floor kitchen, its big E fireplace provided with a stone seat on the S side. The main block's centre door opens into a vaulted guardroom; in the thickness of its W wall, a stair down to a vaulted basement room probably containing the castle's well. At the SE jamb, the house's principal entrance protected by gunloops. In the jamb, a straight stair down to a vaulted room, perhaps a dungeon, and remains of a turnpike to the upper

*Of which the supporters are now at Ackergill Tower.

floors; in the main block behind, another vaulted guardroom. The whole of the main block's first floor has been filled by the hall. Large fireplace in the E wall. At the NE corner, a door to the bretasche outside. Retiring room above the kitchen in the NE wing. Its E gable has a small fireplace. On its l., a door to a turnpike stair in the wall-thickness of the block's NE corner. At the NW corner, another door to a short passage leading to the parapet of the lower building to the E. In the retiring room's floor, a trapdoor into the space above the kitchen's vault. Almost identical second-floor arrangement but with the hall fireplace in the N gable.

E of the NE wing has been a two-storey range, now little more than grass-covered mounds. On the courtyard's S side, a wall whose W part survives, with gunloops set in stepped embrasures; presumably it is C17. At the promontory's E end, a stair cut in the rock leading to a passage down to the sea.

CASTLE OF MEY
5.4km. NW of Kirkstyle

2070

Multi-turreted rubble-built tower house sheltered by trees on the S and looking across the Pentland Firth to Orkney on the N. In 1549 the Bishop of Caithness granted the lands of Mey to George Sinclair, fourth Earl of Caithness, and the house was probably begun soon after. A carving reported in the house in 1914 bore the arms and initials of the Earl and his wife, Elizabeth Graham, together with the date 1566, which may have been the year of the building's completion. The C16 house was basically Z-plan. Four-storey main block. Square NW and SE jambs, the lower NW containing the entrance and main stair, the battlemented SE of five storeys, with a rectangular stair turret in its W inner angle. At the NE, the massive kitchen flue makes a third but shallow projection. Round turrets at all corners, the smaller with chequer-set corbelling, most with crenellated parapets provided in *William Burn*'s alterations of 1819.[*] Wide-splayed C16 gunloops in the S front of the main block and at the SE jamb. The windows are uniformly Georgian, most probably dating from repairs made in the 1790s, but the tall first-floor window l. of the front porch is of 1954, replacing a Tudorish window of 1819. Also of 1954 is the heightening of the E end of the main block's S front. Big two-storey S porch added by Burn, its door and windows roundheaded, the parapet uncrenellated. Before its erection the first-floor S door, probably an C18 insertion, was reached by an open stone stair. Two-storey battlemented W wing of 1954, a larger and turreted version of the wing Burn had placed here. Above its three-light first-floor window, the coat of arms of Queen Elizabeth the Queen Mother (who bought the house in 1952), carved by *Hew Lorimer*. Courtyard at the back, its W range a 1954 remodelling

[*]Before that they had conical roofs.

of Burn's work. Round-arched gateway under a crenellation, probably of 1819, in its N screen wall. Walled garden to the E and W with an early C19 octagonal battlemented gazebo at the NW corner.

On the approach from the S, a harled early C19 LODGE with Gothick windows in its semi-octagonal W end.

CASTLE OF OLD WICK

2.1km. SE of Wick

3040

Isolated and dramatically sited remains of a cliff-top stronghold, very likely Norse in origin but first recorded as the property of Reginald Cheyne † *c.* 1350, from whom it descended to the Sutherlands and Oliphants before being sold in 1606 to the Earl of Caithness and later acquired by the Dunbars of Hempriggs. As late as the 1630s it was noted by Sir James Balfour of Denmylne as one of the 'Castells and Gentlemens housses of most respecte' in Caithness.

The site is a narrow V-shaped promontory rising *c.* 30m. above the sea and cut off from the curve of the coastline by narrow inlets on the W and E. The E side is a sheer drop. On the W, the inlet ends in a beach big enough for a small boat, from which a steep path climbs to the castle's landward approach from the S. Across this end of the promontory has been a low rampart with, behind it, a small building each side of the gateway. Only foundations survive. The next defence is provided by a ditch, *c.* 9m. wide and 3m. deep, cut through the rock and presumably originally crossed by a drawbridge. Immediately across the ditch is the keep, occupying most of the site's width but allowing the path to continue past its W side. The keep is rectangular, *c.* 9.4m. by 7m., its walls of local basalt slabs *c.* 2.1m. thick, still standing to a considerable height on the S and W sides and up to first-floor level on the E. It has been of four unvaulted storeys, the floor joists supported on intakes in the walling. One slit window in the E wall's ground floor, another in the S wall at the second floor, both with wide internal splays. There used to be another ground-floor window in the N wall, first-floor windows to N and E, and a second-floor E window. The ground-floor entrance was at the N wall's E end. Two small recesses in the wall at second-floor level. The thickness of the walls and the architecture's crude simplicity suggest an early date, perhaps C12 or C13. Ranges of outbuildings to the N are now marked only by grassy mounds.

CASTLE SINCLAIR *see* CASTLE GIRNIGOE AND CASTLE SINCLAIR

CASTLETOWN

Village begun *c.* 1830 by James Traill of Ratter in connexion with the adjacent quarry, which produced flagstones for paving the streets of the cities of southern Scotland and England.

OLD OLRIG PARISH CHURCH, 1.2km. S. Long roofless rectangle built of flagstone rubble, the NE skewputt inscribed '1633./31.IVLIE/M/DB', the initials those of the then minister Master David Bruce. This probably gives the date of a rebuilding of the medieval church, but in the S wall is a lancet window with an obtusely arched head, so earlier walling was probably incorporated. On the SE skewputt, the date 1743, presumably for a major repair. C17 chamfered surrounds at doors in the E, S and N walls (the last now blocked) and at the rectangular window near the S wall's E end.

OLRIG FREE CHURCH. Secularized. Built 1843. Double-gable front with a flat-roofed porch.

OLRIG PARISH CHURCH. Built as Olrig United Free Church and opened in 1913. Sturdy, with a hint of Art Nouveau at the front gable's window and bellcote.

CASTLEHILL HARBOUR, 0.8km. N. Small early C19 harbour built of local flagstones. – To the W, an early C19 HOUSE and STEADING, probably erected in connexion with the QUARRY, whose pumps were powered by two WINDMILLS, the tapering circular base of the N still standing.

DRILL HALL. Late C19 with a crowstepped gablet in the centre of the two-storey front; drum towers at the corners.

SCHOOL. Plain late C19 Board school, the long W extension added by *Sinclair Macdonald & Son*, 1938. – Beside it, the OLD SCHOOL, idiosyncratic Tudor dated 1866.

WAR MEMORIAL. By *Percy Portsmouth*, 1925. Tall block of Leggat stone, its upper part hollowed out as a recess for a bronze figure of Repentance (shown as a young man dressed in a toga and laurel wreath).

CORNMILL, 0.7km. NE. Big three-storey crowstep-gabled block, dated 1818 or 1819 at the W gable. Two projecting kilns, now clad in corrugated iron.

CASTLE VARRICH
0.6km. W of Tongue

Built on top of a hill overlooking the Kyle of Tongue. Small and ruinous rubble-built two-storey house, said to have belonged to the Bishops of Caithness; it is perhaps C16. The ground floor has been a vaulted store. No sign of a stair, so presumably the room above was reached by a ladder from outside.

CROSSKIRK

Farm overlooking Crosskirk Bay. Beside the mouth of the Forss Water, a sturdy crowstepped building, probably late C18. Remains of St Mary's Chapel to the W.

St Mary's Chapel. Very simple roofless chapel built of local
whinstone slabs. The nave may be C12. One door in the W
gable, probably original; the other, in the S wall, appears a later
insertion. No window now survives. The chancel was rebuilt,
probably in the C17, as a burial enclosure. On its E wall, a
crudely lettered MONUMENT to Donald Gunn †1778. – In the
surrounding churchyard, C18 and C19 GRAVESLABS, some of
the C18 stones carved with reminders of death.

DALE HOUSE   *1050*
0.5km. N of Westerdale

Big and plain laird's house covered in white harling. The five-bay
centre is of *c.* 1740 with a late C19 gabled porch. L-plan N
addition of 1910, S extension of 1933, both with bay windows.
    DOOCOT to the E. Rubble-built, of beehive type, it is probably
early C18.

DOUNREAY   *9060*

Nuclear power station sitting above the cliffs overlooking the
Pentland Firth.

DOUNREAY EXPERIMENTAL RESEARCH ESTABLISHMENT.
Large industrial complex, the fast reactor housed in a giant eau-
de-nil golfball. The first stage (Dounreay Fast Reactor) is by
Richard S. Brocklesby (Chief Architect to the Industrial Group
of the U.K. Atomic Energy Authority), 1955–8. W extension
(Prototype Fast Reactor) of 1966.

CAIRNS, Cnoc Freiceadain, 2.2km. SE. Two long cairns of the
third or fourth millennium B.C., both on the ridge of a hill and
only *c.* 120m. apart, but at right angles to each other. At each
end of the 71m.-long SOUTH CAIRN, low projecting horns
defining an almost rectangular forecourt, the E the larger. At
the ends, higher round mounds, suggesting that the cairn covers
and joins two originally separate chambered round cairns. –
Much more disturbed NORTH CAIRN, 67m. long, with horns
at its N end, where three projecting slab-tops suggest the presence of a burial chamber. At the S end, a flat-topped circular
mound, presumably originally a separate round cairn.

DUNBEATH   *1020*

Village along the A9, with a small harbour at Dunbeath Bay to
the E.

BERRIEDALE FREE CHURCH. Disused. Plain harled kirk built
in 1856. T-plan with a squat obelisk finial on the jamb's gable.
Porch and round-arched windows at the E end, a vestry at
the W.

DUNBEATH ROSS CHURCH. Built as Berriedale United Free Church, 1907. Three-light rectangular windows in the long sides, a Scots Late Gothic door and window in the N gable.

PRIMARY SCHOOL. By *Highland Regional Council* (project architect: *J. Pottie*), 1989. – Beside it, the late C19 former SCHOOL with obelisk-topped ball finials on the gables.

DUNBEATH CASTLE, 1.1km. S. Standing on a promontory, a substantial laird's house, probably of the early C17 but perhaps incorporating work of *c.* 1530, which was baronialized by *John Bryce* in 1907.* The front (W) block is substantially C17. Symmetrical three-storey façade with tall conical-roofed angle turrets. Central roundheaded and cable-hoodmoulded door, a replacement of 1907 for an earlier door in this position. Corbelled out from the first floor each side of the door is a fat semicircular turret topped by a gabled cap-house served by a small stair turret rising in the outer corner from the second floor. The r. turret is original, the l. an Edwardian replacement for one which had been removed in the early C19. Windows altered in 1907 when the attic windows were inserted, their pedimented dormerheads crowding the elevation. Conical-roofed turret at the SE corner. The NE corner is carried up as a square tower, formerly balustraded but given an aggressive corbelled battlement by Bryce. By Bryce also the large crow-step-gabled but not very martial Baronial additions at the back. Inside the front block, a vaulted ground floor, with the C17 kitchen at the N; at the S, the wine cellar with a mural stair to the first floor.

Flanking the approach from the NE, two rubble WALLED GARDENS, perhaps mid-C19, the S's walls incorporating carved stones, including part of a C17 chimneypiece. – Mid-C19 LODGE with a conical-roofed round tower. – To its N, a mid-C18 lectern DOOCOT.

LAIDHAY. *See* p. 121.

DUN DORNAIGIL *see* ALTNAHARRA

2070   DUNNET

Small village beside the Parish Church.

FREE CHURCH. *See* Barrock.

19 PARISH CHURCH. Harled T-plan kirk with a saddleback-roofed W bell tower. It is all very simple, with rectangular windows. The long body of the church may be of C16 origin. Near the W end of its N wall, in the characteristic pre-Reformation position, a blocked roundheaded door with a chamfered surround. The tower is probably of *c.* 1700. The N 'aisle' was added in

*Perhaps executing the design by *D. & J. Bryce* exhibited at the Royal Scottish Academy in 1881.

1836–7, the lean-to vestry abutting the tower later in the C19. On the S wall, a weathered MONUMENT of *c.*1700, an inept Ionic aedicule, the tympanum carved with a skull, crossbones and hourglass. Plain INTERIOR with box pews of 1837. – To the S, the old MANSE (now KARIBU) by *William Leslie*, 1846, a twin-gabled front with a block-consoled doorpiece in the centre.

HOUSE OF THE NORTHERN GATE. *See* p. 119.

DUNNET HEAD   2070

The most northerly point of the Scottish mainland crowned with a lighthouse.

LIGHTHOUSE. By *Robert Stevenson*, 1831. Squat round tower, the domed lantern rising within a corbelled parapet. – Plain contemporary KEEPERS' HOUSES.

FARR *see* BETTYHILL

FORSE CASTLE   2030
2.5km. E of Latheron

Craggy remains of a castle perched on a promontory high above the sea. The lands of Forse were acquired by the Cheynes through marriage to a Norse heiress. On the death of Reginald Cheyne, *c.* 1350, they passed to his elder daughter Mariota, wife of Sir John Keith, and then to her daughter, who married Kenneth Sutherland, second son of William, fifth Earl of Sutherland, *c.* 1400. The castle seems to have been abandoned in the late C17.

The landward approach from the N is cut off by a ditch, originally spanned by a drawbridge, now by a narrow causeway. At the promontory's broad N end, substantial remains of the 2m.-thick N, E and S walls of a rubble-built keep, *c.* 6.5m. by 3.5m., perhaps dating from the C12 or C13. It has been of at least two unvaulted storeys, the upper floor's joists resting on scarcements in the walls. In the S wall, a small ground-floor gunloop and a first-floor window. There seems to have been a first-floor door in the same wall. In the E wall, a round-headed recess, probably connected with the entrance gate into the castle. Immediately to the E, foundations of a gate-house block, the entrance passage passing through its W side beside the keep. In the courtyard to the S have been late medieval buildings, a fair amount of the W range's walling still standing.

2030
FORSE HOUSE
2.2km. NE of Latheron

Big white harled laird's house built by Captain John Sutherland
of Forse in 1753. The Roman Doric portico is an early C19
addition. Plain Victorian extensions at the back. – To the w, a
large early C18 lectern DOOCOT. Ball finials on the crowstepped
gables; in the centre of the back wall, a thistle finial.

0060
FORSS HOUSE
8km. W of Thurso

Harled early C19 mansion of the Sinclairs of Forss, with huge
chimneys on the wallheads as well as the gables. Lower mid-
Victorian W addition; the E gable's conservatory is also late C19.
On the N front, a crenellated porch added in 1939.

Beside the Forss Water to the w, an early C19 piend-roofed
MILL; at its S end, a small MILLER'S HOUSE with gableted
stone dormers. – On the river's opposite bank, a second MILL,
probably also early C19. – Two-arch BRIDGE with rounded
cutwaters, of c. 1800.

3060
FRESWICK HOUSE
6.5km. NE of Keiss

Tall rendered L-plan laird's house built for William Sinclair of
Freswick, c. 1760, probably incorporating parts of an earlier,
perhaps C17, house on the site. At the five-bay front, a projecting crowstep-gabled and ball-finialled centrepiece. Crowstepped w gable; straight skews on the SE wing. At the back, a
courtyard, its w side formed by a roofless two-storey range. –
To the S, a large U-plan STEADING, probably C18 but altered
and enlarged in the C19. – N of the house, the small rubble-
built ST MADDEN'S CHAPEL, now roofless. Two bullseye
windows in the S wall. Despite the name it has had chimneys;
perhaps it is a late C18 garden house. – On the approach from
the w, a beehive DOOCOT, probably early C17, the rubble
walling broken by two ratcourses.

GARRYWHIN *see* BRUAN

GIRNIGOE CASTLE *see* CASTLE GIRNIGOE AND CASTLE SINCLAIR

HALKIRK   *1050*

Planned village laid out by Sir John Sinclair of Ulbster *c.* 1800, the main street still largely c 19, the remainder c 20.

FREE PRESBYTERIAN CHURCH. Dated 1896. Couthy rubble-built church with a pyramid-roofed tower at the centre of the w gable.

OLD PARISH CHURCH. Disused. Harled T-plan kirk of 1751–3 in a well-stocked graveyard. Birdcage bellcote on the w gable. Segment-headed windows in the long s wall and high up in the gables. Interior gutted, but the segmental arch into the 'N' aisle survives.

PARISH CHURCH. Originally Halkirk Free Church. Broad Italianate box, by *Alexander Ross*, 1884–6. On the l. of the gable front, a big campanile. In the gable's centre, a rose window set in a semicircular overarch carried on squat columns with well-foliaged capitals; below, four small roundheaded lights recessed behind a Romanesque arcade.

PRIMARY SCHOOL. By the County Architect, *W. Wilson*, 1956. Straightforward with pitched roofs but unashamedly of its time.

ROSS INSTITUTE. Baronial, dated 1912. Projecting from the centre, a tall crowstepped tower with pepperpot angle turrets. More pepperpot turrets at the main block's corners, the l. chamfered and corbelled to a right angle, providing a touch of asymmetry.

THURSO COMBINATION POORHOUSE. Now housing. By *W. L. Moffat*, 1854–6. A long harled block, its front barely enlivened by projecting gables.

WAR MEMORIAL. White marble group of a widow and kilted orphan, *c.* 1920. The inscription is from Robert Burns:

> GENTLE PEACE RETURNING,
> WI' MONY A SWEET BABE FATHERLESS,
> AND MONY A WIDOW MOURNING.

BRAAL CASTLE. *See* p. 107.

HOUSE OF THE NORTHERN GATE   *2070*
1.3km. NW of Dunnet

Prominently sited white harled Edwardian shooting lodge sparingly adorned with crowsteps and a turret.

JOHN O' GROATS   *3070*

Scattered village in the NE corner of Caithness, its name taken from the legendary John o' Groats House supposedly built to calm the disputes about precedence among the eight branches of the Groat family in the c 16. It was said to have been an octagon with a window and door in each wall, so that each representative

could enter through his own door to take his place at one side of
the octagonal table inside.

DUNCANSBY HEAD LIGHTHOUSE, 2.6km. E. By *D. Alan Stevenson*, 1921. Small tower with an adjoining two-storey flat-
roofed block of KEEPERS' HOUSES.

JOHN O' GROATS HOUSE HOTEL, 0.7km. N. Designed and
built in 1875–6 by *Thomson Sinclair*, the then owner of the
Duncansby estate. Ragbag Baronial, the main feature an octagonal tower. On each face of the tower, a crowstep-gabled
dormer; SE stair turret. Now much enlarged, but not to the
benefit of its appearance.

KEISS

3060

Small fishing village, most of the housing C 20 and laid out round
a large green, but with a few early C 19 rubble-built houses on the
cliff overlooking the harbour.

FREE CHURCH. Forbidding Gothic, by *Brims*, 1894–5. In the W
gable, three lancet lights under a quatrefoil opening. Big slated
flèche.

PARISH CHURCH. A harled T-plan 'Parliamentary' church (i.e.
to *William Thomson*'s design), built by *James Smith* in 1827.
Tudor arched windows; spikily pinnacled bellcote. One of the
long wall's doors has been built up. Much altered interior.

HARBOUR. Given its present appearance by *Joseph Mitchell*, 1833.
Two basins (an outer and inner) built of rough ashlar. Beside
the harbour, a contemporary early C 19 three-storey WARE-
HOUSE of six bays.

KEISS CASTLE
0.9km. NE

Solid Baronial house by *David Bryce*, 1859–62, incorporating a
plain Georgian block of *c.* 1760. Unusually for a work by Bryce
it is harled. L-plan, the S wing a double pile, its r. half with a
crowstepped gable, the l. ending at the W in a bowed corner
(containing the round-arched entrance) corbelled out to a
square battlemented cap-house with an ogee-roofed turret
rising beside it. Fat candle-snuffered bartizans at the crowstepped W gable.

On the cliff-edge to the E, the roofless shell of OLD KEISS
CASTLE, a tall tower house built for the Earls of Caithness,
probably early in the C 17. It is Z-plan, with towers at the NW
and SE. Round SE tower, a tall chimney corbelled from its
face. The NW tower is roughly D-shaped, its straight N side
continuing the line of the main block's gable; top floor corbelled
out to the square. On the N, at the join with the main block, a
turret carried on tiers of chequer-set corbelling. More chequer-
set corbelling under a bartizan at the main block's SW corner.
Big moulded windows at the upper floors. The entrance must

have been in the mostly missing N gable or E wall. Inside, there has been one tunnel-vaulted room on the ground floor. Stair in the NW tower; a second stair to the top floor in the N turret.

KIRKSTYLE

3070

Place-name on the Thurso–John o' Groats road marking the site of Canisbay Parish Church.

CANISBAY PARISH CHURCH. Cruciform kirk with a bell tower, the harling covering evidence of an apparently complicated development. The long nave probably incorporates walling from the medieval parish church, perhaps built in the C15 and dedicated to St Drostan. A door in the customary late medieval position at the W end of the S wall was blocked and harled over in 1891. The W tower was added in 1704. Repairs costing £1,000 Scots (£83 7s. 6d. sterling) were made in 1706, and twelve years later the Presbytery ordered the church to be repaired or rebuilt at an estimated cost of over £1,500 Scots. This work, probably including the addition of the transeptal S 'aisle', seems to have been carried out in 1724 (the date 1720 appears on one of the nave's skewputts, 1724 on one of the aisle's). Further work, perhaps including the building of the crowstepped N 'aisle', was done at a cost of £1,564 15s. 9d. in 1736; *David Gills elder, David Gills Yr.* and *David Mowat* were the masons. The outcome of all this is quite unpretentious. Saddleback-roofed tower, unadorned except for ball finials. In the church's long S wall, tall rectangular windows with moulded margins rising into gablets. Pointed-arched windows in the gables, the S aisle's with crude Y-tracery. A moulded round-arched doorway is this aisle's entrance.

Inside, the S aisle was converted to a porch in 1891. In the church, E and W GALLERIES, probably made by *Robert Forsyth*, house carpenter in Thurso, in 1831–2. – PEWS and PULPIT of 1891. – On the N wall, an expensive Gothic MONUMENT in grey and white marble with a coat of arms on top to Georgiana, Countess of Caithness, † 1870; it is signed by *Burke & Co.*, of London. – In the porch, GRAVESLAB of Donald Grot † 1768, carved with a cross and a shield bearing a merchant's mark.

Crowded CHURCHYARD containing a number of C18 GRAVESTONES decorated with emblems of mortality.

LAIDHAY

1030

1.4km. NE of Dunbeath

Well-preserved CROFT buildings, now a museum. Long single- 125 storey block built of white-washed rubble, probably early C19. Inside, it contains an end room with a fireplace, a middle room with four boxbeds, a kitchen also with a fireplace, a dairy or scullery, and a byre. The stone wall between the kitchen and dairy and the partition between dairy and byre may be Victorian

insertions. In the roof over the kitchen, a cruck truss. – To the
E, a detached BARN, also rubble-built with a thatched roof
of cruck-frame construction, the timbers mostly of birch but
including reused boat timbers. Opposite the entrance, a second
(winnowing) door providing a through-draught.

LATHERON

2030

Settlement at the junction of the main roads S from Wick and
Thurso.

21 PARISH CHURCH (now Clan Gunn Centre). Rendered T-plan
kirk, the body built in 1725–38,* the N 'aisle' added by *William
Davidson*, 1821–2. At the aisle's gable, a slightly projecting small
tower topped by an octagonal domed cupola with round-arched
belfry openings. Otherwise it is all of the simplest, with rectangular windows. Interior stripped of furnishings for its present
museum use. – Attached to the S wall, the small rubble-built
BURIAL ENCLOSURE of the Sinclairs of Dunbeath, probably
formed from a part of the medieval church here. The S wall
incorporates the head of a lancet window. – Inside, a big MONU-
MENT to Christian Mowat, wife of Sir John Sinclair of Dunbeath, executed by *John Diren* in 1642. Classical, with paired
Corinthian columns; frieze carved with angels' heads, a skull
and bones. – The CHURCHYARD is paved with Caithness slab
memorials. – S of the church, the GRAVESLAB of John Monro
† 1710, with a coat of arms; at the bottom, carved reminders of
death.

49   On the hillside 0.5km. N, a square BELL TOWER, probably
C 17, with thick rubble walls rising sheer to a flattened pyramid
roof of the same stone. Rectangular belfry openings but no
door.

WEST CHURCH. Built as a United Free church in 1909. Bellcote
on the gable front, which contains a segmental arched window.

FORMER SCHOOL. Plain schoolhouse by *William Davidson*,
1821. Attached to its W gable, the late C 19 schoolroom block,
looking faintly ecclesiastical.

LATHERON CASTLE. *See* Latheronwheel.
LATHERON HOUSE. *See* Latheronwheel.
FORSE CASTLE. *See* p. 117.
FORSE HOUSE. *See* p. 118.

LATHERONWHEEL

1030

Planned village, originally named Janetstown, begun in 1853 and
mostly composed of late C 19 housing which forms a single street
pointing towards the sea.

*Work began in 1725 but was abandoned the same year and not resumed until
1735.

CHURCH HALL. Dated 1896 and very simple.

BRIDGE beside the A9. By *Thomas Telford*, 1809–13. A high rubble-built single span.

HARBOUR. Probably begun in the early C19 but altered by *D. & T. Stevenson*, 1851–2. On the NE, a rubble-built pier, most of its stones set vertically or diagonally; concrete SE pier. – Beside it, a rubble BRIDGE of one segmental arch over the Burn of Latheronwheel, built *c.* 1725; it has no parapet.

LATHERON CASTLE, 0.5km. S. Rubble-built corner of a small rectangular keep on the cliff-top S of the harbour. It may be C12 or C13.

LATHERON HOUSE, 0.2km. NE. Plain early C19 farmhouse with late Victorian crowstepped, bay-windowed and segmental-pedimented additions tacked onto the front.

LATHERONWHEEL HOUSE. Scots Jacobean, by *David Bryce*, 1851. Conical-roofed round tower over the entrance at the SE corner. To its r., a two-storey bay window topped by a slated octagonal spire.

LYBSTER

2030

Planned village laid out by Lieutenant-General Patrick Sinclair of Lybster in 1802, but whose development did not begin seriously for another twenty years. It forms one long street broadening out in the centre, the mid-Victorian CLYDESDALE BANK (former Aberdeen Town & County Bank) providing a touch of civic pomp.

LYBSTER AND BRUAN FREE CHURCH. Tall but very plain Gothic, built in 1847–8 and enlarged in 1877.

LYBSTER CENTRAL CHURCH. Originally a United Free church. Staid Gothic box of 1909–10, a bellcote on the buttressed gable front.

LYBSTER CHAPEL-OF-EASE. Disused. By *William Davidson*, 1836. Harled box with two tiers of small Gothic windows; spikily pinnacled bellcote on the W gable. – In the forecourt, a medieval SLAB carved with a Celtic cross.

HARBOUR, 0.8km. SW. Begun in 1833 as a stone quay along the W bank of the mouth of the Reisgill Burn, it was much enlarged by *Joseph Mitchell*** in 1850–4, and again in 1883–5. At the entrance, a small octagonal LIGHTHOUSE of 1884. – Beside the harbour, early C19 STOREHOUSES. – On the hill above, INVER HOUSE of 1815, dressed up with battlements. – Single-span BRIDGE, probably early C19, on the approach. 123

PRIMARY SCHOOL. By *Sinclair Macdonald & Son*, 1934–7, with later additions.

SCHOOL. Now warehousing. The S wing, with round-arched windows, was built as the Free Church School in 1851. Additions of 1877 and 1904 made it L-plan.

SWINEY HOUSE. *See* p. 127.

**With advice from *David Stevenson*.

STONE SETTING, Achavanich, 8.1km. NW. Remains of an elongated U-shaped arrangement of upright stones, mostly 1.2m.–
1.5m. high but many now truncated, their broad faces set at
right angles to the perimeter. They were perhaps erected in the
second millennium B.C.

MELNESS

5060

Straggling settlement beside Tongue Bay.

CHURCH. Built as a Free church in 1900. Dead plain lanceted
box, with a gabled bellcote. – Beside it, remains of the OLD
FREE CHURCH of *c.* 1845, a rubble rectangle with roundheaded doors in the gables.

Former CHURCH OF SCOTLAND. Now a house. By *J. Pond
Macdonald*, 1895. Rubble mission church with depressed-arch
windows. The bellcote is missing.

SCHOOL. Built as a church in 1835–6 and converted to a school
about ten years later. Its present appearance is the result of
alterations and additions by *Andrew Maitland & Sons*, 1892.

MELNESS HOUSE. Plain white harled late Georgian farmhouse. –
To its N, a big mid-C19 L-plan STEADING.

MEY *see* CASTLE OF MEY

MID CLYTH *see* BRUAN

NOSS HEAD

3050

Just the lighthouse standing on the cliff edge.

LIGHTHOUSE. By *Alan Stevenson*, 1849. Standard round tower
with a tall domed lantern. Neo-Egyptian keepers' cottages.

OLDHALL HOUSE
4.3km. NW of Watten

2050

Crowstepped and gableted mid-Victorian mansion house, rather
in the domestic manner of David Bryce.

OLD MAN OF WICK *see* CASTLE OF OLD WICK

OLD WICK *see* CASTLE OF OLD WICK

OLRIG *see* CASTLETOWN

OUSDALE *see* BERRIEDALE

REAY   9060

Small village in the NW of Caithness which acquired the status of
a burgh of barony in 1628. At the E, an informal early C19 group
built round a green, with the Parish Church at the W and the old
graveyard to the E. Further W, C20 housing beside the village hall.

PARISH CHURCH. Harled kirk of 1738–9, T-plan with a long
   main block, the inner angles with the N 'aisle' filled in 1909
   with a vestry and shed. At the E end, a very simple pyramid-
   roofed ball-finialled bell tower with a forestair to its first-floor
   door. In the church's long S wall has been a symmetrical
   arrangement of rectangular doors and windows (checked for
   external shutters). The E door was built up and harled over in
   the C19; the central (minister's) door was also blocked and now
   appears as a recess under an oculus. The W gable's two-light
   Y-traceried window was inserted in 1933. At the 'aisle', a forestair to the gallery's door; ground-floor door with fluted jambs
   and lintel. – Inside, a segmental arch into the 'aisle'. – Hexagonal PULPIT with a Corinthian pilastered back and sounding
   board. – PEWS mostly of 1933.
OLD CHURCHYARD. Gravelled cemetery containing several C18
   GRAVESTONES carved with emblems of death, some with coats
   of arms. – In the NE corner, the MAUSOLEUM of the Mackays
   of Bighouse, apparently added in 1691 to the now demolished
   medieval parish church. – In its W wall, a late C17 TABLET
   carved with the coats of arms of Mackay and Sinclair; it commemorates Angus Mackay of Bighouse and Jane Sinclair, his
   wife. – Beside it is set a medieval GRAVESLAB carved with a
   Celtic cross. – In the N wall, a large MONUMENT to Lieutenant
   Colonel George Mackay of Bighouse †1798. Grey marble
   obelisk with an armorial plaque of white marble, flanked by two
   mourning riflemen.
HALL. Built in 1897 to celebrate Queen Victoria's Diamond
   Jubilee. Small, with a faint Jacobean flavour.
HARBOUR, 1.3km. N. Built by Major William Innes of Sandside,
   c. 1835, the basin tightly enclosed by two L-plan piers. – Beside
   it, contemporary housing, the two-storey blocks having storage
   on the ground floor.

ACHVARASDAL. *See* p. 102.
SANDSIDE HOUSE. *See* p. 126.

UPPER DOUNREAY, 3.5km. E. Mid-C19 courtyard steading. At
the front range, basket-arched openings and a centre gablet.

9060

SANDSIDE HOUSE
1.6km. NW of Reay

Harled mansion begun in 1751 by Harry Innes of Borlum, who
built a five-bay laird's house. Crowstepped gablets; a shaped
chimney gablet in the centre of the E front. c. 1840 the house
was extended to make an H-plan. In 1889 *James Matthews*
infilled the S indentation and shifted the entrance to this side.
But the effect of the crowstepped gabled ends (the r. the original
house's S gable) and off-centre door is bleak. Gablets on the W
front, probably also of 1889, as are the rectangular bay windows
and N extension of the E elevation.

STEADING behind, probably mid-C18, with a long single-
storey S addition of c. 1800. The three-storey crowstepped C18
block at the NW contains a KILN BARN, now rather altered; at
its S gable, a semi-octagonal stair projection.

WALLED GARDEN to the NW. In one corner, a pyramid-
roofed DOOCOT, probably early C19.

1070

SCRABSTER

Little C19 village at the foot of a cliff beside the harbour on the
W side of Thurso Bay, oil storage tanks the dominant feature.

HARBOUR. Begun by *Robert Stevenson & Son*, 1846, and reconstructed in 1891 by *James Barron*. A new quay was built in 1972.
HOLBORNHEAD LIGHTHOUSE. By *D. & T. Stevenson*, 1860–2.
White harled block of KEEPERS' HOUSES. Attached to the SE
end is the tower, square below; above, it is chamfered to an
octagon topped by a domed lantern.
SCRABSTER HOUSE. Prominently sited on the hill above. Late
C19 mansion, dotty but unendearing castellated, incorporating
bits of a late C18 house extended in 1834.

0060

SHEBSTER

Settlement isolated on the edge of moorland.

REAY FREE CHURCH. Disused. Built in 1844. Broad front of
two gables with corbelled turret finials at the outer corners.
Between the gables, a stone-spired octagonal bellcote. Round-
arched ground-floor openings; pointed gallery windows.
REAY UNITED FREE CHURCH. Secularized. Built c. 1910. Late
Gothic window tracery in the gable front.

STONE SETTING, Broubster, 3.4km. SE. Only a few stones still
standing of what has been an elongated U-shaped arrangement

of upright slabs, the tallest *c.* 1.6m. high, with their broad faces at right angles to the perimeter. The setting may date from the second millennium B.C.

SINCLAIR CASTLE *see* CASTLE GIRNIGOE AND CASTLE SINCLAIR

SKELPICK *see* BETTYHILL

STIRKOKE HOUSE
4.4km. W of Wick

3050

Tall but low-key Baronial house dated 1858–9, in the manner of *David Bryce*, possibly incorporating an earlier house at the W. Plenty of Brycean motifs with crowstepped gables, a stringcourse jumping about on the entrance front, conical-roofed angle turrets of one and two storeys, mullioned windows and a canted bay corbelled out to a gabled top. Low crow-stepped office range to the W, perhaps a little earlier.

STRATHY

8060

Scattered village beside the Pentland Firth.

Former CHURCH. Now a house. A T-plan 'Parliamentary' church (i.e. to *William Thomson*'s design), built by *James Smith* in 1826–8. Standard spikily pinnacled bellcote and Tudor windows, but they have lost their lattice glazing, the doors in the front wall have been partly built up and a new door made in the jamb.

FREE CHURCH. Broad box of *c.* 1850. It has lost its bellcote but gained a porch on the long S wall.

PARISH CHURCH. Originally United Free. Built *c.* 1910. A hall which shows its ecclesiastical status by having a small gableted bellcote and a five-light window over the entrance.

SWINEY HOUSE
1.3km. E of Lybster

2030

Harled laird's house of *c.* 1760. Chimney gablet and a pedimented doorpiece in the centre of the front.

THRUMSTER HOUSE
6.3km. S of Wick

Harled model farmhouse of two storeys and three bays, built *c.*
1800 for the then tenant, Captain Brodie. The flanking piend-
roofed wings are probably early additions, as are the endearingly
inept Tudor hoodmoulds. *c.* 1840 a big extension was added at
the back, its central feature a porch projecting from below a
large stair window, the detail Tudorish Gothick. The front
porch probably came a little later, perhaps at the same time as
the E wing's wallhead was lowered and it acquired a battlemented parapet. Plain late C19 NW addition.

THURSO

Town on the N shore of Caithness at the mouth of the River
Thurso. There was a settlement here by 1196, when William I's
army attacked Thurso Castle, but the present town was founded
in 1633 as a burgh of barony under the feudal superiority of the
Earls of Caithness. The lands of Thurso and the overlordship of
the burgh were acquired by the Sinclairs of Ulbster in 1719. In
1798 Sir John Sinclair laid out a 'New Town' SW of the irregular
lanes and streets of the existing burgh. This was 'according to the
most regular plan that could be contrived and in a manner not
only ornamental but also positively well adapted for preserving
the health & promoting the convenience of the Inhabitants.'*
However, development was sporadic; only two of Sinclair's proposed four public buildings were erected‡ and the SW street was
omitted. Since 1950 major expansion and redevelopment has
taken place, much of the Old Town and Fishertown being rebuilt
and new suburbs formed on both sides of the river to house natives
and incomers brought here to work at the nuclear power station
at Dounreay.

CHURCHES

CONGREGATIONAL CHURCH, Castle Street. Plain Gothic of
1875–6. In the gable front, a large rose window with quatrefoil
tracery.
FIRST FREE CHURCH, Olrig Street. Secularized. Ambitious
Dec, by *J. Russell Mackenzie*, 1868–71. The S end fronts the
street, its centrepiece a semi-octagon with a crowstepped gable
on each face; in the middle, a four-light window over the gabled
entrance. On the r., an octagonal stairtower. To the l., a steeple
intaken at the belfry stage, where a conical-roofed turret rises
in one corner; octagonal spire above. On the side elevations,
processions of crowstepped gables for the aisles' transverse

---

*So wrote Captain John Henderson in his *General View of the Agriculture of the
County of Caithness* (1812).
‡St Peter's and St Andrew's Church (on the site earmarked for a Town House)
and the Miller Institution (now Public Library). Sinclair had also specified sites for
a Hospital and Town House.

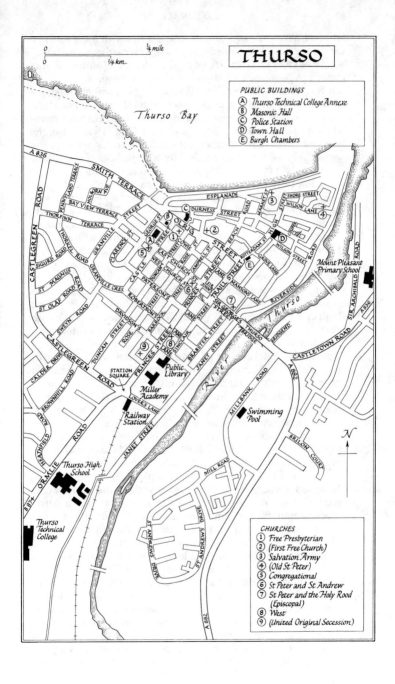

roofs. Interior divided into nave and aisles with a big PULPIT
at the N end. – Fat-bellied GALLERIES on cast-iron columns.

FREE PRESBYTERIAN CHURCH, Olrig Street. Humble Gothic,
built as a Reformed Presbyterian chapel in 1859.

20 OLD ST PETER, Wilson Lane. Roofless agglomeration making a
rough cruciform, built of thin slabs of local rubble. The dedi-
cation to St Peter suggests an early date for the church's foundation, and there seems little doubt that Thurso was one of the
six churches whose parsonage revenues were annexed to the
episcopal *mensa* by Gilbert de Moravia, Bishop of Caithness,
in the early C13. The only part of the present building likely to
date from the C12 or C13 is the FORSS VAULT, the shedlike
chancel projecting at the E end. Externally it is very plain, with
slit windows in the N and E walls, the E round-arched internally,
neither checked for glass. The tunnel-vaulted interior is apsidal-
ended. This combination of a rectangular exterior with a D-plan
interior, common enough in large Anglo-Norman churches, is
found elsewhere on this diminutive scale only at the C12 St
Margaret's Chapel in Edinburgh Castle.

The nave was rebuilt, probably *c.* 1500, with a three-light
pointed window containing crude intersecting tracery placed
high in the crowstepped W gable. Contemporary SW porch with
stone benches inside and an eroded basket-arched door into
the church.

After the Reformation of 1560 the church was rearranged,
the Sinclairs of Forss taking over the now redundant medieval
chancel as their burial place and inserting a door in its S wall.
Lofts were introduced at the E and W ends of the nave, the W
reached by a forestair built against the porch's E side, the E by
a now demolished forestair on the N of the nave.

It was probably early in the C17 that the crowstepped transeptal S 'aisle'* was added, its siting E of centre imposed by the
prior existence of the porch and adjoining forestair. Five-light
S window (its sill raised), again with intersecting tracery.
Moulded rectangular windows, two with roundheaded rear-
arches, in the E and W walls. At the W wall's N end, a partly
blocked roundheaded and roll-moulded door into a passage
which leads under the forestair to a blocked door into the
porch. Big segmental N arch into the body of the church.

At about the same time or a little after the building of this S
'aisle', a session house (used also as the burgh court room) was
added above the chancel.‡ It had a door (now blocked) from
the nave's E gallery, but the main access was from a stair
contained in the contemporary tower awkwardly attached at an
acute angle to the chancel's SW corner, its position perhaps
determined by the need for it to be entered from inside the
church but not from the Forss Vault and without blocking any
existing door or window. The tower's walls have a pronounced

---

*This was the communion aisle by the C19, and was probably built as such.
‡The lintel of the door into this room is said to have had the date 1638 or 1640
carved on it.

batter; on the s and e faces, circular buttresses. It used to have a pyramid roof.

In 1664 a second transeptal 'aisle' was added on the nave's N side. In its crowstepped gable, the remains of a three-light window with intersecting tracery. In the side walls, moulded rectangular windows lighting a gallery to which a door in the SE corner gave access from the forestair on the nave's N side. All this is clearly C 17, but the windows under the gallery have pointed arches; so are the lower parts of the aisle's E and W walls the remains of a late medieval chapel?

St Peter and St Andrew, Sir John's Square. Huge Perp box filling the site reserved for a Town House on the New Town's layout plan of 1798. It was built in 1830–2 to a design by *William Burn* and is a simplified version of his St John's (Episcopal) Church, Edinburgh, of 1815–18. s tower with pinnacled octagonal buttresses; in the inner angles, parapeted projections housing the vestibule and disguising the width of the gable. Foliaged finialled buttresses along the sides, their vertical droving a contrast to the main walling's polished ashlar. Round three sides of the interior, a U-plan gallery whose cast-iron columns rise into plaster ribs which attempt to suggest that the flat ceiling is vaulted. The area was refurnished in 1914. At the N end, a Gothic PULPIT and ELDERS' PEWS. – Behind them, a contemporary ORGAN by *Norman & Beard*. – STAINED GLASS in the N wall below the gallery. On the l., a window (the Sower) by *Oscar Paterson*, 1921–2. – On the r., a more lushly pictorial scene (the Maries at the Tomb), after 1915.

St Peter and the Holy Rood (Episcopal), Sir George's Street. By *Alexander Ross*, 1883–4, with a chancel added in 1906. SW porch; in its inner angle, a tall conical-roofed round tower. Big Geometric W window. – Wooden REREDOS carved with reliefs of the Ascension and Pentecost. – Late C 19 STAINED GLASS W window (the Good Samaritan).

Salvation Army Hall, Market Street. Big box, now dry-dashed and rather altered, built as an Independent chapel in 1799. Tall round-arched windows intended to light the pulpit in the centre of the s wall.

United Original Secession Chapel, Princes Street. Now a drill hall. Small, Geometric Gothic, by *Alexander Ross*, 1875.

West Church, Sinclair Street. By *David Smith*, 1859–60. Gothic box, the gable front broken by a steeple, its tower's corner buttresses now bereft of pinnacles; above, a gableted octagonal belfry surmounted by a lucarned spire.

PUBLIC BUILDINGS

Burgh Chambers, Rotterdam Street. Georgian-survival of *c.* 1850, with a heavy console-corniced doorpiece.

Drill Hall, Olrig Street. *See* Masonic Hall, below.

Drill Hall, Princes Street. *See* Churches, above: United Original Secession Chapel.

Dunbar Hospital, Ormlie Road. Quiet Baronial of 1882–5.

Big entrance tower with copper-spired angle turrets of differing heights and an octagonal slated roof.

HARBOUR. Stone wharfs and short piers on both sides of the River Thurso. By *James Barron*, 1890–1.

MASONIC HALL, Olrig Street. Originally a drill hall. By *David Smith*, 1873. Formidably castellated, with a big round tower in the centre of the front and machicolated turrets at the corners.

MILLER ACADEMY, Princes Street. By *Sinclair Macdonald & Son*, 1934. Utilitarian, with a few neo-Georgian touches to give civic dignity. It incorporates a one-storey Jacobean board school block of the late C19.

MILLER INSTITUTION. *See* Public Library, below.

MOUNTPLEASANT PRIMARY SCHOOL, Castletown Road. By *George Watt & Stewart*, 1966.

PENNYLAND PRIMARY SCHOOL, Trostan Road. By *George Watt & Stewart*, 1960.

POLICE STATION, Olrig Street. Small and busy, in drydash with slate-hung 'mansard' roofs; by *Highland Regional Council*, 1975.

PUBLIC LIBRARY, Davidson's Lane. By *William Smith*, 1859–60, it was built as the Miller Institution, a boys' school. Single-storey ashlar-faced cruciform, a pedimented portico at the front's slightly projecting centrepiece. Behind and above the portico, a cupola of two stages, the round belfry with Doric columns, the upper stage octagonal with clock-faces on four fronts; low dome on top.

RAILWAY STATION, Station Square. 1872–4, by *Murdoch Paterson*, virtually identical to his contemporary station at Wick. Large shed with faintly Italianate detail.

SWIMMING POOL, Millbank Road. By *Sinclair Macdonald & Son*, 1967, with a broad pitched roof and glazed end wall.

THURSO BRIDGE. By *Macbey & Gordon*, 1885–7. Four segmental arches with pacifist-looking semi-octagonal cutwaters.

THURSO HIGH SCHOOL, Ormlie Road. By *Basil Spence*, 1958, with timber-clad curtain walling.

THURSO TECHNICAL COLLEGE, Ormlie Road. By *Alison & Hutchison & Partners*, 1961, looking like a curtain-walled office block.

THURSO TECHNICAL COLLEGE ANNEXE, Castle Street. Built as a Board school in 1892; *Donald Leed* was the architect. Long shallow U-plan, a square tower in one inner angle, a larger octagonal one in the other.

TOWN HALL, High Street. Flemish civic Gothic, by *J. Russell Mackenzie*, 1868–70. Five pinnacle-buttressed bays, a gabled door in the centre under a pointed window. Basket-arched hoodmoulds over the first floor's mullioned and transomed outer windows; below them, carved coats of arms. On top, a parade of gablets pierced by quatrefoils in Gothic overarches.

DESCRIPTION

At the junction of the roads from Wick and Castletown, a white harled TOLLHOUSE of *c.* 1815 with a semi-octagonal front. In MILLBANK ROAD to the SW, the SWIMMING POOL (*see* Public Buildings, above). At the road's end, an early C19 U-plan complex, its S part a former MILL, its N a FOUNDRY. Projecting from the SW corner, the old MILLER'S HOUSE with a pointed-arched window in the massively crowstepped gable. On the r. side of BRIDGEND immediately before the river, a pair of two-storey houses, No. 2 dated 1880 with a Tudorish doorpiece, the rendered No. 1 dated 1854.

Across Thurso Bridge (*see* Public Buildings, above), a formal vista along Sir George's Street to St Peter's and St Andrew's Church (*see* Churches, above) in the centre of the Georgian New Town's gridiron layout. In SIR GEORGE'S STREET itself, St Peter and the Holy Rood (Episcopal) Church (*see* above) contributes villagey Gothic to the r. side. On the l., a former CINEMA of 1922, bouncy English Baroque. SIR JOHN'S SQUARE is dominated by the huge St Peter's and St Andrew's Church ('quite a little cathedral', proclaimed Catherine Sinclair in 1840; *see* above). In front, a line-up of monuments. WAR MEMORIAL by *Percy Portsmouth*, 1920–2, a big bronze of a large Victory patting the head of a small boy symbolic of Peace. Behind, a weathered stone STATUE of Sir John Sinclair of Ulbster in the uniform of Colonel of the Rothesay and Caithness Fencibles, by *Francis Chantrey*, 1835. Memorial FOUNTAIN of 1894 to Sir George Sinclair of Ulbster; gableted Gothic with a marble relief bust.

JANET STREET overlooking the river was designed *c.* 1800 for 115 smart two-storey three-bay villas joined by single-storey links set behind colonnades. The early C19 No. 1 observes the intended size but not the elevation.* Its ground floor is conventional enough, with a tall pilastered doorpiece, but the first-floor windows are set between roundheaded niches with blind crosslet arrow-slits at the ends. Pilastered link to the contemporary No. 2, less ambitious but with a tripartite doorpiece under an overall segmental fanlight. Nos. 3 and 4 are much closer to the engraved elevation, with three-light windows in the slightly projecting ends, No. 3's ground-floor windows set in rectangular overarches in accordance with the engraving, No. 4's corniced doorpiece a deviation from it. Then the late C19 No. 6 (THE THURSO CLUB), with a narrow pedimented centre and rectangular anta-pilastered bay windows. No. 7, again early C19, pays only lip-service to the engraved elevation by having its centre marked off by rusticated 'quoins' although it is not recessed; broad pilastered doorpiece. The contemporary No. 8 follows the engraving, i.e. it has rusticated quoins, three-light first-floor windows and overarched ground-floor windows in the slightly projecting outer bays; in the centre,

---

*Illustrated in John Henderson, *General View of the Agriculture of the County of Caithness* (1812), pl. 7.

a round-arched door with blind side-lights under blind oculi,
all heavily renewed in cement. At Nos. 9–10, a mid-Victorian
double house with wrought-iron foliaged finials on the gables
and dormer gablets. No. 11, with a pair of tall shaped gables,
is by *David Smith*, 1878.

BRABSTER STREET behind is humbler. At the corner of Robertson's Lane, the big front garden of FAIRVIEW (No. 24
Sinclair Street), a superior piend-roofed early C19 house with
a roundheaded door in the porch. Its back is to SINCLAIR
STREET, which focuses on the Public Library (*see* Public Buildings, above). Mostly plain early and mid-C19 housing, but set
back on the NW side is a large mid-Victorian DRILL HALL
with thrifty early Renaissance detail. For the West Church, *see*
Churches, above. In PRINCES STREET, No. 30 on the corner
of Sir John's Square is an early C19 rendered house. The
PENTLAND HOTEL opposite, of *c.* 1980, is a concrete block
intrusion trying to fit in. On the N corner of Paterson's Lane,
another large front garden, that of No. 8 BARROCK STREET,
a smart villa of 1832 with a Roman Doric portico at the advanced
centre. (Inside, the dining room has a late C17 stone chimneypiece, carved with a shield flanked by lions, a rose and a
thistle.) Near the Railway Station (for which *see* above), No. 67
Princes Street, a little Jacobean *cottage orné* dated 1868. The
late Victorian Nos. 71–75 form a picturesquely irregular U-plan
almshouse-like group with gabled porches and front gardens.
More mid-C19 cottages in ROSE STREET. At the NE end, No.
1, dated 1856, a triple house on a U-plan with crowstepped
wings and a steep gabled porch in the centre; it was built as the
Thurso Benevolent Institution. Nos. 9–11 are a pair of semi-
detached cottages, each with a pedimented centre. At Nos.
21–25, single-storey terraced cottages with spikily pinnacled
porches.

TRAILL STREET is the New Town's commercial centre, a disappointingly plain Victorian assemblage for the most part. On
the corner of Cowie Lane, the CLYDESDALE BANK (former
Aberdeen Town & County Bank) by *J. Russell Mackenzie*, 1866,
with bowed corners and giant angle pilasters. At the top of
MANSONS LANE to the SE, the MEADOW WELL, enclosed in
a little conical-roofed shelter of 1823. At the lane's other end,
the crowstepped OLD BREWERY of *c.* 1800, a six-bay block
with, attached to its NW end, the contemporary brewer's house
of two storeys in the height of the brewery's three.

OLRIG STREET begins the exit to the NE. On its corner with
Beach Road, the mid-Victorian ROYAL BANK OF SCOTLAND
(former Commercial Bank), dour despite its wealth of crowstepped gables; flat-roofed addition in front. Much better is
the BANK OF SCOTLAND (former British Linen Bank) by *J. M.
Dick Peddie*, 1897, the central Flemish gable carved with a coat
of arms. Beside it, the old First Free Church (*see* above), its
steeple a prominent landmark. For No. 18 Olrig Street, *see* No.
1 Rose Street, above.

Thurso's Old Town and Fishertown lie to the NE. ROTTERDAM

STREET is a mixture of small-scale C19 and C20 redevelopment. NE of the Burgh Chambers (*see* Public Buildings, above) is the gable end of a late Georgian block with a rounded corner to GROVE LANE, where the LEISURE CENTRE has been made out of other late Georgian buildings. HIGH STREET continues the main street line but broadens out in front of the Town Hall (*see* above). TOLLEMACHE HOUSE is a sizeable block by *Sinclair Macdonald & Son*, 1963; murals on the gable and in the courtyard by *Caziel* (*Cazimir Zielemkiewicz*). The rest of this area was mostly redeveloped in the 1950s by *Sinclair Macdonald & Son* to a layout plan provided by *Frank C. Mears*. Straightforward traditional housing with harled or stone walls and pitched slated roofs, but the generosity of the spaces makes it a touch suburban. Incorporated in this, Nos. 16–18 SHORE STREET, a harled house of 1687 (the date appearing with the initials DW, KR on the l. skewputt), a fat conical-roofed stairtower projecting from the centre of the front. At the bottom of WILSON LANE, Old St Peter's Church (*see* above) in its graveyard near the river. On the ESPLANADE to the N, a cast-iron FOUNTAIN of 1898, the basins supported by lion terms; on top of the central column, a small figure of Hercules.

THURSO CASTLE
1.2km. NE

Bleak ruins of the unappealing but dramatically sited Baronial pile built for Sir John Sinclair, third Baronet of Ulbster, in 1872–8; *David Smith* was the architect. The main feature surviving the house's demolition in 1952 is the W tower, very martial, with a machicolated parapet and corner turret.

Contemporary GATEWAY on the SW approach, a round arch 98 under an extravagantly machicolated parapet with turrets at the corners. – Beside it, a LODGE in the same crazily martial manner.

HAROLD'S TOWER on a hillside 1.1km. NE. Landmark built by Sir John Sinclair *c.* 1780 to replace a previously demolished chapel which had served as the burial place of Harald, Earl of Caithness. Hexagonal, with stumpily pinnacled buttresses at the corners.

FARMS ETC.

PENNYLAND HOUSE, Dounreay Road. Early C19 farmhouse, the birthplace of Sir William Smith, founder of the Boys' Brigade. – To the S, a large contemporary STEADING, its crenellated N screen wall with a turret where it joins the house.

PENTLAND LODGE, Granville Street. Built as the Parish Manse in 1770. White harled with a big central chimney-gablet. The pilastered doorpiece and cornices over the ground-floor windows look additions, perhaps dating from the repairs made in 1831. – L-plan STEADING to the S.

TONGUE

Small village on the E side of the Kyle of Tongue.

FREE CHURCH, 3.9km. NE. Disused. Built in 1846. T-plan, with
a pinnacled birdcage bellcote on the jamb whose pointed front
window contains Y-tracery. The other windows are large rectangles. – Small contemporary MANSE behind.

ST ANDREW'S PARISH CHURCH. White harled kirk, almost
entirely rebuilt (but on the old foundations and incorporating
earlier bits) in 1728–9.* It is T-plan, consisting of a crowstepped
main block, the gableted W bellcote probably dating from the
repairs made in 1861–2, with crowstepped NE and SE 'aisles'.
Simple pointed windows. Forestair at the W end to the gallery
inside. Moulded door to the S 'aisle', its lintel dated 1680.
Interior mostly refurnished in 1861–2. – At the W end, the
REAY LOFT with a front of panelled pine. It had a canopied
superstructure carried on Corinthianish columns, perhaps of
1728–9 but looking earlier; this is now in the Royal Museum of
Scotland (Edinburgh). – Below the gallery, the BURIAL PLACE
of the Lords Reay, with a semi-octagonal head to the door.
   MANSE to the S, built in 1841. Tall and crowstepped.

TONGUE HOTEL. 1854, by *Robert Brown*, Inspector of Buildings
for the Sutherland estates. Hugely inflated cottage. Horizontal
glazing in the windows.

CAUSEWAYS AND BRIDGE. By *Sir Alexander Gibb & Partners*,
1971. 3.8km.-long roadway across the Kyle of Tongue carried
on two rock-filled causeways and a 18.3m. bridge of eighteen
spans, the concrete superstructure supported on steel box piles.
At the E end, a small harled octagonal SUMMERHOUSE, probably early C19.

CASTLE VARRICH. *See* p. 114.

HOUSE OF TONGUE
8.8km. N

Rambling and informal harled house developed through a
sequence of accretions and alterations from the C17 to the
C19. Sir James Balfour of Denmylne mentioned the 'castells of
Tunge' in his notes on Strathnaver made in the 1630s, but the
earliest part of the present house was probably built by Donald,
Master of Reay, in 1678. This is L-plan, with a short NW jamb
and crowstepped gables. Now single-storey, with an attic whose
windows are catslide-roofed dormers, but the range seems to
have been lowered and reroofed in 1852. Sturdy buttress of
1859 against the S wall. Three-storey crowstep-gabled SE wing.
The date of 1678 on its NE skewputt is probably a piece of
Victorian misinformation,‡ and this may be the 'House to My
Lord Rea' which the mason *Andrew Scott* contracted to build
in 1723. Chamfered window margins, probably dating from

William Mackay and *William McLeod* were the wrights.
‡The skewputt used to have the date 1750 as well.

the reconstruction of 1852, when outshots, including a big crowstepped porch, were added to the w and a forestair at the E (garden) front. At the NW, a twin-gabled addition of 1836 originally containing the estate office and factor's house. Informal courtyard to the N, its E side a single-storey rubble-built stable range, the N screen wall's basket-arched gateway probably early C18.

Inside the house, in the Mackay Room at the w of the N range, three late C17 pedimented dormerheads, probably removed from the exterior during alterations. One, over the fireplace, is carved with the Mackay arms and the initials DMR for Donald, Master of Reay; on the sides, lions climbing up to grab down-turned thistles. The others are in the E wall, one with the initials AMR for Ann, Mistress of Reay, and scrolls on the sides, the other with a monogram of the initials of Donald and Ann, Master and Mistress of Reay, and hounds on the sides.

Rubble WALLED GARDEN, apparently early C18, to the NW, N and E. Its NW section is crossed by a walled path from the w, its Georgian doorway from the road said to have come from the Old Courthouse at Lochmaddy (Western Isles). In the garden E of the house, a SUNDIAL, dated 1714 on the square shaft, which carries an octagonal cap topped by a truncated obelisk (restored in the early C20). Carved decoration on the shaft, dials on the obelisk. – N of the walled garden, a small crowstepped OUT BUILDING, perhaps C18, with a triangular pigeon-entrance in the E gable. – On the s approach to the house, rusticated ashlar GATEPIERS, probably of the mid-C18, but their finials looking like Victorian embellishments.

ULBSTER see BRUAN

WATTEN   2050

Village beside the bridge which carries the Wick–Thurso road across the Wick River, a TOLLHOUSE of c. 1815 in the centre.

FREE CHURCH. Small harled kirk of c. 1845, a bellcote on the gable.

PARISH CHURCH. Built as Watten United Free Church in 1908 by D. & J. R. McMillan. Simplified Gothic. SW bell tower with a bellcast pyramid roof; tall pinnacles at the corners.

PRIMARY SCHOOL. Harled school and schoolhouse, by Brims, 1875.

BRIDGE. By Thomas Telford, 1812–17. Rubble-built, with three segmental arches; widened to the w in 1933.

MAINS OF WATTEN, 2km. N. White harled laird's house with a centre chimney gablet. It carries the date 1763, together with the initials of Robert Manson Sinclair of Bridgend and his wife, Isabel Sinclair.

WESTERDALE

Hamlet beside the River Thurso.

CHURCH. Built as Westerdale Free Church in 1844. Very simple
   T-plan kirk with minimally pointed broad windows. – Adjoin-
   ing, the contemporary harled MANSE.
BRIDGE. Built in 1834. Two segmental arches of rubble, the
   cutwater's original triangular profile now rounded in concrete. –
   Beside it, a rubble-built MILL of *c.* 1800.

FARM, 0.2km. N. Harled house of *c.* 1840. – Rubble-built STEAD-
   ING on the W.
DALE HOUSE. *See* p. 115.
FORT (BUAILE OSCAR), Ben Freiceandain, 8km. NW. Oval fort
   of the first millennium B.C., *c.* 245m. by 150m., occupying the
   whole flattish summit of the hill, whose steep N and E sides
   provided natural defence. On the S and W, a stone wall, *c.* 2.7m.
   broad, placed, unusually, some way down the hillside, taking
   advantage of a small natural terrace. Inside the enclosure a
   grassy mound marks the site of a Neolithic chambered CAIRN.

WICK

The county town and administrative headquarters of the present
district of Caithness. In the 1390s Robert III granted to Nicholas
Sutherland the town of Auldwick 'with ane burgh of barony', and
the royal burgh of Wick was founded in 1589. However, despite
the advantage of the large natural harbour of Wick Bay (the name
Wick or Vik is Old Norse for 'bay'), development was slow. In
1726 the parish minister described the burgh as 'a small town of
little trade' consisting of one principal street (High Street) on the
N bank of the Wick River. In the late C18 Benjamin Dunbar of
Hempriggs laid out the suburb of Louisburgh (named after his
daughter Louisa) immediately to the N, the half-acre plots let on
99-year leases with the tenants bound to build houses worth at
least £10. More important than Louisburgh was to be Pulteneytown on the S side of Wick Bay. Here a feu of *c.* 400 acres
Scots was granted by Sir Benjamin Dunbar of Hempriggs to the
British Society for Extending the Fisheries in 1801 and the land
thereupon laid out by *Thomas Telford* for a harbour and 'new
town' called Pulteneytown in honour of Sir William Pulteney,
Governor of the Society, plots being offered for sale from 1808.
By the mid-C19 Wick was the largest herring fishing port in
Europe but since the early C20 the town's fishing industry has
declined sharply, the Caithness Glass factory providing only a
partial replacement.

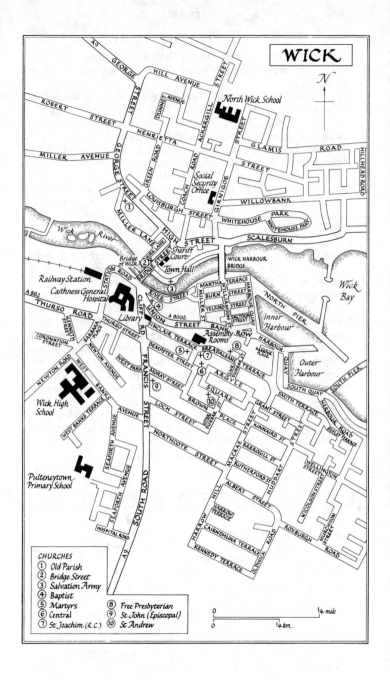

CHURCHES

BAPTIST CHURCH, Union Street. Built in 1868. Simple hall with
a stringcourse forming hoodmoulds over the pointed-arched
windows.

BRIDGE STREET CHURCH, Bridge Street. Originally Wick Free
Church. Flat-fronted Gothic, by *William J. Gray* of Berwick,
1862–3. In the crenellated gable centrepiece, a five-light Perp
window under a cusped roundel. Two-light window to the l.
To the r., a steeple, its barely projecting tower marked off by
big diagonally set buttresses; the octagonal spire's stonework is
relieved by bands carved with trefoils.

CENTRAL CHURCH, Dempster Street. Built as Pulteneytown
Free Church in 1851–3; *James Cormack* was the contractor. Big
bare Gothic box. In 1862 a large steeple was tacked onto the
front, not of much distinction but a welcome townscape incident in the approach to Argyle Square.

FREE PRESBYTERIAN CHURCH, Breadalbane Terrace. A small
Gothic box of 1905. Spired turrets at the corners of the gable
front; on its apex, a solid-spired 'bellcote' finial.

MARTYRS FREE CHURCH, Sinclair Terrace. Built as a Reformed
Presbyterian chapel in 1839. Humble and harled.

24   OLD PARISH CHURCH, High Street. By *John Henry* of Edinburgh, 1820–30.* Prominently sited big box with two tiers of
rather small Tudor windows. At the E gable, octagonal corner
turrets with gableted faces and flat tops. Corner turrets of the
same type at the E tower's battlemented parapet, within which
rises a spire above a gableted octagonal base. Inside, slender
cast-iron columns carry a GALLERY along three sides, the
panelled front cutting across the E corners. The focus is provided by the late C19 PULPIT at the W end. – Behind it, ORGAN
with stencilled pipes, by *Wadsworth*, 1883. – STAINED GLASS.
W window with bright floral motifs, after 1879. – In the other
windows, realistic figures of saints by *G. Maile & Son Ltd*,
1961–71.

E of the church, two fragments of its medieval predecessor.
55   The rubble-built SINCLAIR AISLE is said to have been put up
in the late C16 by George, fourth Earl of Caithness. It was
remodelled as a burial enclosure in 1835, when it acquired a
crudely crenellated parapet, diagonally set buttresses, and
fluted vases on the gables and W wall. That wall's rectangular
moulded windows look late C16, as does the surround of the
large N window infilled with Gothic lights in 1835. In the S
gable, formerly opening into the church, there seems to have
been a big central arch flanked by doors. The l. door's late C16
depressed arch survives; the r.'s is a replacement of 1835. Also
of 1835 is the conversion of the central arch into a two-light
window. Inside, on the E wall, the GRAVESLAB of Jean Chisholm † 1614, wife of Master John Sinclair of Ulbster, with their
initials and impaled arms. – DUNBAR AISLE to the E, brutally

---

*Henry's plans and specifications were drawn up with the assistance of the builder,
James Cormack, and 'particularly examined and approved' by *John Chalmers*.

remodelled with aggressively rock-faced masonry. Inside, the s wall supports an early c18 aedicular MONUMENT of three panels divided by Composite columns. A pair of trumpeting angels sit on the pediment which is broken by the coat of arms of Sir William Dunbar of Hempriggs † 1711 and his wife, Margaret Sinclair. – Set into the N wall, a stone laurel wreath (perhaps a window surround) flanked by carved swags and angels' heads, all probably early c18.

St ANDREW, Argyle Square. Built as Pulteneytown Chapel of Ease, 1841–2. 'Saxon' windows in the gable front, whose minimally projecting centre rises to a gableted bellcote.

St JOACHIM (R.C.), Breadalbane Terrace. By *William Robertson*, 1836–7. Anta-pilastered and pedimented W gable with a corniced doorpiece. More pilasters along the N wall, whose windows are semicircular. – Adjoining on the s, a mid-Victorian CONVENT, again pedimented and pilastered, but it is taller, the stonework exposed not harled, and the front's r. end awkwardly angled to fit the site.

St JOHN (Episcopal), Moray Street and Francis Street. Villagey Gothic, by *Alexander Ross*, 1868–70. Battered stepped buttresses at the corners of nave and chancel; gabled bellcote. Three-light Dec E and W windows, a quatrefoil in the chancel's N wall. Interior with a stone chancel arch. – STAINED GLASS. W window (the Nativity of Our Lord) by *James Ballantine & Son*, 1875. – E window (the Passion, Crucifixion and Ascension), also late c19, as is one light in the nave's s wall (the Light of the World) signed by *C. Taylor* of London.

SALVATION ARMY HALL, Victoria Place. Coursed rubble box built as an Evangelical Union chapel in 1845. Tall ground-floor windows almost continuous with those of the gallery. Truncated finial on the E gable.

PUBLIC BUILDINGS

ASSEMBLY ROOMS, Sinclair Terrace. Built as Pulteneytown Academy in the late c19. Scots Jacobean with semicircular and shaped pediments over the first-floor windows. Interwar extension to the w.

BRIDGE OF WICK. Three segmental ashlar arches. By *Murdoch Paterson*, 1875–7.

CAITHNESS GENERAL HOSPITAL, Cliff Road. By *Baxter, Clark & Paul*, 1983–6.

CAITHNESS WAR MEMORIAL, off Scalesburn. Dated 1909. Tower with a silly little turret at one corner. It must have looked better before it was drydashed.

HARBOUR. The Inner Harbour on the s (or Pulteneytown) side of Wick Bay was built in 1808 by *George Burn* and reconstructed by *Thomas Telford*, 1824–31. It forms a roughly triangular basin. In 1862–7 the Outer Harbour to the se was begun with the building of the South Pier designed by *D. & T. Stevenson*. The protection offered by this Outer Harbour was much improved in 1882–7, when *James Barron* extended the South Pier and added a breakwater to the Inner Harbour's North Pier to cover the Outer's previously open NE side. At the same time the old part of the North Pier was broadened and a new harbour (the River Basin) formed at the mouth of the Wick River by the construction of the South River Pier extending N from the North Pier and of the North River Pier from the river's N bank. Most of what is now visible is Barron's work, concrete the dominant material. LIGHTHOUSE at the end of the South Pier, a tapering octagonal tower.

HILLHEAD PRIMARY SCHOOL, Willowbank. By the Caithness County Architect, *W. Wilson*, 1969.

LIBRARY, Cliff Road and Sinclair Terrace. Domestic Queen Anne, by *Leadbetter & Fairley*, 1896–8. Harled with stone dressings. At the corner, a gabled ashlar centrepiece, from which projects a circular porch, its Doric columns of polished granite. Above, a Roman Doric-columned cupola.

NORTH WICK SCHOOL, Girnigoe Street. Disused. By *Brims*, 1875. Shallow U-plan with hoodmoulded windows in the wings. Three-light Gothic window in the centre gable, whose bellcote has been reduced to a stump.

PULTENEYTOWN PRIMARY SCHOOL, off Seaforth Avenue. By the Caithness County Architect, *W. Wilson*, 1959, with a small brick clocktower.

RAILWAY STATION, Station Road. Faintly Italianate shed, by *Murdoch Paterson*, 1873–4.

SHERIFF COURT, Bridge Street. By *David Rhind*, 1862–6. Small-scale but pompous early Italian Renaissance, but the big central dormer is capped by a Frenchy spire with slate cresting.

TOWN AND COUNTY HOSPITAL, Hospital Road. Built in 1906 and now disused.

TOWN HALL, Bridge Street. Small-scale but determinedly classical of 1826–8. Two-storey block of three bays with block-consoled cornices over the first-floor windows and marked entasis at the sides. In front of the end bays is a balustraded loggia. At the centre, a tower, again with heavy entasis. The main block's cornice is carried round it as a stringcourse below a panelled blind attic. Then an octagonal stage: on four of its fronts, advanced clock-faces under anthemion-finialled block pediments. On top, a dumpy circular cupola with roundheaded arches and a lead dome.

WICK HARBOUR BRIDGE. By *Blyth & Blyth*, 1939. Three segmental concrete spans.

WICK HIGH SCHOOL, West Banks Avenue. By *D. & J. R. McMillan*, 1909. Fag-end Baronial. Additions of various dates but little distinction.

DESCRIPTION

SOUTH ROAD enters the town past the CEMETERY laid out by *W. R. McKelvie* of Dundee in 1872. Set back on the l., the Town and County Hospital (*see* Public Buildings, above). Small Victorian villas in FRANCIS STREET soon establish an architectural norm. This is the W boundary of PULTENEYTOWN, the S development of the burgh, laid out by *Thomas Telford* in 1808 and built up over the next seventy years. In DEMPSTER STREET, plain mid-C19 houses. On the N, a harled late Victorian DRILL HALL, its big first-floor windows' Italian Romanesque glazing giving it a mildly ecclesiastical look. At the top of the street, the Central Church (*see* Churches, above). ARGYLE SQUARE's canted corners make it a long octagon, the centre filled with trees. On the S side but not formally sited, St Andrew's Church (*see* Churches, above). Among the N side's straightforward two-storey houses, Nos. 51–53 are of *c.* 1860 with rusticated pilaster strips and consoled cornices over the doors; incised carving on the window margins to enliven this Georgian-survival detailing. The N boundary of Pulteneytown's formal layout is marked by the one-sided SINCLAIR TERRACE. At its W end, the early C19 No. 18, with a tripartite door and window in the pedimented centre. Another centre tripartite window at the contemporary No. 17, whose doorpiece's tall Doric columns are recessed under a block pediment; distinctly idiosyncratic is the slight projection of the ground floor's wall each side of the openings. At the E end, the Assembly Rooms (*see* Public Buildings, above) opposite the Martyrs Free Church and St Joachim's R.C. Church (*see* above). Beside St Joachim's, the late Georgian Nos. 48–49 BREADALBANE TERRACE, No. 49 with round panes in the fanlight and cast-iron balconies at the first-floor windows. Further up, No. 15 of *c.* 1860, with a pedimented doorpiece. Opposite, the contemporary BREADALBANE CRESCENT, a smart Georgian-survival ashlar-fronted terrace, the gabled dormers recessed in the roof; its front gardens give a touch of luxury. In front of the late Victorian SMITH TERRACE to the E, the OLD MEN'S REST of 1949–50, a harled pavilion, its roof cantilevered out as a canopy on the side overlooking the harbour. Further E, the PILOT STATION built in 1908, a square stone box under a pyramid roof whose eaves sweep out to cover a verandah, its cast-iron columns branching into lacy spandrels at the corners.

LOWER PULTENEYTOWN below is the harbour area (for the Harbour itself, *see* Public Buildings, above). W of the Inner Harbour, pleasantly plain early C19 housing (e.g. in BANK ROW and ROSE STREET). Among this, the WICK HERITAGE CENTRE (Nos. 19–27 Bank Row) presents a harled early C19 house to the street. Behind it, a CURING YARD of *c.* 1830 enclosed by ranges including a cooperage and kiln. In HARBOUR QUAY's N section, two- and three-storey late Georgian warehouses. S of the Inner Harbour, the quay is lined with vaulted ICE HOUSES, presumably early C19, built into the steep bank. In HARBOUR PLACE overlooking the scene is THE ROUND HOUSE designed by *Thomas Telford* in 1807. White rendered double-bow front, the roof taken straight across the recessed centre; big central chimney stack.

At Pulteneytown's NW corner stands the massive but reticent Caithness General Hospital (*see* above). In front, the WAR

MEMORIAL of 1923, a colossal bronze figure of Victory by *Percy Portsmouth*. In STATION ROAD to the W, a marble STATUE of Dr John Alexander †1901, dressed in academic robes. On the path beside the river below, a FOUNTAIN of 1906. Conical cairn with cast-iron lions' heads among the stones; it supports a lotus-leaf basin from which rises a bird-topped finial.

BRIDGE STREET N of the Bridge of Wick (for which *see* above) starts with the ROYAL BANK OF SCOTLAND (former Commercial Bank) of *c.* 1835. Very classical, the first floor's centre framed by a broad screen of Ionic columns *in antis*, the ground floor projecting below to form a plinth. For the dumpier classicism of the Town Hall and the Renaissance Sheriff Court, *see* above. Opposite them, Bridge Street Church (*see* above), followed by the BANK OF SCOTLAND (former British Linen Bank), 1933–5, in a blocky sub-Lorimer Scots manner, by *John Keppie & Henderson*. The CLYDESDALE BANK (former Aberdeen Town & County Bank) is an early Renaissance palazzo by *J. Russell Mackenzie*, 1875. In the spandrels of its round-arched first-floor windows, carved roses, thistles and shamrocks; above, the heads of Scottish historical figures, including John Knox, Mary, Queen of Scots, and Queen Victoria.

HIGH STREET's W stretch passes the harled twin towers of DOMINOES DISCOTHEQUE, built as a cinema *c.* 1930, on its approach to the Old Parish Church (*see* above). E of Bridge Street, the S side starts with a shallowly concave block of *c.* 1820. The stripped classical WOOLWORTHS opposite was built as the North of Scotland Bank in 1886. It is by *A. Marshall Mackenzie*, granite-fronted and pedimented. MARKET PLACE on the S makes a small square, its end filled with the tall and studiously asymmetrical Scots Jacobean POST OFFICE by *W. T. Oldrieve* of *H.M. Office of Works*, 1912. High Street then narrows for its unpretentious and undistinguished descent to the harbour overlooked by a Victorian crowstepped gable and tower added to the early C19 MOUNTHOOLY TERRACE above.

CASTLE OF OLD WICK. *See* p. 113.

YARROWS

3040

Moorland covered with evidence, much of it very ruinous, of prehistoric occupation.

BROCH, South Yarrows. Melancholy remains of a broch, perhaps of the first millennium B.C., on the W shore of Loch of Yarrows. Round wall of *c.* 12.8m. diameter. Entrance from the E, the wall-passage having checks for a door. The inner wall-face to the court has been recased, probably early in the first millennium A.D. On the court's S side, entrance to a stair inside the wall with three vertically arranged openings over the doorway. Entrance to a wall chamber on the W.

CAIRNS, South Yarrows. Two long cairns of the third or fourth millennium B.C. built across the flattish ridge of a hill. The

SOUTH CAIRN is the better preserved, a 78m.-long stony mound. At each end, a pair of horns defining a concave forecourt, the E quite badly altered. E entrance passage leading to a chamber divided by upright slabs into three compartments. On the S side, the entrance to a passage which seems to have led to a second small chamber. – c. 30m. N, the similar but shorter (c. 58m.-long) NORTH CAIRN. Again there have been end forecourts defined by horns. E entrance passage to a three-compartment chamber.

STONE ROWS, Battle Moss. Six (originally at least eight) roughly parallel rows of small stones, c. 43m. long. They were probably set up in the second millennium B.C.

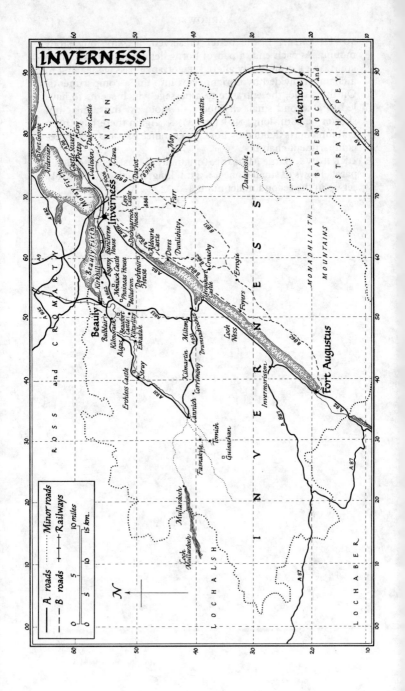

INVERNESS

A district with a fertile coastal plain along the s shore of the Moray and Beauly Firths; to the s, hills and moorland crossed by broad glens, the biggest being the Great Glen, largely filled by Loch Ness. At the mouth of the River Ness stands the burgh of Inverness, the site of a royal castle through the Middle Ages and the undoubted capital of Highland.

AIGAS

Stretch of land on the w bank of the Beauly River, its power station and Aigas House the chief architectural features.

AIGAS POWER STATION. Concrete dam topped by a modern-traditional power station with crazy-paved rubble walling; by *Robert Hurd & Partners*, 1958–63.

AIGAS HOUSE. Superbly sited on a hillside, it is an inflated 93 Baronial-Jacobean villa by *Matthews & Lawrie*, 1877, incorporating a remodelled late Georgian house and with a fairly discreet w addition by *John Allan*, 1988. On the N (entrance) front, a tall tower, its height increased to dotty proportions by a candle-snuffered NW corner turret; huge cannon spouts poking out of battlemented rounds add to the martial effect. Domestic E front to the garden; symmetrical, with a corbelled balcony between canted bay windows corbelled to square caphouses; turrets at the corners. Inside, a two-storey neo-Jacobean hall runs the full length; galleries along the E and W sides, a narrow Imperial stair the focus at the s end. Main rooms (dining room, library and drawing room) off the hall's E side, the drawing room's late C18-revival white marble chimneypiece with cherubs carved on the frieze. W of the hall are the still recognizable rooms of the late Georgian house. – STABLES of 1877 to the NW, a bargeboarded gabled tower over the central pend.

ALDOURIE CASTLE

2.1km. N of Dores

Large and inventively Baronial harled mansion of 1853–61 by *Mackenzie & Matthews* incorporating a C17 house which had been extended in 1839. The C17 house had a rectangular main block with a round tower at the SW corner; corbelled parapet

with angle rounds. The 1839 addition was to its w, a two-storey
wing, perhaps originally quite plain. Mackenzie & Matthews
extended the house in all directions, parading the full repertoire
of early C 17 Baronialism, including a balustraded round tower
cribbed from Castle Fraser (Grampian), oriel windows, scroll-
sided steeply pedimented dormers, candle-snuffered turrets,
corbelling, rope-moulded stringcourses and gunloops. E wing
of 1902–3 by *Robert S. Lorimer*. (Interior mostly of 1853–61. In
the drawing room, an early C 19 marble chimneypiece imported
from the demolished mansion house of Belladrum. In the
former dining room of 1902–3, a coffered plaster ceiling
enriched with Tudor roses.)

7050   ARDERSIER

Village on the Moray Firth, laid out by the Campbells of Cawdor
in the C 18 and formerly known as Campbelltown. Mostly C 19
vernacular houses, of typical fishertown type (some built of clay
and bool) along the shore, more substantial in High Street to the
E. C 20 council housing on the approach from the s.

FREE CHURCH, High Street. By *Alexander Ross*, 1856. Simplified
  Norman detail; a bellcote on the gable front.
PARISH CHURCH, High Street. Originally United Presbyterian.
  Ungainly Gothic by *William Mackintosh*, 1880.
FOUNTAIN, High Street. Late C 19, of cast iron. Lion terms carry
  the quatrefoil basin, its sides decorated with reliefs of flowers.
  Above the basin, an urn-topped pedestal adorned with birds.

FORT GEORGE. *See* p. 174.

5040   BALBLAIR

Rural hamlet.

KILMORACK FREE CHURCH. Disused. Broad red sandstone
  box of 1847. Small birdcage bellcote on the gable; the area
  lighted by roundheaded windows, the gallery by rectangular
  ones.

5040   BEAUFORT CASTLE
                     1.1km. N of Kiltarlity

Large red sandstone Baronial mansion by *Wardrop & Reid*,[*]
1880–6, sadly reduced in size by *Reginald Fairlie*, 1938, after a
fire. The s front's 1880 design was asymmetrical but balanced.
Crowstep-gabled w tower of four storeys and an attic, severe,
with small pepperpot turrets corbelled out at the corners. To

---

  [*]Completed by *Wardrop, Anderson & Browne*, J. M. Wardrop having died in 1882
and Charles Reid in 1883.

its r., a three-storey-and-attic manorial range containing the family rooms, with a central crowstepped gable butting against a chimney; two-storey bay window and carefully varied fenestration. Then a hefty central tower, its top floor's oriel rising into the corbelled battlement, which encloses a crowstepped cap-house. In the tower's s face, the heavy entrance doorway of c 16 type under a tall slimly pilastered aedicule containing an heraldic achievement. At the tower's NE inner angle, a second tower, taller and circular, a battlement round its flat roof, from which rises a conical-roofed cap-house turret. E of this was the range containing the Victorian public rooms, originally with a tall first floor lit from big mullioned and transomed windows flanked by deep conical-roofed round turrets. This E range was destroyed by fire in 1937, and *Fairlie*'s subsequent reconstruction reduced its length by two thirds and substituted for its confident Elizabethan and Baronial manner a style which would be neo-Georgian were it not for an unemphatic corner turret. At the same time he replaced some of the Victorian plate-glass windows in the central tower with small-paned sashes. The result is an unbalanced conflict between the front's boldly Victorian w range and its genteel 1930s E part, the central tower an indecisive referee. At the back, a jumble of turrets and crowstepped gables, but Fairlie's politeness (his turrets at the E end much smaller than had been those of the 1880s) is no match for the starkness of Wardrop & Reid's chapel, with its octagonal NW bell turret, w rose window and tall pointed side-lights.

(Inside, the principal rooms are Fairlie's in his modernized Georgian manner. Tall first-floor chapel of the 1880s with a wooden ribbed tunnel-vault. At its w (liturgical E) end, a white marble ALTAR and crocketed-pinnacled REREDOS, presumably of 1886, both carved with high-relief Biblical scenes.)

BEAULY   5040

Large planned village begun by the Frasers of Lovat, *c.* 1805, with a medieval priory church sitting unobtrusively in one corner.

BEAULY PRIORY

Roofless church of the Valliscaulian monastery founded by Sir John Bisset *c.* 1230. The chancel was completed before 1287, when Sir Simon Fraser of Lovat was buried in front of its high altar. The transepts and E bays of the nave were finished in the early c 14 and the nave's w bays probably some considerable time before Alexander Fraser of Lovat's erection of an oak bellcote on the w gable *c.* 1400. In 1430 Hugh Fraser of Lovat complained to the Pope that as a result of the Prior's maladministration the buildings were becoming ruinous. Presumably as part of the ensuing programme of repairs he added an upper floor to the N transept and built the Chapel of the Holy Cross on the N side of

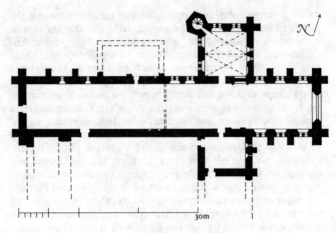

Beauly Priory. Plan

the nave. Reconstruction of the nave's W bays may have taken
place at the same time, but it is more probable that this was part
of the work on the nave, including rebuilding of the W gable,
begun by Robert Reid, Abbot of Kinloss and Prior of Beauly, in
1537. The priory was dissolved after the Reformation, and in 1571
its land and buildings were granted to Hugh, fifth Lord Fraser of
Lovat, in feu ferme. By 1633 the church was 'wholly decayed',
and almost all remains of the cloister buildings had disappeared
by the late C18.

The church's plan, an unaisled Latin cross, is paralleled in early
C12 Cistercian abbey churches in England and, perhaps more
significantly, in Deer Abbey (Grampian),* founded *c.* 1215,
which was originally of almost identical dimensions. Evidence
of the different building phases is provided by the rubble-built
walls, whose masonry's quality deteriorates from W to E; but
the general outline of the design was probably intended from
the start. It consists of a seven-bay nave, transepts of unequal
depth, and three-bay choir. Splayed basecourse all round.
Ashlar buttresses (their stones removed after the Reformation)
marking off each bay except on the nave's S side, where there
was a cloister walk. In the choir and nave's N wall, tall windows.
The nave's S windows and those of the S transept's W face are
curtailed to allow for the roof of the cloister walk below. Sill
courses all round, except at two walls of the S transept and the
rebuilt W gable.

In the C13 choir's side walls, two-light obtuse-arched
windows containing Y-tracery. The E gable was given one huge
window, possibly replacing three lancets; if the statement in
The Wardlaw Manuscript is correct that this window was glazed
at the expense of Julia Ross, widow of Simon Fraser of Lovat,

*Before the addition of its S aisle.

it must be mid-C 14. Unusually in Scotland it has had both an inner and an outer layer of tracery. The wall below was demolished *c.* 1800 but rebuilt later in the C 19 omitting the sill course.

The early C 14 S transept abutted the cloister's E range. In the E wall, two tall lancets, their lower parts blocked probably when a floor was inserted in the C 15. To their S, a small round-arched window lighting the night stair entered from the Dormitory on the upper floor of the cloister through a door in the transept's S gable. Beside the door, a cinquefoil window from the Dormitory into the transept. Otherwise there survives of the cloister's E range only the ground-floor door (probably from the sacristy) into the transept, and one jamb of a pointed-arched window to its E. The transept's W wall evidently suffered settlement in the course of construction. The lower part (below the sill course) leans out, and the hoodmoulded processional door's voussoirs have been shaped to fit in. Bell capitals on the door's attached shafts.

The N transept was heavily restored in 1900–1 by *Thomas Ross*, who added the central buttresses of the E and W walls. The lower part is bonded with the chancel's N wall and must have been begun in the C 13; the upper part is a mid-C 15 reconstruction. In the gable's lower level, two large lancets. The round-arched window above contains awkward Y-tracery inserted by Ross as a not over-accurate replica of the probably late C 16 tracery which was there before. Flanking rectangular lights widened from slit windows in 1900–1. Rounded NE corner, half-hidden by the angle buttress, corbelled out to the square just below the eaves. At the NW corner, an octagonal stairtower, the finial of its stone-slabbed spire decorated with balls. It is clearly an addition built to serve the transept's new upper floor in the C 15.

The nave's three E bays are early C 14. In the S wall, triangular trefoiled windows allowing room for the cloister walk below. The N wall's two E bays have each a large two-light trefoil-headed window. There may have been a third to the W, but if so it was blocked in the mid-C 15 when Hugh Fraser of Lovat added the Chapel of the Holy Cross, cutting out the original basecourse between the buttresses. The only evidence of the chapel now is its segmental-arched doorway into the church and a pointed-arched piscina to its E.

The nave's three W bays were probably reconstructed by Robert Reid after 1537,* with obtusely pointed windows (curtailed on the cloister side) formerly containing Y-tracery. Plain processional doorway in the S wall. At the adjoining W bay, fragments of the cloister's W range, which presumably originally housed the lay brothers. In its N gable, remains of a first-floor fireplace, perhaps part of a C 15 reconstruction, when this range probably became the Prior's lodging.

The W front is mostly Reid's work of the C 16, although the 13

*Their windows bear the same masons' marks as are found at the W gable.

earlier basecourse survives. The door's arch just misses being
semicircular; jambs with two orders of attached shafts with bell
capitals. The hoodmould's labels bore the *Arma Christi* and
IHS monogram, now weathered away. Above the door, an
ogee-arched image niche, its sill bearing worn remains of a
shield carved with Reid's initials and coat of arms, which displays the episcopal crozier and so must date from after his
consecration as Bishop of Orkney in 1541. Beside and above
the niche, a stepped arrangement of three lancets. Off-centre
quatrefoil in the gable's apex.

The INTERIOR was originally divided by a rood screen into
a monastic choir, probably extending as far W as the nave's E
bay, and a lay brothers' church occupying the rest of the nave.
In the C 15, after the monastery had ceased to include lay
brothers, the screen may have been shifted one bay further W,
the new position of the nave altar marked by an aumbry and
trefoil-headed piscina in the S wall.

The nave windows clearly belong to two principal periods of
construction. Those of the W gable and W bays, probably all
dating from Robert Reid's C 16 reconstruction, have wide
internal splays and segmental-headed rear-arches (excepting
the gable's centre lancet, which has a depressed rear-arch).
Wide splays too at the S wall's three early C 14 E lights, but they
are covered by hoodmoulded rear-arches and linked by a sill
course. Hoodmoulded rear-arches again at the N wall's E
windows.

The transepts were cut off from the crossing by walls built
in the later C 15. Round-arched door to the S transept, its
inner face triangular-headed. To its E, the built-up opening
containing the tomb of Prior Alexander Mackenzie (*see* below).
Above, a big arch curtailed just below the springing opens
from the transept's first-floor room into the church. Inside the
transept there is evidence that a vault was begun over the lower
storey and then abandoned or demolished, presumably as a
result of the transept's settlement. The N transept is entered by
a round-arched door. To its E, the monument to Kenneth
Mackenzie of Kintail (*see* below). The transept's lower floor
has been covered by two bays of vaulting. The N wall's ribs
spring from corbel-capitals, the centre carved with stiffleaf
foliage. The ribs on the E and W walls spring from simple points
at a lower level. It looks as if there have been two periods of
vaulting, the second (represented by the E and W walls' ribs)
apparently C 15. The present wooden ceiling was introduced in
1900–1.

In the choir the side walls are decorated with arcading, with
broad arches over the windows and acutely pointed narrow
arches between them, much like the treatment of the early
C 13 choir of Dornoch Cathedral (Sutherland). Presumably
the arcading originally continued across the E gable and was
removed when the present window was inserted. In the gable's
rebuilt centre is an aumbry. If in its original position, it suggests
that the altar was free-standing. Part of the badly weathered

hoodmould and end shafts of a double piscina survive in the s wall.

MONUMENTS. In the wall between the crossing and s transept, the tomb of Prior Alexander Mackenzie † 1479. The moulded round arch has quasi-Gothic mouldings on the face and vaguely classical ornament on the jambs. Are these late C16 embellishments? Not much more than the bases of the flanking buttresses survive. On the tomb-chest's front, trefoil-headed blind arcading. The effigy is now lost and the opening built up. – More complete is the monument to Kenneth Mackenzie of Kintail † 1492 in the wall between the crossing and N transept. Its similarity to the monument sometimes said to be to Bishop John Frisel or Fraser in Fortrose Cathedral (Ross and Cromarty) suggests that they are both by the same designer. Pinnacled buttresses flank the pointed arch, which is decorated with square blocks carved with flowers; solid-looking finial carved with the Mackenzie emblem of a stag's head. On the tomb-chest's front, blind arcading of the same design as on Prior Mackenzie's tomb. Effigy of a knight, his feet resting on a lion. – Inside the transept, table monument (apparently a graveslab later raised on balusters) to Kenneth Mackenzie of Kintail † 1568, his coat of arms carved at the top, skulls and crossbones at the bottom. – Monument of *c.* 1900 to Sir Kenneth Mackenzie of Gairloch, a sheet covering most of the body of the white marble effigy. – In the body of the church, C17 and C18 GRAVESLABS decorated with reminders of death.

CHURCHES

MISSION CHURCH, Croyard Road. Secularized. Plain Gothic of 1875.

PARISH CHURCH, Croyard Road. Originally Beauly Free Church. By *Matthews & Lawrie*, 1877–9. Small and heavily buttressed, with a bellcote. Elaborate wheel window in the w gable.

ST MARY (R.C.), High Street. Austere Dec of 1864, a bellcote on the E gable. – Late C19 bargeboarded PRESBYTERY to one side.

PUBLIC BUILDINGS

BEAULY R.C. PRIMARY SCHOOL, High Street. By *Cameron & Burnett*, 1912.

LOVAT BRIDGE, 1.4km. SW. Slightly humpbacked five-span bridge by *Thomas Telford*, 1811–14, restored by *John Fowler* and *C. R. Manners* in 1893, when two arches were rebuilt. Triangular cutwaters topped by buttresses.

MASONIC HALL, Croyard Road. Authoritarian, by *John G. Chisholm*, 1924.

PHIPPS INSTITUTE, High Street. By *J. Russell Burnett*, 1901–3. Pacific Baronial, but the doorpiece attempts a note of Vanbrugh drama.

School, off Croyard Road. School Board Gothic by *Matthews & Lawrie*, 1875–6.

DESCRIPTION

Beside the bridge at the village's S end is NETHERDALE, a picturesque cottage of *c.* 1840, U-plan with an off-centre porch and horizontal glazing. Then pleasant Victorian villas. The centre is announced by the Phipps Institute (*see* Public Buildings, above). Beyond it, the LOVAT ESTATES OFFICE by *Alexander Ross*, 1865, with a steep centre gablet, and the LOVAT ARMS HOTEL, small-scale French Renaissance pomposity by *Matthews & Lawrie*, 1871–2. HIGH STREET now widens to the E, forming a long rectangle called inaccurately THE SQUARE. In its centre, the LOVAT SCOUTS MEMORIAL by *Edward Stourton*, 1905. Tall stone pedestal with cannon spouts at the parapet's corners; steep Frenchy spire above. On the W face, bronze relief of an officer looking through a telescope while a private holds his horse. Late Georgian and Georgian-survival is now the architectural norm, broken by the would-be tactful PRIORY HOTEL and the SE corner's horribly suburban ROYAL BANK of *c.* 1970. More welcome is the W side's Italianate villa provided for the BANK OF SCOTLAND by *Matthews & Lawrie*, 1871–2. Beside the entrance to Beauly Priory Churchyard (*see* above), the stump of the C16 MERCAT CROSS. At The Square's NW corner, a mid-C19 house militarized by *Matthews & Lawrie* in 1872 with a battlemented oriel window and ogee-roofed bartizans. High Street continues out to St Mary's R.C. Church (*see* above) at the N end.

TOMICH HOUSE, 1.6km. N. Ashlar-fronted laird's house of 1831 with a pedimented porch. *Hugh Chisholm* and *Simon Fraser* were the masons, *Alexander Fraser* the wright.

5040

BELLADRUM
1.3km. E of Kiltarlity

The Georgian mansion house enlarged and remodelled by *David Bryce* in 1858 has been demolished except for a pair of garden pavilions. – Broad-eaved LODGE of *c.* 1860. – Big STEADING of *c.* 1805. Eleven-bay S front; at its centre, a battlemented tower decorated with mock arrowslits, its steeply pitched roof perhaps an addition of *c.* 1860. – Beside it, a picturesque row of COTTAGES of 1914. – To the NE, a battlemented late C18 round gazebo TOWER of rock-faced rubble; ogee-arched door and windows under rectangular hoodmoulds. – S of the steading, THE TEMPLE, designed as a chapel by *Reginald Fairlie*, 1935. Ogee-roofed elongated ashlar octagon. Wheel window over the door. The other windows are tall rectangles with traceried heads; on their lintels, the carved names of four of the cardinal virtues. – To its E, a large WALLED GARDEN, probably late C18.

BOGROY   5040

Church prominent beside the A862.

KIRKHILL UNITED FREE CHURCH. Secularized. By *R. J. Macbeth*, 1909. Large, blocky Gothic with a hint of Art Nouveau; bellcote on the N gable.

BUNCHREW HOUSE   6040
3.9km. w of Inverness

Sizeable house of no great distinction but enjoying its position on the s shore of the Beauly Firth. Bunchrew was described as a mansion house in 1841, and a plain late Georgian house is still visible at the NE corner. In the later C19 this was converted to a substantial L-plan by the building of tepid Baronial harled additions to the s and w. In the inner angle, a big octagonal tower, with a slated spire rising inside its balustrade and a balustraded porch projecting from its sw corner. In 1898 *W. L. Carruthers* added a two-storey rubble-built w extension (its ground floor a dining room). Baronial again, with an oriel window on the s front, a slim conical-roofed tower at the sw corner, and bay windows to the w and N. In its s wall, a pair of 'gunloops'.

CAMPBELLTOWN *see* ARDERSIER

CANNICH   3030

Nondescript village near the w end of Strathglass.

CANNICH CHURCH. Broad-eaved mission church by *John Robertson*, 1898–9; obtusely pointed windows and a bold porch.

CHURCH OF OUR LADY AND ST BEAN (R.C.). Sturdily severe by *Joseph Hansom*, 1866. NW tower topped by a slate-spired octagonal belfry. Priest's house at the SE, plain with some Gothic touches. Inside the church, the wagon roof's stencilled gold stars on a blue ground survive from the DECORATION designed by *Father Paulinus* of Fort Augustus, 1893. – Canopied oak REREDOS of 1938, by *Reginald Fairlie* in the late Lorimer manner.

To the SW, SCHOOL built in 1873 with red sandstone dressings and trefoil-pierced bargeboards.

CANNICH BRIDGE PRIMARY SCHOOL. Broad-gabled and broad-eaved, by *Matthews & Lawrie*, 1875.

GLENAFFRIC HOTEL. By *Matthews & Lawrie*, 1862, refaced in reconstituted granite blockwork, *c.* 1950, so as to be in keeping with the *moderne* roadhouse extension to the w.

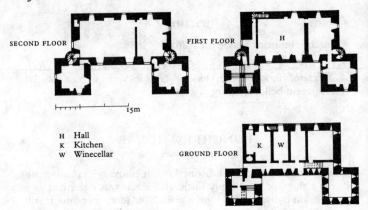

SECOND FLOOR

FIRST FLOOR   H

|←————————————| 15m

H   Hall
K   Kitchen
W   Winecellar

GROUND FLOOR   K   W

Castle Stuart. Plan
(Redrawn from MacGibbon and Ross, *The Castellated and Domestic
Architecture of Scotland*, 1887–92)

7040

CASTLE STUART
2.5km. W of Petty

73 Very smart villa-tower house built for James Stewart, third Earl
of Moray, and his wife, Anne Gordon. It had been begun by 1619
and was probably completed in 1625 (the date on the
dormerheads). Repaired in 1718, it was abandoned later in the
C18 and the roof timbers and floor joists were removed *c.* 1800.
c. 1830 the E jamb was made habitable again and the rest reroofed. Major reconstruction was carried out by *Brown & Wardrop*
in 1869, and further repair and internal alteration began in 1978.

The house is a U-plan built of harled red sandstone rubble.
Crowstepped four-storey main block with taller square towers
projecting both forward and laterally at the S corners. In the
towers' N inner angles, round stair turrets corbelled out from
just above the ground. Slicing across the main block's N corners
are two-storey diagonally set crowstepped rectangular turrets.
The general impression is of wilfully disturbed symmetry. On
the main block's N and S fronts the windows are grouped
2/1 either side of a tall off-centre wallhead chimney, which is
balanced on the S by the front door.* The S towers both rise
unbroken by stringcourses, but the E has crowstepped gables
and conical-roofed round corner turrets corbelled out well
below the wallhead. At the SW tower, a ribbon-moulded corbel
course round the wallhead and corbelled angle rounds con-
jecturally restored above in the 1869 alterations with a battlemented parapet from which project large cannon spouts.‡ Also
of 1869 is the open crown spire on top of the adjoining stair

---

*MacGibbon and Ross describe the door as an insertion but it pre-dates the work
carried out in 1869, and its moulded architrave looks C17.
‡Replacing a late Georgian pyramidal roof.

turret. The treatment of the stair turrets themselves differs, the W rising unbroken to the wallhead, the E's ascent twice fattened by corbel courses jettying out the walling.

Restrained detail. All windows have chamfered margins except those of the SE tower, where there are roll mouldings. Simply chamfered door surround at the SW tower; the front door makes more impact, with a roll-moulded architrave and an accompanying (now empty) frame for an armorial panel. Wide-mouthed gunloops making a martial display at the front and round the towers. Originally all the ground-floor windows were narrow slits, but bigger windows and doors were inserted in the C19 in the E side and back. On the SE tower and the main block's principal elevations, curvaceously pedimented dormerheads carved with the date 1625 and the arms and initials of James, Earl of Moray, and Anne, Countess of Moray.

Inside, a ground-floor corridor across the front of the main block, its E end now filled with a C19 stair. Behind the corridor, a vaulted kitchen at the W end; adjoining winecellar with a narrow stair in the thickness of the N wall leading to the hall above. The other ground-floor rooms, all vaulted, have been stores. In the SW tower, a broad scale-and-platt stair to the first floor. Here the main block contains a (W) hall and (E) retiring room, with a bedroom in the SE tower. At the hall's W end, a recreated screens passage with a plaster tunnel-vault and late C20 panelling of neo-Edwardian type. In the centre of the hall's S wall, a moulded fireplace with a tall stone overmantel topped by a cornice. E of the fireplace, part of a moulded jamb. Was a larger fireplace originally intended? Access to the upper floors is by turnpike stairs in the turrets of the towers' inner angles. On the second floor, the same arrangement of rooms as on the floor below but without a screens passage and with a second bedroom in the SW tower. The provision of two near-identical suites of rooms is rare outside royal palaces. Was the first floor intended for the Earl and the second for the Countess? The hall is now fitted up as a drawing room with panelling of 1978–80 in a late C17 manner. Close garderobe in the W wall. The main block's top floor is a gallery. In each of the N turrets, a closet with its own fireplace and a plaster floral frieze, restored and completed from what had survived from the C17.

CLACHNAHARRY see INVERNESS

CLAVA

7040

Scattered rural settlement beside the River Nairn.

PRIMARY SCHOOL. L-plan school and house, by *William Mackintosh*, 1874. Bellcote on the schoolroom's front gable.

119 RAILWAY VIADUCT. By *John Fowler* and *Murdoch Paterson*, 1893–
8. Immensely long (549m.) and high (39m.) red sandstone
viaduct of twenty-nine roundheaded arches, the S end built on
a curve, straddling the Nairn valley.

CLAVA LODGE. By *Robert Black*, 1897. Tall and plain, with mean
bargeboards.

CAIRNS. Three round cairns of the third millennium B.C. standing
in line. The outer two are very similar, each *c*. 15m. in diameter,
with a kerb of upright stones diminishing in height from those
beside the passage entrance at the SW to the smallest at the NE
behind the chamber. Round each cairn, a stony platform and,
beyond that, a circle of tall standing stones, the circle round
the SW cairn partly rearranged in deference to the road on
its SE side. Inside each cairn, a passage from the SW to the
circular central chamber, its walls constructed of boulders
and upright slabs supporting slightly corbelled drystone
masonry. Both cairns are now roofless. The central cairn
is about the same size, but more oval than round. Again
a kerb of boulders decreasing in height from the SW to the
NE, but there is no passage to the nearly circular chamber,
which must have been entered from above. Like the other
cairns it has a surrounding circle of monoliths, three of them
linked to the platform by cobbled causeways. Just to its W,
a small ring of stones, perhaps the surviving kerb of a Bronze
Age cairn.

CORRIMONY

3030

Handful of houses beside the River Enrick.

CAIRN. Well-preserved round cairn of the later third millennium
B.C. Kerbstones round the edge, the tallest near the SW
entrance, which is marked by two massive upright stones placed
in front of the kerb. *c*. 6.7m.-long entrance passage, its inner
part still roofed with slabs less than 1m. above the cobbled
floor. Central round chamber of *c*. 3.65m. diameter, its walls
constructed of boulders supporting drystone masonry corbelled
inwards to carry a capstone, perhaps the large cup-marked slab
now lying on top of the cairn. Round the cairn, a circle of eleven
standing stones (the four nearest the entrance C19
replacements) and space for a twelfth.

CROACHY

6020

Hamlet in Strathnairn.

ST PAUL'S CHURCH (Episcopal). By *Alexander Ross*, 1867–9.
Very simple lanceted granite-built nave ending in a semi-octagonal apse. Rose window in the W gable, which is topped by a
gableted bellcote. SW porch. Inside, a wooden hammerbeam

roof strengthened with metal ties. – STAINED GLASS. The three apse lights (the Conversion of St Paul; the Crucifixion; the Good Samaritan) and the W rose window (the Sermon on the Mount), like plates from a cheap illustrated Bible, are by *O'Connor*, 1869. – In the S wall, one light (Christ in the House at Bethany) in the C16 Flemish manner, after 1900. – Two lights (St Paul and St Michael) in the N wall of *c.* 1920.

SCHOOL. Now a house. By *Ross & Macbeth*, 1888, with round-arched windows lighting the schoolroom.

TOMINTOUL, 1.3km. NE. By *William Robertson*, 1841 (the date-stone of 1861 refers to its acquisition by E. C. Sutherland Walker). White harled cottage-style laird's house, with brack-eted eaves and horizontal glazing.

CROY 7040

Small village composed mostly of C20 council housing.

PARISH CHURCH. Long harled box built in 1764, the date inscribed on a stone in the ball-finialled E gable. On the W gable, a plain birdcage bellcote. Pointed-arched windows in the S wall, their wooden Y-tracery dating from *John Robertson*'s alterations of 1894.

Piend-roofed late Georgian SESSION HOUSE at the church-yard's S gate. – Some C18 TABLESTONES. – Much smarter are two early C19 MONUMENTS. The one for John Rose of Holme † 1803 has an urn on a tall pedestal, the pedestal's front carved with curtains framing the inscription panel. – The other com-memorates David Davidson of Cantray † 1803. Truncated obelisk carved with an urn and bearing a marble coat of arms; on top, an urn finial.

MAINS OF CROY immediately to the SW, a small mid-C19 STEADING with segmental arched cartshed openings. – MANSE to the N, by *William Lawrie*, 1855, with tall shaped gables.

PRIMARY SCHOOL. By *William Mackintosh*, 1875. Bellcoted school with schoolhouse attached, almost swamped by utili-tarian additions.

DALCROSS CASTLE. *See* p. 161.
HOLME ROSE. *See* p. 275.
KILRAVOCK CASTLE. *See* p. 276.

CULLODEN 7040

Late C20 village, a dormitory for Inverness.

THE BARN CHURCH. Harled U-plan group containing the church and hall. The E range, a former barn, its skewputt dated 1799, was converted to a church by *J. M. Lawrie*, 1978; it is now used mainly as a hall. Forestair at the s gable. Catslide dormers now filled with 'Gothic' windows. It is joined by a glass-walled and slate-roofed N link to the simple church on the W, added by *Betty L. C. Moira*, 1981–2.

CULLODEN HOUSE

85 Self-assured but rather provincial mansion house built for Arthur Forbes of Culloden in 1780. Main block of two storeys and a mansard-roofed attic above a basement. It is joined by slightly recessed screen walls to low two-storey-and-basement pavilions. The walls of the main block and pavilions are of cherrycock-pointed red sandstone rough ashlar, but their basements and quoins are of rusticated yellow ashlar and the links of polished yellow ashlar. At the main block's deep sides are shaped gables, a curiously old-fashioned touch. Its five-bay balustraded W front is quite smart, the centre slightly advanced and pedimented with a coat of arms carved in the tympanum. Open-pedimented doorpiece with attached Roman Doric columns, set in a broad roundheaded overarch; above, a Venetian window (the outer lights blind). At each screen wall, a segmentally overarched corniced door placed between close-set attached Roman Doric columns *in antis*; urns on the parapet. The pavilions are piend-roofed, with small first-floor windows. The E (garden) front has the same massing but considerable differences in detail. The main block is of seven bays, not five. In the centre of its ground floor, a pedimented window with balustered apron; above it, a simple corniced window. Attached Ionic columns *in antis* divide each screen wall into a regular three bays, the centre containing a corniced and overarched door, the others overarched niches. In the niches, statues of Zenonia, Odenatus, Cato and Scipio. In the centre of each pavilion is a Venetian window.

The principal rooms are all on the ground floor (the first-floor Venetian window lights only a dressing room, now a bathroom). Kitchen (much altered) in the S pavilion, a billiard room (its simple panelling late C 19) in the N, both linked to the main block by corridors across the courtyards. In the main block the entrance hall is flanked by a breakfast-parlour on the N and library on the S. Along the house's E side, drawing room and dining room *en suite*. The decoration is expensive. In the entrance hall, a swagged frieze with tipsy urns. Venetian screen into a groin-vaulted back hall with the stair hall to its S. In the breakfast parlour at the NW, a white marble chimneypiece, its frieze bearing a panel carved with a classical scene. Above, another classical scene in a plaster roundel. Late C 18 wooden chimneypiece in the library (now office). The drawing room is lavish. On the walls, plaster swags from which hang roundels containing classical reliefs. Between the windows, reliefs of urns flanked by back-turned sphinxes. On the ceiling, more classical figures surrounding the big central rose, and rinceau and urn decoration in the end panels, all in rather shallow relief.

Attached Adam Corinthian columns at the white marble chimneypiece. Foliage and urns on its frieze, the centre panel carved with a procession of jolly putti. The dining room's sideboard recess is set in an Adam Corinthian columned screen. On the recess's back, a swagged plaster roundel containing a mirror. Another roundel, with a relief of two goddesses, over the white marble chimneypiece, its frieze carved with a large urn.

To the w and N of the house, late C18 rusticated ashlar GATEPIERS topped with vases, those on the w pair carved with swags. – Brick WALLED GARDEN, probably also late C18, to the N. – To the SW, the late C18 STABLES, now roofless. Seven-bay fronts to E and W with the ends advanced and pedimented (the E front's N pediment containing an elegantly carved coat of arms). Round-arched doors at the centre and ends, Diocletian windows in the other bays. – On a knoll a little further SW, an octagonal DOOCOT, probably late C18 again. Rubble-built with rusticated quoins and a single ratcourse; oculus above the door. The pigeon entries are contained in three gableted dormers. Inside, stone nesting boxes and a (restored) wooden potence.

DALAROSSIE 7020

Isolated church in Strathdearn.

PARISH CHURCH. Humble harled rectangle of 1790, the N porch probably added by *W. L. Carruthers* in 1904, when he divided the w end off as a vestry and added the pedimented chimney gablet to the N wall. In this is set an C18 armorial stone. Inside the church, a segmental vaulted plaster ceiling of 1904. – FONT. A roughly worked gneiss boulder.

DALCROSS CASTLE 7040
2.3km. SW of Croy

Tower house built for Simon, sixth Lord Fraser of Lovat, in 1619–21. After a long period of dereliction it was reroofed and restored in 1897–8 by *W. L. Carruthers*. Walls of red sandstone rubble. L-plan, the crowstep-gabled main block of four storeys and an attic, the third-floor windows rising into 1890s dormerheads. C17 iron grilles at several other windows. Round ashlar turrets at the corners, their conical roofs restored by Carruthers; stepped wallhead chimney on the w side. Tenuously attached to this block's SE corner and projecting to the S and E is the crowstepped jamb. Five storeys and an attic, its fourth-floor dormerheads and corner turrets' roofs again of the 1890s. In the w inner angle, a shallow lean-to roofed projection containing a service stair. In the E inner angle, the tall square crowstep-gabled main stairtower, with a corner turret whose roof provided Carruthers with a model for the restoration of the others.

In this stairtower's N face, the entrance, surmounted by a jumpy stringcourse which encloses a panel carved with the date 1720 and the arms of the Mackintoshes, who had acquired the estate eighteen years before. Wide-splayed gunloops and narrow windows at the ground floor; comfortably sized windows at the upper floors, where the only hint of defence is provided by a couple of round shotholes. Low three-storey N extension of 1897–8 on the site of and probably incorporating walling of a building (perhaps a barn) put up here in 1703. Stabling at its end, also by Carruthers.

(Inside, a ground-floor vaulted passage curved behind the main turnpike stair and running along the main block's E side. Off it in the main block are two tunnel-vaulted cellars, the S the wine cellar with a narrow stair to the hall. Tunnel-vaulted kitchen at the N with a large fireplace and a drain in the W wall. On the first floor the main block is filled by the hall, the jamb by a private room. The main stair continues to the upper floors supplemented by a tight stair in the thickness of the NE corner's walling and entered from a door at the dais end of the hall.)

7030   DAVIOT

Small village set in moorland and forestry.

FREE CHURCH. *See* Farr.

26 PARISH CHURCH. A charmingly innocent landmark built in 1826 by *Thomas Macfarlane*, mason, and *Donald Macphail*, wright, to a specification by *Alexander Grant*. Tall harled three-bay rectangle with stumpy pinnacles at the corners of the crenellated parapet. In the long sides, Venetian centre windows flanked by roundheaded lights. At the S gable, an endearingly flimsy steeple, its five-stage tower squashed by a fat cornice with ball finials on the corners; then an octagonal belfry under a stone lid on which sit sharp obelisks; octagonal spire with a large weathercock. Interior recast in 1935.

PRIMARY SCHOOL. Broad-eaved, gableted and gabled school and schoolhouse, by *Alexander Ross*, 1875. Round-arched windows lighting the schoolroom.

DAVIOT HOUSE, 1.3km. NE. Built for Alexander Mackintosh of Mackintosh in 1821 by *Thomas Macfarlane*, mason, and *Lachlan Mackintosh*, wright. Rough granite ashlar front of two storeys above a basement. Three bays, the outer two canted with three-light first-floor windows. At the centre, a Roman Doric portico. – To the N, very scanty remains of DAVIOT or STRATHNAIRN CASTLE, said to have been built by David, Earl of Crawford, *c.* 1400 and to have formed a courtyard with a tower at each corner. – To the W, large courtyard STEADING built by *Thomas Macfarlane* in 1822, an octagonal HORSEMILL on its S side.

DOCHFOUR HOUSE

6030

8km. SW of Inverness

Large and smart Italianate villa designed by *William Robertson* and built for Evan Baillie of Dochfour in 1839–40, incorporating an unpretentious harled laird's house put up by Alexander Baillie of Dochfour *c.* 1770. That house still stands at the centre of the E front. Two storeys and five bays, the outer windows paired. Robertson wrapped broad-eaved additions round its back. At their NE corner a square two-storey Italianate tower with a balustraded and urn-topped porte cochère; panel carved with a coat of arms at the tower's first floor. Large and variegated ranges on the NW, some of the windows set in roundheaded overarches. SW of the C18 house is the two-storey range containing the principal new rooms (library, drawing room and dining room) added in 1839–40. Broad piend-roofed ends, each with an open-pedimented gablet to the front. At each floor, three-light windows with broad ashlar mullions. Recessed centre, again with a broad-mullioned three-light window at each floor; first-floor balcony carried across between the ends. Rising behind the centre, a big tower with a shallow pavilion roof of two stages. This range was extended W in 1871 by *Matthews & Lawrie,* who made its end a replica of one of Robertson's. Linking block with a pilastered and balustraded loggia-like ground floor, the first floor deeply recessed.

STABLES to the N by *Matthews & Lawrie,* 1872. Courtyard of single-storey and attic ranges, not very picturesquely gabled and gableted. In the centre of the S range, a tower with a shallow pyramid roof, its generally Italianate appearance belied by a jumping stringcourse. – To its E, the late C19 hexagonal DAIRY, its shallow-pitched roof carried out over cast-iron rustic columns to form a verandah. – Beside the drive from the NE, a small late C19 BURIAL GROUND. In it, a tall grey granite early C19 OBELISK on a panelled plinth; it commemorates Evan Baillie † 1835. – At the drive's entrance, ball-finialled GATE-PIERS of *c.* 1840.

DOCHGARROCH HOUSE

6040

5.9km. SW of Inverness

Picturesque harled and broad-eaved villa, probably by *William Robertson,* 1839. Asymmetrical E front of three bays, the E shallowly advanced, the W's ground-floor window now two-light. At the centre, a pedimented porch, its pilasters topped by tiny pediments and anthemion finials, a motif recurring at the outer windows of the first floor. Horizontal glazing in the first-floor windows. Cast-iron anthemion finials at the gables, where the eaves turn in to suggest open pediments. Recessed single-storey W wing added as an office for the factor of the Dochfour estate in 1869.

DORES

Small village laid out in 1820 beside Loch Ness, now mostly composed of neat c 20 housing, the white harled DORES INN a late Georgian survival.

PARISH CHURCH. Tall harled box built in 1827–8, the diamond-paned windows rising into stone-finialled gablets. Angular spired bellcote on the w gable. The sw vestry is an addition by *Thomas Munro*, 1910.

ALDOURIE CASTLE. *See* p. 147.

DRUMNADROCHIT

Village at the mouth of Glen Urquhart.

OLD URQUHART PARISH CHURCH. Built or repaired in 1630. Only the E gable still stands, its outer face incorporated in a small burial enclosure. In this gable, a central lancet under a shield carved with a crown and the initials A^{M}G for Mr Alexander Grant, minister of Glenurquhart from 1624 to 1645. Also in the gable, a TABLET commemorating Æmilia Fraser † 1759, with an angel's head at the top and a skull, hourglass and bell at the base. – To the s, MONUMENT to the Rev. Alexander Mackay † 1908, a polished granite column topped by a collection of balls. – Further w, similar monument to John Grant † 1899, with an assemblage of urns on top.

URQUHART PARISH CHURCH. By *William Robertson*, 1836–8. A tall harled and crowstepped box but not without pretension. Stone Y-tracery in the long sides' minimally pointed windows. In the s gable, blind 'Saxon' windows flanking the Tudor door; a small pointed window above. On top of the gable, a bellcote whose pointed arches support a heavy foliaged finial, its appearance more classical than Gothic. Inside, a gallery round three sides. – Late Victorian FURNISHINGS. – STAINED GLASS N window (the Sower) by *A. Ballantine & Son*, 1906.

URQUHART SECONDARY SCHOOL. By *Matthews & Lawrie*, 1876–7. Multi-gabled, long and symmetrical, like a row of almshouses.

DESCRIPTION. On the approach from the s, Urquhart Parish Church (*see* above) is the first incident. Then the road to the school and the old parish church (for both, *see* above). Between them, the white harled BENLEVA HOTEL, built as the manse in 1800, its block-pedimented doorpiece probably part of the alterations made in 1867. On the main road, interwar council housing followed by a less formal group of c 19 vernacular cottages making a rough triangle round a green. Plain early c 19 BRIDGE, widened by *Mears & Carus-Wilson*, 1933. To its NW, the LOCH NESS LODGE HOTEL, a mid-Victorian villa with an Italianate tower and large recent additions. On the exit towards Inverness, the sub-Baronial DRUMNADROCHIT HOTEL by *Matthews & Lawrie*, 1881–2, U-plan with bows projecting from the ends of the wings. Flashy detached block on the W by *Hector Macdonald Associates*, 1985–6.

URQUHART CASTLE. *See* p. 216.

DUNLICHITY
6030

Church and shooting lodge isolated in Strathnairn.

PARISH CHURCH. Humble harled box of 1757–9 incorporating earlier walling, probably medieval. The 1750s work included lengthening the building 3.66m. and the contraction of a (?chancel) arch in the E gable to form a door (now blocked). The rectangular windows may date from this period. On the W gable, the stump of an ashlar bellcote, perhaps added in the repairs of 1829, now surmounted by an iron cross. This gable's pointed windows probably date from *William Lawrie*'s alterations in 1859.

At the CHURCHYARD's S entrance, a harled two-storey early C19 WATCH HOUSE. – Attached to the church's E gable, the rubble-built BURIAL ENCLOSURE of the Shaws of Tordarroch, their ownership commemorated by an armorial PANEL by *C. d'O. Pilkington Jackson*, 1968. – On the ground, an over-grown heraldic GRAVESLAB, perhaps C17. – At the grave-yard's E end, the late Georgian BURIAL ENCLOSURE of the MacGillivrays of Dunmaglass and Dalcrombie, with urns on top of the corniced gatepiers. The gates look original, but the wrought-iron overthrow is by *Robert M. Hadden*, 1968. On the N wall, another armorial PANEL, carved by *Jackson* in 1967.

ERCHLESS CASTLE
4040
1km. NE of Struy

Tall harled and crowstepped early C17 tower house with a late C19 Baronial addition. When the lands of Erchless were granted by Simon, Lord Fraser of Lovat, to John Chisholm in 1606 there was no mention of a tower here,[*] and the house was probably begun almost immediately afterwards. It is L-plan, with a four-storey main block and a five-storey SE jamb. In the W inner angle and at the main block's NW corner, round stair turrets corbelled out from the first floor; slate-roofed bartizans at the main block's NE and SW corners. C17 gunloops in the S front. The upper windows are Georgian, probably dating from the repairs made in 1787–93; swept dormerheads, probably late C19, over the top windows on the S. At the W gable, a two-storey battlemented bay window of 1895. Door in the jamb's S face, its moulded surround looking like C17 work recut in 1787–93, when this entrance was made, perhaps replacing one in the inner angle. Large but soggy Baronial addition to the N, by

---

[*]Although permission to build a castle on the barony of Erchless had been given to Hugh, Lord Lovat, in 1529.

Duncan Cameron, 1895. Scots Jacobean detail at the E front's first-floor windows; round conical-roofed NE tower. (Inside, a turnpike stair in the C17 house's jamb; it is of 1787–93, presumably replacing the original, which would have risen only to the first floor. Otherwise, a mixture of late Georgian and late Victorian.)

Courtyard of crowstep-gabled STABLES AND COACH HOUSES to the N, by *Cameron & Burnett*, 1899, incorporating unassuming work of 1805–6 by *James Smith*. Over the off-centre N entrance, a pedimented clocktower with Venetian windows to front and back; over the S, a cupola on top of a crowstepped gable.

5020   ERROGIE

Scattered moorland hamlet on the line of General Wade's road down the Great Glen.

STRATHERRICK FREE CHURCH. Big harled box by *William Mackintosh*, 1871. Pointed windows; bellcote on the N gable.

STRATHERRICK FREE PRESBYTERIAN CHURCH, 1.5km. SW. Built in 1899. Harl-pointed, with a porch and bellcote; tiny N apse.

STRATHERRICK WAR MEMORIAL, 1.9km. SW. Boldly sited above Loch Mhor. Octagonal granite column with a finial of stylized foliage; *c.* 1920.

4030   ESKADALE

Just the church and a couple of houses set in trees beside the Beauly River.

ST MARY'S CHURCH (R.C.). Chunky harled church built in 1825–6, with 'Saxon' windows and doors. Double-pitch-roofed N and S aisles either side of the nave, which projects one bay to their W. In 1881 *P. P. Pugin* extended the chancel (its E end originally flush with the aisles' E walls) E by one bay, providing narrow pointed lights in its side walls and a large idiosyncratically traceried rose window in the E gable. Bandcourses to suggest pediments at the aisle gables; a hint of open pediments at the nave's ends.

Inside are roundheaded arcades carried on fat circular columns. W gallery over the porch, its front carved with interlacing Romanesque arcading. Simple arch into the two-bay chancel, its W bay flanked by the organ chamber on the N and a wall of the sacristy on the S. – Stone ALTAR of 1881 designed by *P. P. Pugin*, its back carved by *Boulton* of Cheltenham with angels and a pelican in piety. Its REREDOS has high reliefs of the Annunciation and Nativity. – Late C19 STAINED GLASS (angels and saints) in the E rose window. – MONUMENT on the chancel's N side to Thomas Alexander, Lord Lovat, † 1875 and his wife Charlotte Georgina † 1876, probably part of Pugin's alterations of 1881. Neo-medieval tomb recess, the arch's cusps ending in roses; heraldry on the sarcophagus' front. – BRASSES on the sacristy wall at the W aisle's E end to the Hon. George Stafford Fraser † 1854 and to Mrs Amelia Fraser of Strichen † 1860, both with floriated crosses, one with angels. – ORGAN by *James Conacher & Sons*, probably of 1881.

In the GRAVEYARD, good-quality Victorian monuments. Among them, a Celtic cross of red Dumfriesshire sandstone, carved by *D. & A. Robertson*, 1883, commemorating John Sobieski Stolberg Stuart and his brother Charles Edward Stuart, the authors of *Vestiarium Scoticum* and purported children of Bonnie Prince Charlie.

CHAPEL HOUSE. Early C19 *cottage orné* with fretted bargeboards and horizontal glazing.

EILEANAIGAS HOUSE, 2.4km. NE. *Cottage orné* on an island. It was built in 1839 by Lord Lovat for the brothers John Sobieski Stolberg Stuart and Charles Edward Stuart, the antiquarians and reputed children of Bonnie Prince Charlie. Two storeys and plentifully crowstepped. At the front, three gables, the centre taller and further advanced. From it projects a crowstep-gabled porch, an armorial shield above its segmental-arched door. Lattice glazing in the mullioned and transomed windows. Rambling and varied wings to the back, some added in 1858. When the Stuart brothers occupied the house it was fitted up 'in imitation of the style in which Highland chieftains were wont to decorate their rooms in times of yore.'

ESKADALE HOUSE, 1.7km. NE. Small mansion house of *c.* 1800. Two storeys and a basement; piended platform roof. Five-bay polished ashlar front, the Roman Doric portico flanked by windows set in overarches joined by bandcourses. Moulded sill course across the first floor. Discreet E wing added in 1880.

FARR   *6030*

Place-name for scattered housing in Strathnairn.

DAVIOT FREE CHURCH. Cheaply detailed Gothic box, by *James Matthews*, 1858.

FREE PRESBYTERIAN CHURCH. Built in 1938, an ecclesiastical air given by shallow stepped buttresses and pointed windows.

PRIMARY SCHOOL. By *Alexander Ross*, 1875. Broad-eaved display of gables and gablets; round-arched windows lighting the schoolroom.

FASNAKYLE   *3020*

Small settlement at the junction of Glen Affric and Strathglass.

FREE CHURCH. By *Matthews & Lawrie*, 1868. Broad Gothic box with pinnacled corner buttresses. In the gable front, a Tudor-

arched door under a window of three pointed lights, the centre
arch stilted.

BRIDGE. Single arch built in 1793.

FASNAKYLE POWER STATION. Modern-traditional by *James
Shearer*, 1952, the low reliefs of Celtic beasts by *Hew Lorimer*.

FASNAKYLE HOUSE. Large and plain in white harling, mid-C19
in origin but recast by *Cameron & Burnett* in 1899 and 1911.

3000   FORT AUGUSTUS

Victorian village on the Caledonian Canal at the S end of Loch
Ness, the site of its C18 fort now covered by the buildings of St
Benedict's Abbey.

ST BENEDICT'S ABBEY

Victorian monastery on the site and incorporating substantial
parts of a Hanoverian fortress built to command the narrow
centre of the Great Glen between Loch Ness and Loch Oich
and Loch Lochy to the S.

A barracks on the higher ground to the W had been built in
1718–21 (for its remains, *see* Description, below), but as early
as 1724 General Wade thought it 'situate at too great a distance
from Lake Ness' (presumably for ease of supply by water from
Inverness) and suggested building a new fort and barracks on
a promontory at the Loch's W end. Preparations for building
this fort were underway in 1727; construction began in 1729 to
a design by *Captain John Romer* and was completed in 1742,
when it was named Fort Augustus in honour of George II's
third son, Prince William Augustus, Duke of Cumberland.
Four years after its completion, the fort was captured by the
Jacobite army of Prince Charles Edward ('Bonnie Prince
Charlie'), its N bastions largely destroyed and the barrack blocks
badly damaged. In 1747–8, after the collapse of the rising,
Colonel William Skinner repaired the fort and its buildings and
strengthened the defences with the construction of a dry moat
and glacis. Fort Augustus lost much of its military significance
after 1818, when the outer defences were largely dismantled and
the ordnance, together with most of the garrison, transferred to
Fort George. In 1867 the buildings were sold to Thomas,
fourteenth Lord Lovat, who used them partly to house tenants
and partly as a shooting lodge. His son, Simon, fifteenth Lord
Lovat, gave the fort to the English congregation of Benedictines
in 1876, and its conversion from Georgian fort to Gothic abbey
was begun immediately. The first architect employed was *Joseph
A. Hansom*. He designed the reconstruction and extension of
the existing buildings to provide a guesthouse in the W range,
a school for eighty boys in the N, and a monastery for twenty
monks in the E. The C18 S range was demolished and its site
filled with the S walk of the cloister, which was built round the

old barrack square. To the s it was intended to erect a chapter house and abbey church. The guesthouse, school and monastery were completed in 1880, when Hansom had already been replaced by *P. P. Pugin*. The church, designed by Pugin, was begun in 1890, but work stopped three years later for lack of money, only part of the s side having been built and with only the sw St Andrew's Chapel usable. Work on the church resumed in 1914, now with *Reginald Fairlie* as the architect. He retained most of Pugin's plan and massing but substituted a Romanesque style for his Gothic. In 1917 the monastic choir and the Chapel of the Blessed Sacrament to its s were opened for worship, but work then stopped. It did not begin again until 1949, when the nave was started. Fairlie was still architect but replaced his design of 1914 with a new one. The shell of the nave was completed in 1956.* Ten years later, Fairlie's former partner *Charles W. Gray* added the w narthex, baptistery and porch. The church was finally completed in 1980 by *W. W. Allan*, who added a shallow E apse to the choir, plastered the nave walls, paved the floor, and reordered the interior in accordance with the new liturgical practice introduced after the Second Vatican Council.

A surprising amount of the c18 buildings survives, although now disguised in monkish vesture. The fort was a quadrangle whose four ranges enclosed a barrack square, *c.* 30.5m. by 42m. From the outer corners projected polygonal bastions, each provided with emplacements for six cannon to enfilade the walls and cover all approaches; at the bastions' tips were pepperpot sentry boxes. In the centre of each bastion, partly sunk below the terreplein and reached by a passage through it, was a conical-roofed round structure, the NE containing the magazine, the SE the meal girnel, the sw the necessary house or latrine, and the NW the well. Of the two-storey-and-attic blocks round the quadrangle, the w was the gatehouse, the N a barrack with subalterns' quarters in the projecting wings, the E a second barrack, and the s the governor's house with captains' quarters in the wings, all built in a plain Vanbrughian manner.

In remodelling the three c18 ranges he retained (the w, N and E), *Hansom* gave each an extra floor, its windows rising into gablets, and a double-pitch roof‡ enlivened by small gabled dormers and bands of grey and green slates, some in a chevron pattern. The w range (the c18 gatehouse, and now the guesthouse) has a slightly craggy Gothic feel. Central gable in place of the c18 open pediment and a big window instead of the original first-floor Venetian. Hansom's long single-storey porch is carried over the dry moat on the segmental arches of *Skinner*'s bridge of 1747; in the porch's gable, a high relief of monks engaged in building. To the l. of this block, the projecting Calder Wing of 1958–60, a reinforced concrete frame faced with 'Fyfestone' built on the site of the NW bastion. Over

A. R. Conlon acted as executant architect after Fairlie's death in 1952.
‡The c18 blocks had M-roofs.

its entrance, a bronze STATUE by *Arthur Fleischmann* of St Benedict holding two kilted boys.

To the C18 N barrack (now school) block, Hansom added boldly projecting N wings, the E having armorial roundels in the gable. In the centre of the N front he placed a lower wing, which extends to a tall tower whose ground floor forms a *porte cochère*. Oriels at the two floors above; statue of St Benedict below the machicolation carrying the deep shallowly crenellated parapet. On top, a battlemented octagonal cap-house of two stages, the lower a belfry, the upper with round clock-faces. At the range's E end, a dreary interwar addition. To its E, part of the NE bastion rebuilt in 1747 but now lacking its sentry box, a boiler chimney inadequate compensation.

Hansom recast the E front of the E block (C18 barrack, now part of the monastery) with segmental-arched two-light windows filled with Dec tracery. At its N end he added the projecting refectory wing, again with Gothic ground-floor windows. In the inner angle, a tower with canted corners rising to support a conical-roofed circular top stage above the main eaves. N of this, a semi-octagonal-ended block whose top floor housed the Abbot's Chapel. S of the C18 block *Pugin* takes over with a tall tower. The sides of its lower stages are battered; above, it rises sheer to a steep pavilion roof. Below the tall belfry openings, a tabernacled niche containing a statue of St Columba. To the S, the bay-windowed Calefactory.

The three C18 ranges remodelled by *Hansom* present institutional Gothic faces to the cloister quadrangle. Round its four sides is the cloister walk. Heavy buttresses between the big four-light windows, their tops a varied display of Gothic tracery, their hoodmoulds' labels carved as heads. Gargoyles under the quatrefoil-pierced parapet. Inside the cloister, each quadripartite-vaulted bay is marked off by a transverse arch; encaustic tiles on the floor.

The C18 interiors have almost all gone except in the W range where the guardrooms' brick tunnel-vaults survive. The NE guardroom is now the RELICS CHAPEL, its floor still with C18 brick-paving, its walls painted in the C20 with figures of saints in a manner reminiscent of the Roman catacombs by *Father Luke Cary-Elwes*, the ceiling by *Father Lawrence Mann*. Built into the S wall of this range's central passage, a fragmentary Roman SCULPTURE of three mother goddesses, probably C2 or C3. It was found at Colinton (Edinburgh), but its original provenance is unknown. The other interiors worth mention are Victorian. In the old Abbot's Chapel on the top floor of the N range, STAINED GLASS (the Joyful Mysteries of the Rosary) by *John Hardman & Co.*, *c.* 1880. – In the Refectory, a dado of linenfold panelling copied from that of *c.* 1500 in the Hall of Magdalen College, Oxford; high pulpit at the W end. – The windows contain heraldic STAINED GLASS commemorating the Abbey's more aristocratic benefactors. – *Hansom* converted the ground floor of the main E block to a Library with pointed arches punched through the walls of the C18 barrack rooms

and their ceilings heightened. – To the S is *Pugin*'s Great Staircase, with stone arches springing from immensely sturdy squat
columns, their square bases and capitals having chamfered
corners. – Calefactory at the Abbey's SE corner, its hooded
stone chimneypiece carved with a Pelican in Piety. – CHAPTER
HOUSE to the SW by *Pugin*, 1896, with a semi-octagonal W
apse. Walls of ashlar above a plaster dado; attached piers carry
the wooden beams of the roof. Brown and yellow encaustic tiles
on the floor. – Opening off the cloister's S range is a vaulted
vestibule with an arcade opening into the Sacristy. This is of
five bays with apsed ends. Encaustic tiled floor. A short cloister
provided by *Fairlie* in 1916 joins it to the Abbey Church to
the S.

The ABBEY CHURCH, built over a ninety-year period, is a
witness to changing architectural and liturgical fashions. *P. P.
Pugin*'s design of 1890 was for a six-bay aisled nave, an aisled
choir and sanctuary, each of three bays, with the Lady Chapel
to the E and other chapels S of the nave and choir and at the E
end of the sanctuary aisles, and with a tower *c.* 80m. high on
the S. The detail was Dec. During the building work of 1890–
3 all the foundations, except those of the Lady Chapel, were
laid, but the only parts built were the SW St Andrew's Chapel
and the shell of the Blessed Sacrament Chapel S of the choir.
Grey granite walls, heavily buttressed (a structural necessity on
the steep site). Double-pitch roof over St Andrew's Chapel,
whose buttresses have gablet finials. On the Blessed Sacrament
Chapel, a corbelled crenellated parapet.

Reginald Fairlie's contribution in 1914–17 was the design and
erection of the choir, completion of the Blessed Sacrament
Chapel and the building of the first stage of the intended tower
on its W. Pugin's Dec was replaced by simplified Romanesque.
Clearstorey lights in the choir. At the tower, roundheaded
windows containing loop tracery suggestive of C15 Scottish
architecture.

The design of Fairlie's nave, built in 1949–56, is almost as
far removed from his proposals of 1914 as from Pugin's of 1890.
The plan was still that of 1890, but the flat-roofed aisles were
carried up to the nave's eaves and the clearstorey consequently
omitted. Very tall windows, round-arched punctuations in the
walling without hoodmoulds or architraves, filled with Geor-
gian-pattern glazing. The masonry of the new N and W fronts
is more cheerful than the craggy grey granite of the earlier work.
It is of pink and grey granite, rough ashlar with cherrycock
pointing. No buttresses to break the flat planes; not even a finial
on the gable. The effect is of some hugely inflated hall church
translated from a post-war suburb.

Charles W. Gray's gabled W narthex and porch mark a return
to grey granite. In the porch's open front, a cross to support
the roof. Neo-Georgian bowed baptistery projecting N of the
narthex.

W. W. Allan's completion of the E end in 1980 disregarded
Pugin's and Fairlie's earlier schemes for a big sanctuary of a

type made redundant by the liturgical changes following the
Second Vatican Council. Plain 'Fyfestone' walling with a semi-
octagonal apse at the end of the choir.

Inside, the nave arcades of 1949–56 are roundheaded, carried
on immensely tall octagonal ashlar piers for which Fairlie
claimed Palma Cathedral (Majorca) as his inspiration; simplified capitals. Transverse concrete arches to delineate the bays
of the nave and support its concrete segmental vaults. Over the
aisles, a procession of semicircular concrete vaults at right
angles to those of the nave. Tall roundheaded chancel arch of
1914–17 springing from cushion-capitalled responds. In the
choir, conventional though simple Romanesque arcades under
a clearstorey. Hammerbeam roof with painted figures of angels,
made by *Nathaniel Grieve & Co*. The stone sanctuary arch of
1914–17 is a replica of the chancel arch. Beyond, the plain
plaster walling of Allan's apse broken only by high-set slit
windows and a narrow cross-window. – The FLOOR of black
and green Coniston slate, polished in the choir, riven elsewhere,
was provided in 1980.

In *Pugin*'s ST ANDREW'S CHAPEL of 1890–3 at the SW,
two bays of elaborate sexpartite vaulting. – Plain Norman arches
of 1914–17 into the ANTE-CHAPEL at the base of Fairlie's
intended tower and the BLESSED SACRAMENT CHAPEL to
its E. In the chapel, a panelled wooden ceiling of 1914–17 by
Nathaniel Grieve & Co.

FURNISHINGS. Central HIGH ALTAR of 1980, a free-standing stone table. – Above it, a square TESTER of cylindrical metal
lampshades hanging from a wooden butterfly-roof canopy, also
of 1980. – CHOIR STALLS of 1914–17, of walnut and American
black birch. – In the choir arcades, contemporary SCREENS
with two tiers of arcading, Romanesque but with Celtic detail,
the N of oak, the S of Brazilian hardwood, both made by *Robert
Thompson*.

The Blessed Sacrament Chapel furnishings were all designed
by *Fairlie* in 1914–17. – BALDACCHINO with painted wooden
columns carrying a deerskin canopy, its front slope decorated
with embossed harts (an allusion to Psalm 41: 'Like as the hart
desireth the water brooks . . . '). At each corner, a carved Pelican
in Piety; on the pelmet, painted ravens (symbols of St
Benedict). – Gilded ALTAR CROSS and CANDLESTICKS, neo-
Celtic. – Wrought-iron SANCTUARY LAMPS, again of Celtic
inspiration.

Above the ALTAR OF THE HOLY CROSS in the S nave
arcade, a bronze Calvary by *Arthur Fleischmann* on a mosaic
background by *Cecile Fleischmann*.

ORGAN by *Bryceson Brothers*, 1875, originally built for a
private house in London, moved to the Albert Palace in Bat-
tersea Park in 1884, and bought by St Benedict's Abbey in
1894. Part was installed in the choir in 1917; the whole was
rebuilt in 1936–8 by *Lawton*, and again by *Rushworth & Dreaper*,
1980.

STAINED GLASS. Boldly coloured abstract lights in the E wall of the choir and its aisles, by *Michael Farrely*, 1980. – In the Blessed Sacrament Chapel's Ante-Chapel, s w window (Melchisedech and Abraham) by *Moira Forsyth*, simplified realism. – In St Andrew's Chapel, colourful figures of saints, by *Paul Woodroffe*.

CHURCHES

FREE CHURCH. Disused. Built in 1844 on a hill to the w of the village. Harled rectangle with a gableted Gothic bellcote; pointed windows.

PARISH CHURCH. Late Georgian in origin but the present appearance dating from *Henry Burrell*'s reconstruction of 1866–7. Sneck-harled lanceted box. On the roof, a Gothic ventilator; iron bellcote at the gable. The broad-eaved s vestry is presumably of 1866–7; the harled N porch of 1949. Interior recast in 1960.

UNITED FREE CHURCH. Now a shop. Of corrugated iron, with triangular-headed windows and a little spired bellcote; it was opened in 1906.

DESCRIPTION

On the approach from the N, the main road (A82) crosses the Oich on a BRIDGE of 1934 for which *Robert Bruce* was the supervising engineer, *Blyth & Blyth* consultant engineers, and *Mears & Carus-Wilson* consultant architects. It is built of concrete faced with rubble masonry. Upstream, the surviving castellated piers of the former RAILWAY VIADUCT by *William Roberts*, 1897–1903. Downstream, a wooden BRIDGE by *C. R. Manners*, 1902. On a spit projecting E between the Oich and the Caledonian Canal, the old United Free Church (*see* Churches, above). Beside it the WAR MEMORIAL HALL designed as a drill hall by *Alexander Ross & Son* in 1913, with broad eaves and round-arched windows; battlemented porch incorporating the memorial of *c.* 1920. The road crosses the Canal by a SWING BRIDGE, probably C 20. To its w, the six LOCKS, made in 1817–21 and rebuilt by *Walker & Burges* in 1843–7. On the Canal's s side, a row of unpretentious late C 19 houses. At their E end, a canopied cast-iron DRINKING FOUNTAIN of 1897 decorated with reliefs of Queen Victoria, whose Diamond Jubilee it commemorates. To its s, a piend-roofed pavilion built in 1817 as a PUMPING HOUSE in connexion with the making of the canal. E of the bridge, on the Canal's s bank, a small HALL by *John Robertson*, 1891, with broad eaves and Gothic windows. Then the wall of St Benedict's Abbey (*see* above) and, at the entrance to the Canal from Loch Ness, a pepperpot LIGHTHOUSE. s of the Canal bridge, the main road swings w and climbs to leave the village past the LOVAT ARMS HOTEL, harled with large gables, by *Cameron & Burnett*, 1903. At the back of the hotel, part of the w wall, of KILIWHIMEN BARRACKS designed by *James Smith* and built by his son-in-law *Gilbert Smith* in 1718–

21, and mostly demolished after 1746. It is of rubble with square gunloops, their mouths splayed externally; the round-arched gate is a later insertion. Further w, the Parish Church (*see* above) set back from the road on the N. Also set back is the late C19 LOVAT TERRACE, a pretty row of single-storey-and-attic cottages with mansard roofs and bargeboarded dormers; roundheaded panes of glass in the windows and doors.

7050   FORT GEORGE
                          2.4km. NW of Ardersier

76 Isolated on a windswept shingle spit, this massive demonstration of Hanoverian military power is the largest and last of the C17 and C18 forts built in Scotland to house what was virtually an army of occupation.

Fort George is the direct successor of Inverness Castle, a royal stronghold since the C12 guarding the NE end of the Great Glen. Between 1690 and 1727 Inverness Castle had had its defences strengthened and barrack accommodation enlarged, but it was badly damaged during the Jacobite rising of 1745–6. Immediately after the Battle of Culloden the Government decided that its main concentration of military force in the Highlands should be based at Inverness, but the castle there overlooked by higher ground had been shown to be indefensible against serious attack. Instead it was proposed to build a new fort near the mouth of the Ness on the site of the Cromwellian citadel which had been demolished after the Restoration of 1660. *Dugal Campbell* produced one design in 1746 and *Colonel William Skinner* another in 1747. Skinner's plans were accepted and the contract for masonwork and brickwork awarded to *William Adam*, but, before work had begun at the citadel site, the Inverness Burgh Council demanded compensation for loss of the use of its recently extended harbour. The proposal to build the new fort at Inverness was then abandoned and towards the end of 1747 Skinner surveyed the Ardersier peninsula 14.5km. E of the town. This spit of land commands the narrow entrance (1.2km. across) from the Moray Firth into the Inverness Firth, has a sheltered anchorage on its S side, and lies close to the main road from Inverness to Elgin, Banff and Aberdeen. Skinner drew up plans for a new fort to be built at the tip of the peninsula, the cost estimated with suspicious precision at £92,673 19s. 11d. (the eventual figure was more than double). This scheme was accepted and work began in 1748. William Adam's death in the same year led to his sons *John, Robert* and *James* taking over the building contract. When the fort was finally completed in 1769 it was already considered a very expensive white elephant. In 1795 the fort contained only a garrison of 'Invalids' (soldiers unfit for active service) and an artillery unit. By 1815 it was doubtful if Fort George could withstand a modern artillery attack and it was considered as a place of confinement for Napoleon, but the idea was abandoned, as was the proposal of 1835 for its conversion to a prison. After the 1850s scare of a

French invasion, a coastal-defence battery was erected on the fort's seaward-facing N side but it was only with the army reorganization of 1881, by which each regiment was provided with a territorial depot, that Fort George acquired a settled function as the depot of the Seaforth Highlanders, replaced in 1967 by the Royal Highland Fusiliers. Since 1964 it has been open to the public as an Ancient Monument.

The site is naturally defensive, the 300m.-wide tip of a peninsula surrounded by water on the N, W and S sides. To the E the land is flat for 1.4km., a small hill having been removed (as intended earlier) in 1766–7, allowing an attacker neither shelter nor a commanding height within the range of C 18 artillery.

The fort itself is a vast barracks complex designed to hold two battalions, totalling 1,600 men, together with a resident artillery unit. Accommodation for these men and their stores is contained in a formally planned small town surrounded by a strong defence. This defence was designed according to the principles of artillery fortification developed in Europe since the C 16. The main walls were defended by projecting polygonal bastions and demi-bastions from whose outer sides or salients artillery could fire at an approaching enemy, and from whose inner sides or flanks more guns could cover the walls against close attack. At Fort George the general outline is of a rough rectangle but narrowing with the site towards the W, where it ends in a broad triangular projection (the Point Battery), on which were placed guns commanding the sea channel; at the battery's outer corners are demi-bastions (Prince Frederick William's* and the Duke of Marlborough's). About halfway down the fort's long N and S sides are flattened bastions (Prince William Henry's on the S, Prince Henry Frederick's on the N). To their E, the main wall is pierced on each side by a gateway or sally-port protected by a low triangular parapet or place of arms guarding the approach from the shore. At the NE and SE corners, boldly projecting bastions (the Duke of Cumberland's and the Prince of Wales's). Main entrance in the centre of the E front.

The walls are broad ramparts constructed of packed earth excavated from the site alternating with stone cross-walls, all covered with turf. The strongly battered outer faces are fronted with rough ashlar of red Munlochy sandstone from the Black Isle; near the top, a semicircular stringcourse, the parapet above broken by wide splayed cannon embrasures. Behind is a platform (the terreplein), c. 21–27m. wide, high above the level of the fort's interior, from which it is reached by ramps across the retaining walls. At the terreplein's outer side, a continuous firing step on which musketeers could stand to shoot down across the broad downward-sloping ledge on top of the main parapet, whose inner side, like the cannon embrasures, is brick-faced. At each corner, a projecting stone pepperpot sentry box.

*Each bastion or demi-bastion except the Duke of Marlborough's demi-bastion is named after a son or grandson of George II.

The E front facing the landward approach was given massive additional defences. In front is a ditch *c.* 9.7m. deep which could be flooded at high tide through sluice gates in its end walls (or *batardeaux*). In the centre of the ditch opposite the straight E wall of the fort is a triangular island or ravelin, its NE and SE sides protected by side channels (the ravelin ditch) opening off the main ditch. The ravelin is of the same stone-fronted earth construction as the main rampart walls but is less high, so as not to impede the field of fire of the guns behind. Its two outer faces have parapets with cannon embrasures, but its W front is open, so that any attacker who gained possession of this island would be exposed to fire from the main fort. On the E side of the main ditch and ravelin ditch is the covered way, a platform set below the level of the top of the ravelin and open to the W and so, were it to be captured, exposed to guns mounted on the ravelin and the bastions of the fort. On the covered way's E side is a firing step and brick parapet (originally topped by a wooden palisade). Corbelled out from the covered way's end walls like machicolations were latrines (the N surviving). From the top of this parapet the ground outside slopes down in an artificial bank (the glacis) to the flat terrain beyond.

These C18 fortifications are wonderfully little altered (in some places tactfully restored) but not quite intact. One major change is natural, the growth of the shingle bank on the S side, so that water no longer comes up to the tip of the place of arms at high water and the position of the fort's pier is now marked by a land-locked pool. This pier was used both by soldiers and by civilian ferry passengers crossing the firth from Chanonry Point on the Black Isle. Until *c.* 1790 the only access to and from the pier was through the fort itself, but a road was then made along the shore and cutting through the place of arms. Soon after, this road became the workday access to the fort and, as a result, the S sally-port was widened in the C19. *c.* 1861 Prince Henry Frederick's Bastion and the Duke of Cumberland's Bastion on the N side and the Point Battery at the W end were remodelled for coastal-defence batteries, the bastions having part of their parapets rebuilt in indented form, the Point Battery losing its sentry boxes. Also in the C19, windows were made in the E ends of the N and S rampart walls to light casemate rooms behind. A necessary consequence of Fort George becoming the Seaforth Highlanders' depot in 1881 was the subsequent adaptation of the N place of arms as a cemetery for officers' dogs.

On the approach to the fort from the E, two passages are cut through the glacis, the N originally the road to Nairn, the S to Inverness. Each enters the covered way opposite a lunette, an L-plan fighting platform and firing step with a place of arms behind, an effective protection for this first entry into the fort's defences. Just N of the S entrance is the bridge (originally a drawbridge) from the covered way to the ravelin. The entrance in the ravelin's rampart is through an open-pedimented round-

headed arch, its boldly projecting keystone and imposts a fore-
taste of the severe masculine architectural detail of the Fort's
buildings. A brick tunnel-vaulted passage with groined half-
vaults and iron-studded doors at the ends leads through the
rampart. On the ravelin's platform below the rampart is the
piend-roofed Ravelin Guardhouse, completed in 1753. Projecting brown stone ends gripping a red sandstone loggia. In
the centre of the ravelin's W side is a bridge across the main
ditch. It was restored in 1980, with its third span made a
drawbridge operated by upper counterpoise beams, as it had
been when Skinner's bridge here was erected in 1765–6; the
C18 construction of the E span as a second drawbridge opening
to cover the fort's main gate has not been reproduced.

The main gate in the fort's E rampart is another roundheaded 77
arch with a projecting keystone, grandly framed in an aedicule
with paired rusticated Doric pilasters, the pediment's tympanum carved with the arms of George II. The aedicule and
the voussoirs of the arch are of grey stone, the rest of red. Inside
the gate, another brick-vaulted passage through the rampart.
After its second (inner) gate the passage is flanked by groin-
vaulted aisles, their brick arcades springing from ashlar piers.
On each side of the aisles is a guardroom, the officers' to the
N, the soldiers' on the S. Inside the Officers' Guardroom, a
basket-arched chimneypiece; the soldiers' fireplace is quite utilitarian. N of the Officers' Guardroom and entered from the W
is a tunnel-vaulted prison, lighted only from the fanlight over
the door. This guardroom block is built into the rampart which
extends unbroken across its flat roof. Ponderously smart W
front, the projecting three-bay centrepiece having round-arched
entrances to the aisles and centre passage and a small bracketed
open pediment, the outer bays round-arched windows under
blind bullseyes. Stylized urns at the ends, where concave wing
walls sweep out to the main line of the rampart's retaining wall.

W of the Guardroom is the Parade, a turfed area c. 177m. by
95m. intended for ceremonial purposes (ordinary drill being
carried out on the Barrack Square). It is bounded on the N and
S by the rampart walls, which here contain casemate rooms,
each intended to hold up to forty men in shell-proof conditions
during a siege. Originally, each casemate had only a narrow
shuttered window each side of the door and a bullseye above;
most have now had their windows enlarged and openings
punched through the outer wall. On the Parade's W side, two
three-storey blocks (the Artillery Block for the fort's artillery
unit, and the Staff Block for its staff and storekeepers), built in
1761–6. They make a palace front, but its centrepiece is the
axial E–W road through the fort. Like most of the fort's other
buildings, their walls are of cherrycock-pointed rough ashlar
with boldly projecting window sills. At the outer end of each
block, an advanced five-bay house (the S for the Governor, the 78
N for the Lieutenant-Governor and Fort-Major), with a Roman
Doric portico at the pedimented centre. Plain houses designed
as officers' quarters at the inner end of each block. The nine-bay

links (the soldiers' quarters) have ground-floor loggias whose
segmental-headed arches spring from square piers. Inside the
Governor's House (now Officers' Mess), the Great Dining
Room chimneypiece was designed by the *Adam* brothers, *c.*
1766, the fluted frieze's centre panel decorated with circles and
swags of husks. On the stair wall in the Lieutenant-Governor's
and Fort-Major's House (now Regimental Museum) is a stone
fireplace lintel of 1662 imported from the demolished Brahan
Castle (Ross and Cromarty), its front divided by lyre-shaped
pilasters into three panels carved with strapwork, coronets and
the impaled arms and initials of Kenneth, third Earl of Seaforth,
and Isabel Mackenzie, his Countess. Venetian windows lighting
the stairs of these grand end houses.

The fort's road runs between the Artillery and Staff Blocks
to bisect Barrack Square behind. This is a rectangle, *c.* 90m.
by 45m., its two halves bounded by identical U-plan three-
storey barrack blocks of 1753–64. On the short N and S sides,
five-bay centrepieces (officers' quarters), their overall pediments containing the crowned initials GR (for *Georgius Rex*)
and the dates 1757 and 1763. They abut the three-bay jambs of
the soldiers' quarters, whose seven-bay main blocks along the
E and W sides are halted against slightly advanced but
unadorned five-bay pavilions (housing more officers) to which,
as to the centrepieces, the soldiers' quarters piend their roofs in
salute (a deviation from Skinner's original elevation). Rainwater
heads stamped with the cyphers of George II and George III.

The road continues W to separate two identical two-storey
ranges of Ordnance Stores (of 1759–61), each of nine bays with
a bracketed open pediment over the centre three. Circular
ground-floor windows (most restored since 1964); segment-
headed windows above. At the gables, vestigial open pediments.
Bracketed open pediments again on the back elevations, which
look into yards (the N built over *c.* 1955). To the W, what
Skinner intended as a second Parade, *c.* 60m. deep, the N side
now filled by a NAAFI block of 1934, its neo-Georgian feeble
in this Georgian context. On this Parade's W side, a range of
Provision Stores of 1760–2. Smart centrepiece with an open
pediment with bold guttae; it surmounts the roundheaded and
keyblocked pend arch under a blind Diocletian window whose
central light is now filled with a clock-face (originally an hexagonal wooden belfry stood behind the pediment). Five-bay
links, originally with segmental-headed windows (the S side's
fenestration altered in 1952), to three-bay piend-roofed pavilions (the N originally the brewery, the S the bakehouse). In
the yard behind the brewery, a well.

W of the Provision Stores and closing the long axis through
the fort is the Chapel, built as an afterthought in 1763–7. Dumpy
box enlivened by a semi-octagonal E apse projecting from the
pedimented gable and bowed stairtowers on the sides. Segmental-headed windows lighting the area, round-arched upper
windows for the gallery. The W gable is almost covered by a
battlemented low tower. This makes no impact on the formal

approach from the E. Was the chapel designed to face the other way and turned round for a 'correct' orientation?* Interior 28 divided into a nave and aisles by Roman Doric columns supporting piers from which spring roundheaded arcades; gallery in the aisles and across the W end. Segmental-headed ashlar chancel arch under the inscription 'GEOR-GIVS III DG . . M . BRI . FRA . ET HIB . REX . MDCCLXVII.' Groin-vault over the apse. – On the N of the chancel arch, an C18 three-decker PULPIT, formerly under the arch and now bereft of its sounding board. – Some BOX PEWS survive in the gallery, the front one at the W end recording that it is reserved for officers' ladies. – STAINED GLASS in the apse. Centre light (the Crucifixion) of 1950. – The flanking lights (saints) are by *Herbert Hendrie*, 1943. – In the SW corner, a marble TABLET to Major Henry Balfowr (*sic*) † 1776, 'unfortunately cut off By an Accident much to be regretted'. At the bottom, a coat of arms; on top, an urn above a pair of clasped hands.

In the rampart of the Point Battery behind the Chapel, two casemates each side of a magazine whose bracketed open pediment encloses a stone dated 1757. – In Prince Henry Frederick's Bastion on the fort's N side, lean-to workshops of 1752. – In Prince William Henry's Bastion on the S side is the Grand Magazine built in 1757–9, its masonry bulk minimally relieved by open pediments at the door and gables. Ventilation slits in the walls, the vents making right-angled turns inside to prevent the entry of a bullet. Brick-vaulted interior, the narrow centre passage flanked by broad side aisles. Low C19 addition at the E.

FOYERS 4020

Village built to serve the aluminium works founded here in 1896 and closed in 1970.

CHURCH, Upper Foyers. Solid little Gothic lump, by *John Robertson*, 1904–6. Utilitarian iron bellcote on the N gable; pinnacled flèche at the crossing of the nave and S transept. Inside, a broad roof, open over the centre, wooden ceiled with small transverse vaults at the sides.

BOLESKINE GRAVEYARD, 1.6km. NE. Standing by itself high above Loch Ness. At the N end, ENCLOSURE of the Frasers of Leadclune and Balnain, probably C18, its short S wall ashlar-built, the rest of rubble. In the E wall, remains of a Georgian doorway; to its N a blocked roundheaded window which has contained intersecting tracery. Most of the memorials inside are C19, but in the W wall two very similar tablets with heraldry at the top and reminders of death below; one (dated 16··) commemorates James Fraser of Culduthel † 1670 and his wife

---

*As understood by the Church of England but not by the Church of Scotland.

Isabel Fraser, the other Alexander Fraser, who was still living at the start of the C18. – On the ground, the GRAVESLAB, again with heraldry and grisly emblems, of Thomas Houston † 1705 and his wife Marie Fraser. – Just to the S, a large urn-topped MONUMENT erected to Lieutenant-Colonel Thomas Fraser in 1822. – At the graveyard's centre, the big idiosyncratic classical MONUMENT of Alexander Fraser of Dell † 1814. – In front, GRAVESLABS to Donald Fraser of Ericht † 1722 and John Fraser † 1751, both with vigorously carved symbols of mortality. – On the W side, a small WATCH HOUSE, probably early C19.

DESCRIPTION. UPPER FOYERS on the approach from the S begins with harled workers' housing of Edinburgh 'Colonies' type* by *Cameron & Burnett*, 1897, surrounding three sides of a green at whose centre stands a granite FOUNTAIN by *D. & A. Davidson*, erected in 1901 to commemorate Queen Victoria's Diamond Jubilee of four years before. To the N, contemporary rubble-built cottages with gabled dormers. Then interwar council housing. More council housing at LOWER FOYERS beside Loch Ness at the foot of the steep hill. On the E side of the River Foyers, a surviving fragment of the old ALUMINIUM WORKS of 1896, presumably by *Cameron & Burnett*. Very sturdy in hammerdressed rubble, the front a parade of round-arched windows in crowstepped gables.

WHITEBRIDGE HOTEL, 4.8km. S. By *Duncan Cameron*, 1898. White-painted harl-pointed rubble.

GLENMORISTON see INVERMORISTON

GLENURQUHART

FREE CHURCH. *See* Milton.
ST NINIAN'S CHURCH (Episcopal). *See* Kilmartin.
UNITED FREE CHURCH. *See* Milton.

GUISACHAN
2.7km. SW of Tomich

Roofless ruin of the laird's house built by William Fraser of Culbokie, *c.* 1755, transformed into a mansion *c.* 1860 with the addition of a large E block by *A. & W. Reid & Mackenzie*, and further altered later in the C19. The Georgian house at the W is a long and unpretentious single-storey-and-basement range, the centre bay projecting to N and S with a three-light ground-floor window in each front. The late C19 remodelling gave each

---

*i.e. 'flatted cottages', the ground floor entered from one side, the first floor from the other by means of outside stairs; gardens on both sides.

centrepiece another floor, with a Venetian window and French pavilion roof. The E block of *c.* 1860 was of two storeys with a basement and attic under an iron-crested Frenchy roof. Without the roof it now looks very plain, barely enlivened by bay windows to N and W and a semicircular portico on the S.

HOME FARM, 2.5km. NE. Huge courtyard steading by *A. & W. Reid & Mackenzie,* 1860 (probably incorporating some work of 1850 by *James Ross*). Two-storey S range with bracketed broad eaves through which break the gableted dormerheads of the round-arched first-floor windows. Central pend under a clock tower, its main pyramid roof truncated to support a steep pyramid-roofed cupola. – To the NW, former DAIRY by *A. & W. Reid,* 1876, small and picturesque with jerkin-head gables, a tree-trunk verandah, and a spired ventilator. Inside, the S room was the dairy, with a mosaic floor, abstract stained glass and a coved ceiling. – To its N, the broad-eaved FACTOR'S HOUSE, also of 1876 by *A. & W. Reid,* with bay windows and plenty of gablets. – Down the hill to the W, a string of three small single-storey-and-attic COTTAGES joined by porches. Fretted bargeboards; lattice glazing in the mullioned and transomed windows. Canted bay window at the centre.

INVERMORISTON   *4010*

Hamlet at the mouth of Glen Moriston where the A887 to the west coast joins the main Inverness–Fort William road up the Great Glen. The junction is marked by the GLENMORISTON ARMS HOTEL, C19 in its present white harled and gabled form.

GLENMORISTON FREE CHURCH, 8.6km. W. Disused. Rendered rectangle, by *William Munro,* 1857. Wooden Y-tracery in the pointed windows; pilastered birdcage bellcote with a tall obelisk finial. – Adjoining MANSE by *John Rhind,* 1880.

GLENMORISTON PARISH CHURCH. Small-scale Tudor, by *Alexander Grant,* 1911–13. Sturdy battlemented W tower with a turret in the inner angle. Small chancel at the E end.

GLENMORISTON ROMAN CATHOLIC CHAPEL, 11.8km. SW. Disused. Simple sneck-harled box built in 1841. The triangular-headed windows in the long E side may date from a late C19 alteration.

BURIAL GROUND, 0.3km. E. Isolated walled graveyard. At its highest point, an early C19 ashlar OBELISK commemorating Alexander Grant and his wife, Anne Mackenzie. – In the NW corner, MONUMENT to Patrick McDonell †1825, a Roman Doric pilastered sentry box housing an urn-topped pedestal, the inscription recording that

BY HIS BEREAVED FATHER THIS MONUMENT IS ERECTED SIMILAR TO THE TOMB PLACED OVER HIS REMAINS BY HIS BROTHER OFFICERS IN INDIA AT THE TIME OF HIS DEATH.

– To its SE, GRAVESLAB of John Gray and Elizabeth McKenzie, dated 1764, with well-preserved emblems of death. – At the E,

MONUMENT of 1818 consisting of a bit of crude gabled walling with a ball finial on the apex; inset early C19 tablets commemorating McLeods, including Finlay McLeod, piper to Glenmoriston. – Beside it, a large classical TOMB-CHEST carved with dowsed torches commemorates James Grant of Burnhall † 1864.

DUNDREGGAN DAM, 6.3km. W. By *Sir William Halcrow & Partners*, 1947–52. Purposeful, three heavy concrete buttresses the main features.

INVERMORISTON BRIDGE. By *Mears & Carus-Wilson* with *Blyth & Blyth* as engineers, 1933. Rubble-fronted single span. – Immediately up-river, remains of its two-span predecessor, probably C18.

INVERMORISTON PRIMARY SCHOOL. By *Matthews & Lawrie*, 1876.

TORGYLE BRIDGE, 11.8km. SW. 1825–6, by *Joseph Mitchell*. Three spans, of ashlar. Over the cutwaters rise round towers pierced by crosslet arrowslits and finished with a suggestion of battlements.

6040   **INVERNESS**

3 The undisputed capital of Highland and, with a population of *c.* 45,000, by far its largest town. The site was of major strategic importance from the Middle Ages until the C18, enjoying sheltered anchorage at the mouth of the Ness, commanding the N entry into the Great Glen and the main landward route from Moray to the fertile lands of The Aird immediately to the W and of Easter Ross. A royal castle had been built here, on the hill now occupied by the Sheriff and District Courts, by the C12 and almost certainly before the reign of David I (1130–53), who founded the royal burgh of Inverness. That burgh, a prosperous centre for foreign trade with Highland, developed on the E bank of the Ness, stretching N from the castle along Castle Street, Bridge Street, High Street and Church Street, the present Academy Street to the E marking the line of its old wall.

A harbour was begun in 1648, and in 1652–7, during the period of Cromwellian military rule in Scotland, a fort was built beside it, the old royal castle being abandoned. That fort was largely destroyed after the Restoration of 1660, and the castle again became a military centre, a use given up after its partial destruction in the Jacobite rising of 1745–6 and the subsequent building of Fort George 15km. NE of the town.

The burgh grew little in the C17 and earlier C18, although thatched huts 'of the worst class' were constructed E of the old wall and on the W side of the Ness. In 1758 Sir William Burrell

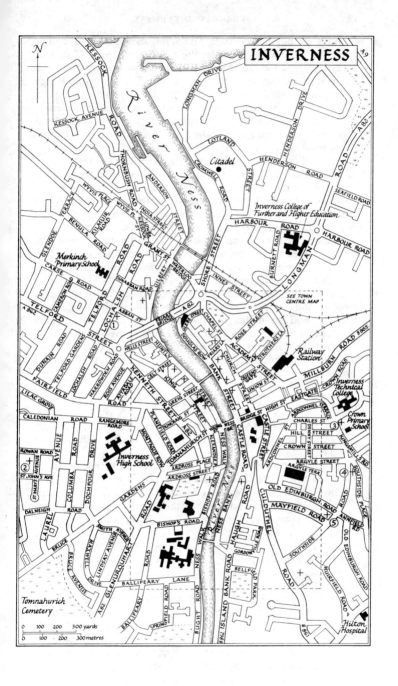

found it 'a long, dirty, ill built Town, remarkable for nothing but being the Place w[hi]ch divides the N & S Highlands'. However, Inverness shared in the growth of Highland prosperity at the end of the C18, acquiring in the 1790s a new Town Steeple, Burgh Courthouse, Academy and Assembly Rooms, and in 1794 Sir William Forbes thought it 'neat, well-built, & remarkably clean'.

Expansion of solidly built housing w of the river began from 1803 with the construction of the Caledonian Canal, its overseers being housed in a new terrace (Telford Street) near the canal's intended N end, the area between the Ness and the canal being gradually filled during the rest of the C19. At the same time much land outside the old burgh boundary on the E of the river was developed, largely for villas catering to the many members of the middle classes who found Inverness a congenial place for retirement, its relative isolation much lessened by the advent of the railway in 1855. A still-present belief in the town's essential civility shared by Invernessians and outsiders alike may explain why its expansion for housing has continued through the C20 with little sign of abatement.

Industry has long been present (malting in the C17, linen, woollen and hemp manufacture in the C18; shipbuilding, iron-founding and saw-milling in the C19; brewing and distilling in the C20), but the chief characteristics Inverness conveys to the visitor are those of a market town serving the whole of Highland and of a bed-and-breakfast honeypot attracting buzzing swarms of tourists.

CHURCHES

ASSOCIATE PRESBYTERIAN CHURCH, Chapel Street. By *Ross & Macbeth*, 1899. Georgian-survival box but with a Gothic bellcote.

BAPTIST CHURCH, Castle Street. By *Stewart & Paterson*, 1932.

CROWN CHURCH, Kingsmills Road. Originally United Free. Powerful blocky lanceted Gothic, by *J. R. Rhind*, 1900–1. Cruciform, the N inner angle filled by the base of an intended tower, the S by a transeptal stairtower. From these, porches project to the line of the main gable.

DALNEIGH AND BONA CHURCH, St Mary's Avenue. By *Stocks Bros. Ltd Buildings*, 1979. Pyramid-roofed square, the walls made up of alternating drydashed and glazed panels. To the N, hall church of 1953.

EAST CHURCH, Academy Street. Opened as a chapel of ease in 1798 but almost entirely rebuilt in 1852–3. The broad front was added in 1897–8 by *Ross & Macbeth*, who provided a gable window with Scots late Gothic tracery; on each side, a gableted stairtower, the l. topped by an octagonal belfry whose crenellated and pinnacled parapet encloses a dumpy slate spire. – ORGAN probably by *Forster & Andrews*, rebuilt here in 1948 by *Rushworth & Dreaper*.

42 FREE NORTH CHURCH, Bank Street. Large and boldly detailed Dec by *Ross & Macbeth*, 1890–3, its grey stone a cool contrast

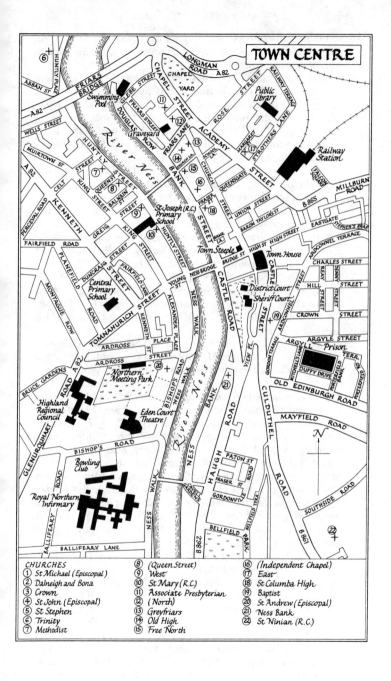

TOWN CENTRE

CHURCHES
① St Michael (Episcopal)
② Dalneigh and Bona
③ Crown
④ St John (Episcopal)
⑤ St Stephen
⑥ Trinity
⑦ Methodist
⑧ (Queen Street)
⑨ West
⑩ St Mary (R.C.)
⑪ Associate Presbyterian
⑫ (North)
⑬ Greyfriars
⑭ Old High
⑮ Free North
⑯ (Independent Chapel)
⑰ East
⑱ St Columba High
⑲ Baptist
⑳ St Andrew (Episcopal)
㉑ Ness Bank
㉒ St Ninian (R.C.)

to the prevalent pinky sandstone of the town. On the r. of the gable front, a stairtower; on the l. a massive pinnacled steeple with a lucarned spire.

GREYFRIARS FREE CHURCH, Church Street. Built as the Gaelic Church by *Hugh Suter*, mason, and *William McDonald*, wright, in 1792–4, it was heightened by 0.9m. in 1822, when *Donald Macphail*, wright, rebuilt the front wall to a specification by *James Smith*. Piend-roofed coursed rubble box with round-headed windows, the end ones carried down as doors. (Interior recast by *Matthews & Lawrie*, 1885–6.)

HILTON PARISH CHURCH, Druid Road. Thrifty hall church of 1958, the bell hung in a recess in the crowstepped gable.

INDEPENDENT CHAPEL, Bank Street. Secularized. Built in 1826. Tall segmental-headed windows in the long elevation; a Venetian window in the s gable.

METHODIST CHURCH, Huntly Street. By *Kenneth Finlayson* of *John R. Chisholm & Co.*, 1964–5. Timidly modern, the church linked by a glass-fronted vestibule to the bell tower. – STAINED GLASS. The w window on each side (a portrait of John Wesley on the N, War Memorial window on the S) is by the *G. Maile Studios*, 1965. – Four other contemporary lights (the Passion, Crucifixion and Resurrection of Our Lord). – ORGAN by *Rushworth & Dreaper*, 1965.

NESS BANK CHURCH, Haugh Road and Ness Bank. Originally United Free. By *William Mackintosh*, 1900–1. Stolid pink sandstone box dressed up with Dec detail, transepts, pinnacles and tracery, but the result is lumpy. Inside, a broad nave and aisles, the arcades carried on red sandstone colums. Panelled wooden wagon roof. Big stone arch into a shallow chancel housing the ORGAN by *James F. Binns*, 1903, altered in 1980 by *Rushworth & Dreaper*. – STAINED GLASS. In the E wall, three windows, Jesus rebuking the Scribes and Pharisees (1967), St Paul (1965), and David and Solomon (1959), all by *Gordon Webster*, with small figures in primary colours. – In the w wall, naturalistic N window (the Risen Lord with His disciples) by the *St Enoch Studios*, 1950. – In the centre, a window (SS. Christopher, Martha and Mary Magdalene) by *Isobel Goudie*, 1930, pale in this company. – To its S, a bright window (the Adoration of the Magi) of 1948 by *William Wilson*.

NORTH CHURCH, off Chapel Street. Secularized. Boxy chapel of 1837 with a classical bellcote.

23 OLD HIGH CHURCH, Church Street. Austerely commanding on its site above the river. The w tower is probably C16, its massive solidity lightened only by a single intake in the rubble walling. Small obtusely arched windows; on the w front, round-headed doors to the ground and first floors. The balustered parapet, carried on corbels mixing with rainwater spouts, may date from the repairs made in 1649. Inside the parapet, an octagonal belfry capped by a lead-clad bellcast spire. The apse-ended vestry on the S face was added by *W. L. Carruthers* in 1899.

The rubble box of the church itself was built in 1769–72,

according to a plan and estimate provided by George Fraser, Depute Auditor of Excise in Edinburgh.* In 1891 *Ross & Macbeth* added porches to the ends of the s front and an apse to its centre. *Carruthers* provided the dormer windows and flèche eight years later.

The interior is a Georgian and Victorian mixture. Braced-collar ROOF by *Carruthers*, 1899, the principals resting on stone corbels. – Late Georgian semi-octagonal GALLERY, perhaps of 1840, grained in 1899. – PEWS by *A. & W. Reid*, 1877. – The stone CHANCEL ARCH in the centre of the s wall is of 1891 by *Ross & Macbeth*, the capitals carved with vigorous foliage. – In the chancel, an ORGAN by *Henry Willis & Sons*, 1895, rebuilt by *H. Hilsdon Ltd*, 1923.

STAINED GLASS. In the chancel, two colourful lights (St Michael on the E, Our Lord blessing little children on the W) by *Douglas Strachan*, c. 1925. – The s wall's E window (Our Lord carrying His Cross; the Maries at the Tomb) is of 1914, competent but routine. – Beside it, darkly coloured scenes (Our Lord with the Doctors in the Temple; St Paul on Mars Hill) by *Stephen Adam & Co.*, 1893. – W of the chancel, memorial window to Lord Gordon (Moses and Samuel) by *A. Ballantine & Gardiner*, 1899. – Cochrane memorial window (Our Lord at the Well; the Adoration of the Magi), after 1916. – In the N wall, a two-light window (the Risen Christ with the Disciples on the Emmaus Road) of 1958 by *Gordon Webster*, with his characteristic strong colours. – Large E window above the gallery (the Nativity of Our Lord) signed by *E. P. Howden*, c. 1890.

MONUMENTS. On the N wall, three marble tablets worth noting. James Smith Baillie, younger, of Dochfour, † 1796, gently polychrome, with a coat of arms hanging from an obelisk; in front, an urn, its pedestal carved with the Baillie crest of a boar's head. – William Inglis † 1801, a shattered Ionic column, signed by *Henry Wood* of Bristol. – John Inglis † 1781 in America, 'WHO WAS MURDERED BY A BAND OF RUFFIANS WHILE ON A VISIT AT A FRIEND'S HOUSE'; with an urn.

The GRAVEYARD's cast-iron GATEPIERS were provided by *John McPherson*, square wright, and *Hugh Suter*, slater, in 1796. – In the SE corner, the ROBERTSON BURIAL ENCLOS- 52 URE built by *James Gordon* and *William Durham*, masons, in 1664–5. Ashlar screen walls surmounted by would-be classical columns with fleshily foliaged capitals. On the columns flanking the moulded entrance, spiralling vines. Emblems of mortality on the frieze. – Inside, a wall MONUMENT to Hugh Robertson † 1703, an aedicule (the columns now missing) mixing inept classicism, heraldry and symbols of death. – On the ground, GRAVESLAB of William Robertson † 1682, carved with a coat of arms and more grisly reminders of death.

QUEEN STREET FREE CHURCH, Huntly Street. Secularized as

---

*The plan was a larger version of that of the Buccleuch Church in Edinburgh.

a funeral parlour. Fussy Palladian by *J. Pond Macdonald*, 1893–6, with plentiful columns and pediments. On the front's l., a tower with an elongated slated dome.

ST ANDREW'S CATHEDRAL (Episcopal), Ness Walk and Ardross Street. By *Alexander Ross*, 1866–9. A large pink sandstone Gothic box planted on the w bank of the Ness, the site giving it an importance which its stodgy outline and routine Dec detail fail to match. It might have looked less earthbound if the w* towers had received their intended 30 m.-high spires or the originally proposed six-bay choir and chancel had not been curtailed. The plan is that of a parish church correctly arranged along Tractarian lines.‡ Four-bay nave, its low buttressed aisles held between the w towers and the equally minimally projecting transepts. Semi-octagonal-apsed chancel, the octagonal chapter house sticking out at its NE. Continuous roof of green Westmorland slate (the iron cresting now missing) over the nave and chancel, the crossing marked by a copper Celtic cross which *William Glashan* substituted for Ross's flèche in 1963. The NW tower is a porch, its N entrance's capitals and arch mouldings realistically foliaged, the crocketed gablet carried on corbels carved with angels (all this carved work by *D. & A. Davidson*). Empty image niches in the flanking buttresses. In the w gable, a five-light window. Below it, the great w door under an open-traceried gablet has more of the Davidsons' naturalistic foliage. The tympanum was filled by *Thomas Earp* in 1875 with a high relief of Our Lord commissioning the Apostles to preach the Gospel. Also by Earp, the contemporary figures of SS. Peter, Paul, Andrew and John the Baptist in the buttresses' canopied niches.

39   The interior looks decidedly prosperous. Narthex between the w towers (the s containing the baptistery), its stone screen's arched openings into the church filled with glass. Nave arcades carried on monolithic Peterhead granite piers, the capitals carved with more naturalistic foliage. The hoodmoulds above the arches spring from corbels sculpted in 1876 with heads of Apostles by *Andrew Davidson* (except for the head of St Philip, which is credited to *Alexander Ross*), Episcopalian worthies, and Queen Victoria (a surprising subject in view of her hostility to the Episcopal Church). The roof's wooden pointed tunnel is marked out with black patterns intended to be covered with coloured stencilling. The transepts (the s containing the organ, the N the Lady Chapel) provide stops to the side-aisles but no interruption to the nave's E thrust into the choir and chancel.

Expensive FURNISHINGS. – Caen stone ALTAR of 1869, its alabaster panels (the centre containing a white cross set with crystals, the l. the Pelican, the r. the *Agnus Dei*) framed in marble-columned arches. – Contemporary Caen stone REREDOS carved by *Earp* with lumpy high reliefs of the Passion, Crucifixion and Resurrection of Our Lord. – SEDILIA S of the

_____

*Actually N. Liturgical directions are given in this description.
‡Perhaps owing something to *Slater & Carpenter*'s unexecuted designs of 1855.

altar made by *D. & A. Davidson* to Ross's design, 1871, the moulded Gothic arches carried on pillars of Cawdor granite. – CHOIR STALLS of Austrian oak designed by *C. Hodgson Fowler* and *Alexander Ross*, 1909, competent but pedestrian. – More exciting is the BISHOP'S THRONE made by *Andrew Fraser*, 1869, with carved angels at the canopy's corners. – Encaustic TILES by *Minton*, 1869. In the sancturary they depict the Passover Sacrifice, the Lifting up of the Serpent in the Wilderness, and the Sacrifice of Abel. – Oak CHOIR SCREEN by *Robert S. Lorimer*, 1923, with thin barley-sugar columns carrying cusped ogee arches, lavishly carved with fruit. – PULPIT of Caen stone designed by *Ross*, 1869, its crude reliefs of St John the Baptist, the Good Shepherd, and St Andrew Preaching from his Cross by *D. & A. Davidson*. – In the SW baptistery, a white marble copy by *James F. Redfern*, 1871, of Thorwaldsen's Kneeling Angel FONT at Copenhagen, but the angel's face is a portrait of Mrs Learmonth of Dean, whose husband paid for the work. – ORGAN by *Hill & Son*, 1869.

STAINED GLASS. All by *John Hardman & Co.*, clearly drawn archaic designs in bright colours. In the nave and chancel, a didactic scheme of 1869–70 showing scenes from the life of Our Lord, starting with the Annunciation at the E end of the S aisle and progressing clockwise (the Baptism of Christ in the baptistery) to the Crucifixion in the chancel's E window. Hardman filled the N transept window with the Ascension in 1877, and ten years later the S transept window with the Feeding of the Five Thousand and the great W window with an expressionist Last Judgement.

MONUMENTS. In the Lady Chapel, a small TABLET to Bishop William Hay † 1707 in a surround of tasselled marble drapery. – At the S aisle's W end, a bust of Bishop Robert Eden, by *Andrew Davidson*, 1900.

ST COLUMBA HIGH, Bank Street. Originally the Free High Church. Tall Perp box by *Mackenzie & Matthews*, 1851–2. Gable front dressed up on the r. with buttresses to suggest an aisle behind. On the l., a tower with diagonally set buttresses intaken at each stage; the spire looks naked without the flying buttresses removed in *Leslie Grahame Thomson*'s restoration of 1948–53 after a fire in 1939. Transept at the rear added by *John Rhind*, 1866. (Inside, STAINED GLASS rose window by *Gordon Webster*, 1957. – ORGAN by *Ingram & Co.*, c. 1920.)

ST JOHN THE EVANGELIST (Episcopal), Southside Road. Broad-eaved villagey church with a slate-spired W bellcote and a harled and half-timbered SW porch. It was built as St Columba's Mission Chapel in 1890–1 to a design by *Ross & Macbeth*. In 1902–3, after the chapel had been taken over by the congregation of St John's, Church Street,* the same architects added transepts (the N for the organ, the S for the vestry) and a chancel, in which they placed the elaborately traceried upper part of the old St John's (liturgical) E window, some of its lower

*Which was by *William Robertson*, 1839–40.

part being used as a new W window. Inside, an open wooden roof over the nave. Stone chancel arch. – Mid-C19 FURNISHINGS from the old St John's. – STAINED GLASS. Five-light E window (Scenes from the Life of Our Lord) signed by *F. Holt & Co.*, *c.* 1910. – Three-light W window (SS. John, Margaret and Columba), after 1910. – ORGAN rebuilt by *Wadsworth*, 1889. – In the chancel, two identical Perp wall TABLETS. The S one, to Jane Shirreff, was designed by *James Ross* and executed by *Batchen*, 1843. Presumably they were also responsible for the other, to Charlotte Robertson † 1842.

32 ST MARY (R.C.), Huntly Street. Carpenter's Perp by *William Robertson*, 1836–7. Ashlar gable front, its main feature an ogee-hoodmoulded and traceried window. Lavishly foliaged spires on the fat octagonal corner buttresses, which are joined by tracery-parapeted canted screen walls to smaller and plainer free-standing buttresses. All the detail is enjoyably outsize. The interior with an almost flat Tudor Gothic roof was tactfully extended to the W (liturgical E) by *W. L. Carruthers* in 1893–4. Less tactful have been the alterations of 1979 by *W. W. Allan*, who added a S aisle and transept with utilitarian rectangular openings to the nave. – Spikily detailed ALTAR and REREDOS of 1893–4 (by *Carruthers*, following suggestions by *P. P. Pugin*). On the reredos, figures of the Sacred Heart, Our Lady and St Joseph stand in front of panels filled with mosaics of angels. – Stone PULPIT (now painted), probably of 1837, with pinnacled angle buttresses and a shield on each face. It has been deprived of its pedestal and consequently of its dignity. – ORGAN by *E. J. Johnson & Son*, 1981. – STAINED GLASS. The S aisle's Baptistery window (the Baptism of Our Lord) is of *c.* 1950. – In the N wall, one light (Our Lady), later *c* 20.

ST MICHAEL AND ALL ANGELS (Episcopal), Abban Street. By *Ross & Macbeth*, 1903–4, incorporating stonework from the Chapel of the Holy Spirit (by *Alexander Ross*, 1886). Long and low, Scots late Gothic. Tall W flèche; large NE vestry. Inside, a W organ gallery above the narthex. The nave and sanctuary, formerly divided by a rood screen, are now a single space. – 3m.-long ALTAR of 1904, its riddel posts topped by gilded angels. – Above the altar, a gilded TESTER carved with a dove,
47 by *J. Ninian Comper*, 1928. – Stone FONT with a steepled oak canopy, by *Comper*, *c.* 1910. – STAINED GLASS. E window (Angels), again by *Comper*, 1928. – Small C15 brass CHANDELIER with a Madonna and Child on the stem. – ORGAN by *John Whiteley*, 1895.

RECTORY attached to the E end. Asymmetrical Jacobean by *Alexander Ross & Son*, 1911–12.

ST NINIAN (R.C.), Culduthel Road. By *W. W. Allan*, 1977. Box-like, its roof very shallow-pitched to the E, almost vertical on the approach from the W, where it comes nearly to the ground and is broken by three tall and narrow gableted windows.

44 ST STEPHEN, Southside Road. By *W. L. Carruthers*, 1895–7. Carefully detailed Arts and Crafts Gothic in coursed rubble with a red-tiled roof ridge for colour. Nave, N transept, and a

low chancel. In the transept's E inner angle, a tower whose parapet has a shallow triangular merlon in the centre of each face; on top, a tiny needle spire. Round-arched nave windows with trefoil-headed lights. Small chancel windows set high up under a widely crenellated parapet. Inside, a braced collar roof. Pointed stone arches into the chancel and transept. – STAINED GLASS. Three-light w window (the Martyrdom of St Stephen) by *A. Ballantine & Son, c.* 1905. – In the N wall of the nave, a portrait of the Very Rev. Norman Macleod, after 1911. – In the S wall, a Prophet, after 1901. – Two-light window (the Maries at the Tomb) in the N transept, by *A. Ballantine & Son,* 1906. – Strongly coloured chancel lights of *c.* 1895. – ORGAN by *Wadsworth & Bros.,* 1902.

TRINITY CHURCH, Huntly Place. Originally West Free Church. Bare lanceted Gothic, by *James Matthews,* 1863, with a bellcote astride the gable front.

WEST PARISH CHURCH, Huntly Street. By *Robert Caldwell,* 1837–40. Temple front with a narrow pedimented centre, its Ionic columns uncomfortably close to the *antae.* At the back gable, a square tower with an octagonal cupola. (STAINED GLASS. E window (St Columba) by *William Wilson,* 1950.)

CEMETERIES

CHAPEL YARD, Chapel Street. Graveyard surrounding the site of the medieval Chapel of St Mary of the Green demolished after the Reformation. Ball-finialled GATEPIERS of *c.* 1800. – Near the entrance, TABLE STONE to Donald Fraser, erected in 1819, its sides carved with swagged drapery. – Large collection of heraldic GRAVESLABS, mostly C18. – On the NE wall, late C17 and early C18 TABLETS carved at the top with initials and emblems (angels' heads, hearts and rosettes), at the bottom with reminders of mortality. – Broad open-pedimented MONUMENT to Hector Scott † 1776. – Long, ineptly classical MONUMENT erected for Thomas Watson in 1674, divided into panels by atlantes and caryatids; bands of thistles and grapes enclose a sort of frieze carved with high-relief bells, skulls, hourglasses, and angels' heads; crossbones and gravediggers' tools in the side panels. – In the SE corner, MAUSOLEUM of the Forbeses of Culloden, late C17 with a corniced doorpiece. Inside, a big Corinthianish aedicule commemorating Duncan Forbes † 1654, put up by his son in 1684; above the inscription panel, the monogrammed initials of Forbes and his wife under a halo carried by two angels. – On the graveyard's SE wall, an aedicular early C18 MONUMENT to William Duff, with skulls sitting on the sides of the curvy pediment; the inscription is on a cloth held in a lion's jaws. – Near this wall's SW end, a weathered late C17 two-panel MONUMENT with caryatids supporting a steep pediment. – Free-standing ashlar ENCLOSURE built round the grave of Norman MacLeod of MacLeod by *Andrew Scott,* 1720, the walls topped by balusters. In the middle of the E side, a contemporary obelisk, its base carved with the MacLeod arms.

GRAVEYARD, Friars Street. The site of a Dominican convent founded by Alexander II in the early C13. Of the monastic church there survives one octagonal pillar with springers for stone vaults over the nave and an aisle. This may be of *c.* 1436, when a papal indulgence was granted to those who gave money for the church's restoration. – Some C17 and C18 GRAVE-SLABS carved with heraldry and reminders of death, the best-preserved (now in the E wall) commemorating Donald Baillie † 1779 and his wife, Margaret Baine. – Built into the S wall, the headless and armless EFFIGY of a knight, probably early C15 and perhaps representing Alexander, Earl of Mar, who was buried here in 1435.

TOMNAHURICH CEMETERY, Glenurquhart Road. Laid out on land acquired in 1863, with the steeply rising and well-wooded Tomnahurich Hill a dominant natural feature. – ENTRANCE LODGE by *Alexander Ross*, 1877, broad-eaved and steep-gabled. – Near the S end of the flat ground on the E, MONU-MENT to Mary Anne Lyall † 1852, with a version of Thor-waldsen's Kneeling Angel font signed by *Andrew Davidson, c.* 1870. – On the hill's S side, the rocky MAUSOLEUM of Henry Christie † 1879, its marble door guarded by an armed angel; figure of a scantily draped youth (the risen soul) on top.

54

PUBLIC BUILDINGS

BOWLING CLUB, Bishop's Road. By *T. H. Scott*, 1909. Cottagey picturesque, in white harl and green-painted half-timbering.

CALEDONIAN CANAL. By *Thomas Telford*, the stretch between the Beauly Firth and Loch Ness constructed in 1803–18. At the N end, an artificial peninsula carrying the canal into the deep water of the Firth. Two pairs of LOCK GATES, their gates of Welsh oak (resistant to salt water) designed by *Thomas Rhodes*. Beside the canal entrance, a neat rendered early C19 LOCK-KEEPER'S HOUSE and a BEACON. – To the E, CLACH-NAHARRY RAILWAY BRIDGE of 1909, a 37.5m.-long plate-girder swing bridge. – Then, two more pairs of LOCK GATES and the CANAL WORKSHOPS of *c.* 1850, rubble-built on an irregular V-plan with a small bellcote at the SE corner. – At the SE end of Muirtown Basin, MUIRTOWN BRIDGE carrying the A862, a swing bridge by *Sir William Arrol & Co.*, 1935, replacing a bridge of 1816. – Above it, five pairs of cast-iron LOCK GATES made by *Outram's Butterley Ironworks*. – TOMNAHURICH BRIDGE, carrying the A82, is another swing bridge, by *Crouch & Hogg*, 1937. – Beside it, a BRIDGE-KEEPER'S HOUSE of 1813.

CAMERON BARRACKS, off Perth Road. Baronial, in bull-nosed rubble, by the *Royal Engineers' Office* at Edinburgh, 1880–6. Long two-storey ranges round three sides of the parade ground, all with plenty of crowstepped gables and gablets. Main gateway at the NE under a square tower. At the centre of the NW and w ranges, paired drum towers, forcefully machicolated and linked by balconies over the round-arched doors.

CASTLE. *See* Sheriff Court and District Court, below.

CAULDEEN PRIMARY SCHOOL, Mackay Road. By *Inverness County Council*, 1968. Boxy, with a prominent boiler chimney.

CENTRAL PRIMARY SCHOOL, Kenneth Street. By *Highland Regional Council*, 1976. To its N, the former school, by *Ross & Macbeth*, 1900–1. School Board Gothic, with a spiky bellcote; fleshily foliaged capitals to the doors.

CHARLESTON ACADEMY, Charleston View. By *G. R. M. Kennedy & Partners*, 1975–6. Straightforward main block with bands of glass and render.

CITADEL, Cromwell Road. A large pentagonal Cromwellian fort, designed by *Joachim Hane*, was built in 1652–8 but demolished after the Restoration of 1660. All that survives is a two-stage rubble CLOCKTOWER, now almost surrounded by oil-storage tanks. Round openings in the E and W faces. The tall slated ogee roof is a conjectural restoration.

CLACHNAHARRY RAILWAY BRIDGE. *See* Caledonian Canal, above.

CLACHNAHARRY SCHOOL (former), High Street, Clachnaharry. Small, School Board Gothic, by *William Mackintosh*, 1876.

CRAIG DUNAIN HOSPITAL, Leachkin Road. Built as the Northern Countries District Lunatic Asylum in 1860–4; the architect was *James Matthews*. Long and bare in red sandstone rubble. Five-bay Gothic-windowed centrepiece on the E front, with a centre gable gripped by boldly advanced wings which break forward from iron-crested French pavilion towers. Further out on each side, slender square and round towers. Big W additions by *Matthews & Lawrie*, 1881. N extension by *Ross & Macbeth*, 1896–8. – CHURCH to the NE, by *W. W. Mitchell* of *Alexander Ross & Son*, 1961–3. It is a hall, the walls drydashed with artificial stone dressings. Big neo-Georgian birdcage bellcote on the S gable.

CRAIG PHADRIG HOSPITAL, Leachkin Road. By *Alison & Hutchison & Partners*, 1967–70. Large scattered collection of dark brick buildings, most with flat roofs.

CROWN PRIMARY SCHOOL, Kingsmills Road. By *John Rhind*, 1878–80. Institutional Gothic with a steeple. Single-storey rear extension by *William Mackintosh*, 1899.

CULDUTHEL HOSPITAL, Culduthel Avenue. The main block is a harled early C19 house, enlarged to one side. Single-storey cottagey pavilions by *Alexander F. Mackenzie*, 1930–2.

DISTRICT COURT. *See* Sheriff Court and District Court, below.

DR BELL'S SCHOOL. *See* Public Library, below.

DRUMMOND SCHOOL, Drummond Road. By *Inverness County Council*, 1963.

DUNBAR'S HOSPITAL. *See* Description, below (Church Street).

EDEN COURT THEATRE, Bishop's Road. Late C20 theatre 108 attached to a Victorian bishop's palace. The palace, built for Robert Eden, Bishop of Moray, Ross and Caithness, in

1875–8, was designed by *Alexander Ross*. It is a large villa of purplish granite. Ecclesiastical Gothic detail at the NE entrance, above which rises a tower. A bow-ended chapel (now green room) projects at the SW. The theatre itself is by *Law & Dunbar-Nasmith*, 1973–6. Heavy core housing the auditorium and fly-tower, built of loadbearing concrete blockwork faced with dark flint aggregate. On its E side, overlooking the river, project two tiers of timber and glass pavilions housing the foyers and restaurant, the upper tier with down-pointing double-pitch roofs, the lower pyramid-roofed hexagons. Are these perhaps too insubstantial for the solid mass behind? Interior of carefully detailed simplicity. Horseshoe-plan auditorium, with a can-tilevered circle and upper circle.

FORBES FOUNTAIN, Ladies Walk. Designed by *A. R. Henderson* and executed by *D. & A. Davidson*, 1879–82, but now deprived of its canopy. Solid but colourful in pink and grey granite. Sturdy flying buttresses on the octagonal basin support a round basin from which rise columns carrying the quatrefoil upper basin.

FRIARS BRIDGE, Telford Street and Shore Street. Three-span concrete bridge by *JMP Consultants Ltd*, 1984–6.

GREIG STREET BRIDGE. Suspension footbridge designed by *C. R. Manners* and made by the *Rose Street Foundry*, 1880–1.

HIGHLAND REGIONAL COUNCIL REGIONAL BUILDINGS, Glenurquhart Road and Ardross Street. By *J. L. Gleave & Partners*, 1961–3. Facing Ardross Street, a collegiate Tudor range (the former Northern Counties Collegiate School) by *Alexander Ross*, dated 1873 but built in 1875–6. Two-bay W extension, also by Ross, 1885.

HILTON HOSPITAL, Old Edinburgh Road. Originally the Poorhouse. By *James Matthews* and *William Lawrie*, 1859–61. White harled and steep-gabled, now rather altered and with additions at the back. Gabled and buttressed gatehouse in front.

HILTON PRIMARY SCHOOL, Temple Crescent. By *Inverness County Council*, 1957, lightweight with an Art Deco entrance. To the S, a heavy block by *Highland Regional Council*, c. 1980, with monopitch roofs.

HOLM PRIMARY SCHOOL, Ardholm Place. By *Inverness County Council*, 1973.

INFIRMARY BRIDGE. Suspension footbridge designed by *C. R. Manners* and made by *W. Smith & Sons* of the *Ness Ironworks*, 1881–2.

INVERNESS COLLEGE OF FURTHER AND HIGHER EDU-CATION, Longman Road. 1960, by the County Architect, *D. M. W. Calder*. Five-storey extension of 1969–70.

INVERNESS HIGH SCHOOL, off Montague Row. Long and horizontal Art Deco spread, by *Reid & Forbes*, 1934.

INVERNESS ROYAL ACADEMY, Culduthel Road. By *Highland Regional Council* (project architect: *S. Grant*), 1977–8. A large assemblage of rendered and curtain-walled blocks.

INVERNESS TECHNICAL COLLEGE, Stephen's Street. Formerly Royal Inverness Academy. By *Ross & Macbeth*, 1893–5. Free François I with prettily sculptured low reliefs, a big wooden cupola the central feature. SE addition by *Robert J. Macbeth*, 1911–13. Further additions on the s by *Inverness County Council*, 1968.

JAIL. *See* Sheriff Court and District Court, below.

KESSOCK BRIDGE. 1976–82, by the *Cleveland RDL Kessock Consortium* in association with *Helmut Homberg* and *Trafalgar House Engineering Services Ltd*. The Rees Bridge over the Rhine near Düsseldorf was the model. 1,052m. continuous steel superstructure, the central span supported by steel cables strung in a harp configuration from four steel towers.

KINMYLIES BUILDING, Leachkin Road. By *Highland Regional Council* (project architect: *J. Alexander*), 1977–8. Long and drydashed; single-storey with monopitch-roofed towers.

KINMYLIES PRIMARY SCHOOL, Assynt Road. By *Highland Regional Council* (project architect: *J. Pottie*), 1977.

LOCHARDIL PRIMARY SCHOOL, Lochardil Road. By *Inverness County Council*, 1964.

MARKET CROSS, High Street. The shaft may be C16, the rest dates from *J. Hinton Gall*'s restoration of 1900. Pink and grey granite base incorporating the Clachnacuddin stone.* Unicorn finial carved by *Andrew Davidson*.

MERKINCH PRIMARY SCHOOL, Telford Road. School Board Gothic with a central bellcote, by *Matthews & Lawrie*, 1875–7.

MILLBURN ACADEMY, Diriebught Road. By *Inverness County Council*, 1959–61, and later extended.

MUIRTOWN BRIDGE. *See* Caledonian Canal, above.

NESS BRIDGE. Three semi-elliptical spans of pale pink concrete; by *Sir Murdoch Macdonald & Partners*, 1959–61.

NORTHERN MEETING PARK, Ardross Street. Of *c*.1930. Grandstand presenting a polite harled backside to the street; wide neo-Georgian console-pedimented entrance.

POST OFFICE. *See* Description, below (Queensgate).

PRISON, Duffy Drive. By *H.M. Office of Works*, 1903. Behind the unsurprisingly high wall, main block whose big octagonal chimneys sport machicolated tops. Lower crowstepped and bellcoted range in front.

PUBLIC LIBRARY, Farraline Park, off Margaret Street. Originally Dr Bell's School, one of several such institutions founded in various Scottish burghs under the will of Dr Andrew Bell, the deviser of the 'Madras' system of education.‡ Greek revival by *William Robertson*, 1839–41. Tetrastyle pedimented Doric portico with Empire garlands on the frieze. Channelled rustication under the windows, whose corniced architraves are given an extravagant entasis. At each end, a recessed low porch containing a pedimented door.

---

*'Stone of the tubs'. It used to stand in the centre of the street and servant girls rested tubs on it when passing from the river.

‡By which the master taught the cleverest boys, who imparted their new knowledge to the less bright, who in turn passed it down to the least bright, ensuring that those identified as the stupidest received the worst education.

RAIGMORE HOSPITAL, Perth Road. By the *Matheson Gleave Partnership*, 1983, studiously avoiding any attempt to decorate or disguise its bulk. Very tall main block with vertical strips of buff brick and glass, the most prominent landmark on the S and E approaches to the town.

RAILWAY STATION, Station Square. Bland front box by *Thomas Munro & Co.*, 1966–8. Over the platforms behind, straightforward roofs by *Joseph Mitchell*, 1855, extended in 1876 by *Murdoch Paterson*.

ROYAL INVERNESS ACADEMY. *See* Description, below (Academy Street).

ROYAL NORTHERN INFIRMARY, Ness Walk. Stolid late Georgian hospital, altered and extended in the late C19 and C20. It was begun in 1799–1804 by *John Smith* of Banff as a three-storey five-bay main block linked by single-storey three-bay straight quadrants to two-storey three-bay pyramid-roofed end pavilions. At the main block, a rusticated ground floor; pedimented and Corinthian-pilastered three-bay temple-front centrepiece. In 1864–6 *Matthews & Lawrie* heightened the quadrants to three storeys and gave the pavilions piended roofs. In 1896–8 *Ross & Macbeth* overlaid the centrepiece with a two-storey open pedimented porte cochère (its upper floor housing an operating theatre) of faintly Italian inspiration. The original main block's outer windows have since been enlarged as bipartites. A Festival of Britain porch was added to the S pavilion in 1954.

The TWEEDMOUTH MEMORIAL CHAPEL was tacked on to the S end by *Ross & Macbeth* in 1896–8. Dumpy lanceted cruciform exterior. Expensively finished inside. Panelled wooden wagon ceiling. – Wrought-iron GATES into the transepts, their overthrows topped by IHS monograms under coronets. – Contemporary stylized STAINED GLASS.

Cheap neo-Georgian EXTENSIONS behind the main building by *John Burnet, Son & Dick*, 1928–36. – To the N, a small Baronial NURSES' HOME of 1898–9, by *Ross & Macbeth*. – PORTER'S LODGE at the NE entrance by *Mackenzie & Matthews*, 1854–5, cottagey but with Georgian detail (e.g. the panelled aprons under the windows). – NE and SE GATEPIERS, sturdy and corniced, of 1804, their stepped concrete tops added later.

ST JOSEPH (R.C.) PRIMARY SCHOOL, King Street and Huntly Street. The earliest part is in Huntly Street beside St Mary's R.C. Church. Plain Tudor by *Matthews & Lawrie*, 1869, a hint of excitement given by steep carved bargeboarded dormers and a slate-spired flèche. Large extensions by *Reid & Forbes*, 1938–43, with a polite neo-Georgian front to the river.

SHERIFF COURT AND DISTRICT COURT, Castle Street. The town's two most prominently placed buildings, standing on the site of the medieval castle of Inverness, which was demolished after being wrecked by the Jacobite army in 1745. – ENCLOSING WALLS, martially bastioned, by *Joseph Mitchell*, 1839.

The SHERIFF COURT, by *William Burn*, 1833–5, is a solid

ashlar-fronted toy fort with big towers at the corners (the SW round, the others square) and smaller round towers on the E and W sides, all with machicolated parapets. On the S front, a three-bay battlemented centrepiece. Roundheaded windows linked by continuous hoodmoulding make it clear that the towers and crenellations are only a dress. Inside, a central stairhall, the Imperial stair rising under a coffered tunnel-vault. N of the stair, Court No. 1 with a coffered ceiling and S gallery; original furnishings including a Tudor Gothic canopy over the bench.

The DISTRICT COURT, designed as Inverness Jail by 103 *Thomas Brown Jun.*, was built in 1846–8. Castellated again but of rubble and more frivolous, the octagonal NW tower extravagantly machicolated and with a very slim round turret rising high above its face to the river.

Between the two buildings, the medieval castle's WELL, restored in 1909. – In front of the Sheriff Court, a huge bronze STATUE of Flora Macdonald, by *Andrew Davidson*, 1896–9; an accompanying Highland collie looks anxiously up as she gazes down the Great Glen.

SWIMMING POOL, Glebe Street. Drydashed shed by *Alexander F. Mackenzie*, 1935, mercifully disguised by the red-brick extensions added by *Inverness District Council* in 1980.

TOMNAHURICH BRIDGE. *See* Caledonian Canal, above.

TOWN HOUSE, High Street. By *Matthews & Lawrie*, 1876–82, a 105 large version of G. Gilbert Scott's Albert Institute at Dundee of 1864. Two-storey Flemish-Baronial with *tourelles* at the corners and flanking the centre gablet; flèche, now truncated. *The Builder*, in puristically functional mood, did not approve:

The effect does not appear to us a successful one. The square corbelled angle-turrets are forced, and the gablets which flank the tower are apparently useless pieces of constructed decoration, which do not help the composition, merely introduced as tit-bits which the designer could not part with.

Dec Gothic detail. Cusp-headed ground-floor windows; large two-light first-floor windows linked by continuous pointed-arch hoodmoulds. Prominent relief of the burgh arms in the centre. In the W gable, another carving of the burgh arms, in the E the arms of Charles II, both of 1686 reused from the former Ness Bridge (built by *James Smith* in 1682–9, demolished 1849). S extension by *James R. Rhind*, 1904, in 'strict harmony with the architectural character of the present Hall', said the *Inverness Courier*, but the detail is much coarser.

TOWN STEEPLE, corner of Bridge Street and Church Street. 101 Designed by *Alexander Laing* and built by *Alexander Stevens*, 1789–92. Tall (47.3m. high) and confident, a last tribute to James Gibbs's influence on C18 architecture. Blind Venetian windows on the first floor; second-floor round-arched windows rising into open pediments on the two exposed faces. Then, clear of adjoining buildings, a Doric-pilastered belfry surmounted by a smaller stage with pediments over clock-faces and swagged urns at the corners. Ionic-pilastered octagonal second belfry surmounted by a smaller octagon, panelled with blind ovals, which serves as a base to the spire.

WAR MEMORIAL, Ness Bank. By *J. Hinton Gall*, 1921–2. Tall Celtic cross, the stepped base carved with the burgh arms.

WATERLOO BRIDGE. Designed by *John A. Mackenzie* with *Murdoch Paterson* as consultant, and built by the *Rose Street Foundry*, 1894–6. Five-span, with steel trusses on iron piers, and very utilitarian-looking.

DESCRIPTION

MILLBURN ROAD leads into and under the EASTGATE SHOP-PING CENTRE, by *Hugh Martin & Partners*, 1983, a towered defence faced with pinky concrete blockwork housing shops above car-parking; glazed stairtower on the s. Inside, a toplit mall. The road now becomes EASTGATE. On its s side, a long shantytown block of 1986, unredeemed by a sub-Baronial gablet. At the w end, a couple of late Georgian vernacular buildings (Nos. 2–8). For the much grander Georgian-survival building opposite, *see* Inglis Street, below.

109 HIGH STREET'S s side after Market Brae starts with Nos. 54–60, built as the Post Office in 1841–4. Severe classical with giant Ionic columns *in antis* at the recessed centrepiece; slab-like end bays barely relieved by the console-corniced first-floor windows. Georgian vernacular at Nos. 26–34, club skewputts making an appearance. No. 22 introduces Victorian commercial Renaissance on a small scale next to the neo-vernacular block by *J. & F. Johnston & Partners*, 1989, which marks the Castle Street corner with a glazed oriel. For the Town House to the w, *see* Public Buildings, above.

On High Street's N side, after Baron Taylor's Lane, a big Renaissance block by *Alexander Ross*, 1870. At its pedimented centrepiece, ladies' heads peeping out from the foliage of the pilasters' Corinthianish capitals; Vitruvian scrolled bandcourse under the second-floor windows. Much plainer but with considerable presence is No. 39, designed as the UNION HOTEL by *William Robertson*, 1838–9. Shallow pediment over the recessed centre; in the end bays, pedimented three-light windows, their lintels supported by consoles. METROPOLITAN HOUSE next door is a late C20 intruder. Then a large Flemish-Baronial block (Nos. 21–23) by *Matthews & Lawrie*, 1878–9, with turreted corners and the royal arms carved on the centre gablet; first-floor windows set in basket arches carried on polished granite columns. Pend to the large back wing in Lombard Street. Balustraded parapet on Nos. 17–19, *c.* 1845. WOOLWORTH is of 1961–4.

110 Next door is the magnificent BANK OF SCOTLAND, built as the head office of the Caledonian Bank in 1847. *Mackenzie & Matthews* were the architects. The ground floor's channelled piers carry a balcony in front of the set-back upper floors; on its ends, huge vases carved with the garlanded portraits of

Queen Victoria and the Prince Consort. In the centre, a pedimented Corinthian portico, the tympanum carved by *A. Handyside Ritchie* with allegorical figures of the wealth of land and sea; on the channelled stonework behind, panels carved with swags of flowers, with *putti* heads in the centre. Then a severe block of 1812, with a bowed corner to Church Street and incised Biblical texts giving moral purpose to the polished ashlar stonework.

BRIDGE STREET continues the street line down to the river. On its l., a development by *Ian Burke, Martin & Partners*, 1963–5; continuous podium of shops carrying three aggregate-faced blocks placed at right angles to the street. Opposite, the Town Steeple (*see* Public Buildings, above) is followed by a block of 1853. Console-pedimented first-floor windows with pilastered shopfronts and overall parapet. Then a large shopping development by *Scott, Brownrigg & Turner*, 1968–70.

CASTLE STREET leads uphill past the side of the Town House to the Sheriff and District Courts (for all these, *see* above) on the site of Inverness Castle. The E side starts with late C20 buildings followed by C18 vernacular at Nos. 33–53, Nos. 35–37 with large crowsteps, dated 1774; segmental-arched and keyblocked pend at Nos. 39–41.

INGLIS STREET is a short introduction to the town's core to the N. On its NE, Nos. 2–4 of *c.* 1845, classy Georgian-survival with a bowed corner and pedimented first-floor windows. Nos. 6–8 are probably by *James Ross*, 1848; pedimented first-floor windows and a punchy late Victorian shopfront. Flemish-Baronial Nos. 11–12 of 1883, by *William Mackintosh*. Much humbler Nos. 14–16 of *c.* 1805, with another ornate late C19 shopfront. On the SW side, tepid stripped Georgian of 1929.

ACADEMY STREET was Inverness's principal shopping street in the C19. The E side begins with a plain Victorian Italianate block, followed by Nos. 8–10, built in 1812 as the town house of the Mackintoshes of Aberarder but given a huge shopfront *c.* 1900. It is joined by an arch to the STATION HOTEL, which was begun by *Joseph Mitchell c.* 1855 but recast in 1858–9 by *Matthews & Lawrie* as a muddled Italianate composition with towers at the NW and SE; *Alexander Ross* added the assertive Roman Doric portico in 1898. It forms one side of STATION SQUARE in front of the Railway Station (*see* Public Buildings, above). In the middle of the square, the CAMERON HIGH-LANDERS MONUMENT by *George Wade*, 1891, a Portland stone statue of a kilted Cameronian in front of a small sphinx. On the square's N side, the old head office of the Highland Railway Co. (Nos. 28–34) by *Matthews & Lawrie*, 1873–5. It is a big confident palazzo with a Corinthian-pilastered centrepiece to the square. In the Academy Street front, a recessed centre with huge first-floor boardroom windows whose roundheaded overarches spring from Corinthian columns; the overarches' tympana are carved with wheel spokes, the central keyblock with a head; incised foliage on the walling above. All this carved work is by *Thomas Goodwillie* of Elgin. The original segmental-arched shopfronts are still intact.

Academy Street's w side begins with a late C19 Ægypto-Greek block (Nos. 1–9) somewhat in the manner of 'Greek' Thomson, a truncated slate dome on the canted corner. For the understated Renaissance block on Union Street's SE corner, *see* Union Street, below. The CLYDESDALE BANK on the NE corner was designed as the Royal Hotel in 1864 by *John Rhind* and refronted by *William Mackintosh*, 1872–3; quite forceful free Renaissance. At the entrance to the MARKET ARCADE, an ashlar screen by *Matthews & Lawrie*, 1869–70, with three tall round arches, the higher centre one's keyblock carved with the head of a bull, those of the outer arches with rams' heads. In the brick-faced arcade behind, roundheaded shopfronts. The MARKET HALLS were added by the *Burgh Surveyor* in 1890, with timber and glass roofs on cast-iron columns and principals. SE arcade to Union Street formed in 1890 by *Ross & Macbeth*; NW to Queensgate by *Duncan Cameron*, 1897. No. 23 Academy Street, NW of the Market entrance, is small-scale but quite punchy Victorian Renaissance. Then bland infill until No. 33 on the corner with Queensgate. It is by *Ross & Macbeth*, 1895, French Renaissance of a sort, with oriels recessed under curly-topped aediculed gablets, except at the corner where the window projects; prettily carved panels of *putti* and foliage. Coarser foliage, with heads poking out, on the capitals of the shopfronts' pilasters.

Nos. 40–44 Academy Street on the E side were built as the Royal Inverness Academy in 1788–92, a shallow U-plan of rough reddish ashlar with piended roofs. In 1895 *Duncan Cameron* converted the ground floor to shops (since altered) and provided the pompous doorpiece. N of Strothers Lane, a red sandstone Frenchy block with a candle-snuffered corner turret; by *William Mackintosh*, 1897–8. The East Church (*see* Churches, above) is a large and dumpy presence on the corner of Margaret Street, whose vista is closed by the Public Library (*see* Public Buildings, above).

The architecture now becomes bitty. On the w side, the OLD HIGH CHURCH HALL (a former school), Gothic by *A. & W. Reid*, 1876. Further on, the ABERTARFF INN, late Georgian with three-light first-floor windows. On the E side, the roughcast Nos. 92–94, early C19 with heavy pilastered doorpieces. Beside them, the front block of the ROSE STREET FOUNDRY by *Ross & Macbeth*, 1893, the first- and second-floor windows contained in giant roundheaded overarches, their tympana (except one) filled with mosaics of foundrymen at work; carved foliage on the friezes of the first-floor oriels. On the opposite corner, the PHOENIX BAR, early C19 with three-light windows, those of the second floor rising into piend-roofed dormers. In ROSE STREET itself, a foundry building, probably of the 1880s by *Ross & Macbeth*, the three front gables containing fat round-arched entrances.

UNION STREET joining Academy Street to Church Street to the

w was laid out in 1863. Of that year are Nos. 1–17 on the s side, a long but timid Renaissance front by *William Lawrie*; a pediment at the centre of each end section and the hint of a tower in the middle. Much more forceful is No. 19 (the former Royal Bank of Scotland) of 1901–2 by *W. L. Carruthers*. Free Queen Anne, with extravagantly rusticated first-floor windows; long back wing down Drummond Street. The stretch from Drummond Street to Church Street is filled by Nos. 21–39, large but unexciting free Renaissance, again by *Lawrie*, 1863. The street's N side was all designed by *Ross & Joass*, 1863–4. Long E palazzo, its detail more Ægypto-Greek than Italian. More conventionally Italianate w range with large urns flanking the pedimented centre gablet. Between these two was the MUSIC HALL, its surviving ground floor with a massively bracketed entrance now providing the base for a block of 1979.

QUEENSGATE to the N was laid out in 1884 by *Alexander Ross*. For the s side's E block, *see* Academy Street, above. Nos. 15–45 are by *W. L. Carruthers*, 1901–2, plain but confident Queen Anne, the large gablets containing octagonal garret windows set in square dumbbell-balustered recesses. On the N side, two matching blocks, blowsy Renaissance by *Ross & Macbeth*, 1885–94. Between them, the POST OFFICE by the *Ministry of Public Building and Works*, 1965–9, large and flashy in mosaic tile cladding.

CHURCH STREET's entry from the s between Nos. 1–7 High Street (*see* above) and the Town Steeple (*see* Public Buildings, above) shows a promise which is at once broken by the bulk of the CALEDONIAN HOTEL, set back from the street line but with assertive balconies pushing forward over the entrance on the axis of Union Street; it is by *Leach, Rhodes & Walker*, 1965–7. Opposite, YORK HOUSE of *c.* 1900, austerely gableted and pilastered in red and grey sandstone. For the corner buildings on Union Street and Queensgate, *see* above.

N of the Caledonian Hotel, a simple block (Nos. 43–47) of 1843 is followed by a cheap but gutsy palazzo (Nos. 49–53) by *Alexander Ross*, 1882. Then a mid-Victorian Flemish-Baronial building (No. 55), its pend opening into a court whose w side is filled by a very plain early C19 house with smart plasterwork in the entrance hall. On the N corner of Fraser Street, No. 67 of *c.* 1830, a superior house with console-corniced first-floor windows on its ashlar front; the built-out polished granite shopfront is an expensive C20 mistake. Now exposed to the street but formerly concealed behind a front block is the harled and crowstepped ABERTARFF HOUSE built in 1593 as the town 113 house of the Frasers of Lovat. It makes an asymmetrical T-shape. Two-storey main block, the upper l. window with a steep-pedimented dormerhead and *fleur-de-lis* finial. Projecting from the s front, a stairtower, bow-fronted up to the main eaves level and then corbelled to a square cap-house. Unusually, the E chimney is set in from the gable. Inside, the ground-floor E room contains a stone fireplace dated 1681, with incised decoration on the lintel. Built into the exposed gable of the building to the NE, a late C17 stone carved with the initials AS and HP flanking a heart.

CUMMINGS HOTEL on the street's E side is of c. 1840, with basket-arched first-floor windows and aprons under the windows above; unfortunate 'mansard' roof a recent addition. To its N, BOW COURT, a harled and crowstepped block of c. 1725, its ground-floor arcade and two tiny catslide dormers dating from *William Glashan*'s reconstruction of 1972. In its NE wing's wall to School Lane, a heraldic stone (restored in cement) recording the gift of the site to the Incorporated Trades and Masons by Katharine Duff, Lady Drummuir, in 1729. N of School Lane is DUNBAR'S HOSPITAL, built as an almshouse in 1668 by Provost Alexander Dunbar, who is said to have used materials from the demolished Citadel (*see* Public Buildings, above). Harled two-storey-and-attic front, with regular eight-bay fenestration, but there are only seven attic windows. These have scroll-sided stone pediments carved with the date 1668, Biblical texts and, at the l., the figure of a bedesman; the centre pediment used to be at the rear but was placed here in a restoration of 1961. Three more dormer pediments at the back. Above the round-arched entrance, an heraldic stone of 1676 and an inscription to record that the rent of the weighhouse was payable to the Hospital's treasurer. Early engravings show a spirelet on the roof. The hospital may incorporate some part of earlier buildings on the site, a possible explanation for the thick base along most of the front, which is cut into by the ground-floor windows, and for the early C17 appearance of a moulded round-arched door (now a window) decorated with rosettes which gave access from School Lane to a single-storey block in the inner angle with the rear wing, itself altered, with a Georgian-looking piend roof.

Opposite Dunbar's Hospital, Nos. 107–111 Church Street, an informal group of C18 vernacular houses beside the main access to the Old High Church churchyard, entered through cast-iron gatepiers and gates supplied in 1796. Small rendered house (No. 115) of 1770 separating this from Greyfriars Free Church (*see* Churches, above). In FRIARS STREET an unwelcome stop to the vista is provided by the TELEPHONE EXCHANGE, authoritarian by *H.M. Office of Works*, 1949–52.

BANK STREET'S S end is dominated by the bulk of the development in Bridge Stret and the car-park of the Caledonian Hotel. Between these, gallantly resisting the C20, is the INVERNESS COURIER office, built for the Bank of Scotland in 1804, with a shaped chimney gablet on its front. Further N, the DR BLACK MEMORIAL HALL by *R. J. Macbeth*, 1907–8, domestic Queen Anne. More ecclesiastical is the mid-Victorian HALL next door, a prelude to St Columba's High Church (*see* Churches, above). Across Fraser Street, the humble old Independent Chapel (*see* Churches, above). Beside it, MORAY HOUSE (Nos. 16–18) by *Crerar & Partners*, 1977, a brutalist aggregate frame surprisingly topped by a pitched roof surmounted by a glazed attic. At Church Lane, the Free North Church (*see* Churches, above)

overpowering a SALVATION ARMY HALL of *c*. 1900, marked
out only by a slate-spired ventilator.

DOUGLAS ROW is small-scale late C18 vernacular with a few
Victorian intrusions. Some way to the N, beside Waterloo
Bridge (for which, *see* Public Buildings, above), is PORTLAND
PLACE, where Nos. 1–3 were built in 1828, a short terrace of
single-storey-and-basement houses with Roman Doric porticoes and three-light windows; the roof of No. 3 has been raised,
to poor visual effect.

NESS WALK w of Ness Bridge begins with a Baronial tenement
by *Alexander Ross*, 1883–4. Then the COLUMBA HOTEL of
1881, also by *Ross*, with canted oriel windows rising from a
massively corbelled balcony; on the l., an extension of 1938
in its own stripped version of the Baronial manner. PALACE
HOTEL by *Ross & Macbeth*, 1890, with a Fyvie Castle centrepiece of conical-roofed towers linked by an arch. The street now
becomes ARDROSS TERRACE, all by *Alexander Ross*, 1873–81,
a procession of bay windows and gablets with a few touches of
Gothic detail. At the s corner, a tower with a swept slated spire,
half-masking the view of St Andrew's Cathedral (*see* Churches,
above), which is saluted by Nos. 1–2 to the w with a centre
gable flanked by pinnacled rounds and topped by a heraldic
beast. ARDROSS STREET, w of Alexander Place, starts with a
pacific Baronial terrace by *Alexander Ross*, 1872. Then houses,
almost all by *Ross & Macbeth*, 1878–89, No. 10 with scrolls
on the dormer pediments, Nos. 11–13 (of 1887) with steep
crowstepped gablets. The Italianate No. 14 is by *Duncan
Cameron*, 1888. Ness Walk s of the Cathedral leads past Eden
Court Theatre to the Royal Northern Infirmary (for these, *see*
Public Buildings, above).

HUNTLY STREET N of Ness Bridge kicks off with a group of
1970s two-storey blocks. Then the late C18 No. 17, its crowstepped gable end squashed against the PALACE BINGO
HALL, designed as a cinema in 1938 by *F. F. Maxwell,
Stewart & Maxwell*. Nos. 23–25 are a late Georgian pair with
three-light windows and an unsuitable new roof. St Mary's
R.C. Church's gable front (*see* Churches, above) is clasped
between the Presbytery, Tudor collegiate of 1888 by *W. L.
Carruthers*, and the plainer Tudor of the Victorian beginning of
St Joseph's Primary School (*see* Public Buildings, above), which
continues with bland 1930s neo-Georgian. No. 36 was built as
the Inverness Dispensary in 1868. It is by *Matthews & Lawrie*,
a smart villa with a Corinthian-pilastered pedimented centrepiece; keystone over the entrance carved as a woman's head.
Next door, the West Parish Church (*see* Churches, above).
Across Greig Street is the early C18 BALNAIN HOUSE, a
large and plain piend-roofed mansion of considerable presence.
Presence of a fussier kind is provided by the old Queen Street
Free Church (*see* Churches, above). The early C19 Nos. 41–44
Huntly Street begin a small terrace continued by the slightly
later Nos. 45–48. Then the Methodist Church (*see* Churches,
above), giving yet another ecclesiastical marker. N of Friars

Bridge (*see* Public Buildings, above), the SALVATION ARMY
HOSTEL by *Inverness District Council*, 1985, a yellow blockwork
bully to the quietly well-detailed Nos. 3–5 of 1818, whose mut-
uled-corniced doorcases recur at Nos. 8–9 of *c.* 1820. Trinity
Church (*see* Churches, above) guards the boundary between
this late Georgian gentility and the 1950s flats along GILBERT
STREET.

In TELFORD STREET to the W, Nos. 26–38 form a terrace of
houses built by *John Simpson* and *John Cargill*, *c.* 1806, for the
more important of the workers employed to build the Caledonian Canal; of droved red ashlar (No. 32 now harled), the
entrances paired under pedimented porches. Further out, No.
60 is an austere villa of 1815, with consoled cornices under the
ground-floor windows and a piered portico. In CLACH-
NAHARRY ROAD, W of Muirtown Bridge across the Caledonian
Canal (*see* Public Buildings, above), the early C19 MUIRTOWN
COTTAGE (No. 50), diminutive Gothick, the wooden porch an
addition.

CLACHNAHARRY itself is a three-street village (HIGH STREET,
MID STREET and LOW STREET) of C19 fishertown vernacular
cottages, many harled but some with ill-considered rear
additions. For its former School, *see* Public Buildings, above.
In Mid Street, a late C19 lattice-girder FOOTBRIDGE over the
railway.

MANSIONS

AULTNASKIACH, off Culduthel Road. The approach now filled
with small late C20 houses. Harled early C19 mansion, plain
except for a Roman Doric portico.

INSHES HOUSE, off Old Perth Road. Gawky harled laird's house
built for the Robertsons of Inshes in 1767. Three storeys and a
basement, three bays. Keyblocked bullseye windows flanking
the rusticated doorpiece, its buckle quoins a C17 rather than
C18 detail.

To the SW, a tiny three-storey harled TOWER, perhaps an
early C17 fragment of the house which was burned in 1664.
Small gunloops at the ground floor; more shotholes above. On
the N gable, a late C19 bellcote (minus its bell).

KINMYLIES HOUSE, Kinmylies Way. Originally a plain early
C19 T-plan farmhouse. In 1860 *William Lawrie* added the
broad-eaved front block, its bay windows projecting from
beneath gables. Rear additions by *Ross & Macbeth*, 1905, after
it became a lunatic asylum.

86 MUIRTOWN HOUSE, Charleston Place. An unexpected apparition among the surrounding speculative housing. Villa of
hugely dotty charm, the complexity of its building history quite
disproportionate to its size. It was put up and almost certainly
designed by *Major Hugh Robert Duff* of Muirtown, of whom
Joseph Mitchell recalled that

He was an able man but somewhat eccentric. He had been one of
Bonaparte's *détenus*, and was confined in a church in France for six

months, which he gave as an excuse for not afterwards attending divine
service at home. He occupied his time in building his house and laying
out the plantations around it ...

The house was begun in 1800 by *Hugh Suter*, mason, and
Alexander Miller, wright, who produced a single-storey-and-
basement villa of Palladian derivation. Simple main block with
round-arched niches flanking the centre; pedimented wings
with overarched Venetian windows. The next year *Miller* raised
the main block's centrepiece by another floor and gave its end
bays tall screen-wall parapets relieved by blind windows. *Miller*
resumed work in 1804–5, now in company with the masons
Lewis Yule, *John Yule*, *John McWatt* and *Colin Nicolson* of Nairn,
adding a large rear extension; above the front's centre bay they
skied a pediment carved with Duff's arms, supplied by *Robert
Burn* of Edinburgh. The Yules and McWatt added a martial
tower behind the main block in 1806, and in 1811 *Hugh Suter*
returned to provide a Doric portico in front, its metopes carved
with alternating rams' heads and harps. Eleven years later, work
resumed when *William Symon*, mason, and *Lachlan Mackintosh*,
wright, built a projecting E pavilion with square bartizans at
the corners of its gable front. Then in 1827 Symon, now in
partnership with *Alexander Fraser*, wright, inserted a three-light
Gothick window in this pavilion's gable and heightened its
bartizans. At the same time they built a balancing w pavilion,
plainer Gothick in manner and with lower bartizans, to house
the kitchen. In 1830–1 *Fraser* added a Batty-Langleyish steepled
clocktower (only the lower stage now surviving) to the w pavilion and a cast-iron lion (since removed) to the E. Probably at
the same time a Gothick upper storey was erected above the
portico (its stumpy pilasters now missing). Perhaps as a cover-
up for stonework which disclosed too blatantly Major Duff's
successive enthusiasms, the front was rendered in 1834. Plain
rear additions by *James Ross*, 1851. The interior is now flatted.
From the front door to the stairhall at the back, a groin-vaulted
passage divided by columns from narrow side aisles.

OLD DRUMMOND, Oak Avenue. Unpretentious harled mansion
of *c.* 1770, with a pedimented doorpiece at the chimney-gabled
centre.

VILLAS ETC.

ANNFIELD ROAD. Nos. 1A–3 make a big U-plan double house
of *c.* 1865. Broad eaves and Italianate detail; a large monkey-
puzzle in front of No. 3. – Contemporary No. 9 (CRAIGMONIE
HOTEL), with carved bargeboards and a squat slate-spired
tower, marred by recent extensions. – The U-plan No. 13
(LETHINGTON) was designed for himself by *W. L. Carruthers*,   116
1892, in an asymmetrical Arts and Crafts Tudor manner.
Harled but with an ashlar-faced octagonal stairtower in the l.
inner angle and half-timbering at the gables and gablets. SW
wing dated 1925.
CROWN AVENUE. Nos. 12–14 were begun in 1815 as a three-bay

house with a pilastered doorpiece and three-light windows; a bow at the back. It became U-plan in the mid-c19, when wings with canted bay ends were added, and L-plan in the late c20, when the w wing was demolished.

CROWN DRIVE. At Nos. 24–26, a pair of semi-detached houses, asymmetrical Arts and Crafts Jacobean; by *W. L. Carruthers*, c. 1895.

CULDUTHEL ROAD'S E side begins with ARDKEEN TOWER (No. 5), built in 1834–6 as the Inverness United Charities Institution to house the Inverness Juvenile Female School, Ladies' Female Work Society and Inverness Infant School. L-plan, the two equal-length single-storey ranges joined by recessed one-bay links to an oval block fronted with a Roman Doric portico and surmounted by a little domed tower, its lower stage octagonal, the pilastered upper stage circular; it was originally used as an observatory.* In 1902–6 *Alexander F. Mackenzie* glazed the portico as an adjunct to the room behind, added a bay window to each wing, heightened the E wing to two storeys, and infilled the inner angle with a harled two-storey block. Inside, the ground floor's principal oval room behind the portico contains a white marble chimneypiece, its classical arch enclosing a Tudor-arched fire surround.

Harled No. 7 of c. 1830 with an Ionic columned porch and heavy anta-pilastered window cases. – No. 9, across Mayfield Road, is by *Alexander Ross*, 1860, with a tall Italianate tower. – On the r., VIEWMOUNT HOUSE (No. 10) of c. 1835, with a broad-eaved piended roof; hoodmoulds over the door and windows on the N (entrance) front. Further s, Nos. 14–18 are of c. 1830–40, No. 14 with a pedimented Ionic portico, No. 16 brute-classical with a heavy anta-pilastered doorpiece at the recessed centre and block pediments on the parapet, and No. 18 Jacobean. – BEECHLAWN (No. 20) was built c. 1850, with an open-pedimented centre and Italianate detail; the N wing and small but martial tower were added by *Alexander Ross* in 1890. – HEATHERLEY (No. 22), set well back from the road, is by *Ross & Joass*, 1860–4, large-scale severe parsonical Gothic, barely relieved by carved bargeboards. – On the E side after St Ninian's (R.C.) Church (*see* Churches, above), HEDGEFIELD (No. 23), built in 1821. Large and plain L-plan, the projecting wing pedimented; Ionic portico in the inner angle. The rear block with shaped gables was added by *George Rhind* in 1846. More recent additions have accompanied its present use as a school hostel. Plain Georgian stables to the N; a walled garden to the NW. – For Aultnaskiach on the w, *see* Mansions, above. – No. 48 is by *W. L. Carruthers*, 1912, asymmetrical but balanced Arts and Crafts. – Cottagey ELMBANK (No. 68) by *G. G. Mackay*, c. 1875, with prettily carved bargeboards on the porch and dormers. – Further out, four small villas by *Carruthers Ballantyne, Cox & Taylor*, c. 1935–8, all flat-roofed and blocky

*An earlier scheme is recorded in a watercolour (now in the Inverness Museum) which shows the portico as Greek Doric and both stages of the tower as octagonal, its windows being ovals instead of the present segmental-headed ones.

in a Modern Movement Dudokian manner, No. 87 with an Art Deco door but its white render replaced by drydash, No. 89 more severe, No. 135 with cut-out corners and its metal-framed 118 windows intact, No. 145 towerlike on top of a small hill.

DAMFIELD ROAD. The KINGSMILLS HOTEL incorporates KINGSMILLS HOUSE, probably late c18 in origin, extended and recast in Tudorish dress by *James Ross*, 1853; the tower over the entrance was added by *Ross & Macbeth* in 1906.

DORES ROAD. THE FIRS of *c*. 1860, expensive blowsy Italianate.

DRUMMOND CRESCENT. At the N end, No. 2 of *c*. 1860, Gothic-Baronial with a spired corner turret and gunloops. – No. 11 is gabled Italianate of *c*. 1850. – No. 13 of *c*. 1865, probably by *Matthews & Lawrie*, a big low villa of Germanic-Italianate type with idiosyncratic detail.

ISLAND BANK ROAD. For No. 2 on the W side, *see* Ladies Walk, below. In the long stretch from Bellfield Park to Drummond Crescent, houses only on the E side. No. 11 of *c*. 1850 with twin bows pierced by three-light windows; wrought-iron anthemion finials on the gabled dormers. – Asymmetrical No. 15 of *c*. 1860 with crowstepped gables and iron cresting. – No. 17 is by *Alexander Ross*, 1864, Georgian-survival going Italianate. – Carved bargeboards on No. 19 of *c*. 1865. – Contemporary No. 21 dignified by a small spiretopped tower; roof patterned with grey and purple slates. – The harled and half-timbered No. 20 on the W side looks like the work of *W. L. Carruthers*, *c*. 1900. – To its S, the gabled and gableted INCHMAY (No. 24), late c19 with the bargeboards and balcony making a display of the carpenter's craft. – CARROL (No. 29) and ROSSAL (No. 31) on the E are both by *W. L. Carruthers*, 1888–9, big and relaxed Arts and Crafts. – Faintly Italianate broad-eaved No. 38 on the W side of *c*. 1865. – Cottagey double house of *c*. 1875 at Nos. 42–44, the doors' and windows' angular consoles carrying the eaves; horizontal glazing.

LADIES WALK. Late Victorian villas overlooking the Ness. At the N end, No. 2 Island Bank Road, crowstepped and turreted of 1863. – Then Ladies Walk begins officially with the carved bargeboards of No. 2. – Nos. 3 and 4 are a pair of bargeboarded houses with cast-iron balconies, identical except for their reversed plans. – No. 5 more sedate. – Nos. 6 and 7, another pair of reversed plan houses; carved bargeboards and oriel windows. – For the Forbes Fountain, *see* Public Buildings, above.

MIDMILLS ROAD. Nos. 60–62 are by *W. L. Carruthers*, *c*. 1900. Rambling Arts and Crafts, harled and half-timbered.

NESS BANK. A string of Victorian villas s of Ness Bank Church (*see* Churches, above). Nos. 5–7 are by *Ross & Joass*, 1864, with Tudor hoodmoulds over the doors and steep bargeboarded gables. – Italianate tower on the GLENMHOR HOTEL of *c*. 1865. – Nos. 16–18 make up a long U-plan triple house of *c*. 1840 with bow-ended wings and a pedimented centre. – The GLENMORISTON HOTEL's Georgian-survival manner is belied by a bay window and the large monkey-puzzle tree in front. – Nos. 28–29 are a U-plan double house in picturesque cottage style, the horizontal glazing still intact at No. 29.

NESS WALK. SPRINGFIELD HOTEL. Large single-storey mid-C19 cottage with broad eaves.

OLD EDINBURGH ROAD. At the corner with Gordon Terrace, the harled VIEWHILL GATE (the INVERNESS YOUTH HOSTEL), built for himself by *Joseph Mitchell, c.* 1835. Jacobean, with gables topped by corbelled chimney stacks or spiky finials. – For Ardkeen Tower on the S corner, *see* Culduthel Road, above. – Nos. 2–4 form a late C19 double house sharing a broad centre gablet; No. 4 has been skinned of most of its half-timbering and harling. – No. 9 mid-C19 Georgian-survival with a heavy Roman Doric doorpiece. – Broad-eaved No. 28 (IVYBANK) of *c.* 1860, L-plan, with an Italianate tower in the inner angle. – The white rendered LAMBURN on the corner with Annfield Road is by *L. Carruthers Ballantyne, Cox & Taylor,* 1935, boxy Modern Movement in the Dudok manner.

SOUTHSIDE ROAD. Nos. 19–21 make a long single-storey-and-attic double house of *c.* 1860 with elaborately carved barge-boards on the dormer windows. – Almost opposite, No. 26, a determinedly picturesque late C19 cottage in the American 'stick' style, half-timbered, pargetted and iron-crested. – Nos. 42–46 form a group of *c.* 1870, No. 42 Italianate, No. 44 with carved bargeboards and strapwork, No. 46 mixing Italian detail with cottagey gablets. – No. 37 on the l. side, gentle Italian Renaissance, L-plan with a porch in the inner angle, a large vase on its corner and its door's keystone carved as a bearded head.

STRATHERRICK ROAD. Some large villas set back from the public gaze. On the w side, WESTWOOD, a rambling broad-eaved house of *c.* 1850, given Frenchy embellishments by *A. & W. Reid,* 1874. – BELLE VUE, Italianate of *c.* 1865, with a tower over the entrance. – DRUMMOND HILL, quieter Italianate of *c.* 1860. – DRUMMOND TOWER, an asymmetrical toy fort of *c.* 1835 but with a Venetian window; low Italianate w wing added *c.* 1865. – LOCHARDIL HOUSE (now HOTEL) on the E, by *John Rhind,* 1876–8. Crowstepped villa-Baronial with a large coat of arms above the round-arched door.

BOAR STONE, 4km. S. Badly weathered standing stone slab, over 2m. high, now protected by wire netting. On its face, the incised figure of a boar with spirals rising from its hips; above, a 'mirror-case' symbol. The decoration is probably of the late C7 or C8 A.D., but the stone itself might have been erected in the second millennium B.C.

FORT, Craig Phadrig, off Leachkin Brae. Grassy flat summit of a well-wooded hill fortified in the C4 or C5 B.C. The area is roughly oblong, *c.* 80m. long, and surrounded by a pair of ramparts, the inner very thick, the outer placed some way below. Excavation has revealed that both were built of timberlaced stonework and subsequently burnt. Excavated finds suggest a reoccupation of the fort in the C6 or C7 A.D.

KILMARTIN

4030

Little more than a place-name beside Loch Meiklie.

St Ninian's Church (Episcopal). In a small graveyard sloping down to the loch. By *Alexander Ross*, 1853. Very simple lanceted rectangle with a round-arched N door and a chunky crow-stepped bellcote on the w gable. At the crowstepped E gable the rubble masonry is exposed. The roof, now slated, was originally thatched. Inside, stone ALTAR incorporating an early medieval stone incised with a cross, imported from a demolished church at the E end of Glen Urquhart.* – STAINED GLASS. Coolly Expressionist E window of three lights, abstract except for a swirling cross in the centre; by *Emma Shipton*, 1986. – Early C20 churchyard GATE, Art Nouveau in wrought iron.

KILMORACK

4040

Former church and manse standing together above the Beauly River, which is dammed by the power station; on the S bank, the remains of the former Kiltarlity Parish Church.

Kilmorack Free Church. *See* Balblair.

Kilmorack Parish Church. Disused. Harled rubble rectangle built in 1786, modestly but carefully detailed. Tall round-arched windows with projecting imposts and keyblocks, the Georgian glazing pattern intact. On the w gable, a birdcage bellcote, its ball finial supported on a concave-sided stalk; ball finial on the E gable.

Uphill to the w, late C18 MANSE, white harled with an advanced and gabled centre. The bay window on the r. was probably added as part of the alterations made by *James Ross* in 1846.

Kiltarlity Old Parish Church. A rectangle of boulder rubble built in 1626 but now roofless and with the walls partly demolished. Rectangular windows in the gables, two doors in the E wall, all with chamfered margins.

Kilmorack Power Station. Modern-traditional with a blocky rubble and glass building standing on the concrete dam. By *Robert Hurd & Partners*, 1958–63.

KILTARLITY

5040

Small village, mostly of C20 council housing, the Parish Church and school at Tomnacross to the SE, the Free Church to the SW.

Free Church. Sneck-harled Georgian-survival of 1843–6. On

---

*The surrounding inscription's statement that that church had belonged to the Knights Templar derives from a failure to realize that the Gaelic word 'teampull' means no more than 'church'.

the w gable, a birdcage bellcote, its ball finial skied on a stone stalk. Low vestry projecting from the s side; less happy is the new drydashed e porch.

OLD PARISH CHURCH. *See* Kilmorack.

PARISH CHURCH. Designed in 1829 by *Alexander Sinclair*; *Donald Macphail* was the contractor. Late Georgian kirk, the harled walls enlivened by rusticated quoins and window surrounds; Gothick glazing in the roundheaded windows. At the w end, a low semi-octagonal vestry. On top of this gable, a double birdcage bellcote with Roman Doric columns, just like the one at Wardlaw Parish Church, Kirkhill. In the e gable, a reused stone carved with the Fraser arms, the date 1626 and the initials MWF for Mr William Fraser, the then minister of Kiltarlity; it came from the old Parish Church. Inside, gallery carried on wooden pillars round three sides. The open wooden roof and pulpit date from *John Robertson*'s alterations of 1894.

TOMNACROSS PRIMARY SCHOOL. School and schoolhouse of 1867 by *Matthews & Lawrie*, who designed an extension in 1875. To the e, a block of 1911 by *R. J. Macbeth* with a more recent addition beside it.

RIVENDELL. Originally the Parish Manse. Front block by *John Smith* of Aberdeen, 1838–9, hiding the late C18 house behind. Straightforward, the Tudorish porch with a hint of castellation.

BEAUFORT CASTLE. *See* p. 148.
BELLADRUM. *See* p. 154.
PHOINEAS HOUSE. *See* p. 215.

5040   KIRKHILL

Small village composed mostly of C20 council housing.

KIRKHILL UNITED FREE CHURCH. *See* Bogroy.

WARDLAW CEMETERY AND LOVAT MAUSOLEUM. The site of the medieval Kirkhill Parish Church, onto whose e end was added the Lovat Mausoleum in the C17. Of the CHURCH only the e gable survives, its masonry showing evidence of a large window said to have been inserted in the mid-C14 by Julia Ross, widow of Simon, third Lord Fraser of Lovat.

51   The MAUSOLEUM built by the mason *William Ross* in 1633–4 is of the same width as the church but taller. Buckle quoins peeping through the harling at the e corners. In the s wall, tall round-arched windows and a rectangular door, all with moulded surrounds. The e gable's centre is corbelled out from the wall-face to enclose a stair topped by a belfry. The harled stair projection may be of 1633–4; the ashlar belfry is dated 1722, very old-fashioned for that date but not unlike the near-contemporary Tolbooth at Tain. It is of two stages, the lower square, the upper round, both with rectangular openings. Sitting on top of the lower stage's corners are round turrets, their conical stone roofs with corbelled eaves and ball finials. The turrets themselves project on continuous corbelling carved

with diagonal strings and a sort of egg-and-dart motif. On top of
the belfry's upper stage, a squat stone spire with small gableted
lucarnes; a lead weathercock on the ball finial.

Built against the graveyard's W wall, the mid-C19 BURIAL
ENCLOSURE of the Forbes family, with a balustrade on top. –
The main GATEWAY's moulded round arch looks C17.

Harled former MANSE to the S, built in 1775. It was extended
at the back in 1825–6 by *James Smith*, who was probably responsible for the addition of a Roman Doric portico to the gabled
centre. The ground-floor windows have been enlarged with
pilastered surrounds, perhaps in 1876, when *Alexander Ross* did
work here.

WARDLAW PARISH CHURCH. Big Georgian box built by *Nicol*
and *Cruikshank*, 1790–2, the plan adapted from that of Dyke
Church (Grampian). Round-arched windows, those in the
gables still with Georgian Gothick glazing, the others altered in
John Robertson's recasting of 1892. The W gable's Roman Doric
columned birdcage bellcote for two bells was added in 1818 by
James Forsyth.

MONIACK CASTLE. *See* p. 212.

REELIG HOUSE, 1.8km. S. Gently neo-Greek laird's house built
for the Persian scholar James Baillie Fraser in 1837–8; *William
Robertson* was the architect. Two storeys and a basement. Polished ashlar front, the centre slightly advanced with a tetrastyle
Ionic portico. Tall ground-floor windows; panelled pilasters at
the corners. Low service wing of 1901 on the E. The back wing
may have been part of the 'very pretty box' built here by James
Fraser of Reelig, *c.* 1750, but was remodelled in 1901.

LEYS CASTLE   6040
4km. s of Inverness

Castellated and turreted mansion house designed by the London
  theatre-architect and playwright *Samuel Beazley* for Colonel
  John Baillie *c.* 1833, and described in 1841 as 'a princely residence ... all that wealth, skill, and taste could render it.' Two
  storeys over a basement with paired stringcourses marking off
  the first floor. E (entrance) front stepped forward from octagonal end turrets past a pair of slim turrets to a porte cochère in
  the centre. Rising up above the roof is the house's central tower.
  On the sides and garden (w) front, full-height canted bay
  windows, an oriel in the garden front's centre. A variety of
  detail, mixing Romanesque and Tudor. Windows mostly hoodmoulded, some with four-centred arches or Y-tracery.

  (In the entrance hall, a stone chimneypiece carved with
  chevron decoration. Imperial stair rising in the tower, its balustrade and that of its corbelled first-floor gallery decorated
  with cusping. At the half-landing, a tall chimneypiece with
  chevron and ball enrichment. Gothick drawing room with ogee-
  arched doorcases and a white marble chimneypiece. Ribbed
  ceiling with a central boss. Octagonal library, its walls and

ceiling grained; on the ceiling, gilded festoons and a central boss. The dining-room walls are also grained. Ogee-arched doorcases and a coffered ceiling.)

MILTON

Hamlet in Glen Urquhart.

GLENURQUHART FREE CHURCH. Built in 1844, a long rectangle, white harled with red sandstone dressings. Minimally pointed windows. On the gables, small obelisk-and-ball finials.

GLENURQUHART UNITED FREE CHURCH. Disused. Late Gothic by *J. G. Falconer*, 1910. At the broad gable front the door (flanked by cusped niches) and five-light window above are contained in a giant segmental overarch. On top of the gable, a corbelled stone bellcote. Dumpy pagoda ventilator on the roof.

MONIACK CASTLE
1.8km. s of Kirkhill

Harled laird's house begun, probably in the early C17, as an L-plan with the main block at the N and a SW jamb. In the inner angle, a big bowed stairtower, its top floor jettied to the square and containing a tunnel-vaulted room reached by a turret stair at the tower's NW corner. Over the tower's moulded door, an empty panel-frame. At the S end of the three-storey jamb's W front and in its E gable are early C17 windows with chamfered margins. Also early C17 are the tower's cannon spouts, but its original parapet was harled over in 1804, when *James Smith* added an ashlar battlement with little square bartizans at the NE, SE and SW corners and a round battlement to the NW turret. This was the prelude to a remodelling of the house in 1807–8, when the mason *James Forsyth* and carpenter *William McDonald* altered the SW jamb and largely rebuilt the N block, giving piended roofs to both. Their smart new entrance front was to the N, where they placed a portico with etiolated Roman Doric columns between two-storey bow windows. These light their new drawing room on the W and dining room on the E, whose plain marble chimneypieces are respectively liver-coloured and black.

Additions to the E were built by *James Forsyth* in 1813–14. They link the main house to a formerly detached harled two-storey-and-attic house of three bays with a rusticated doorpiece, probably the farmhouse built by William Grant, tenant in Moniack, c. 1760. This made an informal U-shape open to the S, its courtyard partly filled c. 1920 by a two-storey block on the E side, a shaped gablet its main adornment.

MOY

No village, just the church and manse of a hill parish.

PARISH CHURCH. Simple harled box built in 1765. The round-arched windows and pinnacled birdcage bellcote could be of that date but are more probably of 1829, when substantial repairs were made.

Protruding from the W wall, a pedimented MONUMENT to Aeneas Mackintosh of Raigmore † 1768, the two panels framed by attached Tuscan columns. Inscription recording that

HE SERVED WITH CREDIT IN GERMANY AS FIRST LIEUT^T WITH KIETHS [*sic*] HIGHLANDERS BUT WAS PUT ON HALF PAY IN EARLY YOUTH BY THE REGIMENT BEING DISBANDED AT THE PEACE OF 1763.

– At the churchyard's NW corner, a roofless late Georgian MAUSOLEUM. – Early C19 piend-roofed SESSION HOUSE beside the gate.

MANSE to the N, its harled back part built in 1765. Ashlar front block added by *Thomas Macfarlane*, 1838–40; quite smart, with a recessed centre and two-light windows, still with horizontal glazing.

MOY HALL, 1km. N. A very plain house of Covesea stone, by *Gordon Gunn* of *George Gordon & Co.*, 1955–7. It replaced a house which had been remodelled in the 1870s in dotty Baronial style by *John Rhind*, whose LODGE of 1868 still stands beside the road to Inverness. – On an island in Loch Moy to the S, a 21m.-high granite OBELISK erected in 1824 to commemorate Sir Aeneas Mackintosh of Mackintosh.

MULLARDOCH

Dam at the E end of Loch Mullardoch, part of a major hydro-electricity scheme.

DAM. By *Kennedy & Donkin* and *Sir William Halcrow & Partners*, 1947–52. Impressive for its size (727m. long and 48m. high) and purposive functionalism.

NESS CASTLE*
4km. S of Inverness

Cottage-villa built *c.* 1820 for Lady Anne Maitland, wife of Robert Fraser of Torbreck. H-plan, the long main block and lower wings all with piended roofs. To the front the main block is of two storeys above a sunk basement. Pedimented Doric portico at the centrepiece, whose ashlar face contrasts with the rather mean rubble walling of the rest. The upper windows have been

*Originally Darrochville.

heightened with pedimented dormerheads pushing up through the eaves, probably as part of *William Lawrie*'s alterations of 1855. The principal rooms facing the garden occupy the whole height of the main block above the basement. Generous bow in the centre; semi-octagonal ends to the wings. To the E, a service court with a Victorian greenhouse on its S and a faintly Italianate tower, probably of 1855, at the NE corner.

The interior is distinctly smart. A small vestibule opens into a square top-lit central hall covered with a shallow ribbed dome on pendentives, the spandrels with enriched plasterwork. Behind, a bow-ended library with the dining room to the l. and drawing room to the r., all with shallowly coffered ceilings, the library and dining room still having austere marble chimneypieces.

7050   PETTY

No more than a place-name for a rural parish, its present church standing beside the A96, the old Parish Church 2.8km. W, near Castle Stuart (for which *see* p. 156).

OLD PARISH CHURCH. Disused. T-plan kirk built in 1836–9, perhaps to a design by *Robert Caldwell*.* Extravagantly tall rectangular windows with hoodmoulds perched on top; horizontal glazing in the wooden mullions and transoms. The W bellcote is now represented only by its corbelled base. Thinly detailed Gothic interior by *John Robertson*, 1903–4.

Attached to the church's E gable is the harled rubble MAUSOLEUM of the Mackintoshes. It was built *c.* 1686, its Gothic detail a surprisingly late survival. In the S front, a pointed door flanked by Y-traceried blind windows. Standing outside are two cast-iron heraldic cats. The mausoleum's N wing is probably an addition of 1742, the date on its blind Venetian window, whose frieze is carved with high-relief foliage and the initials LM and AD, for Lachlan Mackintosh of Mackintosh † 1731 and his wife, Anne Duff † 1750.

On the church's S side, a low BURIAL ENCLOSURE, probably C18, containing a tablet carved with the Mackintosh cat. – To the S, several C18 GRAVESLABS decorated with heraldry and emblems of death. – At the graveyard's old entrance, a tall WATCH HOUSE dated 1825, built into the hillside, its one room lighted by small windows.

To the E, the former MANSE (now AULD PETTY), by *James Macfarlane* of Doune, 1837–8, a bracketed cornice over the door.

PARISH CHURCH. Originally Petty Free Church. By *George Rhind*, 1848–9. Plain box with round-arched windows and a segmental-topped W bellcote; front wall of rough ashlar, the others harled. It was made a T-plan by *Duncan Cameron*'s

---

*Who was paid five guineas 'for plans'; but plans were also prepared by 'an Architect from Edinburgh'.

addition of a low HALL in 1896–7. – STAINED GLASS. W
window (Christ the Light of the World) of 1949. – In the N
wall, one light (Christ the Good Shepherd) by *Abbot & Co.
Ltd*, 1951. – In the S wall, another light (Our Lord with Little
Children), also by *Abbot*, 1960.

PHOINEAS HOUSE
2km. NE of Kiltarlity

5040

Small harled mansion house of *c.* 1805. H-plan, the main block
and wings all with piended roofs. Flying stair over the high
basement's area to the Roman Doric pilastered door; above it,
a three-light window. At the centre of the rear elevation, a full-
height bow with three-light windows.

STRATHERRICK *see* ERROGIE

STRATHNAIRN CASTLE *see* DAVIOT

STRUY

4040

Straggly hamlet on both sides of the Beauly River.

CHURCH. Small but very Gothic, by *Ross & Macbeth*, 1896–7.
Steep gabled porch and bellcote on the front, whose round
corner buttresses are corbelled out to carry big octagonal pinnacles.

BRIDGE. By *Thomas Telford*, 1812. Rubble-built, with five segmental arches and triangular cutwaters.

ERCHLESS CASTLE. *See* p. 165.

TOMATIN

8020

Small village dominated by a distillery opened in 1898, its buildings now mostly late C20.

CHURCH OF SCOTLAND. Built as a United Free church, *c.* 1910.
Of corrugated iron with pointed windows.

MOY FREE CHURCH, 1.3km. SE. Harled box built *c.* 1845 but
completely remodelled in 1900. Big corniced windows in the
long side walls. At the front gable, a pilastered porch below
a keyblocked roundheaded window. On the gable's apex, a
pedimented bellcote; small urns at the ends.

FINDHORN BRIDGE, 1.1km. S. 1925–6, by *E. Owen Williams*,
with *J. W. Simpson* and *Maxwell Ayrton* as consultant architects.
Two 29.3m. spans of reinforced concrete with a massive central

pier. High concrete parapet pierced by semi-octagonal 'windows'.

RAILWAY VIADUCTS. Both by *John Fowler* and *Murdoch Paterson*,
1894–7. The curved Findhorn Viaduct is over 400m. long and
stands 43m. above the river. Nine spans of steel lattice girders
on tapering stone piers. – The VIADUCT over the Allt na Frithe
to the W has nine semicircular arches, the piers and facing of
bullnosed masonry, the soffits of brick.

3020   TOMICH

Late C19 estate village founded by Sir Dudley Coutts Mar-
joribanks, first Lord Tweedmouth, the owner of Guisachan. Picturesquely gabled and gableted broad-eaved cottages.

TWEEDMOUTH MEMORIAL FOUNTAIN. Erected in 1910 by
the second Lord Tweedmouth and his sister to commemorate
their parents. Large piece of granite walling surmounted by a
stone urn. In the wall, a stylized shell-niche from which projects
the basin. Above the niche, a bronze inscription panel with an
angel's head in relief. At the sides, bronze panels with relief
heads of Lord and Lady Tweedmouth, signed by *R. Tait Mc-
Kenzie*.

GUISACHAN. *See* p. 180.

TOMNACROSS *see* KILTARLITY

URQUHART *see* DRUMNADROCHIT

5020   URQUHART CASTLE
                2.7km. SE of Drumnadrochit

65 Ruined stronghold on a promontory jutting into Loch Ness. The
position is of strategic importance, commanding the landward
route down the W side of the Great Glen and the entrance to Glen
Urquhart and providing a safe anchorage for galleys patrolling the
loch.

The site is shaped like an hourglass, the centre of its N bulge
filled by a knoll, the S bulge rising quite steeply from the low waist
to a craggy hill at the SW corner. Cliffs on the E and N made attack
from the loch almost impossible. On the W and S is a curved ditch,
c. 4.9m. deep and up to *c.* 30m. broad; it is partly artificial, the
manmade excavation perhaps dating from the early Middle Ages.

Stones of a vitrified rampart have been found on the SW hill,
the site's highest point, so it has been occupied and fortified since
the Iron Age. Possibly this was the fort of the Pictish King Buide

whom St Columba visited in the C 6. In 1229 Alexander II granted the lordship of Urquhart to Thomas Durward, Sheriff of Inverness. It was probably Thomas Durward or his son Sir Alan who was responsible for the construction of a castle of motte-and-bailey type, building a shell-keep on the natural motte of the SW hill and dividing the rest of the site into two baileys or courts, one for each bulge of the hourglass. The castle changed hands several times during the first War of Independence, being finally captured by the 'patriot' party c. 1308. After David II's flight to France following the Battle of Halidon in 1333, Urquhart was one of only five castles still flying the Scottish flag. At that time the castle's Constable was Sir Robert Lauder of Quarrelwood, who was succeeded in that office twenty-six years later by his grandson Sir Robert Chisholm. Either Sir Robert Chisholm or his grandson Thomas, who had become Constable by 1390, seems to have undertaken a major reconstruction of the castle. This shifted its centre of importance from the S courtyard (Upper Bailey) to the N (Nether Bailey), whose E curtain, formerly perhaps a palisade, was rebuilt as a buttressed stone wall against which was erected a two-storey range containing a kitchen, hall, great chamber and solar. At the site's N apex was built a detached tower, perhaps to house the Constable.

In 1482 a lease of the lands of Urquhart was granted to John Grant of Freuchie, who obtained a royal charter in 1509. That charter stipulated that he repair or build 'a tower with an outwork or rampart of stone and lime . . . and a hall, chamber, and kitchen, with all requisite offices'. This was followed by a thoroughgoing reconstruction of the N tower, the building of a new gatehouse, perhaps as accommodation for a Keeper, and of a W curtain wall at the Nether Bailey and, a little later, by the rebuilding of the Upper Bailey's curtain. This work was presumably interrupted between 1513 and 1516, when the castle was illegally occupied by Sir Donald Macdonald of Lochalsh, and it seems to have been still uncompleted in 1527, when Hector Boece wrote of Urquhart's 'rewinous wallis'. Further work, probably a remodelling of the N tower, was carried out for Sir John Grant of Freuchie in 1623.

Plundered by a detachment of the Covenanting army in 1644, the castle was repaired in 1676 at a cost of 200 merks. In 1689, after the deposition of James VII, Urquhart was occupied by a Whig garrison who, on leaving, blew up the gatehouse to prevent the castle being used again as a fortress. Despite Parliament's order in 1695 that compensation of £2,000 be paid to the Laird of Grant for the 'damnifying of the house of Urquhart and low buildings by several Souldiers of his Majesty's regular forces when they lay in Garrison there', no repair seems to have been made. In 1708 the castle was being plundered by the local inhabitants, and one wall of the N tower fell in 1715. After that the buildings were used as a quarry until 1912, when they were placed in the care of the Government.

The approach from the W is by a much restored rubble-built causeway over the ditch. The wooden bridge across its central

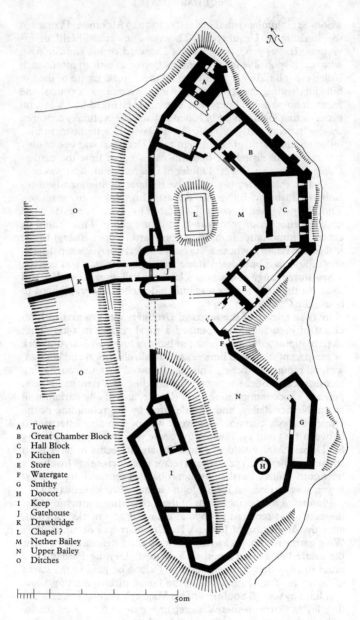

A   Tower
B   Great Chamber Block
C   Hall Block
D   Kitchen
E   Store
F   Watergate
G   Smithy
H   Doocot
I   Keep
J   Gatehouse
K   Drawbridge
L   Chapel ?
M   Nether Bailey
N   Upper Bailey
O   Ditches

50m

Urquhart Castle. Plan

gap is the C 20 replacement of a medieval drawbridge. This was worked from a wooden superstructure whose post-holes are still visible on the gap's E side, where the causeway is strengthened by sloping buttresses to counteract the stress of raising and lowering the bridge. E of the bridge, the causeway is slightly curved and has had stone parapets butting awkwardly against the castle's gatehouse.

The gatehouse itself, now reduced to its two lower storeys, is clearly the forework specified in the charter of 1509. It is of comparable size to the roughly contemporary NW tower of Holyroodhouse (Edinburgh) and the gatehouse of Falkland Palace (Fife). Like them its front has a pair of drum towers but here they are straight-sided bow-ended extensions of the main side walls and of the passage walls, not tenuously attached round corner towers. Round-arched entrance between the drum towers, with slots for a portcullis. Then a short passage to a second roundheaded arch, which has contained two pairs of doors, the first opening out, the second inwards. The passage continues as a tunnel-vault through the gatehouse into the courtyard. On each side of the passage, a tunnel-vaulted guardroom, the N entered from the passage's E end, the S from the courtyard. In the natural stone floor of the S guardroom has been cut a corn-drying kiln. In the N guardroom's N wall and c. 1.8m. above the ground, the entrance to a prison built in the inner angle of the gatehouse and curtain wall; garderobe vents in the prison's outer walls. On the gatehouse's first floor there are two rooms over the passage. The W room housed the portcullis. Its N wall's upper part is corbelled out, perhaps for a stair in the wall-thickness. In the E room, a small aumbry at the NW corner and a sizeable rectangular window to the courtyard. Above each guardroom is a single chamber. In the still partly vaulted S room, slit windows to the E and S, the latter with a garderobe in its embrasure; press in the N wall. The N room has an E fireplace and an aumbry in the S wall. Above the prison to its N, a large garderobe.

A wall from the gatehouse's S side has cut across the waist of the site's hourglass shape to divide it into two irregular courtyards. On the W side of the N courtyard (the Nether Bailey), a curtain wall contemporary with the gatehouse and pierced by three big rectangular slits. Immediately E of this curtain, a rocky knoll is topped by the foundations of a rectangular building, perhaps a C 14 chapel. Built end-on to the curtain's N end, and probably contemporary with it, is the surviving ground floor of a rectangular building, with a fireplace in each gable but lighted only from a small W window and the N door.

On the E side of the Nether Bailey a thick and heavily buttressed curtain wall is angled to the cliff-top overlooking the loch. This is probably late C 14, as are the buildings against it, which form a roughly U-plan range that seems to have comprised a trapezoidal store and kitchen block at the S, a rectangular hall block in the centre, and another trapezoidal block containing the great chamber and solar at the N. The windowless s store has an entrance only on the E side from the loch; perhaps it was used to house boat gear. The adjoining kitchen probably rose through two storeys. In its W wall to the courtyard, two windows and a door, whose chamfered jambs may date from a C16 remodelling. Inside, a stone fireplace-platform at the s end. In the N wall, a service door into the hall's undercroft, whose main entrance is from the courtyard. In the undercroft's E wall overlooking the loch, two pairs of slit windows with splayed ingoes, stepped sills and corbelled lintels. A scarcement has supported the floor of the hall above, which has had four E windows. Less survives of the undercroft of the great chamber to the N. In its SW corner, a triangular platform of masonry may mark the position of a stair. Joist holes show that the great chamber's floor was on a level with that of the hall. Outside the SE corner, a small semicircular platform on the curtain wall may have supported a beacon or a hoist. In the solar's basement, a N door and a small W window.

The inner N corners of the block built against the W curtain and the E range almost touch, the gap between allowing access to a small cobbled court in front of the tower on the site's N apex. This tower, the most nearly complete of the castle's buildings, has been built in three distinct stages, the basement probably in the late C14, the three main storeys above in the early C16, and the parapet and attic dating from an early C17 remodelling, probably part of the work for which the master mason *John Moray* contracted in 1623. It is rectangular (except for the SE corner, which is canted to fit the site) and is built of coursed rubble, the walls rising unbroken to the C17 wallhead, whose main parapet is carried on a stringcourse. At the NE, NW and SW corners, rectangular gabled turrets have been jettied out on corbels. The corbels carry across the short E wall with machicolation holes between them as a defence for the basement's postern gate. Much more forceful machicolation above the main W door, where four tall and boldly projecting moulded corbels have carried a platform. An additional defence at this entrance is provided by a small ditch over which a drawbridge gave access to the tower's segmental-arched doorway. Inside, the ground floor is occupied by a hall; in its s wall, a fireplace with moulded jambs. In the canted SE wall, a C16 rectangular window has been broken through the upper part of an older loophole; another sizeable window in the N wall. In the thickness of the E wall, two turnpike stairs side by side, one going down to the basement, the other up to the floors above. At the basement the down-stair debouches into a short wall-passage leading from the E postern to a store whose C14 W window's rear-arch voussoirs are partly masked by the tunnel-vault, introduced probably in the C16. In the first-floor room, big windows to the N, W and SE, but no evidence of a fireplace. The second-floor room has been vaulted. Big windows again, with a double shot-hole under the N; beside this window, a segmental-arched fireplace. In the NE and SW corners, vaulted wall-closets. Enough survives of the attic to show that each of its three turrets has contained a fireplace, a window with a shot-hole below, and a garderobe. In the thickness of the main walls under these turrets are wall-chambers made redundant by the early C17 remodelling.

In the castle's s courtyard (Upper Bailey) much less survives. Near the N end of its C16 E curtain wall, a watergate with a rough segmental arch. Fragmentary remains of a smithy near the NE corner. On a low hill to its W, the base of a round doocot. On the courtyard's highest point or motte at the SW, remains of a shell-keep, the walling looking C13. It is now almost featureless but appears to have had N and S towers.

WHITEBRIDGE *see* **FOYERS**

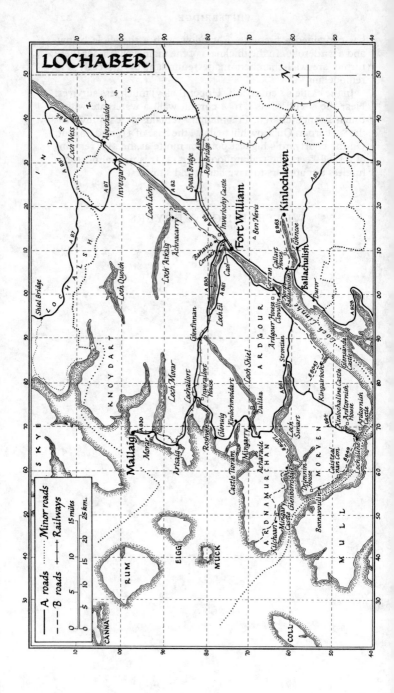

LOCHABER

Mountainous and little-populated district, deeply indented by sea lochs which made travel by water the easiest method of travel until relatively recently. Mallaig is a fishing port, Fort William a tourist centre, its views of Ben Nevis and Loch Linnhe distracting the eye from its architecture.

ABERCHALDER 3000

Place-name at the N end of Loch Oich.

BRIDGE OVER CALEDONIAN CANAL. Swing bridge, probably C20. – Beside it, an early C19 single-storey LOCK-KEEPER'S HOUSE.

BRIDGE OVER RIVER OICH. Built in 1930–2, with *Robert Bruce* as supervising engineer, *Blyth & Blyth* as consultant engineers, and *Mears & Carus-Wilson* as consultant architects. Concrete, with pointed arches and stepped triangular cutwaters.

SUSPENSION BRIDGE OVER RIVER OICH. By *James Dredge* of Bath, 1850. Double cantilever chain bridge with pedimented granite pylon arches at the ends.

ACHARA *see* DUROR

ACHARACLE 6060

Village at the W end of Loch Shiel.

FREE CHURCH. Dated 1878. Small and thrifty Gothic, with a birdcage bellcote to match.

PARISH CHURCH. Built in 1829–33 as a 'Parliamentary' church, i.e. to *William Thomson*'s design,* but varying Thomson's standard pattern by having large windows in both long elevations. Original diamond-pane glazing, with wooden mullions and transoms in the Tudor-arched windows; spikily pinnacled birdcage bellcote. E front of coursed granite rubble, the other elevations harled. The interior was recast *c.* 1930. – At the front of the graveyard, a castellated WAR MEMORIAL arch of *c.* 1920.

*Thomson was also the contractor here.

To the s, the MANSE of *c.* 1900, and to its s the white harled 'Parliamentary' manse of 1829–33, of the single-storey U-plan type designed probably by *James Smith*.

SHIEL BRIDGE. Built in 1899, carefully aping the late Georgian idiom of Thomas Telford and Joseph Mitchell. Three-span, with battlemented parapets and cutwaters. – Downstream, its early c 19 single-span predecessor.

ACHNACARRY

1080

Place-name denoting the neck of land separating Loch Arkaig from Loch Lochy.

ST KIARAN'S CHURCH. Rubbly Early Christian by *P. MacGregor Chalmers*, 1911. Four-bay nave and a slightly lower chancel, both with narrow pointed windows. Square w tower of three stages, all with round-arched openings, those at the top tall and two-light with polished ashlar mullions. Tall slated pyramid roof. Rubble-walled interior with a semicircular chancel arch and a wooden-ribbed tunnel-vault. – STAINED GLASS. War Memorial window of *c.* 1920. – One light by *Gordon Webster*, 1953. – Window in tower of 1931.

87 ACHNACARRY CASTLE. Castellated mansion by *James Gillespie Graham*, begun in 1802 and the shell finished soon after but not finally completed until 1835–7 under the direction of *Peter Manual*. Two storeys, seven bays by five. Parapet crenellated at the sides and rear, pierced by quatrefoils at the s front's outer bays. Angle rounds with crosslet 'arrow-slits' at the outer corners and the front's slightly advanced centrepiece, whose parapet has a wide central merlon flanked by broad crenelles. Ball-finialled and strapwork-pedimented door of 1835–7 flanked by very narrow windows with Gothick glazing; above, three round-arched windows, the outer two narrow, again with Gothick glazing. At the rear, a three-storey central bow. Hood-moulds over the upper windows. Single-storey battlemented wing of the late c 19 on the w.

ARDGOUR *see* CORRAN AND CLOVULLIN

ARDGOUR HOUSE

9060

2.1km. W of Corran

Plain Georgian mansion house of the MacLeans of Ardgour. The three-storey five-bay main block was built in 1765 by *John Menelaws* of 'Kirkmichael in Nether Coul' and *David Girdwood*, wright in Glasgow. It is harled, with rusticated quoins and a moulded eaves course. This house was gutted by fire in 1825, and an ensuing reconstruction and enlargement were carried

out by the builder-architect *Alexander Squair** in 1826–30.
Squair gave a blocking course to the centre of the main block,
remodelled the roof in piended form, and provided a balustraded Roman Doric portico. At the same time he added
two-storey wings to the gables, each piend-roofed and with
Tudor hoodmoulds over the front windows.

ARDNAMURCHAN *see* KILCHOAN

ARDTORNISH CASTLE   6040
2.2km. SE of Lochaline

Prominently sited but architecturally unrewarding stronghold of
the Lords of the Isles, placed on a steep promontory jutting
into the Sound of Mull.

The house, built on the summit of this naturally defensible
position, appears to be late C13, a rectangle *c.* 17.2m. by 8.8m.,
constructed of basalt blocks brought to rough courses by flat
pinnings. At the NW corner, a buttress-like garderobe projection. Door in the E wall; it is in the original position but dates
from a restoration of 1910–15. In the S wall, the sills of two
ground-floor slit windows. The segmental-arched first-floor
window is of 1910–15. Interior now filled with grass-covered
debris, but sockets in the long N and S walls suggest that the
upper floor was carried on wooden joists.

STEADING 0.6km. N, early C19, extended in 1846 by *James
Ross* to form a courtyard. Just missing formality, the W gables
of the N and S ranges respectively straight and piended. In the
E range's S gable, flightholes for pigeons. Segmental-arched
cartshed openings.

ARDTORNISH HOUSE   7040
3.8km. NE of Lochaline

Victorian mansion on a lushly planted hillside overlooking Loch
Aline, the bare hills of Morvern rising behind. A house was
built on the site in 1856–66 for Octavius Smith, who had bought
the Achranich estate in 1845. After his purchase of the adjoining
lands of Ardtornish from 1860 Smith decided to transfer the
name to his uncompleted new residence. In 1884 Smith's son
Valentine demolished almost all his father's building (a victim
of dry rot), except for its free-standing campanile, and a new
and larger mansion designed by *Alexander Ross* was built in
1885–91.

The campanile of 1856–66 stands higher up on the hillside
to the N. Italian Romanesque, built of whin with stugged sand-

*John Pender was the wright.

stone dressings. Four stages; the clock-face in the third stage
of the s front surrounded by a dogtooth moulding. At the top
stage, three-bay belfry arcades with louvres in the openings.
Tall slated pavilion roof added after 1885.

Ross's house, a suburban villa afflicted with elephantiasis, is
of fireproof construction, built entirely of concrete, the main w
(entrance) and s (garden) fronts faced with narrow sandstone
ashlars, the rest rendered. Rough T-plan, with the tail projecting
N. On this jamb's w front, a loggia of four-centred arches
retained from the earlier house but extended from three bays
to four and given an upper storey and attic. To the l., a pend
arch to the service court behind; above the pend, a hoodmoulded three-light window. The principal rooms are all,
except the billiard room, in the crossbar. Wrapped round its
NW, W and s faces is a glass-roofed verandah. Cast-iron columns
with chevrons round the shafts and tall but soggy acanthus
capitals bearing individual entablatures, their soffits decorated
with rosettes. On the s front, a couple of towers, neither
especially martial. The l., in the w inner angle of the projecting
centrepiece, is narrow, its top floor jettied out on a continuous
corbel course; tall slated pavilion roof with bellcast eaves. Much
bigger tower over the dining room at the centrepiece's E end.
Five storeys, with hoodmoulded windows at the upper floors. In
the jettied top stage, a row of five small windows. On the l. side
of the bellcast pavilion roof, a big chimneystack decorated, like
the other stacks, with Lombardic detail. NE of the house is the
service court, its back wall a segmental curve of concrete offices.

The internal plan is Ross's but most of the decoration was
provided in a remodelling of 1908–10 by *John Kinross*, his
designs executed by *Scott Morton & Co.* and *Morison & Co.*
Ross's finishings had been neo-Jacobean. They partly survive in
the Stairhall's blind-arcaded walls and foliage-capitalled granite
columns. The rest is by Kinross, an eclectic introduction to his
other interiors, all carried out in very best Grand Hotel manner.
Elaborately carved stair balustrade in the style of *c.* 1700 (e.g.
as at Hamilton Palace). Adam-revival cornices and plasterwork
on the beams of the trabeated ceilings. Mid-C18 style doorcases,
pedimented when giving access to the principal rooms. On the
ground floor, w of the Stairhall, is the Library, decorated in the
manner of *c.* 1760, the radiators placed in white marble cases
with grille fronts just like those Kinross provided at Manderston
(Borders) a few years before. The s front's centrepiece is filled
by the Drawing Room and Dining Room. The Drawing Room
is a consistent evocation of the manner of *c.* 1700 (e.g. as at
Melville House, Fife). Panelled with carved Grinling-Gibbonsish reliefs of foliage and musical instruments. Foliaged
plasterwork on the ceiling beams. Simple veined marble chimneypiece. In the Dining Room to the E the ceiling's late-C18-
style decoration is clearly by Kinross, but the Jacobean chimneypiece looks a left-over bit of Ross's work. Study at the SE
corner, a reversion to Kinross's manner of *c.* 1700.

On the first floor, the main suite of principal bedroom, dressing room and boudoir is above the dining room and drawing room. Kinross gave the Boudoir a ceiling decorated with reliefs of goddesses in oval compartments. Marble walls and floors in the Bathrooms. Billiard Room at the jamb's NW corner. Kinross transformed it from hammerbeam-roofed Baronial to swishest Adam-revival, with alcoved ends. Lights over the table, their shades helds by rams' heads.

Luxuriant GARDEN, well stocked with species rhododendrons and midges. – KITCHEN GARDEN to the W, its late C19 walls partly of concrete and partly of brick. – On its S side, a broad-eaved concrete COTTAGE designed by *Samuel Barham*, the estate clerk of works, in 1874. – To the SE, the concrete-built ACHRANICH (ARDTORNISH ESTATE OFFICE) by *Barham*, 1880. Broad eaves and bargeboarded gables; consoled canopy shading the ground-floor windows. – Concrete POWER HOUSE, probably early C20, to its E, the interior tiled, the turbines in working order. – Then, beside the Rannoch River, a big WOOL STORE dated 1851, with bracketed eaves and Gothic upper windows lighting accommodation for farm servants; a lean-to on the N has been demolished. – The store is connected by a concrete link to the COACHHOUSE (by *Samuel Barham*, 1871), its detail similar to that of the wool store but simpler and more sparing. Again it is of concrete, perhaps the first such building in Scotland. – Across the road to the SW, an M-roofed late Victorian concrete byre, its gables partly glazed under louvres. – The road crosses the river by a humpbacked rubble BRIDGE, perhaps of *c.* 1850. – Beside the river, RIVERSIDE, another example of *Barham*'s broad-eaved concrete estate architecture, built in 1894–5.

On the shore of Loch Aline S of the mansion house, first the broad-eaved OLD BOATHOUSE built of rough ashlar in 1852–3. T-plan with Gothic windows and a pointed-arch boat entrance. It was too high up the loch for its purpose and was superseded later in the C19 by the BOATHOUSE to the S, built of basalt blocks and again with broad eaves.

W of the mansion house, BRIDGE over the River Aline, slightly humpbacked, of two unequal arches, by *Alexander Ross*, 1888. It leads to Kinlochaline Castle (*see* p. 251) and CASTLE COTTAGES on the lochside, by *Barham*, 1873, with his characteristic concrete walls and broad eaves. – At LARACHBEG, beside the main road to the NW, a two-storey terrace of six estate workers' concrete houses (by *Barham*, 1875). Carved bargeboards; consoled canopy above the ground-floor windows. To their N, a contemporary twin-gabled LAUNDRY, its fittings intact.

ARISAIG

One-sided street of vernacular C19 housing ending in an hotel along the shore of Loch nan Ceall; C20 houses behind.

FREE CHURCH. Now a house. Built in 1879–80; its corbelled bellcote has been reduced to a stump.

PARISH CHURCH. Built as a Roman Catholic chapel in 1810–11; the architect was *James Gillespie Graham*. Very simple, with wooden Y-tracery in the pointed windows; wooden bellcote on the W gable and a deep S porch.

ST MARY'S CHURCH (R.C.), 0.4km. N. By *William Burn*, 1849. Very tall buttressed and lanceted nave and chancel poking into the steep hillside at the E. Battlemented W tower. Inside, a braced coved wooden ceiling over the unaisled nave. Tall pointed arch into the narrow chancel. – STAINED GLASS. Three-light E window (the Crucifixion), after 1900.

In the graveyard to the S, roofless remains of ST MAEL-RUBHA'S CHURCH, built, according to *The Book of Clanranald*, by John Moydartach, Captain of Clanranald, †1574. The church itself is a rubble-built rectangle, *c.* 15.2m. long and 7.5m. broad, its E gable rebuilt to a low height in the C19. Near the E end of the N and S walls, but at different heights and not immediately facing each other, rectangular slit windows with deeply splayed ingoes. Door in the S wall. The W wall is pierced by a window from the small (*c.* 4.8m. by 4.5m.) W chapel adjoining. In each of its S and W walls, a small slit window with a deep splayed ingo. Below the S window is a round hole serving a rectangular recess inside; perhaps it was a drain of some sort. Beside it, a low rectangular doorway under a semicircular relieving arch.

Inside the chapel, opposite the door, a round-arched TOMB RECESS, presumably C16. Set into its back, a stone carved very crudely with impaled arms (the dexter those of Macdonald), initials and the date 1641 or 1671. – Above, a MONUMENT, probably late C17, its four panels divided by attached columns decorated with spirals of stylized foliage. – Inside the church have been placed C15 GRAVESLABS, one carved with two panels divided by a sword, the l. showing the Crucifixion, the r. the figure of a bishop. – Another has a foliaged cross at the top; below, a sword placed in a border of foliage growing from the tail of a dog. – The upper half of a third survives, its top panel carved with a foliaged cross, the remaining part below with a sword and a hunting scene. – Fragment carved with a human figure above a hind and hound. – On the church's N window sill, a hollowed stone, perhaps a FONT.

ASTLEY HALL. Elegant box, by *Philip Webb*, 1893. Weather-boarded walls on a rubble plinth; tall slated piend roof. Lower NW wing (originally the Club Room) added by *George Jack* in 1910, with a straight N gable and flat-topped dormers.

BORRODALE BURN RAILWAY VIADUCT, 3.5km. E. By *Simpson & Wilson*, 1897–1901. Central arch of mass-concrete, its 38.9m. span the largest in the world when built; a rubble-faced arch at each end. Crenellated parapets.

ARISAIG HOUSE
3.4km. SE

Tame Arts and Crafts manor house by *I. B. M. Hamilton & Orphoot, Whiting & Lindsay*, 1936–7, incorporating much of the structure, but little of the architecture, of a house designed by *Philip Webb* which had been built here in 1863–4 and was burnt out in 1935. Webb's house, later dismissed by him as 'a product of his ignorance', was in the manner of G. E. Street's parsonages, picturesquely composed with prominent and sturdy chimneys, a wealth of gables and gablets, and a few ecclesiastical touches. Its surviving and little-altered SE (kitchen) wing is austere, with a pair of colliding gables on the N elevation and a huge chimneystack at the E end. The rest of the house is a 1930s interpretation of a gentleman's house in the Cotswolds but of grey not honey-coloured stone. Webb's Gothic windows survive on the E (entrance) front, as does his clocktower (but lopped and given an ogee roof) beside the pend to the NE service court. The house's size was reduced by the removal of Webb's w-facing drawing room and business room, and this garden front is now a demure L-plan with the former library (now drawing room) projecting as a SW jamb. Interior all of the 1930s. Main stair with a neo-Caroline balustrade. Simple groin vaulting in the drawing room.

WALLED GARDEN of the 1860s to the SE. Triangular buttresses along the N wall. On the E, a range of wooden sheds with simple arched openings; at its S end, house with a jettied attic.

FARMS ETC.

BORRODALE FARM, 3.7km. SE. Long white harled late Georgian farmhouse of two storeys. Its attic's stone-fronted piend-roofed dormers and the ground-floor outshots might be additions of 1864 but look more like work of *c.* 1900. – L-plan STEADING by *Philip Webb*, 1864. High main range, its roof replaced after a fire in 1981. In each of the E and W gables' ashlar tops, a pair of loft openings under an ogee hoodmould. Low SE jamb, with a S pend whose head is made up of a pair of stone corbels supporting a rectangular stone opening containing a semi-circular wooden arch.

KEPPOCH HOUSE, 0.3km. NW. Unassuming mansion house of *c.* 1800. Two-storey main block; single-storey wings, the r. (originally a byre) longer than the l.

BALLACHULISH 0050

Village, now mostly composed of C20 council housing, which developed to serve the slate quarries first opened *c.* 1693 and finally closed in 1955.

BALLACHULISH UNITED FREE CHURCH. A thrifty Gothic box built as Ballachulish South Free Church in 1874.

St John's Church (Episcopal), 1.2km. w. Stark granite-built cruciform, the bellcoted nave and transepts put up in 1842, the low chancel added by *David Mackintosh*, 1888, in the same lanceted style. – The gilded and painted oak and walnut ALTAR and REREDOS inside were designed by *J. W. M. Wedderburn*, 1888.

St Mun's Church (R.C.). Built in 1836; the mason was *William Gray*. Simple rectangle with big lancet windows; small obelisk pinnacles on the corner buttresses.

St Munda Glencoe Parish Church. Opened as a mission church in 1845 and then a plain Georgian box with Tudor-arched windows. In 1881 the NE transept and battlemented E tower were added. w hall of 1935. The interior looks mostly of 1881, with a scissors roof and E gallery.

Ballachulish Hotel, South Ballachulish, 3.2km. NW. By *John Honeyman*, 1877. Strong Gothic villa with ecclesiastical detail and conical-roofed tourelles.

BANAVIE *see* CORPACH, BANAVIE AND CAOL

5050   BONNAVOULIN

Small settlement overlooking the Sound of Mull.

Fernish Church, 1.3km. s. Small and unexciting but quite dramatically sited above the road; built in 1892. Three stepped lancets in the bellcoted w gable; paired lancets in the side walls. sw porch. Low vestry to the E.

St Columba's Church (R.C.), 1.7km. NW. Disused. Built and designed by the Edinburgh wright-architect *James Anderson*, 1838, on the site of Drimnin Castle overlooking the Sound of Mull. Harled box with an E tower. Forceful detail. Crowstepped gables and battlemented parapets, the tower's rising above a corbelled blocking course. Rusticated quoins at the corners and at the round-arched windows and door; big bullseye in the tower's top stage.

Drimnin House. *See* p. 235.

5040   CAISTEAL NAN CON
                      5.5km. SE of Bonnavoulin

Grandly sited ruin of a late C17 house standing on top of a promontory, the site of a prehistoric fort, overlooking the Sound of Mull. The fort had an outer wall, now very fragmentary, across the w neck of the promontory and continuing along a natural low crest on the N. Inside this the ground rises steeply to form a knoll, whose summit was defended by a second wall, which survives on the w side as a low stony bank; two massive blocks were probably the jambs of its gateway.

The house, on the knoll's N side, may have been built for Ewan MacLean, who is recorded as tacksman of the lands of Killundine in the 1670s. The first impression, heightened by the rubbly cragginess of what remains, is of a very defensive structure, but the only martial detail is a pistol hole on the first floor of the stairtower (now mostly demolished). The S gable still stands, as do quite a lot of the E and W walls, the bottom of the N gable, and the first steps of the stair. It has been a long, roughly rectangular three-storey block, with the bowed stairtower projecting towards the W wall's S end, its off-centre position balanced by that of the door to its N. Inside, the ground floor's small N room, probably a store, has deep-splayed windows in the gable and E wall. The big centre room has no fireplace and was perhaps originally divided into stores and a passage. S room with a fireplace in the gable and an aumbry to its r. The S rooms on the upper floors have each been entered from the stair but with no door directly from them to the rest of the house. In each, a fireplace. The second-floor room's windows have been carried up into dormerheads.

At the house's NE corner, remains of a wall, presumably a barmkin.

CALLART HOUSE   0060
3.9km. E of North Ballachulish

Laird's house of two storeys and five bays built for Sir Duncan Cameron of Fassifern in 1835–7. *William Fraser* was the mason and *William Cameron* the wright. Roman Doric columned door-piece; rusticated quoins. Recessed wings, probably also of the 1830s. Long two-storey SE addition of *c.* 1900 in a joyless seaside villa manner.

CANNA   2000

Small island, partly quite rocky and hilly, although nowhere very high; now the property of the National Trust for Scotland.

CHURCH OF ST EDWARD THE CONFESSOR (R.C.), Sanday. Disused. Designed by *William Frame* and built by the Marchioness of Bute as a memorial to her father, Lord Howard of Glossop, 1886–90. Boxy nave and chancel. Small roundheaded windows, the three in the W gable under a rose window. Saddleback-roofed S tower with a two-stage belfry. N porch. Inside, a neo-Romanesque chancel arch; bandcourse round the nave carved by *Thomas Nicholls* with the heads of knights, priests and acolytes.

CHURCH OF SCOTLAND. By *P. MacGregor Chalmers*, 1912–14. Beautifully simple lancet-windowed rubble rectangle. Pencil-like W tower of Brechin Cathedral type. Inside, a pointed tunnel-vault.

CANNA HOUSE. Georgian-survival of *c.* 1865. Shallowly pedimented front with canted bay windows and a parapeted porch.
COROGHAN CASTLE. On the top of a rock stack, reached by a
very steep path. Rubbly remains of a roughly rectangular small
tower, probably of the C17.
CROSS, A'CHILL. Worn shaft and one arm of a cross, perhaps of
the C8 or C9, the W face carved with intertwined figures and a
panel of key pattern, the E more robustly with figures including
animals, a horseman and perhaps the Holy Family.

CAOL *see* CORPACH, BANAVIE AND CAOL

6070   CASTLE TIORAM
                             4.3km. N of Acharacle

63 Lonely ruin of the C13 castle built for the Lords of the Isles, from
whom it passed to the Macdonalds of Clanranald in 1493. The
site is a rocky island in Loch Moidart joined to the shore by a
sand spit at low tide. The castle on this island-promontory's
highest point is an enclosure whose curtain walls, *c.* 2.4m. thick
and now 9.1m. high, form an irregular heptagon with rounded
external corners. The masonry is of random rubble brought to
courses by flat pinnings. Under the battlement, holes with
projecting spouts to drain the wall-walk. The parapets themselves have slit-like crenelles like those in the C16 battlement
at Mingary Castle (*see* p. 257) and putlock holes for a wooden
hoarding; presumably they were reconstructed in the early C16,
although they are innocent of gun- or musket-loops. The main
entrance is a crude arch in the N wall. Above it, the remains of
a corbelled stone bretasche. Near the E wall's S end, a postern
gate (built up), originally reached by a wooden stair whose
landing is represented by the stumps of beams in the wall.
Patched masonry above may indicate the former position of a
bretasche. A second postern (also now blocked) in the S wall
may be the E gate's later replacement.
   The courtyard inside the enclosure rises irregularly from N
to S. In the long W wall, a stone stair which returns to the N to
give access to the wall-walk.
   Built against the N two-thirds of the courtyard's SE wall is a
keep, perhaps of the C14. It is a plain rubble-built rectangle,
probably originally of three storeys, the jettied third floor and
attic possibly added in the C16. Ground-floor door from the
courtyard into a vaulted cellar. The segmental-arched main
door is on the first floor, formerly reached by a wooden stair
and defended by a stone bretasche. On the first floor, a hall
with a fireplace in the S gable; in the thickness of the N wall, a
garderobe whose E end is hollowed out of the curtain wall. At
the NW corner and also in the wall-thickness, a turnpike stair
to the floors above. One room on each of the two upper floors,

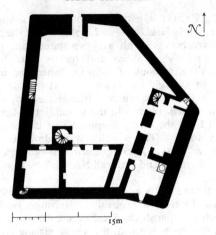

Castle Tioram. Plan.
(Redrawn from MacGibbon and Ross, *The Castellated and Domestic Architecture of Scotland*, ii, 1887)

both with fireplaces, the second-floor room having also a garderobe in the N wall.

The s range may also have been begun in the c 14. It seems originally to have been of two storeys with an attic. At its E end, a tunnel-vaulted passage to the s postern. In the w ground-floor room, a slop sink, so this may have been a kitchen when the range was first built. At the sw corner, a tight turnpike stair, probably a c 13 access to the wall-walk but converted to a service stair for this building. This range's w end was given a further two floors, *c.* 1600; corbelled round turrets with cannon-spouts at the SE, SW and NE corners, a gabled stairtower at the NE. The big segmental-arched windows in the tower's s front and in the range to its E probably all date from the remodelling of *c.* 1600. In the castle's SE corner between the E and s ranges, a two-storey building. Its ground-floor room has a well in the w wall and an oven in the NE corner.

CILLE CHOIRILL *see* ROY BRIDGE

CLOVULLIN *see* CORRAN AND CLOVULLIN

CORPACH, BANAVIE AND CAOL

0070

Just a few buildings beside the Caledonian Canal until the late c 20, when Caol was developed as a suburb of Fort William and a pulp and paper mill was built at the w end of Corpach.

KILMALLIE PARISH CHURCH, N of the A830. Simple harled
rectangle by *Archibald McPhail*, 1781–3. On the W gable, a
tall birdcage bellcote with a crown-spired top. The roundheaded windows' mullions and tracery date from *David
Mackintosh*'s alterations of 1889–90, when the interior was
recast. – Brass eagle LECTERN. – STAINED GLASS. In the
W gable, a three-light window (the Resurrection) by *James
Ballantine & Son*, 1890. – In the N wall, a two-light narrative
window ('I am the Good Shepherd') by the *St Enoch Glass
Works*, c. 1935. – The S wall's W window depicts flowers
and fruit, c. 1895. – Accomplished two-light window to its
E ('Go ye therefore and teach all Nations') by *Gordon Webster*,
1952.

In the GRAVEYARD to the W, BURIAL ENCLOSURE of the
Camerons of Fassifern, probably a surviving N jamb or chapel
of the early C16 parish church. Rectangular windows in the N
and W walls, the W blocked, the N with glazing grooves. Late
Georgian roundheaded S doorway. On the enclosure's W wall,
a well-lettered slate TABLET to Colonel John Cameron of Fassifern † 1815.

S of the church, a big sandstone OBELISK also commemorating Colonel John Cameron † 1815, the inscription
recording that

> During twenty years of active military service
> With a spirit which knew no fear and sham'd no danger
> He accompanied or led
> In marches in sieges in battles
> The gallant Ninety Second Regiment of Scottish Highlanders
> Always to Honour almost always to Victory . . .

ST JOHN'S CHURCH (R.C.), St John's Road, Caol. By *Charles
W. Gray & Partners*, 1970. Octagonal, the felt roof having a
broad gable over each wall-face, the ridges meeting at a central
cross.

BANAVIE PRIMARY SCHOOL, S of the A830. By *Inverness County
Council*, 1965.

CAOL PRIMARY SCHOOL, Glenkingie Street, Caol. By *Inverness
County Council*, 1954.

CALEDONIAN CANAL. Corpach is the W end of *Thomas Telford*'s
canal. CORPACH LOCKS at the entrance from Loch Linnhe
were built in 1804–6. On the N pier, contemporary harled
LOCK-KEEPERS' HOUSES and a round LIGHTHOUSE. –
At Banavie, 1.7km. E, a massive bow-truss SWING BRIDGE
by *Simpson & Wilson*, 1901, carrying the railway to Mallaig
over the canal. Beside it another swing bridge, of the usual
Caledonian Canal type, for the main road. – Immediately NE,
NEPTUNE'S STAIRCASE, a ladder of eight locks built in
1807–11.

CORPACH PAPER MILL, S of the A830. By *Dennis Ramsbottom*
of *W. S. Atkins & Partners*, 1963–6. Built as a pulp and paper
mill; the pulping activity was abandoned in 1980. Buildings
covered in aluminium sheeting above a black brick base.

CORRAN AND CLOVULLIN 0060

Two hamlets, Corran with a harled hotel at the w end of the ferry across the pinch-point of Loch Linnhe, and Clovullin 1.4km. to the w.

ARDGOUR PARISH CHURCH, Corran. A 'Parliamentary' church (i.e. to *William Thomson*'s design), with Tudor-arched windows and a spikily pinnacled birdcage bellcote. It was built by *John Davidson* and *Thomas Macfarlane* in 1829. The doors have been blocked and a castellated porch added at the E end. – Inside, ELDERS' STALLS, PULPIT and COMMUNION TABLE of 1931, stylized Jacobean with some Lorimerian touches. – Late C19 STAINED GLASS in the W window, showing flowers within abstract borders.

ARDGOUR MEMORIAL HALL, Clovullin. Dated 1932; harled.

CORRAN LIGHTHOUSE. By *D. & T. Stevenson*, 1860. Short round tower with a cupola. – Contemporary white painted two-storey KEEPERS' HOUSES. – Adjoining, a mid-C19 crow-stepped brick STORE.

SCHOOL, Clovullin. Later C19, broad-eaved, like a small alms-house.

ARDGOUR HOUSE. *See* p. 224.

DALILEA 7060
4.8km. E of Mingarry

Small three-bay harled mansion house built for Alexander Mac-donald, tacksman of Dalilea, *c.* 1800, the back block probably part of a previous house on the site. The front's present appear-ance dates from the alterations made in 1907 for Lord Howard of Glossop, who added the top floor, enlivened with a pair of crowstepped gablets and corner turrets; crowstepped porch of the same date.

DRIMNIN HOUSE 5050
1.5km. N of Bonnavoulin

Gawky Elizabethan manor built in the 1850s for Sir Charles Gordon and probably incorporating walling of the previous house on the site, which was destroyed by fire in 1849. Two-storey-and-attic, five-bay W front, all rendered. At the corners, little square bartizans topped by spiky finialled urns. In the centre, the Gordon coat of arms above a battlemented porch. The second and fourth bays have shaped gablets rising above the crenellated parapet. At the second bay, a two-storey canted bay window. Surprisingly there is no matching projection at the fourth bay, whose two-light windows are disconcertingly off-centre in relation to the gablet above.

The interior has been opulent and still retains much of its original decoration. Engraved glass doors from the porch to the hall. The walls of the hall, the stair beyond, and the first-floor landing are all painted in imitation of large slabs of yellow marble, each 'slab' a just perceptibly different shade from those of its neighbours. Cornice studded with identical female heads. Between the hall and the stair, a screen of Corinthian columns, their scagliola shafts darker than the walls' marbling. Painted glass (the paint now fragmentary) in the stair window. On the ground floor, dining room to the l. of the hall, severely masculine, with a black marble chimneypiece and heavy cornice. Breakfast room beyond. On the hall's r., library with a vine cornice. On the first floor, interconnecting drawing rooms above the dining room and breakfast room and their feminine counterpart. Walls decorated with painted panels, the lines sprouting foliage at the upper corners. Ceiling plasterwork picked out in white and gold.

OFFICES to the N, probably contemporary, with a spired square tower at their SW corner.

MONUMENT to Allan McLean of Drimnin † 1792, on a hill 0.4km. NW. Plain classical reredos in a small enclosure.

For St Columba's R.C. Church, *see* Bonnavoulin.

9050   DUROR

Just an inn and two churches.

DUROR CHURCH. Rubble-built T-plan 'Parliamentary' church (i.e. to *William Thomson*'s design), completed by *J. Gibb* and *W. Minto* in 1827. Spikily pinnacled bellcote on the S gable, which deviates from the standard plan by being windowless. The other walls' windows are of the usual Tudor-arched type with lattice glazing. Interior now without a gallery and with Victorian furnishings. – To the E, contemporary single-storey MANSE (i.e. probably designed by *James Smith*). Its back wings have been enlarged and bay windows added to the front.

ST ADAMNAN'S CHURCH (Episcopal). The three-bay nave was built in 1848. Plain, with lancet windows; on the S gable, a birdcage bellcote whose obtusely pointed openings only hint at Gothic. *Donald Rankine*, the incumbent, designed the small S porch in 1871. The crowstep-gabled chancel was added by *Eden & Hodgson* of London in 1911. Rubble-built like the nave, but narrower and lower. Two-light E window. The N (liturgical E) window is of three lights under a loop-traceried top.

Inside, a boarded wagon roof over the nave, wooden tunnel-vault in the chancel. – Granite PULPIT of 1911 integral with the W jamb of the chancel arch. – CHAMBER ORGAN, said to be of c. 1730 and to have come from Germany, the case decorated with painted foliage. – STAINED GLASS. The N (liturgical E) window (Our Lady, St Patrick and St Columba) is of 1919 by *J. Ninian Comper*, with characteristic strong blues. – The chancel's E window (SS. Adamnan and Brigitta) of 1929 also looks like Comper's work. – More routine the nave's SE window (the Good Shepherd) signed by *Abbot & Co. Ltd* of Lancaster, *c.* 1920.

ACHARA, 0.9km. SW. Cream harled laird's house of the mid-C19, reconstructed *c.* 1900. Main front of three storeys and four bays, the windows grouped 2/2, those on the second floor rising into shaped and triangular-pedimented dormerheads; bay window on the l. Pepperpot turrets at the corners.

STANDING STONE, 180m. NW. Tall (3.7m. high) and tapering to a pointed top.

EIGG

4080

Island with two conspicuous hills separated and surrounded by flat land. It was cleared of many of its inhabitants in the C19.

CHURCH OF SCOTLAND. Lanceted rubble box of 1862.

OLD ST DONNAN'S CHURCH, Kildonnan. Roofless remains of a simple kirk said to have been built by John Moydartach, Captain of Clanranald, shortly before his death in 1574. Rubble-built, with small rectangular windows. Inside, at the N wall a segmental-arched tomb recess; it contains a panel carved with a coat of arms, the date 1641 and the initials $D^M R$.

In the graveyard, a tall slate CROSS SHAFT of the C14 or C15, its faces carved with scrollwork vine patterns stemming from opposed animals, the motifs taken from pattern books of the Iona school of carvers.

To the NW, harled OLD MANSE of 1790, its side wings probably additions of 1889.

ST DONNAN'S CHURCH (R.C.), Cleadale. Built in 1910. Modest, with a gableted bellcote.

THE LODGE, Galmisdale. By *Mauchlen & Weightman* of Newcastle, 1926–7. White harled neo-Georgian with a gentle Cape Dutch inflexion. At the two-storey main block, a recessed centre providing a ground-floor loggia and first-floor sleeping balcony.

FORT WILLIAM

1070

Town at the SW end of the Great Glen, squeezed between steep hills and Loch Linnhe. The right to found a burgh of barony here was granted in 1618 to the Marquess of Huntly, who called it Gordonburgh after his family name. In 1654 a Cromwellian fort was built, and when this was reconstructed as Fort William in 1690 the adjoining settlement was renamed Maryburgh in honour of Mary II. The burgh was largely destroyed during the Jacobite rising of 1745–6, and, despite the subsequent rebuilding, Bishop Pococke found it 'a very poor town' when he visited in 1760. In 1834 the superiority over the burgh was acquired by Sir Duncan Cameron of Fassifern, who tried unsuccessfully to get it known as Duncansburgh, a name which has stuck only to the parish church. The C19 brought modest prosperity as a local centre, marked by the town becoming a police burgh under the name of

Fort William in 1874, but a railway link to the s was not opened for
another twenty years. In 1928 operations began at the aluminium
works, still the burgh's single biggest source of employment. In
summer Fort William is filled with tourists, through-traffic being
carried on the road begun in 1973 between the town and the loch,
its siting a topographical necessity but destroying any chance of
a happy holiday atmosphere.

CHURCHES

45 CHURCH OF THE IMMACULATE CONCEPTION (R.C.), Belford
Road. Massive Early Christian edifice, by *Reginald Fairlie*, 1933–
4. Nave of well-pinned squared grey granite blocks, a plain box
with round-arched windows; triangular dormer ventilators on
the roof. At the N end, the narrower chancel is covered by a
strong tower of pink and grey granite, its walls rising sheer to
the sloping parapet; the lines of its side walls are carried on by
big stepped buttresses at the N corners. Giant roundheaded
overarches containing the tall rectangular side windows, their
tops filled with late Gothic tracery, and the belfry openings
above. In the SW inner angle of the tower and nave, a copper-
roofed octagonal stair turret.

46   The strength and simplicity continue inside. Over the plaster-
walled nave, a concrete ribbed tunnel-vault. Small apsidal SW
baptistery. At the NE, a two-bay arcade of fat columns, their
capitals carved with Celtic motifs and carrying roundheaded
chamfered arches, opens into the Lady Chapel, whose flat
ceiling is panelled in wood. At the nave's N end, a semicircular
chancel arch, its attached columns' capitals again carved with
Celtic work. Chancel walls of ashlar with tall blind roundheaded
arches containing painted figures of saints standing on corbels;
beamed wooden ceiling. – In the chancel, a huge black and
gold wrought-iron BALDACCHINO with a big squat spire, by
Thomas Bogie. – In the Lady Chapel, a gently Lorimerian oak
REREDOS. – ORGAN by *Griffen & Stroud*.

DUNCANSBURGH PARISH CHURCH, The Parade. By *Ross &
Mackintosh*, 1881. Big Dec box with shallow transepts at the E
end. NW tower of three inset stages; at the top stage, large
pointed-arch belfry openings with well-foliaged capitals. Inside,
a braced kingpost roof, the braces diagonally set over the crossing. The focus is on the ORGAN, by *Forster & Andrews*, 1906. –
STAINED GLASS. Rose window in the E gable (the Last Supper),
brightly coloured expressionist, by *A. Carrick Whalen*, 1969. –
In the N wall, two lights ('Suffer Little Children to Come Unto
Me'; Ruth) by *Whalen*, 1976 and 1973. – More conventionally
realistic War Memorial window (a Christian Knight and the
Archangel Raphael) by the *Abbey Studio*, 1949. – In the S wall,
another window (Our Lord Bearing His Cross) by *Whalen*,
1979. – Two narrative windows (Our Lord and Nathaniel; Our
Lord and the Centurion), unattributed but by the same artist,
both apparently of 1882.

FREE CHURCH, High Street. Put up in 1846, an unpretentious

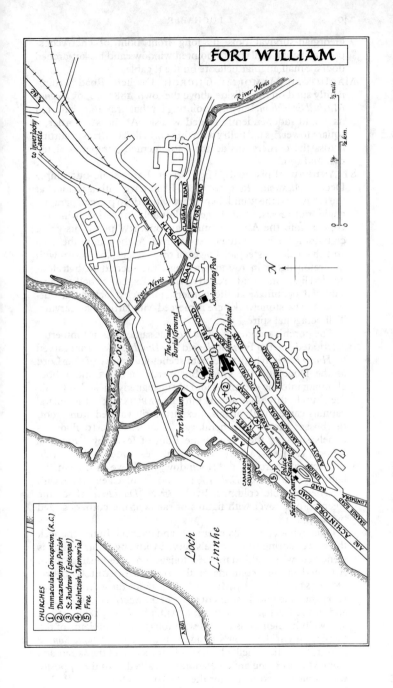

FORT WILLIAM

to Inverlochy Castle

River Nevis

River Nevis

River Lochy

NORTH ROAD

CLAGGAN ROAD

BELFORD ROAD

Swimming Pool

The Craigs Burial Ground

BELFORD ROAD

Station ①

Belford Hospital

Fort William

FREE PRESS ROAD

VICTORIA ROAD

② +

③

KENNEDY ROAD

CAMERON ROAD

ABRACH ROAD

HIGH

A 82

ARGYLL

UNION ROAD

Police Station

⑤ +

④ +

A 82 ACHINTORE ROAD

CAMERON SQUARE

Sheriff Court

GRANGE ROAD

LUNDAVRA ROAD

Loch Linnhe

A 861

½ mile

½ km.

N

CHURCHES
① Immaculate Conception (R.C.)
② Duncansburgh Parish
③ St. Andrew (Episcopal)
④ Macintosh Memorial
⑤ Free

Georgian-survival box, its long front built of cherrycock-pointed rough ashlar with pointed windows and basket-arched doors. Small angular bellcote on the N gable.

MACINTOSH MEMORIAL CHURCH, Fassifern Road. Prominently sited on the hillside above the town. 1887–90, by *Sydney Mitchell & Wilson*, but disappointing for that firm. Bare lanceted nave and independently roofed W aisle. At the SW corner, a square tower, its tall belfry with thin corbelled buttresses cutting across the corners; inside the battlemented parapet, a slated pyramid roof.

ST ANDREW (Episcopal), High Street. Large-scale but simple Dec, by *Alexander Ross*, 1879–84. Plain nave with a chancel at the E.* Across the W end, baptistery with a deep pierced parapet, angle buttresses, and large elaborately traceried windows copied from the Abbey Church at Iona. NW porch, its gable containing a stone statue of St Andrew. At the join of the nave and chancel, a N steeple. Tower of three stages, the lowest with quatrefoil lights in round openings, the second with trefoil-headed lights in round-arched openings. Expensive belfry stage: gabled openings; at the corners, pinnacled octagonal buttresses. The stonework here is pierced with lattice-like carving. Tall octagonal spire.

The porch's wooden DOORS ('of the same class as Ghiberti's celebrated gates at Florence', said *The Building News*) are carved by *Harry Hems* in high relief with scenes illustrative of Our Lord as the Door and the Good Shepherd, the thief and robber climbing into the sheepfold looking engagingly wicked. – Inside the church, three-bay arcade into the BAPTISTERY, the pillars' capitals carved with angels. Sexpartite rib-vaulted stone roof, the bosses carved with heraldry. – Marble MOSAIC floor, its panels showing the Tree of the Root of Jesse, by *Salviati* of Venice, 1884. – STAINED GLASS (the Beatitudes in the W wall, the Acts of Mercy in the N window, the Dove in the small S light) by *Clayton & Bell*, 1884. – FONT of Caen stone with attached marble columns, by *D. & A. Davidson*, 1880, the steepled oak cover with figures of saints at the corners added by *Hems* in 1884.

Open wooden ROOFS over nave and chancel. In the chancel, the braces spring from corbels carved with angels; its ceiling is stencilled with gold stars and foliage on a reddish ground. Attached granite columns at the stone CHANCEL ARCH. – ENCAUSTIC TILES by *Minton & Co.*, 1880, those in the sanctuary showing Old Testament types of the Sacrifice of Our Lord and of the Eucharist. – CHOIR STALLS by *Hems*, 1880, of oak and walnut, their ends carved with foliage and emblems of the Passion. – On the choir's N side, ORGAN by *Bryceson, Son & Ellis*, 1880, with stencilled pipes. – In the S wall of the sanctuary, stone SEDILIA, the arches elaborately carved. – In the opposite wall, a big arched recess for the BISHOP'S THRONE. – Rather low ALTAR of Caen stone: three roundheaded blind arches with

*Really NE, but E for convenience and in keeping with liturgical convention.

green Connemara marble shafts and 'ballflower' embellishment enclosing reliefs of the *Agnus Dei*, saltire and Pelican in Piety. – REREDOS by *D. & A. Davidson*, 1880, across the full width of the E wall. Gableted stone panels carved with painted reliefs of incidents in the Passion of Our Lord; in the centre, a mosaic of the Crucifixion by *Salviati*. – PULPIT also by *Davidson*, 1880, of Caen stone with dwarf shafts and steps of Connemara marble. – Brass eagle LECTERN by *Jones & Willis*, 1880. – STAINED GLASS all of 1880 by *Clayton & Bell*, with depictions of the forerunners of Christ in the W window, scenes from His Ministry in the nave, and His Passion, Crucifixion, Resurrection and Ascension in the chancel. – At the W end of the nave floor, a memorial BRASS of *c.* 1905 commemorating the Rev. Hugh MacColl, a full-length figure in eucharistic vestments.

LYCH GATE at the churchyard entrance designed by *Alexander Ross* and executed by *Harry Hems*, 1881; of Devonshire oak, the gambrel roof covered with red Ruabon tiles.

CEMETERY

THE CRAIGS BURIAL GROUND, Belford Road. Laid out in the C18 as a graveyard for soldiers at the fort. At the main ENTRANCE, an open-pedimented semicircular arch with projecting imposts and keyblock; it was built in 1690 at the landward entrance to the fort and moved here in 1896. – Inside, at the highest point, a granite OBELISK to Ewen Maclachlan, erected in 1847. – To its N, in an iron-railed enclosure, the TOMB-CHEST of John Jaffray † 1831, its sides carved with draped urns.

FORT

FORT WILLIAM, off the A82. Remains of the fort from which the town takes its name, now isolated by car-parks and the road to the harbour and heliport. The fort (known then as Inverlochy) was begun in 1654 by General Monk's engineers to house troops engaged in overawing the Royalist clans of the area. The position was a promontory at the confluence of a branch of the River Nevis and Loch Linnhe, this natural protection given by the river on the N and the loch on the W strengthened by a bog and a burn on the S. These natural defences were reinforced by a ditch cut on the W to give security from the only easy approach, and the site was surrounded by a rampart, probably of clay and wattle, enclosing an irregular pentagon with a three-pointed bastion at the SE and demibastions (enfilading only one wall each) at the other four corners.

In 1690 William III's general Hugh Mackay of Scourie reconstructed the Cromwellian ramparts as stone walls built of boulders taken from the river or the loch, the fort being rechristened in honour of the new King. Besieged during the Jacobite risings of 1715 and 1745, the fort was reconstructed in 1746 by *Dugal Campbell*, who erected new barracks and was probably responsible for a partial rebuilding of the main walls using roughly squared stones in coursed layers. However, in the late C18 part of the rampart was destroyed by a flood of the River Nevis and the fort was not repaired subsequently. It was sold to Mrs Cameron Campbell of Monzie in 1864 and then in 1889 bought by the West Highland Railway, who used part of the site for a goods yard.

Substantial parts of the N and W ramparts survive, together with the NW demi-bastion. In the N wall, rectangular musket-loops and a round-arched gateway, probably of 1690 but on the site of the river-gate of 1654. The main gateway was in the demolished S wall; it has been rebuilt at the Craigs Burial Ground (*see* Cemetery, above).

PUBLIC BUILDINGS

BELFORD HOSPITAL, Belford Road. Large but lightweight, by *J. L. Gleave & Partners*, 1962–5.

LOCHABER HIGH SCHOOL, 2.6km. NE on the A830. By *Inverness County Council*, 1960. Four-storey extension by *Inverness County Council* (County Architect: *Douglas Calder*; job architects: *A. M. Fulton* and *W. Watson*), 1967. Further extension by *Highland Regional Council*, 1976.

POLICE STATION, High Street. By *Inverness County Council*, 1958.

SHERIFF COURT, High Street. Lump of bare institutional Gothic, by *Matthews & Lawrie*, 1876.

SWIMMING POOL, Belford Road. By *Crerar & Partners*, 1973; extended by *T. Harley Haddow & Partners*, 1988.

DESCRIPTION

NORTH ROAD's approach to the centre is marked by the old GLEN LOCHY DISTILLERY's maltings, brick-built with tall pagoda roofs, by *Duncan Cameron*, 1898–1900. They stand beside the NEVIS BRIDGE of 1932–3, a single span faced with hammer-dressed red granite ashlar. In BELFORD ROAD, VICTORIA COURT on the r. is of *c.* 1985, in a sort of late C20 Queen Anne manner, with big red-tiled roofs above the brick and rendered walls. For the Swimming Pool opposite *see* Public Buildings, above. Then the Craigs Burial Ground (*see* Cemetery, above). On the path up to it, the Victorian MACLAREN FOUNTAIN, with a version of a mercat cross rising from its basin. The Church of the Immaculate Conception (*see* Churches, above) is a powerful presence, the Belford Hospital (*see* Public Buildings, above) a large but weak one. Beside it, FAS-SIFERN ROAD climbs the hill. On its S side, ST ANDREWS HOUSE by *Alexander Ross*, 1880, built as an Episcopalian school and very ecclesiastical. At the r., a Gothic porch to the school; conical-roofed tower over the schoolhouse door. Higher up

106

the road on the r., a tall granite OBELISK put up in 1847 to commemorate Captain Peter Cameron. In UNION ROAD past the MacIntosh Memorial Church (*see* Churches, above), the HIGHLAND HOTEL by *Duncan Cameron*, 1895, a big symmetrical U-plan with parapeted bay windows in the gables of the wings, which are linked by a cast-iron balconied verandah across the centre.

HIGH STREET's N side starts with 1970s shantytown shops. The ALEXANDRA HOTEL opposite, dated 1876, is decently gabled and gableted. Beside it, Duncansburgh Parish Church (*see* Churches, above) and its grey harled MANSE (by *G. MacRitchie*, 1936), followed by the plain GOVERNOR'S HOUSE built in the early C18 for the officer commanding the fort and made L-plan by the addition of a r. wing in the mid-C19. The parade ground in front is now covered by grass and overlooked by monuments. First, a stone WAR MEMORIAL of *c.* 1920, the statue of a kilted soldier. Larger and much more accomplished is the bronze STATUE of Donald Cameron of Lochiel, by *W. Birnie Rhind*, 1909, standing on a craggy granite pedestal. Then a PEACE MONUMENT of 1985, its main feature the bellcote from the old Duncansburgh Church (later Town Hall) by *Henry Burrell*, 1860. St Andrew's Episcopal Church (*see* Churches, above) establishes the building line of High Street. Across Bank Street, the crowstepped ROYAL BANK OF SCOTLAND (former National Bank) by *T. P. Marwick*, 1911, in pink and grey granite. Further on, on the r., the MASONIC HALL by *J. G. Falconer*, 1903, spindly classical in bright red sandstone. No. 38 High Street, bowing the corner to Cameron Square, was built as the British Linen Bank, *c.* 1860. Renaissance, with a pedimented centre on the s front. CAMERON SQUARE's E side was filled in 1983 by the CAMERON CENTRE, a lightweight pavilion lacking the *gravitas* required by its position. On the square's s side is the WEST HIGHLAND MUSEUM built *c.* 1840 as the British Linen Bank's first Fort William home, small but pompous, with aediculed doorpieces (the r. now a window) in the pedimented end bays, and segmental pediments over the recessed centre's ground-floor windows. Inside, mid-C18 panelling from the demolished Governor's House at the Fort.

In High Street's final stretch, the red sandstone STAG'S HEAD HOTEL on the r., late Victorian Renaissance of a sort, with an off-centre oriel. On the l., the Tudor gable-fronted BANK OF SCOTLAND of *c.* 1860 on the corner of Monzie Square. Opposite, the harled and half-timbered QUEEN ANNE HOUSE (Nos. 111–115) of *c.* 1900, a pair of bargeboarded gables containing two-storey oriel windows. For the Free Church, Police Station and Sheriff Court, *see* Churches and Public Buildings, above.

INVERLOCHY CASTLE
off North Road

Unloved ruin of the C13 castle of the Comyn lords of Lochaber,

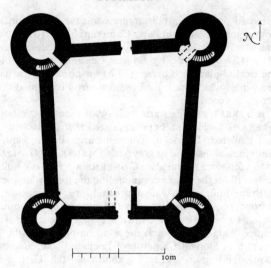

Inverlochy Castle. Plan.
(Redrawn from MacGibbon and Ross, *The Castellated and Domestic
Architecture of Scotland*, 1887–92)

strategically placed at the mouth of the River Lochy commanding the sw entrance to the Great Glen. The low-lying site
is bounded on the N by the Lochy, whose water formerly filled
the ditch surrounding the other three sides.

The castle is built of random rubble brought to a level course
about every 1.8m. by flat pinnings, a standard C13 masonry
technique. Also typical of the third quarter of the C13 is the
plan, a curtain-walled quadrangle, *c.* 30m. by 27m., with a
boldly projecting round tower at each corner, the sw, se and
NE towers *c.* 10m. in diameter, the NW (the donjon or keep) *c.*
12m. Entrances in the centre of the N and s walls, the s still
segmental-arched, the N (the watergate) robbed of its dressings.
Each has contained a portcullis with a double-leaf door behind.
These were originally the curtain walls' only openings, but
windows have been inserted, perhaps in the C16, in the N wall.
The w wall's crude battlement is an embellishment of *c.* 1905.

The corner towers have battered bases. Well-preserved long
fish-tailed slit windows at the donjon. Each tower was entered
through a door in its straight gorge wall cutting diagonally
across a corner of the courtyard. Inside each entrance, a curved
stair in the thickness of the walls led to the upper floors. Off
the NW donjon's first-floor room, a dog-leg wall-chamber
extending into the N curtain. Above this chamber, a second-
floor garderobe overhanging the curtain wall, which is thickened
to take the chute. The donjon's gorge wall is intaken at the
second floor, giving a ledge outside this floor's door, the ledge
being reached also by steps from the wall-walks of the N and w

curtain walls and so providing a link between them without passing through the tower. Above this upper door, the walling is corbelled out to the round. From the N curtain's wallhead, steps up to the wallhead of the donjon, which has putlock holes for a hoarding over its outer face.

The foundations of stone barbicans project from each entrance, and there has been a stone passage or porch inside the s doorway. These probably date from soon after 1506, when Alexander, Earl of Huntly, was granted a charter of the castle, with permission to strengthen its defences and add outworks.

INVERLOCHY CASTLE, 3.6km. NE. *See* p. 249.

GLENBORRODALE   *6060*

Hamlet beside Loch Sunart.

GLENBORRODALE CASTLE. Magnificently sited, making the most of its steep hillside site; by *Sydney Mitchell*, 1898–1902. Large-scale but bare Baronial in red Dumfriesshire sandstone, with thin Renaissance detail. Massive battlemented SW tower, a cap-housed turret in the inner angle, overpowering the short main block, whose *piano nobile*'s rooms open onto a terrace down to the gardens. Over the low E service range, a small but martially angular tower. – To the E, a detached U-plan COACHHOUSE block. Crowstepped gables; in the centre of the roof, a half-timbered gabled doocot.

GLENCOE   *0050*

Small C19 and C20 village on the shore of Loch Leven at the mouth of Glen Coe.

ST MARY'S CHURCH (Episcopal). Very simple Gothic in grey granite; by *Alexander Ross*, 1880. Nave and chancel; a spired bellcote on the W gable. Inside, an open roof. – Wooden REREDOS of *c.* 1920, carved in high relief with the Crucifixion and flanking saints. – Victorian Gothic brass GAS STANDARDS. – Brass eagle LECTERN, consecrated in 1932. – STAINED GLASS. In the S wall, three-light window (Our Lady and saints), Comperish of *c.* 1935. – W window (Our Lord as the Good Shepherd, with Our Lady and St John) by *Gibbs*, 1890. – Round polished granite FONT of *c.* 1890, its prickly steepled oak cover of *c.* 1935.

At the SE, a plain SCHOOL (now hall) by *Ross & Mackintosh*, 1883.

GLENCOE HOSPITAL, 0.7km. NE. Built for Donald Alexander Smith, later Lord Strathcona, in 1896–7; the architect was *R. Rowand Anderson*. Scottish Jacobean, the grey granite walling relieved by red sandstone dressings. Crowstepped gables; segmental-pedimented stone dormerheads. Two wings were demolished in 1965.

DESCRIPTION. At the village's E end, an early C19 humpbacked BRIDGE. Then, C19 vernacular cottages, one (now the GLENCOE AND NORTH LORN FOLK MUSEUM) still thatched, followed by timber-clad housing of *c.* 1955. To the W, at TIGH-PHUIRT, whitewashed or harled C19 cottages and the remains of a rubbly PIER.

9080

GLENFINNAN

Hamlet at the head of Loch Shiel, best known for the raising of the Young Pretender's standard there in 1745.

CHURCH OF OUR LADY AND ST FINNAN (R.C.). Big, Geometric Gothic, by *E. W. Pugin*, 1873, with a fully aisled clearstoreyed nave and iron-crested chancel. In the E gable, a statue of St Michael under the angular-traceried rose window. Inside, a scissors roof. The columns carrying the nave's pointed arcades are of polished granite, those of the chancel of sandstone, all with foliaged capitals. – Stone FONT with a steepled wooden canopy. – High-relief plaster STATIONS OF THE CROSS.

1 GLENFINNAN MONUMENT. A battlemented 18.3m.-high round tower built by Alexander MacDonald of Glenaladale in 1815 to commemorate the start of the Jacobite rising here seventy years before. In 1834 Angus MacDonald of Glenaladale removed ancillary buildings from round the foot of the tower and placed on its top a stone statue by *John Greenshields* showing Prince Charles Edward looking E to the pass along which came Lochiel and the Camerons to join the cause.

RAILWAY VIADUCT. By *Simpson & Wilson*, 1897–1901. At 380m., the longest concrete railway bridge in Scotland. Twenty-one semicircular arches, built on a curve.

GLENGARRY *see* INVERGARRY

8040

GLENSANDA CASTLE
7.8km. S of Kingairloch

Roofless remains of the unsophisticated tower house said to have been built for Ewan MacLean, fifth of Kingairloch, in the later C15. The site is a rocky outcrop on the N of the Glensanda River at its entry into Loch Linnhe.

The house is roughly rectangular (*c.* 12.9m. by 8.8m.), the walls built of pink granite, probably quarried locally, and formerly harled. In places, because of the uneven site, they are carried on a rough plinth; crude buttresses at the NE and SE corners. Only two storeys, perhaps originally with an attic inside the now fragmentary crenellated parapet. Slit windows, with a larger first-floor one in the E wall. Entrance roughly in the centre of the E front, its granite lintel a replacement. The door is now reached by stone steps, but a beam-socket each side shows that there was originally a wooden platform in front; above the door's relieving arch, another pair of sockets, probably for the framework of a pulley to raise and lower a drawbridge.

Inside, a dog-leg stair in the thickness of the walls, entered through an opening in the door's N ingo. Ground-floor store. The floor above has been of wood, the joists supported on rough corbels and one end of each runner slotted into the walls. First-floor hall with a large fireplace (much mutilated) in the W wall. To its N, a garderobe with its own window and lamp recess. E window with a stone seat surviving in its N ingo. Stair to the parapet walk inside the walls at the NW corner.

GLENUIG   6070

Coastal hamlet with a white harled inn.

ST AGNES' CHURCH (R.C.). Minimal Gothic of 1861. – STAINED GLASS. Two-light E window (Our Lady and St Agnes), probably late C19. – In the nave's S wall, two windows (Saints) and in the N, one light (the Sacred Heart), all early C20.

INVERAILORT HOUSE   7080
0.7km. S of Lochailort

Ungainly shooting lodge which has developed by a process of accretion. The nucleus is a late Georgian harled farmhouse of two storeys and three bays, its l. windows now enlarged as bipartites. The octagonal-roofed two-storey bay window on the r. is probably part of the additions made in 1875. So too is the r. extension, tame Baronial with big dormerheads and a small conical-roofed corner tower. Tall and bleak Baronial addition on the l. by *J. Pond Macdonald*, 1891.

INVERGARRY   3000

Estate village at the mouth of Glen Garry where the river enters Loch Oich.

GLENGARRY PARISH CHURCH. By *Alexander Ross*, 1864–5, the chancel, transepts and tower added in 1896–7. Plain villagey Gothic in local granite with red sandstone dressings. In the inner angle of the chancel and N transept, tower with a squat slated broach spire. Inside, open roof of stained and varnished local larch. Stone arches into the transepts and chancel. – Victorian COMMUNION TABLE, the legs carved as satyrs. – ORGAN by *Ingram & Co.*, 1898, rebuilt by *George Sixsmith* in 1985.

ST FINNAN'S CHURCH (R.C.), 0.6km. SE. Couthy crowstepped and bellcoted kirk of white-harled brick, by *Ian G. Lindsay*, 1938.

SCHOOL. L-plan school and schoolhouse with a wallhead bellcote, by *William Paterson*, 1868.

WELL OF THE HEADS, 1.8km. S. Beside the road along the w shore of Loch Oich. Obelisk with panelled sides commemorating a grisly C16 event. On the pedestal's faces, inscriptions in Latin, French, Gaelic and English relating that it was erected by Colonel Macdonell of Glengarry in 1812

AS A MEMORIAL OF THE AMPLE AND SUMMARY VENGEANCE, WHICH IN THE COURSE OF FEUDAL JUSTICE INFLICTED BY THE ORDERS OF THE LORD M^CDONELL AND AROSS OVERTOOK THE PERPETRATORS OF THE FOUL MURDER OF A MEMBER OF THE KEPPOCH FAMILY ... THE HEADS OF THE SEVEN MURDERERS WERE PRESENTED AT THE FEET OF THE NOBLE CHIEF IN GLENGARRY CASTLE AFTER HAVING BEEN WASHED IN THIS SPRING.

DESCRIPTION. On the approach from the E the village starts with the INVERGARRY HOTEL by *John Rhind*, 1885, quietly picturesque with a verandah across the front. Then the Parish Church and School (*see* above), followed by cottages of the 1860s and 1870s by *William Paterson*, with rustic porches. C20 housing to the S.

GLENGARRY CASTLE, 0.7km. E. Formerly Invergarry House. Baronial-manorial by *David Bryce*, 1866–9, the low stable block at the NW added by *J. Macvicar Anderson* in 1875–6. This makes the house an irregular L-shape; conical-roofed tower in the inner angle. On the E front, overlooking the terraced garden, canted bay windows corbelled out to square gabled tops. Inside, a Frenchy marble chimneypiece in the entrance hall. Suite of main rooms along the E front.

INVERGARRY CASTLE, 1.2km. SE, within the grounds of Glengarry Castle. Tall gaunt ruin on the edge of a cliff overlooking Loch Oich. The house was built in the early C17 for Donald Macdonell of Glengarry † 1645 or his grandson and heir Æneas. In 1654 General Monk reported that his troops had burned 'Glengaries new House' and that 'the remaining structure I order'd to be defaced by the pyoneers.' However, the building had been repaired by 1691, when it was described as 'ane extraordinary strong house. It is fortified and cannot be taken without great cannon.' But in 1746 a corner of the house was blown up by the Duke of Cumberland's forces and the building abandoned.

It has been a rubble-built Z-plan; round stairtower at the NE and a rectangular SW jamb with a rectangular tower in its inner angle. Corbelled turrets in the inner angles of these towers. Chamfered or moulded margins at the windows. The lower part of the jamb's moulded-arched door survives. This enters the jamb's W part, perhaps a late C17 addition, since the masonry is not bonded with the rest; it is now very ruinous but contained a scale-and-platt stair to the first floor, from which the floors above were reached by a similar stair in the W tower. Another stair (a turnpike) in the NE tower. Tunnel-vaulted ground-floor rooms in the jamb's E part and the W tower. The main block has been unvaulted. Its ground floor probably contained the kitchen; first-floor hall with a big N fireplace.

INVERLOCHY CASTLE   *1070*
3.6km. NE of Fort William

Large but not very exciting castellated-manorial house built of bull-nosed rubble for the third Lord Abinger in two stages, the first in 1863 to a design by the London architect *Robert Hesketh*, the second by *J. Macvicar Anderson* in 1889–92. E (entrance) front with a two-storey battlemented S tower of 1863, a turret corbelled out at its SW corner; projecting porte cochère, its battlement topped by carved angels (the Abinger supporters). The rest of this front is Anderson's, with broad two-storey canted bay windows breaking forward from crowstepped gables. At the N end, a big square tower, battlemented again and with a tall octagonal turret at its SE corner. The garden fronts to the S and W are mostly by Hesketh, in a resolutely asymmetrical castle style, stolid despite the low towers, battlements and hoodmoulded four-centred-arched windows. Near the W front's N end, another of Anderson's bay windows projecting from a crowstepped gable.

(Inside, in the hall an opulent plaster ceiling, its centre painted with cherubs. Wooden barley-sugar balusters at the broad staircase.)

INVERLOCHY CASTLE, FORT WILLIAM *see* FORT WILLIAM

KENTALLEN   *0050*

Hamlet on Loch Linnhe with now disused granite quarries to the NE.

ST MOLUAG'S CHURCH (Episcopal). Diminutive Gothic-picturesque of 1868. Bellcote on the N gable; diamond panes in the windows.

ARDSHEAL, 1km. W. Victorian in its present form. Rambling white-harled lodge with a little W tower enjoying the view over Loch Linnhe.

KILCHOAN   *4060*

Straggling settlement near the W end of the Ardnamurchan peninsula.

ARDNAMURCHAN FREE CHURCH, 0.5km. NW. Perfunctorily

Gothic buttressed box of 1876–7, a metal bellcote on the gable. – Contemporary MANSE adjoining.

ARDNAMURCHAN PARISH CHURCH (ST CONGAN). Now a roofless ruin. It was built in 1762–3 as a galleried kirk of the same dimensions as the preceding medieval church. Some of that building's stonework has been retained in the gables. In the W, a blocked deeply splayed slit window below the C18 gallery window. In the E, medieval quoins in the lower part, whose window contains part of a rebated daylight opening, apparently C12 or C13.

s of the church, two Iona School GRAVESLABS of the C14 or C15, carved with elongated nailhead borders containing swords surrounded by intertwined plant-scrolls joined at the top by animals and galleys, one with a hunting scene, the other with a foliaged cross.

The white harled house (MEALL NA CHRIDHE) beside the graveyard was built as the Manse, c. 1790. In 1828–30 *William Ross* added the front block, with three-light ground-floor windows flanking the door (now a window). Also of 1828–30 the U-plan offices behind, with elliptical-arched gig-shed entrances.

ARDNAMURCHAN PARISH CHURCH. By *William Burn*, 1827–9. T-plan Tudor, the jamb's s end topped by a belfry suggestive of a tower, its ashlar stonework contrasting with the granite rubble of the rest. From the E view the effect is compromised by the juxtaposition of two big chimneys. Inside, segmental tunnel-vaulted plaster ceilings, the jamb's narrower vault cutting into the main one. – Pine-fronted GALLERIES at the ends and in the jamb, where there is a retiring room behind. – Tall PULPIT, also of pine, with a spikily pinnacled sounding board.

DUN, Rubha na h'-Uamha, 10.7km. NE. The site, at the end of a rocky headland, is provided by a crag of three parallel spines with gullies between, the E spine's stack-like s end divided off by what seems an artificial cleft. Sheer rock-faces on the s and W, the only easy approach being from the sea on the N and up along the gullies. This crag has been defended by a drystone wall, probably of the first millennium A.D., its thickness varying from 1.2m. to 4.3m. and still standing on the W to a height of 2.4m. Slight batter on each wall-face. Entrances at s and N, the s checked for a door.

MINGARY CASTLE. *See* p. 257.

KILMONIVAIG *see* SPEAN BRIDGE

KINGAIRLOCH

Hamlet beside the shore of Loch Linnhe, the broad-eaved late C19 cottages beside the church trim in estate livery of white harl and red-painted woodwork, their tree-trunk porches a picturesque touch.

CHURCH. Late C19 mission church. Simple harled box with porches flanking the S gable and a semi-octagonal apse at the N. – Inside, an extensive but uninspiring scheme of pictorial STAINED GLASS (in the apse's three lights, the Good Shepherd, the Last Supper, Our Lord with Little Children; in the nave's NW window, the Stilling of the Storm; in the nave's NE window, the Miraculous Draught of Fishes; in the S window, the Light of the World), all signed by *A. Ballantine & Son*, 1906.

KINLOCHALINE CASTLE

6040

3.6km. NE of Lochaline

Unpretentious tower house on top of a rocky ridge at the head of Loch Aline. Built for the MacLeans of Duart, probably in the C15, remodelled *c.* 1600, and repaired *c.* 1890 after a century and a half's dereliction, it is a three-storey rubble rough rectangle of 13.2m. by 10.5m. Originally it seems to have had parapets flush with the walls, their walks drained by slate weeper-gargoyles like those surviving on the N face. At the S (entrance) front was a ground-floor door on the l. (blocked *c.* 1600 and again *c.* 1890, but visible from inside) and a first-floor door (repaired *c.* 1890) on the r., now reached by a Victorian stone stair. Above this second door, a weathered sandstone panel carved with a dog, a deer and a salmon. In the alterations of *c.* 1600 the S front's parapet was rebuilt in more obviously martial form, being projected on corbels, given rectangular openings for musketry defence, and provided with angle rounds. Box machicolation over the first-floor door, probably reused C15 work. The Victorian repair reconstructed most of the windows, which had been robbed of their freestone dressings, to improbably large sizes and with rubble surrounds. At the same time a garderobe chute at the W end of the N parapet was remodelled to look like a box machicolation.

When the tower was first built, its ground floor seems to have been one unvaulted* store, with a slit window in the centre of the E wall and the S door to the outside, but with no communication with the rest of the house. In the alterations of *c.* 1600 the door was built up and a skin-wall built against the S wall's inner face, the original entrance passage becoming a pit-prison. At the same time the store was converted into two tunnel-vaulted cellars, with a second E window inserted to light the N room. Each cellar was provided with a stair awkwardly hollowed out of the W wall for access to and from the floor above.

The first floor contained the hall. In the S wall, on the r. of the entrance, a porter's lodge with a slit window overlooking the approach. At this wall's W end, a second slit window, its

---

*One corbel to support a wooden floor above survives in the E wall.

embrasure above the pit-prison. In the centre of the s wall, a well-shaft, probably extended upwards *c*. 1600, when its lower part was encased in the ground floor's s skin-wall. Big w windows, the s's embrasure segmental-arched, the N's rectangular. In the N wall, a fireplace, now missing its lintel. Above it, a weathered sandstone panel carved with a kneeling naked woman holding a bowl in her right hand and with a flask under her left arm. To the r., a semicircular-arched window embrasure muscling into the E wall. Rectangular embrasure at the reconstructed E window. In the long E and W walls, stumps of two tiers of massive corbels, the upper presumably to carry runners under the second floor's joists, the lower perhaps for braces. Turnpike stair in the SE corner.

Another single room on the second floor. Fireplace in the w wall. One window in each of the side walls, both with tall round-arched embrasures. In the E window's ingo, entrance to a wall-chamber at the NE corner; it has a slit window and an aumbry. s window with a lower arched embrasure. Scarcements in the E and W walls, presumably for an attic floor. It would have cut across the window embrasures, so are these part of the Victorian remodelling? At the SW corner, a dog-leg stair rising in the wall-thickness to a passage inside the s wall. This passage has been much altered and now leads to steps connecting with the turnpike stair and also to a flight up to the parapet walk. Probably there used to be a door from the passage to the former attic.

1060 KINLOCHLEVEN

Village founded to provide housing for the workers at the aluminium factory opened here in 1909.

PARISH CHURCH. Long and harled, with an apse at one end, a bellcote at the other. By *J. Jeffrey Waddell*, 1930.

ST PAUL'S CHURCH (Episcopal). By *Alexander Ross & Son*, 1954.

SECONDARY SCHOOL. Begun in 1927. Large extension by *Inverness County Council*, 1970, and canteen addition of 1986.

ALUMINIUM WORKS. Built in 1905–9 and extended in the 1930s. Near the street, tall aggressively rubbly Edwardian blocks, their sides patterned by round-arched openings.

7070 KINLOCHMOIDART

Small settlement beside Loch Moidart.

ST FINAN'S CHURCH (Episcopal). Secluded in woodland above the main road. Simple lancet Gothic, by *Alexander Ross*, 1857–60. Crowstepped nave and chancel, both with steep slated roofs; porch, also crowstepped, at the SW. Corbelled out from the W gable, a chunky bellcote, crowstepped again. Inside, an open wooden roof. Pointed chancel arch. – Wooden ALTAR and REREDOS decorated with stencilled motifs. – The chancel's ENCAUSTIC TILES are of 1860. – STAINED GLASS. Late C19 E window (Our Lord, St Finan and St Columba). – In the S wall, two windows (the Annunciation of the Shepherds; the Crucifixion) by *Jemima Blackburn*, one after 1859, the other of 1873, both in a brightly coloured picture-postcard manner. – In the N wall, a routine light (Our Lord), after 1883. – Two lights in the W gable (SS. Maurice and Michael), after 1883.

KINLOCHMOIDART HOUSE
0.7km. E

A tautly vertical apparition among the hills of Moidart, the house designed by the Glasgow architect *William Leiper* and built for the distiller Robert Stewart in 1885 is almost identical to the same architect's Dalmore at Helensburgh (Strathclyde). The materials are local whinstone, with red Ballochmyle sandstone for the dressings. The style is Scottish Baronial but of the late Victorian type, unencumbered by the historicist references of its earlier practitioners.

Three-storey-and-attic main block at the S. Secondary N block set back from the W front and protruding to the E; single-storey service wing extending further N. The entrance front faces E. Its crowstep-gabled S bay contains the door to the *piano nobile* approached by a flight of steps rising from between ball-finialled piers. Doorpiece with fluted pilasters. Over its plain entablature, a large panel carved with *putti*, who flank a car-touche bearing the initials SS (for Stewart and Stevenson, the surnames of the first owner and his wife) and hold a scroll proclaiming 'PAX INTRANTIBUS SALUS EXEUNTIBUS'; above, a label inscribed 'SALVE'. The main block's centre bay is slightly recessed, its principal feature an off-centre oriel. To this win-dow's r., a diagonal ascent of stair windows, all three-light, with convex-sided top corners, stepping up to the round-arched mullioned and transomed window of the second-floor landing. Below the oriel, the unobtrusive ground-floor entrance; to its r., windows of the adjoining lavatory and washroom, one with an ogee-arched panel above, the other two-light, its top carved with the relief of a woman's head. The main block's crowstep-gabled r. bay is taller and broader than the l., with an attic room corbelled out at the centre. The secondary block to the N is unassertive, its crowstepped r. gable overlaid by the single-storey service wing, which stretches N under a battlement to a quiet crowstepped gable. Plain addition of *c.* 1900 to the N ending in another crowstepped gable.

The main block's S end is gently diversified. Big gable on the l. without crowsteps. Narrower and crowstepped centre gable, its r. part projected on a corbelled segmental arch providing a shelter for a seat. To the r., a big mullioned and transomed window lighting the end of the first-floor entrance hall.

The garden front to the W displays baronial status but quite

pacifically. The big crowstepped gable of the N bay is half-
covered by a massive round tower, its top corbelled out under
the conical roof. To the S, a symmetrical range, its centrepiece
a semicircular tower topped by a semi-octagonal attic and
octagonal roof. Each side of this tower, a broken segmental-
pedimented dormerhead carved with armorial motifs. The secondary block on the N is set slightly back. Two gables. The r.
contains the mullioned windows of the back stair, the top
window crowned with a scroll-sided pediment. To the l., a plain
crowstepped gable, its centre corbelled out from the first floor.
The single-storey service wing to the N ends with a heavy
chimney and small pepper-pot tower.

The internal arrangement is of carefully delineated zones,
little altered by the division of the house into two dwellings as
part of *Simpson & Brown*'s repairs begun in 1989. On the main
block's ground floor are grouped the less formal public rooms
(library at the SE, morning room at the SW, a small gunroom,
a NW billiard room). On the *piano nobile* above, the drawing
room and dining room fill the W part of the main block, with
the hall and principal staircase on the E. Principal guest bedrooms on the second floor. In the secondary block the ground
floor is occupied by the kitchen and scullery, servants' hall and
servants' bedrooms, the first floor by the family bedroom and
dressing room, and the second floor by nurseries. The ground-
floor rooms are simply finished. In the billiard room, a fret-
carved ventilator panel above the table. Original tiles in the
kitchen. The main block's *piano nobile* contains a stunning
display of 1880s decoration. Over the hall and main stair, panelled wooden ceilings. On their walls, a deep panelled dado
below green, yellow and red embossed wallpaper. A broad ogee
arch at the hall's S end delineates a sitting area, where the
dado is omitted. On the hall's W wall, a simplified Gothic
chimneypiece of red and buff sandstone. Opposite, a wooden
screen, its outer compartments rectangular openings under
little balustered arcades which give access to the entrance lobby
and the stair down to the ground floor; the central compartment
is a cusped arch to the main stair. At the house's SW corner,
the drawing room. Bay window to the W. In the E wall, a wooden
neo-Jacobean chimneypiece with coupled Ionic columns
topped by lions' masks and a strapworked lintel. White painted
wooden ceiling of simple Jacobean type. Walls with a wooden
dado and wallpaper embossed with flowers. Dining room to
the N, with a bow window projecting from the NW corner.
Another panelled wooden ceiling of Jacobean character. In the
S wall, a broad but shallow inglenook with a canopied half-vault
wooden ceiling and built-in benches. The chimneypiece is neo-
Jacobean again, with lions' masks on the lintel.

On the second floor of the main block, the principal stair
opens into a hall, the lower part of whose walls are covered with
the stair's embossed paper, the upper part with a stencilled
paper. In the NW bedroom, a segmental-arched alcove in the S
wall containing a bath; to its l., a built-in tallboy.

In the secondary block's sw corner, the dog-leg back stair rising round a lift enclosed by a balustered screen.

LODGES. To the w, a lodge contemporary with the house, one gable crowstepped, another with just a single step; porch placed diagonally in the sw inner angle. – Another lodge to the SE, of c. 1900, piend-roofed with tile-hung walls.

STEADING, 0.9km. NW beside the A861. Harled courtyard, probably of the mid-C19. S front with three gables, the outer two containing paired round-arched windows; in the centre, a round-headed pend under flight-holes for pigeons.

LAGGAN DAM see ROY BRIDGE

LOCHAILORT   7080

Little more than a place-name with a telephone kiosk at the head of Loch Ailort where the A861 joins the A830.

CHURCH (R.C.), 1.7km. w. Disused. Proudly isolated on top of a hill. A tall white harled and buttressed nave and chancel, built in 1874.

LOCH NAM UAMH VIADUCT, 4.2km. w. By *Simpson & Wilson*, 1897–1901. Mass-concrete railway viaduct, the eight arches each of the West Highland Extension Railway's standard 15.2m. (50 ft) span.

INVERAILORT HOUSE. *See* p. 247.

LOCHALINE   6040

A small village at the mouth of the eponymous Loch Aline and one end of the ferry from Morvern to Mull. It was laid out by John Sinclair of Lochaline, c. 1830, but little formality of Georgian planning has survived and the buildings are now mostly late C19 or C20.

KEIL CHURCH. Built in 1898, probably to a design by *P. Mac-Gregor Chalmers*. A plain kirk, the Early Christian detail of the simple round-arched windows almost flush with the walls, picked out by the contrast of the red-painted sandstone dressings against the harling. Buttress bisecting the w gable. sw porch. Simple gabled bellcote on the nave's E wall, from which projects the lower chancel. Interior with braced kingpost roofs over both compartments. Roundheaded chancel arch; deep-splayed window jambs. – STAINED GLASS. In the narrow E window, four tiers of oval panels containing portraits of Our Lord and SS. Columba, John and Paul, c. 1900, in good dark colours. – The nave's NE window (The Sower) is by *Roland Mitton*, 1983, tepidly Expressionist. – NW window (Abraham) by *Stephen Adam & Son*, 1899.

Stacked round the nave's w end, a magnificent array of medieval GRAVESTONES, probably C14 and C15, brought inside from the churchyard. Several demand individual mention. – Upper portion of a slab carved with a relief of a galley below two tabernacle niches, one containing the figure of a knight, the other of a man dressed in a tunic and wearing a sword. – Slab, now in two bits, carved with a big floriated cross above a sword; in the flanking foliage, the figure of a horseman on the l. – Five slabs, each carved with foliage and a sword. – Shaft of a cross-slab, its front bearing the relief of a bishop, its back foliaged scrolls. – Slab carved with three panels, each containing a floriated cross. – Weathered upper part of a slab with a floriated cross below reliefs of what may be a priest and a woman.

CHURCHYARD to the s and w of the church. In its SE corner, a mid-C18 HEADSTONE for the eleven children of John and Florans Cameron, the front carved with an angel's head and wings above the parents' initials and a crowned hammer (the insignia of the hammermen or smiths, of which John Cameron was one), the back with a skull and thighbone. On the top of the inscription panel, eleven little heads. – To its w, the TABLE STONE of John Livingstone † 1816, the top ornamented with a coat of arms, the bottom with emblems of death. – Further w, two fairly ruinous BURIAL ENCLOSURES, both perhaps on the site of transeptal 'aisles' built against the body of the demolished C13 St Columba's Church. The N enclosure's s wall incorporates a pointed arch with rounded soffits carried on semicircular responds; this looks late medieval. Just behind it, a second wall with a blocked roundheaded arch, its soffit chamfered; it is probably a late C16 alteration to the 'aisle'. – The rubble-built s enclosure is much more fragmentary.

DESCRIPTION. At the village's SW end, a concrete PIER, built in 1883, overlooked by the PIERMASTER'S HOUSE AND POST OFFICE of 1898–9, broad-eaved and with some Tudor hoodmoulds still surviving above the windows. Small and much altered late C19 HOTEL to the E. At the mouth of Loch Aline, a concrete ramped FERRY PIER with a harled mid-C19 house beside it. In HIGH STREET on the brae above, a row of five concrete houses of c. 1899 designed by *Samuel Barham*, master of works at Ardtornish, with broad eaves and oversailing chimney copes.

LOCHALINE HOUSE, 6km. w. Sleeping Beauty of a ruin hidden among trees and rhododendrons. A 'very handsome and substantial mansion-house' was built for John Sinclair soon after he acquired the Lochaline estate in 1821. In the 1870s it was remodelled and extended. Victorian front of five bays, the centrepiece a gabled Italianate tower. In the flanking bays, windows of two basket-arched lights under consoled cornices. Consoled pediments over the outer windows.

ARDTORNISH CASTLE. *See* p. 225.
ARDTORNISH HOUSE. *See* p. 225.

Kinlochaline Castle. *See* p. 251.

MALLAIG   *6090*

Large fishing village overlooking the Sound of Sleat. It developed
after the opening of the railway to Fort William in 1901 with a
main street (bypassed in 1988) leading to the harbour and C20
housing on the hillside across the bay to the NE.

St Columba's Parish Church. By *J.G. Falconer*, 1903.
Buttressed harled box with a small apsidal s chancel and a N
bellcote. – STAINED GLASS. One light in the chancel (Christ
Walking on the Water) signed by *Abbott & Co.* of Doncaster,
probably of 1903.

St Patrick's Church (R.C.). Simple Early Christian, by
Reginald Fairlie, 1935. Ventilator with a Central European spire.
In the N transept's gable, a statue of St Patrick. Small SE bell
tower.

United Free Church. Now a hall. By *J.G. Falconer*, 1911.
Humble except for a big stone bellcote; half-timbering in the
porch's gable.

West Highland Hotel. By *Duncan Cameron*, 1898–1900.
Harled with brick dressings.

MINGARRY   *6060*

Place-name marking the position of the church standing on a
hillside N of Loch Shiel.

Church of Our Lady of the Angels (R.C.). Large but
austere lanceted Gothic of 1862. Battered base to the sneck-
harled granite walls. Tall gableted w bellcote. Inside, an open
wooden roof. – STAINED GLASS. In the sanctuary's N and S
walls, two cinquefoil lights, the N showing Our Lady of the
Angels, the s St Hyacinth, both of the late C19 by the same
hand. – Two late Victorian w windows (SS. Finnan and
Columba). – In the N transept, one light (Our Lady) of after
1927. – In the nave, one N window (the Assumption of Our
Lady) and one s (Christ the King), both early C20.

MINGARY CASTLE   *5060*
1.6km. SE of Kilchoan

Substantial remains of a castle guarding the entrance from the   61
open sea to Loch Sunart and the Sound of Mull. The site, a
low rock promontory sticking s into the sea, was fortified in the
C13 by a descendant of Somerled, Lord of the Isles. The N
approach from the land was severed by a ditch, *c.* 7.5m. wide
and 3m. deep, cut through the rock. The promontory's summit,
an area *c.* 19.7m. by 17.9m., was enclosed by a curtain wall

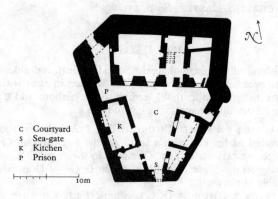

C Courtyard
S Sea-gate
K Kitchen
P Prison

⊢ ⊣ ⊣ ⊣ ⊣ ⊣ 10m

Mingary Castle. Plan of ground floor.
(Redrawn by permission of the RCAHMS)

forming an irregular hexagon with rounded corners, a bowed
garderobe covering the join of the E and SE sides, and a shallow
rectangular garderobe projecting from the SE side. The walling,
c. 2.7m. thick and originally 12m. high on the NW and E landward sides but only 1.8m. thick and c. 8.5m. high on the four
sides to the sea, is built of rubble brought to courses by flat
pinnings. At the top, the landward-facing walls have been finished with crenellated parapets above square holes which
drained the wall-walk behind, the original arrangement most
clearly visible, despite blocking of the crenelles, in the E wall's
S part. Evidence of the C13 parapet on the S walls was destroyed
in a late C16 remodelling.

The short NW wall contained the entrance from the landward
side, perhaps defended originally by a bretasche.* Under the
present threshold of c. 1700, three massive corbels which carried
the pivot beam of the C13 drawbridge spanning the ditch; slots
in the door jambs may have housed the bridge's chains. In the
S wall was a sea-gate approached from the landing place below
by steps cut in the rock.

The C13 buildings inside the courtyard included a block built
against the N and E sides which contained a hall above an
undercroft. The hall had one lancet window in the curtain's E
wall and two (now blocked) in the N, all with deep-splayed
ingoes (the E's remodelled in the C18). S of the E window, a
passage in the wall-thickness but below the level of the hall
floor,‡ so it was probably reached by a wooden stair. This
passage, lighted by a (blocked) window to the courtyard, led to
a garderobe in the semicircular projection at the join of the E
and SE walls. The garderobe's C13 window has been built up;

*A corbel slightly below and to the l. of the early C17 bretasche may have been for
a C13 bretasche.
‡Its level is shown by beam-sockets below the E window and in the present E room.

its two small gun-holes are C16 or C17 embellishments. At the passage's N end, remains of a stone stair in the thickness of the E wall. On the W side of the stair's second-floor landing, a chamfered door into a narrow chamber (infilled, c. 1700), c. 8m. long and 1m. broad, in the N wall. On this chamber's N side, two C13 windows (both blocked) through the curtain, the E a single lancet, the W of two lights, similar to but a little smaller than the hall windows below.

Door from the courtyard to the SE side's outward-projecting rectangular garderobe. Lamp-recess in its N wall. Slots for a wooden seat over the latrine.

At the N end of the curtain's long W side, a stone stair (its lower treads removed c. 1700) has led from the courtyard up to the wall-walk on the landward side. At the foot of the stair was a door, blocked c. 1700, when a new door was made to the N, but the C13 S jamb still visible inside the wall-passage to which it gave access. On the passage's W side, a window (now blocked) through the curtain wall. At its S end, a small garderobe, originally with a window to the courtyard. At the passage's N end, a windowless pit-prison, originally entered by a hatch.

In 1588 Mingary Castle, then held by the MacIans of Ardnamurchan, was besieged by Maclean of Duart, and the defences were probably strengthened at about the same time. The N front's C13 parapet was thickened internally (reducing the width of the original wall-walk) to provide a new wall-walk 2m. above the old and screened by a new battlement. The C13 crenelles were converted to splayed gunloops for use by defenders standing on the old wall-walk. Regular putlock holes under the new parapet suggest that the high-level wall-walk was a wooden hoarding partly projecting inwards and presumably supported by posts on the old wall-walk, and partly cantilevered outside the curtain, where it was reached through the crenelles and a corbelled opening near the castle's NE corner. At the same time the wall-walks and parapets of the SE, S and SW walls were rebuilt, the battlement provided with tall slit-like crenelles, an assortment of splayed gunloops of various widths, and both horizontal and downward-pointing musket-loops. At the SE and SW corners, jettied round turrets, now missing their roofs, were entered from the wall-walk. The better-preserved SE turret has two rectangular windows. At the floor-level of each turret, a pair of musket-loops, the SW's pointing down to cover the foreshore below. Abutting the SE turret, remains of a contemporary box machicolation above the sea-gate. This entrance seems to have been remodelled at the same time with rounded jambs; rybats for a door and yett, an aumbry in each ingo.

Slightly later than these late C16 alterations, perhaps c. 1612, when the seventh Earl of Argyll gave custody of the castle to his brother-in-law, Donald Campbell of Barbreck-Lochow, the top of the NW wall was rebuilt as a covered wall-walk or chamber giving access to a wooden bretasche over the landward entrance.

The bretasche's stone corbels survive under the parapet door; to its r., a window.

In 1696 the lands of Ardnamurchan, including Mingary, were granted to Alexander Campbell of Lochnell. Either he or his son, Sir Duncan, seems to have been responsible for a major internal reconstruction of the castle before its sale to Alexander Watson in 1723. An austere three-storey-and-attic block, its s front an almost regular four-bay elevation, was built on the site of the C13 hall, the C13 curtain providing its N and E walls, the new 1.4m.-thick s and w walls topped by a continuation of the C13 wall-walk, within which rose the attic; a line of stone spouts along the s wall to drain water from the wall-walk into the courtyard. The C13 hall's surviving windows were blocked and the second-floor chamber in the N wall was filled in with masonry. The E wall's C13 stair was converted to cupboards. Probably at the same time a lean-to two-storey block (now ruinous) was built against the courtyard's w wall. Its large N room seems to have been the castle kitchen, with fireplaces at the ends; in the w wall, recesses cut into the curtain, its upper walling supported on wooden beams. Apparently also C18 but probably a little later is a single-storey lean-to built on the courtyard's SE side and now fragmentary. Presumably also a Georgian improvement was the building of a stone causeway across the ditch to the NW entrance.

MORAR

6090

Hamlet on the isthmus between Loch Morar and the Sound of Sleat.

CHURCH OF OUR LADY AND ST CUMIN (R.C.). Built in 1889. A big austere granite Gothic box with an apsidal E end; a statue of Our Lady in the w gable. At the sw, a round conical-roofed bell tower of the Brechin Cathedral type. Inside, a scissors roof. – STAINED GLASS. In the apse, two folksy windows (SS. Columba and Margaret) of c. 1950. – In the nave's s wall, two lights (the Annunciation of the Shepherds, after 1954; the Annunciation of Our Lady, after 1958). – Contemporary PRIEST'S HOUSE at the NE, plain with gabled first-floor windows.

NORTH BALLACHULISH

0060

Hamlet at the N end of Ballachulish Bridge.

ST BRIDE'S CHURCH (Episcopal). Very simple lanceted nave and chancel, by J. Garden Brown, 1874–5. w bellcote; sw porch. Inside, an open roof over the nave, a wooden wagon roof in the chancel. – ORGAN by Wadsworth & Bros., originally on the N side of the chancel, moved to a small w organ loft in 1898. –

STAINED GLASS. Three-light E window (Christ in Glory with SS. Bride and Columba and angels) by *Clayton & Bell*, 1875. – In the chancel's S wall, a single light (St John the Evangelist) by *Margaret Chilton, c.* 1935. – In the S wall of the nave, a pictorial window ('I Am the Good Shepherd') of *c.* 1890. – Much more accomplished the adjoining two-light window (the Annunciation), very painterly in rich dark colours broken by a lot of white glass, by *Shrigley & Hunt*, 1896. – In the N wall, four lights (Our Lady and SS. Columba, Bride and Patrick) of *c.* 1910. – Outside the door, MONUMENT to Bishop Alexander Chinnery-Haldane † 1906, a large Celtic cross with a Calvary on its E face.

RHUM *see* RUM

ROSHVEN   7070
6km. N of Kinlochmoidart

Victorian holiday home overlooking the Sound of Arisaig, approachable by road (as well as sea) only since 1966. The nucleus is a late Georgian laird's house, possibly built for Major Allan Nicolson Macdonald, who bought the lands of Moidart from Clanranald in 1827. It was of two storeys and five bays, the centre of the W front projecting as a semi-octagon. In 1854 the estate was sold to Professor Hugh Blackburn, husband of the painter Jemima Blackburn, and three years later *David Bryce* provided designs for a partial reconstruction and large addition. This was completed in 1859. In the alterations of 1857–9 the two S bays of the Georgian house were remodelled as a big crowstepped gable, its ground floor a segmental-arched porch. S of this Bryce added a three-storey-and-attic block beginning with another crowstepped gable and ending with a conical-roofed turret at the SW corner. At the back, Bryce's addition has another big crowstepped gable, this time with rounded corners. Bryce also joined the Georgian house to its detached NE office range by the provision of a scullery and filled this inner angle with a kitchen.

Further remodelling and extension were made later in the C19, probably in 1896 (the date on part of the work). This recast and enlarged the Georgian house N of its centre as a frontage of three plain gables, the third set back and ending with a pepperpot tower at the NW corner. Segmental-arched mullioned and transomed windows with concrete surrounds. At the back, a second NE service wing which combines with the Georgian back wing to enclose three sides of a small court-yard. On the Victorian wing's S elevation, roundheaded arches. The Georgian wing was remodelled at the same time. Its court-yard front now has reliefs of a cow above the dairy door and of a horse beside the mounting block. Its S elevation was given a

fishscale-slated round tower, the upper stage designed as a
doocot. Another tower, largely built of concrete, with roundheaded windows, was added to the back of the Georgian house's
main block. To its s, a window of two Gothic lights, the surrounds and mullions of concrete; presumably it is also of the
1890s.

Inside, the principal rooms are in *Bryce*'s extension of 1857–
9. Plain neo-Jacobean main staircase. The s ground-floor room,
shown on the plans as a barrack room (dormitory), was converted to a chapel, probably early in the c20, its altar's tabernacle painted with a praying angel. *Jemima Blackburn* made
the design for the oakleaf, acorn and thistle cornice in the
drawing room above. The room to its N, originally the dining
room, became a library in the late c19 or early c20, with built-
in bookcases and panelling under the egg-and-dart cornice.

₂₀₈₀ ## ROY BRIDGE

Small village, most of its houses c20.

CILLE CHOIRILL* (R.C.), 3.5km. E. Perched high up on the
Braes of Lochaber, a little medieval church, roofless by the
c19 but heavily restored in 1933. Sneck-harled granite walling,
swept eaves at the roof, small bellcote on the w gable. The E
gable's two round-arched windows under a slit light and the
rectangular openings in the s and w walls are all of 1933. Near
the s wall's E end, a moulded round-arched window; it could be
c13. – Outside the E gable, GRAVESLAB of Ranald Macdonhill
†1729, carved with grisly intimations of death. – To the sw,
MONUMENT to Ian Lom Macdonald (the 'Bard of Keppoch')
designed by *John Rhind* and executed by *D. & A. Davidson*,
1873; an upright slab carved with an elaborately decorated
Celtic cross.

ST MARGARET'S CHURCH (R.C.). Large and very simple
Gothic by *Reginald Fairlie*, 1929, built of dressed granite
blocks with prominent pinnings filling the wide joints. The
sw tower rises unbroken, save for a statue of St Margaret, to
the set-back pyramid-roofed belfry. The simplicity continues
inside. Open wooden roof over the nave. Panelled wooden
ceiling in the chancel, which is entered through a roundheaded stone arch. Low transepts, the N (Lady Chapel) with a
STAINED-GLASS window (Our Lady of Fatima) of *c.* 1940.

SCHOOL. By *Henry Burrell*, 1876. Broad eaves and round-arched
windows.

LAGGAN DAM, 10km. E. By *C. S. Meik & Halcrow*. Built as one
of a chain of dams to provide water power to the Fort William
aluminium works; opened in 1934. Huge stone-faced curve, the
water channelled through segmental arches. The machinery is
housed in two towers.

*St Cyril's Church.

RUBHA NA H'-UAMHA *see* KILCHOAN

RUM   *3090*

Hilly island largely occupied by red deer.

BULLOUGH MAUSOLEUM, Harris. Rather stolid early C20
Greek Doric temple with plain crosses on the pedimented ends,
enjoying a spectacular cliff-top view. Inside the peristyle, three
table tombs, the earliest (in the centre) of sandstone, the others
of pink granite.

KINLOCH CASTLE. Large castellated Tudor mansion designed
by *Leeming & Leeming* of London for the Lancashire indus-
trialist George Bullough, 1897. It is square, nine bays by nine,
built round a centre court. Only two storeys, the ground floor
encircled by a castellated semi-elliptically arched verandah.
Round corner towers, their battlements strongly corbelled. On
the E (entrance) front, three full-height bay windows and a tall
off-centre entrance tower with a still taller turret corbelled out
at one corner.

Inside, the vestibule opens into a two-storey living-hall, neo-
Jacobean Artisan Mannerist, with a gallery round three sides.
Panelled ceiling with strapwork decoration and pendants. Fireplace in an inglenook. In the windows, panels of stained glass.
To the s, the drawing room, originally Jacobean but partly
remodelled in 1906 after Bullough's marriage, the formerly dark
carved woodwork painted white and a broad arch framed by
Ionic pilasters opened into the adjacent boudoir. Also of 1906
are the Adam-revival white marble chimneypieces. On the
house's E side, the dining room and billiard room, both also
Jacobean. In the billiard room, both a dais for spectators and
an arch into a sitting area for those bored by the game. Two-
storey high ballroom, the detail again Jacobean but the walls
covered in gold damask set off by white painted woodwork and
plasterwork. Shallow tunnel-vaulted plaster ceiling. Musicians'
gallery at one end.

At the s edge of the garden beside Loch Scresort, a harled
concrete octagonal GAZEBO of *c.* 1900, castellated and with a
strongly corbelled bartizan at one corner.

SOUTH BALLACHULISH *see* BALLACHULISH

SPEAN BRIDGE   *2080*

Hamlet beside the bridge over the Spean.

KILMONIVAIG FREE CHURCH, 3.5km. NW. Small rendered
box of 1860. Pointed windows; a low vestry has been added to
one gable.

KILMONIVAIG PARISH CHURCH, 0.9km. NW. Built in 1812 as
a harled rectangle with round-arched windows and a W bellcote.
The bellcote was renewed (except for its ashlar base) with a
lead-spired top and the windows acquired fat glazing bars in
alterations of 1891. In 1928 *J. Jeffrey Waddell* added the low E
chancel and SE vestry. Interior now mostly of 1928. Wide
tunnel-vaulted wooden ceiling over the nave; straight-coved
ceiling in the chancel, entered through a semicircular stone
arch. – STAINED GLASS. In the chancel's gable, three lancet
lights (Faith, Hope and Charity) of 1928. – In its S wall, two
small but strongly coloured windows (SS. Ninian and John) by
Gordon Webster, 1967.

ST JOSEPH'S CHURCH (R.C.). By *Charles W. Gray*, 1967. Triangular plan, the roof rising above low harled walls to a tall
tapering metal spirelet finished with a cross. Gabled porch
projecting from the long W wall.

BRIDGE. By *Thomas Telford*, 1813. Three-span, with a big segmental arch flanked by two smaller ones; widened in concrete,
1932.

60 COMMANDO WAR MEMORIAL, 1.6km. NW. Dramatic moorland setting. Bronze group of three commandos on a stone
pedestal; by *Scott Sutherland*, 1949–52.

SCHOOL, 0.9km. NW. By *J.G. Falconer*, 1912.

8060   STRONTIAN

Village at the entrance of the Strontian River into Loch Sunart.
Intermittently a lead-mining centre between 1724 and 1871, it
was largely rebuilt as a three-sided quadrangle round a green in
the 1960s.

FREE CHURCH, 1.5km. W. Built in 1869–73. Five-bay buttressed
and lanceted granite rectangle, the gable's birdcage bellcote
still with a Gothick accent belied by its High Victorian wrought-
iron finial.

PARISH CHURCH, 0.8km. N. Built in 1827–9 as a 'Parliamentary'
church and presumably to the standard design by *William
Thomson*, who was also the contractor. The present broad-eaved
and blocky bellcoted appearance dates from a reconstruction of
1924.

Former SCHOOL. Small but tall Gothic, by *Henry Burrell*, 1875.

STRONTIAN HOTEL. Built, *c.* 1808, as a trim white harled three-
bay piend-roofed block with a projecting semi-octagonal centre.
Lower piended wings added soon after, the recent additions
less happy.

NAIRN

Small but prosperous agricultural district with a broad and fertile plain bordering the Moray Firth. Nairn, its only town, was the seat of a sheriff and the site of a royal castle in the Middle Ages; it is now better known as a resort for golfers.

ARDCLACH
9040

No village. The old Parish Church sits in a ravine beside the Findhorn; its bell tower, school and the present Parish (former Free) Church are strung out along the high ground to the N.

OLD PARISH CHURCH. Plain T-plan kirk built by *Donald McAndrew* in 1765 and reconstructed with roundheaded windows by *George Dunbar* and *John Wilson*, 1836–8. (Galleried interior recast by *Alexander Reid*, 1892.) – In the GRAVEYARD, C18 and C19 monuments. Among them, S of the church, the TABLE TOMB of David Rose †1772, with angels carved on the supports.

BELL TOWER standing alone on top of the hill 0.3 km. N, a two-storey harled square. Datestone of 1655 on the W gable, which is topped by a rudimentarily pedimented stone bellcote. First-floor shotholes in both gables. Inside, a tunnel-vaulted ground-floor store. Straight stair to the first floor, above whose fireplace is a stone inscribed with the monogram MGB, presumably for Master George Balfour, minister of Ardclach from 1642 to 1680.

PARISH CHURCH, 1.1km. NW. Built as Ardclach Free Church c. 1845. Broad nave with a birdcage bellcote on the W gable. The piend-roofed aisles look like early additions. Lattice glazing in their roundheaded windows. A ball finial on the E porch, a chimney on the W vestry. Inside, FURNISHINGS of 1892 from the old Parish Church, the suspended ceiling a late C20 introduction.

SCHOOL, 0.7km. NW. Disused. Mid-C19 ball-finialled schoolroom, the schoolhouse at right angles to it.

GLENFERNESS HOUSE. *See* p. 275.

AULDEARN
9050

Small village which was made a burgh of barony in 1511.

PARISH CHURCH. Long harled box built in 1754–7.* Birdcage
bellcote on the W gable. The round-arched and keyblocked
windows probably date from the alterations made in 1816–18,
their Gothic glazing pattern and the metal roof ventilators from
John Robertson's reconstruction of 1898. On the S wall, a tablet
commemorating John Inglis † 1650 and his wife Janet Burnet,
with two shields and their initials; a skull and crossbones in the
steep pediment. On the W gable, an early C17 heraldic tablet
to James Sutherland of Kinsteary and his wife, with a skull and
crossbones at the bottom.

The interior is all of 1898, when *Robertson* placed the pulpit
at the W end, a very deep gallery at the E, and Gothicized the
walls and roof. – STAINED GLASS. In the round W window, 'I
Am the Good Shepherd' of *c.* 1900, mercifully unattributed. –
In the N wall, memorial window to Ewen James Brodie † 1914
('Be Thou Faithful unto Death'), a competent depiction of Our
Lord with a knight. – In the S wall, a characteristic work (St
Luke and Angels) by *William Wilson*, 1948. – ORGAN by the
Positive Organ Co. Ltd, c. 1900.

Attached to the church's E end is the roofless chancel of its
late medieval predecessor taken over after the Reformation as
the burial place of the Hays of Lochloy and the Dunbars of
Boath. Ashlar-built N wall, its moulded stringcourse not continued across the gable, whose two-light Y-traceried window
looks early C16. The gable's door is a Georgian insertion.
Rubble-built S wall, perhaps a rebuild of *c.* 1600, the date
suggested by the moulded jambs of its doorway. Inside, the
small aumbry near the N wall's E end is presumably pre-Reformation. – Excellent display of post-Reformation MONUMENTS.
At the W end of the N wall a large but plain Roman Doric
pilastered frame for inscriptions to the Dunbars of Boath; it is
dated 1837. – Next to it, an ambitious but illiterately classical
tablet commemorating Alexander Hay of Kinnudie † 1616 and
his wife but also recording that this is the grave of John Hay of
Lochloy † 1563; aedicular, the attached columns composed of
superimposed foliaged balusters, the join masked by a rosette. –
Memorial to the Rev. Thomas Gordon † 1793, with small
emblems of death in the segmental pediment. – In the SE
corner, a long C17 tomb, its front divided into panels by bal-
uster-shaped pilasters. Monogram in the centre; in the other
panels, a trophy of gravediggers' tools, an angel trumpeting the
Resurrection, and a skull and crossbones.

PRIMARY SCHOOL. Asymmetrical with a spired bellcote, by
A. & W. Reid & Wittet, 1895.

DESCRIPTION

On the approach from the E, an oblique view up to the Parish

---

*A datestone on the S front says 1751, but the Presbytery ordered the building of
a new church in 1754, and according to *The Statistical Account of Scotland*, xix (1797)
it was built in 1757.

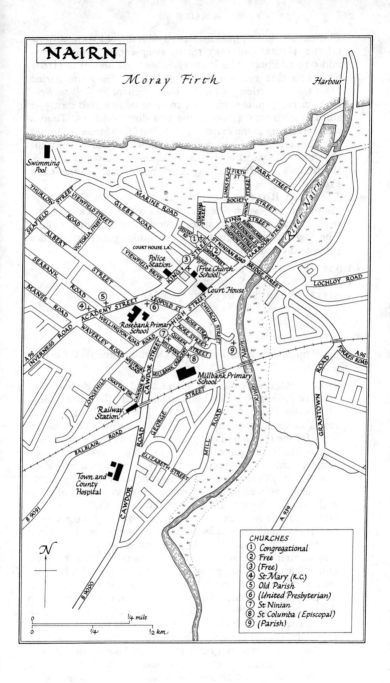

NAIRN

Moray Firth

Harbour

Swimming Pool

THURLOW STREET
VIEWFIELD STREET
SEAFIELD ROAD
ALBERT STREET
VICTORIA STREET
MARINE ROAD
GLEBE ROAD
LINKS PLACE
FIRTH ST
PARK STREET
SOCIETY STREET
UNION STREET
CUMMING STREET

SEABANK ROAD
MANSE ROAD
INVERNESS ROAD
ACADEMY STREET
WELLINGTON ROAD
WAVERLEY ROAD
COURT HOUSE LA.
VIEWFIELD DRIVE
KING STREET
LEOPOLD ST
HIGH STREET
ROSE STREET
CHURCH STREET

KING STREET
ST NINIAN ROAD
GORDON STREET
ALTON STREET
WILSON STREET
SIMPSON STREET
HARBOUR STREET

BRIDGE STREET
LOCHLOY ROAD

River Nairn

Police Station

Free Church School
Court House

Rosebank Primary School

LONGHILL
CHATTAN DR.
CAWDOR STREET
MILLBANK STREET
CRESCENT RD
QUEEN STREET
ACRE STREET

St Columba (Episcopal)

A.96
FORRES ROAD
GRANTOWN ROAD

Millbank Primary School

Railway Station

BALBLAIR ROAD
CAWDOR ROAD
GEORGE STREET
ELIZABETH STREET
MILL ROAD

Town and County Hospital

A.939

B 9090
B 9091

N

0   ¼ mile
0   ¼   ½ km

CHURCHES
1 Congregational
2 Free
3 (Free)
4 St Mary (R.C.)
5 Old Parish
6 (United Presbyterian)
7 St Ninian
8 St Columba (Episcopal)
9 (Parish)

Church (*see* above), its ridge shared with the old MANSE (now GLEBE HOUSE) of 1817–18, its steep-gabled centre bay a mid-C19 addition. The Primary School (*see* above) is HIGH STREET's first major incident. Beside it, the white harled JAMESMOUNT, designed as the Infant School by *William Robertson* in 1841, quite smart with an open-pedimented centre; it still has horizontal panes in the first-floor windows. Then a road forking up to the Parish Church, but High Street continues downhill lined with C19 vernacular houses. Near its end, the DUNBAR MEMORIAL HALL by *Duncan Cameron*, 1885–6. 'Italianate', said *The Building News*, but its main element is a Frenchy spire.

96 Off DOOCOT ROAD to the N, the late C17 BOATH DOOCOT,* built on a medieval motte site. Round with a conical roof, the moulded rat and eaves courses a contrast to the white harling. The flight holes are grouped in an ashlar panel, its cornice supported by consoles.

BOATH HOUSE. *See* p. 269.
INSHOCH CASTLE. *See* p. 276.
KINSTEARY HOUSE. *See* p. 277.

8040   BAREVAN

Isolated hillside graveyard in a forest clearing, formerly the centre of a parish.

CHURCH. Roofless remains of the medieval church dedicated to the little-known St Aibind and abandoned after the building of Cawdor Parish Church in 1619. The Church of Evein is mentioned in a papal bull of 1255, and an early C13 date seems likely for the erection of the present building, its side walls still largely intact, the gables reduced to a few courses. It is very simple, a rubble-built rectangle with a pointed-arch nave door near the S wall's W end and a narrower chancel door further E. The nave has been lit by two lancet windows in each of the N and S walls. The N wall's W light and the S wall's E are both intact, but the N wall's E window's jambs have been renewed and the S wall's W window, which lacks the deeply splayed internal daylight and obtusely pointed rear-arch of the others, may be an insertion reusing an original window head from one of the church's missing parts. In the chancel's S wall, a big two-light window, its Y-tracery cut from a single stone (cf. Rait Castle), with moulded jambs and a hoodmould. Inside, a double piscina at the S wall's E end. Immediately W of the N wall's W window, a corbel. Its position would seem to preclude its having supported a rood beam, unless the nave was windowless, and it may not be *in situ*. – The floor is covered with mossy GRAVESLABS, mostly C18, some with crudely incised carving of skulls and crossbones, looking as if they were copied from a child's drawings.

---

*Property of the National Trust for Scotland.

BOATH HOUSE

0.3km. N of Auldearn

9050

Neat neo-Greek pinky ashlar box designed by *Archibald Simpson* 88 for Sir John Dunbar of Boath, *c.* 1830. Five-bay S (entrance) front of two storeys, its pedimented portico with giant Ionic columns. At the back, a broad central bow and deep ground-floor windows in segmental overarches. Beautifully finished but austere interior. Big entrance hall with a coffered ceiling and Ionic columned screen at its N end, a prelude to the double bow-ended drawing room, off which opens a second smaller drawing room to the E, both with white marble chimneypieces. A door at the hall's NE corner gives access to the D-plan stairhall. Segmental-arched recesses for statuary in its walls. Cast-iron stair balustrade with anthemion uprights. From the first-floor landing, a cupola-lit passage divided into two sections by roundheaded arches. Greek key decoration on the bedroom doors. In the basement's SE corner, a groin-vaulted kitchen.

BRACKLA HOUSE

2km. NE of Cawdor

8050

Villa of 1835, by *Robert Caldwell.* Two storeys over a sunk basement, and three bays. Portico with coupled Roman Doric columns; a broad fanlight over the door. Victorian additions at the back.

CAWDOR

8040

Picturesquely informal village of C19 vernacular houses, the surprisingly smart late Victorian lamp-standards a reminder of the proximity of Cawdor Castle (*see* below).

PARISH CHURCH. A crowstepped cross built in 1829–30 by *John Wilson*, mason, and *John McIntosh*, wright, incorporating bits of the church erected here in 1619. That church seems to have been T-plan. At the end of its S jamb, the gable's centre is carried up as a tower, its broadly battlemented parapet projected on diagonal stone strips and enclosing a pyramid-roofed belfry, perhaps an C18 addition. In each face of the tower are slit windows. Its main S window's intersecting stone tracery probably reproduces C17 work. Also of 1619 is the flat-roofed porch across the SE inner angle, its fat attached columns topped by moulded square capitals from which springs an obtusely pointed arch. For the rest, thin Georgian Gothic detail. Inside, the S arm has been partitioned off as a vestry. The body of the church was recast with plenty of pitch-pine by *John Wittet* in 1904. 'So complete has been the transformation', wrote the *Inverness Courier*, 'that one could hardly imagine he was within the walls of an ancient church.' Gallery in each arm; roomy pulpit against the S wall.

Primary School. Dated 1892* and plain.

CAWDOR CASTLE

Medieval tower surrounded by later additions, the complex making an ordered Victorian Baronial vision from the approach, a largely C17 jumble when entered. In 1310 Robert I granted William, Thane of Cawdor, a charter of the thanage and lands of Cawdor to be held on the same conditions as they had been in the reign of Alexander III (1249–86). In 1454 William, sixth Thane of Cawdor, was granted a licence to crenellate the castle of Cawdor, and the castle's general plan and earliest surviving parts are still recognizably C15.‡

The site, at the top of a bank which falls almost sheer to the Calder Burn on the w, has been cut off by a ditch on the N, E and S sides. This defensible 'island' was surrounded by a wall, with a gateway in the middle of its E side reached by a draw-bridge. Some stonework of the C15 wall of enclosure survives, incorporated in later work, e.g. the lower courses of the wall at the entrance, and a blocked segmental-headed archway near the E wall's N end.

It is probable that the interior of the enclosure was divided from the start into two unequal-sized courts, the S perhaps containing the chapel founded here in 1467, the smaller and lower N court housing domestic accommodation. There may also have been, as there now is, a small entrance court between the two main courtyards. Projecting S from the N court is the C15 tower. This is a severe rubble-built rectangle (c. 10.4m. by 13.7m.) of four storeys, its roof, perhaps originally flat, drained by boldly projecting spouts. Above the spouts and flush with the walling below is an ashlar battlemented parapet, probably a replacement of the early C17, when the attic is likely to have been added. At the parapet's corners are small turrets, their round lower parts possibly C15, the octagonal upper stages C17, their conical roofs restored in 1854–5.§ On the S and w faces, heavily corbelled machicolations, both at parapet level and presumably C17. A third machicolation on the N side is C15; it is entered from the third floor and guarded the ground-floor entrance (now hidden inside a C17 addition). The tower's principal entrance has been at the first floor on the E side, presumably reached by a removeable wooden stair. Its round-headed arch survives but the door itself was built up in the C17, when the present large rectangular windows were inserted in the tower's upper storeys. C15 window slits lighting the ground floor and the stair at the NE corner remain.

The castle's outer ranges built against and on top of the C15

---

*The datestone of 1855 is reused from its predecessor.

‡MacGibbon and Ross (*The Castellated and Domestic Architecture of Scotland*) mention payments for work at 'Calder Castle' in 1398, but this refers to Calder House, Midcalder (Lothian), not, as they assumed, Cawdor Castle.

§The turrets are shown as having conical roofs in survey elevations of 1748 but had lost them before 1800.

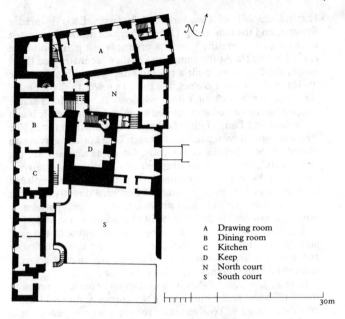

Cawdor Castle. Plan of ground floor.
(Redrawn from MacGibbon and Ross, *The Castellated and Domestic Architecture of Scotland*, 1887–92)

A   Drawing room
B   Dining room
C   Kitchen
D   Keep
N   North court
S   South court

30m

wall of enclosure are substantially of the C17 and early C18, but their development has been far from straightforward. The entrance and adjoining walling in the centre of the E front seems above its lower courses to be early C17, with a crude little ball-finialled bellcote above the segmental-arched gateway. The N range was almost entirely rebuilt in the C17. Before then it had a 'lytill tour' at its E corner and a kitchen at its W. Probably at the beginning of the C17, the space between the little tower and kitchen was filled with a two-storey-and-basement block containing vaulted cellars below a ground-floor hall and first-floor gallery. In 1639–43 *Robert* and *George Nicolson*, masons, added an attic to the hall and gallery block and rebuilt the kitchen to its W, creating a big and regular crowstep-gabled range. Projecting from the NW corner, awkwardly placed because the N and S walls meet at an obtuse angle, is a slab-roofed first-floor closet (serving the room above the new kitchen) jettied out above moulded corbels and a frieze studded with cannon spouts. The contract of 1639 specified that on this range's N side were to be four dormer windows 'withe armes names and siferis upone the said windockis'. If provided, they had disappeared by 1748; the present dormers carved with beasts climbing their sides towards rose and thistle finials are of 1855, copied from the dormers on this range's S front towards the court. Those dormers are carved with the initials of Sir

Hugh Campbell of Cawdor* and his wife, Lady Henrietta
Stewart, and the date 1674. Did they replace dormers provided
in 1639–43 or were the tympana originally left plain and then
carved in 1674?‡ At the same time as they reconstructed the N
range, the Nicolsons built a tall crowstep-gabled block on the
W side of the N court connecting the C15 tower to the N range.
Between this block's first-floor windows is a moulded frame
containing the carved and painted arms and initials of Sir Hugh
Campbell and Lady Henrietta Stewart and the date 1672. The
frame is topped by a pediment broken by a corbel carrying an
obelisk; more obelisks at the ends. On these obelisks are the
initials SIC for Sir John Campbell of Cawdor, and the tympanum has been carved with the date 1618. Was this first placed
over the door into the hall, originally entered directly from the
court, and moved here and given a new armorial panel as a
minor part of Sir Hugh Campbell's alterations in the 1670s?

The building of the W range behind this block of 1639–43
and the C15 tower is undocumented. A date in the 1660s or
1670s seems likely. It is quite plain, of two storeys above a
vaulted basement which contains the castle's well.

In 1699 *James* and *Robert Nicolson* signed a contract to rebuild
the 'lytill tour' at the enclosure's NE corner and to add the N
court's E range.§ To the N the rebuilt tower appeared as a
straightforward continuation of the main N range; to the E it
presented a crowstepped gable. The four-bay E range was of
two storeys, flat-roofed and with a balustraded parapet. A small
jamb, probably contemporary, containing the pend into the N
court, joined its S end to the medieval tower. About the same
time or a little later an unassuming block was built along the S
court's S side.

Between Sir Hugh Campbell's death in 1716 and the mid-
C19, Cawdor Castle received only occasional visits from its
owners, who had inherited estates in Wales of much greater
value than their Scottish property. John Campbell was made
first Baron Cawdor in 1796, and his son first Earl Cawdor in
1827. It was perhaps from a desire to make the neglected castle
worthy of his title that the first Earl employed *Mackenzie &
Matthews* in 1854–5 to carry out a gentle baronialization of the
buildings, giving them a more obviously C17 appearance. A
short crowstepped block of offices was added to the S end of the
W range, its tall W front adorned with very steeply pedimented
dormers and a round tower topped by a cap-house. On the N
range's N elevation were added dormers copied from the C17
ones on its courtyard front. This range's E end of 1699 was

*The lands of Cawdor had passed to the Campbells after the marriage of Muriel
Calder, daughter and heiress of John, eighth Thane of Cawdor, to Sir John Campbell
in 1510.

‡In 1639–43 Cawdor was under the tutelage of Colin Campbell, whose elder
brother had been declared a lunatic in 1638, and whose father, Sir John Campbell
† 1642, had resigned the lands in 1622.

§A very similar contract had been signed in 1684 with *James Smith Sen.* and *James
Nicolson.* Clearly the work was not executed at the time, perhaps because of Smith's
death.

heightened to make it again a 'lytill tour' with a semicircular turret crowned by a crowstepped cap-house projecting boldly from its N front. The contemporary wing to its S was recast, the balustrades being removed, the first-floor windows carried up into dormerheads of C17-type, the flat lead roof replaced with a pitched and slated roof, and a fat candle-snuffered turret added at the SE corner. Baronialization was resumed in 1884 by *Alexander Ross*, who added a wing S of the entrance, its height and detail carefully matching that of the wing to the N as it had been remodelled in the 1850s, but Ross's wing is of three bays not four. The S range's plain E gable was hidden behind a front block which combines a semicircular stair turret and cap-house with a pedimented dormer of 1702, possibly reused from the E end of the N front. The work was completed by the provision of iron yetts at the main entrance and N postern of the 'lytill tour'.

The interior is entered through a simply moulded door (its doorplate dated 1716) into the block of 1639–43 on the W side of the N court. Inside, a big scale-and-platt stair to the first floor, with a massive stone pillar in its centre and heavy-handed vaulting. To the S is the C15 tower constructed of two super-imposed stone vaults, the semicircular lower one covering the ground floor, the upper a pointed tunnel subdivided hori-zontally by wooden floors into three storeys. Inside the ground floor's door, an iron yett said to have been brought here from Lochindorb Castle (Badenoch and Strathspey) after that stronghold's dismantling by William, Thane of Cawdor, in 1456. Unusually, it incorporates a wicket gate. In the thickness of the N wall, a straight stair leads to a turnpike in the NE corner, serving the upper floors. The ground-floor Thorn Tree Room (named after the stump of a thorn around which the tower was built) has deep-splayed and round-arched embrasures to its window slits. In the S wall, a dungeon, its access originally by a trap door from the hall above; up a few steps to its W is a privy. On the tower's upper floors, garderobes and wall chambers in the N and S walls, the third floor's N wall containing a passage from the stair to the machicolation above the ground-floor entrance.

The C17 N range's ground floor is occupied by the hall (now drawing room), its beamed ceiling perhaps a C19 replacement. At the W end, where there may originally have been a screens passage, a little musicians' gallery of 1921. The chimneypiece in the E wall is presumably the one which *James* and *Robert Nicolson* contracted to provide in 1699, its keystone carved with a buckle and hart's head (armorial bearings of the Calders and Campbells of Cawdor). The floor above, reached from either the main stair at the SW or a private stair in the 'lytill tour' to the E, was filled by a gallery until *c.* 1700, when it was divided into a W drawing room (the Yellow Sitting Room) and E bed-chamber (the Tapestry Bedroom), both with simple heavy cor-nices, the bedchamber hung with Flemish tapestries (episodes in the life of Noah, the Flight into Egypt, hunting scenes)

imported from Oudenaarde in 1682. In the Blue Room above
the C17 kitchen to the W, panelling made by *John Brembder* in
75   1717–18. Its massive stone chimneypiece, dated 1667, is an
overpowering display of Artisan Mannerism, the jambs carved
as hirsute caryatids, the lintel with little boys perching on tasselled swings; in the centre, the heraldic supporters and initials
of Sir Hugh Campbell of Cawdor.

On the ground floor of the W range, the two N rooms may
have been intended as a drawing room and bedchamber; they
are now the dining room and kitchen. In both, thin-com-
partmented Jacobean ceilings, probably of 1855. In the dining
room's S wall, a large stone chimneypiece of *c.* 1670. It commemorates the marriage in 1510 of Muriel Calder, the heiress
of Cawdor, to Sir John Campbell, so it bears that date and their
arms and initials. Frieze carved with huntsmen, toucans (?),
goats, a mermaid, a dog smoking a pipe, and a cat playing a
fiddle, all probably copied from woodcuts. On the cornice's
soffit, human heads linked by vine branches.

BRACKLA HOUSE. *See* p. 269.

8050   GEDDES HOUSE
                    3.6km. s of Nairn

Sizeable laird's house built in 1801–5 for William Mackintosh,
who had made a fortune in India. It is of cherrycock-pointed
rubble with rusticated quoins. Two storeys over a sunk basement; three bays by four, the NW wing an addition of *c.* 1830.
At the S (entrance) front, advanced centre under a pediment
containing an oval panel. Are the corniced Roman Doric portico
and the fanlit front door with side lights original or an alteration
of *c.* 1830?

Inside the front door, a vestibule with a ceiling rose of faintly
Gothick inspiration, its petals ending in little thistles. Down
the centre of the house, a hall with Roman Doric columned
screens at the ends. Swagged frieze and big ceiling rose. On the
hall's W side is the stair to a first-floor hall in the same position
as the one below but lower and with fluted columns at its
screens. The ground floor's N front is occupied by the drawing
room and dining room. In the drawing room, very smart
Frenchy decoration of *c.* 1830. Wallpaper of a light grey background adorned with curvy-topped panels, their stiles gilt, filled
with naturalistically coloured foliage and flowers; at the top of
the panels, grisaille roundels containing cherubs. Doors painted
with stylized sprigs. Plaster rinceau enrichment on the frieze of
the ceiling. In the centre of its flat, a large oval painted with
cherubs frolicking among clouds. This is bordered by panels
containing sprays of flowers. At the ends, caryatids flanking
roundels painted in grisaille with classical scenes. Empire garlands on the white marble chimneypiece. The adjoining dining
room's stiff acanthus cornice seems to be of *c.* 1800, but its vine
frieze probably belongs to the redecoration of about thirty years

later, as must the plain black marble chimneypiece. In the
billiard room at the house's SE corner, a pine and composition
chimneypiece of *c.* 1805, its frieze with a scene showing a house,
dog and church. Plain grey marble chimneypiece of *c.* 1830 in
the morning room at the SW.

GLENFERNESS HOUSE

9040

2.8km. SW of Ardclach

Gentle broad-eaved Italianate villa of 1844–5 by *Archibald
Simpson*, the rubble walls formerly harled as a contrast to the
granite dressings. E (entrance) front of seven bays, the broad
gabled ends advanced, their bracketed eaves combining with
bandcourses to suggest pediments. In these ends, console-
corniced tall ground-floor windows. Across the centre, a Roman
Doric columned screen (now glazed), its porte cochère added
in 1869 by *A. & W. Reid*. Asymmetrical W front to the garden
with a three-storey shallowly pyramid-roofed tower, a window
of three round-arched lights in its W face. The inner angle of
the tower and the S wing was filled by a piend-roofed block in
1869. Low N additions, also of 1869, one range linking to a
Norwegian single-storey wooden house built here in 1890, its
twin sitting across the forecourt to the S.

STABLES probably also of the 1840s and by Simpson. Shallow
H-plan, the centre range of the main E front with a round-
arched and keyblocked entrance flanked by giant pilasters;
consoled cornices over the outer windows.

HOLME ROSE

8040

1.3km. SE of Croy (Inverness)

Quadrangular house of the later C18 but with the front (S) range
deepened and recased in the early C19, its pinky droved ashlar
(perhaps from Tarradale) a contrast to the local red sandstone
rubble of the rest. Seven-bay front, its two storeys divided by a
band course and with a sill course linking the first-floor
windows. Slightly advanced broad centre, from which projects
a semicircular portico with coupled Roman Doric columns;
overall fanlight over the door and side lights behind. Above
the portico, a semicircular overarch containing the first-floor
window. This front block's back part, visible from the courtyard, is the C18 house of three storeys with a bowed stairtower.
The three other C18 ranges are two-storey and quite unassuming.

Inside, large but plain drawing room and dining room,
respectively W and E of the entrance hall, the dining room with
a pilastered sideboard recess. The lower part of the early C19
stair in the centre of the main block was removed in the 1930s
to create a large sitting hall extending to the house's W side, in
which large windows were inserted.

To the S, a rubble-WALLED GARDEN, perhaps late C18, the S ends of the E and W walls scooped down.

INSHOCH CASTLE
2km. NW of Auldearn

9050

Prominently sited ruin of the late C16 house built for the Hays of Lochloy. Z-plan, with round towers at the SE and NW corners, the SE tower, which contained the stair, now very fragmentary, the NW still rising for four storeys to a corbelled parapet. Both have ground-floor gunloops. Round turrets corbelled out at different heights in the inner angles. The ground floor was vaulted, with a passage along its S side. The first-floor hall's moulded E fireplace survives. In the NE corner, a wall chamber, possibly a garderobe.

KILRAVOCK CASTLE
1.7km. E of Croy (Inverness)

8040

Massive medieval tower of the Roses of Kilravock, softened by the addition of a harled laird's house. Hugo de Rose is said to have acquired the lands of Kilravock through marriage c. 1280. In 1461 his descendant Hugh Rose was granted a licence by John Earl of Ross 'to fund, big, ande vpmak a toure of fens [defence], with barmkin ande bataling'. A 'castell off Kilrawok' had been built by 1482, when it was claimed by the Mackintoshes, who soon after captured it and did damage to a value estimated in 1499 at over £100. This late C15 tower is a big square rubble-built keep, purposefully martial, with a corbelled battlement and angle rounds; square turret at the SW corner. Inside the battlement, a cap-house.

In 1665–7 the masons *Robert Nicolson* and *James Smith Sen.* added what was effectively a self-contained three-storey house joined to the C15 tower's SW corner by a square stairtower. Entrance to this stairtower on the N (now hidden by later additions), its moulded doorpiece carved with stars and rosettes. The C17 main block is a tall harled rectangle with a square stair turret corbelled out at the SW corner and a round turret, also containing a stair, almost in the centre of the S face. Catslide dormerheads over the second-floor windows. This C17 house was thickened to the N and a low NW range added or reconstructed in 1759–61,* the new N front giving the appearance of an unassuming laird's house. Piend-roofed projecting centre, its small battlemented porch a C20 addition. Probably rather later in the C18 was the insertion of a Venetian window in the remodelled W gable of the C17 block. Mid-C20 addition on the tower's N side balancing the low mid-C18 NW wing.

(Inside, the C15 tower is largely intact, its turnpike stair rising

John Baillie was the wright.

in the wall-thickness at the SW corner. First-floor hall with stone corbels carrying its ceiling's beams. C 20 chimneypiece. The C 17 range's rooms were remodelled in the later C 18. Coved ceiling and an Adamish chimneypiece in the drawing room. In the C 18 entrance hall, a carved stone chimneypiece dated 1662, formerly in the tower's hall.)

To the SW and joined by a surviving stretch of the C 15 or C 16 barmkin wall is a two-storey square tower, probably mid-C 16 and perhaps identifiable as the 'mekell towr of Kilraowk' for whose iron yett *George Robertson*, smith in Elgin, was paid in 1569. It was given a flattened pyramid roof with flight-holes in the early C 19, when the upper floor became a doocot and the ground floor a privy.

KINSTEARY HOUSE 9050
1.2km. S of Auldearn

Unassuming low rubble-built quadrangular house, the S range now demolished. The main (entrance) front is to the N, its weather-vane's date of 1792 likely enough for the house's rebuilding or remodelling to its present form. Three-bay single-storey-and-attic centrepiece, its Venetian ground-floor windows containing intersecting astragals. More intersecting astragals in the segmental attic window of the projecting centre. Long single-storey lateral wings, each with a three-light window. In the W range's S gable, a reset stone carved with the initials IS (for Isobel Sutherland) and the date 1698. Round the courtyard's sides, glazed corridors, probably added *c.* 1940, when the house was used as an army hospital. – To the E, a WALLED GARDEN, perhaps of the 1790s, with three walls of brick and one of stone.

LETHEN HOUSE 9050
4km. SE of Auldearn

Stolid late Georgian mansion house built for Miss Anne Brodie of Lethen in 1788. Three-storey main block of five bays, its columned doorpiece sheltered by a balustraded porte cochère of *c.* 1865. At each side, a slightly recessed two-storey wing with a first-floor Venetian window. One wing originally linked to a pavilion, removed together with a Victorian balancing pavilion in 1970. Bowed stairtower at the back, its D-plan flat roof given a balustrade and ball finials *c.* 1865.

To the W, the rubble-built and crowstep-gabled GRANARY, its main part early C 18. Crowstepped gablet on the W front; stone forestair to an off-centre first-floor door. At the S gable, a lower addition, probably C 19, joining the main block to a crowstepped cottage, perhaps also C 18. – To the S, a low crowstep-gabled C 18 lectern DOOCOT with one ratcourse; flight-holes in a gabled dormer.

NAIRN

A royal burgh at the mouth of the River Nairn, founded, together with a long-vanished castle,* by William the Lion, *c.* 1200. By the late C18, buildings stretched the length of High Street and there was an informal fishertown to the N. In the C19, villas were put up for those attracted to Nairn by its reputation for healthy air and bracing bathing, development aided by the opening of the railway from Inverness in 1855 and its subsequent extension to Aberdeen, golf being a further attraction by the 1890s.

CHURCHES

CONGREGATIONAL CHURCH, King Street and Crescent Road. Simply detailed but quite ambitious Gothic, by *James Matthews*, 1860–1. SW steeple with a broached lucarned spire in the manner of the Hays of Liverpool.

FREE CHURCH, King Street and Court House Lane. Now Community Centre. A galleried box built in 1844. The minimally Romanesque N gable dates from *James Anderson*'s remodelling of 1862. The windows were blocked and an E extension built on its conversion to its present use.

FREE CHURCH, King Street and Gordon Street. By *James Strang* of Falkirk, 1908–9. Sturdy buttressed box with a broad-eaved tower.

43 OLD PARISH CHURCH, Academy Street. 1893–7, by *John Starforth* and almost a replica of his earlier Trinity North Church at Kelso (Borders). Big and confident Transitional in hammer-dressed rubble. D-plan body with two pairs of transepts, the E set diagonally back towards the bowed end, against which is clamped the four-stage martially parapeted tower; in the inner angles, low pinnacle-buttressed circular stairtowers. The only hint of friendliness is given by the carved angels holding upended jars each side of the entrance's gablet. Behind, a vestry and hall whose flèche echoes that of the main block.

Inside, pitch-pine gallery following the shape of the D. Wooden braces pierced with *fleurs-de-lis* spring from foliaged stone corbels to strengthen the coombed ceiling. The focus is the wooden Gothic PULPIT, the arched recess behind filled with an ORGAN by *H. Hilsdon Ltd.* – White marble FONT with green marble columns, their capitals massively foliaged; by *Andrew Davidson*, 1899. – STAINED GLASS. Five-light W window (the Last Supper) by *A. Ballantine & Gardiner*, *c.* 1900 – In each transept, below the gallery, a three-light window, again by *Ballantine & Gardiner*. In the N, the Ascension of 1901; in the s, Faith, Hope and Charity, *c.* 1900. – Above the gallery, the transepts' W walls have two-light War Memorial windows (the Faithful Warrior and Eternal Victory in the N, the Agony in the Garden in the s) by *James Ballantine II*, *c.* 1920. – In the

*Which perhaps stood on or near the site of Constabulary Gardens, High Street.

s transept's gable, a three-light window (the Crucifixion) by *Douglas Strachan*, 1946, bittily Expressionist.

PARISH CHURCH (former), Church Road. Roofless remains of the broad piend-roofed box built in 1809–11. Lunette gallery window in the w gable. Above the w door, an armorial TABLET to the Rev. James Dunbar †1660 and his wife, Margaret Hay, their impaled arms set in a strapwork frame. – At the graveyard's s edge, two large but plain pilastered monuments. One, dated 1835, commemorates William Grant; the other, to Hugh Robertson, is pedimented and dated 1866.

ST COLUMBA (Episcopal), Queen Street. Begun by *Alexander Ross*, 1857, as a lanceted two-bay chancel and three-bay nave. Ross intended the addition of a fourth bay to the nave and a NW tower, but *John Robertson*'s enlargement of 1898 provided two extra bays, a NW porch, but no tower. In the w gable, two-light windows with quatrefoiled heads under a rose window. Inside, elaborate open roofs. – Complete scheme of STAINED GLASS. E window (the Crucifixion and Resurrection, flanked by SS. Andrew and Columba) of *c.* 1870. It looks like *Hardman*'s work. – Late C19 and early C20 glass in the side lights of the nave and chancel, but only the figure of St Ninian in the chancel is of note. It is by *J. Ninian Comper*, 1914, characteristically well drawn and coloured. – Routine but competent w windows (the Nativity, Presentation of Our Lord in the Temple, and Annunciation) by *John Hardman's Studios*, 1932–42. – ORGAN with stencilled pipes, by *Forster & Andrews*, 1889.

ST MARY (R.C.), Academy Street. Crowstepped L-plan group of church and presbytery built in 1864, the church with plain Gothic lights. N chancel added by *John Robertson*, 1901. Inside, neo-Jacobean ALTAR CANOPY of carved and gilded oak by *Reginald Fairlie*, 1952.

ST NINIAN, High Street and Queen Street. Originally Nairn Free Church. By *Andrew Maitland & Sons*, 1880–2. Big preaching box, its gable front diversified by a steeple on the l. and a gallery-stair 'transept' on the r. Mechanical Dec detail.

UNITED PRESBYTERIAN CHURCH, Academy Street. Disused. By *Mackenzie & Matthews*, 1852. Cheap Romanesque, a bellcote on the gable front.

PUBLIC BUILDINGS

BRIDGE, Bridge Street. Built by *George Burn*, 1803, and reconstructed in 1829, 1868 and 1936. Three segmental arches, their size diminishing to the E; round panels in the spandrels. – To the N, a late C19 metal FOOTBRIDGE with cast-iron lamp-posts at the ends.

COURT HOUSE, High Street. Plain two-storey ashlar-fronted block built in 1817–18. The centre is advanced and carried up another two storeys as a battlemented tower with a hoodmoulded first-floor window and a roundheaded second-floor

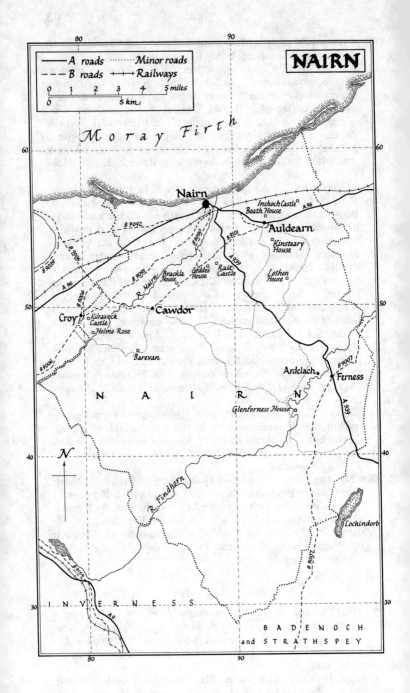

niche. Inside the parapet, a lead spire, its top sliced off and replaced by a bellcote in 1868–70, when *A. & W. Reid* added the lucarned clock-faces. Also of 1868–70 the back wing, with high-set cell windows at the ground floor. – Outside, the MERCAT CROSS of 1757, a round shaft (much patched with cement) carrying a defaced sundial, now missing its ball finial.

FREE CHURCH SCHOOL, Court House Lane. Now offices. By *Mackenzie & Matthews*, 1847–8. Italianate *cottage orné*, the batter-sided porch rising into a belfry.

HARBOUR, Harbour Street. Formed in 1818–25 by *Thomas Telford*, who straightened the mouth of the River Nairn. Its present appearance dates from 1930. Very roughly rectangular basin with concrete quays; concrete embankments along the river.

MASONIC HALL, Millbank Street. By *J. Young*, 1913. Small but heavily classical with a pedimented Roman Doric portico.

MILLBANK PRIMARY SCHOOL, Millbank Crescent. By *William Mackintosh*, 1908.

NAIRN ACADEMY, Duncan Drive. Mannered assemblage of rhomboids with a metal boiler chimney at the centre. By *G. R. M. Kennedy & Partners*, 1975.

POLICE STATION, King Street. By *Moray and Nairn County Council*, 1970.

RAILWAY STATION, Cawdor Road. By *Murdoch Paterson*, 1885. Long single-storey block with thrifty Baronial detail. – Standard Highland Railway lattice-girder FOOTBRIDGE over the line.

RAILWAY VIADUCT, off Mill Road. 1856–7, by *Joseph Mitchell*. Four segmental arches; the rounded cutwaters support politely martial semi-octagonal refuges.

ROSEBANK PRIMARY SCHOOL, Academy Street and Lodgehill Road. E block by *William Mackintosh*, 1901–3, Wrenaissance with a broad portico and small cupola. – W block of *c.* 1930, a larger plainer version of the Edwardian original.

SWIMMING POOL, Marine Road. By *Highland Regional Council*, 1983.

TOWN AND COUNTY HOSPITAL, Cawdor Road. Small but stodgy Wrenaissance, by *William Mackintosh*, 1904–6.

WAR MEMORIAL, Cawdor Road. By *A. Marshall Mackenzie & Son*, 1922. Fluted Ionic column with a wreath on the front.

DESCRIPTION

Entering from the W, the Old Parish Church (*see* Churches, above) in ACADEMY STREET is a huge landmark. WELLINGTON ROAD to the r. gives a taste of well-heeled villadom. Nos. 10–12 of *c.* 1860, tall with broad eaves. No. 8, dated 1856, is a dotty mixture of the *cottage orné* and the toy fort. Bargeboards carved with wheat-sheaves and shields; sculpted human heads above the porch's pilasters and again on the tower, where lotus-flower chimneypots stand at the corners of the battlemented parapet. Much staider the contemporary Georgian-survival No. 6, with an absurdly stumpy portico. Georgian elements

again at No. 2, but with canted bay windows linked by a
verandah, the chimneys by arcading; a pediment on the
central dormer. LODGEHILL ROAD leads past the back of
Rosebank Primary School (*see* Public Buildings, above) to
HIGH STREET, its beginning marked by the steeple of St
Ninian's Church (*see* above). In front, a squat CENOTAPH
on a Doric base commemorates John Straith, the parish
schoolmaster. It was put up in 1816, the design based on a
sketch by *Sir Thomas Dick Lauder*. Beside it, a fussy Jacobean
FOUNTAIN of 1897 to mark Queen Victoria's Diamond
Jubilee.

The street's commercial buildings start on the r. with the STAF-
FORD HOTEL, dated 1893, its open pediment supported by
scrolls. Next door, Nos. 3–9, English baroque of 1902, the first
of the palace plums in the C19 vernacular and freestyle mixture.
A second appears with the Italianate WAVERLEY HOTEL,
dated 1877, followed by the timidly French HIGHLAND
(former STATION) HOTEL, by *Duncan Cameron*, 1896, its red
sandstone bulk a bully to the small Jacobean CLYDESDALE
BANK of *c.* 1860 opposite. On the E corner of Leopold Street,
the ROYAL BANK OF SCOTLAND (former National Bank),
smooth Greek of *c.* 1830 with giant angle pilasters and a very
shallow pediment. Then a Venetian Gothic block of *c.* 1870
looking across to a single-storey Victorian shop, its architecture
an urn-topped frame for plate glass. On the Church Street
corner, the VICTORIA HOTEL, early C19, with a channelled
ground floor and recessed bowed corner, spoilt by a later
mansard roof. Beside it, No. 61, a late C18 survivor with a gable
to the street and an architraved door to the close. The Court
House (*see* Public Buildings, above) makes a solidly civic break
in the procession of shopfronts. WOOLWORTH opposite is late
C19 commercial classical, its columned entrance still intact.
The set-back but very grand BANK OF SCOTLAND is by
William Mackintosh, 1874, a Renaissance palazzo but with
Gothic capitals at the end porticoes. Slightly later Jacobean
block (Nos. 75–77) next door, with crowstepped gablets above
oriel windows. It faces the severe late Georgian ROYAL
HOTEL, whose ground-floor windows (their glazing pattern
altered in the early C20) are set in roundheaded overarches.
On the corner with Douglas Street, MACKINTOSH'S BUILD-
INGS by *John Rhind*, 1869, uninspired baroque but with an
iron-crested truncated corner dome to give a hint of gaiety. No.
88, built as the BRITISH LINEN BANK, *c.* 1840, is the last of
the palazzi, its bay windows' keystones carved with human
heads. Across Gordon Street, No. 94, smart late Georgian with
an arcaded shopfront; first-floor pilasters at the ends and the
recessed bowed corner. CONSTABULARY GARDENS opposite
is set well back from the street, a late C19 house with a steep
pedimented dormerhead between crowstepped gables; on the
porch, a big armorial panel in a segmental-pedimented aedicule. To its E the crowstepped gable-front of the old PUBLIC
HALL of 1865; a bust within the first-floor window's overarch.

VILLAS ETC.

ALBERT STREET. The WINDSOR HOTEL has been made from two late C19 villas (both much altered), the l. Gothic, the r. with dotty mason's detail (blind quatrefoils, label stops carved with the heads of royalty). TARLAND is by *W. R. Davidson*, 1906–7, large and harled, of Voyseyish simplicity, but mechanical.

ALTONBURN ROAD. ACHAREIDH HOUSE. Early C19 double-bow-fronted villa with a late Victorian porch. The large N additions are by *W. R. Davidson*, 1907.

CAWDOR ROAD. HERMITAGE HOTEL. Jacobean villa of *c.* 1860, its front built with two shaped gables and extended a little later with a more delicate third.

CAWDOR STREET. MILLBANK. Very smart ashlar-fronted early C19 villa; urns on the pedimented centre. It was extended at the back by *Mackenzie & Matthews* in 1846, and a new 'front' door was later made in the harled side. Acorn finials on the garden gatepiers.

CRESCENT ROAD. The white harled BLENHEIM HOUSE is of *c.* 1840, with a very pretty cast-iron verandah with gableted ends across the front. KINGILLIE at the NW end is a harled single-storey-and-basement villa of *c.* 1810. Two bows on the front, with a Roman Doric portico between them; Tudor hood-moulds over the windows. The castellated rear wing looks like an afterthought but is shown on Wood's map of 1821.

INVERNESS ROAD. NEWTON HOTEL. Large and complicated house, its s block begun *c.* 1830 as a two-storey-and-basement centre with lower semi-octagonal fronted wings. Crenellated parapet studded with gargoyles; heraldic beasts on top of the portico's balustrade. In 1874–7 *Alexander Ross* added big Baronial extensions to the N, with a tower over his new entrance. The original house was remodelled in 1896 by *Ross & Macbeth*, who added one storey to the centre and two to the wings. The parapet was reused but its central coat of arms left at the original level. To the w, early C19 office courtyard (now hotel bedrooms). s entrance flanked by pyramid-roofed doocots; basket-arched pend at the N.

MANSE ROAD. MANSE. Heavy-handed Gothic by *William Mackintosh*, 1898, the corner turret just hinting at levity.

MARINE ROAD. On the Links, a late Victorian cast-iron BANDSTAND with lacy spandrelled sides and the roof swept up to a finialled dome. Many-gabled ROYAL MARINE HOTEL begun by *James Matthews*, 1860, and extended in 1867, 1890 (by *John H. Gall*) and 1934 (by *Carruthers Ballantyne, Cox & Taylor*); large and plain.

SEABANK ROAD. Towards the s end, CRIANICH of *c.* 1900, white harled and crowstepped with a scrolly pediment over the door. The late Victorian HEBRON HOUSE is opulent Italian, the curvaceous pediments broken by urns; stone swags at the centre and at the sliced-off l. corner, where a bay window projects. Near the N end, two harled houses by *W. R. Davidson*:

BROOMHOLM, of 1903, is strongly composed with prominent chimneys and full-height bay windows to the garden; the crow-stepped LINKSIDE, built in 1900 and enlarged in 1905, is more overtly Scottish, with a gabled tower in the inner angle and a round corner turret. Much less appealing is the GOLFVIEW HOTEL of *c.* 1890, probably by *Duncan Cameron*, who designed additions in 1897; plain except for half-timbering in the gables.

VIEWFIELD DRIVE. VIEWFIELD HOUSE. Smart piend-roofed villa of *c.* 1800 with rusticated quoins and a pedimented centre. Rosettes at the ends of the doorpiece's fluted frieze. On the door's architraves are consoles supporting stone blocks as if a lower cornice was originally intended. The lined render and flat-roofed dormers are C20 alterations. In front, bronze statue of Dr Grigor, the propagandist of Nairn's healthy virtues, dressed for a walk; by *John Hutchison*, 1890.

VIEWFIELD STREET. WASHINGTON HOTEL. Big Italianate villa of *c.* 1880, with stilted segmental-arched windows. Lower wings of differing sizes. Iron cresting on the roofs.

8050
RAIT CASTLE
4.1km. S of Nairn

62   Roofless but substantial remains of a hall house built probably *c.* 1300 for Sir Gervase de Rait, Constable of Nairn Castle, or his younger brother Sir Andrew. The site, enclosed by a partly surviving barmkin wall, is not naturally defensive, being low-lying and overlooked by a steep wooded hillside on the S. The house itself appears more of a *dacha* than a castle. It is a big rubble-built rectangle, *c.* 19.5m. by 10m., presumably originally covered with a steep-pitched roof containing an attic opening onto continuously corbelled wall-walks at the gables (some of the E wall-walk still visible). At the SW corner, a round tower of *c.* 6.4m. diameter, with a battered base. A rectangular garderobe tower projects from the N wall's W end. On the ground floor of the main block, rectangular windows set quite high; the door was presumably in the largely demolished E gable. The main block's pointed first-floor windows have been two-light with moulded jambs, their Y-traceried heads cut from single blocks of stone. Near the S wall's E end, a hoodmoulded pointed door (originally reached by a wooden forestair), its outer arch chamfered, the inner moulded; it has contained a portcullis with a wooden door behind. Immediately W of the door, a small pointed window, probably lighting a porter's room. In the SW tower, sizeable slit windows and a two-light NW-facing first-floor window like those of the main block but its head built of several stones and the whole set in a rectangular chamfered frame. Inside, the ground floor probably contained storage. The main block's first floor, its timbers supported on a scarcement of the walls, has been the hall. Presumably there was a screen across the E end. At the W (dais) end, a hooded S fireplace with a sconce each side. Stone seats in the window embrasures. The

sw tower contained a private first-floor room but without a fireplace. Stone seats in its NW window; the roof is a stone saucer dome. There is some evidence of further buildings against the E gable, the likely position of the kitchen.

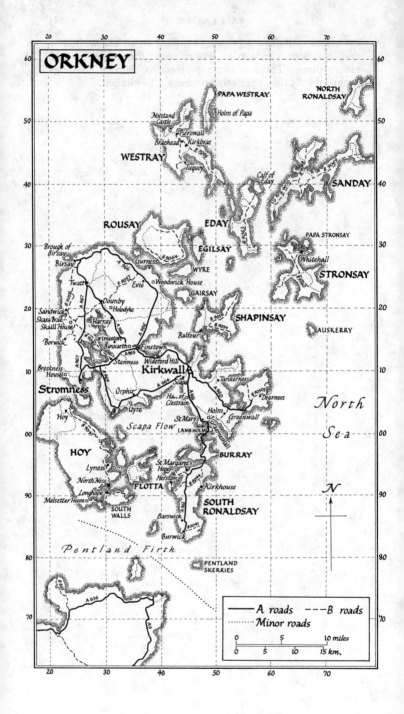

ORKNEY

NORTH
RONALDSAY

PAPA WESTRAY

Holm of Papa

Noltland
Castle

Pierowall
Kirkbrae

Bræhead

WESTRAY

Tuquoy

Calf of
Eday

SANDAY

ROUSAY

EDAY

EGILSAY

PAPA STRONSAY

Brough of
Birsay

Gurness

WYRE

Whitehall

Birsay

Evie

Woodwick House

GAIRSAY

STRONSAY

Twatt

Dounby
Holodyke

SHAPINSAY

Sandwick
Skara Brae
Skaill House

Harray

Balfour

AUSKERRY

Borwick

Grimeston
Binscarth

Finstown

Stenness

Wideford Hill

Breckness
House

Kirkwall

North
Sea

Stromness

Orphir

Scapa

Tankerness

Deerness

Gyre

Ha. of
Clestrain

Holm

Greenwall

Scapa Flow

St.Mary

LAMB HOLM

Hoy

BURRAY

N

HOY

St Margaret's
Hope
Herston

Lyness

Kirkhouse

NorthNess

FLOTTA

Longhope

SOUTH
RONALDSAY

Melsetter House

SOUTH
WALLS

Barswick

Pentland Firth

Burwick

PENTLAND
SKERRIES

—— A roads   --- B roads
.... Minor roads

0   5   10 miles
0   5   10   15 km.

ORKNEY

Archipelago just N of the Scottish mainland, its islands mostly flattish and fertile. They were first colonized by the seventh millennium B.C., early inhabitants leaving the most impressive collection of monuments in Scotland. Viking invasions from c. A.D. 800 led to the establishment of a Norse earldom, which became part of the kingdom of Scotland only in 1469.* After a brief period of supposedly tyrannical rule by the Stewart Earls of Orkney in the late C16 and early C17, the land was divided into small estates, many of the lairds doubling as merchants.

AUSKERRY 6010

Small island c. 5km. S of Stronsay, its medieval chapel now a mere fragment.

LIGHTHOUSE. By *D. & T. Stevenson*, 1865–7. Tapering round brick tower, 34.2m. high.

BALFOUR CASTLE *see* SHAPINSAY

BARSWICK (SOUTH RONALDSAY) 4080

Quite rural, with just the church and school.

CHURCH. Built as South Ronaldsay Free Church in 1873. Tall box, harled except for the snecked rubble E gable. On this front, a birdcage bellcote with a spire roof and cross finial. Intersecting astragals in the pointed windows.

TOMISON'S SCHOOL. Now a house. Built in 1850–1, its foundation financed by a bequest from William Tomison, a native of South Ronaldsay who had made a fortune in the service of the Hudson's Bay Company. U-plan group of three piend-roofed pavilions (originally containing classrooms and teachers' houses), the centre with tall chimneys. Flat-roofed porches in the inner angles; horizontal glazing.

---

*It was received by James III in pledge for 50,000 crowns owed him in dowry as a result of his marriage to Margaret of Denmark.

3010

BINSCARTH (MAINLAND)
1.2km. w of Finstown

Well sited on a hillside amply planted with trees. Harled Jacobean
manor built for Robert Scarth in 1850, his monogram and the
date carved on the Artisan Mannerist doorpiece. – GARDEN
WALL and COTTAGE in the same style to the w.

Downhill to the SW, a big rubble-built STEADING, probably
also mid-C19, with pyramid-roofed towers (now covered with
blue metal sheeting). – WALLED GARDEN S of the steading.

2020

BIRSAY (MAINLAND)

Small village dominated by the ruins of the Earl's Palace.

FREE CHURCH. *See* Twatt.

ST MAGNUS CHURCH. Harled rectangular kirk built in 1664
and enlarged in 1760. Roundheaded S windows, probably of
1760. The W gable's crude birdcage bellcote may be of 1664.
Small SW porch, probably dating from the alterations made in
1867, as may also the three-light Gothic E window. In the N
and S walls, traces of medieval work. Near the N wall's W end,
a very narrow round-arched door (blocked) and to its E a small
lancet window (also blocked) which can hardly be earlier than
the C13. Another small lancet (again blocked) high up in the S
wall, its sill formed by part of a reused lintel inscribed 'S
BELLVS' for Monsbellus, a name given to Birsay in the late
C16.

Inside, a small red sandstone FONT, perhaps late medieval,
one face of its octagonal bowl carved with a coat of arms,
perhaps those of Tulloch (Thomas and William Tulloch were
Bishop of Orkney in the C15) or of Craigie. – STAINED-GLASS
E window (the Crucifixion and scenes from the life of St
Magnus) of 1904, in the manner of Douglas Strachan. – Set
into the floor at the NE corner, a worn GRAVESLAB crudely
carved with the initials NN (probably for Nicol Nisbet) and the
date 1645; coat of arms above, a skull and crossbones below.

In the churchyard, S of the church, rustically inscribed
GRAVESTONES of the mid- and late C18, some with low-relief
emblems of death.

71 EARL'S PALACE. Substantial ruin of the courtyard palace begun
by Robert Stewart, Earl of Orkney, *c.* 1574, and completed by
his son Earl Patrick † 1612. Earl Robert's design was for a
quadrangle, *c.* 39m. by 31m. externally, with two-storey ranges
along its S, W and E sides and towers projecting at the SW, SE
and NE corners and presumably also at the NW. The N side was
to be closed either by a wall or by a fourth range. Earl Patrick
added the N range but with its S front on the line of the originally
intended N wall of the courtyard and its N front projected N of
the already existing NE corner, which was consequently
deprived of its ability to provide an enfilading defence against
attack from the N.

Much of the N and W ranges, less of the E and only a little of the S range, together with most of the three corner towers, survive, all rubble-built. Ground-floor gunloops in every face, plain with splayed rectangular embrasures, even those of the N range eschewing the decorative treatment provided at Earl Patrick's other houses at Kirkwall and Scalloway (Shetland). Some small ground-floor windows to the outside in Earl Robert's ranges; larger (blocked) ground-floor windows in the N range. Big first-floor windows with moulded margins (where not robbed of their dressings), those of the N and E ranges having risen above the wallhead to finial-pedimented dormerheads. Tall wallhead chimneys on the W range.

The courtyard's main entrance was in the centre of the now fragmentary S range. On each side of the passage was a room, the W having a door and large window to the courtyard. Fireplaces in both rooms, the W's brutally restored to avoid confusion with original work.

At each floor of the W range's courtyard elevation, big windows with segmental rear-arches. Gunloops, one splayed, covering the doors at the centre and W end. The centre door opens onto a passage which led through the block but had its outer door built up by the early C17. Opening off this passage is one room on each side. The other ground-floor rooms were entered from the courtyard, the S room giving access to the vaulted store in the SW tower. The whole first floor formed a gallery, with a fireplace near the W wall's N end. In the N gable, a big window converted c. 1600 into a door to the N range. To its W, a close garderobe, perhaps made from a doorway provided in the C16 for access to the intended but unbuilt NW tower.

The E range seems to have contained ground-floor stores, all entered from the court. At its N end, a room now entered through the N block's stairtower, with a fireplace in the S wall. At this room's NE corner, a small projection, possibly for a narrow stair to the first floor, which probably contained the C16 hall, withdrawing room and lord's chamber.

The N range of c. 1600 is L-plan, with a SE jamb containing the stair. Ground-floor gunloops commanding the courtyard. The central entrance opens into a passage running along the S front. To the N and W of this passage are two large stores, the W with a second entrance from the courtyard, both with sizeable (blocked) windows. At the passage's E end was the kitchen. In the gable wall, part of the fireplace's N jamb. The first floor was divided into a hall and W chamber.

BRIDGE. Dated 1872. Two arches with triangular cutwaters. Fat stone cones at the ends of the parapet.

BOARDHOUSE MILL, 0.7km. E. Complex of three rubble-built mills on the S side of a burn. Three-storey NEW BARONY CORN MILL at the E, built in 1873, with a large kiln. – Small OLD BARONY MILL, perhaps C18. – At the W, a large late C19 THRESHING MILL.

KITCHENER MEMORIAL, Marwick Head, 3.2km. SW. Built in 1926 overlooking the scene of Lord Kitchener's death ten years before, when H.M.S. *Hampshire* was sunk. 13.6m.-high tower, its battered rubble walls barely relieved by two stringcourses. Battered bartizans with panelled sides at the corners of the battlement, from whose N and S sides project big stone spouts.

STANE O' QUOYBUNE, 1.5km. SE. Tall standing stone, nearly 4m. high, erected in the second millennium B.C.

2010   BORWICK (MAINLAND)

Place-name for an area on the W shore of Mainland.

BROCH. Ruin of the broch built *c.* 100 B.C.-100 A.D. The site is a high promontory whose cliffs dip down on the S towards an inlet ending in a sandy beach. Across the promontory's landward side has been a wall, *c.* 18m. E of the broch itself. The broch's W half has been destroyed by coastal erosion, but the E half still stands to a height of almost 3m., its semicircular wall's battered outer face built with massive boulders surmounted by smaller stones. Over the entrance passage's first part, roofing slabs, which provide the floor for a small cell in the wall above. Then door checks formed of superimposed upright slabs. Just beyond them, on the passage's N side, a guard cell in the wall.

4040   BRAEHEAD (WESTRAY)

Just a church and a few houses.

WESTRAY UNITED FREE CHURCH. Built as a United Secession meeting house, 1823. In the long sides, two tiers of windows, the lower rectangular, the upper roundheaded with intersecting astragals. Foliage finial on the E gable, whose door and windows are all roundheaded. Attached to the W gable, a mid-C19 session house with a gableted bellcote. – Inside, a gallery round three sides, the pulpit at the W end.

BROUGH HOUSE, 0.4km. NE. Harled and crowstepped laird's house, probably late C18. The gabled porch and single-storey W wing look C19 additions.

2000   BRECKNESS HOUSE (MAINLAND)
2.8km. W of Stromness

Roofless and derelict two-storey mansion house of quite pacific character built by George Graham, Bishop of Orkney, in 1633. Walling of honey-coloured rubble with the surviving dressings of grey sandstone. The windows have had rounded margins with glazing grooves. The plan is an L, but unusually the entrance is placed not in the inner angle (now filled with the remains of lean-to additions) but at the centre of the long E wall in a shallow porch whose doorpiece has had moulded jambs.

Inside the door, a small vestibule with the remains of a straight stone stair rising from it. The N room on the ground floor was the kitchen, its gable containing two segmental arches, the r. for the fireplace, the l. for a deep recess. The ground floor's s room seems to have been the C 17 hall. Large W fireplace; to its N, an aumbry with a moulded frame. In the N wall two doors (both blocked), the l. to a closet under the stair, the r. to the vestibule. This room has been subdivided (the partition wall since removed) in the C 18 or C 19, when a small fireplace was inserted in the E wall and an outside door made in the S. Two rooms on the first floor, the N with a fireplace in the gable and a close garderobe with window and lamp recess to its E.

BROUGH OF BIRSAY   2020

Ruins of a church and settlement on a small island joined (at low tide) to the mainland by a causeway.

CHURCH. Standing in a roughly rectangular rubble-walled enclosure whose s part has been used as a graveyard. The church, probably erected in the early C 12, is traditionally said to have been dedicated to St Peter.* The lower part of its walls survive, built of good-quality rubble. It has comprised a nave, c. 9.7m. by 5.7m., choir and apse. Tusking shows that a rectangular W tower was intended if not built. In the N walls of the choir and apse (better preserved than the rest), two windows, both splayed. Inside, a stone bench along the sides of the nave and across its W end. The entrance to the choir is a doorway, 1.3m. wide, flanked by semicircular recesses in the nave's E wall, probably intended to contain small altars. The high altar in the choir is a reconstruction of 1934. Behind it, a cross-wall, probably late medieval, cutting off the apse.

N of the church and within the enclosure are the coursed rubble bases of the walls of buildings which have formed an irregular U. They are clearly associated with the church and may have been monastic.

Immediately s of the enclosure, the CAST of a late C 7 Pictish stone‡ incised with 'mirror-case', 'crescent and V-rod', 'swimming elephant', and eagle symbols. Below, three low-relief figures of warriors, each dressed in a long belted tunic and carrying a shield and spear, the leader with smartly curled hair. – To the s, an early medieval GRAVESTONE, now set upright, its face incised with a cross which has a circle at the intersection of the arms.

SETTLEMENT. N, W and SW of the church enclosure are the foundations of oblong houses with rounded corners, built from the C 9. – NE of the enclosure, on the edge of the cliff, foundations of a rectangular Norse SMITHY standing by itself. – E

*Or, less authoritatively, St Colm. The suggestion, first made in 1958, that this was Christ Church, Orkney's first cathedral church, built by Earl Thorfinn in the mid-C 11, seems unlikely.

‡The original is now in the Royal Museum of Scotland, Edinburgh.

of the enclosure, foundations of small rooms, probably late
medieval. On the edge of the cliff, truncated fragments of two
substantial Norse buildings. The N, with a central fire-pit in its
paved floor and stone benches round the wall, may have been
a bath-house. The S was a large hall. – To their S, remains of a
contemporary paved PASSAGE, perhaps a boat slip, which
seems to have led down to the shore, its lower end now vanished,
a victim of coastal erosion.

BURRAY

One of a chain of islands linked to the S coast of Mainland by the
Churchill Barriers.

OLD PARISH CHURCH, Kirk Taing. Roofless rubble rectangle
built in 1621 (the date formerly visible on the NW skewputt).
High up in each gable a window, the E (built-up) with a roll
moulding, the W with chamfered margins. Near the S wall's W
end, a door whose roll moulding is interrupted before the top
of the jambs but reappears on the lintel. Roll-moulded window
in this wall's centre and another window with chamfered
margins to its E. Small SW vestry, probably a late Georgian
addition.

ST LAWRENCE'S CHURCH, Burray village. Plain harled box
built for the United Presbyterians in 1856. In the side walls,
tall rectangular windows; basket-arched windows in the gables
which are topped by pinnacled stone balls. W porch.

SCHOOL, Burray village. Harled L-plan, dated 1868.

BURRAY VILLAGE. Group of C18 and C19 vernacular buildings
along the shore, with C20 houses behind. At the W entry, WEST
END, a late Georgian two-storey house, now drydashed and
with a C20 conservatory across the front. To its E a harled
rubble STORE HOUSE, dated 1645 on its moulded SW skewputt.
Two storeys, with a stone forestair to the first-floor door. Chamfered window margins; a chimney on the W gable. For St
Lawrence's Church and the School, *see* above. At the village's
E end, a mid-C19 PIER built of coursed blocks of stone. Behind
is the SANDS MOTEL, converted from a plain twelve-bay warehouse of 1860.

BU OF BURRAY. Substantial farmhouse, now drydashed, built *c.*
1790 by the island's principal tenant, Captain Balfour, to
replace a C17 laird's house. Three storeys and three bays, with
small second-floor windows. The porch is an addition, as is
probably the single-storey N wing.

Immediately NW of the house, a small rubble-built and flag-
stone-roofed OUTBUILDING, perhaps early C19. On top of its
N gable is part of a mid-C17 lintel, set on its side; it is carved
with the initials BS for Barbara Stewart, the daughter and
heiress of James Stewart of Burray. – To its N, a contemporary
rubble-walled BARN with a roof of stone slates. In the W gable,
flight-holes for pigeons. – To the N and W, an extensive col-

lection of late C18 and C19 FARM BUILDINGS, rubble-built with stone-slate roofs.

CHURCHILL BARRIERS. *See* p. 294.

BURWICK (SOUTH RONALDSAY) *4080*

Church overlooking the eponymous bay.

ST MARY'S CHURCH. Harled and crowstep-gabled kirk of *c.* 1788. Rectangular windows in the s wall and a door in each gable. Sturdy crowstepped w bellcote. The interior, reordered in 1898, is very plain. MONUMENTS. At the N wall's E end, GRAVESLAB of James Kynnaird of Burwick † 1624, with two coats of arms under his initials and those of his wife, Janet Balfour. – In the vestry, GRAVESTONE of Sir Hugh Halcro, Rector of Ronaldsay, † 1544, carved with his coat of arms, a cross and a chalice. – Also in the vestry is the GREY WHIN or LADYKIRK STONE, a roughly oval block of water-worn whinstone, its top's central ridge flanked by foot-shaped hollows.

sw of the church, a small free-standing GABLE containing a rectangular door, perhaps part of the previous church.

BURNT MOUND, Liddel, 2.4km. E. Excavated remains of a cooking shelter of the early first millennium B.C. The lower courses of the walls survive, forming a rough oval. Inside, a paved floor and upright slabs making compartments, probably for storage, round the walls. In the centre, a sunk watertight trough, its sides and bottom formed of thick slabs. It was used to boil water heated by stones taken from the hearth, of which traces were discovered to the SE, where it was recessed into the wall.

CAIRN (TOMB OF THE EAGLES), Isbister, 3km. E. Oval cairn built *c.* 3000 B.C. The tomb inside is a hybrid, a stalled chamber with Maes-Howe-type side cells. Chamber just over 8m. long, divided into three compartments by upright slabs; at each end, a compartment with a stone shelf. Three small cells opening off.

FORT (CASTLE OF BURWICK), 0.5km. w. Cliff-edged peninsula joined to the mainland by a very narrow neck. On the mainland, three ramparts with ditches between, a fourth rampart on the promontory, all probably of the late first millennium B.C. Inside the enclosure, grass-covered foundations, presumably of houses.

CALF OF EDAY *5030*

Uninhabited island N of Eday, now used for grazing but on whose w shore John, Earl of Carrick, attempted to establish a saltworks in the early C17.

SALTWORKS. Roofless ruins of two buildings of *c.* 1632 associated with the saltpans. Each has a bowed gable into the sea and a straight gable built into the hillside behind. In their thick centre walls were fireplaces, of which one survives in the s building.

CAIRNS. Three cairns placed close together near the shore at the island's sw, all probably dating from the third millennium B.C. The SE cairn is a low mound, c. 10m. in diameter, covering an entrance passage cut into the s slope of the hillside and a roughly oval underground chamber with side compartments formed by upright slabs. – Just to its NW, a second cairn, again covered by a mound, c. 7.6m. in diameter, its centre removed for access to the chamber below. This is divided by upright slabs into a central space and four compartments, which seem to have had stone benches. At the backs of the N and W compartments the drystone masonry is built on top of the cut rock-face of the hill. Another cut rock-face supporting masonry on the W side of the entrance passage from the s. – A little further to the NW, a long cairn, c. 20m. by 8.2m., left open after excavation. Its covering stones have been retained by a drystone wall which stands to a height of 0.6m. Inside are two chambers. The earlier and smaller drystone-walled W chamber, its SE entrance passage blocked, has pairs of upright slabs at its entrance and back wall and at the centre to divide it into two compartments. The cairn was extended when the long E chamber was added. Side and end walls of drystone masonry. Pairs of upright slabs forming four compartments; against the sides of the slabs, edge-set small stones which have supported stone shelves. Entrance passage at the E.

CARRICK HOUSE *see* EDAY

4090
CHURCHILL BARRIERS

Four causeway-topped dams of concrete blocks stringing together the islands of South Ronaldsay, Burray, Glimps Holm and Lamb Holm. They were built in 1940–4 by *Balfour Beatty*, with the labour of Italian prisoners-of-war, to block the E entry to Scapa Flow, where H.M.S. *Royal Oak* had been sunk by a German U-boat in 1939.

5000
DEERNESS (MAINLAND)

Flat peninsula with a narrow link to the sw corner of Mainland.

CHAPEL, Brough of Deerness. Remains of an early medieval chapel and settlement isolated at the top of the Deerness peninsula. The site is a roughly triangular fragment of land, with steep cliffs on all sides, now accessible only by a perilous descent from the mainland down to a beach and a climb up the s front.

Formerly it seems to have been reached by a narrow neck of rock near the W end of its S side, where there is an entrance in the flagstone wall (now grass-covered) defending this approach. Near the centre of the brough is a stone-walled rectangular enclosure, which has been entered through a gateway near the SW corner. Inside the enclosure the lower courses of the chapel's walls survive. They are built of a mixture of flat slabs and larger blocks. Door in the centre of the W gable. Lower part of an altar against the E wall. Excavation has shown that this chapel, perhaps of the C12, replaced an earlier one, probably C10, which was timber-framed and stone-clad.

S of the enclosure, a round WELL. – To the N and W are the grassy foundations of a sizeable group of stone HOUSES, mostly rectangular. Possibly they were monastic. Round depressions on the W. Some at least seem to be shell-holes dating from the First World War, when the brough was used as a target for artillery practice, but others may be the foundations of beehive huts, perhaps associated with the C10 chapel.

ST NINIAN'S CHURCH, Skaill. By *Joseph Mitchell*, 1829. Harled kirk with roundheaded windows. Solid-looking birdcage bellcote on the E gable. The vestry and porch look like additions. Interior altered in 1924.

WEST CHURCH, 1.7km. W of Skaill. Built by *John Dick*, mason, 1843–4. Harled box; roundheaded windows. The spired ventilator on the roof is probably late Victorian.

COVENANTERS MEMORIAL, Scarva Taing. Rubble-built tapering pier, 12.2m. high, with a cushion capital. It was built in 1888 to commemorate two hundred Convenanters who died in 1679 when the ship transporting them to the Colonies was wrecked off Orkney.

DOUNBY (MAINLAND)   *2020*

Small village.

UNITED FREE CHURCH. Pebble-dashed cruciform, dated 1947. Basket-arched windows; E porch with a deeply splayed door and spire-topped birdcage bellcote of concrete.

PRIMARY SCHOOL AND COMMUNITY CENTRE. By *Orkney County Council*, 1976. Single-storey and flat-roofed, the walls covered in drydash with blue metal trim.

CLICK MILL, 3.7km. NE. Built c. 1825. Small rough rectangle, its walls of flagstone rubble, the roof of flagstones covered with turf. Tirl of two six-paddle rows.

NISTHOUSE, 1.9km. SE. Prosperous early C19 farmhouse of two storeys and three bays, with a big chimney stack on the centre of its piend roof. – Beside it, a smaller farmhouse, probably late C18.

SABISTON MILL, 0.6km. N. C19 two-storey L-plan mill, the kiln vent now mostly removed. Wheel at the N gable.

HOLODYKE. *See* p. 308.

EDAY

Narrow island with heather-covered low hills on its w side, cattle pasture on the E.

BAPTIST CHURCH. Secularized. Dated 1881. Unambitious, except for the pointed windows and door in the front gable.

Former PARISH CHURCHES. There are three. The earliest, in a rubble-walled enclosure on a hillside s of the present Parish Church, was built *c.* 1730. The N and E walls largely survive. They are of harled rubble. E door; vestry on the N. – Its successor in the graveyard at Skaill to the E was put up in 1815–16. Harled roofless rectangle with windows in the s wall and a door in the E (the W gable has been demolished). – s of these is the third (now in secular use), which was opened in 1895. Minimal Gothic, a Celtic cross on the E gable.

PARISH CHURCH. Built for the United Presbyterians in 1858. Tall harled rectangle. Depressed arches in the side walls and W gable. Another depressed arch at the E door, but it is flanked by narrow roundheaded windows and surmounted by an obtusely pointed window of three stone-mullioned lancet lights. Projecting keystones at all openings. On the E gable, a small spire-topped birdcage bellcote. – The interior's PEWS and PULPIT are of 1904. – E GALLERY of 1858, with blind Romanesque arcading on its front.

CARRICK HOUSE. Laird's house composed of several tenuously connected units, looking over the sheltered Bay of Carrick to Calf of Eday. The main block is at the N, a harled crowstep-gabled house of two storeys and an attic built by John Stewart, Earl of Carrick, in 1632–3. In its W front one ground-floor window and two at the first floor still have C17 chamfered margins. The other windows are all of *c.* 1830, those of the first-floor drawing room at the N end deeper than the rest. Also of *c.* 1830 the corniced porch in the centre of the E front and perhaps the lean-to single-storey W addition. This late Georgian remodelling further included the building of a short link from the C17 house to a formerly detached single-storey block to the s. This block, still with a crowstepped E gable and now embellished with a mid-C19 stone dormerhead on the s front, may be C16 in origin, built for the Sinclairs, who possessed Eday from 1560 to 1617.

In 1852 Carrick House was bought by Robert James Hebden, who made further additions over a number of years, providing a two-storey morning-room extension W of the s block (by then containing the kitchen and laundry) and short single-storey jambs at its SW and SE, all this work crowstepped and now covered with Caithness stone slates.

WALLED GARDEN to the E. Most of the walling is probably early C19, but at the NW corner is a moulded round-arched gateway with a keystone dated 1633. Above the gateway, a worn panel carved with the date 1662 and the arms and initials of Arthur Buchanan of Sound and his wife, Marjory Buxton, the then owners.

Mid-C19 courtyard STEADING 0.5km. S, rubble-built, the roofs covered with red sandstone flags. In its SE corner, a farmhouse of 1858 with stone dormerheads over the first-floor windows.

CHAMBERED CAIRN, Vinquoy Hill. Low round cairn of Maes Howe type, prominently placed on a moorland ridge. The site slopes gently to the S where is placed the entrance to a passage partly cut into the hill, as is the irregular polygon of the central chamber, whose walls are corbelled gently inwards to support the missing roof slabs. Off this chamber are paired entrances to the four small side-cells. The cairn probably dates from the third millennium B.C.

STONE OF SETTER. Exceptionally tall (4.5m.-high) sandstone monolith, deeply furrowed by weathering. It was probably set up in the second millennium B.C.

EGILSAY
4020

Low island E of Rousay, the site of the martyrdom of St Magnus in 1116.

PARISH CHURCH. Built as a United Presbyterian church in 1885. Very simple harled box, with a pinnacled ball finial on the W gable, a chimney on the E. Only the W windows are round-headed.

ST MAGNUS CHURCH. Roofless C12* shrine church, probably 7 built on the site of the chapel in which St Magnus prayed before his death. A likely date is c. 1135–8, when, according to The Orkneyinga Saga, William, Bishop of Orkney, was in frequent if not constant residence on Egilsay, perhaps to oversee the church's erection. It comprises a crowstep-gabled nave, c. 10m. by 5.7m., a rectangular and crowstepped chancel, c. 5.5m. by 3.8m., and a tapering round tower now of four stages but formerly higher and covered by a conical roof of stone slabs. The masonry is of rubble with putlock holes, the tower being built of smaller stones than the rest.

Near the W end of the nave's N and S walls are doors facing each other (the N now blocked), both with semicircular arches springing from inside the jambs. To their E, a window in each wall, each with a semicircular arch set back from one jamb. The rectangular windows above the S door and at the S wall's E end are later insertions, perhaps of the C17. In the chancel's N and S walls, small windows (now blocked), each with a semicircular arch set back on one jamb like those of the nave. High up in the E gable, a narrow rectangular window to light a room above the chancel.

*An earlier date has been suggested, but it seems more probable that such a smart church was built to commemorate St Magnus than that it was already in existence as if anticipating the martyrdom.

Inside, an unmoulded semicircular chancel arch (its shape slightly distorted by the pressure of the walls) the full width of the tunnel-vaulted chancel. Above the arch is a door to the room over the chancel, its round arch again set back from the jambs; the sill seems to have been lowered. At the E end of each of the chancel's N and S walls, a small rectangular recess. They are both c. 3.9m. above floor level and almost but not quite directly opposite each other. What was their purpose?

In the outer faces of the W tower, tall slit windows. To the E the tower has doors at two levels opening into the nave, the upper presumably giving access to a gallery. The lower door's roundheaded arch springs directly from the jambs, the upper door's arch is set back. Clear of the nave roof, a second-floor basket-arched window; big slit window at the third floor.

MONUMENT. By *John Firth*, 1938. Diminutive snecked rubble tower with strongly battered sides and a stepped top. It marks the site traditionally held to be that of the martyrdom of St Magnus in 1116.

SCHOOL. Late C19 school and schoolhouse, built of rubble, partly harled. Recent hall addition.

HOWAN. Derelict group of buildings round a courtyard. The main house, probably late C17, at the S range's W end, is of two storeys, built of rubble (formerly harled). Chamfered margins at the windows. Crowstepped gables with moulded skewputts, the NW having been carved with the initials of William Douglas and his wife, Marjorie Monteith, heiress of the island of Egilsay. At the S wall a (roofless) lean-to porch. Inside the porch, a C17 first-floor door with a later door beside it. Two ground-floor doors, the r. checked to open outwards. The inner face of this door's lintel is carved with a crowned heart flanked by *fleurs-de-lis* whose tendrils end in thistles and roses and with the inscription

16. AMICIS.ET.GENIO.81

In the W ground-floor room, a stone fireplace with fluted jambs.

At the E end of the main house, a now roofless single-storey building. Inside it, a moulded stone fireplace, now much weathered but whose lintel (probably reused) used to bear the arms and initials of Robert Monteith and his wife, Katharine Nisbet, together with the date 1635.

On the courtyard's short E side, a drystone store. Fragmentary N range. The W side has been closed by a screen wall running N from near the main block's W end. In the wall's surviving S stub, one jamb of a roll-moulded and roundheaded arch.

KIRBIST. Plain mid-C19 two-storey FARMHOUSE tacked on to the W end of its late C18 single-storey-and-attic crowstep-gabled predecessor. – Rubble-built mid-C19 L-plan STEADING. – Also mid-C19 is the CORNMILL, with a water wheel at the W wall.

EVIE (MAINLAND)   3020

Hamlet with a church.

OLD PARISH CHURCH, 1.6km. SE. Now a garage and with a corrugated iron roof. Harled box built in 1799. Roundheaded windows in the long sides, bullseyes in the gables. The sloping buttresses are probably additions. At the W gable, corbelling for a vanished late Victorian bellcote; porch of *c.* 1900. Big garage door in the E gable. SE vestry addition.

PARISH CHURCH. Originally Evie Free Church. By *Samuel Baikie & Son*, 1885–6. Tall lancet-windowed rectangle. Small bellcote with a lucarned spire at the N. Rose window in the S gable.

HOWE, 0.7km. NW. C19 rubble-built cornmill with the wheel on the W wall.

WOODWICK HOUSE. *See* p. 376.

EYNHALLOW   3020

The name (*Eyin-helga* in Old Norse) means 'Holy Isle', and *The Orkneyinga Saga* implies that it was occupied in the C12 by monks, possibly a Benedictine community. If there was a monastery here, it seems to have been abandoned before the Reformation. The island was cleared of its cottagers in 1851 and its only house is now the late Victorian LODGE, used as a base for ornithological research.

CHURCH. Substantial remains of an early medieval church, probably of the C12. After the Reformation it was converted to three houses, these being abandoned and their roofs removed in 1851. The ruin was consolidated by *W. R. Lethaby* in 1897. Nave, rectangular chancel and porch, all built of split slabs of grey whinstone. Square W porch, possibly the base of an intended or partially demolished tower. Narrow (0.46m.) W door, inclined slabs forming a triangular head. N door just as narrow but with a semicircular head cut out of a block of red sandstone. These both look early or mid-C12. The rectangular S door is probably a post-Reformation insertion. Putlock holes in the W and S walls. Round-arched doorway into the nave, its springing set back on the jambs. Each side of the door, a putlock hole. In each of the nave's side walls, a door near the E end and a window, all rectangular and probably inserted when the nave became a house. Also dating from its period of domestic use are the large blocked cupboard in the N wall and the three aumbries in the S. In the E wall, the entrance to the chancel, fractionally narrower than the nave doorway but with a would-be pointed arch ingeniously constructed of the unsuitable local flags by the use of dressed red sandstone triangular blocks for the keystone and springers. That the arch is pointed suggests a date not before the last few decades of the C12. Putlock hole to the S of the arch. The chancel was used as a house after the

church fell out of use, its s wall being thickened externally, the
E gable largely rebuilt and provided with a first-floor fireplace,
and a door made through the N wall to a new room built against
it. In the N wall, a splayed window, probably of the late C12,
and an aumbry.

Remains of a s addition at the nave's w end. It seems to have
contained a passage next to the church. s of the passage, a
moulded late medieval door to the bottom of a staircase. Was
this a belfry? s of that and w of the church the lower portions
of the walls survive of an agglomeration of buildings. Their
position relative to the church suggests they may have been
monastic in origin, perhaps originally making a T-shaped block
immediately w of the porch, with the tail protruding to the N,
and later remodelled and extended to the w, s and SE.

3010   FINSTOWN (MAINLAND)

Substantial village laid out in the early C19 and reputedly named
after an Irish soldier called Phin who settled there *c.* 1822. Much
of the present housing is mid-C20.

FIRTH PARISH CHURCH. Drydashed Gothic cruciform, built
as a United Free church in 1902. Jerkin-head roof with red-tile
cresting. It may have looked less dumpy before the removal of
its flèche.
FIRTH FREE CHURCH. Now a church hall. Built in 1870.
Lancet-windowed box in sneck-harled rubble, a pyramid-
roofed birdcage bellcote on the N gable.
GRAVEYARD. The former Firth Parish Church of 1813 has been
demolished. Well-stocked rubble-walled graveyard with a mid-
C19 crowstep-gabled SESSION HOUSE.
PIER. Long rubble-built C19 pier.

BINSCARTH. *See* p. 288.
BURNESS, 3.3km. NE. Harled and crowstepped house of two
storeys and three bays, perhaps early C18; late C19 gabled
porch. At each side and attached to the main block by a short
screen wall is a lower projecting wing, again crowstep-gabled.
The E wing extends back behind the main block, its rear portion
earlier than the rest. – Extensive collection of rubble-built
STEADING buildings, mostly C19.
CHAMBERED CAIRN, Cuween Hill, 1.1km. SE. Round grass-
covered cairn of Maes Howe type, probably built in the third
millennium B.C. Entrance passage on the E, its outer part a
stone-walled trench, its inner length curving and rising slightly
and roofed at a height of 0.6m. with lintel slabs set on edge
except at the ends, where they are laid flat, those at the outer
end probably dating from a repair. Roughly rectangular central
chamber, *c.* 1.65m. by 3.35m., with the long E and W walls
slightly curved and the N wall angled. The walls, still standing
to a height of *c.* 2.3m., are superbly constructed of very long
thin slabs, with a gentle inward corbelling to carry the roof (a

replacement). Smooth rock floor. In each wall, a small doorway into a cell *c*. 1.7m. high, the N and W doorways each with a step up, the entrance to the E crossed by a kerb of horizontal slabs. The S cell's floor is level with the main chamber's, the lower part of its side walls of the same build as the chamber's and the lower part of the partition wall apparently an insertion. Above the level of its entrance lintel the partition is bonded into the chamber walls, so the formation of this cell may have resulted from a change in the design during construction. The W cell has two compartments, the outer roofed with flat slabs (probably a reconstruction), the inner with slabs on edge. Slabs on edge form the roofs of the N and E cells.

EARTH-HOUSE, Rennibister, 3.5km. E. Souterrain of the first millennium B.C., originally entered from the NW by a narrow drystone-walled passage, only *c*. 0.7m. high, but now through a hatch in the chamber's roof. Roughly hexagonal chamber *c*. 1.5m. high, its drystone walls corbelled inwards to carry the roofing lintels, which are given extra support by four stone pillars. In the corners, five small recesses, one divided by a stone shelf.

FIRTH *see* FINSTOWN (MAINLAND)

FLOTTA 3090

Flattish island between Hoy and South Ronaldsay, its N part now the site of an oil terminal.

PARISH CHURCH. Harled rectangle, possibly C17 in origin, but reroofed with heather thatch (since replaced by slates) *c*. 1782, when it probably acquired its roundheaded windows.

GAIRSAY 4020

Small island with a sheltered anchorage, strategically sited on the approach to the Bays of Firth and Kirkwall. In the late C12, according to *The Orkneyinga Saga*, it served as the winter quarters of the Viking raider Svein Asleifarson, who kept there a retinue of eighty men and 'had a drinking hall so large that there was not another to match it for size in the Orkneys.' Now there is a small but smart mansion house.

LANGSKAILL. Not improbably on the site of Svein Asleifarson's drinking hall (the name means 'long hall'), but nothing of the present building is likely to be earlier than the later C16. A 'maner place' existed on Gairsay by 1588, when the island was sold by William Muirhead to William Bannatyne, and may perhaps be identified as the present house's E range. A major extension of the building took place in the late C17, probably

begun soon after the marriage of William Craigie of Gairsay to
Margaret Honeyman, daughter of the Bishop of Orkney, in
1673* and completed in 1676, the date carved on a skewputt.
By the 1790s the house was 'almost in ruins' and it was later
partly demolished, only the E range being remodelled for occupation in a restoration of c. 1900.

The late C17 remodelling produced a U-plan house, with W,
N and E ranges of two storeys, probably with attics; the court's
open S side was closed by a screen wall. All the surviving work
is rubble-built and was originally harled. The S front was and
still is the showpiece, approached by a straight perron stair from
the shore. At this front the gables of the E and W ranges (the E
now cut down and crowstepped, the W's top removed) grip the
formerly balustraded screen wall, this combination of gable
ends and a balustraded flat-roofed centrepiece or screen wall a
recurring motif in Scottish post-Restoration classicism. The
screen wall rises to the uncorbelled corniced parapet, whose
front is pierced by square gunloops. More gunloops below, but
of oval shape. They flank the roundheaded pend arch, its simple
moulding enriched with carved vines. Over the arch and rising
well above the parapet, a large but weathered armorial panel
set in an aedicule, its now missing columns having stood on
corbels whose soffits are carved with human heads, their sides
with foliage; on the wall between the corbels, more carved heads
flanking a garland of fruit. The aedicule's cornice is enriched
with egg-and-dart ornament and surmounted by a steep pediment, its scroll sides carved with human figures, its tympanum
with the monogrammed initials of William Craigie and Margaret Honeyman under worn carved figures.

Of the W range only the truncated S gable and part of the W
wall survive. SE skewputt carved with the initials MH and the
date 1676. Large moulded ground-floor windows, with grooves
for fixed glazing above shutters. In the gable's centre, a badly
weathered panel in a moulded frame. The N range has been
demolished.

The E range is still roofed and inhabited but its present single-
storey-and-attic crowstep-gabled appearance dates from its
reconstruction c. 1900, when the upper floor which must have
given access to the screen wall's parapet walk was replaced by
an attic with a big crowstepped stone dormer to the court. In
the S gable, two small ground-floor windows with chamfered
margins; they could be C16. The bigger window to their l. is of
c. 1900. In the centre of the gable, a moulded frame containing
a panel carved with a lion rampant, probably late C17 but not
in situ. In the long elevation to the courtyard, three doors, the
plain outer two perhaps C16 but converted to windows c. 1900.
Above the r. door, a moulded frame containing a very worn
carved panel. The moulded and corniced centre door is late
C17. Its lintel-frieze has been inscribed with a monogram of the

*Craigie was still under-age in 1668, and 1673 was the year of both his marriage
and his registration of arms.

initials of William Craigie and Margaret Honeyman and a
motto. The l. and r. doors each gave access to a sizeable room,
the N (now subdivided) probably the kitchen, the S the hall,
and the C17 centre door to a straight stair to the upper floor,
this stair replaced and the wall on its S rebuilt much more thinly
c. 1900. There seem in the C17 to have been two rooms (the
Blue Room and the Yellow Room) on the first floor. Their late
C17 chimneypieces survive in the present attic. (In its S room,
a large moulded stone chimneypiece, its lintel decorated with
a guilloche pattern enriched with *fleur-de-lis* and bunches of
grapes under the inscription (partly a conflation of lines from
Virgil's *Georgics* and the *Elegies* of Tibullus):

FOELIX OPES QVI CVM SAPIENTIA [DIRIGERIT?]
FOELIX [QVI] POTUIT CONTENTUS VIV[ERE PARVO]

(Happy he who has ordered wealth with wisdom
Happy he who has been able to live content with little)

In the N room, another moulded stone chimneypiece, its lintel
bearing the WCMH monogram flanked by hunting scenes.)

GRÆMESHALL (MAINLAND)   4000
1.3km E of St Mary's

Low-key Jacobean manor house built for and largely designed by
Alexander Malcolm Sutherland Græme and his wife, Margaret
Isabel Neale (their initials carved on two window pediments on
the W front), in 1874–98 to replace a laird's house. That house
had consisted of two main blocks separated by a courtyard, the
S range possibly late C15, the N built in 1626 for Patrick Smyth
of Braco, who had acquired the estate through his marriage to
Katherine Graham, daughter of George Graham, Bishop of
Orkney. The first phase of rebuilding took place in 1874–6,
when the existing S block was demolished and its two-storey-
and-attic replacement built on its site and over the courtyard.
The second phase in 1896–8 added pedimented and scroll-
sided dormerheads to the 1870s S block, replaced the C17 N
block, and provided a small service courtyard on the E, with a
single-storey chapel forming its S range. This C19 work is
unexciting, with mullioned and transomed windows the principal features, but it incorporates a surprising amount of early
C17 features. The main (W) door was the C17 E entrance to the
courtyard, a round-arched and roll-moulded gateway of red
sandstone, heightened and given a transom of yellowish stone
in 1874–6. Another C17 gateway E of the chapel. In the service
courtyard's N range, quite a lot more. Its gabled porch came
from the N of the old house; it was rebuilt on the site of the
chapel in the 1870s and moved here in 1896–8. Above its roll-
moulded doorpiece (heightened in the 1870s), a red sandstone
panel, inscribed

16   26
PATEAS AMICIS

A small slitlike window in this block's front wall looks C17. Certainly C17 is the stone carved with the arms and initials of Bishop George Graham which used to be above the old courtyard's E entrance. In a C19 stone dormerhead is reset a C17 pedimented dormerhead with scrolls on its sides; tympanum carved with a rosette and the date 1644, the year in which it was added to the old S block.

More C17 work is reused inside. In the library at the SE, an oak chimneypiece incorporating panels of c. 1630 from Bishop Graham's gallery in St Magnus Cathedral, Kirkwall. They are carved with the arms of the Bishop and his sons-in-law and stylized foliage. In the dining room N of the entrance hall, armorial panels on the back of the sideboard recess. The l., bearing Patrick Smyth's arms, is again from Bishop Graham's gallery, the others are of the 1890s. In the stair window, late C19 heraldic STAINED GLASS (the arms of Sutherland and Graham).

The CHAPEL's interior is very simple. In the S wall, STAINED GLASS (St Margaret of Antioch and St Margaret of Scotland), probably of 1898. – Against the N wall, a weathered medieval GRAVESLAB from Holm Parish Church, carved with a Celtic cross. – Against the W wall, another medieval GRAVE-SLAB from Holm churchyard, incised with three swords (the arms of the Orkney family of Magnuson or Manson).

In the garden, colossal STATUES of Faith, Hope and Charity (1868), from the demolished Y.M.C.A. in Inverness.

5000 GREENWALL (MAINLAND)
1.2km. E of Holm

Tall two-storey-and-attic laird's house built for Patrick Graham, a son of Bishop George Graham, in 1656. Rubble walls; roof still partly covered with stone slates. Crowstepped gables with moulded skewputts; rounded window margins. At the front, a shallow stone porch with a moulded doorpiece and steep pediment enclosing a worn stone, presumably once carved with a coat of arms. The front's E first-floor window (originally lighting the drawing room) is deeper than the others. Lean-to addition of c. 1840 along the back; another small lean-to at the W gable. Inside, an inglenook fireplace in the W ground-floor room (originally the hall).

Rubble-built FARM BUILDINGS, probably early C19, to the N and W.

3010 GRIMESTON (MAINLAND)

Small scattered hamlet E of the Loch of Harray.

CONGREGATIONAL CHURCH. Secularized. Built in two stages, 1817–23. Humble, with a crude bellcote. – Early C19 single-storey T-plan MANSE adjoining.

BUCKQUOY. C19 single-storey steading, built of flagstone rubble with roofs of stone slabs. Among the buildings, a small MILL dated 1876 on its E gable.

GURNESS (MAINLAND)   3020

Site at the N end of the Aikerness peninsula where the substantial remains of a broch and late Iron Age houses were uncovered by excavation from 1930.

BROCH AND SETTLEMENT. The broch and its defences, standing on the edge of low cliffs overlooking Eynhallow Sound, were probably built c. 100 B.C. – A.D. 100. Defences consisting of three ditches, the outer 2.44m.–4.57m. broad, the middle c. 1.7m. broad, and the inner 2.44m.–5.18m. across, each with a rampart, the innermost still standing to a height of c. 3m. They enclose what was a circular platform of c. 40m. diameter before its N part fell into the sea. Across the inner ditch are narrow walls built of flat stones, their purpose unclear. On the E side the ditches are crossed by a causeway, the ramparts of the outer ditches curved in to meet it. Roughly in the centre of the enclosure is the drystone-walled broch, probably originally a tall round tower but now reduced to not much more than the height of one storey. Overall diameter of c. 19m., the outer wall battered. Internal court of c. 10m. diameter. Entrance passage on the E, its first part narrow as far as the position of the door, whose pivot stone and bar-hole survive. Immediately beyond the door, a mural guard chamber each side of the passage. The broch's inner wall to the court still has part of a scarcement on the S, and above it a door which gave access to a lobby and an internal stair up to the wallhead. At this level there have been the usual galleries between the inner and outer wall-thicknesses. In the court's centre, a rectangular hearth and, to its E, steps down to an underground spring-filled tank cut out of the rock.

Perhaps in the second or third century A.D. the broch was reconstructed and the surrounding enclosure built over. In the remodelling of the broch its height was apparently lowered, a new floor (with two new hearths) was laid over the court, whose interior was divided by partitions of flagstones and rubble, and two narrow stairs were provided from the court, the W giving access to the new wallhead. At the same time two small rooms were added to the exterior, flanking the broch's entrance. The area of the enclosure was enlarged, except at the SW, where the original rampart remains, by rebuilding the rampart wall as a series of bastion-like projections encroaching on the inner ditch. These projections formed the outer gables of a ring of dwellings, housing a community of perhaps thirty to forty families, which were built over the enclosure, only a path from the causeway and encircling the broch and a space at the SW being left undeveloped.

Some time after, the settlement seems to have been abandoned and the remains of these houses and of the broch were covered with debris which formed a new ground level. On this new level by the C9 there had been built a substantial Pictish house containing a long centre room surrounded by five round cells, and, to its NE, a large oblong house which may also have been Pictish, although it is as likely to have been a product of early Viking settlement. These two houses were removed in the course of the 1930s excavation and rebuilt immediately W of the broch defences, beside the present museum. Remains of a smaller rectangular house survive to the S in the partly infilled outer ditch.

3000   GYRE (MAINLAND)
1.2km. S of Orphir

Small mansion house of some complexity. The estate was bought by the Halcros of Coubister in 1737 and there probably then existed a U-plan house on the site. The main (W) range of this house was rebuilt in the late C18, and a W wing was added to it in 1851. In 1886 *C. S. S. Johnston*, brother of the then proprietor, replaced the late C18 main block but retained the E and W wings. Not surprisingly, the result is disjointed. The single-storey E wings, built of flagstone rubble, are perhaps late C17 or early C18. Crowstepped gable on the longer S range. Their short higher links to the main block may have been part of the late C18 work. The present two-storey-and-attic main block of 1886 is of snecked rubble. In the crowstepped front gable, an off-centre canted bay window to the r. of the door; above the door a carved coat of arms. At the back, Johnston's main block projects as a sturdy tower, its battlement bristling with big cannon spouts. The effect would be very martial were not the harled two-storey W wing of 1851 a model of domesticity.

To the N, a mid-C19 STEADING built of flagstone rubble with stone slated roofs.

2000   HALL OF CLESTRAIN (MAINLAND)
4.9km. NW of Orphir

Smart but now derelict villa built for Patrick Honyman of Graemsay in 1769. Three bays by three, of one storey and an attic carried on a tall basement which projects slightly as a plinth. Harled walls, but with the ends slightly recessed and of ashlar. At the door, a lugged architrave under a big corniced rectangular fanlight, its effect that of a panel frame filled with glass instead of carved heraldry. Bandcourse marking off the attic. Cavetto cornice under the eaves.

HARRAY (MAINLAND)

A few houses in the centre of a rural parish.

FREE CHURCH, Brough. Now a house. Tall lancet-windowed box of 1874. On the s gable, Victorian version of a birdcage bellcote looking almost Gothic.

ST MICHAEL'S CHURCH, Brough. Harled kirk built in 1836 and heavily restored in recent years. Solid-looking birdcage bellcote on the w gable; roundheaded windows. The vestry and hall are additions.

BARROWS (KNOWES OF TROTTY), 2.3km. E. Group of twelve burial mounds of the second millennium B.C. ranged along the flat ground at the foot of the w slope of the Ward of Redland. The largest, at the N, *c.* 18m. in diameter and 3m. high, has been excavated and was found to contain, as well as cremated remains, gold discs, perhaps covers for buttons, and amber beads and pendants. The others are 9m. to 13.7m. in diameter and up to 1.5m. high.

HERSTON (SOUTH RONALDSAY)

Small village on the s shore of Widewall Bay, the houses mostly C19, several with crowstepped gables.

CHURCH. Built as a mission chapel in 1884–5. Pointed windows. w gable with a rudimentary bellcote and projecting vestry.

HOLM (MAINLAND)

Hardly even a place-name for a rural parish at the s end of Mainland.

OLD PARISH CHURCH, Howes Wick, 1.4km. SE. Disused church in a graveyard beside Howes Wick. Broad harled rubble kirk built in 1818 and very old-fashioned for that date. Almost solid pyramid-roofed birdcage bellcote on the w gable. Five-bay s front, with tall round-arched windows in the outer bays; in the centre, a low round-arched window, perhaps originally a door, with an oval recess above. In the gable of the vestry at the E, a weathered C17 heraldic GRAVESLAB.

PARISH CHURCH. Built as an Antiburgher meeting house in 1814. Harled rectangle, with roundheaded windows in the long sides. The jerkin-head roof dates from a restoration following a fire in 1920, as probably do the porch and vestry.

Early C19 harled MANSE to the E, piend-roofed with a central chimney-stack; ball-finialled s porch.

GREENWALL. *See* p. 304.

HOLM OF PAPA

Small almost flat island just off the E coast of Papa Westray. Perhaps never inhabited, but its chambered cairns of the third millennium B.C. show that it then had some importance as a burial place and presumably for religious ceremonies.

CAIRN, N tip of island. Remains of a low rectangular cairn, c. 12m. by 9m. Passage from the N end to the rectangular central chamber, which has been divided by thin upright slabs into four stalled compartments. Wall cell to the S.

CAIRN, E side of island. Long turf-covered mound, c. 38m. by 20m., built on the island's highest part. Drystone-walled entrance passage in the centre of the long E side, its outer stretch roofless, its inner section covered with lintel slabs, all laid on edge except the W, which is flat. The passage enters the middle of the chamber. This is very long (c. 20.5m.) and narrow (c. 1.5m.). Each end is divided off by a cross-wall containing a doorway. Side walls of drystone masonry, the upper courses corbelled inwards to support the roof, now of C 20 concrete and with an access hatch. In each of the main compartment's side walls, three not very regularly disposed low entrances to small cells, two of them double. Three more cells open off each end compartment. In all the cells, walls corbelled inward from the base. In the central compartment's E wall, carved stones, one with a circle, another with conjoined ovals, a third with a double circle, pecked dots and an inverted V-motif. In the S compartment the lintel stone above the entrance to the E cell is carved with pecked dots and arcs, some combined in 'eyebrow' motifs. In the W wall, one stone with a zig-zag motif, another with circles.

HOLODYKE (MAINLAND)
1.6km. SE of Dounby

Prominently sited harled L-plan house which has grown from humble beginnings into a small mansion. The earliest part, probably early C 19, is at the SE and was originally a single-storey cottage. This became a school in the mid-C 19, with a gable-fronted schoolroom added to its W end. In 1888 the psychiatrist and antiquarian Sir Thomas Clouston remodelled the existing buildings as a holiday house, adding to the cottage an upper floor with windows rising into gableted dormerheads, and to the schoolroom's gable a semi-octagonal bay window. In 1896 Clouston commissioned *T. S. Peace* to extend the house by adding a dining-room wing at the NW with a porch in its inner angle with the existing house. Peace's work is pacific Baronial but with exaggeratedly tall crowsteps and much vertical emphasis. Over the porch, a saddle-backed tower with a shaped gablet at the top. Stepped chimney projecting under the harling of the dining-room wing's gable. A further extension N of the 1890s work but in the same style was made *c.* 1920. Single-storey late Victorian service court to the N.

HOY (HOY)   *2000*

Little more than a place-name marking the position of the Parish Church near the island's N end.

Former PARISH CHURCH, 0.9km. NE. Roofless rubble rectangle of *c.* 1790. Symmetrical six-bay S front, all the openings rectangular. – Inside, against the N wall, MONUMENT to Jacoba Baikie, dated 1733, with incised Ionic columns framing the inscription; an angel's head at the top, reminders of death at the bottom. – Similar but badly weathered monument on the churchyard's W wall.

PARISH CHURCH. Broad box of snecked rubble built in 1891–2. Pointed windows. On top of the E porch, a corbelled-out squat pyramid supporting a ball.

ROCK TOMB (DWARFIE STANE), 3.5km. S. Chambered tomb of the third millennium B.C., cut out of a roughly rectangular sandstone block which lies at an angle on a hillside, its N end partly buried. Small entrance near the W side's S end opening into a hollowed-out rectangular chamber off which are two side cells, the roof of the S showing the peck marks of the makers' tools. Plenty of incised names also, the earliest dated 1735. Large boulder lying outside, the original blocking stone of the entrance.

FARMS ETC.

BU OF HOY, 1km. NE. Low two-storey harled and crowstepped house built *c.* 1615 for Hugh Halcro of that Ilk, whose initials are inscribed on the SW skewputt. The upper floor and roof were much altered in the C19, when the first-floor windows acquired dormerheads.

BURRA HOUSE, 0.5km. E. Harled and crowstep-gabled house of two storeys and three bays, built as Hoy Manse in 1798. – At the rear, a rubble-built single-storey BARN with a kiln at one end.

HOY LODGE, 0.3km. NW. Long two-storey U-plan laird's house; probably C18 in origin, but its present admirably unpretentious appearance dates from *W. R. Lethaby*'s reconstruction of *c.* 1900.

KIRKBRAE (WESTRAY)   *4040*

Little more than the Parish Church.

WESTRAY PARISH CHURCH. Built in 1845–7. Harled box with a jerkin-head roof and small E porch. Roundheaded windows in the w gable, the rest rectangular. – Inside, a deep e gallery (the space below partitioned off). – PULPIT with an ogee-topped sounding board.

FRIBO HOUSE, 1.5km. SW. Laird's house of c. 1840. Two storeys and three bays, the gabled porch probably an addition. Piended roof with a central chimney-stack. Horizontal glazing in the windows. – To the w, a two-storey STEADING, probably contemporary.

GALLOWHILL, 1.4km. w. Mid-C19 U-plan steading, rubble-built with a roof of stone slates; house at the sw corner.

CAIRN, Point of Cott, 1.5km. NE. Cairn of the third millennium B.C., placed on the edge of a low cliff. Low mound of grass-covered flat slabs, c. 30m. long. At the broader s end, remains of a projecting sw horn; presumably it was balanced by one at the SE. Protruding from the cairn's centre, the tops of upright stones, the partitions of a long stalled chamber of five or six compartments.

4090   KIRKHOUSE (SOUTH RONALDSAY)

Church and farm overlooking the Pool of Cletts on the e coast of South Ronaldsay.

ST PETER'S CHURCH. Long harled rectangle built in 1642 and reroofed in 1801, the two dates carved on stones over the s door. Roundheaded windows and doors, probably of 1801. The w gable's pyramid-roofed birdcage bellcote may be contemporary, but its crudity may point to a C17 or early C18 date. The lean-to e porch is Victorian. Interior mostly of 1801. – Shallow end GALLERIES, each of the panelled fronts embellished with a late Victorian band of stencilled flowers. – PULPIT with an octagonal sounding board and brass baptismal bracket. – Three COMMUNION PEWS. The one in front of the pulpit has benches round its four sides and a central table. Much longer pews to e and w, each with benches facing each other across a narrow table. – Elaborately worked late Victorian OIL LAMPS of brass and iron.

MONUMENTS on the s wall's exterior. One, with conjoined coats of arms and a long inscription, commemorates Mr Alexander Graham † 1717, minister of South Ronaldsay and Burray, and his wife, Barbara Baikie. – The other, to someone † 1724, is a weathered aedicule with would-be Ionic columns; angel's head in the curvy pediment, which is topped by a surprisingly sophisticated urn.

KIRKHOUSE. Mid-C19 harled farmhouse with a contemporary rubble-built STEADING behind. – Late C18 CORNMILL to the w.

KIRKWALL (MAINLAND)

4010

The metropolis of Orkney, first given importance in the mid-C 12 when Earl Rognvald moved the site of the cathedral church of Orkney and the bishop's residence here from Birsay. Seventeen years after the incorporation of the Northern Isles into the Scottish kingdom in 1469, the status of Kirkwall as a city and royal burgh was recognized by a royal charter, although the town was not enrolled in the Convention of Royal Burghs until 1669 or represented in Parliament until 1670. By 1701 Kirkwall was experiencing a decline in trade and population, but it seems to have regained a modest prosperity by the late C 18, its relative affluence rapidly increased by the development of the kelp industry in Orkney, whose rewards were such that it was reported in 1813 that:

Country Gentlemen have thus acquired from their bleak estates, sums of money, great beyond all former experience. This has gradually induced many of them to abandon, especially during winter, their lonely and dreary habitations in the Isles, and to draw together in Kirkwall ... During winter, there are dancing assemblies and card assemblies, alternately every week: and popular Lectures on Chymistry were lately delivered twice a week ... and the profits generously given to the Poor.

Sir Walter Scott, who visited the next year, found less to admire:

'Tis a base little borough, both dirty and mean –
There is nothing to hear, and there's nought to be seen,
Save a church where of old times, a prelate harangued,
And a palace that's built by an earl who was hanged.

Collapse of the kelp industry after c. 1830 brought a stop to the town's expansion and redevelopment, but later in the C 19, as Kirkwall strengthened its position as the main market town of Orkney, development began again. Until then almost all the houses had stood on or behind the town's one long main street, with warehouses and stores beside the harbour, but by 1900 villas were spreading to the S, and this expansion has continued in the C 20.

ST MAGNUS CATHEDRAL
Broad Street

The grandest and largest building in Orkney, dominating the town and a landmark from the sea. Earl Magnus was killed on the island of Egilsay in 1116 when pressing his claim to half the earldom of Orkney. That claim was revived by his nephew

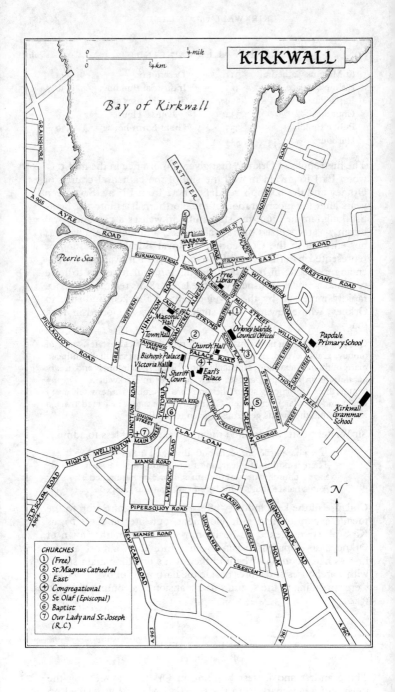

KIRKWALL

Bay of Kirkwall

Peerie Sea

GRAINSHORE ROAD

A 965

AYRE ROAD

EAST PIER

WEST PIER

HARBOUR ST.

SHORE ST.

ST. CATHERINE'S

CROMWELL ROAD

EAST BERSTANE ROAD

BURNMOUTH ROAD

MOUNTHOOLIE

BRIDGE ST.

ST OLAF'S WYND

Free Library

WILLOWBURN ROAD

WILLOW ROAD

MILL STREET

PICKAQUOY ROAD

GREAT WESTERN ROAD

JUNCTION ROAD

CASTLE ST.

BROAD STREET

ALBERT ST.

STRYND

JUNCTION ST.

Masonic Hall

Town Hall

TANKERNESS LANE

① Church ②

Orkney Islands, Council Offices

KING ST.

③

Papdale Primary School

Bishop's Palace

Victoria Hall

PALACE ROAD

Church Hall

④

Earl's Palace

DUNDAS CRESCENT

ST ROGNVALD STREET

THOMS STREET

BAXTER STREET

WHITE STREET

Kirkwall Grammar School

Sheriff Court

VICTORIA ST.

Victoria Road

⑤

BUTTQUOY CRESCENT

GEORGE STREET

⑥

UNION ST.

MAIN STREET

CLAY LOAN

LAVEROCK ROAD

⑦

HIGH ST.

WELLINGTON ST.

JUNCTION ROAD

MANSE ROAD

BIGNOLD PARK ROAD

CRAIGIE CRESCENT

HOLM ROAD

OLD SCAPA ROAD

A 964

PIPERSQUOY ROAD

QUOYBANKS CRESCENT

N

NEW SCAPA ROAD

MANSE ROAD

A 963

A 961

A 964

CHURCHES
① (Free)
② St Magnus Cathedral
③ East
④ Congregational
⑤ St Olaf (Episcopal)
⑥ Baptist
⑦ Our Lady and St Joseph (R.C.)

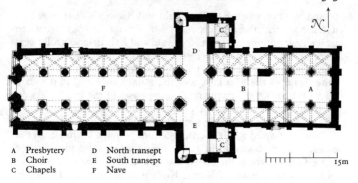

A	Presbytery
B	Choir
C	Chapels
D	North transept
E	South transept
F	Nave

15m

Kirkwall. St Magnus Cathedral.
(Redrawn from a plan by G. Mackie Watson)

Rognvald in 1129, and the acceptance of Magnus' sanctity by the powerful Bishop William the Old in 1136 may have assisted Rognvald in gaining control over the whole earldom the next year. Almost immediately Rognvald decided to move the site of the cathedral church of Orkney from Birsay to Kirkwall, whose new cathedral was to enshrine the relics of his saintly uncle. Supervision of the work was undertaken by Kol, father of Rognvald and brother-in-law of Magnus.

The c 12 design of St Magnus Cathedral has striking parallels with two other major churches, Durham Cathedral and Dunfermline Abbey (Fife), and it seems almost certain that masons of the Durham school who had worked previously at Dunfermline and perhaps elsewhere in Fife were employed at Kirkwall. In size St Magnus was very close to Dunfermline, at the time the largest church in mainland Scotland, and was little smaller than the then metropolitan cathedral at Lund in Norway. In comparison with Durham, it is tiny, but the plan is very close to that of Durham on its completion c. 1130. Indeed the cathedral at Kirkwall appears to have been designed almost as a scale model of the huge English cathedral. St Magnus was designed with a nave of eight bays (but with a bay width of c. 3.96m. compared to Durham's 7.62m.), probably with w towers, N and S transepts, each with a chapel (probably apsidal) projecting E, and a three-bay choir, its aisles probably straight-ended (unlike Durham's originally apse-ended choir aisles), the central vessel extending E as an apse. Like both Durham and Dunfermline, there was a tower over the crossing, and, again like Durham, the outer w corners of the transepts seem intended to have had turrets. Like the two prototypes, St Magnus appears to have been originally designed to serve as the church for a community of monks or canons regular, the provision of processional doors in the nave's first and sixth bays from the E strongly indicative of an intended cloister in the same position as at the two more southerly churches.

As usual with large medieval churches, building work at St Magnus began at the E end. The first phase was probably com-

pleted by 1153, when Earl Rognvald and Bishop William went on
a crusade, and the church was certainly usable by 1155, when
peace negotiations between Rognvald and Earl Erlend's followers
were held there. This phase comprised the three-bay choir, the
transepts and lower part of the crossing, the lower part of the
outer walls of the four E bays of the N nave aisle and of the six E
bays of the S. Of the nave arcades, the bases of the five E piers on
each side seem to have been begun at this time, but only the E
pier of the N arcade and the S arcade's two E piers were completed.

There followed a halt in construction, perhaps lasting from the
death of Earl Rognvald in 1158 to his canonization in 1188, the
same year in which the diocese acquired an apparently forceful
bishop in the person of Bjarne Kolbeinsson, the son of Kolbein
Hruga, an important landowner in both Orkney and western
Norway. The resumption of work was accompanied by a change
in the cathedral's plan, seemingly the result of deciding that it be
staffed not by a monastic community but by a chapter of secular
canons* such as was in existence at St Magnus by 1247. The
introduction of secular canons made necessary the lengthening of
the choir by a further three bays to accommodate them during
their corporate services, which they preferred to hold E of the
crossing rather than under it, as was the fashion of monks. At the
same time it was decided to remodel the crossing and replace the
small transept chapels (possibly not yet completed or even begun)
with larger rectangular chapels, perhaps inspired by the chapels
in this position at Nidaros Cathedral at Trondheim.‡ Work was
also resumed on the nave, and the construction of its W front
began to a design which omitted towers. In the course of this
second stage of building work, the design was again changed when
it was decided to construct stone vaults over the central vessels
of the choir and nave as well as over their aisles, necessitating a
heightening of the clearstorey. A further change was the omission
of the originally intended full triforium storey over the aisles and
its replacement by pitched roofs rising from a lower wallhead. By
c. 1250, when work stopped, the extended choir, new transept
chapels, the remodelling of the crossing, the six E bays of the nave
aisles, the five E of the nave's central vessel, and the lower part of
its W front had all been completed. Early in the C14 the crossing
tower's belfry stage was added, as was probably its spire.

A final and thrifty completion of the nave's W bays and W front
was not undertaken until the late C15 or early C16. Reform of the
cathedral chapter in 1544 possibly marks the ending of work.

St Magnus suffered little direct damage, except the destruction
of furnishings, as a result of the Reformation of 1560, but worship
was thereafter confined to the choir, which was divided from the
crossing by a wooden screen and provided with galleries from c.
1630, the nave, still roofed, being used as the burgh graveyard. In
1671 the central spire, which had been of wood, probably covered

---

*In 1152 Cardinal Nicholas Breakspear had ordered the provision of such a chapter
for each cathedral in the newly formed province of Trondheim, of which the diocese
of Orkney was part until 1472, when it was transferred to the province of St Andrews.
‡But rectangular transept chapels were also built in England at this time.

with lead, was destroyed by lightning and then replaced by a pyramidal roof.

In 1847–50 a restoration of the cathedral was carried out by *William Nixon* on behalf of the Government, which mistakenly believed itself to own the building. Internally, post-Reformation furnishings were removed; externally, the church was reroofed, parapets were renewed and pinnacles added. After the Burgh Council's ownership of the building had been established, the choir was again fitted up as a parish church in 1855–7, *Richard Spence*'s* furnishings being described by the antiquarian Sir Henry Dryden as 'most barbarous outrages', and the upper part of the S transept's gable was rebuilt. Further work, including the restoration of windows and the replacement of many of their nook-shafts and the removal of whitewash from the nave's interior, was done later in the C19. Between 1913 and 1930 *George Mackie Watson* carried out another and more far-reaching restoration, bringing the whole church back into use, and replacing the crossing tower's C17 roof with a copper-covered spire. Further repair, including replacement of medieval carved stonework, is now in progress.

DESCRIPTION

The WEST FRONT was begun in the early C13, completed probably in the early C16, altered in the C19 and again in the early C20. Except for its three boldly modelled doors it appears penny-pinching. The nave and aisles are marked off by buttresses (the N and S set in from the outer corners), each crossed low down by a band enriched with pearl ornament and with nook-shafts rising from waterholding bases. Their lower parts are C13. The tops broached to octagons are presumably of *c.* 1500 but quoting from the buttresses of the E front. On top of the inner buttresses, round conical-capped pinnacles; octagonal pinnacles on the outer buttresses. All these pinnacles are of 1847–50, copied from surviving medieval pinnacles at the E end, but *Nixon* placed the octagonal pinnacles on the corners of the aisle parapets and they did not reach their present homes until *Watson*'s C20 restoration. Strangely, the decorative effect of using alternating bands of red and white stone up to the bandcourse on the two N buttresses is not repeated at the S pair, an anomaly which looks pigheaded but may suggest that the C13 work was staggered.

Gripped between the buttresses are the C13 W doors to the nave and aisles, the aisle doors contained in the wall-thickness, the nave door projecting boldly. At each aisle entrance, a splay-sided arch of three outer orders carried on detached shafts (mostly replacements) and an engaged order flanking the narrow pointed door. The N doorway's outer order is carved with dogtooth enrichment, its third order with nailhead. At the S doorway, orders decorated with dogtooth and chevron, the

*David Bryce was consulted about the work but disclaimed responsibility for it.

jambs with pellet ornament. Shaft bases of waterholding type. The capitals of the N doorway are conventional enough, with stiffleaf foliage, but at the S doorway they merge into each other to provide a surface for continuous carved tendrils. At both aisle doorways red and white stones are used in deliberate contrast, but at the N they are employed on alternate orders, at the S on alternate voussoirs. The impression is of two rival masons at work, each sticking resolutely to his own design. The much grander nave door's details suggest that it may occupy a position intermediate in date as well as site between the aisle entrances. Like them it is splay-sided, with an engaged order framing the pointed door, but this is followed by no fewer than seven orders carried on staggered shafts; at each outer corner are three more detached shafts intended to carry tall pinnacles (only their bases surviving or executed). Undercut relief carving on the tops of the door jambs; the stones below are hollowed in preparation for carving. The outer orders' carved surfaces have mostly weathered away.* Like the N doorway, the centre door's orders are alternately of red and white stone. Closer in spirit to the S doorway are its capitals. Those at the sides are carved with tendril foliage running from cap to cap. The capitals at the outer corners form continuous unbroken blocks carved with denser foliage and grotesque animals. The gablet above this door, probably intended from the start of the C13 work, may have been at least partly rebuilt c. 1500, when it acquired a shield which probably bears the arms of Robert Pictoris or Painter, Bishop of Orkney from 1477 to c. 1506.

The nave's pointed W window is of c. 1500 and rather small for its position. Four-light with a transom, the sub-arches trefoil-headed, the upper arches with simple intersecting tracery. Below the window's sloping sill, a stringcourse across the nave front; a second stringcourse above the window. A small lancet window in the gable's apex lights the roof space above the internal vault. In each aisle gable, a small trefoil-headed pointed window to light the triforium gallery behind. At the bottom corners of the nave roof, mid-C19 gargoyles.

The history of the NAVE's S side is largely told by its masonry. In the six E bays the aisle walls are built of red-coloured flagstone rubble up to the top of the windows. Above this mid-C12 work is red sandstone ashlar of the early C13, perhaps a little earlier than the white sandstone corbels which carry the plain mid-C19 parapet. The clearstorey's five E bays and the beginning of the sixth bay are of the early to mid-C13, built of white ashlar. By contrast the walls of the aisle's two W bays and the W end of the clearstorey, built c. 1500, are all of red ashlar. The medieval corbels under the clearstorey's C19 parapet are of white stone at the C13 E part, of red at the W.

The C12 design is clear enough. Two-storey aisles, the bays divided by pilaster strips, and a clearstorey. Round-arched aisle

*These were replaced with new carved stone, 1990–1.

windows, the hoodmoulds carried on shafts, and with a
stringcourse joining their sills. Processional doors to the cloister
in the first and sixth bays from the E. The biggest change to the
design took place early in the C 13, when it was decided to finish
the aisle wallheads at a lower level than originally intended, so
that the triforium gallery became an attic under a lean-to roof
rather than an upper storey to the aisle. The pilaster strips
dividing the aisle's six E bays have been overlaid with sturdy
stepped buttresses, probably *c.* 1500, when the two W bays were
built with stepped buttresses in place of pilaster strips. In the E
bay there survives the nook-shafted E jamb of the mid-C 12 E
processional door, built up in the C 13. The much restored
round-arched window above, larger than the windows to its W
and with a plain moulded surround, looks like a C 13 replacement. The next five windows (heavily restored in the C 19 and
C 20) are of mid-C 12 type, the second and third decorated with
billet and chevron enrichment. In the sixth bay, the last of the
C 12 and C 13 bays, a door thought to have been erected by
Bishop Reid in the mid-C 16 to replace the mid-C 12 W processional door. The badly weathered shafts' big capitals and
the polygonal top could well be of the supposed date; on the
lintel, a worn shield carved with the arms of a bishop. In the
two W bays of *c.* 1500, small trefoil-headed pointed windows,
like the triforium windows of the W front. Perhaps as the result
of a feared foundation weakness, the lower part of the W bay's
walling is thicker than the rest and intaken to the general wall-
plane at the top of the buttresses. All the clearstorey windows,
whether C 13 or of *c.* 1500, are small lancets, linked by a
stringcourse which jumps over each to form a hoodmould.

The nave's N elevation is similar to the S but without the later
buttresses added to the C 12 and C 13 work, so the pilaster strips
of the aisle's six E bays are unobscured. The walling between
them is topped by corbelling with trefoil pendants, probably an
elaboration of the original design made when the upper part of
the aisle walls was completed early in the C 13. In the aisle's
five E bays, round-arched windows, all with nook-shafts and
hoodmoulds, but the three E windows, which are larger, have
cushion capitals, indicating that they belong to the mid-C 12
work. Presumably also of the mid-C 12 is the fourth window's
cushion-capitalled E side, but its W side, with a stiffleaf capital,
must have been constructed in the early C 13. C 13 stiffleaf
capitals again at the fifth window. In the next bay, a smartly
gabled C 13 door (much restored in the C 19 and by *Watson*
in the C 20), intended as the principal entrance for laity into the
church. Round-arched doorway, its three orders carried by
shafts standing on waterholding bases; the round capitals with
stiffleaf carving look like replacements. Carved branch enrichment on the hoodmould and the gablet's eaves. In the gablet,
a lozenge frame decorated with dogtooth ornament; it was
probably intended to contain a relief. The two C 15 or C 16 W
bays repeat the red ashlar, stepped buttresses and small pointed
windows of the corresponding bays on the S. The clearstorey is

another repeat of the s elevation, the junction of the C13 work's yellow sandstone with the red stone of *c.* 1500 in the middle of the sixth bay from the E all too evident. The parapets are C19 restorations.

The TRANSEPTS are substantially of the mid-C12 but remodelled and heightened in the course of the building programme of *c.* 1188–1250, the alteration marked by a change in the stonework from red rubble to yellowish ashlar and with the original wallhead level disclosed by one corbel on the s transept's w face and another on the N transept's E. Much of the C12 design is clear. Three-storey elevations, the windows' sills and the springing of their arches joined by stringcourses. These are carried round the big clasping buttresses (the w buttresses larger and containing stairs), which may have been intended to rise into turrets like the similar transept buttresses at Durham. C12 windows (some much restored) with nook-shafts and hoodmoulds survive at the two lower storeys. At the w triforium window of the s transept, a restored chevron decoration. The blocked overarches of openings from the transepts' triforium galleries into those of the nave and choir reprove the decision to place the aisle wallheads at a lower level than originally intended. The clearstorey windows of the E and w fronts disclose a partial remodelling of the transept together with the crossing, *c.* 1200. Three of the four outer windows are of the same mid-C12 Romanesque type as those of the triforium, but the four inner windows are all Transitional, with waterleaf capitals. The outer window of the s transept's w front, of yellowish stone with a chamfered surround and no hoodmould, looks a C17 replacement. The C12 design for the top of the gables can only be conjectured – perhaps blind arcading as at Durham. Both were rebuilt on a grand scale in the early C13 heightening of the transepts. The N gable then acquired a pair of tall round-arched windows with crocketed foliage on the capitals of their banded nook-shafts. Above, a round window of two orders, the inner of alternating red and white stones and enriched with dogtooth ornament. The s gable's upper part was rebuilt in buff-coloured stone in the restoration of 1856 by *Richard Spence*, who probably followed the general lines of the C13 design.* Big rose window at the clearstorey level; above it, a round window, the outer order decorated with sawtooth. Grotesque gargoyles at the eaves. At the bottom of this s gable, a door inserted at the beginning of the C13 as an entrance for the cathedral's canons into the crossing. It is built of red and white stones set chequer-wise. Four orders, the outer and third with dogtooth enrichment. Some of the shafts' weathered waterleaf capitals have been replaced recently with elided caps. Parapets again looking C19.

The early C13 TRANSEPT CHAPELS, built of red sandstone ashlar and with their outer walls butted awkwardly against the

---

*But work had been done on the medieval rose window in 1671, and it was further 'renewed and ornamented' *c.* 1810.

transepts' buttresses, are obvious deviants from the mid-C12 design, which must have intended much smaller chapels, prob- ably apsed, to project here. On their inner sides the chapels are joined to the choir by low links which were originally designed to leave the choir windows unobscured; the S chapel's link was given an upper storey probably in the C17. At the chapels' gable, clasping buttresses, their present octagonal pinnacles dating from 1847–50, but the N chapel had pinnacles in 1818 and they may have been medieval. At the ends of the gables, grotesque heads which look Victorian. The parapets are carried on C13 corbelling carved as human heads. In each outer wall and gable, a tall pointed C13 window with nook-shafts on waterholding bases and with (restored) waterleaf capitals. Hoodmoulds joined by stringcourses. In the apex of each gable, a hoodmoulded lancet. Under the N chapel's N window, a round-arched light in a shouldered surround. Is this a Victorian alteration of an inserted Georgian window?

The CROSSING TOWER is all of red ashlar. The lower part must be of *c.* 1200. On its W and E faces, raggles showing that the nave and choir roofs were pitched more steeply before *Nixon*'s restoration in the 1840s. The belfry stage above is early C14. In each face, a pair of tall pointed two-light openings containing Y-tracery. Each is of four orders, the outer three with hollow chamfers, the inner order with a plane and chamfer; clustered shafts with moulded capitals and bases. The corbelled parapet with small gableted openings and big dragon gargoyles dates from *George Mackie Watson*'s restoration of 1913–30. So too does the copper-clad broached and lucarned spire. It replaced a late C17 pyramid roof, itself replacing a spire destroyed by lightning in 1671.

The CHOIR as designed in the mid-C12 was to have been of three bays, with two-storey aisles and a clearstorey at the central vessel. As at the nave, the design of the aisles, their walls perhaps not yet completed, was changed when it was decided in the early C13 to finish their wallheads at a lower level with the triforium gallery squashed under a pitched roof. The aisle walls of these three mid-C12 bays (the W bay on each side now hidden largely or wholly by the transept chapels) are of red-coloured rubble, the bays delineated by pilaster strips, the pilasters at the choir's original E corners broader than the others, the N side's partly covered by a late medieval stepped buttress from which is corbelled a Victorian chimney. Round-arched windows, orig- inally with nook-shafts and hoodmoulds; they are joined by stringcourses at the sills and springing level. The S side's centre window has been replaced in a simplified form, probably in the C16. Some medieval corbels survive under the C19 parapets. On the S aisle the corbels are of C13 character. On the N, where they are carved with human and animal heads (three of these, depicting a man, a sheep and a pig, recently renewed), they seem to be reused C12 work, perhaps reset when the aisle wallhead was lowered from its originally intended height. The ashlar-walled clearstorey of these three W bays is substantially of the mid-C12, a stringcourse at springing level linking the windows. These are all round-arched with nook-shafts and hoodmoulds, but the capitals at the windows next to the crossing have waterleaf foliage, so they were presumably rebuilt as part of the C13 remodelling of the crossing. A couple of uncarved corbels at the W end of the N side show the original wallhead level before the C13 decision to vault the central vessel and its consequent heightening in yellow stone.

The aisles of the PRESBYTERY extension begun c. 1190 are, except for one ashlar-walled bay, of yellowish rubble with stepped buttresses. Windows set higher than those of the choir, whose sill course is continued inconsequentially below them. All three N windows and the two E windows of the S aisle are pointed, but the N windows are large, with chamfered surrounds, the S quite small, with moulded jambs and waterholding bases. In the S aisle's ashlar-built W bay, an early C13 priest's door, placed off-centre. Its nook-shafts rise from bases that are almost waterholding; the hoodmould labels are carved with tightly curled foliage. Above this door but in the centre of the bay, a contemporary round-arched window containing two pointed lights, its slender nook-shafts crossed low down by the E continuation of the choir's upper stringcourse. Obtusely pointed clearstorey windows. Above them, at the original wallhead level, corbels carved with human heads.

The presbytery's C13 EAST FRONT makes an almost clean break from the cathedral's original Romanesque character. Ashlar clasping buttresses with octagonal pinnacles at the aisles' outer corners. As at the W front, the centre is marked off by nook-shafted buttresses with waterholding bases, the buttresses being broached to octagons and finished with conical-capped round pinnacles. In the rubble-walled end of each aisle, an obtusely pointed window; above, a small roundheaded window with chamfered jambs lighting the triforium gallery. The great E window fills the whole width of the centre and must, before the heightening of the roof for the choir vault, have risen almost to the apex of the gable. It is a huge stilted arch containing a very large wheel window above paired pointed sub-arches. Each of these sub-arches was divided into two pointed lights in the 1840s, but some such division may well have been the case originally. The wheel window's bar tracery is also of the 1840s, apparently reproducing a similar C13 plate-traceried design. C13 plate tracery with trefoils survives in the spandrels between the wheel window and the sub-arches. At the top of the gable, a moulded round window of the mid-C13 lighting the roofspace above the internal vault. Over the centre, a crocketed parapet with grotesque gargoyles at the ends. Nailhead ornament on the aisle parapets; carved heads at the ends.

The NAVE INTERIOR looks at first glance to be of a piece, and indeed most of the essentials of the mid-C12 design were respected in its execution, the major alteration being the vaulting of the central vessel. Each side of the central vessel is a three-storey elevation of arcade, triforium passage and clear-

1. Glenfinnan (L) and monument of 1815–34

2. Stenness (O) with standing stones of the third millennium B.C.

3. Inverness (I), east bank of the River Ness

4. Cromarty (R & C), Church Street

5. Mousa (Sh), broch, first century A.D.

6. Callanish (WI), Stones of Callanish, third or second millennium B.C.

7. Egilsay (O), St Magnus Church,
twelfth century

8. Kirkwall (O), St Magnus Cathedral, crossing,
twelfth to thirteenth century

9. Dornoch (Su), Cathedral, thirteenth century, restored by Alexander Coupar, 1835–7

10. Dornoch (Su), Cathedral, choir, thirteenth century

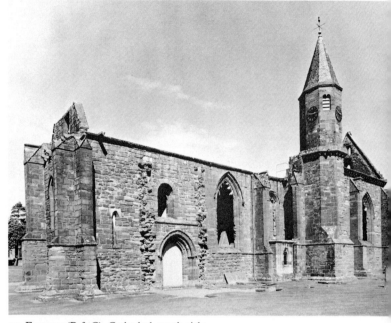

11. Fortrose (R & C), Cathedral, south aisle, fourteenth to fifteenth century

12. Tain (R & C), St Duthus Memorial Church, late fifteenth century

13. Beauly (I), Priory, west end, thirteenth century, reconstructed in the early sixteenth century

14. Rodel (W I), St Clement's Church, early sixteenth century

15. Nigg (R & C), Parish Church, cross slab of *c.* 800

16. Arisaig (L), St Maelrubha's Church,
graveslab, fifteenth century

17. Rodel (WI), St Clement's Church, tomb of Alasdair Crotach MacLeod, 1528

18. Rodel (WI), St Clement's Church, tomb of William MacLeod, 1539

19. Dunnet (C), Parish Church, probably sixteenth century

20. Thurso (C), Old St Peter's Church, *c.* 1500
with early seventeenth-century south 'aisle' and east tower

21. Latheron (C), Parish Church (Clan Gunn Centre),
1725–38, with north 'aisle' by William Davidson, 1821–2

22. Portmahomack (R & C), Tarbat Old Parish Church,
rebuilt in 1756 incorporating west gable and bellcote of *c.* 1700

23. Inverness (I), Old High Church, 1769–72, with sixteenth-century tower

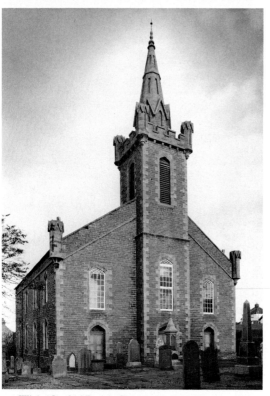

24. Wick (C), Old Parish Church, by John Henry, 1820–30

25. Kilmuir Easter (R & C), Parish Church, belfry, 1616

26. Daviot (I), Parish Church, 1826

27. Dingwall (R & C), St Clement's Church,
by George Burn, 1799–1803

28. Fort George (I), Chapel, by William Skinner, 1763–7

29. Thurso (C), St Peter's and St Andrew's Church, by William Burn, 1830–2

30. Cromarty (R & C), East Parish Church, sixteenth century, enlarged in the eighteenth century

31. Poolewe (R & C), Parish Church, by William Thomson, 1828

32. Inverness (I), St Mary's R.C. Church, by William Robertson, 1836–7

33. Rosskeen (R & C), Old Parish Church, by James Smith of Edinburgh, 1830–2

34. Edderton (R & C), Parish Church, by Donald Munro, 1841–2

35. Grantown-on-Spey (B & S), Inverallan Parish Church,
early seventeenth-century panelling

36. Golspie (Su), St Andrew's Church, Sutherland Loft,
by Kenneth Sutherland, 1738

37. Tain (R & C), St Duthus Memorial Church,
Trades Loft, eighteenth century

38. Cromarty (R & C), East Parish Church,
Cromartie Loft, 1756

39. Inverness (I), St Andrew's Episcopal Cathedral,
by Alexander Ross, 1866–9

40. Dingwall (R & C), Free Church, by John Rhind, 1867–70

41. Fort William (L), St Andrew's Episcopal Church,
by Alexander Ross, 1879–84

42. Inverness (I), Free North Church, by Ross & Macbeth, 1890–3

43. Nairn (N), Old Parish Church, by John Starforth, 1893–7

44. Inverness (I), St Stephen's Church, by W. L. Carruthers, 1895–7

45. Fort William (L), Church of the Immaculate Conception (R.C.),
by Reginald Fairlie, 1933–4

46. Fort William (L), Church of the Immaculate Conception (R.C.),
by Reginald Fairlie, 1933–4

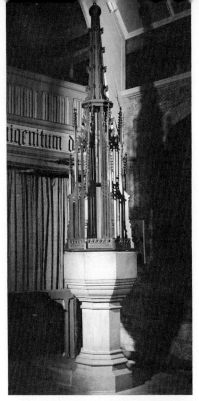

47. Inverness (I), St Michael and
All Angels' Episcopal Church,
font, by J. Ninian Comper, *c.* 1910

48. Grantown-on-Spey (B & S), Inverallan Parish Church, pulpit, 1886,
reusing carved woodwork of 1639

49. Latheron (C),
Parish Church (Clan Gunn Centre),
bell tower,
probably seventeenth century

50. Ardclach (N), Old Parish Church, bell tower, 1655

51. Kirkhill (I), Lovat Mausoleum, by William Ross, 1633–4, with belfry of 1722

52. Inverness (I), Old High Church, Robertson Burial Enclosure, by James Gordon and William Durham, 1664–5

53. Duthil (B & S), Seafield Mausoleum,
by William H. Playfair, 1837

54. Inverness (I), Tomnahurich Cemetery,
Christie Mausoleum, c. 1880

55. Wick (C), Old Parish Church, Sinclair Aisle,
late sixteenth century, remodelled in 1835

56. Hill of Fearn (R & C), Fearn Abbey, Lockhart Ross Monument,
by John Baxter Jun. and A. Farquhar, c. 1790

57. Fortrose (R & C), Cathedral,
monument to Sir Alexander Mackenzie of Coul, *c.* 1800

58. Golspie (Su), Sutherland Monument, Ben Bhragaidh, the statue
by Joseph Theakston and Francis Chantrey, the base by William Burn, 1836–8

59. Glenelg (S & L),
War Memorial,
by Robert S. Lorimer and
Louis Deuchars, 1920

60. Spean Bridge (L),
Commando War Memorial,
by Scott Sutherland,
1949–52

61. Mingary Castle (L), thirteenth century, remodelled in sixteenth century

62. Rait Castle (N), *c.* 1300

63. Castle Tioram (L), thirteenth to fourteenth century

64. Castle Girnigoe and Castle Sinclair (C), fifteenth to seventeenth century

65. Urquhart Castle (I), begun in the thirteenth century

66. Urquhart Castle (I), tower, early sixteenth century
on late fourteenth-century base, remodelled in early seventeenth century

67. Castle Craig (R & C), early sixteenth century

68. Cawdor Castle (N), fifteenth-century tower

69. Kirkwall (O), Earl's Palace, 1606

70. Kirkwall (O), Bishop's Palace, tower, *c.* 1550

71. Birsay (O), Earl's Palace, late sixteenth to early seventeenth century

72. Scalloway Castle (Sh), probably by Andrew Crawford, 1600

73. Castle Stuart (I), *c.* 1619–25

74. Ruthven Barracks (B & S), by James Smith, 1719–24

75. Cawdor Castle (N), chimneypiece of Blue Room, 1667

76. Fort George (I), by William Skinner, 1747–69

77. Fort George (I), main gate, by William Skinner, 1753–6

78. Fort George (I), Governor's House, by William Skinner, 1762–6

79. Foulis Castle (R & C), *c.* 1740–54 with alterations of 1777

80. Castle Grant (B & S), north front, by John Adam, 1753–6

81. Embo House, Embo (Su), *c.* 1785

82. Poyntzfield (R & C), 1757

83. Cromarty House, Cromarty (R & C), *c.* 1775

84. Tarbat House (R & C), by James McLeran, 1787

85. Culloden House (I), 1780

86. Inverness (I), Muirtown House, Charleston Place,
by Hugh Robert Duff, 1800–34

87. Achnacarry Castle (L), by James Gillespie Graham, 1802–37

88. Boath House (N), by Archibald Simpson, *c.* 1830

89. Geanies House (R & C), 1742–*c.* 1765,
with early nineteenth-century west wing

90. Dunvegan Castle, Dunvegan (S & L), entrance front,
early nineteenth century

91. Dunrobin Castle (Su), by the second Duke of Sutherland,
Charles Barry and William Leslie, 1845–51;
north-east tower remodelled by Robert S. Lorimer, 1915–21

92. Kinlochmoidart House, Kinlochmoidart (L), by William Leiper, 1885

93. Aigas House, Aigas (I), by Matthews & Lawrie, 1877

94. Melsetter House (O), by W. R. Lethaby, 1898

95. Cadboll (R & C), doocot, *c.* 1700

96. Auldearn (N), Boath Doocot, late seventeenth century

97. Conan House (R & C), steading, 1822

98. Thurso Castle (C), gateway and lodge, by David Smith, 1872–8

99. Tain (R & C), Tolbooth, by Alexander Stronach, 1706–8

100. Cromarty (R & C), Court House, 1782

101. Inverness (I), Town Steeple, by Alexander Laing, 1789–92

102. Grantown-on-Spey (B & S), Speyside Orphan Hospital, 1824

103. Inverness (I), District Court (former Jail),
by Thomas Brown Jun., 1846–8

104. Cromarty (R & C), Primary School, by A. Maitland & Sons, 1875–6

105. Inverness (I), Town House,
by Matthews & Lawrie, 1876–82

106. Fort William (L), St Andrews House (former Episcopal School),
Fassifern Road, by Alexander Ross, 1880

107. Inverness (I), Public Library (former Dr Bell's School),
by William Robertson, 1839–41

108. Inverness (I), Eden Court Theatre, by Law & Dunbar-Nasmith, 1973–6

109. Inverness (I), Nos. 54–60 High Street, 1841–4

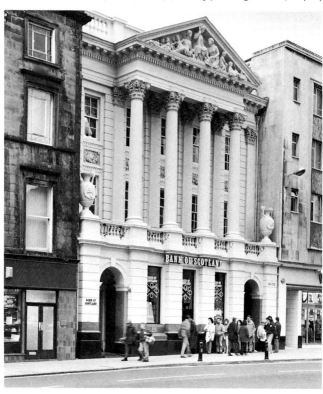

110. Inverness (I), Bank of Scotland (former Caledonian Bank),
High Street, by Mackenzie & Matthews, 1847

111. Wick (C), Royal (former Commercial) Bank of Scotland,
Bridge Street, *c.* 1835

112. Dingwall (R & C), former National Bank of Scotland,
High Street, by William Robertson, 1838

113. Inverness (I), Abertarff House, Church Street, 1593

114. Cromarty (R & C), St Anns, Church Street, c. 1800

115. Thurso (C), Janet Street,
early nineteenth century

116. Inverness (I), Lethington, Annfield Road, by W. L. Carruthers, 1892

117. Strathpeffer (R & C), Heatherlie, off The Square,
by Duncan Cameron, 1895–7

118. Inverness (I), No. 135 Culduthel Road,
by Carruthers Ballantyne, Cox & Taylor, *c.* 1937

119. Clava (I), railway viaduct,
by John Fowler and Murdoch Paterson, 1893–8

120. Kylesku (Su), bridge, by Ove Arup & Partners, 1984

121. Portmahomack (R & C), store houses, by Alexander Stronach, 1699, and of 1779 enlarged in the early nineteenth century

122. Fortrose (R & C), Chanonry Lighthouse, by Alan Stevenson, 1846

123. Lybster (C), Harbour, 1833, enlarged in 1850–4 and 1883–5

124. Glendale (S & L), mill, perhaps mid-eighteenth century

125. Laidhay (C), croft buildings, probably early nineteenth century

storey (also with a passage). Unlike the nave at Durham but like that at Dunfermline, the three storeys are firmly marked off from each other like the layers of a cake, with intervening stringcourses providing filling, the horizontality only slightly weakened by the ribs and corbels of the C 13 vault dropping through the clearstorey into the triforium stage. Again like Dunfermline and unlike Durham, the arcades' piers are all circular, giving an uninterrupted visual thrust to the E, the effect accentuated by the piers at St Magnus being undecorated ashlar cylinders. Differences in the pier's capitals and bases testify to changes of fashion during the long period of construction and not to the first architect's desire for variety. Scalloped capitals on the N arcade's E pier and the two E piers of the S arcade, probably the only ones completed by c. 1150. All the others have moulded capitals, the mouldings of the two W bays' piers of c. 1500 very little different from those of the C 13 piers; but the late medieval W piers have moulded bases, the others all chamfered bases of the mid-C 12. Roundheaded triforium arches of three chamfered orders. Pointed clearstorey arches of two chamfered orders. The C 13 vaulting is quadripartite, with chamfered stone ribs springing from fluted cone corbels which hang down from the clearstorey's stringcourse. Rosetted bosses at the intersections. The three W bays' vaults, doubtless intended from the C 13, were not erected until the later C 19; their interstices were replaced in glass-fibre in the 1970s.

The NAVE AISLES' quadripartite vaults are also early C 13 (late C 19 in the two W bays), but the decorative glory of these aisles is the blind arcading which covers the lower part of the walls of the five E bays on each side. Its coupled shafts and intersecting arches are probably derived ultimately from the arcading in Durham Cathedral's aisles, but a more direct source may be Leuchars Parish Church (Fife), perhaps also a product of the Durham-Dunfermline school, which has blind arcading on the exterior of its choir and apse. St Magnus shares with Leuchars the motif of a triangular spur between the coupled shafts, although at Leuchars this appears at the single arches of the apse and not at the choir's intersecting arches. All the S wall's arcading and that of the N wall's four E bays has shafts with cushion capitals, strongly suggestive of a mid-C 12 date. The shafts at the N side's fifth bay have waterleaf capitals, indicating a date of c. 1200 for this part of the nave wall.

The aisles' two W windows on each side are late C 15 or early C 16, quite plain with roundheaded rear-arches. In the next bay on each side is a door, the N being the principal entrance for laity in the C 13. The S door was the W processional door. Despite its C 16 exterior, to the inside it presents engaged shafts with mid-C 12 cushion capitals (one having a volute). All the nave windows in the five E bays, except the S aisle's E window, which is probably a C 13 replacement and plain, have round-headed rear-arches of several orders and nook-shafts. Cushion capitals of the mid-C 12 at the second window from the E on the S side and at the three E windows and the fourth window's

E jamb on the N side. Crocketed capitals on the shafts of the third to sixth windows of the S side suggest that these were completed c. 1200. Slightly later seems to have been the construction in the N aisle of the fourth window's arch and W jamb and of the fifth window, their shafts having capitals carved with stiffleaf foliage. The arches from the aisles into the transepts are of c. 1200, the S roundheaded, the N pointed. Each springs from a crossing pier of c. 1200 on its inner side but on its outer from mid-C12 corbels carved with human heads. Round-arched triforium and clearstorey openings to the E.

8   The CROSSING's tall and pointed arches are of c. 1200. Compound orders with waterleaf capitals, the arches' inner orders carved with chevron, the hoodmoulds with sawtooth decoration. Flat wooden ceiling.

In each of the TRANSEPTS, triforium and clearstorey passages across the E and W walls. At the lower part of the W walls and gables is blind arcading. Intersecting arches as in the nave aisles, but the arch heads are only recessed minimally. Presumably an impression of greater recession was originally obtained by painting. At the S transept's gable, the canons' door inserted c. 1200, its shafts' capitals carved with crockets, the pointed rear-arch made up of alternating red and white stones. The round-arched window above is mid-C12, with nook-shafts and voluted capitals, but its rear-arch again alternates red and white stone, apparently the first use of this decorative device in the cathedral. Nook-shafts at the other transept windows. Waterleaf capitals at the clearstorey windows next to the crossing rebuilt with it c. 1200. The open wooden roofs were renewed in *Watson*'s C20 restoration. The doorways into the transept chapels are again of the mid-C12, with corbelled roundheaded arches of two orders, the hoodmoulds carved with sawtooth ornament.

In each TRANSEPT CHAPEL built in the early C13, the main space is covered by a quadripartite vault with a central boss. In each outer wall, a pointed window, its capitals carved with deeply undercut waterleaf foliage. Tunnel-vaulted recess between each chapel and the choir. Above each chapel and entered from the triforium gallery is a room, the S vaulted.

The CHOIR is entered from the crossing and transepts through arches rebuilt c. 1200. In its mid-C12 three bays, the central vessel's elevations have a three-layered arrangement generally similar to those of the nave, but there is not the same regular procession of equal bays. The centre arch is slightly wider than the W. This may be the result of the rebuilding of the crossing piers and consequently of part of this W arch c. 1200, so perhaps the choir's two W arches on each side were intended originally to read as a double bay, followed to the E by walling through which the narrow third arch is cut, the walling extending on into the apse which housed the high altar and the associated shrine of St Magnus. All these main arches are of three orders, the outer enriched with a billet moulding, the hoodmould with sawtooth. Each of the two W arches on each side shares a central round pier and springs from a respond on its other side. The narrow arches of the E bay on each side spring from corbels carved with heads. Hoodmoulded triforium arches of three orders, those on the S side with piers of rectangular section, the piers on the N of stepped section. Clearstorey arches of two orders with nook-shafts, the windows next to the crossing having waterleaf capitals, indicating that they were reconstructed together with the crossing c. 1200. In the choir aisles, round-arched mid-C12 windows with nook-shafts and hoodmoulds. The aisles' quadripartite vaults were intended from the start, their ribs springing from the arcade piers on their inner side and from corbel heads on their outer. The central vessel's vaulting, quadripartite again, was introduced in the C13 as an afterthought, the triplets of stone ribs springing from wall shafts which rise from corbel heads above the clearstorey stringcourse. The vault of the broad E bay is very awkwardly related to the off-centre openings of its arcade, triforium and clearstorey.

The PRESBYTERY was begun c. 1190. Its three bays' elevations continue the layering of the work to the W, with stringcourses again separating the three storeys, but the greater length of the bays and the relative elaboration of the arcades' compound piers relax the urgency of the thrust to the E. At the piers, waterholding bases. Their capitals are either moulded or decorated with foliage of crocketed or stiffly cut trefoil type; in the foliage, figures of humans and snakes. Arches of four orders with roll and hollow mouldings. The triforium openings courteously reproduce the design of those to the W, but the clearstorey windows are pointed. At the central vessel's E end, the wall under the window has three blind pointed arches. In their spandrels, round panels, the outer two (the N a restoration) carved with foliage, the inner panels decorated with foliaged capitals at the springing of the mullions and moulded capitals at the arch head. The central mullion's capital is carved with figures; at the mullion's base, a carved head. The central vessel's quadripartite vaulting, although an afterthought, appears less of an intrusion into the design than the vaulting of the nave and choir. Shafts coming down as clusters into the clearstorey, then as thick single shafts down to the triforium's imposts, and below that as pencil shafts disappearing into the springing of the arcades, this lowest stage of wall shafts perhaps designed independently of the decision to provide vaulting. The aisle vaults spring from wall shafts.

FURNISHINGS almost all designed by *George Mackie Watson* and executed in Scottish oak by *Scott Morton & Co.* in the 1920s; their design was inspired by the early C16 furnishings of King's College Chapel, Aberdeen, and a few early C16 fragments in St Magnus. – SCREENS at the nave doors. – PULPIT at the crossing's NE pier. Late Gothic with Lorimerian touches. Small statues of the four Evangelists and the Good Shepherd in tabernacled niches at the corners; angels on the octagonal sounding board. – LECTERN on the crossing's S side, with angels holding shields. – Round FONT, carved with more angels. – SCREENS to the choir aisles, decorated with vines. – CHOIR STALLS with linenfold-panelled fronts; elbow-rests carved with beasts, birds and crowned saints. – ORGAN SCREEN dividing the choir from the presbytery. Elaborate late Gothic, with a large centre cross and symbols of the Evangelists and the Eucharist; small statues of two bishops, St Magnus and St Columba. – ORGAN by *Henry Willis & Sons*, 1925; restored by *Henry Willis IV*, 1971. – In the door to the organ chamber off the S aisle are set two wooden PANELS carved with the monogram MHC and the date 1620.

In the medieval presbytery (now the St Rognvald Chapel), HOLY TABLE, PULPIT and LECTERN designed by *Stanley Cursiter* and executed by *Reynold Eunson*, 1965. In the table's front, early C17 panels carved with stylized foliage. Two C17 fluted panels in the lectern. More late C16 and early C17 panels, probably from pews, at the pulpit. In its sides and front, three armorial panels: one has the initials ES and VF (for Edward Sinclair of Essenquoy † *c.* 1641 and his wife, Ursula Foulzie), a second the date 1593, and the third the initials DMC and MG. Another panel is carved with stylized foliage, and yet another with the head of an anxious angel. – In the E wall's blind arcading, wooden STATUES of Kol, St Rognvald and Bishop William the Old, again carved in 1965 by *Eunson* from designs by *Cursiter*.

MARKET CROSS at the N transept's E wall, moved there from Broad Street in 1954. Dated 1621. Crude cross, its arms ending in *fleurs-de-lis*.

STAINED GLASS. Very extensive scheme, mostly of the early–mid-C20 by *Oscar Paterson*, with figures of saints, Old Testament worthies and people connected with Orkney; armorial glass in the S transept chapel. A few windows are by other artists. – Strongly coloured W window (Our Lord with emblems of St Magnus, St Luke and St John) by *Crear McCartney*, 1987. – In the N nave aisle, two windows, one (David) by *Douglas Strachan*, 1912, the other (Elijah) by *James Ballantine & Son*, 1887. – In the middle of the S nave aisle, two lights (the Good Samaritan, and the Sower) by *A. Ballantine & Gardiner*, 1898 and *c.* 1905. – Great E window (the Crucifixion and Ascension) by *James Ballantine II*, 1918.

MONUMENTS. At the E end of the S choir aisle, recumbent Portland stone effigy of the Arctic explorer John Rae, his gun beside him; by *Joseph Whitehead*, *c.* 1895. – At the N choir aisle's E end, a sarcophagus with coats of arms commemorating the African explorer William Balfour Baikie † 1864.

In the N aisle, late C17 HATCHMENT (or MORT BROD) of Robert Nicolson, its W side painted with a shrouded skeleton, emblems of death, and the monogram RNID (for Robert Nicolson and his wife, Jean Davidson); above, angels sticking arrows into a heart, and the motto MEMENTO MORI. On the E side, a painted inscription.

GRAVESLABS AND WALL MONUMENTS. Large collection of stones, many removed from the cathedral's floor and placed against the walls in the mid-C19. In the s nave aisle they begin at the w with George Liddell of Hammer † 1681. At the top, a mantled helm and coat of arms; symbols of death at the bottom. – Patrick Prince, merchant in Kirkwall, † 1673. Weathered stone with a prominent skeleton and emblems of death and resurrection. – T. Murray † 1577. Very worn, with a low relief of a cross under a coat of arms. – Wall monument to Elizabeth Cuthbert † 1685. Etiolated Ionic columns at the sides. In the centre, high relief of a lady kneeling in front of a skull, crossbones and hourglass, whilst a hand holds out a crown to her. Angels' heads on the top. Inept but endearing. – Jean Grahame † 1694. Impaled coats of arms at the top; grisly emblems in high relief at the bottom. – Mary Young, dated 1750. An even cruder version of Elizabeth Cuthbert's monument, omitting the crown and angels' heads. – John Edmonstone † 1682, with a long inscription above a high relief of symbols of death. – Aedicular wall monument marking the burial place of Captain Peter Winchester and his wife, Jean Baikie † 1674. On the starved Ionic columns, spirals of vine leaves. Two bunches of grapes on the frieze and angels' heads at its projecting ends. Steep pediment (dated 1675) with birds on its sides and a thistle on top. At the bottom, a trophy of emblems of death. – James Bakie of Burnes † 1679. Under the inscription, a relief showing a naked man who stands on a skull and crossbones while, above him, angels point to a crown and sceptre, the symbolism explained by a caption at each level

AD HOC
AB HOC
PER HOC

– Thomas Baikie Yr † 1740. Long inscription and a few grisly reminders of death. – Paplay Monument. Segmental-arched tomb recess, probably C14, its gablet bearing a stone carved with the Paplay arms. In the recess has been placed a medieval graveslab, also bearing the Paplay arms. – Wall monument to Nicola Traill † 1688. High relief of a woman (looking very like Elizabeth Cuthbert) who stands on a ball labelled 'VANITAS', with a skull and crossbones in front, and appeals to a figure of Our Lord in glory holding a crown. The scene is framed by etiolated Ionic columns from which springs a pointed arch inscribed 'HEAVEN OPENED'. – Barbara Irvine † 1682, with a long inscription and reminders of death. – In a recess, William Maine † 1592. Pointed-arched slab carved with a coat of impaled arms. – Edward Pottinger, perhaps C16. Crude, with an angel at the bottom. – Elizabeth Irving † 1681. Long inscription and plenty of grislies.

At the N nave aisle's w end, the late C17 monument to George Drummond † 1653 and his grandchildren, with the dates 1653, 1660 and 1662; coat of arms at the top. – Wall monument to John Cuthbert † 1650, his wife and daughter, probably of *c.* 1670. Unpedimented aedicule, the columns' capitals would-be Composite; angels' heads on the entablature's ends. Above

the inscription tablet, another angel with outspread wings. –
Catherine Craigie † 1612, with a coat of arms and an incised
skull and crossbones. – Robert Richen of Linklater † 1679. Not
very skilful reliefs of a coat of arms and emblems of mortality. –
John Sinclair † 1676 and James Adamson † 1682, carved by
Patrick Adamson, 1689. Two foliage-bordered cartouches. Thistles in the stone's bottom corners, roses in the top. – Elizabeth
Elphinstone † 1680. Border decorated with rosettes; a copious
display of grisly emblems at the bottom. – James Black † 1675,
with more grislies. Inscription including the injunction

> CORPS.REST.IN.PEACE.WITHI[N]
> THS.GROVND.VNTIL.ARC[HAN]
> [GELS.] TRUMPET.SOUN[D.]
> SOUL[.] IOY.ABOVE.
> TIL.THY.CREA[T]ORS MIGH[T]
> BOTH.RE[UNI]TE.
> TO.REIGNE WTH SANTS.IN.LIGHT

– Margaret Henderson † 1683, with a vine border and emblems
of death. – John Kaa † 1679, and very similar. – John Richen
† 1679. Similar again, but with a chequered border. – Thomas
Sandison † 1656, with a blank shield and a skull and crossbones,
all in shallow relief.

s choir aisle. At the w end, a stone to Marjorie and Beatrix
Smyth † 1666 and 1669, its top carved with a coat of arms
flanked by emblems of death. – Two mid-c 16 fragments
cemented together, both carved with the Sinclair arms and one
with a sword hilt and the initials ES said to be for Edwin Sinclair
of Strome. – George Sinclair of Rapnes † 1643, with a coat
of arms. – Two more stones cemented together. The upper,
commemorating Thomas Reid † 1603, has a coat of arms and
an incised skull and crossbones. The lower, to Laurence Sinclair
† 1564, has a coat of arms flanked by the initials IS (for his wife,
Janet Strang). – Worn heraldic slab, perhaps c 16, to AB. –
Patrick Murray † 1687, with a mantled helm and coat of arms
at the top and a skull and crossbones at the bottom; placed
above, but clearly belonging to another monument, is the
carved head of an angel. – Stone dated 1612 to RC and WC,
with a coat of arms; at the bottom, a crude skull and crossbones.
The date March 16 1705 is an obvious addition. – Lord Adam
Stewart † 1575, heraldic. – William Urving † 1614. Coat of arms
and a skull and bone, all in very shallow relief. – William Halcro,
c. 1600. Worn, with coats of arms and the initials VH and IS. –
William Henryson † 1582, heraldic. – Red sandstone slab of *c.*
1600, with a coat of arms and the initials MF above a cross.

n choir aisle. At the w end, James Traill of Woodwick † 1733
and other Traills, including Mary Balfour † 1794, wife of John
Traill of Westness. Pedimented sandstone slab bearing a marble
panel carved with the arms of Traill and Balfour, so presumably
it is of *c.* 1795. – Thomas Tayleor † 1666, with a big coat of
arms at the top and a skull and crossbones at the bottom. –
David Monroe † 1684, with a coat of arms at the top and

emblems of death at the bottom, vigorous but crude. – Isobel Calcrit, dated 1612. Narrow red sandstone slab (probably trimmed) with a coat of arms at the top and an incised skull and crossbones at the bottom. – Worn slab, perhaps C 13, carved with a sword and with a cross with a floriated top. It has been reused, probably in the C 17, and the initials P C added. – William Peterson, of 1522, with a coat of arms. – Andrew Gilbert † 1652 (?) and Elene Yenstay † 1663, with an incised skull and crossbones. – Marjorie Potinger † 1669, with a coat of arms. – Sir Nicol Halcro, parson of Orphir, of *c.* 1550. Weathered, with a coat of arms surmounted by a chalice. – Robert Irving. Late C 17, a coat of arms at the top, emblems of death at the bottom. – William Kincaid † 1594, smith to Robert Stewart, Earl of Orkney. Worn, a hammer for crest above the coat of arms.

N of the cathedral, the pink granite WAR MEMORIAL GATEWAY of 1923 into the graveyard. Round arch with foliaged capitals on the nook-shafts. This is enclosed in a stepped gable topped by a victorious-looking angel.

BISHOP'S PALACE
Watergate

Unprepossessing ruin but of considerable importance, as it incorporates the undercroft of one of the earliest stone-built halls in Scotland. That hall certainly existed by 1263, when King Haakon Haakonsson took up residence there after his defeat at the Battle of Largs, and was large enough for both the king's house carls and those of the bishop to dine simultaneously, although at separate tables, whilst the king ate his meals in apartments on the floor above. It is possible the hall had been built by Bishop William the Old soon after the site of his cathedral church and episcopal residence was transferred from Birsay to Kirkwall, *c.* 1140, but the use of decoratively contrasting red and white stone finds a parallel in the second phase of work on St Magnus Cathedral (*see* above), suggesting that the hall may have been put up *c.* 1200 during the episcopate of Bjarne Kolbeinsson. *c.* 1550 Bishop Robert Reid remodelled the undercroft, rebuilt the upper floors and added a NW tower. About fifty years later the palace was again remodelled and extended S, apparently as part of a scheme by Patrick Stewart, Earl of Orkney, to create a great courtyard palace with his new Earl's Palace at its SE corner and the Bishop's Palace forming the W range.

Much of the walling of the early medieval hall's ground floor or undercroft survives. It is a long rectangle, *c.* 34.4m. by 8.2m., built of coursed flagstone slabs, the masonry pierced by putlock holes. Narrow loopholes with chamfered margins (the S one, of inverted keyhole shape, a late medieval replacement) in the long W wall; near its N end, the opening of a chute from a first-floor garderobe. The internal quoins of these loopholes' embrasures and the sides of the garderobe vent are all built of alternating red and yellow stones, a decorative device used at St Magnus Cathedral (*see* above) from *c.* 1200. At the E wall's S end, three small square windows, the outer two still with their dressings, which are checked for shutters but without glazing grooves. Inside, their embrasures have come down to the floor and been later infilled up to sill level.* There has been a door in the N gable, its red sandstone E jamb still visible. Inside the gable to its E is an aumbry. Three more early medieval aumbries (two blocked) in the S gable.

In his reconstruction of *c.* 1550 Bishop Reid not only rebuilt the upper floors and added the NW tower but remodelled the existing undercroft. The N door was converted to a window, and a new door (perhaps replacing an existing one) was made in the E front. On the W front, all the loopholes except the S were blocked. Inside, he inserted a tunnel-vault over the N two-thirds, thickening the side walls to support it, blocked two of the aumbries in the S gable, and rebuilt the NW corner abutting his new tower. This work was partly undone *c.* 1600, when the vault was removed and sturdy stepped buttresses were added on the W.

Reid's rebuilding of the upper floors of the hall block provided two new storeys and an attic, their rubble masonry less regularly coursed and with a greater variety of stones than the earlier work below. At the first floor, decently sized windows, some of those in the W wall set high up and of horizontal proportion. Near the E wall's S end was a door, presumably reached by a forestair. At the S end of the W wall, the shallow rectangular projection of a first-floor garderobe, carried on big moulded corbels. On the E front, another shallow projection for a first-floor fireplace and, to its S, a corbelled projection from the second floor.

70   Reid's NW tower is round, of five storeys and an attic, the walling rising sheer from a splayed basecourse to the parapet, whose individual corbels have small corbels set chequer-wise between them. Inside the parapet, an L-plan cap-house, its SE jamb covering the stairhead. Unusually, the parapet walk was roofed. On the tower's E side, a double gunloop at the ground floor. Big gunloop (perhaps enlarged) pointing W to enfilade the main block's W wall. Gunholes in the breasts of the upper floors' windows. Above the first floor and facing NW, an arched niche containing a white freestone statue, perhaps of St Olaf. To its W, an ogee-arched panel frame.

In the alterations of *c.* 1600, two big first-floor windows were inserted in the W wall; in the E, one window was enlarged and the first-floor door converted to a window. At about the same time was added a S extension, its S end now lost in the Old Manse (*see* Description, below). What is exposed of this addition is a two-bay block of two storeys, perhaps originally with an attic. On the E front, a ground-floor arcade (now

---

*It is possible that they were infilled completely *c.* 1550 as a preliminary to building a vault and then partly unblocked *c.* 1600, when the vault (if ever built over the ground floor's S end) was removed.

infilled with a door and window) with square ashlar piers and semicircular arches. At the centre of each front, a cone of continuous corbelling for a second-floor oriel window, like those on the w front of the Earl's Palace. At the sw corner, a first-floor garderobe projection on big moulded corbels. Probably of the same date as this s addition was the erection of a wall extending e from the palace's N gable. It was demolished in 1877 and the unmoulded semicircular arch of its gateway (the Water Gate) rebuilt in a stretch of masonry with deeply recessed pointing which fills a gap in the first-floor e wall of the palace.

Inside the palace's main block the first-floor level was lowered, except at the N end, *c*. 1600, when Bishop Reid's tunnel-vault was removed and replaced by a wooden floor, the corbels for its joists surviving in the s gable. This first floor seems to have been divided into three or four rooms, two with close garderobes (their floors lowered *c*. 1600) in the w wall. Stone seats at the SE window.

The NW tower's interior is of *c*. 1550. Trapezoidal ground floor, awkwardly covered by a tunnel-vault. The first-floor room, entered from the main block, is roughly rectangular, *c*. 4.3m. square. In its NE wall, a fireplace with moulded jambs flanked by a window and an aumbry. NW and SW windows, both with stone seats and the NW with an aumbry in its l. jamb. Beside the SW window, a close garderobe with a lamp recess. At the SE corner, the door to the tight turnpike stair which gave access to the upper floors of both the tower and the main block. The tower's second-floor room has another moulded fireplace and window seats. No fireplace in the third-floor room, but there is one on the floor above.

EARL'S PALACE
Watergate

Partly ruined but still sophisticated Franco-Scottish lodging built 69 for Patrick Stewart, Earl of Orkney, the quasi-royal ruler of the Northern Isles, in 1606.* Grand though this is, it seems likely that it was intended only as the SE corner of a great quadrangle, its w side formed by the Bishop's Palace (*see* above) and with ranges for retainers on the s and perhaps the N.

The palace is an irregular U-plan, its rubble-built walls intended to be harled. Main e block of two storeys, the first floor very high, with an attic above. Three-storey sw wing, its second-floor windows rising above the wallhead. Tenuously attached short three-storey NW jamb. The primacy of the e range (containing the hall and chamber) is marked by mullioned and transomed oriel windows. Each is of an individual show-off design. Of the two corbelled out from the w front's wall-face, one is bowed, the other semi-octagonal. On the e, where they are linked by a stringcourse, they are much bigger and are

*The date reported as still visible in 1774.

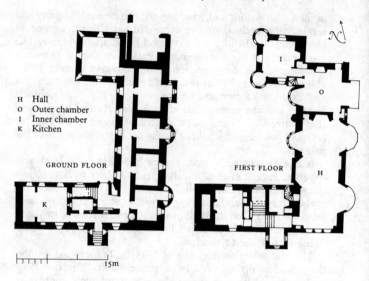

H Hall
O Outer chamber
I Inner chamber
K Kitchen

GROUND FLOOR

FIRST FLOOR

15m

Kirkwall, Earl's Palace. Plans of ground and first floors.
(Redrawn by permission of the RCAHMS)

corbelled out from stems rising from the ground. Both stem
and oriel are bowed at the s end, semi-octagonal in the middle,
and rectangular at the N. In the s gable, a transomed window
of three roundheaded lights. At the w corners of the N jamb
and s wing are round turrets, of one storey at the wing but at
the jamb of two storeys, with their upper floors jettied out
on corbelling. More corbelling at the massive chimney which
projects from the main block's w front. All this corbelling also
displays a zest for variety. Chequer-set corbels at the chimney.
Widely spaced individual corbels carry the N jamb's top floor
and the upper parts of its turrets. Cones of continuous corbelling, but of different profiles, at each of the main block's w
oriels. Continous corbelling again at the s porch's jettied upper
floor, the E oriels and the SW turret of the s wing. This wing's
NE turret also has continuous corbelling, but it is topped by
chequer-set corbels with dummy shotholes placed between
them. Plenty more shotholes at the ground floor and window
breasts, all either quatrefoils or moulded circles of the same
patterns as used at Earl Patrick's Scalloway Castle (Shetland)
and his uncle's Muness Castle (Shetland) a few years before.
Moulded panel frame (formerly containing an inscription) on
the w front's chimney. The principal door at the E end of the s
wing's N elevation is flanked by semi-octagonal piers, their
corners with quirked rolls, their sides fluted. Tapering capitals,
their bottom course carved with upside-down egg-and-dart
ornament, their upper part with weathered foliage which twines
across the door's lintel. Above, three panels, the lowest hori-

zontal and flanked by very worn human figures. The two upper panels are framed by baluster columns. Both have been carved with heraldry, the top panel still showing part of the royal arms circled by the Order of the Thistle.

Inside the principal door, a tunnel-vaulted vestibule with the stair to its W. Immediately E of the door, a rectangular recess or guardroom with the deeply splayed embrasure of a gunhole in its N wall. Beside this recess is a segmental arch into the tunnel-vaulted passage which runs along the W side of the main block and the S side of the S wing. At the passage's SE corner, a vaulted recess in the wall containing the well. S of the passage in the wing is a porch with a flight of steps up to its outer door. N of the passage, an opening (perhaps a service hatch) into the vestibule and, W of this opening, the door to a guardroom under the stair. In this guardroom's S, E and W walls are small windows into the passage and vestibule and a larger one into the tunnel-vaulted kitchen which occupies the wing's W end. In the kitchen's N and S walls, good-sized windows (two blocked). W of the S window is a saltbox recess; directly opposite, in the N wall, a window. It is clear from a constructional joint in the vault and part of the abutment for an arch in the N wall that these were originally intended to be within the fireplace and that it was decided as an afterthought but while construction was in progress to extend the S wing by the depth of the present segmental-arched fireplace. Inside this fireplace, a (blocked) N window.

On the ground floor of the main block and NW jamb, tunnel-vaulted stores. Both they and the passage have windows of quite generous size and no shortage of gunholes.

The stair up to the first floor is a stone dogleg with a tunnel-vault over each flight. W of the half-landing, a small lobby with a close garderobe to its N. W of the lobby, a room (probably the principal guest chamber) above the kitchen. On the l. of its W fireplace, a moulded stone cornice; double aumbry in the E wall. S of the stair's main landing, a big segmental arch into the ante-room above the porch. Large windows in its three outside walls and a gunhole at the NW corner. Moulded stone ribs divide the upper part of the walls and the tunnel-vaulted ceiling into panels, the effect still one of restrained luxury. Tunnel-vaulted steward's room on the N of the landing. Beside its fireplace, two large and deep recesses, presumably to house files.

The hall, c. 16.7m. by 6.1m., occupies the greater part of the main block's first floor. It has been wonderfully well lit from its great S window and the oriels on the E and W. At the SW corner, just inside the entrance, an aumbry. In the centre of the W wall, a huge fireplace, c. 4.57m. broad, framed by octagonal piers like squat versions of those at the palace's entrance, topped by chunky finials carved with the initials PEO (for Patrick, Earl of Orkney). Straight lintel surmounted by a segmental relieving arch. Opposite, a buffet recess. A second fireplace, robbed of its dressings, in the N wall. Just S of the W fireplace is the door

to a turnpike stair serving the s wing's second floor and the
main block's attic. E of the N fireplace is the door into a tiny
tunnel-vaulted lobby with a garderobe on its E. N of the lobby
is the outer chamber, almost all its side walls taken up by oriel
windows. On the r. of the N fireplace, a door to a N extension
(now almost entirely demolished). At the NW corner, two doors,
the l. to a stair giving access to the second floor of the jamb and
the main block's attic, the r. opening into a little lobby under
the stair. N of this lobby, another close garderobe. In the jamb
to the W, the inner chamber with big windows in its N, W and
s walls, and a plain fireplace in the E. At its W corners, doors to
the round closets in the turrets. The second-floor room above
the inner chamber seems to have been almost identical. The
plan of the main block's attic floor is now hard to reconstruct.
The sill of the N stair's door is set below the level of the top of
the outer chamber's window embrasures. In the s gable, a
rectangular window lighting a room above this end of the hall.
At the s wing's W end has been a comfortable room with good-
sized N and s windows, a W fireplace, and closets in the angle
turrets.

CHURCHES

BAPTIST CHURCH, Victoria Street. By *T. S. Peace*, 1888. Cheap
Romanesque, the carved detail eroded by stone cleaning.

CONGREGATIONAL CHURCH, Palace Road. Built in 1876.
Humble Gothic, a big rose window in the s gable.

EAST CHURCH, School Place. Built for the United Presbyterians
in 1847–9. Big box, its innocent Romanesque detail almost
'Saxon'. The W gable front is dressed up with a parapet and
buttresses to suggest a 'nave' and 'aisles' behind, the 'nave'
window of four lights with etiolated columns and an overall
round-arched fanlight filled with interesting tracery. On top
of the buttresses, cupolas topped by crocket-finialled spires.
Similar but much taller bellcote corbelled out at the centre.
Inside, a U-plan GALLERY with *fleur-de-lis* decoration on its
cast-iron columns' capitals; Romanesque blind arcading on the
front. – Roomy PULPIT of 1871 with the ORGAN behind.

FREE CHURCH, King Street. Disused. Big buttressed Gothic
box of 1892–3. Above the front gable's porch, a four-light
window with a rose head reminiscent of the E window of St
Magnus Cathedral. Spired and gableted bellcote.

OUR LADY AND ST JOSEPH (R.C.), Junction Road. Low buttressed Gothic rectangle of 1877, a priest's house at the E end. –
The interior was reordered by *McClure*, 1986.

ST OLAF (Episcopal), Dundas Crescent. By *Alexander Ross*,
1875–6. Long rectangle with paired trefoil-headed lights in the
side walls. At the W gable, three stepped lancets under a little
rose window. NE vestry. The SW tower, intended from the start,
was added by *Thomas S. Peace* in 1886. Three stages marked by
stringcourses; sturdy battlement and pyramid roof, the general
shape faintly reminiscent of the crossing tower of St Magnus

Cathedral before its C20 alterations. – Attached to the S, plain
RECTORY of 1889.

Inside, a braced kingpost roof over the nave and chancel.
Stone arch on the chancel's N housing the ORGAN by *G. M.
Holdich*, 1881. – In the chancel's S wall, a two-seat SEDILIA,
the pointed arches springing from corbels. – To its E, an ogee-
arched SACRAMENT HOUSE formerly in the C16 St Ola's
Church in St Olaf's Wynd (*see* Description, below). – Panelled
REREDOS, late Gothic revival of *c.* 1920. – Wooden CHANCEL
SCREEN made in 1897 mostly from remains of the Bishop's
Loft and Throne erected by Bishop George Graham in St
Magnus Cathedral *c.* 1620. Faceted blocks on the uprights;
fluted frieze. At the bottom, panels carved with reliefs of stylized
foliage. – Similar panels on the contemporary PULPIT and
BISHOP'S THRONE. – Late Victorian LECTERN carved with
emblems of the Evangelists. – FONT, a roughly shaped octag-
onal bowl from a pre-Reformation chapel on Rousay.

Complete scheme of STAINED GLASS. Three-light W window
(Faith, Hope and Charity) by *Heaton, Butler & Bayne*, 1931,
and rather insipid. – In the nave's S wall, a line-up of saints, *c.*
1894–1900. – In its N wall, the window in the W bay (Our Lord
with Little Children) is of 1880. – Two other windows (SS.
Paul and James; SS. Matthew and Mark) are by *James Ballantine & Son*, 1883 and 1888. – The fourth window (SS. Gabriel
and Michael) signed by *A. Ballantine & Gardiner*, after 1906. –
In the chancel, one late C19 window (Our Lady and St Margaret
of Scotland) on the S side. – Another (SS. Olaf and John) on
the N of 1876. – Contemporary floral designs in the sedilia's
arches. – E window (the Ascension) of *c.* 1930.

PUBLIC BUILDINGS

CHURCH HALL, Palace Road. Late C19 Gothic, quite plain
except for the S window's wooden tracery.

COVENANTERS MEMORIAL, Broad Street. By *James Hutcheon*
of Aberdeen, 1890. Pedestal with dogs' drinking troughs, supporting an urn-topped shaft; of polished red and grey granite.

FREE LIBRARY, Laing Street. Small but pompous Italianate by
J. M. Baikie, 1909. Pedimented portico with coupled Roman
Doric columns. The first-floor windows rise into pediments,
the outer two segmental, the centre triangular.

HARBOUR. *See* below.

KIRKWALL GRAMMAR SCHOOL, Willow Road. By *M. M. Gilbertson*, 1970–5. Long and low, the precast concrete frame filled
with aggregate panels.

MASONIC HALL, Castle Street. Free Renaissance, by *T. S. Peace*,
1884–5. Just two storeys and three bays. At the ground floor,
rusticated pilasters, their cavetto capitals carved with
anthemions; hoodmoulded door with masonic symbols in its
tympanum. At the first floor, a pedimented centre window, the
outer windows corniced.

ORKNEY ISLANDS COUNCIL OFFICES, School Place. Large

but rather utilitarian complex built as Kirkwall Grammar School. The earliest part at the NW is by *T. S. Peace*, 1873–4. Single-storey L-plan; in the inner angle, a square tower, its upper (belfry) stage corbelled out and topped by an iron-crested Frenchy roof with bargeboarded dormers. This is overwhelmed by the extensions of 1890, 1904 and 1914. Mid-C20 additions at the back.

PAPDALE PRIMARY SCHOOL, Willow Road. By *Orkney County Council*, 1962. Lightweight in the Festival of Britain manner.

SCHOOL HOSTELS, Berstane Road. By the *Property Services Agency*, 1970. Three-storey aggregate-clad blocks with triangular skylights rising from the flat roofs.

SHERIFF COURT AND POLICE STATION, Watergate. By *D. & J. Bryce*, 1875–7. Peaceful Baronial of two storeys on a T-plan. Asymmetrical N block (the Sheriff Court) with two crowstepped gables on the l., a slightly advanced entrance bay with a jettied gable, and steep pedimented dormerheads with rose finials over the two r. bays' first-floor windows. In the E and W gables, three reset early C16 stones, two with the arms of Bishop Robert Reid and one with those of Bishop Edward Stewart. The downstroke is the Police Station. Steep pedimented first-floor dormerheads with rose and thistle finials. In the NW inner angle, a conical-roofed round tower without martial pretension. Plain cell block to the SE.

TOWN HALL, Broad Street. Tall Baronial, by *T. S. Peace*, 1884–6. In the centre of the three-bay front, a crowstepped gable with corner tourelles. The r. bay's corner is canted below, then corbelled out to a bow and finally corbelled out to the square. Entrance framed by fluted columns supporting figures of C18 pikemen; over the door, the carved burgh coat of arms in a neo-Jacobean unpedimented aedicule. High up on the front's l., a panel of 1682 carved with the burgh arms; it came from St Ola's Bridge. – In the first-floor hall, a three-light W window filled with STAINED GLASS (Henry St Clair, Earl of Orkney; James III; and King Haakon Haakonsson) by *A. Ballantine & Gardiner*, 1892.

VICTORIA HALL, Victoria Street. By *T. S. Peace*, 1889–90.

HARBOUR

Basin formed by two piers, the E first built by *George Burn*, 1809–11, the W by *James Allan* in 1813. In 1865–7 the WEST PIER was replaced with an iron pier designed by *Robert Davison*. This was cased in stone and extended by *John Miller* in 1875. Its fat N end has since been replaced in concrete. The long EAST PIER, mostly of concrete, is by *T. S. Peace*, 1883–5. At its S end, the single-storey HARBOUR OFFICE, dated 1871.

DESCRIPTION

BIGNOLD PARK ROAD starts at the junction of the A960 and A961 on the entry from the S. On its r., the single-storey LAINGBRAE, dated 1862, with a block-consoled stone canopy over the door and canted bay windows; pinnacled ball finial on the centre gable. DUNDAS CRESCENT to the N has C20 housing on the l. Its r. side is solid late Victorian, including St Olaf's Episcopal Church and Rectory (*see* Churches, above). Then comes SCHOOL PLACE, its beginning dominated by the East Church (*see* above). Chunky crowstep-gabled range of one and two storeys at Nos. 4–8, probably early C19. The harled No. 5 opposite is of *c.* 1800, its attic lit by windows in the gables. No. 3 with a crowstepped gable to the street looks a little later. For the Orkney Islands Council Offices, *see* Public Buildings, above. On the l. side of KING STREET to the NE and set well back in a garden, No. 11, a Baronial villa of 1880 with a conical-spired turret beside the entrance. Opposite, the late Georgian No. 10 with a pilastered doorpiece and Nos. 6–8 with inept Roman Doric columns at their doors. Then the former Free Church (*see* Churches, above) and the early C19 No. 9, with a very tall corniced doorpiece. A glimpse of the Free Library's portico (*see* Public Buildings, above) down LAING STREET to the W. (Diversion up MILL STREET to the E, where the PAPDALE MILL of 1856, altered by *T. S. Peace*, 1880, is now housing.) In QUEEN STREET, another pilastered doorpiece at No. 14, of *c.* 1840. In EAST ROAD to the E, some plain late Georgian houses on the S and a small crowstep-gabled MILL on the N. The main route continues along ST CATHERINE'S PLACE, with late Georgian ranges pushing crowstepped gables towards the street on its E. At the beginning of CROM-WELL ROAD, a line of crowstep-gabled houses, perhaps of *c.* 1800.

SHORE STREET is the entry to the harbour area. On its built-up S side, a couple of crowstepped gable-enders, perhaps late C17. Its line is continued by HARBOUR STREET, again with buildings only on the S. At its start, the KIRKWALL HOTEL, by *T. S. Peace*, 1889–90, free Renaissance, the carved detail badly weathered. French pavilion roofs over the centre and E corner. At the far end, No. 20 with a broad crowstepped gable, one of its skewputts carved with the date 1643 and the initials IC and MC for John Cuthbert and his wife, Margaret Chalmers. Beside it, the GIRNELL HOUSE (now ORKNEY SAILING CLUB) with a forestair; perhaps also early C17, and built for the storage of rents paid in grain. In JUNCTION ROAD to the S, the former ZETLAND ESTATES OFFICE of 1866, a small T-plan with a pediment on the tail's gable. A little further S, a big and badly altered block, dated 1887. Tall battlemented entrance tower; round-arched and keyblocked windows in the main gable.

BRIDGE STREET, exiting S from Harbour Street's E end, contains several gable-ended houses, probably of the C18. Among them, No. 25, refronted in 1882, with a reused and perhaps recut datestone of 1628 bearing the initials MCEP (for Magnus Craigie of Papdale and his wife, Elizabeth Paplay) and WCMH (for their son, William Craigie of Gairsay, and his wife, Margaret Halcro). In an outshot at the back, another reused early

C 17 stone with the initials M.C./E.P. In ST OLAF'S WYND on the E, a roll-moulded and round-arched door, all that remains of ST OLA'S CHURCH, said to have been rebuilt by Bishop Robert Reid *c.* 1550. At Bridge Street's SW corner, a block dated 1904, its canted corner rising into a narrow shaped gable topped by pinnacles. The S vista is closed by a broad stepped gable of 1860 at the beginning of Albert Street.

ALBERT STREET is a mixture of buildings from the C 17 to the C 20 but with little of distinction. On its S side, the HYDRO-ELECTRIC BOARD (former Commercial Bank) by *David Rhind*, 1859, a big three-storey palazzo. Further on, on the N, the CUSTOM HOUSE built for Captain Balfour of Trenaby in the early C 19. Two storeys and attic, but only two bays wide, with a pilastered doorpiece. No. 34 on the S is Victorian Gothic, with a gablet over the door and pointed shop windows. Then a small L-plan group on the N composed of Nos. 41–43. No. 41 with a crowstepped gable to the street is probably early C 18; No. 43, set behind a forecourt, appears to be of *c.* 1740. To the l. of its fluted doorpiece, a basket-arched pend opening. This gives oblique access to the pilastered and corniced porch at the back of No. 45, *c.* 1800, this house's five-bay front to Albert Street dignified with a central pediment. Another mid-C 19 palazzo housing the BANK OF SCOTLAND at No. 56. Consoled cornices over the doors; shell-headed niches at the attic. On Albert Street's SW corner, No. 60, probably C 18, with a crow-stepped gable to the street and a five-bay rendered side extending up STRYND to join a two-storey row, dated 1703, but heavily 'restored' in 1979 by the Orkney Heritage Society with concrete window sills and lashings of harl.

BROAD STREET is Kirkwall's civic and ecclesiastical centre, with St Magnus Cathedral and the Town Hall (*see* above) looking across at each other. As well as St Magnus, the E side has a pair of early C 19 two-storey houses (Nos. 4 and 6), each of three bays with a pilastered doorpiece; the back slope of No. 6's N gable is crowstepped. In front of the cathedral, the replica erected in 1954 of the C 17 MARKET CROSS (now in the cathedral) and the Covenanters Memorial (*see* Public Buildings, above). On Broad Street's W side, the harled No. 5 is probably mid-C 18. L-plan, the N jamb's gable with straight skews, the W gable crowstepped. Corniced gatepiers at the entrance to its forecourt. To the S of Tankerness House (for which, *see* Town Houses and Lairds' Houses, below), a harled and crowstep-gabled house of the early C 18, its canted SW corner to Tankerness Lane scooped up to the square. Opposite, on the corner of PALACE ROAD, a group of three buildings, their gable-fronts (the two S crowstepped) staggered in an irregular U-plan. The N is early C 19, the centre may be C 16, the S perhaps C 17. All were given concrete sills and thickly harled in their conversion to sheltered housing by *Sinclair Macdonald & Son*, 1970, which the Saltire Society hailed with an award for 'reconstruction'. For the Earl's and Bishop's Palaces in WATERGATE, *see* above. Attached to the S end of the Bishop's Palace, and probably incorporating some masonry of its addition of *c.* 1600, is the harled and crowstepped OLD MANSE of *c.* 1700, L-plan, with a catslide roof on the NE jamb.

VICTORIA STREET'S W side begins with the neo-Georgian ROYAL BANK OF SCOTLAND, by *Dick Peddie, Todd & Jamieson,* 1938. On the E, a crowstepped gable-ender (No. 14), perhaps early C18, and the rubble gable of the Victoria Hall (*see* Public Buildings, above). Quality appears with the harled two-storey No. 19; its door has a lugged architrave whose lintel bears the date 1743 and the initials RMK and MM separated by a heart. Rope moulding and flowers on the scrolled skewputts. More scrolled skewputts on a house, probably of the late C18, at the corner of Whitechapel Lane. The ROYAL HOTEL on the E is unpromising C19, but in its front is a reset red sandstone lintel carved with birds and vases of flowers together with the monogram ITHS (for John Traill and Helen Stewart), flanked by the date 1679. On the hotel's S side, the fragment of another lintel, bearing the initials IL (for Janet Louttit) and the date 1670. Opposite are more gable-fronted houses, probably C18. The street now declines into shantytown shopping before the reappearance of earlier vernacular at the harled and crowstepped No. 54. No. 60, a small gable-ender perhaps of the C17, has a canted NW corner scooped up to the square. In GUNN'S CLOSE opposite, a low terrace of harled two-storey houses, looking early C19 in their present form. More harling on the early C19 No. 62 Victoria Street. Nos. 72 and 74 form a small courtyard, its W side closed by a screen wall. Both look C18 and have been heavily restored, but at the L-plan No. 72 the W gable's N skewputt is carved with the monogram VM, probably for the late C16 owner William Main † 1592, and the S with the head of a bearded man wearing a cap and ruff. Another harled and crowstepped gable-ender, perhaps early C18, at No. 76. Just before the street's end, the Baptist Church (*see* Churches, above) set discreetly back on the E. The corner blocks, probably late C18, at Union Street are quite different in height, but both are crowstepped and have canted corners scooped up to the square.

MAIN STREET kicks off with crowstep-gabled C18 houses. More sophisticated is the WEST END HOTEL built for William Richan of Rapness in 1824. Again harled and crowstepped, but of three storeys and four bays, with a light cast-iron portico in front of the door, its balcony-parapet topped by little urns. After the garden of a large but cottagey villa of *c.* 1840, more C18 gable-ended houses, giving way to plain Victorian. In WELLINGTON STREET and HIGH STREET to the W, C18 and C19 vernacular on the S, C20 bungalows on the N. In OLD SCAPA ROAD, No. 8 is early C19, with chimneys flanking its piend roof's platform. On each side, a projecting outbuilding, the N with pigeon-entries at the side. On the r., ANDERSQUOY SHELTERED HOUSING by *T. S. Peace,* 1881. U-plan, with a two-storey centrepiece. Monopitch-roofed extension (ST ROGNVALD'S HOUSE) by *Moira & Moira,* 1975.

INDUSTRIAL BUILDINGS

AYRE MILL, Ayre Road. Late C19 twelve-bay range, built of rubble (now partly harled). Three-storey centre. Taller crowstep-gabled ends, the E with a little ball finial, the W with a chimney.

HIGHLAND PARK DISTILLERY, Holm Road. Established in 1798, but most of the buildings are of the mid- and late C19, with a fair number of C20 additions. The main complex is E of the road, a rubble-built procession of gable-ended bonded stores with pagoda-roofed kilns behind. More bonded stores W of the road.

KIRKWALL POWER STATION, Great Western Road. Built in 1951. Utilitarian, with a few neo-Georgian touches.

TOWN HOUSES AND LAIRDS' HOUSES

BERSTANE HOUSE, off Berstane Road. Single-storey-and-basement broad-eaved cottage-villa, by *David Bryce*, 1850. A pair of canted bay windows on the E front overlooking the Bay of Berstane. – To the S, a crowstepped lectern DOOCOT, perhaps of *c.* 1700.

DAISYBANK, Berstane Road. Big piend-roofed house of *c.* 1840, with horizontal glazing.

GRAINBANK HOUSE, Grainbank. Smooth and sophisticated villa built for Lord Dundas of Aske (later first Earl of Zetland) in 1829. Two-storey S front, a fully exposed basement at the E side and back. It is of three bays by three, built of rubble with freestone dressings. Central chimneystack on the piended platform roof. On the front, stone canopies over the ground-floor windows, including one in the centre of the broad gabled porch. Stone canopies again on the E elevation, whose N bay is recessed, with corbels supporting the straight line of the eaves above. In this section, the drawing-room window comes down to floor level; in front of it, a balcony with stone corbels and an iron railing. Horizontal glazing in the windows. Well-finished interior, its plasterwork and chimneypieces intact. Attached to the W side is an L-plan coach-house range; in the gable of its SW jamb, an ogee-arched pigeon entrance under a datestone of 1829. – Further W, a detached STABLE and BYRE, dated 1715 over the built-up door but remodelled in the early C19, when a dummy keyhole gunloop was inserted in the front. At the back, more late Georgian 'gunloops' together with blind pointed arches.

TANKERNESS HOUSE, Broad Street. Harled ranges round a roughly rectangular courtyard, the product of building, rebuilding and remodelling from the late C16 to the early C19. The earliest part is the N range and the gateway from the street to its S, apparently erected by Gilbert Fulzie, minister of Kirkwall and Archdeacon of Orkney, in 1574. The crowstep-gabled three-storey N range is an irregular T-plan, its short S tail (containing a turnpike stair) placed near the E end. The door from the courtyard into this stairtower has moulded jambs. So too has the window in its W face, but there are chamfered

margins at the stairtower's first-floor window. On the tower's
S skewputt, the initials MGF and EK for Mr Gilbert Fulzie and
his wife, Elizabeth Kinnaird. In the N range's E gable, ground-
floor windows with rounded margins (one also moulded);
chamfered margins (much restored) at the first floor. The
range's other windows all seem to belong to a remodelling of
c. 1820 made by the Baikies of Tankerness, the family which
owned the house after 1641. Over the narrow window W of the
early C19 entrance in the centre of the S front, a reused C16
lintel inscribed 'HEIR BE GOD'. On the range's SE skewputt,
the sacred IHS monogram; IHS again, but as individual letters
together with the initials MGF, on the NE skewputt. Screen
wall to the S with a wall-walk corbelled out towards the street
on the E. On its parapet, the coats of arms of Fulzie and
Kinnaird and the initials MGF and EK. Between them, a
panel inscribed 'PATRI[A]E ET POSTERIS / NISI DOMINVS
CVSTODI / ERIT FRVSTRA SEMEN / NOSTRVM SERV[I]ET
IPS[I] / ANNO SALVTIS 1574'. The main gateway is roll-
moulded and round-arched. To its N, a moulded door and
window to a single-storey lean-to filling the inner angle between
the N range and its stairtower. It now has a door into the tower
but seems originally to have had access to the street. If it is an
addition it cannot date from much after 1600. Access to the
screen wall's parapet walk by a forestair built against the N gable
of the C18 crowstep-gabled five-bay block S of the gateway.

The courtyard's two-storey W range eschews crowsteps.
Chamfered window margins. The date of 1722 provided on its
SW jamb's S skewputt is likely enough for its rebuilding or
substantial remodelling. On the N skewputt, a monogram seem-
ingly of RBMS (for Robert Baikie of Tankerness and his wife,
Margaret Sinclair).

The S range's present appearance, with a three-light window
in the S front, is early C19 but may incorporate work of the C18
or earlier.

The interior shows evidence of various remodellings. The N
range's rooms are of c. 1820, contemporary with the introduction of its main stair. In the W range, a stone stair newel at
the ground floor is probably of 1722 but could be late C17, as
could also be the segmental-arched kitchen fireplace in its S
ground-floor room. On its first floor, panelling of the earlier
C18 in the N and S rooms. The S range's W first-floor room has
a basket-arched stone chimneypiece, apparently of the early or
mid-C18, and belying this block's general early C19 character.
In the centre first-floor room, fluted piers of c. 1820 at the three-
light window.

GRAIN EARTH-HOUSE
Scotts Road

Excellently preserved deep souterrain of the first millennium B.C.
Access is by a stair, its upper part restored in 1912, the lower
steps original, leading down from the W to the S end of a narrow

gently curved passage, its walls lined with drystone masonry, the roof of flat lintels *c.* 0.9m. above the floor. At the passage's other end, an oval chamber, *c.* 1.6m. high, its walls again of drystone masonry, additional support for the roofing lintels provided by four stone pillars.

KNAP OF HOWAR *see* PAPA WESTRAY

4000   LAMB HOLM

Small island joined to Mainland and Glimps Holm by the Churchill Barriers.

ITALIAN CHAPEL. A piece of ingenious kitsch constructed in 1943–4 by and for Italian prisoners-of-war when they were building the Churchill Barriers; *Domenico Chiochetti* was responsible for the design. The chapel consists of two Nissen huts (now covered with felt) joined end-to-end and dressed up with a showpiece w front modelled in cement. This façade is a gable screen, its parapet and bellcote crocketed; *fleur-de-lis*-finialled pinnacles at the ends. Pedimented portico with more crockets and another *fleur-de-lis* finial, the columns having Romanesque capitals. In the tympanum, a low-relief head of Our Lord, by *Pennisi*.

The interior is lined with plasterboard to make a tunnel-vault, painted in *trompe l'œil* imitation of stone, with a traceried dado. – Wrought-iron SCREEN (by *Palumbo*) dividing off the chancel, whose ceiling DECORATION (by *Chiochetti*) has symbols of the Holy Spirit and the four Evangelists; on the E wall, a version of Nicolo Barabino's Madonna of the Olives. – STAINED GLASS. Two lights (St Catherine of Siena and St Francis) in the E wall, *c.* 1944.

Outside, STATUE of St George by *Chiochetti*, 1943, modelled in cement on a barbed-wire framework, rather archaic in manner.

CHURCHILL BARRIERS. *See* p. 294.

LANGSKAILL *see* GAIRSAY

LONGHOPE *see* SOUTH WALLS

2090   LYNESS (HOY)

Scattered handful of buildings around Ore Bay where a naval base, now disused, was developed from 1917.

WALLS FREE CHURCH, 1.5km. S. Secularized. Minimally

Gothic rubble box of 1877. Angular bellcote with a short spirelet on the w gable.

NAVAL CEMETERY. Laid out *c.* 1920 with neat rows of head-stones to sailors who died in the First World War. At the centre, WAR MEMORIAL by *Reginald Blomfield,* 1925. Tall granite cross with a bronze sword fixed to its E face. Contemporary rubble-built small pavilions with round-arched openings to the N and W.

MARTELLO TOWER, Crock Ness, 2.1km. SE. Built *c.* 1812–18. Squat tapering ashlar tower of two storeys. Small round-arched windows; the first-floor door was reached by a ladder. Inside, domical-vaulted barrack room on the upper floor. Stairs in the wall-thickness, one leading down to the tunnel-vaulted ground-floor stores, the other up to the roof.

FARMS ETC.

MILLHOUSE, 0.9km. N. C19 rubble-built cornmill, a kiln at the s end.

RYSA LODGE, 2.4km. N. Beautifully restrained version of a long two-storey laird's house, by *W. R. Lethaby, c.* 1900. Harled, with crowstepped gables and tiny first-floor windows.

MAES HOWE *see* STENNESS (MAINLAND)

MELSETTER HOUSE (HOY)   2080
4.2km. sw of North Ness

Large but decidedly unostentatious country house of 1898 by 94 *W. R. Lethaby,* who incorporated a humdrum Georgian haa or laird's house. Lethaby's clients, a Birmingham bicycle-seat manufacturer, Thomas Middlemore, and his wife, the embroid-erer and weaver Theodosia Mackay, were disciples of William Morris, whose daughter May found Melsetter 'the embodiment of some of those fairy palaces of which my father wrote with great charm and dignity. But, for all its fitness and dignity, it was a place full of homeliness and the spirit of welcome, a very loveable place.' The Georgian house, a product of accretion and alteration, comprised a long main block, basically L-plan, with a crowstepped sw jamb dated 1738, but with a low s extension and three outshots on the E, the s larger than the other two. Lethaby heightened the main block and broadened it to the line of its two N outshots, wrapped an L-plan addition round the s outshot's N and E sides, and added a sizeable N extension which joined on the w to an existing crowstep-gabled outbuilding; it was remodelled as a wing containing the gunroom and smoking room. The reconstruction produced a gently inventive fiction of organic growth, unified by harling and the consistent use of local sandstone for dressings. For the window and door surrounds of his new work Lethaby used a roll moulding of traditional Orkney type but which had not previously existed at Melsetter.

Low-key entrance court on the w composed of the sw jamb and w side of the Georgian house, with the gunroom wing on the n, this nw wing and the main block provided by Lethaby with broad eaves, those of the main block supported by heavy unmoulded corbels. At the house's s end, informal diversity. On the l., the plain late Georgian s extension projecting from the main c18 block, whose 1890s heightening is marked by the provision of a stone stringcourse which bellies out where it crosses a downpipe. At the r., the crowstepped gable of Lethaby's se wing with tall windows marking the *piano nobile*. On this wing's e front, a tall broad gable covering the width of the Georgian outshot and of Lethaby's n widening of it. In the gable, a pair of heart-shaped attic windows below panels carved with a star and a moon. At the *piano nobile*, a French window from the drawing room opening onto a stone landing carried on an arch, its l. side's straight jamb rising into the beginning of a semicircular head, which then flattens on the r. into a long ellipse carrying a stair down to the garden. To the n, the side of the Georgian main block reconstructed by Lethaby with closely spaced windows, followed by his n addition, its windows far apart and its centre breaking up through the broad eaves to an attic, whose small mullioned windows are surmounted by an ashlar triple gablet carved with the initials of Thomas and Theodosia Middlemore and the date 1898. At the straight-skewed n gable, projecting corbels supporting nothing.

The interior is expressive of the simple life based on high ideals and cushioned by financial security. From the main entrance, steps up to the large hall, most of its walls covered with white-painted simple panelling. On its s side an admirably simple wooden stair to the floor above. At the n wall, elliptical-arched stone doorways to a passage and the dining room. To their r., a broad ashlar chimney breast. Elliptical-arched fireplace in a wavily moulded stone surround; above, a stepped arrangement of five big conical stone corbels intended to carry candles under a straight frieze of five stone shields. Dining room to the n, again with white-painted panelling. Plaster low reliefs of Orcadian wild flowers on the frieze and ceiling beams. Very broad inglenook containing a large stone fireplace, its lintel's soffit shallowly curved at the centre, its ingoes tiled in dark green. e of the hall, the L-plan drawing room, the walls again panelled, the frieze decorated with more flowers. Simple moulded stone chimneypiece containing Delft tiles decorated with coloured birds. French window to the garden in the e wall. At the house's sw corner, a vaulted morning room, presumably of 1738. In the nw wing's smoking room, a heavy stone chimneypiece of 1898, its corbels supporting the ceiling.

The Georgian steading was immediately w of the house. Lethaby provided a new steading further w, demolishing or reconstructing the old farm buildings. Near the house, on the s of the road to his steading, he designed a CHAPEL OF ST

COLM AND ST MARGARET, which was consecrated in 1900. Externally very simple, with random rubble walls (partly C18) and roofed with Caithness slabs. Slanting buttress against the N wall; narrow round-arched entrance. In the W gable, two tiers of stubby lancet windows. Inside, a pointed tunnel concrete vault, the nave marked off from the sanctuary by a bridge-like arch. – Cubic stone ALTAR on a low plinth. – Cylindrical sandstone FONT carved with bands of wave decoration. – Late medieval ivory RELIEF of the Adoration of the Magi on the S wall. – STAINED GLASS. In the S wall, two lights (St Margaret and St Colm) by *Christopher Whall*, c. 1900. – N window (the Crucifixion) by *Morris & Co.*, 1900, from a design of 1865 by *Edward Burne-Jones*. – E window (the Nativity of Our Lord), again of 1900 by *Morris & Co.*, following a design of 1863 by *Ford Madox Brown*.

S of the chapel, the C18 WALLED GARDEN. Square pavilion-roofed Georgian DOOCOT in the SW corner. The balancing TEA HOUSE at the SE was added by Lethaby.

On the N side of the road to the steading, a line of buildings. The E was the S range of the Georgian courtyard steading but converted by Lethaby to house a packing room, museum, spinning room and manservant's room. To its W, a crowstepped building converted by Lethaby to a HALL. Beyond that and effectively all by Lethaby, the harled FACTOR'S HOUSE, with big sash-and-case ground-floor windows and horizontal casement windows at the first floor; heavy stone porch shaped like the up-ended stern of a boat. N of these, on the site of the old steading, Lethaby formed a ROSE GARDEN. In its E screen wall, a reused C17 roundheaded arch. In the W wall, segmental-arched cartshed openings, reminders of the steading. Harled LAUNDRY COTTAGE on the N, Lethaby's reconstruction of the steading's N range, the relieving arches over the openings left exposed.

NOLTLAND CASTLE (WESTRAY)
0.8km. W of Pierowall

4040

The ruin of one of Scotland's strangest C16 creations, a smart house sitting on top of two floors of purposeful artillery fortification. In 1560 lands on Westray were granted by Adam Bothwell, Bishop of Orkney, to his brother-in-law Gilbert Balfour. Balfour, a political thug involved in most of the violent episodes of the reign of Mary, Queen of Scots, became at the same time, or soon after, Constable of Kirkwall and Sheriff of Orkney. Probably he set about the construction of Noltland immediately after receiving his charter of the lands. The castle seems to have been habitable by c. 1572, when it was taken by Lord Robert Stewart (later Earl of Orkney), who had exchanged his temporalities of the abbey of Holyrood for those of the see of Orkney in 1569. In March 1574 the Privy Council was told that the castle had been returned to the Balfours, in whose hands it remained* until 1598, when it was besieged and captured by William Stewart of Egilsay on behalf of his half-brother, Patrick, Earl of Orkney. Earl Patrick held Noltland for at least five years. In 1606, perhaps fed up with the disputatious violence of Orkney, Sir Andrew Balfour of Mountquhanie sold the lands and castle to Sir John Arnot, Treasurer-Depute of Scotland and Lord Provost of Edinburgh, who was made Sheriff of Orkney in 1611 after Earl Patrick's imprisonment for treason. The castle, never completed, seems to have been abandoned by the late C17.

The site is a low hill just W of the Bay of Pierowall, the best anchorage in the north isles of Orkney. Formerly marshy ground on its E and the Loch of Burness to the S provided a measure of natural defence.

The castle's layout on a Z-plan, with a main block, c. 26.4m. by 11m., and NE and SW jambs, each c. 8.2m. square, must have been intended from the start, but the stonework suggests there may have been several phases of construction. All is of local flagstone rubble with red sandstone dressings, probably from Eday, but the masonry of the lower storeys is of thin stones, giving place to almost cubical blocks above; at the top of the main block's E end and the NE jamb, smaller stones reappear.

The design may have altered with the different phases of construction, but what was intended at the time that work was abandoned seems clear. The castle's main block and jambs were all to have risen to the same height and been finished with a simply corbelled parapet and angle rounds. The two lowest floors were to have served as an artillery fortification, the upper floors (two and an attic in the main block, three and an attic in the NE jambs) to have provided spacious accommodation for the lord. Of this were completed the NE jamb and the E third of the main block. The remainder was built only to the height of three storeys.

The two lowest floors are stark. Except for the door in the SW jamb's E face, the only openings are provided by a profusion of wide-splayed rectangular and oval gunloops set in an irregular chequer pattern to cover every approach and enfilade the walls; gunloops are placed even in the corners. Sparse decoration is given by the door's rounded jambs, an adjacent moulded circular gunhole of late C16 type (cf. Muness Castle, Shetland), and a stringcourse (its decoration weathered into bumps) across the SW jamb's E face and with a very short return along the main block's S elevation as if it was originally intended to have gone right across this front.

To the N and W the castle's upper floors, so far as they were completed, are just as stark, quite without ornament and broken only by gunloops. Canted projection splayed out across the NE jamb's inner angle. The S and E elevations disclose the presence

*Gilbert Balfour's son Archibald sold the lands on Westray to his uncle Michael Balfour of Mountquhanie in 1589.

of the living quarters of a lord's house. Here the upper floors are marked off from the gun battery below by a stringcourse running round the NE jamb's N, E and S faces and across the main block's S front and the SW jamb's E face. At its corners the stringcourse has mouldings like full ice-cream cones; over the second-floor windows it jumps up to form hood-moulds. In these fronts, generous-sized windows. Chamfered margins at the SW jamb's S window. At all the others the surrounds are moulded, very boldly at the corniced windows of the NE jamb's top floor. In the centre of the S front, an empty panel-frame.

The interior, like the exterior, juxtaposes military purpose and domestic grandeur. The main block's two bottom floors, lighted by gunloops, are covered by a single tunnel-vault, the dividing wooden entresol now gone. Hatches in the vault, perhaps to allow ammunition to be hoisted to the hall floor above. Mountings for small cannons in the gunloops' embrasures. At the ground floor's W gable, a large segmental-arched kitchen fireplace, with an oven on its N side. This provided the only heat for these two floors, although they must have been intended to house, at least on occasions, a sizeable garrison. The only other hint of normal domestic arrangements is the N service stair rising behind the curve of the vault to the second floor. On each of the NE jamb's lower floors, a tunnel-vaulted store, perhaps for ammunition and powder.

In the SW jamb, a ground-floor entrance vestibule; to its W, a guardroom under the principal stair. This stair is a broad and comfortable turnpike, but, disconcerting for a visitor, its newel is pierced by a broad-mouthed oval gunloop pointing from the guardroom to the entrance. Second-floor stairhead covered with a tunnel-vault. Here the stair's newel is finished with a tapered round capital, its top now missing but said* to have been pyramidal. What remains is showy enough, the lower part fluted, the upper carved with weathered reliefs. What is the date of this capital? Directly above is a hatch which must have been intended for hoisting materials from the landing to the third floor but is made useless by the projection of the newel's top courses and capital, their greenish stone contrasting with the red sandstone below. The closest stylistic parallel to the capital is the stair capital of 1595–1603 at Fyvie Castle (Grampian). It looks as if the upper part of Noltland's stair newel was an afterthought, and it probably dates from the very end of the C16. A second and slightly later afterthought seems to be the guardroom S of the landing, the arch which provides the abutment for the segmental vault supporting its floor obviously inserted into the stair newel, its walls interrupting the line of the main vault and hiding the carved back of the newel's capital from view. In the guardroom's walls to the stair, quatre-foil-shaped gunloops of the type used at Muness Castle and

*By Robert W. Billings, *The Baronial and Ecclesiastical Antiquities of Scotland*, iv (1852).

Scalloway Castle (Shetland) and the Earl's Palace at Kirkwall *c*. 1598–1606. In the sills of this room's N and E windows, lockers with secret compartments, so it may have served as a steward's room as well as protecting access to the hall. N of the stair landing, the beginning of a small turnpike stair built against the flue of the kitchen chimney.

The main block's second floor is occupied by the hall and private chamber. Muscling into the hall's NW corner, a lobby at the head of the service stair. Gunloops in the N and S walls. In the centre of the S wall, a fireplace with lockers in its ingoes. It is flanked by windows, each set in a segmental-arched embrasure, the E still with stone window seats. At the hall's NE corner, a pair of doors sharing a central jamb. The N, now a window, presumably opened into a passage to the NE jamb which contains what may have been a guest room, with stone seats at the windows, a S fireplace and a gunloop to the N; at the room's NW corner, two close garderobes, each with a gunloop. S of the line of this passage and entered by the S door from the hall was the lord's private chamber, its S and W walls pierced by both gunloops and windows, again with stone seats. Aumbry beside the S window; fireplace in the W wall. At the chamber's NE corner is the entrance to a turnpike stair contained in the wall-thickness. This stair gave direct access to the jamb's third- and fourth-floor rooms, each with a fireplace and a close garderobe; possibly they were closets for the lord. At the level of the jamb's third floor, another stair curves off to give access to the lord's bedchamber above the private room in the main block. Attic room on top of the NE jamb, entered from the parapet walk.

COURTYARD to the S. The castle forms its N side. On the W and E, rubble-built screen walls, the W aligned with the SW jamb's E face, the E with the E gable of the main block. In the E wall, a C17 round-arched and roll-moulded gateway. On the courtyard's S side has been a single-storey block containing three habitable rooms. Its outer S wall has had a cornice, probably topped by a parapet. At the SW corner, the conical base of a turret. All this seems early C17. Foundations of later extensions to E and W.

2090

NORTH NESS (HOY)

Place-name with a telephone kiosk on the N shore of North Bay.

NORTH WALLS PARISH CHURCH, 0.8km. W. Built as a mission church in 1883. Harled box with small pointed windows, a gableted and spired bellcote on the W gable. Porch at the W, vestry at the E.

THE GARRISON, 0.6km. N. Two-storey Art Deco villa built as the front block of a Nissen hut theatre, *c*. 1942. Blocky symmetrical composition, the horizontals strongly emphasized.

NORTH RONALDSAY 7050

Almost flat island, the NE of the Orkney group.

FREE CHURCH. Built in 1845–52 and plain.

PARISH CHURCH. Harled and crowstepped box of 1812; rectangular windows. E tower added in 1906; square merlons on its minimally corbelled parapet.

MANSE to the NE. A single-storey U-plan 'Parliamentary' manse (i.e. probably designed by *James Smith*) built by *John Davidson* and *Thomas Macfarlane* in 1829–30.

BEACON, Dennis Head. The first lighthouse built in Orkney; by *Robert Kay*, 1786–9. Circular rubble tower with a corbelled walkway (missing its parapet) round the low conical roof, all topped by a big ball finial. It has been disused since 1809.

LIGHTHOUSE. By *Alan* and *David Stevenson*, 1851–4. Tapering brick tower painted in horizontal bands; at 42.4m. high, the tallest land-based lighthouse in Britain. Single-storey keepers' houses.

MILLS, Peckhole. Group of mills showing changes in technology. The earliest, perhaps C18, has been a windmill, its conical stone base still standing. Then a watermill, probably early C19 but reroofed in 1853 after a fire. Rubble-built, of two storeys with a large kiln vent. Finally, an engine-powered mill of 1908. Again rubble-built, with a lean-to outshot.

BROCH, Burrian. Shaggy ruin of a broch of *c.* 100 B.C.–A.D. 100. It has been circular, *c.* 14m. in diameter. Battered outer wall-face, the buttressing at the NW presumably an addition. Solid-walled base with a scarcement in the inner wall-face towards the court and a cell at the NE.

ORPHIR (MAINLAND) 3000

Small village by the Parish Church on the A964.

PARISH CHURCH. Originally Orphir Free Church. By *C. S. S. Johnston*, 1885–6. Big snecked-rubble box with a roof of purplish slate. Roundheaded side windows; a small rose window in the top of the E gable. Spired flèche with bellcast eaves. Gableted bellcote on the E porch. W vestry.

To the W, the harled piend-roofed MANSE (now CAIRNTON) of 1845–6.

ST NICHOLAS CHURCH, 1.6km. SW. Rather scanty remains of the only medieval round church in Scotland. Round churches, rare anywhere, were apparently all based on the Church of the Holy Sepulchre at Jerusalem and associated with crusading expeditions to the Holy Land. The church at Orphir, seemingly in existence by 1135,* may well have been erected by Earl Haakon after his pilgrimage to Jerusalem *c.* 1116–18 and before his death in 1122 or 1123.

The foundations of the nave (only fragments of its rubble

---

*A 'magnificent church' here in 1135 is recorded in *The Orkneyinga Saga*.

walling surviving on the E) are marked out in gravel. It has
been of *c.* 7.1m. diameter. In the fragment of wall at the SE,
a small square window, probably an insertion. Much more
intact is the apse-ended chancel, *c.* 2.2m. long, with an unmoulded entrance from the nave. It is tunnel-vaulted.
Round-arched E window, with glazing grooves cut in the
jambs. The two small square windows again look like
insertions.

Immediately N of the graveyard, grassy foundations of the
EARL'S BU, probably the drinking hall described in *The Orkneyinga Saga* as being next to the church in 1135. It has been a
long rectangle, the door probably near the S end of the E wall.

FARMS ETC.

KIRBISTER MILL, 2.8km. E. Built in 1889 of flagstone rubble.
Big three-storey-and-attic T-plan; lean-to wheelhouse at the
NE.

OLD SCHOOLHOUSE, 2.6km. E. Harled and crowstepped two-
storey main block, with small first-floor windows and two large
buttresses added at the rear; it looks C18. Single-storey schoolroom, also harled and crowstepped, at the S end, perhaps an
early C19 addition. Stone slated roofs.

YARPHA, 2km. E. Dated 1903. Harled laird's house with tall
crowsteps at the gables; small shaped gablets above the first-
floor windows. – Mid-C19 rubble STEADING, with a little pyramid-roofed tower.

PAPA STRONSAY

6020

Flat little island just NE of Stronsay.

PAPA STRONSAY HOUSE. Probably early C19. Crowstep-gabled
farmhouse of two storeys and an attic.

PAPA WESTRAY

4050

Low island which belonged to the Traills of Holland from 1636
to 1886.

PARISH CHURCH, Village. Harled rubble box of 1841. Rectangular windows in the N wall; the S windows are big and
roundheaded, with intersecting astragals. In the W gable a
stepped arrangement of three small roundheaded windows, the
centre with horizontal glazing. The bell hangs inside the E
porch.

Early C19 old MANSE to the w, piend-roofed and harled.

ST BONIFACE'S CHURCH, Kirkhouse. Small crowstep-gabled
kirk built of harled rubble, perhaps in the C12, but extended W
by *c.* 2.4m. in 1700. Domestic Georgian windows to N and S.
In the N wall there is also a blocked slit window, which looks
medieval. Stone forestair at the W gable to a door (built-up) to

the gallery. The site of the medieval chancel at the E end is marked by the low BURIAL ENCLOSURE of the Traills of Holland. Interior now derelict, but the pulpit has stood against the S wall.

E of the church, a C12 hogbacked red sandstone GRAVE-STONE.

VILLAGE. Not much more than the Parish Church (*see* above) and school. At the W end, a long single-storey C19 rubble-built terrace of cottages. PIER, o.4km. NE, probably C19, built of coursed rubble. At its landward end, a pair of small two-storey rubble-built STOREHOUSES, the N (roofless) with crowstepped gables. They look early C19.

HOLLAND HOUSE. Harled two-storey-and-attic laird's house built for the Traills of Holland in 1810–14. Crowstepped gables; a corniced porch in the centre of the main block's three-bay front. At the W gable, a single-storey wing joined by an outshot to a low two-storey crowstep-gabled block, whose tiny first-floor windows suggest it may be C17. Crowstepped outbuildings at the back. – WALLED GARDEN of *c.* 1832 to the E.

Extensive STEADING to the W, mostly C19 and rubble-walled, but with late C20 concrete additions. At the N range, a conical-roofed circular HORSEMILL. – To its W, a barn with a large round kiln at the N end. – To the SW, a harled lectern DOOCOT (now roofless) with a single ratcourse; it is probably C18.

SETTLEMENT, Knap of Howar. Substantial remains of a farmstead occupied, according to radiocarbon dating, from *c.* 3700 B.C. to *c.* 2800 B.C. Two buildings, both oblong with rounded corners, built alongside each other but touching at only one point. Presumably there was an earlier farmstead here, since they stand on a layer of midden material. Thick walls constructed of two faces of drystone masonry with a core of midden, probably scraped from the floor of the houses when they were built. The larger (S) building, *c.* 10m. by 5m. internally, was the dwelling, its walls still standing to a height of 1.6m. Entrance at the W end, its lintels, door jambs and sill still intact. The windowless interior was divided by a line of upright slabs and two posts (their holes still visible) into two rooms, the W with a low stone bench along the S wall. The inner (E) room, presumably the kitchen, had a hearth; still in this room are two querns found during excavation. The N building seems to have been a workshop-cum-barn. Access near the W end from the dwelling, the passage through the walls having jambs which show that the door was at the workshop end. Another doorway in the W gable, now without its lintels. Inside, three rooms divided by upright slabs. The W may have been a barn. The centre room has been the main working area, with a central stone hearth. Inner (E) room, apparently a store, well-provided with wall cupboards and aumbries and three pits in the floor.

4070
PENTLAND SKERRIES

Group of islands s of South Ronaldsay, Muckle Skerry the only one of any size and the site of a pair of lighthouses.

LIGHTHOUSES, Muckle Skerry. By *Thomas Smith* and *Robert Stevenson*, 1833. Two tapering round towers, *c.* 52m. and 46m. high, both with corbelled walkways, the shorter with a round building wrapped round its base.

4040
PIEROWALL (WESTRAY)

Village, mostly C19, built in three sections round the Bay of Pierowall.

BAPTIST CHURCH. Built in 1850. Harled box, its jerkin-head roof covered with stone slates.

LADY KIRK. Roofless rubble-walled church of 1674, built partly on the foundations of its C13 predecessor and incorporating its nave's s wall. Roughly rectangular nave, the w gable surmounted by a simple ball-finialled birdcage bellcote with round-arched openings in its short N and s sides. Rectangular windows. The medieval chancel's site is occupied by the low C17 laird's aisle, its E gable crowstepped and with a transomed window. Inside, the nave's s wall has a deep scarcement. C17 arch into the aisle with chamfered jambs and soffit. The round arch itself is set back on the jambs, possibly in deliberate reminiscence of the medieval chancel arch, which seems to have been of the same width.

MONUMENTS in the laird's aisle. Set into its N wall, a big GRAVESLAB to Michael Balfour and others, including George Balfour of Pharay †1657 and his wife, Marjory Baikie †1676. High-relief emblems of death at the bottom. Inscription ending

DEATHS.TROPHEES.OVER OUR.BODYS STAND
OUR SOUL^S.ABOVE.AT.CHRISTS.RIGHT.HAND
AND.HALELVIA.STIL.DOTH.SING
UNTO.THE.LAMB.THAT.HEAVENLY.KING

– On the E wall, the GRAVESLAB of Helen Alexander, wife of George Sinclair of Rapness, and of Malcolm Sinclair. At the top, a coat of arms, the initials MS and the date 1676. Inscription at the bottom:

DEATH^S.BUT.A.SERVANT.PALE.
THAT.LEADS.THE.LITL^E.FLOCK.
INTO.THE.GLORIOUS.VAILE

DESCRIPTION. At the NE, two PIERS, with light beacons on their ends. GILL PIER on the E may have been begun *c.* 1800 but was much extended in 1897 and has been altered since. The w pier is utilitarian C20. On the shore, a three-storey rubble-built C19 STOREHOUSE. A few C19 vernacular houses to the w. The main part of the village is on the w side of the bay, s of Lady Kirk (*see* above). Mostly C19 two-storey vernacular houses, but some discreet C20 infill, all pleasant and unassuming. At the S end and set back from the street, the big rubble-built three-storey TRENABIE MILL of *c.* 1885. At BROUGHTON to the E, single-storey C19 cottages, most still roofed with stone slabs.

NOLTLAND CASTLE. *See* p. 343.

POINT OF COTT *see* KIRKBRAE (WESTRAY)

QUANTERNESS *see* WIDEFORD HILL (MAINLAND)

QUOYNESS *see* SANDAY

RENNIBISTER *see* FINSTOWN (MAINLAND)

RING OF BRODGAR *see* STENNESS (MAINLAND)

ROUSAY

4020

Sizeable island, unusually hilly for Orkney, the buildings scattered round the coast.

CHURCH, Skaill, Westside. Roofless rubble rectangle, probably of the late C16. Rectangular windows with splayed ingoes. Buttresses, probably Victorian, have been added inside and out.

OLD PARISH CHURCH, Brinian. Disused in a graveyard. Early C19 harled box, the W gable now missing its bellcote. Rectangular windows. In the centre of the S wall, a small crow-stepped vestry.

PARISH CHURCH, Brinian. Built as a United Secession meeting house *c.* 1835. Harled, with pointed windows. On the gables are ball finials, the E with a pinnacle. Small crowstepped vestry on the S.

NOUSTIGER MILL. Apparently built in 1880 and reconstructed in 1937, the dates placed in the centre of the S gable. This gable's other datestones, of 1776 and 1862, probably belonged to a previous building on the site. Three storeys, with the SE corner canted at the base and splayed to a right angle above. Wheel at the N gable.

TRUMLAND HOUSE. Unexciting mansion house by *David Bryce*, 1872–3, built for Lieutenant-General Frederick Traill-Bur-roughs. Tall harled (originally exposed-rubble) double-pile, with crowstepped gables and Jacobean gableted dormers. In the N front's entrance bay, a round-arched door under a rope moulding; coats of arms high above and to the r. On the s (garden) front, a big M-shaped gable, with a canted bay window to its l. The sw corner is bowed below the second floor, where it is corbelled out to the square.

Neo-Jacobean GATEPIERS with spiky pinnacles at the entrance to the drive. They are probably contemporary with the house.

Mid-Victorian HOME FARM to the s. Long harled range. In its centre, a roundheaded pend arch under a small tower, the s face of its steep pyramidal roof with a wooden gableted doocot opening.

WESTNESS HOUSE. Harled and crowstepped laird's house of 1792, set among trees. Three-bay main block, with a bullseye attic window in the centre of the w front. Low outshots at the gables.

MIDHOWE BROCH

Sizeable remains of a broch, probably of the C2 B.C., standing at the landward end of a promontory bounded by the Stanchna Geo on the s and the Geo of Brough on the N. Just E of the broch the approach is defended by a massive stone rampart, its inner face battered, flanked by a broad outer ditch and narrower inner ditch. The entrance has been at the rampart's s end.

The broch behind is c. 18m. in diameter, its wall, standing to a height of 4.3m., built of drystone masonry and with a distinct batter. Among its stones, one placed low down at the NE is decorated with cups and rings, probably work of c. 1000 B.C.; it may have been reused from the nearby cairn. On the N, upright slabs have been stacked against the wall as buttressing. Entrance from the w, its passage roofed with flat and edge-set lintels, all with spaces between, some of which towards the court allowed observation of a visitor from a wall cell above. About two-thirds of the way in, door checks and, beyond them, the entrance to a guard chamber on each side, the N narrowing at its end where it joins a ground-floor gallery (partly blocked, probably at the same time as the external buttressing was added), which originally ran almost the full circumference of the broch. From inside the court a doorway c. 1.75m. above the ground has given access to a staircase inside the wall. On the court's E side, a scarcement ledge to support the beams of a wooden gallery c. 3m. above the ground.

Perhaps in the C2 A.D. the court was converted to a double house by the erection of a wall of up-ended slabs which crosses it from a lobby just inside the entrance. The two semicircles thus formed have each a hearth, the s house's flanked by post-holes to carry a spit, and stone-slabbed water tank. Part of the court's N wall-face was recased, probably at the same time. In the casing, an alcove formed of upright slabs supporting a corbelled roof. Both houses have had slab partitions forming cells and cupboards. Near the centre of the N house, a cellar quarried out of the rock, probably pre-dating the reconstruction of the court.

To the N and W of the broch within the enclosure, some remains of a tight-knit group of houses built partly over the inner ditch. They may be of the C I A.D.

CAIRNS

Semicircle of cairns, probably all of the third millennium B.C., most looking out to sea. The entries are arranged in anti-clockwise order, beginning at the NE of the island.

BIGLAND. Remains of a ROUND CAIRN of c. 12m. diameter standing on the lowest terrace of Faraclett Head. The roofless rectangular chamber has been divided by upright slabs into three stalled compartments. – In the valley 0.4km. SW, a low turf-covered LONG CAIRN, c. 24m. by 12m. It contains two chambers, the larger at the NW apparently divided by upright slabs into six compartments, the SE chamber an addition whose construction blocked the original entrance.

KNOWE OF LINGRO. Roughly rectangular turf-covered mound, c. 21m. by 12m., placed on a hillside. The tops of slabs poking up suggest there is a stalled chamber inside.

MIDHOWE. Big cairn excavated in 1932–3 and now housed in a utilitarian shed. The cairn is an oblong, c. 32m. by 13m., with rounded corners. The outer wall-face's stones are placed slantwise in one direction below a stringcourse and, above it, slightly recessed and slanting in the opposite direction. Second wall behind, built of slabs laid flat. SE entrance to the end of the oblong chamber. This is c. 22m. long but only c. 2.4m. across, divided by pairs of transverse upright slabs into twelve stalled compartments. In half the E side's stalls, low benches formed of slabs. There seems to have been another bench across the end of the N compartment.

KNOWE OF ROWIEGAR. Low grass-grown oblong with a few slabs projecting near the centre. Inside the cairn has been a chamber of c. 43m. by 1.8m. divided by slabs into at least ten stalled compartments.

KNOWE OF LAIRO. Sited on the edge of a terrace with the hill rising steeply behind, a big overgrown cairn, its broad concave E façade ending in projecting horns (now truncated). Only the stump of the S horn survives at the narrower W end. Inside, there has been a roughly rectangular chamber, c. 5m. by 2.5m., divided into three compartments by upright slabs.

KNOWE OF RAMSAY. Now appearing as a low mound near the edge of a natural terrace overlooking Knowe of Lairo. Exceptionally long and narrow cairn, c. 31m. by 6m. Inside, a long chamber divided by slabs into fourteen stalled compartments.

KNOWE OF YARSO. Oblong cairn with rounded corners, c. 15m. by 8m., standing on a cliff edge. Entrance at the SE, its passage leading to one end of a roughly paved chamber (its roof C 20), which is divided by upright slabs into three stalled com-

partments, the NW larger than the other two and seeming to
have had a shelf across its end.

BLACKHAMMER. Another terrace site with a slightly convex-
sided cairn, *c.* 22m. by 8m., now turfed over and with a C20
concrete roof. Entrance passage into the long S side of the
narrow chamber, which has been divided by pairs of upright
slabs (two now missing from each side) into seven stalled compartments.

TAVERSOE TUICK. Round cairn of *c.* 9m. diameter, unusual in
that it contained two chambers, one above the other.* The
upper chamber, entered from the N (uphill) side, is at ground
level and divided into two compartments, the smaller E compartment's floor slightly below that of the W, both with rounded
ends. C20 roof, but the floor is original, formed by the lintel
slabs covering the chamber below. This lower chamber, entered
from the S, is entirely underground, its drystone walls only a
lining of the excavated hillside and its roof slabs mostly supported on the solid ground behind the walls. It forms a rough
oval divided by upright slabs into a lobby off which open two
shallow compartments to the N and a deeper round-backed compartment at each end, each compartment containing a shelf.

The cairn stands on a sort of platform of flat stones with a
stone-free path to the W. Leading S from the lower chamber's
entrance is a 5.8m.-long trench which narrows to a width
of only 6.35cm. at its far end. It may have had some ritual
significance. Beside the trench's S end, a tiny underground
chamber in which were discovered three pottery bowls.

ST ANDREWS *see* TANKERNESS (MAINLAND)

4090   ST MARGARET'S HOPE (SOUTH RONALDSAY)

Substantial village developed from the C18 at the head of a bay
of the same name.

ST MARGARET'S CHURCH, Church Road. Built as South Ronaldsay United Presbyterian Church, it seems to have been
begun by 1844 but was not completed until 1856. T-plan, with
an unequivocally Victorian birdcage bellcote on the tail's N
gable and a gabled W porch. The other detail is largely late
Georgian, with roundheaded windows in the gables and a segmental-arched N door. Pinnacled ball finials on the E and W
ends and at the S wall's slightly advanced and gabled centrepiece, from under whose bullseye windows there projects a
plain schoolroom, built by 1858 apparently as an afterthought.
Inside, a straight-coved ceiling with big roses of late Georgian
character. – Shallow N GALLERY. – In the centre of the S wall,
a late C19 baroque PULPIT, with a round-arched back.

---

*The only other two-storey cairn in Orkney is at Huntersquoy on Eday, where
there is now little to see.

Adjoining, a harled piend-roofed MANSE of 1844.

SCHOOL, Erland Terrace. Dated 1875. L-plan, with a birdcage bellcote on the E gable, the schoolhouse making a N jamb.

DESCRIPTION. At the top of the hill to the S, a crowstep-gabled double house, perhaps late C18, with the WAR MEMORIAL, a stone kilted soldier, c. 1925, to its E. CHURCH ROAD leads downhill past the church and manse (*see* above). Near its foot, BACK ROAD's straightforward C19 vernacular houses make a departure to the W. Church Road continues for a short stretch down to the shore, where it ends with crowstepped early C19 houses. More crowstepped late Georgian houses in the E part of FRONT ROAD overlooking the bay. OLD BANK HOUSE on the N has a forestair at the front and a jetty behind. Then the street becomes one-sided, the villa-like BANK OF SCOTLAND of 1878 being followed by the white-painted late Georgian BELLEVUE HOTEL, before houses reappear on the N side. At the W end, crowstepped houses on the l. mark the junction with Back Road at CROMARTY SQUARE. On the square's E side, a dour HALL dated 1878. At the NW corner, a smart early C19 house with a block-pedimented porch. A road goes past it along the bay to a three-storey early C19 WAREHOUSE and the C19 PIER, whose rough ashlar masonry is protected by wooden rubbing strakes. From Cromarty Square's SW corner, a second exit is made by ERLAND TERRACE, its l. side beginning with two crowstepped C19 buildings, the first a single-storey smithy (now the BLACKSMITHS MUSEUM). On the r., ST CLAIR VILLA of 1893, very Baronial but not very big, and then the School (*see* above).

CARA, 2.7km. NE. Late Georgian farmhouse of two storeys and five bays, harled with crowstepped gables.

ROEBERRY, 2.3km. W. Tall crowstepped house of 1865, proudly sited on a hilltop. – More sensibly sheltered to the S, a mid-C19 rubble-built courtyard STEADING, with segmental-arched cartshed openings.

ST MARY'S (MAINLAND) 4000

Village laid out along the Bay of Ayre in 1828. One- and two-storey houses, the earliest built in the 1830s, some with stone slate roofs.

PIER. Long rubble-built pier begun in 1877 and extended later.

STORE HOUSE. Built in 1649. Two storeys and attic, of harled rubble. Rounded margins to the windows and doors; moulded skewputts at the crowstepped gables. In the W gable, a first-floor door approached by a stone forestair.

GRÆMESHALL. *See* p. 303.

SANDAY

Long low island, its shape that of an irregular star.

CROSS AND BURNESS PARISH CHURCH, Broughtown. Opened 1862. Harled box, with round-arched windows. On the W gable, a birdcage bellcote with a steep pyramid roof and *fleur-de-lis* finial. Bow-ended vestry at the E; gabled W porch.

Former CROSS PARISH CHURCH, How. Roofless rubble-built (formerly harled) rectangle, perhaps of *c.* 1700. The N wall has been demolished. In the long S wall, three windows and a door (built up). A door under a window in each gable. The interior has had end galleries.

Former LADY PARISH CHURCH, Silverhall. Tall harled T-plan kirk, now roofless. It is dated 1773 on the main block's NW skewputt but may incorporate earlier walling. In the W gable (masked by a porch of 1902), a door with a roll-and-fillet moulding which looks C17. Rectangular Georgian windows, either of 1773 or dating from the repair of 1814. There has been a gallery, approached by an external stone forestair in the N 'aisle'.

In the graveyard, SE of the church, a rubble-built BURIAL ENCLOSURE, perhaps early C18, the W entrance with chamfered margins. – Smarter ENCLOSURE to the SW, probably late C17, with a bolection-moulded cornice; S door with rounded margins and a panel frame above.

SANDAY UNITED PRESBYTERIAN CHURCH, Roadside. Disused and partly demolished. Simple Dec of 1881. Big buttressed rectangle, with two tiers of windows in the long E and W walls. SE tower, its hoodmoulded windows' labels carved with flowers. Two-storey vestry block at the NW. The interior has had a braced kingpost roof and galleries.

SCHOOL, Broughtown. By *Orkney County Council*, 1964.

START POINT LIGHTHOUSE. By *D. & T. Stevenson*, 1869. Tall round tower, its brickwork painted with black-and-white vertical stripes.

VILLAGES

KETTLETOFT. Small village of C19 vernacular houses. PIER of coursed stone blocks built in 1833; extended in concrete, 1883.

ROADSIDE. Dominated by the former Sanday United Presbyterian Church (*see* above). Small group of plain C19 houses. Opposite the church, a crowstep-gabled mid-C19 farmhouse with a small steading.

FARMS

BEAFIELD. Roofless early C19 house of two storeys and three bays, with a pilastered doorpiece at the advanced centre. – Contemporary LODGE to the N with semi-octagonal ends and stone canopies over the windows.

GALLOW HILL. Piend-roofed rubble-walled house of *c.* 1840, the windows still with horizontal panes.

LOPNESS. Plain crowstep-gabled farmhouse, probably early C19. – Contemporary rubble-built STEADING to the S. – To the E, remains of a lectern DOOCOT, probably C18.

QUIVALS. Built as the island's school, perhaps in the late C18. Harled and crowstepped, with very small first-floor windows.

SAVILLE. Harled rubble T-plan farmhouse, probably late C18. Three-bay front; crowstepped gables.

SCAR. Built for the Traills of Westove. The rendered house is probably early C19. Four-bay front; three gableted stone dormers at the attic. Lower two-storey crowstepped W wing. – To the W, a single-storey range of FARM BUILDINGS, probably of the C18 and early C19, ending in a MILL. – More rubble-built farm buildings to the W and N form a courtyard. – To the SW, a lectern DOOCOT, probably C18. – Across the road to the E, the round rubble stump of a WINDMILL.

STOVE. Piend-roofed farmhouse and steading, built in 1857. At the steading's NW corner, a MILL with a brick chimney.

WARSETTER. Plain mid-C19 farmhouse, with a contemporary rubble-built steading making an informal courtyard. – On a hill to the E, a rubble lectern DOOCOT with a piend-roofed top. Above the flightholes in the W gable is a datestone of 1613, but the doocot is more likely to be C18.

CHAMBERED CAIRN, Quoyness. Large cairn of the Maes Howe type, probably built *c.* 3000 B.C.,* its site just above the high-water mark on the E shore of the Els Ness peninsula. The cairn is surrounded by a roughly oval boulder-strewn platform constructed as a sandwich with a filling of mixed stones, earth and refuse between layers of horizontal slabs. At the platform's edge on the S and W, remains of a kerb of stones set on their sides. At the SW, kerbstones of a projecting 4.9m.-long horn; there seems to have been a second horn at the platform's N.

The cairn itself is built of concentric rings of stone (now partly exposed), the two inner rings original, the innermost battered, the second vertical. The low third ring seems an addition, since, unlike the others, whose line it follows with little accuracy, it is built on the platform and also blocked the cairn's entrance. This entrance is at the SE, its slab-floored outer section between the cairn's two inner walls now a trench,‡ its side walls heightened with C20 walling. Clay-floored inner section, its roof made of slabs on edge except at the inner end, where they are laid flat. Roughly rectangular chamber, *c.* 4m. by 2m., the walls still standing to their full height of almost 4m., carefully constructed with the side and end walls bonded and an angled slab crossing each corner, and corbelled inwards to narrow the chamber's top to a width of under 0.9m. At the S end, three lintel slabs, perhaps not original, form a roof. Small

---

*Objects found in and around the cairn include bone and stone implements similar to examples from Skara Brae.

‡Formerly roofed with slabs on edge.

trench, its purpose unclear, running across the chamber's clay floor from the passage doorway to the centre of the N wall. Low entrances, two on each of the long sides and one at each end, into cells with inwardly corbelled walls and lintel slab roofs.

SANDWICK (MAINLAND)
2010

Place-name for a rural parish on the W side of Mainland.

OLD PARISH CHURCH. Disused. Harled kirk of 1835–6. Round-headed doors and windows in the gables and flanking the pulpit at the centre of the S wall; the other openings are rectangular. Almost solid ogee-roofed and ball-finialled birdcage bellcote on the W gable. Inside, GALLERY round three sides. – PULPIT with fluted pilasters on the back.

PARISH CHURCH, Quoyloo, 1.5km. NE. Plain harled box; it was built as a United Secession meeting house in 1828 but heightened and reconstructed by *Samuel Baikie*, 1911–12. The roundheaded windows look late Georgian. Gothic W bellcote dating from 1911–12, as does the small hall at the E.

MILL OF RANGO, 3.6km. SE. C19 rubble-built range, a tall pyramid-roofed kiln at the E end.

SKAILL HOUSE. *See* p. 362.
SKARA BRAE. *See* p. 363.

SCAPA (MAINLAND)
4000

A handful of houses between the distillery and the pier on the N side of Scapa Bay.

PIER. P-plan, the narrower E end built of coursed sandstone blocks by *Shearer & Budge*, 1878–80. The fat W end of concrete was added by *Heddle*, 1912. – STORE AND DWELLING HOUSE to the SW. Two storeys, with segmental-arched store openings.

SCAPA DISTILLERY. Some single-storey rubble-built warehouses of 1885, the rest late C20.

SHAPINSAY
5010

Substantial flattish island, *c.* 4km. E of Mainland. Its agricultural improvement began after Major Thomas Balfour's purchase of the Elwick estate in 1782 and was continued by his son William, who had acquired the whole island by 1844. One small village at Balfour, one large country house (Balfour Castle), and a good number of well-tended small mid-C19 farmhouses.

Former PARISH CHURCH. Roofless harled rectangle built in 1822, the doors and windows (except a small one in the N wall) roundheaded.

To the E, a roofless C17 BURIAL AISLE, rubble-built with

moulded skewputts. Originally it formed a N jamb of the now demolished late C16 parish church. Round-arched N window, rectangular E and W windows and W door, all with chamfered margins. On the door's lintel the date 1656. The S arch, originally into the church, has chamfered arrises; round head placed well back on the jambs. On the arch the initials MGB, for Master George Buchanan of Sound, who then owned Shapinsay. Inside, at the N gable, a moulded square panel frame, probably C17, and the recess for a second panel.

PARISH CHURCH, Brecks. Originally United Presbyterian. By *T. S. Peace*, 1891–2. Romanesque but with Y-tracery in the side windows. At the W gable, porch with a nook-shafted door; it is flanked and surmounted by windows linked by hoodmoulds. On top of the gable, a corbelled and gableted bellcote.

SCHOOL, Balfour. By *Orkney County Council*, 1970. Concrete frame containing glass and blue-coloured panels.

BALFOUR VILLAGE. Founded *c.* 1785 by Major Thomas Balfour of Elwick. At its S end, the HARBOUR, with an L-plan pier of coursed rubble, probably early C19 but extended in 1861 and again to the E (in concrete) in 1969. Late C20 ferry pier to its N. Overlooking the harbour, the S gateway to Balfour Castle (*see* below). Then a single long row of terraced single-storey cottages, with two-storey buildings at the ends and just S of the centre. One of these nearly central buildings is THE SMITHY, with stone gablets over the first-floor windows and a forestair to the crowstepped gable's first-floor door. It all looks early C19 rather than late C18. At the N end of the row, the mid-C19 gatepiers and lodges to Balfour Castle (*see* below).

Just to the NE beside the shore, the late C19 former GAS-WORKS, a squat round tower built of rubble with a corbelled brick parapet. Broad slit openings in the tower and narrower slits in the parapet. Set into the tower's N side are three panels. One, of red sandstone, is said to have been removed from Noltland Castle on Westray. It is carved with the Balfour coat of arms flanked by the initials GB, presumably for Gilbert Balfour † 1576. On it have been added the date 1725, together with the initials of John Balfour of Trenabie and his wife, Elizabeth Traill. – Above, a C17 yellow sandstone scroll-sided dormerhead carved with a rose and thistle. – To the l., another C17 pedimented dormerhead bearing the relief of a unicorn.

ELWICK MILL. Three-storey rubble-built mill of 1883. At the front, a segmental-arched cart opening and a gableted stone dormerhead. Wheel at the E gable.

BROCH, Burroughston. Ruined circular broch of *c.* 500 B.C.– A.D. 500, its site beside the shore enclosed by a broad ditch and rampart. The broch itself is *c.* 17m. in diameter. Entrance at the E, its passage provided with door checks and a bar-hole; off its S side, a tapering guard chamber. Scarcement in the inner wall-face to the court. The court was converted to a wheel house later in the first millennium A.D.

BALFOUR CASTLE

Confidently relaxed but inventive Baronial mansion of 1846–50, designed by *David Bryce* for Colonel David Balfour of Balfour and Trenabie. The house was not entirely new. Colonel Balfour's grandfather, Major Thomas Balfour, who had bought the Elwick estate in 1782, had built a house here which he christened Cliffdale. That house was said in 1790 to have 'rather the appearance of a neat little villa in the vicinity of some opulent city, than of a gentleman's house recently raised in a remote sequestered part of the kingdom.' Part of that house is still visible on the W. It seems to have been a quite straightforward harled and crowstep-gabled building, with a gabled centrepiece at its three-storey main block and with recessed two-storey wings. Bryce retained the N wing and about two-thirds of the main block, refacing its E front. On the S he added a big new block extending W of the original house and containing the principal rooms. At the NE he added a service court. A later C19 NW addition hid the Georgian N wing from view.

The appearance of the E and S fronts is entirely due to Bryce. The E builds up from the low crowstep-gabled service block projecting at the NE. On its S front, a thistle-finialled steeply pedimented dormerhead. At its inner angle with the main house, a round conical-roofed tower jostled by a square projection, its upper floor corbelled out to a diagonally set crowstepped gable with an oriel window. The main block begins quietly with a broad crowstepped gable (the refaced back of Cliffdale) followed by the vertical jolt produced by a martially battlemented four-storey tower. Corbelled out from the tower's SE corner, a pencil-like three-storey turret, its stone-slabbed conical roof rising between gablets. Three-light mullioned first-floor window in the tower. Below that, a battlemented porch, the Balfour arms carved above the lugged-architraved door. l. of the tower another crowstepped gable but narrower than the one on the r. and with a two-storey, shallowly battlemented rectangular bay window, its upper floor corbelled out and its window mullioned and transomed.

The E front flirts with symmetry but refuses to espouse it. At each corner a square bartizan derived from the C17 Pinkie House (Lothian). Fractionally off-centre narrow round tower, its conical slated roof emphasizing the nervous verticality. To its r., a canted bay, corbelled out at the second floor and again, but now to a rectangle, at the crowstepped attic. It is joined to the tower by a narrow two-storey arch inspired by Fyvie Castle (Grampian) topped by a narrow window under a steep pedimented dormerhead. To the l. of the tower, a twin crowstepped gable bisected by a stepped chimney. Projecting from the gable, a broad two-storey canted bay window, its upper floor corbelled out and shallowly battlemented. At the W gable of Bryce's S range, a two-storey block, the ground floor pierced by a shouldered pend arch, the upper floor a conservatory with tall mullioned and transomed windows. At its SW corner, a boldly projecting low octagonal tower, a crocketed finial on its shallow spired stone-slab roof. Quieter but still muscular Baronial detail on the W front of Bryce's addition. To its N the harled front of Cliffdale. The two-storey canted bay window at the l. of its main block seems to be of the 1780s but remodelled by Bryce as a version of a bay window at Pinkie House. Late C19 single-storey wing to its N, gently Baronial.

The interior's main rooms are all by Bryce. Entrance hall with a rib-compartmented Jacobean ceiling and encaustic-tiled floor. To its S, the billiard (now morning) room, with a raised dais in the S bay window. N of the entrance hall, a Jacobean stair, its newel posts' finials strapworked and foliaged, their bases carved as pendants. From the stair's first-floor landing, a door S into a broad passage. Its ceiling is simple Jacobean. At the E end, an Artisan Mannerist wooden chimneypiece, the jambs carved with naked men holding bowls of fruit; caryatids, cherubs and the Balfour arms on the overmantel. Off the passage, at the house's SE corner, the dining room. Grained plaster ceiling, Jacobean again, with small pendants. Black marble chimneypiece of simple C17 type but with a brutalist keystone. Immediately to the W in the central tower was the dinner service room. Drawing room at the house's SW corner, again entered from the passage. Another Jacobean plaster ceiling with small pendants. Its compartments are enriched with strapwork, seal heads (from the Balfour arms) and hands holding batons (the Balfour crest). Another seal's head carved on the white marble Frenchy chimneypiece and seals rampant (the Balfour supporters) at the ends of its grate. Mirror over-mantel in a lugged and pedimented marbled frame. Another mirror in a 'doorcase' of the same type at the centre of the E wall. In the W wall, entrance to the conservatory. Here is a double-pitch glass roof and encaustic tiled floor. End door onto steps down to the garden. N of the drawing room and at the passage's W end is the library, its NW corner breaking into a bow window. Another Jacobean plaster ceiling with small pendants. Oak bookcases, their tops decorated with grotesque heads. In the oak overmantel above the veined marble chimneypiece are panels, perhaps C16 German, carved with depictions of Adam and Eve, the Presentation of Our Lord in the Temple, and St Luke with an angel. N of the passage and overlooking the garden on the W were the family's private rooms, Mrs Balfour's dressing room or boudoir, the family bedroom with a bathroom behind, Colonel Balfour's dressing room, and, at the N of this suite, Colonel Balfour's business room, with its own stair from the service court.

Terraced GARDEN to the W and S of the house laid out by *Craigie Halkett c.* 1850. Projecting from the S ha-ha wall are low parapeted bastions. Extensive woodland to the N, probably planted in the late C18. At the end of the walk W of the house, an aedicular late C17 GATEWAY, presumably a fragment of the demolished House of Sound, which stood near this site, its roll-moulded arch now filled with a stone seat. Coupled would-be Composite columns, the l. shafts carved with spiralling vines. Frieze carved with figures of human, animal and mermaid musicians and with the Honours of Scotland (the crown, sword and sceptre). Above, a smaller aedicule, its pediment bearing the monogrammed initials of Arthur Buchanan of Sound and his wife, Margaret Buxton, and the date 1674, and supported by an atlantis and a caryatid in C17 dress who frame a mantled coat of arms (Buchanan impaling Buxton); scrolled sides carved with unicorns.

GATE LODGES, 0.4km. NE at the N end of Balfour village, of c. 1850 and presumably by *Bryce*. Canted corners heavily corbelled out to form rectangular gables. In front, octagonal ashlar GATEPIERS with tall obelisk tops, Pinkie House again the inspiration. – GATEWAY 0.3km. E of the house and overlooking the harbour, in the most heavily defensive early C19 castellated manner. Drum towers with inverted keyhole gunloop windows flanking the gate, its corbelled parapet carved with the Balfour coat of arms. Forecourt in front, its retaining wall provided with parapeted bastions, again equipped with gunloops. Doors in the wall give access to stores under the forecourt. – On Point of Dishan to the S, a round rubble-built TOWER rising from a battered base to a corbelled parapet. It looks early C19, but the parapet's merlons appear to be Victorian, as does the crowstep-gabled doocot cap-house on top, its segmental-arched doorway made of brick.

BALFOUR MAINS, 0.8km. NE of the house. Mid-C19 courtyard steading, the W range now replaced, the S side a screen wall. Short wing projecting S from the centre of the N range, its gable topped by a corbelled bellcote. In the courtyard's centre, a three-bay block with gableted stone dormerheads.

2010
SKAILL HOUSE (MAINLAND)
1.2km. S of Sandwick

Rustically smart harled laird's house placed on a low hillside between the Bay of Skaill to the NE and the Loch of Skaill to the SW. The earliest part of the main house is the narrow crowstep-gabled N range, probably built for Bishop George Graham *c.* 1620, apparently as a free-standing block, its slightly off-centre S door from the present stairhall provided with a bar-hole and clearly the original entrance from outside. In the late C17 the Bishop's grandson, Henry Graham of Breckness, converted the house to a U-plan by adding a SW link to a broader straight-gabled S range, the two W gables being joined by a screen wall. In this wall, a roll-moulded round-arched doorway, its weathered keystone decorated with a cherub's head surmounting the Honours of Scotland (crown, sword and sceptre). Above this, a reused lintel, probably from a fireplace, carved with a monogram of the initials of Henry Graham and his wife Euphemia Honeyman and the inscription

WEAK THINGS GROW STRONG [B]Y VNITIE AND LOVE
BY DISCORD STRONG THINGS WEAK AND WEAKER PROVE
ANNO 1676

The date may be that of the additions.

The S range was damaged by a fire *c.* 1800, and subsequent remodelling of the house introduced late Georgian windows, including a big ground-floor bullseye window in the S range's W gable. Probably at the same time the open centre was partly filled by a piend-roofed stairhall with a three-light first-floor window looking over to the sea. In the mid-C19 further alterations took place, two gabled stone dormerheads being added on the S side and a flat-roofed porch built on the E, providing a resting place for early C17 carved stones. In the porch's S side, a panel taken from Breckness House bearing the arms and initials of Bishop George Graham. In the porch's E front, a dormerhead, its strapworked cartouche again containing Bishop Graham's initials. At one corner of this front, a skewputt carved with a shell, at the other a skewputt bearing a rosette.

Office courtyard attached to the house's N side, its present appearance largely informal late Georgian. Tall crowstepped N range. On the E range's E front, shaped dormerheads, perhaps mid-C19. Over the entrance through the single-storey W block, a reset C17 dormerhead carved with a cherub's head under a star. Mid-C20 courtyard to the NE with a battlemented screen wall on the S. W and N ranges, the N with shaped armorial dormerheads, forming two sides. The fourth side is closed by the N end of the C19 crenellated WALLED GARDEN.

To the SE, a rubble-built lectern DOOCOT, probably late C18. – At SKAILL HOME FARM to the SW, a mid-C19 single-storey L-plan STEADING, a pyramid-roofed tower (now covered with metal sheeting) in the centre of its N range.

SKARA BRAE (MAINLAND)   *2010*
1.2km. S of Sandwick

Remarkably well-preserved farming settlement which was occupied from *c.* 3100 B.C. until *c.* 2500 B.C. The site, on the S side of the Bay of Skaill, is now beside the shore but was originally set well back, its natural defences and some of the settlement itself having been eroded over the centuries.

The bulk of the settlement, representing the final form of its long development, consists of a tight-knit group of six houses linked by passages; to the W, a detached workshop. The houses were subterranean, the first stage in their construction having been the making of a heap of previously decayed midden material. After that had been consolidated, the houses and their linking passages were built in holes which had been left or excavated in the midden (much of it removed during excavation in 1928–30). The house walls have unmortared facings of local flagstone slabs enclosing midden cores, the masonry of no great sophistication. Lintelled roofs over the passages. Each house is

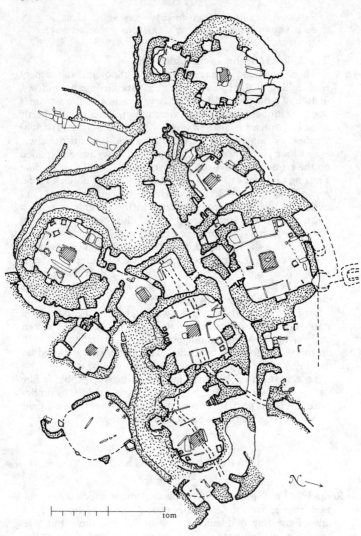

Skara Brae. Plan

self-contained and entered directly from the passage through a low and narrow door provided with a bar-hole. Inside, each has one squarish room (varying in size from *c.* 5.2m. by 5.5m. to *c.* 6.7m. by 6.1m.) with rounded corners. Striking use of built-in stone furniture arranged to a standard plan. In the centre of the floor of each house, a large stone-lined hearth. At the wall directly opposite the entrance, a chunky stone dresser, either projecting or recessed, perhaps intended to display pottery. At the side walls, box-beds, their sides and ends formed by slabs and with slab pillars at the end corners, perhaps to support canopies. Aumbry recesses in the walls, the largest usually above the beds. Also in the wall-thickness, one or more small cells. Some of these were probably for storage, but others seem to have been made deliberately hard to enter and may have been safes. One cell in each house was provided with a drain joining to a main drain which ran to outside the settlement; these seem to have been lavatories. Set into each house's floor are three or four clay-luted stone-slabbed tanks, some perhaps intended to hold shellfish. It is not known how the houses were roofed but mid-C19 excavation produced evidence that they may have had whalebone rafters. These houses stand on the remains of others, and four of these earlier houses are wholly or partly exposed at the E and S, the best-preserved in the centre of the settlement's S side. They are smaller but seem to have been planned in the same general way, except that they had rounded bed-recesses set into the walls instead of projecting rectangular box-beds.

The workshop to the W was not placed in the midden heap but stood above ground on a bedding of blue clay. Its walls' bottom course is of large edge-set slabs with horizontal masonry above. 6m.-long pear-shaped main block with a horse-shoe-plan S porch. The opening at this building's N end may represent a flue. Inside, the S end is largely partitioned off by upright slabs. Central hearth, wall cupboards and cells but no dresser nor beds. Burnt stones and chips of chert (the Orkney substitute for flint) were found here, so it seems to have been used by a tool-maker.

SOUTH WALLS

3080

Low-lying crofting island joined to the SE tip of Hoy by a cause-way.

SOUTH WALLS CHURCH, Longhope. Built in 1832, a harled box with a S vestry and N porch. Roundheaded windows, with intersecting astragals. On the W gable, a sturdy birdcage bellcote with corner pinnacles; a ball-finialled obelisk on its truncated pyramid roof. – Inside, a gallery on thin fluted piers round three sides; pulpit in the middle of the S wall. – Brass OIL LAMPS.

GRAVEYARD, Osmondwall. This was the site of a medieval chapel removed in 1887. In the graveyard's older part, the C17 BURIAL VAULT of the Moodies of Melsetter. It is a rubble-walled crow-stepped rectangle. Small windows with chamfered margins in the S wall. At the W gable, a roll-moulded round-arched doorway, its worn inscription having read 'SOLI DEO LAVS HONOR ET GLORIA'. Above the door, a triangular-headed window under a weathered armorial panel. In the E gable, two moulded panel frames, the N with a steep pediment. – Lying on the ground to the S, the bottom part of a GRAVESTONE, probably C18, carved with a skull and crossbones in high relief. –

To the NE, headstones of sailors killed in the First and Second World Wars and a WAR MEMORIAL cross of *c.* 1925 to the standard *Blomfield* design. – In the graveyard's more recent part, MONUMENT to the crew of the Longhope lifeboat, a bronze statue of a lifeboatman by *Ian Scott,* 1970.

CANTICK HEAD LIGHTHOUSE. By *D.* & *T. Stevenson,* 1856–8. Tall tapering round tower of white-painted brick. Corbelled walkway below the octagonal lantern. – Pitched-roofed KEEPERS' HOUSES and STORES.

MARTELLO TOWER, Hackness. Built *c.* 1812–18. Squat tapering ashlar tower of two storeys. Small round-arched windows; tall round-arched first-floor door reached by a ladder. Inside, the first floor, covered by a shallow dome vault, was the barrack room, with one part, which has its own fireplace, partitioned off as a non-commissioned officer's cubicle. Stairs in the thickness of the walls, one down to the ground floor's tunnel-vaulted stores, the other up to the roof. On the roof, a circular iron track for the 68-pound gun which replaced the original 24-pounder in 1866. Segmental-arched recesses in the parapet for storing cases of shrapnel and shot.

LONGHOPE VILLAGE. The village was laid out 'according to a regular plan' in 1800 but is now largely late C20. Harled ROYAL HOTEL of *c.* 1900, picturesque Orcadian vernacular revival, with tall crowsteps and a roof of stone slates. Coursed rubble PIER, probably C19. At the E end, the OLD CUSTOM HOUSE of *c.* 1840. Seven-bay front of sneck-harled rubble. At the slightly recessed three-bay centre, a portico whose columns have drum-capitals.

3010   STENNESS (MAINLAND)

Place-name at the S end of the Lochs of Stenness and Harray, the standing stones more notable than the buildings.

PARISH CHURCH. Unambitious box of *c.* 1910, with pointed windows. At the E end, a tall gableted bellcote and large porch.

BRIDGE OF WAITHE, 3.2km. W. Dated 1859. Rubble-built; three segmental arches with rounded cutwaters.

MILL OF EYRLAND, 3.2km. SW. C19 L-plan rubble-built cornmill, now a house.

TORMISTON MILL, 0.7km. E. Now a restaurant and craft shop. Built in 1884–5. Three storeys, of rubble, with a twin-vent kiln. Wheel at the S gable, its lade carried on a stone aqueduct.

CAIRNS, HENGES AND STANDING STONES

Ceremonial and burial complex of the third millennium B.C. stretching in a line from the Stenness promontory NW to the Ring of Bookan, the cairn at Maes Howe an outlier to the E. The monuments are described on a circuit from the SE to the NW.

CAIRN, Maes Howe. Turf-covered mound, 35m. in diameter and

7m. high, made up mostly of clay and stones. The cairn, datable to *c.* 2700 B.C., sits on an artificially levelled circular platform ringed by a broad ditch and a low bank, the latter rebuilt in the C9 A.D. The cairn's entrance at the SW opens into a low passage, its outer end a reconstruction. After 6.9m. there is a door-check each side and a step down. Beyond the check on the l., a triangular niche containing the boulder which was used to close the entrance. From here the passage is original, its walls and roof constructed of huge slabs. Just before its inner end, a pair of tall stones projecting like door jambs. The main chamber is *c.* 4.5m. square and probably originally the same in height; its present stone and concrete roof is C20. In each corner, a buttress built of flat slabs but with a tall upright slab facing the side parallel to the axis of the entrance passage. Walls of beautifully laid long slabs, their edges broken with a slight slant so that the walls' inward curve is smooth up to a height of 2.6m., above which the slabs oversail more noticeably. In the centre of each wall is a rectangular opening, that in the S the entrance to the passage, the others set above the ground and giving access to small side cells. On the chamber's walls, about thirty C12 runic inscriptions, three referring to hidden treasure. On the NE buttress, contemporary carvings of a dragon or lion, a walrus and a serpent knot.

BARNHOUSE STONE, 0.7km. SE of the Stones of Stenness. Standing stone, *c.* 3.2m. high, tapered towards the bottom. It is aligned to the NW.

STONES OF STENNESS. Henge monument dated by radiocarbon analysis to the early third millennium B.C. The circular ditch and bank have been almost removed by ploughing, but the bank's line is visible as a band of clay, *c.* 6.5m. wide, and the ditch inside has been at least 7m. wide and over 2m. deep, its lower part cut into the rock. Causeway on the N. These enclose an area *c.* 44m. in diameter, in which upright stones have formed a circle of *c.* 30m. diameter. Four stones, the tallest over 5m. high, still stand (two re-erected in 1906–7), and the stumps or holes of seven others are known; probably there were twelve originally. In the circle's centre, excavation has uncovered a rectangular setting of four flat slabs and, running N towards the causeway, the holes for a pair of standing stones, followed by the bedding trench of what may have been a timber structure and the holes for three more upright stones.

WATCH STONE, 150m. NW of Stones of Stenness. The tallest standing stone in the neighbourhood, *c.* 5.6m. high. The stump of a similar stone was found just to the S on the shore of the Loch of Stenness and perhaps they were part of a formal setting.

STANDING STONES, 470m. NW of Stones of Stenness. Pair of stones, the N 2.7m. high, the S 1.7m., standing in a line pointing NW and SE.

COMET STONE, 150m. E of Ring of Brodgar. 1.75m.-high standing stone, its main axis aligned NW to SE. Its site is a low circular platform on which have been found the stumps of two other uprights, so there was probably a stone circle.

RING OF BRODGAR. Round henge monument, its rock-cut ditch
c. 10m. wide and over 3m. deep, but with no trace of a bank;
causeways at the NW and SE. This encloses a perfect circle of
103.7m. diameter composed originally of about sixty standing
stones, of which twenty-seven are now in place (thirteen re-
erected since the mid-C 19); the positions of another thirteen
are known. Carved on the third stone (now a stump) N of the
NW entrance are twig runes of the C 12, spelling the name Bjorn
above a small incised cross.

SALT KNOWE, 137m. W of Ring of Brodgar. Burial mound of *c*.
18m. diameter and 6m. high.

FRESH KNOWE, 90m. E of Ring of Brodgar. Long burial mound,
35m. by 20m. and over 6m. high.

PLUMCAKE MOUND, 73m. NE of Ring of Brodgar. Low circular
burial mound, *c*. 19m. in diameter. Excavation has uncovered
two burials, probably of the second millennium B.C.

MOUNDS, SE of Ring of Bookan. Low burial mounds of uncertain
date.

RING OF BOOKAN. Roughly circular henge on top of a low hill.
Flat platform of *c*. 44.5m. by 38m. enclosed by a ditch 13.5m.
wide and at least 2m. deep. No sign of an outer bank or of a
causeway, but this might have been on the E, where the ground
has been disturbed. On the platform, scattered stones and an
irregular mound, probably the vestiges of a cairn.

CHAMBERED CAIRN, Unstan. Large turf-covered round cairn of
the third millennium B.C., standing on a promontory jutting
into Loch Stenness. Entrance at the E, its passage rising by one
step halfway along, its roof a recent reconstruction. The passage
enters the oblong chamber near the S end of its long E wall.
Chamber walls of concave section. From them project pairs of
upright slabs (the two central slabs on the W now truncated)
dividing the space into five compartments or pairs of stalls with
a central passage. In each end compartment, projecting stones
to carry a shelf. The S compartment's floor is divided down the
centre by two low upright slabs. In the middle of the chamber's
W wall, a small entrance into a side cell. Its lintel, carved
with a short runic inscription, was placed here during the C 20
restoration and later acquired more decoration, including a
bird. C 20 concrete roof over the chamber.

2000

STROMNESS (MAINLAND)

Long thin town along the W shore of the narrow and sheltered
bay of Hamnavoe. Feus of land here were granted by the Bishop
of Orkney in the 1620s. In 1701 John Brand reported the village
as 'daily increasing as to Houses and number of Inhabitants', their
chief occupation being to service ships, including those of the
Hudson's Bay Company, which called before crossing the Atlantic
or en route to the Baltic. By 1760, when Bishop Pococke visited
Stromness, there were over two hundred families resident, 'all
(except one Factor), Publicans and shopkeepers'. The village's

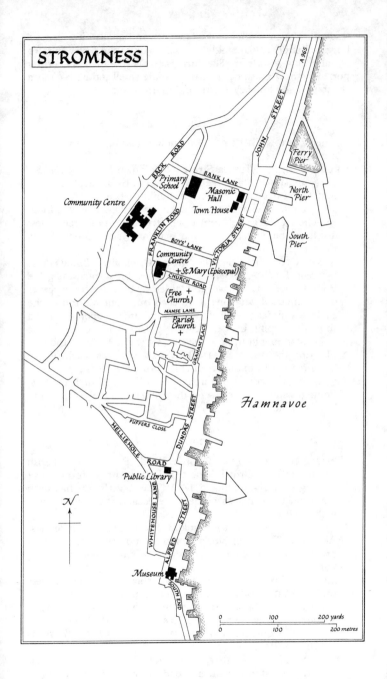

STROMNESS

Community Centre

Primary School

BANK LANE

BACK ROAD

Masonic Hall

Town House

FRANKLIN ROAD

BOYS' LANE

Community Centre

+ St. Mary (Episcopal)

CHURCH ROAD

(Free + Church)

MANSE LANE

Parish Church +

VICTORIA STREET

JOHN STREET

A 965

Ferry Pier

North Pier

South Pier

GRAHAM PLACE

Hamnavoe

PUFFERS CLOSE

HELLIEHOLE ROAD

DUNDAS STREET

Public Library

WHITEHOUSE LANE

ALFRED STREET

Museum

SOUTH END

N

| 0 | | 100 | | 200 yards |
| 0 | | 100 | | 200 metres |

trade developed further in the late C 18, and in 1817 it became a burgh of barony. Boat building was a major C 19 industry and, for about twenty years from 1888, Stromness also boomed as a herring port. It is now a fishing town with some small industries and a reputation as a low-key artistic and tourist centre.

CHURCHES

Former PARISH CHURCH. *See* Public Buildings, below: Community Centre.

FREE CHURCH, Victoria Street. Now Town Hall. By *William Robertson*, 1890–2. Big rectangle covered by a steeply pitched roof. Gable front with pinnacled chunky bartizans at the corners and a continuous fat hoodmoulding over the lancet windows. Attached to the gable's centre, a battered tower of three stages; inside its battlement, a slated octagonal spire topped by a weather cock.

PARISH CHURCH, Victoria Street. Originally United Presbyterian. By *Richard Spence*, 1862–3. Big broad box, the gable front divided into a 'nave' and 'aisles' by buttresses, the corner ones pinnacled octagons. Corbelled out from the top of the gable is a birdcage bellcote with round-arched openings and a short stone spire. Inside, a U-plan gallery. The focus is on the pulpit standing in front of the ORGAN (by *J. J. Binns*, 1906). – Flanking the organ, STAINED-GLASS windows, each of two lights (scenes from the life of Our Lord), after 1922.

ST MARY (Episcopal), Church Road. Mission church of 1888. Pointed windows, a cross on the rendered S gable. It used to have a flèche.

PUBLIC BUILDINGS

COMMUNITY CENTRE, Church Road. Built as the Parish Church in 1814. Broad pedimented front with a central tower bearing a clock-face dated 1826. The tower's top has been removed, the windows crudely altered and the walls covered with drydash.

COMMUNITY CENTRE, Franklin Road. Former Stromness Academy. The main block is of 1937 and utilitarian. From it project three gableted two-storey wings dated 1896, 1904 and 1912.

HARBOUR. Private JETTIES along the shore of Hamnavoe were built in the C 18 and early C 19. – The deep-water SOUTH PIER, constructed of flagstones and fronted with wooden piles, is by *William Robertson*, 1879, extended S in concrete by *James Barron* in 1893. – Concrete NORTH PIER by *James A. Liddle*, 1923–5.– FERRY PIER of 1972.

MASONIC HALL (LODGE MERCANTILE MARINE), Victoria Street. Two-storey, with a broad crowstepped gable, dated 1869.

MUSEUM, Alfred Street. Built in 1854–8, the ground floor intended as a town hall, the first floor to house the collection of the Orkney Natural History Society. Rendered front of two storeys and three bays, the sw corner canted at the ground floor and splayed to a right angle above. Superimposed anta pilasters carrying plain entablatures. Pedimented centre porch.

POLICE STATION, North End Road. Dated 1928. *Retardataire* Scots Jacobean on a small scale.

PRIMARY SCHOOL, Franklin Road. By *Orkney County Council*, 1970. Lightweight Modern Movement. Steel frame, the E front a curtain wall.

PUBLIC LIBRARY, Helliehole Road. Plain Tudor, dated 1905.

STROMNESS ACADEMY. By *Orkney Islands Council*, 1988. Dour and sensible, with drydashed walls, pitched metal roofs, and windows of domestic character, all suggesting a model prison.

TOWN HOUSE, Victoria Street. Late C19, with crowstepped front dormer, porch and gables.

DESCRIPTION

WAR MEMORIAL of *c.* 1920 on the entry from the N, a grey granite lady on a battered plinth of hammerdressed grey granite. A little S, FERRY ROAD, made in 1972 as an approach to the ferry pier, goes off to the SE. The main road is NORTH END ROAD. On its W side, a late C19 former MILL, utilitarian, but its warm-coloured rubble introduces the town's main building material. Then appear large stone slabs forming the pavements. A little beyond the Police Station (*see* Public Buildings, above), diversion up BACK ROAD to the piend-roofed BELLEVUE of *c.* 1840, with a shallow block pediment on its anta-pilastered doorpiece.

JOHN STREET is the real start of the town, and the roadway's tarmacadam gives place to concrete slabs. On the l., the early C19 rubble-built SPEDDINGS or LIEUTENANT'S HOUSE, half-buried below the road, to which it presents a gable. There soon follows continuous C19 development on both sides of the street, the houses mostly two-storey, their rubble walls often harled or cement-rendered. The gable of the OYSTER GALLERY (No. 55) on the r. is bounded by the first closes to step up the sheltering W ridge. In the close S of the early C19 gable-ended No. 15 is the MILLARS' HOUSE with a grandly Artisan shallow stone porch, its pediment carved with the arms of Millar and Nisbet, the date 1716 and the inscription

.GODS. PROVIDENCE. IS. MY. INHERETANCE

VICTORIA STREET's appropriately Victorian N side provides a little civic and commercial centre, with the flat Scots Jacobean ROYAL BANK OF SCOTLAND of 1864, the Masonic Hall and Town House (*see* Public Buildings, above). Much bigger is the STROMNESS HOTEL by *Samuel Baikie*, 1902. Scots Jacobean of a sort, with three-storey canted bay windows and diminutive pepperpot bartizans. Across the street to the E, the crowstepped WAREHOUSE (now TOURIST OFFICE) built in the 1760s by

James Gordon of Cairston. Further s, a cast-iron FOUNTAIN made by *Walter Macfarlane & Co.* of the *Saracen Foundry* and erected in 1901 to commemorate Alexander Graham, who in 1743 had led the fight to free Stromness merchants from paying tax to the royal burgh of Kirkwall; the drinking trough stands on cows' feet. Victoria Street narrows and the E houses, many with their own jetties, are set between closes running down to the shore. The prevalent idiom is c 18 and c 19 vernacular, with a good proportion of gables fronting the street. A weathered stone, perhaps c 17, incised with the initials RG, has been reset in the late c 20 single-storey No. 96, which looks up the steep ascent of Church Road to the Community Centre (*see* Public Buildings, above). The carriageway's slabs now change from concrete to stone. Ecclesiastical and civic excitement on the r., beginning with the old Free Church (*see* Churches, above), set well back between gable-ended houses. Then the BANK OF SCOTLAND by *William Henderson*, 1871, authoritarian Georgian-survival in yellow and red sandstone, and the Parish Church (*see* Churches, above). No. 112 opposite, probably early c 19, has a corniced doorpiece to its close; its SW corner's lower part is canted to allow access to the close between it and its crowstep-gabled neighbour, which repeats the trick at its SW corner. GRAHAM PLACE makes an informal square. In LESLIE PLACE to the W, HAMNAVOE, perhaps c 18 but with a mid-c 19 block-pedimented doorpiece.

DUNDAS STREET brings another narrowing of the main street. Wedge-shaped close between the early c 19 gable-ended Nos. 4 and 8 on its E, their corners intaken below corbelling to allow access to the sides. After more gable-ended late Georgian houses, an unexciting stretch to the corner with Helliehole Road, the vista half closed by the Public Library (*see* Public Buildings, above). Diversion up HELLIEHOLE ROAD to the YOUTH HOSTEL (former Drill Hall), single-storey and cottagey, by *T. S. Peace*, 1888. Dundas Street jinks l. into a tiny square. On its E side, the mid-c 19 No. 90, with consoled eaves.

ALFRED STREET is mid-c 19. On the r., Nos. 15–17, a pair of English-Regency-survival houses, their flagstone rubble curiously reminiscent of London stock brick. Each has a round-arched door, No. 17's framed by Tuscan pilasters and a hood. They stand on the W side of another tiny square. On its S, No. 27, with a block-consoled and corniced doorpiece. Probably rather earlier c 19 houses on the E, No. 8 with a crowstepped gable, No. 10 with rusticated quoins and bandcourses across its rendered front. The street jinks and narrows again. Still mostly mid-c 19 vernacular but the harled No. 20, down a close on the l., looks earlier, with small windows and crowstepped gables. Then closes leading to jetties. Another square in front of the Museum (*see* Public Buildings, above).

SOUTH END begins the exit from the town, its shore-side houses with jetties. Nos. 10–12 of *c.* 1800 present a twin gable to the street; at No. 10's E end, a Gothick-windowed store. On the r., a covered stone stair to LOGIN'S WELL, which was used to

supply water to the ships of the Hudson's Bay Company from
1670 to 1891 and to Captain Cook in 1780 and Sir John Franklin
in 1845. NESS ROAD follows, the Victorian villas on its w side
enjoying views over the bay. At the s end, the early C19 DOUBLE
HOUSES, a long crowstep-gabled double pile with its own pier.
To the w, STENIGAR, the austere mid-C19 building of Stan-
ger's Boatyard, converted to a house for the painter Stanley
Cursiter by *Robertson & Hendry*, 1948.

BRECKNESS HOUSE. *See* p. 290.
GARSON, 0.8km. E. Harled early C19 laird's house, the main
block of two storeys and three bays; a lower wing each side. –
To the E, contemporary STEADING built of flagstone rubble
and with a circular horsemill.

STRONSAY   *6020*

Sizeable flattish island with a sheltered anchorage at Papa Sound
on the NE.

CHAPEL, Whitehall village. Secularized and altered. Built in
1937. Tall harled box with small obelisk finials on the gables.
MONCUR MEMORIAL CHURCH, 0.6km. SE of Wardhill. By
Leslie Grahame Thomson, 1950–5. Tall harled cruciform, the
chancel higher than the nave and the transepts lower. Sloping
buttresses against the nave walls. W wall of the s transept carried
up to a Cape Dutch bellcote. Round-arched windows, all with
projecting chamfered sills of red sandstone and all tall except
the paired lights high up in the chancel's side walls. Gabled sw
porch. Lean-to vestry against the E end. Attached to the N
transept a HALL of 1900, given a low wing in the 1950s.
    Spacious interior with an open kingpost roof. Roundheaded
arches into the transepts and chancel. Parquet flooring in the
nave and transepts, stone in the chancel. – Scoto-Catholic
arrangement of FURNISHINGS, the pulpit, lectern and font
flanking the chancel arch, the holy table in the chancel, all
of wood decorated with carved reliefs of sacred emblems. –
STAINED-GLASS E window (the Good Shepherd) by *Marjorie
Kemp*, 1955, expressionist, with strong blue the dominant
colour.
WESLEYAN METHODIST CHAPEL, near Sandybank. Now a
barn. Built in 1837. Small rubble rectangle with a jerkin-head
roof. Pointed windows in the N gable.
Former MANSE, 1.1km. SW of Whitehall village. Now derelict.
Harled late Georgian three-storey house. Corniced doorpiece
with side-lights. Ball-finialled back gable.
Former NORTH SCHOOL, Clestrain. Harled school and schoolhouse of *c.* 1875, a spiky finial on the N gable.
Former ROTHIESHOLM SCHOOL, Rothiesholm. Diminutive
rubble-built late C19 schoolroom with *fleur-de-lis* finials on the
gables and porch. To the NW, a small lavatory block looking
like a lectern doocot.

Former SOUTH SCHOOL, Scoulters. Rubble-built school and schoolhouse of *c.* 1875, a spiky finial on the S gable. At the back, two monopitch-roofed lavatories, like little lectern doocots.

SCHOOL, Wardhill. By *Orkney County Council, c.* 1960.

STRONSAY MILL, Millfield. Probably of the earlier C19. Three storeys; rubble-built, the N wall harled. At the W gable, a rubble outshot housing the wheel.

WHITEHALL VILLAGE. Founded as a fishing village in the early C19. At Whitehall proper, a one-sided street of two-storey houses, mostly mid-C19 but several with early C20 gabled porches. At this row's W end, the early C20 concrete OLD PIER; at its E end, the NEW PIER built in 1913, coursed rubble with a concrete extension. Then some late C20 housing and the former Chapel (*see* above) before LOWER WHITEHALL, a one-sided row of plain two-storey houses (one dated 1914) followed by single-storey cottages (one dated 1887). Coursed rubble PIER, probably late C19, to the E.

TANKERNESS (MAINLAND)

5000

Place-name marking the ecclesiastical centre of the rural parish of St Andrews.

ST ANDREWS NORTH CHURCH. Sturdy harled and buttressed box built in 1801 and enlarged in 1827. Big gableted W bellcote. Roundheaded windows, the E of three lights with intersecting stone tracery. – STAINED-GLASS E window (the Crucifixion), after 1927.

OLD MANSE (now a barn), 0.9km. NE, built in 1756 and heightened in 1793. Harled and crowstepped house of two storeys and an attic. Three bays, the centre advanced with a chimneyed gable.

ST ANDREWS SOUTH CHURCH, 1.2km. S. Built as a Free church in 1886 and desperately plain.

HALL OF TANKERNESS, 1.6km. NE. Harled laird's house, the product of growth from the C16 to the C20. The earliest part is the narrow crowstep-gabled SW wing of two storeys, probably built for William Groat, who acquired the lands of Tankerness in 1550, and perhaps extended N in the 1730s.* The house was made Z-plan *c.* 1830, when a single-storey NE wing containing new public rooms, with horizontal glazing in their windows, was joined to the existing house by a short battlemented link. The NE wing acquired a canted bay window and upper floor *c.* 1910.

At the back, a COURT OF OFFICES of *c.* 1830. Curved single-storey W range ending in a round dairy (formerly conical-roofed), all with Gothick windows. The buildings at the court's N corners (the E a laundry) have battlemented outer faces.

---

*When it was let to a tenant, but James Baikie of Tankerness reserved part of the house for his own use.

STEADING to the S, perhaps early C19, forming an informal courtyard. Crowstepped two-storey W range. Lean-to buildings against a battlemented wall on the E. Crowstepped smithy in the middle. – W of the steading, a FARMHOUSE, probably late C18. Main block of two storeys and three bays; slightly lower N and S wings.

SEBAY MILL, 2.6km. SE. Rubble L-plan, built in 1854. Main block of three storeys and four bays, the N gable's wheel now missing. Two-storey SW wing.

TANKERNESS MILL, 0.8km. NE. Early C19. Long two-storey rubble-built block with a kiln at the E end. The wheel is housed in a low outshot (now roofless) at the W.

TUQUOY (WESTRAY)   4040

Ruined church on a cliff-top site overlooking the sea.

CROSS KIRK. Roofless remains of a small mid-C12 church enlarged later in the Middle Ages, much of the rubble walling now reduced to its lower courses. As first built it comprised a nave, c. 5.7m. by 4.2m., and a rectangular chancel, c. 3.8m. by 2.9m., slightly out of alignment with the nave. The later extension added c. 8.2m. to the length of the nave, with a door near the W end of its S wall. The nave's C12 S door, now just E of centre, has a roundheaded arch set back from the jambs. To its E, a small roundheaded window, its arch again set back from the jambs internally. Between this door and window, a putlock hole.

The chancel arch is again roundheaded, with the arch set back from the jambs. Over the chancel, a low segmental tunnel-vault.

LANGSKAILL, 1.8km. W. Built as a manse in 1813–14. Harled and crowstepped main block of two storeys and an attic, with a stone slate roof. Lower piend-roofed wing projecting from the front, clearly an addition. Plain rear wing. – Mid-C19 rubble-built STEADING to the E, the E range with a two-storey centrepiece.

TWATT (MAINLAND)   2020

Church and a few houses.

CHURCH. Originally Birsay Free Church. Tall flagstone-rubble-walled box of 1874. Pyramid-roofed birdcage bellcote on the E gable; two tiers of pointed windows containing intersecting astragals.

BARROWS, Kirbuster Hill, 1.5km. NE. Scattered group of eleven unexcavated low burial mounds of the second millennium B.C. placed on the SE slope of the hill. They are from c. 5.2m. to 9.1m. in diameter.

BARROWS, Ravie Hill, 0.9km. NW. Eight burial mounds of the second millennium B.C. beside Loch of Boardhouse. A ninth has been excavated and was found to have a stone kerb and a central cist which contained the cremated remains of two people and a deer.

UNSTAN *see* STENNESS (MAINLAND)

4010
WIDEFORD HILL (MAINLAND)
3.9km. W of Kirkwall

225m.-high hill overlooking the Bays of Firth and Kirkwall. One chambered cairn is halfway up on the W side, the other at the foot on the N.

CHAMBERED CAIRN, W side. Big round cairn of Maes Howe type, probably erected in the third millennium B.C. The stonework is now partly exposed to show its construction of three abutting concentric walls. The resulting profile is stepped, but it is likely that the original appearance was rounded or perhaps conical, the masonry having been covered with clay and turf. The cairn is built on a steep slope with the entrance placed, unusually, in the lower W side. From it a slightly curved passage, its outer third probably always open, the inner two-thirds roofed with lintel slabs, leads to an oblong stone-walled chamber cut into the hillside. The chamber's roof is a C20 reconstruction. Low doorways off the chamber into oblong cells, their walls corbelled inwards to roofs *c.* 2.1m. high, now formed by single flat slabs but originally by stones set on edge.

CHAMBERED CAIRN, Quanterness. Large grassy mound of *c.* 30m. diameter. The entrance passage led from the E into the side of a long chamber, 6.5m. by 1.9m., and 3.5m. high, off which opened two cells on each side and one at each end, i.e. the cairn is of Maes Howe type. Radiocarbon dating has placed its construction at *c.* 3400 B.C.

3020
WOODWICK HOUSE (MAINLAND)
2.7km. SE of Evie

Almost hidden by trees, the harled and crowstepped country house built for William Traill in 1912 in the manner of an Orkney laird's house of a century before. Crowstep-gabled entrance tower for pretension; battlemented bay window and conservatory on the E front for comfort. Attached to the N gable, an early C19 battlemented rubble screen wall and archway with big 'gunloops' in its round piers.

Immediately S of the house, a lectern DOOCOT (now a chapel) built of drystone rubble with stepped gables and a pigeon entrance over the door. This door's red sandstone lintel bears a coat of arms, the initials D M C (for David McClellan of Woodwick) and the date 1648, but the doocot itself looks C 18 and the lintel has probably been reused. Stone nesting boxes inside. – More early C 19 battlemented rubble GATEPIERS to the s.

WYRE   4020

Small island SE of Rousay. In the C 12 it was occupied by Kolbein Hruga, who built its castle and probably also the adjoining chapel.

CHAPEL. Small roofless church built of local whin-rubble, probably in the mid-C 12, the walls partly restored in the late C 19. Nave and a narrower chancel, both rectangular. W door, its semicircular arch set back from the jambs just like the doors of St Magnus Church on Egilsay. In the nave's S wall, a rectangular window with a stepped sill.* The chancel arch is a doorway only 0.75m. wide, its semicircular arch again set back from the jambs. Rear-arch of the same type at the chancel's S window, which is deeply splayed to its small external slit.

CUBBIE ROO'S CASTLE. Rubbly ruin on top of a small hill. According to *The Orkneyinga Saga*, in *c.* 1145 there lived on Wyre a Norseman 'called Kolbein Hruga, and he was the most outstanding of men. He had a fine stone castle built there; it was a safe stronghold.' This stronghold can be identified with the central surviving building. It is almost square, 7.8m. by 7.9m., with most of the ground-floor walls still standing, built of good-quality coursed rubble. Rectangular windows with splayed ingoes in the W and S walls, but no door, so presumably the entrance was at first-floor level. This tower stands in an oval enclosure surrounded by an earth rampart, a ditch, a rough stone wall, and an inner ditch. At the E side, stone piers, perhaps not original, which seem to have carried planks or slabs across the outer ditch. Additions were made to the tower at various times later in the Middle Ages, the S extension covering part of the enclosure's original defences. In the N extension, a fireplace and an oven.

*A second window was recorded in 1866.

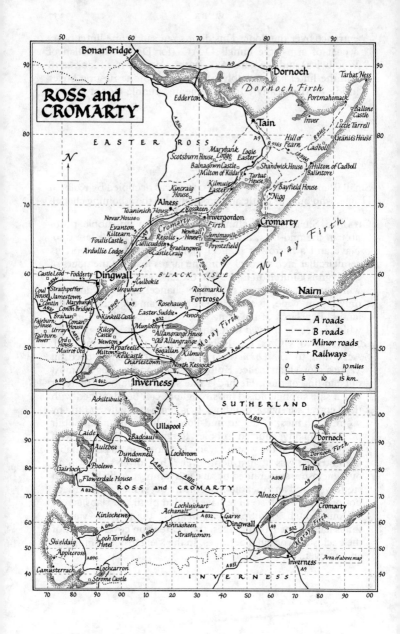

ROSS and CROMARTY

Bonar Bridge

Dornoch

Dornoch Firth

Tarbat Ness

Edderton

Portmahomack

Balline Castle

Little Tarrell

Tain

Inver

Geanies House

EASTER ROSS

Hill of Fearn

Cadboll

Scotsburn House

Marybank Lodge

Logie Easter

Shandwick House

Hilton of Cadboll

Balnagown Castle

Milton of Kildary

Tarbat House

Balintore

Kincraig House

Kilmuir Easter

Bayfield House

Alness

Bosskeen

Nigg

Teaninich House

Novar House

Invergordon

Cromarty

Moray Firth

Evanton

Kiltearn

Foulis Castle

Ardullie Lodge

Resolis

Cullicudden

Newhall House

Jemimaville

Poyntzfield

Braelangwell

Castle Craig

Castle Leod

Fodderty

Dingwall

BLACK ISLE

Nairn

Coul House

Strathpeffer

Jamestown

Culbokie

Contin

Maryburgh

Conon bridge

Urquhart

Rosemarkie

Fortrose

Fairburn House

Brahan

Kinkell Castle

Easter Suddie

Conan House

Rosehaugh

Avoch

Fairburn Tower

Urray

Ord House

Kilcoy Castle

Newton

Munlochy

Allangrange House

Muir of Ord

Arpafeelie

Old Allangrange

Milton

Redcastle

Gogallan

Kilmuir

Charlestown

North Kessock

Inverness

A 831

A 862

	A roads
	B roads
	Minor roads
	Railways

0 5 10 miles

0 5 10 15 km.

SUTHERLAND

Achiltibuie

Ullapool

Dornoch

Dornoch Firth

Laide

Badcaul

Aultbea

Dundonnell House

Lochbroom

Tain

Gairloch

Poolewe

Alness

Flowerdale House

ROSS and CROMARTY

Cromarty

Kinlochewe

Lochluichart

Achanalt

Garve

Achnasheen

Dingwall

Moray Firth

Loch Torridon Hotel

Strathconon

Shieldaig

Applecross

Inverness

Camusterrach

Lochcarron

Strome Castle

INVERNESS

Area of above map

ROSS AND CROMARTY

A large district stretching from the E coast to the W with plenty of low-lying and prosperous farmland on the E; the interior and Wester Ross are mostly mountainous moorland. From the C12 to the C15 it was governed almost independently of the Crown by the Earls of Ross. After the forfeiture of that earldom in 1476 a number of estates were formed on the fertile E side, each quickly acquiring a tower house, of which some survive. In the late C18 some of the earliest clearances of population in Highland to make way for sheep-walks took place in the NE of the district, some of the dispossessed finding employment in new industries then being established in the burgh of Cromarty. The later C20 has seen attempts, not all successful, to set up industrial complexes along the Cromarty Firth.

ACHANALT   2060

Place-name in Strath Bran marking the position of the former church and Achanalt House.

CHURCH. Tiny Gothic box of 1891, now converted to a house. – Rubble-walled GRAVEYARD on the hill above.
ACHANALT HOUSE. Small white harled shooting lodge of c. 1835.
POWER STATION. See Lochluichart.

ACHILTIBUIE   0000

Strung-out late C19 crofting township.

FREE CHURCH. Very plain harled T-plan built in 1854, its roof now of corrugated iron.
HYDROPONICUM. Functional but of makeshift appearance, designed by *Robert Irvine*, 1984, to grow quantities of unusual plants at unexpected times.
MILL. Small rubble-built C19 mill of three storeys with circular second-floor windows. Remains of the lade, but the wheel is missing from the N gable.

ACHNASHEEN   1050

Railway halt and hotel at the head of Strath Bran where the roads from Lochcarron and Gairloch converge.

LEDGOWAN BRIDGE. Single segmental arch of c. 1815.

RAILWAY STATION AND HOTEL. The railway line from Dingwall to Attadale was begun by *Murdoch Paterson* in 1868 and
opened in 1870. At the station, a lattice-girder footbridge of
the usual Highland Railway type. – Lattice-girder RAILWAY
BRIDGE over the river. – White painted HOTEL by *Alexander
Ross*, 1871, extended by *William Roberts* in 1898 and again more
recently.

ACHNASHELLACH LODGE, 14.7km. SW. Shooting lodge of *c.*
1870, mixing steep pitched and jerkin-headed gables.

LEDGOWAN LODGE, 3.3km. SW. Built in 1904. U-plan, with a
cast-iron-columned verandah across the centre.

ACHNASHELLACH LODGE *see* ACHNASHEEN

ALLANGRANGE *see* OLD ALLANGRANGE

6050   ALLANGRANGE HOUSE

By *W. L. Carruthers*, 1907. Long neo-Georgian harled spread with
a projecting bow at each end.

6060   ALNESS

Long village, rather urban in character though not noticeably
urbane. It underwent major expansion in the 1970s, when it
became the chief dormitory for workers at the Invergordon aluminium smelter and the oil-rig construction yard at Nigg.

CHURCHES

ALNESS OLD PARISH CHURCH, 1.1km. SW. Unroofed in 1970.
T-plan kirk of harled rubble reconstructed in 1775 (the date on
its SW skewputt*), and the general appearance is Georgian at
its least pretentious. Two storeys of domestic windows, the
pulpit's position in the middle of the S wall marked by taller
openings. Gallery forestair at the E gable. But earlier work is
incorporated. The thickness of the lower parts of the windowless N wall and the E gable suggests that their masonry is
medieval. Near the NE corner inside, a round-arched recess,
probably for a monument. On the W gable, a birdcage bellcote
(formerly pinnacled), whose date of 1625 is probably that of

*But the *Statistical Account of Scotland*, xix (1793), gives a date of 1780, and Roderick
Maclean, 'Notes on the Parish of Alness', *Transactions of the Gaelic Society of Inverness*,
xiv (1887–8), 223n., the date of 1782 and names the wright responsible as *Thomas
Macdonald*.

the whole gable. The long N jamb (formerly the 'aisle' of the Munros of Novar) is clearly of two periods. In its narrower N part, a door to the W with chamfered margins suggesting a C17 date, apparently confirmed by the lintel formerly in its S door (now inserted in a window in the church's S front) inscribed

MORTIS.MEDITATIO.VITA.EST
16.WML.IMT.72

Was this originally a detached mausoleum linked to the church by the addition of the 'aisle's' S part in the late C18, when it was reconstructed with an upper floor (equipped with a fireplace) to serve as the 'aisle's' retiring room? – In the church's S wall, a rustic classical MONUMENT, probably late C17, carved with emblems of death. – Against the E gable, a BURIAL ENCLOS-URE, the entrance surmounted by a tablet bearing the Munro arms and the date 1671.

To the W, the OLD MANSE of 1795 with a bullseye window in the centre gable and three-light ground-floor windows.

ALNESS PARISH CHURCH, Kirkside. Originally Free. Red sand-stone box dated 1843. S belfry tower with clumsy Romanesque detail. The round-arched windows' glazing pattern and the roof's tiled ridge presumably date from the renovation of 1893. – To the E, polished granite MONUMENT to the Rev. Alexander R. Munro, by *J. & A. Fraser*, 1904.

ROSSKEEN PARISH CHURCH, Perrins Road. Originally United Free. Sturdy lanceted rectangle by *Andrew Maitland & Sons*, 1909–10. Ornamental metal ventilator flèche on the roof; pro-jecting wooden bellcote at the E gable.

PUBLIC BUILDINGS

ALNESS ACADEMY, 0.3km. S. By *Ross and Cromarty County Council* (project architect: *W. E. McWhirter*) in association with *T. Hartley Haddow & Partners*, 1977–8. Metal clad box over-sailing a blockwork ground floor.

AVERON COMMUNITY CENTRE, High Street. By *Ross and Cro-marty County Council* (project architect: *C. Porteous*), 1973.

AVERON YOUTH CENTRE, High Street. Originally Public Hall. 1898, by *Andrew Maitland & Sons*. Agreeably old-fashioned Georgian castellated detail on the gable front.

BRIDGE, Novar Road and High Street. By *Thomas Telford*, 1810. A segmental arch with two stringcourses under the parapet.

COULHILL PRIMARY SCHOOL, off Coul Park. By *George Bennett Mitchell*, 1974–5.

DALMORE DISTILLERY, 1.1km. SE. By *Andrew Maitland & Sons*, 1893–6. Pagoda-roofed kilns; stark bonded warehouses to the E.

MASONIC HALL, Invergordon Road. Mid-Victorian Dec box, very ecclesiastical-looking, with elaborate carved cusping at the door.

PERRINS CENTRE, Invergordon Road. By *Henman & Cooper* of Birmingham, 1903–4. Single-storey free Scots Renaissance.

Above the porch, a metal lion; flowery metal finial on top of the conical-roofed reading room.

RAILWAY VIADUCT. By *Joseph Mitchell*, 1861–3. Two large segment-headed arches; smaller semicircular arches at the ends. The piers between are enlivened by gunloops and machicolated battlements.

DESCRIPTION

NOVAR ROAD is the w entry. The first impression is of vernacular drabness, but the creeper-covered No. 28 on the l. is late Georgian, with three-light ground-floor windows. Mid-C19 Nos. 20–26 with a basket-arched pend in the centre. On the r., No. 3 of *c.* 1840, with fluted Doric pilasters at the door. Across the Bridge (*see* Public Buildings, above) HIGH STREET begins with the set-back Averon Community Centre quelled by the more aggressive Averon Youth Centre opposite (*see* Public Buildings, above). Standing out from the Victorian vernacular is the ROYAL BANK OF SCOTLAND of *c.* 1900, solid but pacific Baronial. More low-key Baronial at the STATION HOTEL, begun by *William C. Joass*, 1867, but recast in 1902 by *William Mackintosh* with a spired corner tower. At the end of the street, big Celtic cross WAR MEMORIAL of *c.* 1920 marking the exit of Invergordon Road to the r., for whose Perrins Centre and Masonic Hall *see* Public Buildings, above.

DALMORE, 0.6km. s. Built *c.* 1935. Large but very low-key Baronial.

TEANINICH HOUSE. *See* p. 463.

7040   APPLECROSS

Site of a long-vanished monastery founded by St Maelrubha in 673. The village now consists of a row of mid-C19 cottages, mostly harled and with big gableted dormers, looking over the Inner Sound to Raasay.

OLD PARISH CHURCH. Disused. Georgian preaching-box of 1816–18, with Tudor windows. The w gable's bellcote is a late Victorian replacement. Inside, the plaster has been stripped to expose rubble walls. – Early C19 canopied PULPIT with fluted pilasters at the back and a precentor's seat below. – In the porch under the w gallery, sizeable bits of Dark Age CROSS-SLABS. The largest has been carved in relief with a Celtic cross. In the panel to the r., spirals ending in birds' heads; interlaced work below. On the edge, more spirals and interlacing topped with the figure of a bowlegged naked man, his hands hiding his genitals. – More interlaced carving on the two smaller fragments.

Beside the GRAVEYARD entrance, a Dark Age standing SLAB, its front incised with a Celtic cross. – At the E end, a roofless rubble-built BURIAL ENCLOSURE with rectangular door and

windows (now blocked), perhaps a s 'aisle' of a previous church
(the orientation makes it unlikely to have been a chapel).

To the w, the harled OLD MANSE built by *William* and
John Cumming in 1796. The top floor was heightened and
dormerheads added to its windows by *Alexander Ross*, 1858–9,
perhaps the date of the ground floor's three-light windows.
Projecting single-storey wings built by *George Russel,* mason,
and *Roderick Finlayson,* house carpenter, in 1816, almost but
not quite touching the house.

PARISH CHURCH. *See* Camusterrach.

PRIMARY SCHOOL. *See* Camusterrach.

APPLECROSS HOUSE. Large but unpretentious mid-c18
mansion house built for the Mackenzies of Applecross. The
main block is a harled three-storey-and-attic double pile with
crowstepped gables. Single-storey-and-attic wings projecting N
to enclose the entrance court. On the s front, a large mid-c19
iron-balustraded porch, its flat top projecting over columns to
form a verandah each side. Above its cornonced door, a reset
stone with the date 1675. Late Victorian bargeboarded attic
windows.

APPLECROSS MAINS. Among the farm buildings are three vernacular barns. One, probably early c19, has segmental-arched
openings filled with wooden louvres in the front wall and with
wattle in the back; roof now of corrugated iron. – The other
two, on a knoll to the w, may be late c18. Battered drystone
rubble walls, the wide openings filled with halved wooden
staves. One roof is heather-thatched, the other now covered
with corrugated iron.

ARDROSS   *6070*

Hamlet on a wooded hillside above the Cromarty Firth.

CHURCH. By *Ross & Macbeth*, 1899–1900. Simple buttressed
rectangle; late Gothic detail. sw porch; gableted w bellcote.

ARDROSS CASTLE, 0.5km. sw. Large Baronial house with wide
views over to the Black Isle. It was created in 1880–1 by *Alexander Ross* for the opium trader Alexander Matheson, who had
bought the estate thirty-five years earlier and employed *George
Rhind* in 1846 to enlarge an existing house, all this now swallowed up in the 1880s additions. Mostly quite low and rambling,
with Jacobean detail, but the E (entrance) front given strong
vertical accents. Very tall off-centre tower over the entrance
with plentifully corbelled candlesnuffer-roofed round corner
turrets and crowstepped gables. The peaceful Jacobean porte
cochère projecting at its base is an addition of *c.* 1900. Corbelled
out at the SE corner, a tall candle-snuffered turret. Telescopic
turret to the r. of the entrance tower. At the main block's NE
corner, a round tower corbelled out to a square saddleback-
roofed and crowstepped cap-house, its martial effect lessened
by the broad crowstepped gable to its l., from which projects a

two-storey canted bay window, both gable and bay window built *c.* 1900, replacing a tauter earlier design.

(Very grand interior, mostly Jacobean. Entrance hall opening onto the main stair, its newel posts topped by heraldic beasts. At the house's SE corner is the drawing room with a *pâtisserie* plaster ceiling and woodwork whose design veers between being Jacobean and Frenchy. N of the entrance hall, a billiard room of *c.* 1900 with a crowded strapwork ceiling and coupled Ionic attached columns at the broad overmantel. In the Oak Room above, more lavish Jacobean display and a stone chimneypiece with terms on the jambs. At the house's N side, the Great Hall of 1880–1 with a steep-pitched elaborately carved and decorated hammerbeam roof. The walls' linenfold panelling of *c.* 1900 is a little too conscious of good taste.)

Formal TERRACED GARDEN to the E laid out by *Edward Whyte, c.* 1909.

ARDULLIE LODGE
4.2km. SW of Evanton

5060

Small harled and crowstep-gabled laird's house of *c.* 1700. Two storeys and five bays, the windows grouped 2/2/1; steep-pitched roof. The lean-to porch and catslide dormer windows are C20 additions. Inside, a panelled dining room with a sideboard recess.

ARPAFEELIE

6050

Isolated hamlet, the church its main feature.

ST JOHN (Episcopal). Built in 1816, but its present appearance is almost all due to *Alexander Ross*'s reconstruction of 1879. Very simple Gothic with a gableted W bellcote (for two bells) and SW porch; minimally projecting apse at the E end. Inside, a coved pitch-pine ceiling. – Late C19 STENCILLING in the apse. – STAINED-GLASS E window (the Crucifixion) of *c.* 1880. – Oak ALTAR and REREDOS designed by *John Robertson* and made by *Maciver & Co.*, 1890. Altar front divided into three arched panels, the centre carved with a high-relief *Agnus Dei*, the side panels with Melchizedek and Moses. In the reredos's five gableted arches, scenes from the life of Our Lord, all this carving by *Robert Smith.*

PARSONAGE to the W. Small and plain by *Ross & Joass*, 1863, extended in 1895 by *John Robertson.*

AULTBEA

8080

Scruffy village on the edge of crofting land.

CHURCH OF SCOTLAND. By *J. Hinton Gall*, 1889. A sturdy

buttressed box with hoodmoulds over the round-arched windows in the bellcoted gable front.

FREE CHURCH. Minimal Romanesque, by *Andrew Maitland & Sons*, 1888. Transeptal stairtowers and a gableted bellcote at the gable front.

UNITED FREE CHURCH. Disused. By *William Mackenzie*, 1914. Small and harled, with an apsed w end; big Celtic cross on the E gable.

BUALNALUIB PRIMARY SCHOOL. School and schoolhouse of *c.* 1875, with broad eaves and a gableted bellcote.

AVOCH   7050

Substantial village which developed from what in the C18 were three separate small settlements of Seatown (at the SW), Kirktown and Milntown. Planned expansion to the E on a gridiron layout began early in the C19 when the harbour was built. Later in the C19 the High Street acquired its small-town commercial character.

CHURCHES

CONGREGATIONAL CHURCH, High Street. Thrifty Dec by *James Matthews*, 1868. Plain pinnacled buttresses at the corners of the gable front.

FREE CHURCH, Toll Road. Secularized. By *Alexander Ross*, 1872–3. Prominently sited Romanesque box with a wheel window in the S gable and an Italianate NW tower.

PARISH CHURCH, Braehead. By *Alexander Ross*, 1870–2. A broad Dec box articulated by sturdy stepped buttresses. Ambitious but awkward SW steeple, its tower broached to an octagon, gableted belfry and a lucarned spire. Inside, pitch-pine is dominant. Braced collar roof. W gallery. At the E end, a large PULPIT, its back painted with texts from the Sermon on the Mount and the Lord's Prayer. – ORGAN by *John R. Miller*, 1891. – STAINED GLASS. Two brightly coloured lancets (the Adoration of the Magi and the Entombment of Our Lord) flanking the pulpit; in the rose window above, the Ascension. All by *James Ballantine & Son*, 1870. – Contemporary narrative w window (the Beatitudes) by *Henry M. Barnett* of Newcastle.

In the NE vestry, a reset SACRAMENT HOUSE of *c.* 1500, its moulded border stepping up at the top to enclose a rustically carved chalice.

In the graveyard, wall MONUMENT to John Mackenzie of Newton †1759 and Margaret Mackenzie †1783. Piers supporting a ball-finialled pediment. High-relief emblems of mortality under the well-lettered inscription.

HARBOUR, High Street. Straight N pier by *Thomas Telford*, 1814. C-plan S pier, largely of concrete, by *James Fraser*, 1904.

MACKENZIE FOUNDATION SCHOOL, Mackenzie Place. Built as an Episcopalian school but no longer used as such. By *Ross & Joass*, 1863. Parsonage-Gothic with Baronial touches and a tall saddle-back tower.

DESCRIPTION

TOLL ROAD comes in from the W. On the hill to the r., the old Free Church (*see* Churches, above), followed by the gabled and gableted STATION HOTEL, dated 1892. On the hill to the l., the Mackenzie Foundation School (*see* Public Buildings, above) in MACKENZIE PLACE. In BRAEHEAD, the Parish Church (*see* above) and, beside it, HILL HOUSE built as the Manse in 1820–2 by *Thomas Murison*, mason (who also produced the design), and *John More*, wright. Cherrycock-pointed ashlar front with three-light windows flanking the meanly corniced door; segment-headed dormer windows.

HIGH STREET begins promisingly with the CONGREGATIONAL MANSE, a mid-C19 cottage embellished *c.* 1900 with an outsize carved shell over the front door. Then the Congregational Church (*see* above), followed by vernacular tedium. At the Harbour (*see* above), a harled warehouse of 1813, now converted to other uses. S and W of High Street, an extensive display of C19 vernacular cottages (some probably of clay and bool construction under their render), not much spoilt but not very exciting.

ROSEHAUGH. *See* p. 447.

0090
BADCAUL

Hamlet above Little Loch Broom.

CHURCH. Mission church of sneck-harled rubble built in 1917.
SCHOOL. Late Victorian and cottagey.

8070
BALINTORE

Much altered fishing village with new housing on the hill behind.

UNITED FREE CHURCH, New Street. Rectangular hall church of *c.* 1910.

HARBOUR. By *D. & T. Stevenson*, 1890. L-plan pier and straight breakwater, both of concrete.

CROSS SLAB (CLACH A'CHARRIDH), Shandwick, 0.6km. SW. 2.7m.-high slab, erected *c.* 800 and rather crudely mended after being blown down and broken in 1846. E face decorated with a cross outlined by high-relief bosses. Beneath each arm, a little

angel equipped with two pairs of wings; below, two beasts
(?lions) above interlaced groups of scrawny animals and snakes.
At the bottom have been four large bosses, the two on the l.
surviving, carved with interlace decoration and circled by face-
to-face snakes. On the slab's w face, five panels, their relief
decoration rather shallower. In the top panel, a spiral-patterned
'double-disc' symbol. Below it, a 'Pictish beast' symbol with
diminutive animals underneath. In the third panel, a crowd of
people, some mounted, engaged in drinking, fighting and stag
hunting. In the fourth panel, an abstract design of interlocking
spirals. The bottom panel is damaged but two of its four abstract
patterns are visible.

BALLONE CASTLE   *9080*
1.6km. E of Portmahomack

Substantial remains of the large and smart cliff-top tower house
built by the Dunbars of Easter Tarbat in the mid-c16. Z-plan,
the NW tower round, the SE square. In the w inner angles, tall
stair turrets corbelled out from the first floor and finished with
shallow pitched stone roofs. Roofs of the same type on the
bartizans, which project on machicolated corbelling from the
NE and SW corners at second-floor level, not the wallhead, as
is usual. In both towers and the main block's w wall, plentiful
large gunloops with the same rectangular splay as those at

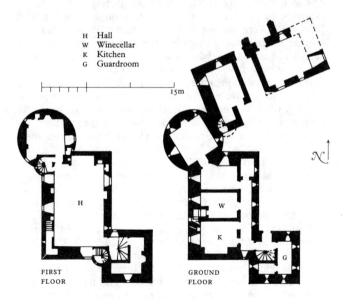

H   Hall
W   Winecellar
K   Kitchen
G   Guardroom

15m

Ballone Castle. Plans of ground and first floors.
(Redrawn from MacGibbon and Ross, *The Castellated and Domestic
Architecture of Scotland*, 1887–92)

Fairburn Tower. Shotholes in the bartizans. The window margins are chamfered except at the main block's first-floor hall and what were apparently the principal private rooms on the first floor of the NW tower and the second floor of the SE tower.

The round-arched main entrance in the SE tower's N face gave access to the principal stair. Behind it has been a guard-room with a small prison off it. Opening off a passage along the main block's E side are three tunnel-vaulted rooms. The S has been the kitchen, with its own external door to the W. Next to it, the winecellar, with a service stair to the hall in the thickness of the W wall. The whole of the main block's first floor has been occupied by the hall, its ceiling joists' moulded stone corbels still in position.

At the main block's N end and extending E to the cliff edge, a small addition, probably early C17 from the look of the pediment over the entrance. Two tunnel-vaulted rooms, the E with doors to N and S, with a passage between. The lower part of a stair to the upper floor survives at the SW corner.

7070   BALNAGOWN CASTLE
                     0.9km. N of Milton of Kildary

Tall mansion developed by accretion and reconstruction from the C15 to the C19, endearingly lighthearted despite the present exposure of previously harled rubble walling. The lands of Balnagown were granted by William, Earl of Ross, to his half-brother Hugh Ross *c.* 1350, but the first mention of a castle here is not until 1490, when the W range of the present house may have been newly built; the placing of its stair in a barely noticeable projection at the NE corner suggests a C15 date. The range seems to have been reconstructed and possibly extended in 1593, when the master mason *James Nicolson* was paid for his part in the 'new wark of Balnagown', perhaps including the provision of the conical-roofed bartizan at the SE corner and a SW turret corbelled out from above the ground floor. In 1668 David Ross of Balnagown began to make the house L-plan by adding a plain NE wing with a stairtower in the inner angle, *Alexander Ross*, carpenter in Inverness, being employed for some of the work, which may not have been completed until 1672, the date on a stone in the W range's S gable.

Transformation of this simple tower house into a building of some architectural pretension began when Admiral Sir John Lockhart Ross settled at Balnagown in 1763 and immediately commissioned the infilling of the L's inner angle, at the same time removing the late C17 stairtower. His tall three-storey addition, containing a ground-floor dining room and first-floor drawing room, roughly balanced the W range's S gable with a broad full-height bow at the SE. Apparently at the same time he made a new entrance in the centre of the W front. In 1794

Sir William Forbes found Balnagown to be 'a large house, originally a Castle, with a Bow-window pieced to it ...'

The early C19 saw further extensions built for the admiral's grandson, Sir Charles Lockhart Ross. In 1818–27 he employed *George Alexander* to remodel the C15 and C16 house's W front, adding a slim tower at its N corner to balance the existing SW turret, both being given lancet windows, and erecting a ground-floor verandah, its battlement carried on four-centred arches; at the verandah's N end, the gateway to a service court, at its S was a conservatory. Then in 1832–5 the entrance was moved from the W to the S front, a Gothick portico being wrapped round the C18 bow, which was given a battlement and whose straight one-bay link to the W range was balanced by a new one-bay link to an E range projecting boldly to the S. This new range and its linking bay are castellated Gothick, the range's S end gripped by slender conical-roofed drum towers. At this end, hoodmoulded upper-floor windows filled with intersecting tracery; a wheel window at the ground floor. Big round NE tower. *James Rhind* and *Alexander Ross* were the masons employed, *James McBride* the carpenter. Further work, perhaps largely internal finishing, was carried out in 1840–1 by *Alexander Ross* and the carpenter *James Munro*.

(Inside, the W range's ground floor is vaulted. Most of this range's first floor is taken up by the Trophy Room (the C16 and C17 hall), its panelled plaster ceiling an embellishment of *c.* 1840 with a heavy central rose. At the N end, a stone chimneypiece, its overmantel carved *c.* 1670 with strapworked cartouches enclosing the initials, singly and monogrammed, of Baron David Ross and his wife, Lady Anne Stewart; in the centre, their coats of arms. The NW window embrasure is painted with their initials and crude depictions of two wild men (the Ross supporters) and a dragon. The gunroom to the N was the C16 private room. In the late C17 NE range is the first-floor library, redecorated in the early C19 in the best Gothick style. Double doors on the S into the drawing room of 1760, also redecorated in the early C19 but in a post-Adam classical manner. Gothick gallery in the 1830s addition to its E. Off the gallery's S end opens the dining room, Gothick again with a shallow fan-vaulted plaster ceiling with a large centre pendant. Ogee-arched surrounds to the doors and windows, the E window's enclosing the Lockhart Ross coat of arms. The Frenchy chimneypiece is a discordant note. In the Red Bedroom on the second floor, an early C17 stone chimneypiece brought from the demolished Meikle Daan near Edderton. At each end of the lintel, a moulded stone semicircle containing the profile of a bearded human face, perhaps representing the sun and moon. Between them are three circles, the outer two containing coats of arms, the centre the figure of a minister and the initials H^{M}M and ER for Master Hector Munro, minister of Edderton and proprietor of Meikle Daan, and his first wife, Euphemia Ross. To the lintel have been added the initials of their son, Alexander Munro, and his wife, Margaret Forester, and the date 1680.)

BAYFIELD HOUSE
1.2km. N of Nigg

Austere but smart small mansion house of *c.* 1790. Tall piend-roofed centre block of three storeys and three bays, the first-floor *piano nobile* marked off by a bandcourse and sill course, the second-floor windows very small. Each side, a low two-storey link to an equally low pavilion, whose small first-floor windows have been raised above the eaves with gabled dormerheads.

BEN-DAMPH LODGE *see* LOCH TORRIDON HOTEL

BOGALLAN

Church standing by itself.

KNOCKBAIN FREE CHURCH. Dumpy lanceted Gothic, by *John Rhind*, 1888–9. The body is T-plan but with a belltower N of the E transept and a vestry to its E to give the impression that it is cruciform.

BRAELANGWELL
2.4km. SW of Jemimaville

Late C18 laird's house, enlarged and given a new front in 1839–45, probably by *James Ross*, who was responsible for the work's final stages. The C18 front is still visible to the E. Two storeys and five bays. Corniced central door (now a window) with a three-light window above. The ashlar front of 1839–45 faces S. It is of seven bays, neo-Greek on an intimate scale. Giant angle pilasters at the ends. More giant pilasters are used to mark off the third and fifth bays as pylons flanking the recessed and pedimented centre, across whose ground floor is stretched an Ionic screen portico.

BRAHAN
3km. SW of Maryburgh

Brahan Castle, a tower house built for the Mackenzies of Kintail and Seaforth and much enlarged and remodelled in the late C18 and early C19, has been demolished.

MAINS SQUARE, its centrepiece built by *David Aitken* in 1787–8. Segmental pend arch under a shallow pediment containing a bullseye window. On top, an octagonal wooden cupola with a pedimented clock-face on its S front. The rest looks mid-C19.

1.7km. W, MONUMENT to Caroline Mackenzie, dated 1823. Squat Tudorish hexagonal column with a crenellated top and cusp-panelled faces.

CADBOLL

8070

1.5km. NE of Hilton of Cadboll

Harled and crowstepped L-plan laird's house built for Æneas Macleod, Town Clerk of Edinburgh, after he bought the estate c. 1680. Macleod arms and crest carved on the W skewputts. The S wing was extended in a suburban manner c. 1975 by *Robert Hurd & Partners*, who replicated the original flat curvy stair balusters inside.

To the W, remains of the C16 CADBOLL CASTLE, perhaps built for a factor of the Bishops of Ross, who then owned the land. Small rubble-built main block of two storeys above an inaccessible basement. Round NW tower; bartizan at the SE corner. Two decorative arrow loops in the W gable; shotholes in the tower. Tunnel-vaulted rooms inside, but none seems to have had a fireplace. At the NW corner is a ruined stairtower of c. 1600 with the frame for an heraldic panel above the moulded door. This is the surviving fragment of a W wing, probably added by William Sinclair, who acquired Cadboll in 1592.

WALLED GARDEN to the E of the house, probably late C18. In its NE corner, an archway with the Macleod crest. At the S part's NW corner, a reused stone carved with the arms and initials of Æneas Macleod and his wife, Margaret Mackenzie. Fragment of a building, possibly late medieval, in the SE corner. – In a field to the S, large and classy lectern DOOCOT 95 of c. 1700. Ball-finialled parapets on top of the gables.

CAMUSTERRACH

7040

Small coastal settlement beside a rubble pier of c. 1800.

APPLECROSS PARISH CHURCH. A plain harled box built as Applecross Free Church in 1845.

FREE PRESBYTERIAN CHURCH. Built c. 1895. White harled, with a corrugated asbestos roof.

APPLECROSS PRIMARY SCHOOL. Broad-eaved school and schoolhouse, by *Alexander Ross*, 1872.

CASTLE CRAIG

6060

Substantial ruin of a tower house beside the Cromarty Firth. It 67 was built before 1561, when the lands of Craig 'cum fortalicio' were granted by the Bishop of Ross to Thomas Urquhart of Culbo, and an early C16 date seems likely. The site, approached down a gentle slope from the S, is a roughly rectangular promontory with steep drops to the N, E and W. The perimeter has been enclosed by a barmkin wall, the house itself forming part of the enclosure on the S. The barmkin, now very fragmentary except for a N stretch pierced with gunloops, has had a battlement and projecting round towers.

The tower is of four storeys and attic, the rubble walling rising sheer to a cavetto cornice on the long N and S sides. At the NE and SE corners, angle rounds linked by a parapet walk stretched across the E gable at third-floor level. The corbels of the rounds and walk are set between bands carved with dogtooth and cable ornament. In the N wall, windows with chamfered margins, and round gunholes at the ground, first and second floors; also on the ground floor, an inverted keyhole gunloop. The E gable's only opening is the door onto the parapet walk. In the S wall, the main entrance guarded by another gunhole. Almost in line above, a stack of sizeable windows, with chamfered margins like the others. The W gable has fallen, as has the extension built against it.

Inside, a tunnel-vault over each floor except the third, whose ceiling has been provided by a wooden mezzanine below the attic's vault. Ground-floor kitchen with a big fireplace at the E gable. On each of the upper floors, the space S of the kitchen flue has formed a small private room, with a narrow window in the S wall.

4050

CASTLE LEOD
0.9km. N of Strathpeffer

Large red sandstone tower house of the early C17. In the charter of 1608 by which Kenneth Mackenzie of Kintail granted his younger brother Roderick the barony of Coigach and the lands of 'Cultelloud', there was mention of a mansion house here, but not of a tower. The present house was probably begun very soon after the granting of that charter, and a likely date for its completion is provided by two dormerheads on the N elevation which are carved with the initials of Roderick Mackenzie and his wife, Margaret Macleod, together with the date '3 Agvs [August]', 1616. But it must have been very soon after that the building was enlarged, acquiring a fashionable stair to the first floor and additional bedrooms, the resulting external appearance very stolid. The house seems to have been little used in the C18 and was described as 'deserted except by Crows' and 'quite a ruin' in 1814, when repair was begun. In 1851 *Andrew Maitland*, adapting a design by *David Bryce*, placed a single-storey addition on the E and a low wing to the N. This N wing was thickened by a two-storey block on its W in 1874 before being mostly rebuilt in 1904 and extended further N in a gentle Baronial manner by *Donald Matheson*, 1912.

The house as first built was of five storeys, L-plan, with its SE jamb projecting to both S and E. Crowstepped gables. Corbelled parapet walk placed below the wallhead on all sides except the N of the main block, where the top windows rise through the eaves into stone dormerheads. At the walk's corners, round bartizans, those on the N with candle-snuffer roofs and continuous corbelling forming panels. The C 17 enlargement thickened the house to the s, although still allowing the jamb to project slightly. The addition is a little higher than the original building and dispenses with a parapet walk, although it has a conical-roofed turret at the SE corner to give a hint of martial display. Over the top windows, stone dormerheads with scrolls on the sides. Moulded door near the s front's E end; above it, a long stone carved with heraldic panels separated by attached baluster columns.

Inside, the ground floor of the C 17 extension is mostly filled by a vestibule and the stone scale-and-platt stair to its l. Behind the vestibule, in the original main block, a passage off which open three stores; kitchen in the jamb. The main rooms are now plain late Georgian, except for a large C 17 stone chimneypiece in the original first-floor hall.

CHAPELHILL see NIGG

CHARLESTOWN see NORTH KESSOCK AND CHARLESTOWN

CONAN HOUSE
2km. s of Conon Bridge

5050

Harled late Georgian mansion house of the Mackenzies of Gairloch. The three-storey main block was built in 1790–8. Five bays, the pedimented centre minimally advanced and with a Roman Doric columned doorpiece, its frieze carved with rosettes between the triglyphs. Tall first-floor windows marking the *piano nobile*. Steeply piended and bellcast roof. *c.* 1805 the house was made H-plan by the addition of two-storey wings, each with a full-height bow projecting to the front and a first-floor Venetian window at the side. Back extensions by *Andrew Maitland & Sons*, 1904. – Corniced early C 19 ashlar GATE-PIERS at the entrance to the drive from the SE.

Large U-plan STEADING to the SW, dated 1822. In the centre of the long s front, a tower, its lowest stage containing a huge roundheaded pend arch, the second a Venetian window (the outer lights blind) flanked by coupled pilasters topped by crenellations, the top a tall belfry-cupola, its weathervane displaying a plough. Two-storey ranges, their windows much altered. – To the E, a tall octagonal rubble-built DOOCOT, probably late C 18, its pyramid roof now felted. One ratcourse with flight-holes above. At the wallhead, a s-facing small gablet with flight-holes.

97

CONON BRIDGE

Single-street village laid out in 1829, now thickened with C20 housing.

FERINTOSH CHURCH OF SCOTLAND, School Road. Disused. By *W. C. Joass*, 1906. Plain Gothic, a bellcote on the w gable; sw porch.

FERINTOSH PARISH CHURCH, High Street. Originally United Free. By *Thomas Munro*, 1909. Stolid Gothic box with a bellcote on the gable front.

NURSES' HOME, Station Road. Built as a memorial to Sir Kenneth Mackenzie of Gairloch in 1902; *W. C. Joass* was the architect. Two unequal-sized cottage blocks, with fretted barge-boards and red-tiled roofs. The entrance from Station Road is through a lychgate.

PRIMARY SCHOOL, Leanaig Road. Sensible, by *Hugh Crawford*, 1977; extended by *Highland Regional Council*, 1990.

SCHOOL, School Road. Disused. Best School Board Gothic, by *W. C. Joass*, 1875.

DESCRIPTION. Entry from the N across the ROAD BRIDGE by the County Surveyor, *James Arrol*, 1969. To its w at the N end, a TOLLHOUSE by *Joseph Mitchell*, 1828, a two-storey octagon with a ground-floor verandah; quite tactful E addition. Upstream, the RAILWAY BRIDGE by *Joseph Mitchell*, 1860–3, five segmental arches built on a skew. HIGH STREET begins with two early C19 inns, the CONON HOTEL on the l. and the DROUTHY DUCK TAVERN on the r., both rendered and painted white. Then houses, mostly mid- and late C19 small-burgh vernacular, but BEAUFORT HOUSE on the l., dated 1843, is quite elegant though plain Georgian-survival. At the mid-C19 VIEWBANK, a tree-trunk porch. WAR MEMORIAL, a granite Celtic cross of *c.* 1920, to mark the divergence of Leanaig Road to the l. Further along High Street on the r., the early C20 Art Nouveauish harled LARCHFIELD, symmetrical, with red tile-hanging on its two-storey bows, and a late C19 cottage with busts of a man and woman on its porch.

CONAN HOUSE. *See* p. 393.
KINKELL CASTLE. *See* p. 432.

CONTIN

Nondescript village at the approach to Wester Ross, the church and manse standing apart on an island in the Black Water.

PARISH CHURCH. Harled Georgian box incorporating sub-stantial amounts of medieval walling. The church dedicated to St Maelrubha is said to have been burned by the Macdonalds in the 1480s and seems to have then been rebuilt as a simple rectangle. Major repairs were ordered by the Presbytery in 1734, perhaps the date of the s wall's tall rectangular windows (originally flanking the pulpit). In 1760 the roof's heather thatch was replaced by Easdale slates and the birdcage bellcote with an octagonal stone spire was added to the W gable. Further work was carried out in 1832 by *Thomas Macfarlane* and *Donald Mackintosh*, who heightened the walls, inserted small rectangular gallery windows in the gables, made doors in the S wall (the W now a window) and added a vestry behind the pulpit.

Interior recast in 1919, when a vestibule was formed under Macfarlane and Mackintosh's E gallery, their other galleries were removed, and the body of the church was refurnished and reorientated to the W, where the gable window was enlarged in honour of its new importance. – STAINED GLASS W window (I am the Good Shepherd) by *Roland Mitton*, 1981, colourful and sloppy. – In the N wall, evidence of a late medieval round-arched TOMB RECESS. – Also in the N wall under the gallery stair, a very plain pointed-arched SACRAMENT HOUSE of *c.* 1490. – Now in the vestibule are two late medieval carved GRAVESLABS, one decorated with a foliaged cross and sword, the other a fragment carved with the head of a wheel cross.

Harled MANSE to the E, built in 1794 and made a double-pile in 1829 when *George Angus* added the rear block. The front's gablets and porch were provided by *W. C. Joass* in 1894. – Small U-plan STEADING to the E, probably early C19.

WAR MEMORIAL. Battlemented granite toy tower of *c.* 1920.

SCHOOL. Thrifty Gothic, by *W. C. Joass*, 1875, swamped in additions.

BRIDGE OVER THE BLACK WATER. By *Thomas Telford*, 1812–13. Rubble-built, with three segmental arches; triangular cutwaters topped by pilasters at the parapet.

COUL HOUSE. *See* below.

COUL HOUSE

4050

0.8km. N of Contin

Sophisticated cottage-villa built for the mineralogist and connoisseur Sir George Steuart Mackenzie in 1821. Long two-storey block, of whinstone with sandstone dressings. On the entrance (N) front, a build-up from straight-gabled ends to a slightly advanced three-bay centrepiece, its outer bays piend-roofed supports to a broader and higher gable from which projects a single-storey octagonal porch with a pedimented Roman Doric portico. On the garden (S) front, the centrepiece begins as a broad canted bay projection but rises up above the eaves as a pavilion-roofed octagon. On both fronts, segmental-arched first-floor windows. Tall corniced ground-floor windows to the garden. *c.* 1860 the house was extended at each end with a wing projecting to the N and a shallow rectangular bay window added on the S front. Probably slightly later is the small service range at the E.

The interior is grand. Octagonal entrance hall (cut across by a late C19 glazed screen) with pilastered side walls and Roman Doric columns flanking double doors at the S end. Heavy foliaged ceiling rose. Big late c 19 neo-Jacobean wooden chimneypiece. Off the hall's w side, the stair, with pretty husk and garland decoration at its window. Above, a panelled plaster ceiling enriched with anthemions. The principal rooms are along the s front. In the centre, the octagonal dining room (now lounge). Deeply modelled acanthus-leaf ceiling rose, from which radiate wedge-shaped panels with Greek key ornament at their inner ends and acanthus fans in the corners. Black marble chimneypiece, its shelf supported by tall consoles. The room to the w was probably the library (now bar), its ceiling's acanthus-leaf rose set in a large panel with quarter-fans of acanthus at the corners. Greek key ornament in the side panels. Rather small plain chimneypiece, probably late Victorian. E of the dining room, the drawing room (now dining room), with an acanthus border to the ceiling's central fan, which is set in a large circle from which anthemion and palmette enrichment radiates inwards. More anthemion decoration in the end panels. WEST LODGE of c. 1821, harled with a semi-octagonal front.

8040

COURTHILL HOUSE
6.1km. W of Lochcarron

Roofless ruin of a harled early Victorian Tudor mansion house. Mullioned and transomed windows, chimneys corbelled out from the gables. Routine additions by *Alexander Ross*, 1883. These include a single-storey service court on the N, its W range converted by *Ross & Macbeth*, 1901, into a CHAPEL with a pyramid-roofed tower over the N chancel. Inside the chapel, a Romanesque chancel arch. Braced wooden roof over the nave, wagon roof in the chancel. – STAINED GLASS. In the chancel, W (liturgical N) window ('Holy, Holy, Holy'). – N (liturgical E) window (St George). Both look of *c.* 1901. – Marble BUST of a woman, signed by *Henry Weekes*, 1848.

7060

CROMARTY

Small town at the N tip of the Black Isle which had acquired the status of a royal burgh by *c.* 1265 but was dependent on the Earls of Ross from 1315 until the forfeiture of that earldom in 1475. In 1593 Cromarty was granted a new charter of erection as a royal burgh and seems to have experienced a burst of prosperity although not enrolled in Parliament or the Convention of Royal Burghs until 1661. However, only eleven years later, Parliament accepted its 'dimission' or resignation, finding it had 'not onlie become depauperat bot also dispeopled'. Its name was finally expunged from the roll of royal burghs in 1685, when it was made a burgh of barony under the feudal superiority of the Viscount of Tarbat (later first Earl of Cromartie). By 1730 its decline was said to be such that its inhabitants included only one shopkeeper, who doubled as a pedlar during the summer months.

George Ross of Pitkerrie bought the Cromarty estate in 1772 and the next year founded a ropeworks, followed by a brewery and pier, together with a new Townhouse and a second church (the Gaelic Chapel) to accommodate Gaelic-speaking immigrants who had been cleared from lands in the N part of Ross and Cromarty to make way for sheep and were attracted here by the prospect of employment. Still prosperous in the early C19, when solid new houses were built to the NW of the old town, Cromarty declined from c. 1850, the ropeworks and brewery both closing. By 1882 it had 'an appearance of picturesque decay and desolation', which it retained until after the opening of the Kessock Bridge from Inverness to the Black Isle in 1982. Since then buildings have been repaired and 'restored' and the burgh is threatened with becoming the choicest of dormitories for workers in Inverness.

CHURCHES

EAST PARISH CHURCH, Church Street. The epitome of the 30 post-Reformation kirk, but its white harling hides a long and none too simple history. The first church on the site was a long skinny rectangle built in the late C16 and provided with a small vestry at the E gable c. 1700. In 1739 *Alexander Mitchell* and *Donald Robson*, masons, and *David Sandieson* and *John Keith*, wrights, added the N jamb or 'aisle'. Seventeen years later the C16 church's side-walls were heightened by 4 feet, new windows were made, and the jamb roof's sandstone slabs were replaced with Easdale slates. In 1798–9 *Andrew Hossack*, house-carpenter, raised the jamb to the same height as the main block, which was given a new roof and whose windows flanking the pulpit were enlarged as roundheaded openings. Piend-roofed porches were added to the gables, the N and W gables being given ball finials. On the E gable Hossack placed a classy bird-cage bellcote which innocently mixes classical and Gothick detail (a fluted band under the cornice, cusped double-arched openings, stumpy pilasters and a ball finial).

Inside, a few late C16 features are visible. Below the W gallery's present window, a deep splay showing the position of the original. Under the E gallery's window, a roundheaded niche. Was this the head of an earlier E window? At the N wall's E end, just above the present floor level, a plain aumbry, its position suggesting that it might have served an altar. But the predominant character is C18. Galleries at the main block's E and W ends; a third gallery fills the jamb. The N gallery is of 1739, its front painted with initials and the dates 1741 and 1788 (these were repainted and the graining renewed in *Thomas Munro & Co.*'s restoration of 1978–81). The E gallery (the 38 Cromartie Loft) dates from 1756, when the W gallery (the Scholars' Loft) was probably rebuilt.* Simple pilastered fronts, the E with a Doric frieze below, both supported by wooden posts with rudimentary Doric capitals. Above each gallery breast a

---

*A W gallery had been built c. 1715.

semi-elliptical wooden arch frames the view into the church. The w gallery's arch springs from fluted pilasters. The e gallery's is grander, with a screen of Ionic columns *in antis*, the plaster vaulted ceiling running back to a second screen of Tuscan piers. Are these superstructures of 1756 or embellishments of 1798–9? On the e gallery's ceiling, a HATCHMENT painted with the arms of George Ross of Pitkerrie and Cromarty † 1786.

The plain PEWS in the body of the church are mostly mid-C19; the table-pews in the centre look earlier. Narrow pews in the N gallery, probably mainly of 1739, but their tiered arrangement is an alteration, perhaps of 1756. At the front of the e side, a large pew covered with faded painting of an arabesque frieze and panels containing flowers, the Sun in glory, *fleurs-de-lis*, and the Mackenzie coat of arms. It bears the initials KMK (presumably for Sir Kenneth Mackenzie of Grandvale and Cromarty) and HMC and the date 1740. – In the e gallery, fragments of escutcheons painted with the arms of Sir Kenneth Mackenzie and his wife Anne Campbell and dated 1702. – PULPIT by *John Robertson*, 1901, a very simplified version of the C16 pulpit in King's College Chapel, Aberdeen.

In the church, C19 and C20 marble WALL MONUMENTS of routine quality. More enjoyable is the vestry's memorial to Gilbert Anderson † 1656 and Hugo Anderson † 1704, with emblems of mortality carved in relief below the Latin inscription. – In the w porch, a graveslab of *c.* 1500, carved with a cross-shaft topped by the Sun in glory and flanked by swords.

Rubble-walled GRAVEYARD containing a number of C18 TABLE STONES. – On the N wall, a late C17 aedicular MONU-MENT, a coronet in the tympanum and grisly emblems on the frieze.

GAELIC CHAPEL, The Paye. The now roofless chapel built in 1783 by George Ross of Pitkerrie and Cromarty for Gaelic-speaking immigrants cleared from land on the w side of the Cromarty Firth. It is a harled rectangle with tall round-arched and keyblocked windows in the s front. At the e gable, a two-stage tower, its corners chamfered, the belfry stage of cher-rycock-pointed red sandstone ashlar under a pyramidal slate roof. Vestry at the w end.

NW of the graveyard, WAR MEMORIAL of *c.* 1920, a small battlemented tower with cannon spouts sticking out at the corners. – To the e, MONUMENT TO HUGH MILLER, the geologist and writer, erected in 1858–9, a 15.24m.-high Doric column of Davidston stone built by *Thomas Watson*. On top, a colossal statue by *A. Handyside Ritchie* ('The sculptor, it is said,' reported *The Builder*, 'has, on the whole, been successful in transferring to the stone the stalwart form and intellectual lineaments of the late literary, editorial, and geological quarryman'). Pedestal, carved with inverted laurel wreaths, from the Shore quarry, 'the first scene of Mr Miller's labours, and of his geological researches.'

ST REGULUS (Episcopal), Church Street. Plain Gothic, of red

sandstone, by *Ross & Macbeth*, 1906–9. Inside, a hammerbeam roof over the nave, panelled wagon roof over the chancel. Outsize floral carving on the chancel arch's capitals. – STAINED GLASS. Two windows by *J. Ninian Comper*: The Risen Lord (1932), with strong blues and deep reds, and a brightly coloured depiction of St Francis (1951) with Scottish birds and animals, among them a West Highland terrier.

WEST PARISH CHURCH, Bayview Crescent. Originally Cromarty Free Church. Gothic box by *John Rhind*, 1865–7, rebuilt in 1932–3 after a fire. Gable front divided by buttresses into a 'nave' and 'aisles', the l. topped by a gabled belfry, the r. carried up as a stair turret. – In front, polished granite MONUMENT (an urn on a pedestal) to the Rev. Alexander Stewart † 1847. The inscription records that he was 'invincibly attached to the retirement and obscurity ... and when at length chosen to be Minister of Free St Georges, Edinburgh, and about to be translated to that important charge, the Lord, pitying the perplexities of his spirit, put an end to them by suddenly removing him to the upper sanctuary.'

PUBLIC BUILDINGS

COURT HOUSE, Church Street. Set back from the street but quietly dominant, this is Cromarty's chief burghal building, provided at the expense of George Ross of Pitkerrie and Cromarty in 1782. Plain harled box with tall roundheaded windows at the first floor. In the centre, a boldly projecting solid-looking tower, its pinnacled parapet containing a fat octagonal cupola fronted by a contemporary clock (by *William Ross* of Tain). Immediately in front, the MERCAT CROSS, its capital carved with stylized rosettes and supporting a weathered cross-finial. On the shaft, the initials GR (for George Ross) and the dates 1578 and 1772.*
  Inside, the first-floor courtroom's furnishings are of 1844; cast-iron stoves flank the Bench. Cells on the ground floor. Additional cells (with built-in wooden beds) and an exercise yard were added to the rear by *Thomas Brown Jun.* in 1844.

HARBOUR, Marine Terrace. Begun in 1785 with two piers built of rough ashlar. The s pier was extended with an iron bridge to a wooden landing stage by *James Fraser*, 1880.

HUGH MILLER INSTITUTE, Church Street. Florid baroque by *Ross & Macbeth*, 1903–4. – In front, a small granite drinking FOUNTAIN celebrating Queen Victoria's Diamond Jubilee of 1897.

LIGHTHOUSE, George Street. 1846, by *Alan Stevenson*. A round tower embraced by a semicircular store block. On top of the tower, a tall octagonal cupola; in its front, an Egyptian door. More Egyptian detail on the single-storey keepers' cottages to the s.

PRIMARY SCHOOL, Braehead. By *A. Maitland & Sons*, 1875–6.

*The year when George Ross bought the Cromarty estate.

Long single-storey Gothic range in red and yellow sandstone,
picturesquely gabled and buttressed. At the s end, a round
slate-spired bell tower with a two-storey teacher's house
beyond. Rear additions of 1890 and 1904.

VICTORIA HALL, High Street. Single-storey drill hall by *A.
Maitland & Sons*, 1887. In the gable, a wheel window, its glazing
bars radiating from a central clock.

DESCRIPTION

On the approach from Fortrose the descent into HIGH STREET
is stopped by the late Georgian white harled and crowstepped
DENOON VILLA. A little to its N, LAUREL VILLA, dated 1828,
severe but smart with a sill course joining the architraved first-
floor windows. Beside the Victoria Hall opposite (*see* Public
Buildings, above) and set humbly back, a small crowstepped
BARN, probably late C17; the gables' quatrefoil vents are early
C19 insertions. Further on, the BANK OF SCOTLAND, douce
Italianate by *A. & W. Reid*, 1876. (In BANK STREET to the s,
a basket-arched pend at the ashlar-fronted Nos. 14–18 of *c.*
1840. THE OLD BANK HOUSE's painted early C19 front is of
droved ashlar at ground floor, polished above; three-light outer
windows and a pilastered doorpiece.) High Street's N side
continues with Nos. 8–10, dated 1817, with a Doric frieze and
rosettes at the pilastered doorpiece. Elaborate pilastered and
finialled late Victorian iron shopfront at Nos. 2–4 on the Church
Street corner. FORSYTH HOUSE opposite was built as the
manse in 1770; large but plain behind a front garden defended
by ball-finialled rusticated gatepiers.

FORSYTH PLACE continues the line of High Street downhill. At
its head, No. 1 of 1808 with cherrycock pointing to relieve its
austerity. BRAEHEAD curves round to the W with open views
over the Firth. On its r., an early C19 ICE HOUSE, like a turf-
covered air-raid shelter. On the l., the harled No. 7, mid-C19
but with a reset stone carved with a tailor's iron and scissors
and the date 1727. Opposite the Primary School (*see* Public
Buildings, above), a squat obelisk drinking FOUNTAIN of *c.*
1885. BARKLY HOUSE has a low servants' range dated 1825
joined by a screen wall to the late C18 main house, its s gable
partly crowstepped. For the Lighthouse in GEORGE STREET,
see Public Buildings. Beside it, the late Georgian REAY HOUSE
with club skewputts and a pilastered doorpiece. More pilastered
doorpieces at the contemporary Nos. 3 and 5, No. 3 having a
segmental arched pend on the l. Beside the Harbour (*see* Public
Buildings), the ROYAL HOTEL, converted from a short terrace
of early C19 houses, its crisp white harl and black paint diverting
attention from the many alterations. Further s, the three surviving ranges* of the OLD ROPEWORKS built in 1773–6 as a
large quadrangle. Unpretentious two-storey buildings of red
sandstone rubble but impressive for sheer length. The twenty-

---

*The W range was demolished in 1973.

five-bay E block was converted to housing in 1984. In the centre of the S range, a three-bay manager's house.

FISHERTOWN W of Forsyth Place is a picturesque jumble of late C18 and early C19 vernacular with a few gap-sites. Most houses are harled, some crowstepped, several restored, a few tarted up. Old photographs show that they used to be thatched. An inscribed stone on No. 4 SHORE STREET records that it was built by George Hossack and Anny William in 1775.

CHURCH STREET to the S is more urbane. After a simple ver- 4 nacular beginning, St Regulus' Church, the Hugh Miller Institute and the Court House (*see* Churches and Public Buildings, above) provide an informal civic centre. Then, sandwiched between two late Georgian houses, HUGH MILLER'S COTTAGE,* built by John Feddes in 1711 and now dressed in a thick coat of harl and a roof of Norfolk reed thatch. (At the top of THE PAYE to the S, the Gaelic Chapel and Hugh Miller's Monument, for which *see* Churches, above.) BELLEVUE sits well back, decidedly prosperous-looking in the severe Cromarty manner of *c.* 1800; its Gothick-windowed porch and piend-roofed wings are early additions. Diagonally across the street is the contemporary ST ANNS, just as stern but less aloof, facing 114 THE RETREAT, an L-plan house of *c.* 1700, heavily restored in 1979–80. Roughly contemporary ALBION HOUSE with a narrow gable to the street; its steep roof suggests it was originally thatched. After the East Church (*see* Churches, above), half-hidden by its graveyard wall, a red sandstone Gothic CHURCH HALL (by *John Robertson,* 1898) closes the view. In BURNSIDE PLACE to the N, two short back-to-back ranges survive of the BREWERY built by George Ross of Pitkerrie and Cromarty *c.* 1785, and converted to student accommodation by the *Law & Dunbar-Nasmith Partnership,* 1989.

THE CAUSEWAY skirts the walled garden of Cromarty House. On the l., a pair of harled and crowstepped houses, the late Georgian THE KENNELS and CLUNES HOUSE with a skew-putt inscribed 'JOHN CLUNES / ISSOBEL GRAHAM / 1724'. THE GARDENER'S HOUSE‡ opposite is probably early C17. L-plan, with crowstepped gables and a steep-pitched roof (perhaps originally thatched). In the inner angle, a chamfered door to the SE jamb. Moulded ground-floor window on the main block's E face. On the W front, a pair of first-floor doors sharing a jamb. The r. door has been converted to a window. The l. has been built up and partly covered by a small central wing added *c.* 1700, probably contemporary with the lugged-architraved door in the main block's E front. Inside, a large fireplace of *c.* 1700, its lintel inscribed 'IL MC' in the jamb's ground floor. Contemporary moulded chimneypiece in the next room.

*Property of the National Trust for Scotland.
‡Sometimes known as the OLD MANSE.

CROMARTY HOUSE
0.6km. SE

83 Smart but slightly stodgy mansion house of polished ashlar built for George Ross of Pitkerrie soon after he acquired the Cromarty estate in 1772 and demolished Cromarty Castle. Five-bay main block of two storeys and an attic above a half-sunk rusticated basement. On the entrance (S) front, a slightly advanced and pedimented centre marked off by rusticated quoins. Straight flight of steps to the tripartite front door, its attached Roman Doric columns carrying an open pediment; Venetian window above. Roundheaded ground-floor windows in the outer bays, which are topped by an overall cornice and balustrade. The garden (N) front uses several of these elements in a different pattern. The outer bays are identical, except that they have rusticated quoins and solid parapets. At the centre, a D-plan projection with bracketed cornices over its door and first-floor window and a crowning balustrade. Big scooped-up chimney stacks on the ends, emphasizing the double-pile plan. Extending from each end is a low three-bay piend-roofed wing of two storeys, the floor levels not corresponding with those of the main block. The wings' N and S fronts have roundheaded blind arcades at their ground floors; rectangular windows, originally blind but a couple now open, above. Panelled parapets on the S front and ends, balustrading to the N. Punctuation at the ends seems wanting. Were pavilions intended?

The interior is quietly expensive. Octagonal entrance hall; Coade stone statues of two Graces in the short sides, which flank the pedimented doorpiece to the drawing room on the N. The drawing-room ceiling is of elaborate Adamish character, the plaster modelled in shallow relief. Its large central compartment is filled by a neo-classical open umbrella with acanthus leaves in its middle and husks forming the rim and spokes; in the end compartments, foliaged circles, but in the N bow is more naturalistic foliage and a basket of flowers. White marble chimneypiece, its fluted columns' rams'-head capitals joined by swagged husks to more rams' heads on the lintel; anthemion decoration on the frieze, foliage and sea horses on the slip's uprights. The main block's SE corner is filled by the stairhall, quite restrained, with a simple ceiling rose and stylized foliage on the stair's wrought-iron balustrade. In the NE corner is the dining room (now morning room), its S end divided off as a sideboard recess by a beam supported by Adam-Corinthian pilasters with acanthus-leaf capitals. The chimneypiece is again of white marble but with scrolled sides and goats playing in the foliage of the frieze. At the W end of the main block are two simpler rooms (perhaps a parlour and bedroom), both with fluted and rosetted friezes. On the E wing's upper floor, the gunroom (now dining room), its Jacobean ceiling probably part of the alterations made in 1852. The Victorian stone chimneypiece incorporates a lintel carved with thistles, angels' heads, and huntsmen, the central figure blowing a horn; this is probably a relic of Cromarty Castle, perhaps dating from its remodelling in 1631–2.

From the house's E side a late C19 brick-vaulted SERVICE TUNNEL goes NE under the lawn to debouch on the road through a roundheaded arch; it enabled servants and tradesmen to approach the house without disturbing the owners' enjoyment of its garden.

STABLES to the SE, contemporary with the house. The U-plan S elevation is rubble-built and unassuming. The N front faced the principal C18 approach to the house and is ashlar-fronted, the heads of its ground-floor blind arcade filled with Diocletian windows lighting the stalls behind. Twin-aisled interior, the plaster groin vaults carried on wooden Tuscan columns. Restoration from near dereliction is proposed (1992).

CULBOKIE   6050

Long straggle of a village with late C20 bungaloid growths stretching out from its C19 core.

SCHOOL. School Board Gothic, by *W. C. Joass*, 1875.

CULLICUDDEN   6060

A scatter of houses beside the road, the old Parish Church set well back overlooking the Cromarty Firth.

PARISH CHURCH. Only the E gable and fragments of the side walls survive of the church built *c.* 1600 and abandoned after the formation of the parish of Resolis in 1662. In the gable, a moulded door and three panels (now empty) framing a window. – To the S, the late C17 BURIAL ENCLOSURE of the Urquharts of Kinbeachie, its walls topped by balusters. In its E wall, two mid-C17 heraldic stones, one commemorating Thomas Urquhart, the other dated 1658 for John Urquhart and his wife, Isobel Cuthbert. – On the graveyard's S wall, a large worn MONUMENT dated 1745, carved with the arms and initials of Master Thomas Inglis, minister of Resolis, and his wife, Anne Urquhart.

PRIMARY SCHOOL. By *Alexander Ross*, 1875. Small and simple Gothic; thoughtless recent additions.

DINGWALL   5050

A royal burgh since 1227* and the county town of Ross and Cromarty, but overshadowed in importance and prosperity by the larger burghs of Inverness and Elgin. In 1691 Dingwall's trade

---

*But alienated by the Crown to the Earls of Ross in the C14 and C15, its return to the status of a royal burgh after the forfeiture of the earldom marked by a new charter in 1498.

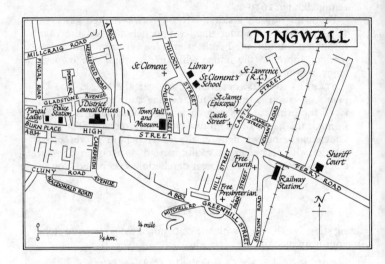

was reported to be almost non-existent, and, although linen manufacture had been introduced by 1760, Sir William Forbes found the town in 1794 'a small, paltry place, with but an indifferent Inn.' However, a harbour made by *Thomas Telford* in 1815–17 at the mouth of the Peffery was the signal for modest early C19 expansion, to which the arrival of the railway in 1862 gave a further gentle push. The central area redevelopment begun in 1963 has deprived the town of much character but provided it with an abundance of car-parking.

CHURCHES

CASTLE STREET CHURCH, Castle Street. Originally United Free. Lumpy Gothic with a SE tower. By *William Mackintosh*, 1909.

40 FREE CHURCH, High Street. By *John Rhind*, 1867–70. A broad buttressed box with Geometric detail. To the r. of the gable front, a gableted stairtower, to the l., a steeple ending in an octagonal domed belfry with tall lucarned openings.* Five-light window over the moulded and nook-shafted entrance. On the side elevations, tall gallery windows climbing into gablets. Huge plate-traceried rose window in the s gable. (Galleried interior. – STAINED GLASS in the s window by *James Ballantine & Son*, 1870.)

  Outside, MONUMENT to the Rev. John Kennedy by *D. & A. Davidson*, 1886. Marble Gothic pillar with a crocketed finial; at the base, a high-relief bust.

FREE PRESBYTERIAN CHURCH, Hill Street. By *J. Lyon* of

---

*The steeple's height was curtailed because of inadequate foundations.

Matheson & Mackenzie, 1959. Harled buttressed box, with a rubbly N gable.

ST CLEMENT, Tulloch Street. Urbane but isolated in its grave- 27 yard; by *George Burn* of Haddington, 1799–1803. A broad piended box with its main front away from the street. On this front, a pedimented three-bay centre topped by an octagonal belfry tower and spire whose blind oval panels give it a look of St Cuthbert's Church, Edinburgh. At the back, a battlemented vestry. Stolid Gothick detail, the s windows' wooden mullions and tracery late C19 replacements. Inside, a semi-octagonal gallery containing a clock by *A. Scott* of Dingwall. – The other furnishings were renewed by *William C. Joass* in 1877–8. – Platform PULPIT with a Jacobean sounding board. – STAINED GLASS. On the l. of the pulpit, a realist greeny-yellow window of 1895 signed by *James Steel & Co.*; on the r., War Memorial window by *A. M. McLundie* of the *Abbey Studio*, 1921. – In the E wall under the gallery, two lights (Blessed are the Merciful; They Shall Sleep No More) of 1938.

In the graveyard, immediately N of the church, a C16 GRAVE-SLAB incised with a skull and crossbones. – Further N, two BURIAL ENCLOSURES. The W is of *c.* 1700, a low wall topped by fat balusters; pediment over the lugged-architraved entrance. – The E enclosure is the roofless remainder of the former parish church's St Clement's Aisle, built in 1510. Inside are built-up arches to the S, N and E. Under the S, which opened into the medieval church, a C15 GRAVESLAB carved in high relief, with blank shields flanking the head of a naked man, who has a sword on his l. side and holds a staff in his r. hand. – On the s wall, a late C18 MONUMENT to the Mackenzies of Fairburn with an oval tablet in a frame of swagged curtains. – Near the churchyard entrance, a Pictish STONE with three symbols carved on one face and two on the other. – In the car-park to the S, stumpy OBELISK to the first Earl of Cromartie † 1714, built in 1923 on the site of a taller C18 obelisk which had been demolished three years before.

ST JAMES THE GREAT (Episcopal), Castle Street. 1851–2, by *J. L. Pearson* with *James Ross* as executant architect, partly rebuilt after a fire by *Alexander Ross*, 1871–2. Very simple sturdy Gothic with a three-bay nave and lower one-bay chancel poking E toward the street. A bellcote over the join was intended. Vestry at the NE; SW porch. Unaisled interior, a braced roof over the nave. – ORGAN by *Bevington & Sons*, 1872. – STAINED GLASS. Complete scheme of *c.* 1872–1920, mostly unattributed. W window (SS. Andrew and James) by *Hardman*, 1873. – E window (the Nativity, Resurrection and Ascension) by *Heaton, Butler & Bayne*, *c.* 1895. – W window on the S side (Christ at the House of Martha and Mary) signed by *A. L. Moore*, *c.* 1912.

ST LAWRENCE (R.C.), Castle Street. Plain Gothic by *William C. Joass*, 1900. – Inside, a recent garish STAINED GLASS W (liturgical E) window (SS. Jude, Lawrence and Anthony).

PUBLIC BUILDINGS

CEMETERY, Mitchell Road. Laid out on a hill-top site by *C. R. Manners*, 1890. It is dominated by the MACDONALD MEMORIAL (the National memorial to Major-General Sir Hector Macdonald) by *James Sandford Kay*, 1904–7. Very tall whinstone tower on a battered base of bull-nosed sandstone. Minimally projecting top stage under a balustered parapet; NW bartizan carried up as an open cap-house.

DINGWALL ACADEMY AND SPORTS CENTRE, Tulloch Park. By *Donald Matheson*, 1929–35. Additions by *George Bennett Mitchell*, 1974–5. Sports centre by *Thomson, Taylor, Craig & Donald*, 1972.

DINGWALL LIBRARY AND YOUTH CENTRE, Tulloch Street. Plain late C19 broad-eaved blocks, formerly the Dingwall Academy.

DISTRICT COUNCIL OFFICES, High Street. By *Ross and Cromarty County Council* (project architect: *C. Porteous*), 1965.

FINGAL LODGE OF FREEMASONS, Burn Place. Dated 1926. Queen Anne with a hint of Art Deco.

POLICE STATION, Burn Place. By *Ross and Cromarty County Council* (project architect: *C. Porteous*), 1972.

PRIMARY SCHOOL, Tulloch Castle Drive. By *Ross and Cromarty County Council* (project architect: *Hugh Crawford*), 1968.

RAILWAY STATION, Station Road. By *Murdoch Paterson*, 1886. A long U-plan with crowstepped gables and a red-tiled roof-cresting. Cast-iron columns carry the platform's glazed awning. Lattice-girder bridge to the up-platform's wooden waiting room.

ROSS MEMORIAL HOSPITAL, Ferry Road. By *William C. Joass*, 1872–3. Single-storey almshouse Gothic in red sandstone. Utilitarian rear additions. To the r., LODGE dated 1895, with a *fleur-de-lis* finial on the gable and a tree-trunk porch.

ST CLEMENT'S SCHOOL, Tulloch Street. By *Ross & Joass*, 1863. Small, with round-arched openings and urns on the gables.

SHERIFF COURT, Ferry Road. Tudor, by *Thomas Brown Jun.*, 1842–5. Broad centre gable gripped by slightly lower gables from which project two-storey bay windows. A martial touch is provided by a tower to the l., its parapet pierced by arrow-slits. The gabled rubble-built range on the r. was added by *Andrew Maitland*, 1864. Inside, the courtroom still has its original furnishings. At the back, a small detached PRISON with horizontal windows lighting the cells.

TOWN HALL AND MUSEUM, High Street and Church Street. Baronial by *William C. Joass*, 1902–6, clasping a remodelled C18 steeple. Dingwall's first Town House was built by the mason *William MacNeil* in 1732–3. In 1773–4 the steeple was added, its design by *John Boog*, architect, *Donald Morrison*, square wright, and *Donald McNeil*, mason, loosely based on the early C18 Tolbooth steeple at Forres (Grampian). It seems deliberately archaic. Big square rubble-built tower, its balustered parapet a replacement of 1902–6. On top, a tall wooden belfry-cupola, also an Edwardian replacement and taller than the original. The stone balcony, its front carved with heraldry, was added by *Joass* when he rebuilt the Town House (now Museum) and added the Library (now Town Hall) behind. On his Town House's E gable, a panel bearing the burgh arms and the date 1730. The Library fronts Church Street with a procession of crowstepped gables, each inscribed with the name of a famous Scotsman (Burns, Scott, Watt, Wilkie, Wallace, Knox and Carnegie). – In front, the MERCAT CROSS of *c.* 1600, a weathered shaft and capital re-erected here in 1985.

DESCRIPTION

HIGH STREET demonstrates how not to impose modernity upon an unpretentious burgh. Predominantly two-storey in scale, with a good number of C18 and early C19 gable-ends, but almost all cut across by shantytown shopfronts, and the closes curtailed for car-parks. The Museum (*see* Public Buildings, above) just manages to retain its civic dignity. To its E, Church Street and Tulloch Street both leading to St Clement's Church (*see* Churches, above). After Tulloch Street, No. 60 High Street is dated 1786; central gablet and a round-arched pend. Across the road, at the corner of Lochiel Place, MANSEFIELD HOUSE's canted corner has a tiled portrait of Queen Victoria to celebrate her Diamond Jubilee. At LOCHIEL PLACE's end is THE RETREAT, built as the Parish Manse in 1789–91, with club skews at the gables and centre gablet. Long back wing added by *John Hay*, mason in Maryburgh, 1826–7. Beyond, in High Street, an early C18 scrolly gable suspended above plate glass. The mid-Victorian ROYAL HOTEL on the Hill Street corner provides a large but gentle Italianate presence.

In CASTLE STREET, a collection of churches (*see* above) and prosperous Georgian and Victorian villas. Among them a small octagonal DOOCOT of *c.* 1825 masquerading as a tower, with big cruciform arrowslits. A little further up, the ROSS-SHIRE JOURNAL OFFICES occupy the former FREE CHURCH of *c.* 1845: T-plan with a stumpy bellcote on the jamb's gable. Opposite is the approach to THE CASTLE, a toy fort built for Captain Roderick MacLennan in 1821, its rear tower demolished after a fire. In the garden, a MONUMENT to Captain MacLennan by *John Hinchcliffe yr.*; a Gothic pedestal, one face carved with MacLennan's ship, the *Dart*. Ivy-covered fragments of the medieval DINGWALL CASTLE, demolished in 1818.

High Street's N side continues with the NATIONAL HOTEL of 1858, broad-eaved with a balconied verandah across the centre. Immediately beyond it, FIRST WORLD WAR MEMORIAL by *J. J. Joass*, 1922, with a bronze figure of a kilted soldier. Further on, the former NATIONAL BANK by *William Robertson*, 1838, 112 austere Greek with broad angle pilasters and a low pediment. On the street's S side, the streamlined pagoda front block of the CLYDESDALE BANK (by the *Lobban & Mullineux Partnership*,

1975) butts against the gable of the late C18 PARK HOUSE whose gable-centred front is hidden down a close. The ROYAL BANK OF SCOTLAND is competent classical by *W. C. Joass*, 1906, the contemporary POST OFFICE less assured, by *Ross & Macbeth*. On the Station Road corner, the Free Church (*see* Churches, above) facing the SOUTH AFRICAN WAR MEMORIAL, a pink granite Iona cross by *A. Macdonald & Co.*, 1904. FERRY ROAD leads to the Sheriff Court and Ross Memorial Hospital (*see* Public Buildings, above). STATION ROAD to the r. is the S exit. After the Railway Station (*see* Public Buildings) a backward diversion down GREENHILL STREET to THE PARK, formerly a smart villa of *c.* 1830, its recessed centre filled by an Ionic screen, now a garage. The BEN WYVIS DISTILLERY's bonded stores (by *A. Maitland & Sons*, 1878) mark the end of the town.

TULLOCH CASTLE
Tulloch Castle Drive

Harled C16 tower house with big C19 and C20 additions. In 1542 Duncan Bain was granted the lands of Tulloch with a stipulation that he build a mansion house there, and the tower was probably put up soon after. It is square, with a chamfer across the ground floor's SW corner. In this chamfer, a large gunhole; another gunhole in the W face. At the NW corner, a round stairtower. Late C18 Venetian window in the W front, the other windows plain Georgian. The corbelled parapet with stone cannon spouts projecting from angle rounds dates from the restoration and alterations made by *Andrew Maitland & Sons* in 1891. Also of 1891 is the E wing, incorporating an earlier extension, perhaps of *c.* 1700. Two-storey bay window. The wing's top floor with steep scroll-sided gablets was added by *Robert S. Lorimer* in 1920–2. Manorial-Baronial NE wing of 1891. Big roundheaded and hoodmoulded arch in a battlemented screen wall, perhaps of the earlier C19, to the service court behind.

FARM STEADING to the E, a large courtyard dated 1774. Thirteen-bay S range with advanced piend-roofed ends. Above the central entrance, a square piend-roofed tower, its upper stage a doocot with gableted flight-holes in three faces. The rubble block on the l. of the centre was reconstructed with bay windows and gableted dormerheads in 1900 by *Cameron & Burnett*. – On the hill to the N, CAISTEAL GORACH, a 'ruinous castle' folly by *Robert Adam*, 1790. Round two-storey tower with low links to square pavilions. In the tower, a round-arched doorway at the ground floor, a quatrefoil opening and two crosslet 'arrow-slits' above.

DUN CANNA *see* ULLAPOOL

DUNDONNELL HOUSE
11km. SE of Badcaul

1080

Built in 1767 (the date over the door) for Kenneth Mackenzie of
Dundonnell. Harled six-bay main block of three storeys. The
small second-floor windows have been heightened to rise
through the wallhead to piended dormerheads, an alteration
probably of *c.* 1820. That is also the likely date of the back wing,
which was heightened and enlarged *c.* 1960. – To the SW, a
piend-roofed and Gothick-windowed GARDEN ROOM by *Neil
Rodger*, 1960. – Early C19 WALLED GARDEN behind the house.

DUN LAGAIDH *see* ULLAPOOL

DUNSKEATH NESS *see* NIGG

EASTER SUDDIE

6050

Isolated group of a churchyard beside a farm.

SUDDIE CHURCH. Of the church abandoned in 1764, only the
E gable and a short stretch of the bottom of the N wall still
stand, both featureless but probably late medieval. In place of
a N transept, crowstepped mid-C19 MAUSOLEUM. – Beside the
church's E gable, two TABLE STONES with almost identical
inscriptions in the same cursive script, both commemorating
Kenneth Logan † 1774, one erected by William, the other by
Robert Logan. – In the churchyard's NW corner, the BURIAL
ENCLOSURE of the Mathesons of Bennetsfield. On its N wall,
a weathered rustically classical tablet, probably late C17. –
Beside it, a much larger tablet to John Matheson † 1768, with
a coat of arms. – On the tablet to Kenneth Matheson, 'late
merchant at Fortrose', and his son John, both † 1769, an inscription beginning:

> HERE.lies the young the friendly
> And.the.Just
> Who.were both quickly.hurried
> Into.dust

EDDERTON

7080

Hamlet near the Parish Church, with a distillery just to the N.

FREE CHURCH, 1km. E. Originally the Parish Church but made
over to the Free Church of Scotland after the Disruption of
1843. Harled kirk of 1743 in a graveyard overlooking the
Dornoch Firth. T-plan with a long low main block and N 'aisle';
the windows are quite domestic-looking. On the W gable, a
corniced bellcote with obelisk finials. The 'aisle's' gallery is

reached by a forestair. Easdale slates replaced the original
heather thatch in 1758. The s front's piended dormers and the
oversize *fleur-de-lis* finial on the gable of the 'aisle' probably
date from the repairs of 1851. Inside, galleries at the ends (now
blocked off) and in the 'aisle'. – Canopied PULPIT of 1794.

BURIAL ENCLOSURES are built against the main gables. The
E, now roofless, is a mausoleum of 1637 with a moulded s
door. The w was built for the Baillies of Rosehall in 1821:
battlemented Tudor Gothic. – MONUMENTS. On the church's
s front, a small armorial tablet put up by Hector Fraser, minister
of Edderton, to his wife, Margaret Watson † 1716. – On the
churchyard's E wall, a large monument to Walter Ross, minister
of Tongue, † 1762, erected by Joseph Munro. It is a pedimented
'gateway' topped by urns, the 'entrance' filled by two inscription
tablets. – Near the graveyard gate, a CROSS SLAB of the C8 or
C9, its E face carved with the relief of a horseman above incised
depictions of two mounted warriors, all framed in a roundheaded arch surmounted by the relief of a plain cross. On the
w face, relief of a Celtic cross.

34 PARISH CHURCH. Ambitious but earthbound Gothick, built and
designed by *Donald Munro* of Tain, 1841–2. Piend-roofed box,
the slightly projecting buttressed ends with pediments containing trefoiled oculi. In the centre of the long s wall, a tower
with a square ground floor (for the vestry) and then two diminishing octagonal stages under a slated spire. Flanking the
tower are large windows, each of three mullioned lancet lights
with lanceted plate tracery in its head. Interior with a semi-
octagonal panelled gallery (now partitioned off) on fluted cast-
iron columns. – The original PULPIT has been replaced, but
its ogee-domed SOUNDING BOARD, decorated with Adamish
stucco duro work on the frieze, survives.

SCHOOL, 0.7km. s. At the N, a mid-C19 house altered in 1876
by *Andrew Maitland & Sons*, who added the ball-finialled school
(itself since altered); metal roof ventilator.

BALBLAIR DISTILLERY, 0.6km. N. By *Charles C. Doig*, 1895–8,
with a pagoda-roofed kiln and tall brick chimney. Some of the
rubble-built bonded stores have been replaced recently.

STANDING STONE, 0.3km. N. Tapering stone, *c.* 3m. high, probably set up in the second millennium B.C. In the C7 or C8 A.D.
one face was decorated with an incised fish and, below it, a
double-disc and rod motif placed vertically.

6060   EVANTON

Planned village laid out in 1807, but almost all the older buildings
are nondescript Victorian. Sizeable but well-hidden late C20
development.

KILTEARN FREE CHURCH, Chapel Street. By *D. Matheson &
Son*, 1953.

KILTEARN PARISH CHURCH, Balconie Street. Thrifty Gothic with a gableted bellcote. By *Andrew Maitland & Sons*, 1893.

SECESSION CHAPEL, Chapel Street. Now a house. Piend-roofed box with roundheaded gallery windows, built in 1824. In the E front's centre, a tower with concave intakes at the sides of each stage and a large birdcage bellcote on top; Tudor hoodmould over the first-floor door.

VICTORIA DIAMOND JUBILEE HALL, Hermitage Street. Dated 1897 but not very festive.

DESCRIPTION

On the bank of the River Skiach just to the S is the old FREE CHURCH MANSE of *c.* 1845, an unpretentious harled T-plan; it was converted to a COMMUNITY CENTRE and given a large breeze-block addition in 1981. BALCONIE STREET is one-sided except for a wooden hall, a concrete garage and Kiltearn Parish Church (*see* above) on the E. On the W it begins with a Victorian house picturesquely adorned with a tree-trunk porch and wooden gableted dormer windows. Nothing else of note except the harled NOVAR ARMS HOTEL, mid-C19, with a small shaped gablet at the centre.

CHAPEL STREET climbing the hill to the W makes the village T-plan. At its top, the grandly sited Secession Chapel (*see* above). In HERMITAGE STREET to the r., a terrace of prettily verandahed Victorian cottages.

FOULIS CASTLE. *See* p. 419.
NOVAR HOUSE. *See* p. 441.

FAIRBURN HOUSE 4050
7.8km. NW of Muir of Ord

Big Baronial mansion designed by *Wardrop & Reid* for John Stirling and built in 1877–8, the studied asymmetry emphasized by stugged rubble walling. Roughly in the centre of the S front, the boldly projecting three-storey entrance bay with a round-arched porch and pepperpot turrets gripping the crowstepped gable. To its r. but only minimally advanced from the main block, a tall square tower, its heavy battlement having angle rounds at three corners; at the fourth (the inner angle with the entrance bay), a corbelled-out round turret capped by a conical roof. The rest is routine, with corner turrets, stone gablets and bay windows.

Inside, a neo-medieval stone chimneypiece in the entrance hall, from which a stair rises to the *piano nobile*. Drawing room with neo-Jacobean pendants at the plaster ceiling and two white marble chimneypieces. In the dining room, a panelled wooden dado and ceiling and a tall wooden chimneypiece, its over-mantel containing a portrait.

4050

FAIRBURN TOWER
6km. NW of Muir of Ord

Roofless remains of the tall rubble-walled tower house probably built for Murdoch Mackenzie soon after 1542, when he received a charter of the lands with the condition that he build a house there. Almost square, it is only *c.* 8.2m. by 7.9m., but five storeys high. Quite plain except for crowstepped gables and round turrets at the NE and SW corners and without a wall-walk. At the ground floor, deeply splayed rectangular gunloops in each face. Quite comfortably sized windows interspersed with round shotholes at the upper floors. The off-centre rectangular stairtower on the S is an addition, probably of the early C17, replacing the original external stair or ladder to the C16 first-floor entrance and blocking two ground-floor gunloops. Door in its S gable instead of the more usual inner angle.

Inside, a tunnel-vaulted ground-floor store, originally with no external access. In its N wall, a straight stair to the first floor, where it ends at a lobby in the E wall. The C16 stair to the floors above was a turnpike in the house's SE corner. The unvaulted first-floor hall, like the room on each of the second and third floors, has a moulded fireplace and small chambers (probably garderobes) hollowed out of the walls. The fourth-floor room lacks these wall chambers but had closets in the corner turrets in compensation.

FEARN *see* HILL OF FEARN

8070

FLOWERDALE HOUSE
2km. SE of Gairloch

Rustically smart white harled C18 laird's house with a big Edwardian addition. The main block was built in 1738 for Sir Alexander Mackenzie of Gairloch and his wife, Janet, their initials and the date carved on the skewputts. Single-storey-and-attic above a fully exposed basement. Slightly projecting crowstep-gabled centre, its corniced door approached by a solid-parapeted T-plan stair and flanked by segmental-headed windows. Segmental-headed windows again in the ground floor's outer bays. Narrow swept dormers, probably a C19 addition. In 1904 *Andrew Maitland & Sons* extended the house W, a big full-height bow and broad crowstepped gable the main features of their front.

At the MAINS farm, 0.6km. E, a large BARN, originally of nine regular bays but with big segmental-arched openings made at the ends of the S front in the C19; small first-floor windows. Grand heraldic panel with the arms of the Mackenzies of Gairloch above the (blocked) centre door, whose lintel is inscribed 1730, a date for the barn's construction confirmed by the initials of Sir Alexander Mackenzie and his wife, Janet, above the first-floor door in the w gable. The roof, probably originally heather-thatched, is now covered with corrugated iron.

FODDERTY 5050

Just the churchyard* and former manse.

FODDERTY AND STRATHPEFFER PARISH CHURCH. *See* Strathpeffer.

PARISH CHURCHYARD. Enclosed by a low battlemented rubble wall. The entrance is through a WAR MEMORIAL ARCH by *A. Marshall Mackenzie & Son* and *Donald Matheson*, 1930, built of grey whinstone, the inscriptions in bronze letters on polished grey granite panels. Elaborate iron gates decorated with wreaths of laurel and thistles; in the centre, a hand holding a flaming torch. – Routine C19 and C20 monuments.

The old manse (now FODDERTY LODGE) behind is dated 1730 on the lintel of its exceptionally broad door (enclosed by a sun-lounge porch). Originally a narrow crowstepped rectangle, it was given a plain two-storey w addition in 1794 and a single-storey office wing in 1835. Bay windows and an E extension provided by *Ross & Joass* in 1861.

FORTROSE 7050

Small town for long known as Chanonry from its having been the property and residence of the canons of its Cathedral, their manses being built round the church. It was granted a share in the burgh privileges of the adjacent Rosemarkie in 1455 and became a royal burgh in 1590, but this did not prelude prosperity, for in 1691 the Town Council reported that the burgh 'have no trade by merchandizeing nor ever hade that wee know or can learne of, being but a litle village.' A new harbour was built in 1813, but by the later C19 Fortrose was best known as a holiday resort.

CATHEDRAL

Ross's first cathedral was the Church of St Peter at Rosemarkie, said to have been founded by St Boniface in the C7 on the site of a Columban monastery and established as the seat of a bishop by the early C12. In 1236 Pope Gregory IX gave Bishop Robert leave to reform and enlarge the cathedral chapter, the change being confirmed twenty years later by Pope Alexander IV. These reforms were accompanied by the building of a new cathedral at Fortrose. Services in the cathedral ceased after the Reformation, and in 1572 the lead from its roof was granted to William, Lord Ruthven. In 1652–3 the stones of its nave and choir were removed for the building of the Cromwellian citadel at Inverness. The s aisle, taken over as the burying place of the Mackenzies of Seaforth

*The church, redundant after the opening of a new parish church at Strathpeffer in 1890, has been demolished.

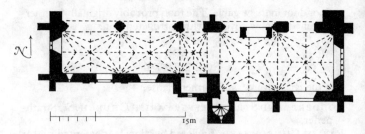

Fortrose Cathedral. Plan.
(Redrawn from MacGibbon and Ross, *The Ecclesiastical Architecture of
Scotland*, 1896–7)

and Coul, and the sacristy, used for meetings of the town council,
survived, and their repair as ancient monuments was begun by
Robert Matheson in 1853.

11 The s aisle is best understood as two chapels, the E markedly
broader and taller than the w and having a protruding sw
tower. It is traditionally said to have been built as the burial
place of a Countess of Ross, almost certainly Euphemia † 1394,
the wife successively of Walter Leslie and Alexander Stewart,
Earl of Buchan (the 'Wolf of Badenoch'), her tomb being
identified as the one occupying the E chapel's E bay. Heraldic
evidence for dating the w chapel is provided by two bosses, one
carved with the arms of Leslie (probably for Euphemia's son,
Alexander Leslie, Earl of Ross, † 1402), the other with the arms
of John Bulloch, Bishop of Ross from 1420 to 1439. A building
period stretching from the last years of the C14 into the third
decade of the C15 is indicated, but was the aisle intended
from its beginning to have its present form, or was the
w chapel either an afterthought or made narrower than at first
envisaged?

w gable built of squared rubble with gableted angle buttresses
of ashlar (the N buttress's N part an addition of 1853–5). Narrow
two-light Y-traceried window, badly off-centre for no obvious
reason. The gable's apex is set back; below it, corbels for a
projecting parapet walk reached by a door (perhaps dating from
the repairs made in 1615) from the space above the internal
vault. The s front's w bay continues the gable's rubble walling.
In it, a narrow obtusely pointed lancet. To its E has been a two-
storey porch (now demolished). Broad-arched door of two
orders into the church. Above, a roundheaded door from the
porch's upper floor opening onto a balcony inside the aisle. At
the next bay the stonework changes to ashlar and there begins
a continuous stringcourse carried under the window sills and
across the buttresses. Tall window with fragments of Y-tracery;
it has been of three lights. On the hoodmould's r. label, a
weathered carved head. This w chapel's E bay is much narrower.
In it, another (blocked) three-light window with fragments of
tracery. Squeezed into the inner angle formed by the projecting

E chapel is a small corniced burial vault built by Alexander Mackenzie of Coul *c.* 1635*; in its S wall, a trefoil-headed window.

The E chapel and its SW tower are clearly of a single build. Above the aisle's continuous stringcourse the tower is broached to an octagon rising to a second projecting stringcourse made by a continuation of the W chapel's wallhead cavetto frieze and (renewed) frieze of corbels. Is the belfry above original or a C17 alteration? Slated-spire roof, probably of the early C18. In each of the E chapel's bays, a four-light window with fragments of intersecting tracery, one containing quatrefoils inside. In the E gable, a five-light window (with fragments of Geometrical tracery). Above the level of the vault, a tall lancet; smaller light at the gable's apex.

The N front now looks like the outside wall of a free-standing building, this effect heightened by the angle buttresses added by *Matheson* in 1853.‡ Incorporated in the N buttress is a cluster-shafted jamb of the demolished choir's SW window. Each chapel opened into the nave through two broad pointed arches spring-ing from clustered shafts with simply moulded caps and bases; the arches' hoodmould labels carved with human faces. In the centre of each pillar's N and S face, a rectangular pro-jection ending in a corbel (carved as a human head). On the S, these corbels carry the vaulting ribs; on the N, they seem merely decorative. The E arch's pillars are integral with the canopied tomb placed within it, so this monument must have been part of the design. The W chapel's narrow E bay seems originally to have been divided from the nave by a solid wall, cut through when a monument was inserted here.

Inside the aisle, sexpartite vaults with tiercerons over each chapel. In the E chapel's E bay, foliaged vault bosses. In the W chapel, the bosses are carved with heads, except for those at the centre of the E and middle bays, which bear the arms of Leslie and Bulloch. In the E chapel's E bay, an aumbry in the N wall; in the S, a trefoil-headed piscina. – Red sandstone FONT, its panelled octagonal basin probably C15; base of 1853.

MEDIEVAL MONUMENTS. Built into the arcade's E arch, a canopied monument, probably that of Euphemia, Countess of Ross, †1394. Broad gableted arch, its hoodmoulds' labels carved with heads, one on the N that of a bishop. On the plain tomb-chest, a fragment of an effigy's draperied torso. – In the next arch, another canopied monument, thought to be that of Bishop Robert Cairncross †1545, its surviving outer order forming a depressed arch. On the foliaged pedestal, the head and torso of the effigy of a bishop. – Inserted in the wall of the W chapel's E bay is a third late medieval monument, possibly to Bishop John Frisel or Fraser †1507.* Heavily restored canopy, its arch carved with oak leaves contained by a crocketed ogee hoodmould.

Lavish display of POST-REFORMATION MONUMENTS. In the floor of the W chapel's two E bays, several C17 graveslabs decorated with skulls and crossbones. – The aisle's W bay became the burial place of the Mackenzies of Seaforth in the C17. On the S wall, a very smart marble obelisk carved with a relief of two Arab slaves sitting under a trophy; its inscription and base, now on the W wall, are signed by *John Bacon*, 1798. – Most of this end wall is occupied by a large but plain Tudor monument to Francis, Lord Seaforth, † 1815; unfortunately the shields' three-dimensional stags' heads have lost their antlers. – In this chapel's centre bay, a C17 tablet on the S wall to John Dunbar of Bennetfield and Agnes Mackenzie. Strapwork inscription cartouche under cherub heads and a coat of arms; on top, a steep pediment carved with a skull and crossbones. – To its E, a huge Ionic screen framing the entrance to the Coul Mausoleum and erected to commemorate Sir Alexander Mackenzie of Coul † 1796. Over the door (originally a semi-circular arch springing from imposts, but partly blocked by the monument) a figure of Father Time sitting among ruins of a castle, church and column. On top of the entablature's ends, flaming incense burners; at the centre, an urn-finialled flat obelisk carved with a cherub floating above a coat of arms. – Inside the mausoleum, C17 graveslabs on the floor and W wall. On the E wall, a stone, probably early C18, inscribed:

> Were not a Hereafter Mans predestinated Lot
> Mans Destiny would be to Revel and to rot
> Natures Shame and Foulest Blote

– Outside, on the aisle's W gable, a would-be classical C17 monument to Thomas Forres, with columns framing the inscription panel; reminders of death above and below. On top, an armorial panel.

On the N side of the demolished Cathedral choir is the old SACRISTY, externally a plain rubble rectangle with a pointed-arched S door into the church. The upper floor, reached originally by an internal stair and now by a W forestair, was rebuilt probably in the C17 and altered in the C18. Inside, the ground floor is covered by a six-bay ribbed groin-vault. On the long walls, stone benches backed by blind arcading; aumbries towards the E end. This looks C13.

The GRAVEYARD was enclosed by a dwarf wall and railings in 1857. – At the N, a Gothic WAR MEMORIAL GATEWAY of 1921, by *J. Pond Macdonald* after a sketch design by *J. Wilson Paterson*. – In the grass a number of C18 GRAVESLABS carved with skulls and crossbones.

*But according to the Wardlaw Manuscript he was buried at Fearn Abbey.

CHURCHES

FREE CHURCH, Church Street. Cream-harled hall with a
wooden cupola-ventilator. By *Donald Matheson*, 1909.

Former PARISH CHURCH (now Town Hall), Church Street.
Built as a chapel-of-ease in 1839–41. Ashlar-fronted rectangle
with Tudor-Gothic detail. Flowery finial on the E gable; on the
W, the base for another.

PARISH CHURCH, High Street. Originally Fortrose Free
Church. Dec, by *John Robertson*, 1895–8. Buttressed pink sandstone box with N transepts. At the S front the breadth is disguised
by a bowed stairtower on the r.; on the l., a darning needle of
a steeple with concave-sided pinnacles and spire. Broad gablet
over the door. Inside, an elaborate hammerbeam roof with
arcading above the collar. Deep S gallery. Refurnished except
for the massive pitch-pine pulpit at the N end. Above it, a small
STAINED-GLASS window (the Risen Lord) by *Father Ninian
Sloan*, c. 1970.

Outside, a granite Celtic cross by *J. & A. Fraser*, 1903,
commemorating the Rev. Charles Falconer.

ST ANDREW (Episcopal), Academy Street. Ashlar box built in
1828, dumpy despite its Gothic detail and pinnacled buttresses
('a horrible conglomeration of pinnacles, without chancel –
without any one good point', thought J. M. Neale[*]). In 1904
Ross & Macbeth gave the W end an apsidal baptistery with
cusped loop tracery in its round W window. The chancel (again
by *Ross & Macbeth*) finally came in 1907, externally masked by
the sacristy of 1913.

The interior is a high-minded celebration of the virtues of
Tractarianism and natural materials. The Georgian plaster has
been stripped to show rubbly walls and an open wooden roof
(but are its pendants of 1828?). Elaborate but hamfisted stone
screen into the baptistery. Wrought-iron chancel screen. –
Wooden ALTARPIECE of 1906 with a relief of the Last Supper
flanked by small figures of saints. – ORGAN with stencilled pipes,
by *E. H. Lawton*, brought here in 1915. – STAINED GLASS. In
the porch, one light (Giving Food to the Hungry) of c. 1900. –
Three lights in the baptistery (the Baptism of Our Lord, the
Descent of the Holy Spirit, and Our Lord at the Well) of c.
1920. – In the nave's S wall, one window (Christ as the Light
of the World and the Good Shepherd, and SS. Andrew and
John) signed by *F. Holt & Co.*, c. 1920. – In the chancel's central
rose, Our Lord in Glory, of c. 1920. To its l., a window of 1912
(Three Women Saints); to its r., two male saints, by *F. Holt &
Co.*, after 1912.

PUBLIC BUILDINGS

ACADEMY, Academy Street. Begun by *John Robertson* in 1890, a
small block with a conical-roofed round tower. A match with

[*]In *Ecclesiological Notes* (1848).

the original reddish sandstone is attempted but not achieved by additions of 1972 by *Ross and Cromarty County Council* (project architect: *M. Kirkwood*).

122 CHANONRY LIGHTHOUSE, Ness Road. By *Alan Stevenson*, 1846, and just like his lighthouse at Cromarty. A round tower embraced by a semicircular store block. On top of the tower, a tall octagonal cupola; in its front, an Egyptian door. More Egyptian detail on the single-storey keepers' cottages.

HARBOUR, The Shore. By *Thomas Telford*, 1813–17. L-plan w pier and a short E pier, both of rough ashlar.

MACKERCHAR HALL, Cathedral Square. Small pink sandstone drill hall with simple Romanesque detail, by *John Robertson*, 1881.

DESCRIPTION

CANONBURY TERRACE is the entrance from the s. Prosperous late C19 villas standing well back on the high ground to the l. to enjoy the view (now marred by bungalows) over the Beauly Firth. CRAIGDHU has a huge cast-iron verandah. KINDEACE LODGE, with a steep piended roof of red tiles and Arts and Crafts touches, was built as the Rosehaugh estate office, *c.* 1900; it may be by *William Flockhart*. (Diversion down HARBOUR ROAD. On its r., an early C19 storehouse (THE MOORINGS) now converted to housing. At the Harbour (*see* Public Buildings, above), the harled QUAY HOUSE, a granary built in 1813, now badly altered, with a long box dormer.) At Canonbury Terrace's N end, two late Victorian houses, THE ANCHORAGE, with spiky Gothic gables, and the broad-eaved and balconied KINGARTH.

HIGH STREET'S E side begins with the gatepiers at the drive to FLOWERBURN COTTAGE, a minimally pedimented little villa of *c.* 1838 with three-light windows flanking the front door. Plain E addition by *Ross & Macbeth*, 1887. More damaging are the large dormers which replaced the small piended originals in 1977. On High Street's w side, the crowstepped mid-Victorian WOODSIDE's front block bears the date 1740 in reference to its earlier back range. Then Nos. 17–21, a pretty Gothic terrace by *John Rhind*, 1869. Contemporary but more prosaic BANK OF SCOTLAND by *A. & W. Reid*, incorporating a recut marriage stone of 1719. On the corner with Academy Street, the stump of the MERCAT CROSS, perhaps of *c.* 1590. High Street now becomes more firmly urban, with plain early and mid-C19 blocks. The focus is the black-and-white paintwork of the ROYAL HOTEL, built *c.* 1835 with a recessed bow at the corner but enlivened by *Matthews & Lawrie* in 1879 with a spired turret and large wallhead chimney. On the house beyond, early C19 skewputts carved with the heads of a man and woman. The Free Church and old Parish Church are in CHURCH STREET to the l., the present Parish Church at High Street's N end (for all these, *see* Churches, above).

UNION STREET back at the Royal Hotel is the entry to

CATHEDRAL SQUARE, a mixed terrace overlooking the mown grass surrounding the Cathedral ruins (for which, *see* above). On the corner, the ashlar-fronted No. 32 High Street, dated 1836, with a flattened rubble bow to the square. Beside it, the early C19 No. 7 Cathedral Square, with battlemented twin bows and a Victorian cast-iron porch. In ACADEMY STREET to the w, the piend-roofed centred back of Flowerburn Cottage (*see* above). SEAFORTH PLACE (Nos. 8–10 Academy Street) fronts a court entered from the side, where one late C18 gate-pier is half-embedded in the gable. Simple front with a panel dated 1783. On Academy Street's l., ST ANDREW'S HALL, small-scale Victorian Gothic incorporating a marriage stone of 1788. On the r., fluted gatepiers at the garden entrance to MEADOW BANK, prosperous late Georgian with scroll skews and a late C19 porch. On the Rose Street corner opposite St Andrew's Episcopal Church (*see* Churches, above) is the smartly harled DEANERY. Crowstepped mid-C18 main block, the centre window round-arched and keyblocked; over-large new castellated porch. The back wing is early C19, with rus-ticated quoins and a fluted frieze. Probably contemporary are the ball-finialled panelled gatepiers. In the garden, a mid-C18 pavilion with a bullseye window each side of the door. For the Academy at the street's end, *see* Public Buildings, above.

In ROSE STREET, a long range (ANGEL COURT and ROSE COURT), early C18, but the roundheaded pend arch looks C16. Main front to the garden, with a carved stone angel on Angel Court's C19 porch, a late Georgian Roman Doric portico at Rose Court.

NESS ROAD at High Street's N end leads to Chanonry Point. On the l., NESS HOUSE, a plain harled block by *William Lawrie*, 1859, was built as the Black Isle Combination Poorhouse. Further down, on the r., a pair of early C19 tunnel-vaulted ICE HOUSES, their pointed gables looking stark now that the roofs have lost their turf covering. At the Point, the Chanonry Light-house (*see* Public Buildings, above). To its s, a ramped PIER built to serve the ferry to Ardersier; it is by *Thomas Telford*, 1819.

FOULIS CASTLE   5060
2.6km. sw of Evanton

Big harled Georgian mansion, quite pacific despite the name but 79 occupying the site, and incorporating parts, of an earlier house. The Munros had acquired the lands of Foulis by the C13, and a tower house here is mentioned in 1587. Rebuilding of that house was begun by Sir Robert Munro *c.* 1740 and seemingly completed by his son Sir Harry in 1754. About twenty years later Sir Harry Munro added bay windows at the sides and finally erected his coat of arms together with the date 1777 on the front pediment.

The main s front is an elongated version of the piend-roofed Anglo-Dutch box introduced to Scotland at the end of the C17.

Two storeys above a full-height basement. Eleven bays, the centre three slightly advanced under an urn-topped pediment. Strip quoins at the corners; sill courses tying together the ground- and first-floor windows emphasize the horizontality. Imperial stair, its balustrades decorated with anthemions and rosettes, to the front door, which is set in a rather skimpy corniced wooden surround. Heavily rusticated basement door below. Poking up behind the pediment like an off-centre cupola is the rear tower's gazebo. Projecting from the sides of the back wings are full-height canted bays, probably of the 1770s, not aligned with each other and the w substantially the larger.

The rear is much less regular. Irregular E-plan, the E wing only about two-thirds of the width of the w, the tower between them off-centre towards the E. In the E corner, a big stepped chimney. Probably this and some of the E wing's walling are C16. So too may be the tower's E wall, which is thicker than its w. The tower is dated 1754 on its second-floor window lintel. Canted N front; the top two stages rise as an octagonal gazebo above the roof. Chunky detail, with bracketed window sills and a lugged architrave and open pediment at the door.

Inside, the planning of the ground floor attempts as much symmetry as the unequal width of the wings will permit. Entrance hall-cum-stairhall occupying the two E bays of the centrepiece, the tower aligned behind. On each side of the hall, a two-bay room (the E now subdivided). Most of the w wing is occupied by the drawing room, most of the E by the dining room, both given their present form, together with their bay windows, in the 1770s. In the drawing room, a fluted frieze with rosettes. The dining-room fireplace contains an C18 cast-iron grate bearing the arms of Sir Harry Munro. Under the dining room is the kitchen, with two fireplaces in its w wall, the N with a straight lintel, the s segmental-arched. In the servants' hall under the entrance hall, a classical cast-iron stove by *Joseph Cooper & Son*, 1796. Acorn finials at the corners of its domed top; on the front, a relief of Justice. In the basement of the w wing, the E wall's s end incorporates the gable of a small earlier building, probably a C16 outbuilding, its door having opened to the E. Straightforward mid-C18 panelling on the first floor. At the top of the tower, an octagonal library.

Courtyard STEADING behind, joined to the wings' outer corners by screen walls dated 1792. At the ranges' s end, harled square pavilions, each with a forestair to the upper floor. The w pavilion's ground floor is C16, tunnel-vaulted, with an inverted keyhole gunloop in each wall. It may have stood at the NW corner of the C16 barmkin. From these pavilions, plain harled ranges run back to a terrace on which sits a pair of castellated pavilions, perhaps of 1792. At this terrace level the courtyard's walls are also battlemented. In the harled N wall, a roundheaded arch; octagonal recesses in its outer face.

On the lawn in front of the house, a polyhedron-headed

SUNDIAL, carved with the Munro crest and the date 1741. – At the end of the E drive, rusticated GATEPIERS topped by stone eagles; they look late C18.

GAIRLOCH 8070

Large village stretching round the N shore of Loch Gairloch, the architecture undistinguished C19 and C20 vernacular.

FREE CHURCH. By *Matthews & Lawrie*, 1878. Big but plain Gothic T-plan, the short arms treated as transepts. Bellcoted E gable front whose pinnacled buttresses hint at a nave and aisles behind.

FREE PRESBYTERIAN CHURCH. Dour box, its roundheaded windows still almost Georgian in character. By *Ross & Macbeth*, 1896.

PARISH CHURCH. Harled rectangle of 1791–3. The long S wall was rebuilt in 1834 with simple roundheaded windows. *Andrew Maitland & Sons* added the lean-to porch in 1894 and the gableted bellcote and hoodmoulded W window in 1908–9, when they recast the interior.

In the OLD BURIAL GROUND to the NW, a roofless rubble-walled L-plan BURIAL ENCLOSURE, perhaps a fragment of the former Parish Church.

GAIRLOCH HOTEL. Very big and very plain Jacobean. It was begun in 1872 by *Andrew Maitland*, enlarged by *Andrew Maitland & Sons* in 1880, and again in 1896 by *Ross & Macbeth*.

MUSEUM. Small C19 rubble steading built round a narrow court-yard. A lighthouse cupola has been added to the SW corner with weird high-tech effect.

DUN, An Dun, 1.5km. S. Small promontory fortified in the first millennium B.C. or the first millennium A.D. by the erection of two stone walls, now grass-grown, cutting across the landward approach. They form an outer and an inner enclosure, both very small.

FLOWERDALE HOUSE. *See* p. 412.

KERRYSDALE HOUSE, 4.8km. S. Early C19 harled laird's house, its roof now covered with asbestos tiles.

GARVE 3060

Hamlet beside the early C19 Parliamentary road and reached by the railway in 1869. Harled lump of an hotel (begun in the early C19 but much enlarged by *Ross & Macbeth* in 1888) and some late Victorian gableted cottages.

FREE CHURCH. Dated 1899 but very old-fashioned, with projecting keystones on the round-arched windows and an innocent Romanesque eaves course. Bellcote on the W gable, porch at the E.

RAILWAY STATION. By *Murdoch Paterson*, 1869. Lattice-sided bridge across the line.

GEANIES HOUSE
5.3km. SE of Portmahomack

89 Undemonstrative but very satisfying Georgian mansion of the
    Macleods of Geanies. The harled U-plan entrance (s) front is
    at the first glance of a piece; at the second it suggests a building
    of some complexity. The E wing is probably of 1742, the date
    given by a stone on its W face which bears the arms and names
    of Hugh Macleod and his wife, Isobel Fraser; it may have been
    an addition to a C16 or C17 house of which there survives only
    the heraldic stone of c. 1650, reset in this wing's E face, carved
    with the arms and initials of John Sinclair of Dunbeath and
    Geanies and his wife, Katherine Fraser. If so, the original house
    was replaced, probably in the 1760s, by a three-storey piend-
    roofed block, its severity relieved by ashlar lintel courses and
    the nicely differentiated hierarchy expressed by the tall first-
    floor windows and small second-floor openings. At the same
    time was built a W wing, a little shorter and broader than the
    E, whose S gable's crowsteps were presumably removed as
    old-fashioned (the N gable's survive). About fifty years later a
    Roman Doric loggia (now glazed) was thrown across the front, a
    bow-centred castellated addition of cherrycock-pointed rubble
    built against the W side, and the C18 W wing extended N.

    Entrance hall at the l. of the centre block. Its floor is covered
    with late C19 tiles, but the Corinthian screen (piers, not
    columns) at the back looks like 1760s' work. The stair behind
    is of c. 1810, with smart plasterwork. On the ceiling over the
    first-floor landing, a hanging rose. Curved second-floor ceiling,
    the centre panel filled with foliage. Basket arches decorated
    with classical motifs, the E springing from large consoles, to the
    adjoining rooms. The dining room on the ground floor of the
    early C19 addition may have been designed as a library–business
    room, since it has an iron door to a safe in one corner. Pilasters
    marking off the bowed end; elegant black-and-white marble
    chimneypiece, perhaps one of those supplied by *Isaac Jopling*.
    High-ceilinged drawing room above, again with pilasters at the
    bow. Its white-marble balustered chimneypiece and the pretty
    floral frieze are embellishments of c. 1900. To its S, a bedroom
    with an elliptically vaulted plaster ceiling. Tunnel-vaulted cor-
    ridor running back down the service wing to the N. In the C18
    main block, first-floor boardroom (former dining room); its
    marble chimneypiece, carved with a central urn, is a replace-
    ment of c. 1810.

    WALLED GARDENS to E and W, dated 1781. – To the S, a
    wooded cliff-top walk leads through two ARCHWAYS, perhaps
    C18 but now topped by C19 stone crosses, to a harled octagonal
    SUMMERHOUSE overlooking the Moray Firth. Rusticated
    doorpiece with blocks on the architrave. Its heraldic lintel,
    carved with the initials of Hugh Macleod and Isobel Fraser, pro-
    vides a date of 1760, which accords with the basket-arched fire-
    place and panelled overmantel inside. – At the drive's N end, late
    Georgian GATEPIERS with spikey obelisk tops to their ball finials.

HILL OF FEARN   8070

There was a village here by the late C 18, but the present buildings
are C 19 and C 20.

FEARN ABBEY
0.8km. E

Parish kirk reconstructed from the remains of a C 14 abbey church,
its stodgy appearance hardly hinting at the complexity of its
building history or that it houses one of Scotland's grandest
late C 18 monuments. A house of Premonstratensian canons was
founded at Fearn near Edderton by Ferquhard, Earl of Ross, *c.*
1225 and moved to the present site (then named New Fearn) *c.*
1238. The first buildings were said to have been built 'bot of clay
and rouch staine'. Between 1338 and 1372 the abbey church was
rebuilt and given a new roof by Abbot Finlay (*c.* 1408–1436) in
the early C 15. In the later C 15, Abbot Finlay McFaed † 1485
added the St Michael's Aisle on the S. S of this aisle he began a
new dormitory, which was completed by his successor, Thomas
McCulloch. In 1541 the abbey was described as ruinous and
neglected, and the SE chapel may have been added as part of
ensuing repairs. After the Reformation the abbey church became
a parish church; its E end was taken over by the Rosses of Balnagown as their burial place and a N mausoleum was added for
the Douglasses of Mulderg. In 1742 the church's stone-slabbed
roof collapsed, an event which so terrified the minister that he
refused to countenance the building being repaired, insisting
instead on the building of a new church to the S. For the construction of this new church, stone was taken from the old church's
W bay* and from the remains of the medieval dormitory and
cloister. By 1771 this new church was in turn ruinous, and in 1772
James Rich reconstructed the old church as a place of worship,
its short-lived successor being then demolished. Alterations
were made by *Hector MacPhail* in 1814, by *William C. Joass* in
1899–1902, and, most recently, by *Ian G. Lindsay & Partners*
c. 1972.

The C 14 church was ashlar-faced, of six unaisled bays, each
  apparently buttressed and containing a pair of lancets. In the
  angle-buttressed E gable, four lancets of equal height. All was
  neatly tied together by a stringcourse running below the sills
  and across the buttresses' intakes. The gable's lancets survive,
  as do most of those in the N wall and three of the four in the S
  side's two E bays. In the S side's present W bay, two small
  blocked lancets placed high up, presumably to allow for the
  cloister roof, to which the corbels below may belong.
     Abbot Finlay's early C 15 reroofing probably included the
  insertion of the (now blocked) pointed window high in the E
  gable. Of Abbot Finlay McFaed's late C 15 additions there

*The W bay was, by the C 18, divided off from the body of the church and known
as Denoon's Chapel.

survives only the featureless lower part of the St Michael's Aisle, refaced with droved ashlar *c.* 1790. The aisle seems to have occupied the N end of the cloister's E range and was originally of the same height as the body of the church, into which it opened through a broad arch (since built up). Hardly less fragmentary is the mid-C16 SE chapel projecting from between the E bay's two buttresses. In each of its E and W walls, a pointed window with tracery fragments; roundheaded E door. Much more survives of the early C17 Douglas mausoleum, built between the buttresses of the second bay from the E on the N side. The C14 stringcourse (its original continuation visible inside) is carried up vertically to the eaves, where it turns into a moulded cornice. In the N gable, three-light window with intersecting tracery under an armorial panel. Pointed window in the W wall; in the E, remains of another window and door. The roof has been carried on pointed stone arches springing from corbels, the two S arches still complete. Perhaps also early C17 is the blocked chamfered arch in the middle of the N wall of the church.

James Rich's reconstruction of 1772 gave the church its present general form. The original W bay having been lost, the W gable was rebuilt one bay to the E. In it three lancets, possibly a quotation from the previous gable but odd company for the birdcage bellcote and (now blocked) Venetian window lighting the W gallery. Rich placed another Venetian window (also now blocked) in the E gable's built-up upper window. At the same time he lowered the tops of the walls and provided a slated roof more shallowly pitched than had been its predecessor.* The pulpit was placed near the centre of the S wall, but its flanking windows were remodelled with Gothic arches by *Hector Mac-Phail* in 1814. Their intersecting tracery came in the alterations of 1899–1902 by *William C. Joass*, who also blocked Rich's Venetian windows and reopened the lancets into the Douglas mausoleum.

Bare interior, the result of the alterations made *c.* 1972 by *Ian G. Lindsay & Partners*, who replaced Joass's lath-and-plaster partition blocking off the W bay with a wall of artificial stone, stripped plaster from the walls and introduced the flat cedar ceiling. – The medieval SEDILIA survives near the S wall's E end, the trefoiled arches' hoodmoulding extended E to cover the PISCINA. Beside it, a small AUMBRY.

MONUMENTS in the E bay, divided off as the Ross of Balnagown 'aisle' in the C18 and opened up again into the church in 1899–1902. On the E wall, a large inscription tablet to David Ross †1711 and his wife, Lady Anne Stewart †1719; on top, their impaled coats of arms under the relief of an angel blowing the Last Trump. – To its l., the hugely grandiose monument to Admiral Sir John Lockhart Ross †1790 designed by *John Baxter Jun.* and signed by *A. Farquhar*. Side panels carrying the

*That roof was said in 1789 to have been 'a very steep high oak roof thatched with very heavy broad flag slates' and may have been the roof provided by Abbot Finlay in the early C15.

inscription beginning 'He possessed, in an eminent degree, The qualities of a hero ...' In the centre, high-relief sculpture of Ross's coat of arms framed by trophies. Above is an obelisk carved with a sarcophagus bearing the relief of a man-of-war in full sail. – On the N wall, baroque marble tablet to Lieutenant-General Charles Ross † 1732, a lugged-architraved frame with a curly segmental top and a plain cartouche above.

More monuments in the roofless side chapels. On the N mausoleum's N wall, a late C 17 aedicule bearing the impaled arms of Douglas and Ross with angels' heads above the leafily capitalled columns and emblems of death at the base. – In the St Michael Aisle's s wall, tomb of Abbot Finlay McFaed † 1485, a boldly moulded segmental-arched recess under an ogee hood-mould topped with McFaed's coat of arms. It contains the worn but largely intact effigy of an ecclesiastic. – On the Aisle's E wall, the C 17 corniced and moulded frame for a tablet. – On the W wall, a badly weathered aedicule, probably early C 18, with stumpy Doric pilasters, a prone skeleton on the frieze and a coat of arms in the segmental pediment. – Inside the SE chapel, segmental-arched tomb recess, the effigy now gone.

In the GRAVEYARD's SW corner, ambitious baroque monument to James Anderson † 1876, signed by *Thomas Goodwillie*, with a hand breaking down through the pediment to hold the inscription between dowsed torches. – In a small wall at the centre of the graveyard's s part, an armorial stone enlivened with emblems of mortality and with the initials AR and MR; it looks early C 18. – More reminders of death on some of the C 18 GRAVESLABS at the E end.

Old MANSE to the S, probably of C 17 origin but given its present plain harled appearance in the reconstruction made by *Donald Munro* in 1825. The W gable's early C 19 Corinthian portico is a recent import from a demolished house in Dingwall.

FEARN FREE CHURCH, 2.3km. E. Disused. Large but economical Dec by *J. Pond Macdonald*, 1896–7. Transepts at the E end. Bellcoted W gable, its breadth disguised by octagonal slate-roofed towers.

FEARN UNITED FREE CHURCH, 1.5km. E. Now a hall. By *Andrew Maitland & Sons*, 1908–9.

HALL. Dated 1887, the porch a recent addition.

PRIMARY SCHOOL. By *Andrew Maitland & Sons*, 1875–6, much extended in 1940.

RAILWAY STATION. By *Joseph Mitchell & Co.*, 1864–5, with broad eaves and a platform-verandah.

HILTON OF CADBOLL 8070

C 19 fishing village overwhelmed by C 20 box dormers.

PRIMARY SCHOOL. By *Sir Frank Mears & Partners*, 1961.

CADBOLL. *See* p. 391.

INVER

Jumble of a fishing village, the altered vernacular cottages jostled
by bungalows.

SCHOOL, 0.4km. SW. White harled school and schoolhouse by
   Andrew Maitland & Sons, 1876. In the school's N gable, three
   Gothic lights.

INVERGORDON

Small town founded as a fishing village by the Gordons of Invergordon in the mid-C18 and enlarged in the C19. It became a
police burgh in 1864. A naval dockyard was established here at
the beginning of the C20. The aluminium smelter opened in 1971
gave expectations of major industrial development but closed ten
years later.

CHURCHES

MISSION HALL, Joss Street. Disused. Humble Gothic of *c.* 1900.
PARISH CHURCH, Castle Road. Originally Invergordon Free
   Church. By *Ross & Joass*, 1859–61. Ambitious but simply
   detailed Dec in the manner of the Hays of Liverpool. The body
   is a big buttressed box enlivened by the deep N transepts and
   the S windows' tall gablets. At the S gable, a buttressed square
   tower broached to a tall lucarned needle spire. In the main S
   window, spiralling mouchettes. – HALL at the N added by
   Sinclair Macdonald, 1895. Inside, braced-collar pitch-pine roofs
   over the nave and transepts. S gallery. At the N end, a Gothic
   canopied platform PULPIT (now bare of varnish). The other
   furnishings have been renewed. – Abstract STAINED GLASS by
   Swaine Bourne & Co., 1898.

PUBLIC BUILDINGS

ALUMINIUM SMELTER. By the *British Aluminium Co.*'s own
   architects, with *Renton, Howard, Wood Associates* as consultants,
   1969–70.
CROMARTY FIRTH PORT AUTHORITY OFFICE, Shore Road.
   By *Thoms & Nairn*, 1982, with balconies and a bowed oriel to
   enjoy the S view.
CUSTOMS AND EXCISE OFFICE, High Street. Small-scale and
   mannered, by the *Property Services Agency*, 1976.
HARBOUR, Shore Road. Begun by Roderick Macleod of Cadboll
   in 1825–8, reconstructed in 1856 and again (by *George Gordon &
   Co.*) in 1894. Rough ashlar piers, the W L-shaped. Long wooden
   C20 pier to the E. To the W, a ramped ferry pier by *Thomas
   Telford*, 1817.
INVERGORDON ACADEMY, off Castle Road. By *George Watt &
   Stewart*, 1964, in the Festival of Britain manner.

PARK PRIMARY SCHOOL, Albany Road. Low and rambling, with a Gothic bellcote, by *Andrew Maitland & Sons*, 1876. W addition of *c.* 1900. Blockwork E extension of 1976.

RAILWAY STATION, off High Street. By *Joseph Mitchell*, 1861–3. Single-storey block with a shaped centre gable. The platform's awning is carried on cast-iron brackets with foliaged spandrels. Lattice-girder footbridge across the line.

SOUTH LODGE PRIMARY SCHOOL, Castle Road. By *Ross and Cromarty County Council*, 1976.

TOWN HALL, High Street. Urn-topped Renaissance palazzo in poor-quality yellow stone, by *William C. Joass*, 1870–1. In the pediment, a carved figure of Neptune by *D. & A. Davidson*.

DESCRIPTION

At the W entry to the town, a Gothic drinking FOUNTAIN in polished pink granite, made by *A. Macdonald & Co.*, 1904, to celebrate the visit of Edward VII and Queen Alexandra two years before. HIGH STREET begins with the HAVEN BAR on the r., *c.* 1820, with later additions to its S front. On the l., an early C19 warehouse with a gableted hoist door at the back. Behind the set-back Railway Station (*see* Public Buildings, above), OIL STORAGE TANKS (a system begun before the First World War and extended before the Second) which stretch in a line behind the burgh. High Street now settles down into workday C19 vernacular, with a few more pretentious accents. On the S, a late C19 crowstepped POLICE STATION sturdily clad in hammer-dressed masonry. A Roman Doric doorpiece on the late Georgian No. 13 opposite. Mid-Victorian MARINE HOTEL, crisp in white harl and black paint, with flowery stone crosses on the gables. Austere but unspoiled late Georgian at No. 22 opposite. After Albany Road (for whose Park Primary School, *see* Public Buildings, above), the street climbs gently. On its N side, the ANCHOR BAR of *c.* 1820, quite grand in a mildly ponderous way. Pilastered shopfront with a centre portico; three-light centre window above. It faces the ROYAL BANK OF SCOTLAND, an unassuming palazzo of 1856. Opposite the Town Hall (*see* Public Buildings, above), the gableted CLYDESDALE BANK by *Andrew Maitland & Sons*, 1873, its ground floor wrecked by a garish late C20 addition. The view up Castle Road is dramatically closed by the Parish Church's steeple (*see* Churches, above). After Castle Street, Nos. 89–91, mid-Victorian, with a heavy segmental-pedimented doorpiece. Then the architecture falters, but the BONE MILL (now a bar) provides no-nonsense mid-C19 industrial muscle. At the E end, the WAR MEMORIAL, a pink granite cenotaph of *c.* 1920. On the way down the hill to the r., OAKES VILLA by *Ross & Joass*, 1860, the house now crushed by box dormers but with immensely grand flowery iron gates.

SHORE ROAD overlooks the Cromarty Firth. At the E end, a long early C19 warehouse with horizontal second-floor windows, now tidily converted to housing. For the Harbour, *see* Public Buildings, above.

FARMS ETC.

HOUSE OF ROSSKEEN, off Strath Avenue. Large villa of *c.* 1930 with a flattened ogee roof over the l. entrance.

INVERGORDON MAINS, off Strath Avenue. Courtyard steading dated 1810. Plain three-bay farmhouse in the w range. In the centre of the piended N range, a pitched-roofed tower with a round-arched pend and first-floor Venetian window.

4050 # JAMESTOWN

Rural hamlet.

CONTIN AND FODDERTY FREE CHURCH. Roofless ruin, its walls (some lowered) enclosing a garden. It has been a tall buttressed and lanceted rectangle; by *Ross & Joass*, 1861–2. – Behind, its former MANSE of 1850, with pendant brackets at the consoled doorpiece.

7060 # JEMIMAVILLE

Small village laid out *c.* 1825 and named after Jemima Graham, wife of Sir George Gun Munro of Poyntzfield.

Former RESOLIS FREE CHURCH. Built in 1844 and now roofless. Roundheaded windows and door; bellcote on the w gable.

KIRKMICHAEL PARISH CHURCH, 1.4km. NW. Remains of the small late medieval church, disused after the formation of Resolis parish in 1662. It consisted of a nave and narrower chancel. In the chancel's s wall and E gable, windows, each of two lancet lights. The moulded s door looks late C17, presumably inserted when the chancel was taken over as the burial place of the Urquharts of Braelangwell. The nave has been curtailed and partly rebuilt, probably in the C18 after becoming the Munro of Poyntzfield mausoleum. Inside, a smart white marble MONUMENT to George Gun Munro † 1805, with a mourning lady clinging to an urn. – To the w, a further fragment of the nave's N wall incorporating part of a late medieval round-arched TOMB RECESS. – To the s, a rustically classical BURIAL ENCLOSURE dated 1680, built by William Grant of Ardoch to house the remains of his first wife, Florence Dunbar. Entrance with blocked columns and a pediment; balustrades on top of the wall. Inside, a MONUMENT with the arms and initials of William Grant † 1728 and both his wives (Florence Dunbar and Kate Mackenzie).

DESCRIPTION. Terraced houses, mostly of the earlier C19, form a single line N of the road. A few club skews carved with rope

mouldings for decoration; some box-dormer additions for C 20
convenience. Surprisingly suave former FREE CHURCH
MANSE of *c.* 1845, a harled single-storey house with twin bows
linked by a continuous straight roof carried by columns over
the open centre.

BRAELANGWELL. *See* p. 390.

KIRKTON, 1.4km. NW. Plain mid-C 19 farmhouse. To its W, a
large contemporary STEADING, its steam-engine house's tall
brick chimney perhaps added when work was done here in
1893.

NEWHALL HOUSE. *See* p. 439.

POYNTZFIELD. *See* p. 446.

KILCOY CASTLE 5050
0.9km. NW of Newton

Smart tower house built for Alexander Mackenzie soon after he
acquired the estate in 1618; it was restored and reroofed by
Ross & Macbeth in 1890. Z-plan, with a crowstep-gabled main
block. At the NW corner, a big round tower, its NW chimney
curved like the wall below; telescope-like stair turret in the S
inner angle. At the SE corner, a slightly thinner tower, its lower
part round, its upper part corbelled to the square above the first
floor and finished with a crowstepped gable. In its W inner
angle, a slim stair turret corbelled out from the first floor. Plenty
of splayed gunloops all round the ground floor. Classy detail,
not all original. High up in the SE tower's N face and at the top
of the NW tower, quatrefoil gunholes. These look early C 17. So
too do the late Gothic panel frames on the S front. On the
NW tower, pedimented dormerheads carved with the arms of
Stewart of Atholl and Sutherland of Duffus, one flanked by the
initials IS, the other by L[?]S; they are probably late C 17
embellishments commemorating Sir James Stewart of Kilcoy,
whose widow married Alexander Mackenzie, and Lilias Sutherland, the wife of Colin Mackenzie of Kilcoy. Another pedimented dormerhead, again probably late C 17, near the S front's
W end.

The original entrance was at the main block's E end next to
the SE tower. *Ross & Macbeth* provided a new entrance in the
centre. Inside, the ground floor is all vaulted. Passage along the
S side of the main block. To its N at the W end, the kitchen,
with an oven in its fireplace's N ingo; water inlet and a drain in
the N wall. The room beside the kitchen was the wine cellar,
with a stair to the hall in the thickness of the N wall. Across the
main block's E end, a large store with an octagonal cellar off it
in the base of the NW tower. In the SE tower, a comfortable
turnpike stair to the first floor, where the W two-thirds of the
main block is filled by the hall. In its W wall, a large stone
chimneypiece dated 1679 on the lintel, which is carved with
mermaid harpists at the ends. Between them, three shields
and sets of initials which commemorate the marriages of three

successive Mackenzie lairds of Kilcoy (of Alexander Mackenzie to Jean Fraser, widow of Sir James Stewart of Kilcoy, in 1611; of Colin Mackenzie to Lilias Sutherland in 1640; and of Alexander Mackenzie to Mary Mackenzie in 1664). Stone cornice along the hall's N wall. At the NW corner, the door to a tight turnpike stair which rises in a turret corbelled out from the corner of the hall. Withdrawing room to the w and bedchamber in the NW tower, these and the hall itself all well provided with cupboards and garderobes.

5040 KILLEARNAN

FREE CHURCH. *See* Newton.
PARISH CHURCH. *See* Milton.

6050 KILMUIR

Ruins of a church set in a graveyard overlooking the Moray Firth. Small Victorian farm steading on the approach.

KILMUIR WESTER PARISH CHURCH. Probably late C15, abandoned in 1764. Both gables and much of the ivy-covered N wall still stand. In the E gable, a pointed three-light window with intersecting tracery; in the w gable, a window of two pointed lights. The E end has been converted into a mausoleum, its round-arched blind s window perhaps late Georgian; early C20 w door with rosettes on the architrave.

7070 KILMUIR EASTER

Just the church and school standing near the shore of the Cromarty Firth.

PARISH CHURCH. Ungainly kirk but not without interest. The main part is a sneck-harled Georgian box, with rusticated quoins and ball finials, built in 1797–8. It was made no prettier by *John Robertson*'s alterations of 1903, which introduced the present round-arched windows but destroyed the symmetry of the main fronts. The E gable abuts a much lower rubble-built burial aisle with a round tower at its end. In the aisle's s wall, a door and built-up window. Slit windows with glazing grooves flank the tower. This is of rubble up to the apex of the gable. Then a continuous course of decoratively carved corbelling jettied out the ashlar belfry stage, its openings surmounted by carved curvy pediments. On the belfry, three stones carved with shields and the information that 'GMR BEIGIT 1616 MD', the arms and initials those of George Munro of Milntown and his second wife, Margaret Dunbar. The tower is finished with a conical stone roof pierced by oval lucarnes topped by carved finials; stump of a finial at the apex. Interior recast in 1903.

In the GRAVEYARD, on the church's N side, a BURIAL ENCLOSURE, its rusticated ashlar walls topped by balustrades; lugged-architraved doorway under a pediment. Inside, an approximate date is given by the heraldic tablet which commemorates James Baylie of Migdale † 1747. – Two other enclosures against the graveyard's E wall, one topped by diagonally set balusters; it may be early C 18.

SCHOOL. Asymmetrical, gabled and gableted, by *Andrew Maitland & Sons*, 1876, with a tall Gothic bellcote.

KILMUIR WESTER *see* KILMUIR

KILTEARN

6060

Just the old Parish Church and Manse in the middle of fields beside the Cromarty Firth.

KILTEARN FREE CHURCH. *See* Evanton.
KILTEARN PARISH CHURCH. *See* Evanton.
OLD PARISH CHURCH. Now roofless, it was rebuilt in 1791 and at first glance appears a standard late Georgian kirk. T-plan, of harled rubble, the S 'aisle' opposite the pulpit, which sat in the middle of the N wall flanked by tall round-arched and keyblocked windows. Roundheaded gallery windows in the E and W gables. On the W gable, a birdcage bellcote; chimney on the 'aisle'. However, the E gable has what look like medieval angle buttresses and an obviously medieval built-up pointed window. But this window is badly off-centre towards the S and the gable unusually broad for a medieval parish church, so was the gable widened in the C 18 and a medieval N buttress rebuilt at the new corner? What is the date of the S 'aisle'? It was first built in 1743 for the Munroes of Foulis and the corniced and lugged-architraved door to the gallery looks mid- rather than late C 18.

In the GRAVEYARD a fair number of C 18 and C 19 TABLE STONES. – Adjoining the church's W gable, the mid-C 18 BURIAL ENCLOSURE of the Munroes of Novar, the wall topped by a dumbbell balustrade; ball finial on the entrance's pediment – there used to be more balls at the corners and the centre of each side. Inside, a tablet to Hugh Munro † *c.* 1760. – Against the churchyard's W wall, the late C 18 ENCLOSURE of the Munroes of Foulis, the ashlar angle pilasters and entablature above the entrance contrasting with the harled walls. – At what used to be the graveyard's NW corner before it was extended, angle-pilastered ashlar walling, the background for three tablets, only the l. (apparently recut) now legible; it commemorated William Robertson of Teaninich † 1770.

Late Victorian MANSE to the NW. – To its E, the minister's STABLE AND BYRE (now a house), built in 1834. – Further E, a late Georgian BARN with a doocot opening in the S gable.

KINCRAIG HOUSE
3.9km. E of Alness

Harled laird's house begun for the Mackenzies of Kincraig probably in 1800, the date on a stone in the S wall, whose Ionic
doorpiece's frieze is carved with urns and rosettes. Baronial
additions of 1872 by *Andrew Maitland*, who gave the S front a
steep gablet flanked by conical-roofed bartizans and dormer
windows; round tower at the SW corner. The coat of arms
above the Georgian entrance is an embellishment of *c.* 1900.

KINKELL CASTLE
1.5km. SE of Conon Bridge

Crisply harled tower house built *c.* 1590 for John Mackenzie of
Gairloch, who had acquired the lands of Kinkell Clarsach in
1582. It is Z-plan, with a conical-roofed SE stairtower and a
round stair turret corbelled out from the first floor at the NW
corner. The tower and turret stick up well above the crowstep-
gabled main block, so the tradition that it had a floor removed
c. 1770* may be correct. It is now of three storeys and an attic,
whose catslide dormers date from *Gerald Laing*'s restoration
of 1969–70.‡ Formidable display of wide-mouthed gunloops
above the projecting base. Two more gunloops of the same type
below first-floor windows on the N and W. In the centre of the
N front, a pair of second-floor pistol holes. On this front, one
ground- and one first-floor window have been enlarged, perhaps
as part of the alterations made by *William Munro* in 1855; like
all the other windows, they now contain small-paned casements
of 1969–70. Above the door in the stairtower's inner angle, an
empty frame for an armorial panel.

Inside the door, the hinge-brackets and bolthole for an iron
yett. A pistol hole in a tread of the turnpike stair above. A short
passage on the ground floor gives access to the N kitchen and
W store. In the kitchen, a segmental-arched fireplace. Both
rooms contain gunloops (one of those in the store is blocked).
Their original windows are slits with wide internal splays. The
first floor is occupied by the hall. Segmental-arched embrasures
to the S windows. Steps up to the gunloops in the sills of two
windows in the N and W walls. The ceiling beams (replaced in
1969–70) are carried on stone corbels. Fireplace lintel carved
with a defaced shield and the date 1594. In the NE corner, a
garderobe. The second floor has a fireplace in each gable, so
presumably it originally contained two rooms. The NE turret
stair continues up above the attic, suggesting that another floor
once existed or was intended.

---

*As reported in Alexander Mackenzie, *History of the Mackenzies* (2nd edn, 1894),
p. 436.
   ‡When an C18 E addition was removed.

KINLOCHEWE

Scruffy West Highland hamlet.

FREE CHURCH. By *W. C. Joass*, 1874. Harled box, the W window
on each of the long sides carried up into a gablet to suggest that
there are transepts. Porch at the W end, vestry at the E.

KNOCKBAIN

FREE CHURCH. *See* Bogallan.
PARISH CHURCH. *See* Munlochy.

LITTLE TARRELL

2.2km. S of Portmahomack

Small tower house built for the Rosses of Little Tarrell, probably
in the late C16, and converted to a bothy and farm store in the
early C19. It was restored by *Sandy Gracie* in 1981–4, with much
use of pink-tinted cement. Harled and crowstepped L-plan.
The approach to the round-arched first-floor door in the inner
angle was defended by a wide-mouthed gunloop (now hidden
by the C19 forestair). More gunloops in the W gable and N wall,
one at first-floor level. In the main block's S front, a window
sill inscribed 'A.R.B.R.Of.Litil.Terrel.155[?]', presumably for
Alexander Ross and his wife; it seems to be a fragment reused
from an earlier house on the site. Round-arched N door, an
early C19 insertion. Interior now mostly of 1981–4, but the
SE jamb's tunnel-vaulted kitchen still has a segmental-arched
fireplace in the S gable and a slop sink in the embrasure of the
E window.

LOCHBROOM

Church and old manse standing by themselves at the head of
Loch Broom.

PARISH CHURCH. By *A. & W. Reid*, 1844–5. Harled box with
two tiers of rectangular sash windows; a hoodmould over the
round-arched E door. The gableted bellcote probably dates
from *Matthews & Lawrie*'s repairs of 1878. Inside, original
fittings. – Panel-fronted GALLERY round three sides. – Two
long COMMUNION TABLES with accompanying BOX PEWS
down the centre. – At the W end, PULPIT with a pilastered back
and sounding board.
In the graveyard, N of the church, a rubble-built BURIAL
ENCLOSURE of 1666, its round-arched entrance apparently a
C19 replacement. On its S wall, MONUMENTS to Alexander
Mackenzie of Ballone †1724 and Kenneth Mackenzie of Dundonnell †1739, with very crudely carved coats of arms and
symbols of death.

To the w, the pink harled old manse (now GLENVIEW) of 1810–11. U-plan, the two-storey-and-attic main block with a bullseye attic window in the advanced centre. Its porch is an addition, as is the N wing's upper floor.

LOCHCARRON

Village laid out c. 1800, and originally named Janetown after the wife of John Mackenzie of Applecross. One-sided street following the shore of Loch Carron, the houses (one dated 1812) predominantly C 19 vernacular, some much altered. Several gaps, some with late C 20 infill.

FREE CHURCH. Big harled T-plan kirk of 1846. Slender round-arched windows with Y-traceried wooden mullions. – Simple original PULPIT. – The GALLERIES, carried on cast-iron columns with acanthus-leaf capitals, were probably introduced as part of Ross & Joass' alterations of 1859.

FREE PRESBYTERIAN CHURCH. Humble harled box, dated 1908.

OLD PARISH CHURCH. Tall harled rectangle built and probably designed by James Smith in 1834–6. Long two-light windows with wooden Y-traceried mullions in the s wall. On the w gable, a spikily pinnacled birdcage bellcote of the 'Parliamentary' church type. Interior recast with a new PULPIT, probably during Alexander Ross's alterations of 1883. – W GALLERY and long COMMUNION TABLE of 1836.

In the well-stocked OLD BURIAL GROUND to the w, the s wall and gables survive of the FORMER PARISH CHURCH, built in 1751 and known as the 'Great Church of Lochcarron'. Rubble-built and apparently very plain, with big rectangular windows, the s wall's openings in a symmetrical six-bay arrangement of doors and windows.

MANSE to the NW, by Alexander Ross, 1867–9.

PARISH CHURCH. Originally United Free Church. By William Mackenzie, 1909–10. Ogee-headed lights in the front gable's window.

NEW KELSO, 4.9km. NE. Long harled block, its main part built in 1755–6 as a linen factory by the Trustees for Encouraging and Improving Linen Manufacture in Highlands of Scotland and named after the home town of its superintendent, Ninian Jaffrey. Originally it consisted of a semi-detached pair of five-bay buildings, each of two storeys with an attic. In 1789 the attempt at linen manufacture here was abandoned and the buildings were sold to the Mackenzies of Applecross, who may have added the low E addition soon after. Service wing at the w, perhaps added as part of the alterations made in 1906 by Ross & Macbeth, who probably also provided the bay windows on the w of the 1750s blocks.

Large FARM SQUARE. On its E and w sides respectively, a byre and hay barn, and a corn barn, both perhaps late C 18, with louvred walls, the corrugated iron on the roofs a replacement for heather thatch. On the square's N and S sides, C19 buildings (a cart shed, stable and byre, and an implement shed) with slated roofs.

TULLICH HOUSE, 3km. N. White harled early C19 tacksman's house.

STRATHCARRON RAILWAY STATION, 4.6km. NE. By *Murdoch Paterson*, 1869–70. – Lattice-girder FOOTBRIDGE by the *Rose Street Foundry*, 1900.

LOCHLUICHART

Handful of randomly disposed houses.

KINLOCHLUICHART PARISH CHURCH. T-plan 'Parliamentary' church, built in 1825–7 by *James Smith* to *William Thomson*'s standard design. Spikily pinnacled birdcage bellcote; diamond-pane glazing in the mullioned and transomed Tudor windows. The N front's two doors have been blocked, their fanlights left as windows, a new door being made at the back. The interior has been recast and reorientated. – In the graveyard, MONUMENT to Louisa, Lady Ashburton, † 1903, a giant table stone, the top supported by granite columns with fleshily foliaged Gothic capitals.

Beside the loch below, a contemporary H-plan MANSE, originally single-storey but heightened in the late C19.

ACHANALT POWER STATION, 1.2km. SW. By *James Shearer*, 1951. Flat-roofed, the walls of crazy-paved grey rubble.

GRUIDIE BRIDGE POWER STATION, 1.1km. SW. Lightweight modern-traditional in red Tarradale sandstone, by *James Shearer*, 1951. On the W gable and porch, low reliefs of a bear and coat of arms.

CORRIEMOLLIE LODGE, 3.9km. NE. Late C19 and faintly neo-Georgian, with a piended roof and central bay window.

LOCHLUICHART LODGE, 1.2km. NE. Overgrown cottage with Baronial touches. It probably began in the early C19 as a very simple two-storey shooting box. In 1840 *William Robertson* made this into a *cottage orné*, adding an Italianate tower at the SE corner and a rear extension. *Alexander Ross* made further additions in 1854, probably the date of the heightening of Robertson's back wing. In 1881 Lady Ashburton, the then owner, commissioned Ross again to adapt a scheme by *W. Eden Nesfield*, raising the main block with a gabled and slate-hung top floor and recasting Robertson's corner tower in Baronial dress. A rectangular bay window was added to the E side in the early C20. – At the back, a harled late C19 STABLE BLOCK; projecting from the SE corner, a SUMMERHOUSE, its octagonal roof topped by a spired cupola. – To the NW, GAME LARDERS with herringbone-patterned wattle walls.

LOCH TORRIDON HOTEL
8.9km. E of Shieldaig

Formerly Ben-Damph Lodge. By *Alexander Ross*, 1884–7. Over-grown cottage dignified by a conical-roofed round tower which bears an inscription commemorating Queen Victoria's Golden Jubilee and the arms of the Earl of Lovelace, who then owned the deer forest.

LOGIE EASTER

A rural parish, its churches and former manse standing alone near the A9.

OLD PARISH CHURCH. *See* Marybank Lodge.

OLD PARISH CHURCH. Disused. In a graveyard on top of a small hill. By *James Gillespie Graham*, 1818–19, replacing the previous church near Marybank Lodge. Broad rectangle of sneck-harled rubble with tall pointed windows. Crocketed finial on the E gable. At the W gable, a shallow porch carried up as a tower of four diminishing stages under a corbelled and cren-ellated parapet with crocketed pinnacles sticking up at the corners. In the tower's narrow N and S sides, big crosslet belfry openings; in the W front, a clock-face under an oculus. On the centre of the church's long S side is a second porch, with clustered shafts (formerly topped by pinnacles) at the corners; the latticed stone parapet has been removed. On the N, a small boiler house added by *Andrew Maitland & Sons*, 1890–1. Inside, the pulpit (removed) stood at the E end. Round the other three sides, a rectangular gallery on Tuscan columns, its pine front given Gothic stencilling in 1890–1. Quatrefoil ceiling roses.

The harled KELTON HOUSE immediately to the NE was built as the manse in 1779–80. Angular-headed attic window in the centre gable. Wings were added by *James McLean*, 1826–7, the W later extended.

PARISH CHURCH. Originally United Free. Unloveable but prominently sited red sandstone box of 1905, buttressed and lanceted. 'Transepts' at the pinnacled gable front, its apex topped by an angular Gothic bellcote.

MARYBANK LODGE. *See* below.
SCOTSBURN HOUSE. *See* p. 451.

MARYBANK LODGE
2km. W of Logie Easter

Built as Logie Easter Manse in 1759 but acquired by Sir John Lockhart Ross of Balnagown in 1780. A narrow* rectangle, harled and crowstepped, with a rusticated window in the central gablet. The E wing and piended porch are mid-C19 additions.

*It was built on the foundations of the C17 manse.

In a small graveyard 0.4km. W are the remains of the former
LOGIE EASTER PARISH CHURCH. It has been a harled rubble
T-plan. Little more than the W gable survives of the main block
rebuilt in 1764 under the supervision of *James Wilson*, mason in
Tain. N 'aisle' of 1730. Two storeys with off-centre rectangular
windows in the gable.

MARYBURGH   5050

Village laid out on a triangular plan in the early C19 by Lord
Seaforth, who named it in honour of his wife, Mary Proby, and
daughter, Mary, Lady Hood. Late C20 development along the
main road to the S joins it to Conon Bridge.

FREE CHURCH, Seaforth Place. Built as a large mission church
by the Mackenzies of Seaforth in 1840–1 and made over to the
Free Church of Scotland after the Disruption. *John Henderson*
was the architect. Broad cruciform of generally Tudor character
but with plain round-arched windows; tall gableted bellcote.
Inside, a sexpartite plaster vault. – Late C19 FURNISHINGS.

PRIMARY SCHOOL, Hood Street. Built as a Free Church school
in 1859. Steeply gabled and gableted.

DESCRIPTION. In PROBY STREET along the main road, mid-
C19 vernacular. SUNNYHOLM on the E side has scrolled skewputts and a pilastered doorpiece. In HOOD STREET, climbing
the hill to the W, the Primary School (*see* above) and, at the top,
the former EASTER LODGE to Brahan Castle, by *W. C. Joass*,
1888, U-plan with a diagonal porch across the inner angle. In
SEAFORTH PLACE, the Free Church (*see* above) and adjoining
big Tudor MANSE by *A. & W. Reid*, 1850.

MILTON   5040

Church and manse beside the Beauly Firth.

KILLEARNAN PARISH CHURCH. Stolid cruciform of sneck-
harled pinkish rubble built in 1745, its heather-thatched roof
replaced with slates and the walls raised *c.* 1800, and again
reroofed and heightened in 1891 by *Ross & Macbeth*, who
provided the plain Gothic bellcote. A built-up roundheaded
door in the S wall recalls its Georgian origin. In the N transept's
W wall, a moulded panel frame, probably early C18. – In the S
wall, a weathered late C17 red-sandstone MONUMENT, the
inscription tablet framed by attached Ionic columns decorated
with vine leaves; at the top, angels' heads, a skull at the base. –
Immediately S of the church, a worn late medieval GRAVESLAB
carved with a Calvary cross. – In the graveyard's NE corner, the
BURIAL ENCLOSURE of the Mackenzies of Kilcoy, built *c.*
1700, its low ashlar walls surmounted by diagonally set balusters
under a corniced cope.

MANSE to the W. Large and plain, by *Ross & Macbeth*,
1891–2.

REDCASTLE. *See* p. 446.

See p. 446.

MILTON OF KILDARY

7070

Small C18 flax-spinning village, almost swamped by late C20 housing.

DESCRIPTION. The core of the old village survives, the vernacular houses grouped informally round a triangular green. On it stands the MERCAT CROSS, a slim octagonal shaft with a ball finial, dated 1779. At the triangle's apex, on the l., the harled late C18 old DROVERS' INN, with two blind bullseye windows in the centre gablet. On the r., MILTON HOUSE, late Georgian with a Victorian wooden porch. Set back is the L-plan MILL, built in 1858 and reconstructed after a fire in 1900, with a pagoda ventilator at one end. At the village's NE end, the harled VIEWHILL, solid early C19.

ARABELLA HOUSE, 3.3km. NE. Early C19, with a crenellated parapet and central bow. Extensive rear additions by *Andrew Maitland & Sons*, 1882.

BALNAGOWN CASTLE. *See* p. 388.

SHANDWICK HOUSE. *See* p. 451.

TARBAT HOUSE. *See* p. 462.

BALNAGOWN CASTLE. *See* p. 388.
SHANDWICK HOUSE. *See* p. 451.
TARBAT HOUSE. *See* p. 462.

MUIR OF ORD

5050

Big late C19 village which developed after the opening of the Inverness–Dingwall railway in 1863 and became the junction for the line to Fortrose in 1894.

EAST CHURCH, Seaforth Road. Originally United Free Church. Solid but thrifty Gothic in pink Tarradale stone; by *William Mackenzie*, 1910.

KILCHRIST CHURCH, 1.5km. SE. Late medieval church burned, with worshippers inside, in a raid by the Macdonalds in 1603 and restored as a shell by *W. C. Joass c.* 1870. In the S wall, a chamfered pointed-arch door and blocked rectangular windows, their varying levels evidence of past alterations. The E gable's three-light window of late Scots Gothic type was provided by Joass. – Immediately E, a late C17 BURIAL ENCLOSURE, with a corniced entrance and diagonally set balusters on the front wall.

URRAY FREE CHURCH, Corrie Gardens. By *George Rhind*, 1861. Confident but plain lancet Gothic. Bellcote on the front gable, which is flanked by transepts containing the gallery stairs.

PUBLIC HALL, Seaforth Road. Cottagey, by *Alexander F. Mackenzie*, 1893. Half-timbered and bargeboarded gables; a red-tiled roof ridge.

RAILWAY STATION. Built in 1894. Humble white harled building with a canopy over the platform. – Behind, the STATION HOTEL by *John Robertson*, 1881, routine Jacobean but the gablets still have their wrought-iron finials. – To the N, a lattice-girder FOOTBRIDGE of standard Highland Railway type.

TARRADALE PRIMARY SCHOOL. A complex of buildings (not all still in educational use). At the NW, the plain Tudor school and schoolhouse, built in 1875. To its S, a larger triple-gabled block by *Thomas Munro*, 1912–14. Behind, big extension of 1954 in a stodgy Festival of Britain manner.

ORD DISTILLERY, 0.9km. NW. Large late C20 industrial complex incorporating mid-C19 maltings with pagoda-roofed ventilators; severe Victorian bonded stores.

EVELIX, 0.8km. N. Built as an Episcopal school in 1860. Single-storey, with a tower-like W pavilion. The porch and E bay were added in 1873.

ORD HOUSE. *See* p. 443.

MUNLOCHY

6050

Village laid out by the late C18. The buildings are now mostly C19 vernacular but include an old mill bearing a marriage stone of 1740; fairly discreet C20 infill.

KNOCKBAIN PARISH CHURCH. Originally Knockbain Free Church. By *John Rhind*, 1884–6. Big lanceted Gothic box, its gable front's slightly advanced centre giving a misleading hint that there might be a nave and aisles behind. On top, a spiky iron-crested bellcote. At the corners, pinnacled angle buttresses.

PRIMARY SCHOOL. Late C19, much altered and enlarged. Wrought-iron finial on the bellcote.

NEWHALL HOUSE
1.9km. W of Jemimaville

6060

Solid classical laird's house built for Donald Mackenzie of Newhall, *c.* 1805. Two-storey-and-basement rectangle of five bays by five under a piended platform roof. At the front, an advanced and pedimented centre building up from a portico with paired Doric columns to an Ionic pilastered and corniced three-light first-floor window and a bullseye in the tympanum. In the outer bays, cornices over the ground-floor windows, moulded architraves at the first floor, all tied together by sill courses. Mutuled corniced and rusticated quoins. (Inside, the entrance hall opens to the stair through a screen of fluted Doric columns placed between consoles instead of *antae*.)

MAINS OF NEWHALL to the W. Big courtyard steading of *c.* 1830. Over the pend in the S front, a pyramid-roofed doocot tower.

NEW KELSO *see* LOCHCARRON

5050   NEWTON

Church making a landmark beside the A832.

KILLEARNAN FREE CHURCH. By *John Rhind*, 1864. Buttressed
Gothic box, the gable front's centre slightly advanced under a
bellcote; octagonal pinnacles on the corner buttresses.

KILCOY CASTLE. *See* p. 429.

8070   NIGG

Parish Church and school sitting together. At Dunskeath Ness to
the s, a late c20 fabrication yard and oil terminal built to serve
the off-shore oil industry.

CHAPELHILL CHURCH, 2.8km. NE. Originally Nigg United
Presbyterian Church. By *Alexander Ross*, 1871–2. Romanesque
rectangle. N tower with a low-pitch slated roof, the eaves
scooped up to form a semicircular gablet on each face. Decoratively carved belfry shutters.

FREE CHURCH. Now Nigg Hall. Red rubble box of 1844–5. The
E tower still has a Georgian feel, rising from a square to an
octagon to a drum topped with a little slated spire.

PARISH CHURCH. Very simple harled T-plan kirk with rectangular windows. The narrow main block was built in 1626,
perhaps on medieval foundations, and given a major repair in
1723–5. Of 1723–5 is the stone birdcage bellcote, with panelled
piers and ball finials on the corners, and the top of the stumpy
spire. N 'aisle' added in 1730. Further alterations were made in
1779–84, when the roof pitch was lowered, its stone slabs were
replaced by Easdale slates, and the s windows flanking the
pulpit were enlarged. The simple interior was refurnished in
1879 and the end galleries partitioned off more recently. Housed
at the E end is a Pictish CROSS SLAB of *c.* 800, its front carved
with a cross decorated with panels of key pattern and interlace
ornament and set against a background of high-relief bosses
placed like fruits among bare tendrils. Rudimentary pediment
on top, its tympanum carved with a representation of St Paul
and St Anthony in the desert, each crouching over a lion;*
above them, a plummetting raven carrying a loaf in its beak.‡
On the back, a broad border with an eagle symbol at the top.
Below, traces of scenes in the life of King David; at the bottom,
a mounted huntsman pursuing a deer and followed by a cym-
balist.

15

*Lions helped St Anthony to bury St Paul.
‡The raven regularly brought St Paul half a loaf but provided a full loaf when St
Anthony visited.

SCHOOL. Plain Gothic school and schoolhouse, by *Andrew Mait-land & Sons*, 1876.

BAYFIELD HOUSE. *See* p. 390.

NORTH KESSOCK AND CHARLESTOWN 6040

Two villages at the SE tip of the Black Isle, now forming a single ribbon along the shore of the Beauly Firth, with recent development on the hillside behind. Both grew during the early C19, North Kessock on land belonging to Sir William Fettes, who built a pier for the ferry to Inverness, Charlestown laid out by the Mackenzies of Kilcoy.

At North Kessock, two ramped ferry PIERS, the E built of rough ashlar in 1821 and extended in 1825, the W now of concrete. MAIN STREET is single-sided, most of its buildings C19 vernacular. Opposite the E pier, a late Georgian GRANARY, converted to a mission church, *c.* 1890. At the W pier, the KESSOCK HOTEL, Georgian in origin but late C19 in its present form with broad eaves and a verandah. Beside it, STABLES of 1819, with a quatrefoil in the pediment over the central pend. More C19 vernacular at Charlestown. CHARLESTON VILLA of 1852, with a pedimented stone porch, may be by *John Shaw*.

NOVAR HOUSE 6060
2km. NE of Evanton

Harled mansion built in 1720 for John Munro of Novar, extended and remodelled by his nephew Colonel (later General Sir) Hector Munro *c.* 1770, again altered by Ronald Munro-Ferguson in 1897, and further recast in 1956.

The house built in 1720 (the date above its centre first-floor window) had a plain two-storey seven-bay main block with service wings running back to enclose a N courtyard divided in two by a cross-range. In the W wing's outer face, a reset stone with the date 1634 and the initials of Robert Munro of Novar and his wife, Helen. Probably soon after his return from India in 1765 enriched with prize-money gained at the Battle of Buxar, Colonel Hector Munro added two-storey piend-roofed SE and SW pavilions with full-height semi-octagonal bay windows projecting to E and W. Much less welcome additions were made in 1897, when an attic was added, the wallhead being raised below a meanly corbelled parapet; a line of inserted carved stones marks the line of the original wallhead. At the same time a porch was added to the front. This porch was removed in 1956, when *Arthur Munro-Ferguson* moved the main approach to the N, providing rusticated gatepiers with ball finials at the entrance into the outer (N) court. Inside this court, rusticated garage openings were made in the side wings. The pend through the cross-range was given an open-pedimented aedicule, its giant pilasters topped with stone eagles. Pedimented shallow portico at the main block's off-centre door on the s side of the inner court. The detail, mostly executed in cement, is of a free early c18 character.

Inside, the full seven-bay s front of the main block is now occupied by the dining room formed in 1897, its doorcases carved with small heraldic emblems, the fireplace's Georgian-revival frame containing an early c18 basket-arched marble chimneypiece. Built into one wall of the stairhall behind is an early c17 fireplace lintel carved with an aphorism and the crest and initials of Robert Munro and his wife, Helen. The drawing room in the sw pavilion has a late c18 pine chimneypiece decorated with swags. The ceiling was made for Rosehaugh as part of *William Flockhart*'s reconstruction of 1893–1903 and moved here after that house's demolition in 1959. It is heavily moulded in the late c17 manner, the centrepiece a genuine late c17 skyscape with cherubs and flowers by *Jacob de Witt*. In the library behind, Corinthian-pilastered and segmental-pedimented bookcases, more early c18 in character, also of *c.* 1900 and imported from Rosehaugh. Above the dining room, the first-floor gallery, apparently formed from three rooms. Ceiling of three coved compartments with a husk-swagged rose in each; shells and feathers decorating the friezes. Swagged friezes on the end chimneypieces. All this looks work of *c.* 1770, but the minstrels' gallery over the door must be of 1897.

At the E drive's s end, late c18 GATEPIERS with ball finials. – 0.5km. NE of the house, MAINS OF NOVAR, a much altered late Georgian courtyard steading, a pyramid-roofed tower in the centre of the s range.

MONUMENT on Cnoc Fyrish, 1.8km. N. Gothick folly built by Sir Hector Munro *c.* 1800. Screen of 'ruined' rubble columns with a three-bay arcaded centrepiece. It is, mist permitting, a prominent landmark.

6050 OLD ALLANGRANGE

Laird's house built for the Mackenzies of Allangrange in 1760, according to a datestone on the centre. Projecting wings were demolished *c.* 1905. The surviving main block is of two storeys above a basement; symmetrical five-bay front, the advanced centre finished with a shaped gable. This centre contains a mason's display piece consisting of a rusticated door surround whose very deep keyblocked top carries brackets supporting the sill of the lugged-architraved first-floor window. Inserted under this sill is an armorial stone carved with the initials of Simon Mackenzie of Allangrange † 1730 and his first wife, Isobel Mackenzie, probably reused from the house's predecessor. The architectural effect must have been much crisper before the harling was extended over the corner dressings and stripped from the centre bay. Inside, original staircase (altered at the ground floor) with turned balusters. Some doorcases have lugged architraves.

These must be of 1760. So too is the basket-arched stone chimneypiece in the first floor's sw room.

CHAPEL to the NE. Probably late medieval, the surviving E gable pierced by three narrow lancets. The Templars' cross on top is a Victorian embellishment.

ORD HOUSE   5050
1.3km. w of Muir of Ord

Unpretentious harled seat of the Mackenzies of Ord, whose progenitor, John Mackenzie, obtained a charter of the lands in 1637. The present U-plan house was probably built *c.* 1810, with three-light windows in the ground floor's outer bays and the first floor's centre. Roman Doric portico. Stubby single-storey-and-attic wings. The building was remodelled in 1850 by *James Ross*, who added the centre gablet, its corbelled chimney decorated with the date 1637 and the arms and initials of John Mackenzie.

POOLEWE   8080

Small village at the head of Loch Ewe. It was laid out by 1804, when building plots were offered for sale or lease.

FREE CHURCH. Stripped Romanesque, by *Andrew Maitland & Sons*, 1889, with a gableted bellcote.

PARISH CHURCH. T-plan 'Parliamentary' church (i.e. to *William* 31 *Thomson*'s design), built by *James Smith* in 1828. It is of the standard pattern, with Tudor doors and windows (containing lattice glazing), and a spikily pinnacled birdcage bellcote. Original furnishings inside, but partitions have been introduced.

ST MAELRUBHA'S CHURCH (Episcopal). By *William Glashan*, 1965. A long low buttressed rectangle, rubble-built with a slate roof. Narrow porch at the E end; concrete bellcote on the W gable. The sturdy simplicity continues inside, with unplastered walls and an open kingpost roof.

BRIDGE. Single large segmental arch of *c.* 1850.

INVEREWE HOUSE, 1.1km. N. The house itself is an undistinguished harled villa of 1936. The interest lies in the GARDENS created by *Osgood Mackenzie*, whose mother bought him the estate in 1862, when he was twenty. Within two years he had built a house with a walled garden to its SE and fenced off Rudhá Ard na Bà promontory to keep out sheep. At that time, 'with the exception of two tiny bushes of dwarf willow about three feet high, there was nothing in the shape of a tree or shrub anywhere within sight.'* Mackenzie began by planting huge shelter belts of Corsican and Scots pines and then from *c.* 1880 made clearings in the belts in which to place a wide range of

*Osgood Mackenzie, *A Hundred Years in the Highlands*, new edn, ed. M. T. Sawyer, London, 1949, p. 196.

exotic trees and shrubs. The 1860s house was badly damaged by fire in 1914 and Mackenzie himself died in 1922, when he was succeeded by his daughter, *Mairi T. Sawyer*, who built the present house and continued to develop the garden, using stone from the old house to make a rockery s of the front lawn. The property now belongs to the National Trust for Scotland, which employed *Elizabeth Beazley* to redesign the planting round the entrance and car-park in 1981. – WALLED GARDEN s of the entrance drive completed in 1864. – VISITOR CENTRE by *W. Schomberg Scott*, 1963; enlarged with a restaurant in 1978.

SRONDUBH, 0.4km. N. White harled two-storey five-bay tacksman's house of *c*. 1800. – STEADING to the N.

TUIRNAIG, 3.4km. N. Gabled and gableted shooting lodge, by *Matthews & Lawrie*, 1878. The conservatory projecting at the s front's E end may date from *Andrew Maitland & Sons*' alterations and additions of 1908.

9080 # PORTMAHOMACK

A stone pier built here by the first Earl of Cromartie in the late c 17 was in ruins by *c*. 1750, and Portmahomack had only three houses in 1798. The present fishing village developed after the building of a new harbour in 1815.

CHURCHES

TARBAT FREE CHURCH, Main Street. Grandly isolated at the village's w end. By *Andrew Maitland & Sons*, 1892–3. Large but plain pinnacled Gothic, with a spiky bellcote on the gable.

22 TARBAT OLD PARISH CHURCH, Tarbatness Road. A long harled kirk, mostly built in 1756 on medieval foundations, but the w gable is older, and so too was the off-centre N 'aisle' which was lengthened and heightened by *Keil*, 'architect', in 1780. Very simple detail, with rectangular windows. Piended off-centre vestry on the s. At the ends of the s front and against the 'aisle', forestairs to the galleries. On the w gable, a stone cupola bellcote of *c*. 1700, its dome studded with tiny lucarnes; on top, a finial carried by four balls, giving an ogee outline to the whole.

The interior is now bare, except for some furnishings provided by *Alexander Annandale* in 1891, and the galleries have been blocked off. In the w gable, evidence of an arch, apparently of a late c 17 columned screen, probably built up in the repairs made in 1739. Under the E end, a late medieval vaulted crypt with an aumbry in the gable.

MONUMENTS. In the N 'aisle', an Ionic aedicule commemorating William Mackenzie † 1642 and his wife. Coat of arms above the top of the inscription, cherubs' heads on the frieze, a skull and bones in the segmental pediment. – Beside it, fragment of an heraldic tablet to someone † 1623.

Well-stocked GRAVEYARD. Against the church's w gable,

BURIAL ENCLOSURE of the Macleods of Geanies, *c.* 1700, with balustraded walls and a lugged architrave at the entrance. Inside it, set into the church gable, a marble obelisk MONUMENT to William and Patrick Macleod † 1805 and 1807, carved with a lady who mourns before two urns shaded by a drooping tree. – On the graveyard's old E wall, a couple of early C18 aedicular MONUMENTS, one with emblems of mortality under the coat of arms, the other with coupled Corinthian columns. – To their N, contemporary three-compartment ENCLOSURE with ball finials on the back and a lugged architrave flanked by balusters at the central entrance. In the l. compartment, a monument to David Ross † 1748. – In front of these, C18 heraldic GRAVE-STONES, some with symbols of death.

TARBAT PARISH CHURCH, off Main Street. Originally United Free. Minimal late Gothic, by *Andrew Maitland & Sons*, 1908.

PUBLIC BUILDINGS

HARBOUR, Main Street. L-plan E pier by *Thomas Telford*, 1813–15. Short ramped ferry pier of *c.* 1865 to the w.
LIBRARY, off Main Street. By *J. Pond Macdonald*, 1899. Single-storey, with bracketed eaves.
TARBAT OLD PRIMARY SCHOOL, Tarbatness Road. By *Andrew Maitland & Sons*, 1875.

DESCRIPTION

At the S end, ecclesiastical competition between Tarbat Old Parish Church on the hill and the Free Church by the shore (for which, *see* Churches, above), each with an accompanying manse, the Parish by *George Burn*, 1801–6, with a later porch and bay window on the front, the Free built in 1845. MAIN STREET, overlooking the Dornoch Firth, is one-sided. Simple early C19 houses for the most part, generally rendered and many now with sun-porches. At the foot of Castle Street, seaside frivolity is given by a Victorian cast-iron FOUNTAIN of *c.* 1890, the water coming from a flagon on which sits a jolly fisherboy. Gaelic inscription on the domed canopy

UISGE TOBAR NA BAISTIAD*

Beside the Harbour (*see* Public Buildings, above), two harled store houses. The first, built by *Alexander Stronach* in 1699, is a low two-storey rectangle with massive buttresses at the S gable. The other was put up in 1779 but enlarged and remodelled in the early C19; it is now severely elegant with ball finials on the gables.

BALLONE CASTLE. *See* p. 387.
LITTLE TARRELL. *See* p. 433.

*The well of Baptism.

7060

POYNTZFIELD
1.2km. SW of Jemimaville

82 Rustically smart small harled mansion built for Sir George Gun Munro in 1757 and named in honour of his wife, Charlotte Poyntz. It is a S-facing U-plan. In the three-storey main block, windows grouped 2/1/2 and a centre pediment projected on blocks carved with the date of the house's erection. Off-centre entrance, its lugged architrave repeated at the corresponding window to the l.; bellcast roof. Low two-storey wings, the E extended N c. 1790 with a semi-octagonal-ended pavilion (one storey in the height of the wing's two) containing the drawing room. At the centre of the back, a tower rising from a square base through curvilinear chamfers to an ogee-roofed octagon; it is a variant on the contemporary and similarly placed tower at Foulis Castle. – At the end of the N drive, corniced and ball-finialled GATEPIERS contemporary with the house.

5040

REDCASTLE
0.5km. E of Milton

Big C17 L-plan house of the Mackenzies of Redcastle, remodelled by *William Burn* in 1840 and now derelict. The site, on the edge of a ravine near the N shore of the Beauly Firth, is naturally defensible, and there was a castle (known as Edradour) here by 1179, when it was strengthened by William the Lion. After the forfeiture of the earldom of Ross in 1455, the lands of Redcastle 'cum castro et fortalicio' fell to the Crown, passing in the C16 to the Mackenzies of Kintail and then to Roderick, third son of Kenneth Mackenzie of Kintail, who obtained a Crown charter in 1599. In the 1630s Sir James Balfour of Denmylne noted Redcastle as one of the 'Castells and Gentlemens housses' in Ross, and some medieval walling may be incorporated in the present house's S jamb. This house was built for Rory Mackenzie of Redcastle c. 1641 (the date given by a stone in the E gable). In 1649 Rory's 'new strong house of Redcastle' was besieged by Covenanting troops who 'brunt the castle to ashes, with all the good furnitur', but it must have been repaired soon after. The estate was sold by the Mackenzies in 1790, and Burn's alterations were made for Colonel Hugh Baillie of Dochfour who had recently bought the lands.

The C17 house is a large three-storey-and-attic rubble-built L. In the inner angle, a rectangular stairtower with a bristle of cannon spouts at the parapet, whose crowning balustrade is now missing. At the main block's SE corner, a second tower, also rectangular except for an awkwardly canted W side, the top corbelled out to a square cap-house. At the jamb's S gable, which is angled to the line of the cliff-top, round angle turrets on two tiers of corbelling. Another corbelled angle turret, but square, on the jamb's NW corner.

Burn's alterations included the addition of a lower tower in front of the C17 stairtower, the building of a loggia (since removed) across the main block's s front and a round NE tower and utilitarian extensions at the rear. At the same time windows were enlarged, the wallhead recast and the turrets reroofed.

STEADING to the NE, its s range presumably of 1790 (the date on the weathervane), with a central octagonal steeple. Smart W range of c. 1820, with giant pilasters and swagged urns.

RESOLIS 6060

Church and manse standing by themselves in the middle of a rural parish.

Former FREE CHURCH. See Jemimaville.

FREE CHURCH, 1.1km. SW. Harled T-plan kirk (the s jamb containing a vestry), by *William Munro* and *Andrew Maitland*, 1865. Round-arched windows with projecting imposts and lattice glazing, large and Georgian-looking in the long sides, small and almost Romanesque in a stepped arrangement at the gables. On the W gable, a ball-finialled birdcage bellcote. – To the S, gableted MANSE by *Andrew Maitland & Sons*, 1880.

PARISH CHURCH. Harled box built by *James Boag* in 1767. Porches at the gables and N wall, where they cover the head of forestairs to the gallery from the steep bank behind, all built in 1787. Alterations were made by *William Robertson* in 1838–40, the likely date of the Tudor-chimneyed s vestry, big lancet windows, and the W gable's foliage-finialled birdcage bellcote. Inside, a rectangular gallery round three sides, its panelled front and Roman Doric columns still grained. This is probably Robertson's work, as must be the PULPIT, with a Tudor Gothic sounding board, in the centre of the s wall. – Simple Victorian PEWS.

MANSE to the s, designed and built* by *John Rose*, of Invergordon, 1830–2. Front of red sandstone coursers, the pedimented centre containing a three-light first-floor window; bullseye in the tympanum. – To its SE, a contemporary U-plan STEADING.

NEWHALL PRIMARY SCHOOL, 1.3km. E. Plain School Board Gothic, by *Alexander Ross*, 1875. W addition of c. 1900.

RHIROY see ULLAPOOL

ROSEHAUGH 6050
2.5km. W of Avoch

Estate buildings disposed in well-planted landscape along a hill-side rising up from the Moray Firth. The mansion house, demolished in 1959, was one of the largest in Highland. It had

*In partnership with *Donald Munro*, of Tain.

been built for Sir Roderick Mackenzie of Scatwell in 1798 and much enlarged in 1872 by *Alexander Ross* for James Fletcher, a native of Avoch who had made a fortune in Liverpool and bought the estate in 1864. His son James Douglas Fletcher employed *William Flockhart* to carry out a complete remodelling and major extension of the house in 1898–1903, producing what *The Builder* acclaimed as 'grandeur in a fine composition, the design of which is based on what is best in the French Renaissance.'

LODGE on the A832, Italianate by *Alexander Ross*, 1870; pompous urn-topped GATEPIERS. – The site of the mansion house on the hill to the NW is marked by massively buttressed RETAINING WALLS, their present appearance dating from the 1890s. – Behind the house was the small Tudor POWERHOUSE of *c.* 1900. L-plan, each wing with a pyramid roof. – Built into the hillside to its E is the contemporary WINE STORE. Tudor again, with concave moulded openings and lozenged panels on the parapet. Door hinges decorated with saltires. – To the N, GRAYS COTTAGE, English Arts and Crafts of *c.* 1900, its mansard roof partly tiled. Big front chimney flanked by the small windows of an inglenook. Half-timbering at the gables and porch. – To the NW, the rendered LAUNDRY, again English Arts and Crafts of *c.* 1900, with a tiled gambrel roof, touches of half-timbering, pedimented dormers and a rustic porch. Sturdy rubble battered buttresses and chimney; deep cavetto cornice, the rhones carried on scrolled cast-iron brackets. – STABLES E of the mansion house, originally a mid-C19 three-sided court but remodelled by *Alexander Ross* in 1874 and again more enjoyably *c.* 1900, when was added the N range with mullioned windows and a large battered chimney. More mullioned windows and battered chimneys of *c.* 1900 at the S range, which acquired an off-centre shaped gable and a squat conical-roofed round tower at the SE corner. – Further E, the DAIRY of *c.* 1910, again English Arts and Crafts, with red-tiled roofs. Cottage at the W end with a tall broad-eaved roof and centre chimney. From it a wooden arcade runs in front of the dairy itself, its small front block pyramid-roofed, its long rear portion piend-roofed, to the gambrel-roofed byre. Behind the byre, a low stone barn with battered buttresses.

ROSEMARKIE

7050

Sizeable village, the first seat of the cathedral church of Ross traditionally founded by St Boniface in the C7. In the C13, when the cathedral was moved to Fortrose, Rosemarkie was made a burgh of the Bishops of Ross, but by 1590 it was regarded only as an appendage of Fortrose. Despite its long history, nothing earlier than the C18 is now visible.

PARISH CHURCH, off High Street. Only glimpsed from the street but a landmark from the sea, it was built by *Charles Falconer* and *John Watson*, masons, and *James McLean*, wright, in 1818–21. The body is a big ashlar-fronted box with extravagant flowery finials at the corners* and a battlemented vestry projecting from the s side. The hoodmoulded windows' Gothic glazing bars are replacements (probably for Y-tracery) by *John Robertson*, 1894. w tower with tall crocketed pinnacles at the corners of its corbelled and battlemented parapet; the second-stage windows' hoodmoulds end in carved human heads. The interior, originally a plain galleried meeting hall, was pitch-pine Gothicized in 1894 by *Robertson*, who provided new gallery fronts, their supporting shafted pillars carried up to support plaster arcades dividing the single space into a nave and aisles. Contemporary collar-braced wood roof under the Georgian coved ceiling. – FURNISHINGS all of 1894, but the massive PULPIT incorporates the Gothick canopy of 1821. – On the w wall at gallery level, two large but chaste early C19 marble TABLETS to members of the Fowler family, both signed by *James Dalziel* of Edinburgh, the top of one carved with cherubs' heads, the other with an urn.

On the graveyard's s wall, a big MONUMENT to the Houston family, dated 1766 but very old-fashioned. Coat of arms and an angel's head in the steep pediment; reminders of mortality on the panel at the base.

GORDON MEMORIAL HALL, Courthill Road. By *J. Pond Macdonald*, 1904.

DESCRIPTION

MANSE BRAE is the s approach. On the r., the OLD MANSE of 1831–3 by *James McLean* and *Donald Mackintosh*; *John Watson* was the mason and *Donald Macphail* the wright. Its back faces the road, with a ground-floor Venetian window in the pedimented centre. Grand E front, the centre pediment opened to receive the top of a round-headed overarch above the first-floor Venetian window. Three-light ground-floor windows flanking the elliptically fanlit door. To the s, piend-roofed office court built by *Charles Falconer* and *John Watson*, masons, and *James Grant*, wright, in 1816. At the road's sharp bend to the r., a long white harled early C19 range (GOLLANHEAD HOUSE and COTTAGE). In HAWKHILL ROAD to the E, the MARINE HOTEL, a huge late Victorian Italianate villa, much altered and extended. HIGH STREET continues the main road with vernacular C19 houses and cottages, some with their gables to the street. A touch of civic dignity is provided by Nos. 12–14's mid-C19 miniature Town Hall shopfront, with Roman Doric columns at the centre door. Entrance to the Parish Church (*see* above) through a gap in the buildings. The harled GROAM HOUSE of *c.* 1800 was heavily restored after a fire *c.* 1978. Closing the vista is the tiny PLOUGH INN, rebuilt in 1907 with twin oriels flanking an inscription plaque. In BRIDGE STREET

*Some replaced in the restoration of 1984–5.

to the l., a row of mid-C19 white harled cottages, FULMAR
COTTAGE and BURNSIDE COTTAGE with decorative club
skewputts.

ROSSKEEN

The Parish Church is cut off from the Cromarty Firth by the
railway; the Free Church stands beside the A9 to the N.

FREE CHURCH. Tall Gothic box of *c*. 1870. Minimally projecting
N 'transepts' with big three-light windows. Four-light window
and pinnacled angle buttresses at the S gable. To its l., an
octagonal steeple; on the r., a transeptal stair turret. Inside,
gallery round three sides, the pulpit at the N end.

33 OLD PARISH CHURCH. Disused. 1830–2, by *James Smith* of
Edinburgh, and very urbane. Piend-roofed harled box, the
windows (many dummies) segmental-arched above, roundheaded below. In the S front the two flanking the pulpit rise
through the two storeys, each of three lights under an overall
fanlight. Between them projects the vestry-cum-belfry tower,
its first stage square, its second with canted corners, its top a
lead-domed octagon. Piend-roofed porches in the centres of
the other fronts. Inside, a semi-octagonal gallery on fluted cast-
iron columns. – Canopied PULPIT with Adamish enrichment.

At the GRAVEYARD's entrance, corniced GATEPIERS of *c*.
1832. – Outside, a MOUNTING BLOCK. – Immediately NE of
the church is the MAUSOLEUM of the Munros of Newmore,
built in 1664, with a moulded cornice and thistle finials on the
gables. Simply moulded S door flanked by roundheaded panels
carved with fruit; on each side a double lancet. The wrought-
iron gate with leafy decoration in a C17 manner presumably
dates from the restoration of 1908. Triple lancet in the W
gable. Interior with a segmental-arched recess in the E wall now
containing a weathered heraldic graveslab. – E of this, remains
of the FORMER PARISH CHURCH* converted into burial
enclosures. The ashlar-walled enclosure projecting at the SW
corner is dated 1675 above its moulded door. In its W wall, a
short window with clumsy intersecting tracery. A late Georgian
enclosure abuts it on the E. The roofless body of the church (its
walls reduced in height) is of harled rubble. C17 moulded
doorpiece in the E gable. The N 'aisle' was added by Sir William
Gordon of Invergordon in 1727 and in 1884 acquired a heavy
Greek temple front with a Celtic cross and anchor carved in
the pediment.

PARISH CHURCH. *See* Alness.

---

*It was probably built in the C17, its roof thatched until covered with slates in
1753.

SCOTSBURN HOUSE
5.4km. w of Logie Easter

7070

Laird's house of 1800–10. Two storeys and a basement, five bays. Corniced door at the centre.

SHANDWICK *see* BALINTORE

SHANDWICK HOUSE
2.1km. NE of Milton of Kildary

7070

Derelict harled front block of a U-plan house built by John Cockburn Ross of Shandwick, *c.* 1790–1805. Two storeys and three bays, the centre a big bow with a rather insubstantial-looking console-corniced door. In the straight outer bays, Venetian windows at the first floor. Crenellated parapet, in contrast with the classicism of the rest. The two back wings were demolished when a new mansion house was built to the s in 1936–7.

SHIELDAIG

8050

One-sided row of houses on the shore of Loch Shieldaig, most of the buildings C19 vernacular, several badly altered.

FREE CHURCH. Disused. By *W. C. Joass*, 1876–7. Broad rectangle with round-arched windows. – Contemporary MANSE adjoining.

FREE PRESBYTERIAN CHURCH. Drydashed box; by *Ross & Macbeth*, 1895.

PARISH CHURCH. Built as the United Free Church, *c.* 1910. White harled and humble, with a tiny bellcote.

STRATHCONON

3050

Hamlet beside the River Conon.

CHURCH. Built as a Free church in 1892. Solid box with a gableted wooden bellcote projected on heavy stone corbelling at the E gable. Also at this gable, a muscular buttressed and gableted porch.

PARISH CHURCH, 1.2km. SW. T-plan rubble-walled 'Parliamentary' church (i.e. to *William Thomson*'s design) built by *John Davidson* and *Thomas Macfarlane* in 1830. Tudor-arched doors and Y-traceried windows with lattice glazing. Spikily pinnacled birdcage bellcote on the W gable. Much altered interior.

Contemporary former MANSE to the E, of the standard single-storey 'Parliamentary' type (i.e. probably by *James Smith*).

HALL. Built *c.* 1900. Of white-painted wood with black trimmings and a corrugated iron roof.

PRIMARY SCHOOL. By *W. C. Joass*, 1876, small and domestic-looking.

STRATHCONON HOUSE. Harled neo-Georgian by *Francis Johnson*, 1986, the exterior hinting at the internal plan. Two two-storey blocks side by side, the piend-roofed front one slightly shorter than the back and with a higher ground floor, since it contains the principal rooms. Bowed centrepiece, its garden door in a heavily rusticated and corniced surround under a coat of arms. At the centre of the back block's N front, a bay window. Rising from behind the front block, an octagonal cupola topped by a stag weathervane. Single-storey E wing stepping back in three stages. The entrance is at the open-pedimented W gable of the back block. Pedimented Roman Doric portico projecting from an overarch which rises to the attic. Ground-floor Venetian window in the slightly recessed W end of the front block.

Inside, to the S of the entrance hall is a corridor running E along the spine of the house. For its progress through the main part of the house it has segmental arches springing from anta pilasters and panelled groin vaults. In the centre of the main house it is interrupted by a double-bow-ended stairhall, the stair rising round the N end, its landing cantilevered out round the other sides; wrought-iron balustrade decorated with thistles and barley. Semi-domes over the ends. At the ceiling's centre, an octagonal glazed opening allowing a view up to the base of the cupola, decorated with compass and an arrow so the house's occupants can see the direction of the wind on their way to breakfast. On the ground floor, N of the stairhall, a semi-octagonal-ended small dining room. S of the stairhall, a little octagonal ante-room with alternating doors and niches and, to its S, a circular garden room. W of the ante-room is the drawing room, its canted corners containing radiators. Enriched plaster ceiling with a central circle and swagged semicircles at the ends; thistle and rose embellishments. More thistles and roses, together with a flaming ewer, on the chimneypiece, carved by *Dick Reid*. E of the ante-room is the dining room, its corners cut out to house radiators. Another enriched ceiling, its Greek-key-bordered centre panel set in a frame of Gothick arcading; armorial crests at the ends. Pedimented chimneypiece, its pulvinated frieze with a central panel bearing a stag's head. In the billiard room at the house's NE corner, a white marble columned chimneypiece of *c.* 1800; carved thistles at its centre and ends.

4050

STRATHPEFFER

A C19 spa, now providing accommodation for coach parties touring the Highlands. In 1772 Dr Donald Munro gave a paper on the 'Castle Leod Water' to the Royal Society, and the sulphurated Strathpeffer waters seem to have enjoyed a limited local popularity in the late C18.* A village was projected in 1800 and plots for lodging houses offered for sale in 1806, but only after the first pump room was built in 1819 were 'a number of respectable-looking buildings ... for the accommodation of visitors'‡ put up. In 1860 *George Devey* produced a layout plan for the village's further development and, although it was not adhered to at all closely, some new houses and hotels came after the rebuilding of the pump room in 1861. The opening of a branch railway line from Dingwall in 1885 was followed by about twenty years of villa building, and then in 1911 by the opening of the railway company's massive Highland Hotel. Spas have lost popularity since the First World War, and Strathpeffer's main pump room was finally demolished in 1950. The railway is now closed and the casual visitor may have difficulty in noticing any village vitality.

CHURCHES

FODDERTY AND STRATHPEFFER PARISH CHURCH. By *William C. Joass*, 1888–90. Large and prosperous buttressed whinstone box with a slate-spired wooden cupola. The S front is gripped by corner towers which are broached to fat octagons covered with shallow-pitched lucarned stone spires. Above the broad entrance doorway, a squat five-light window with elaborate late Gothic tracery.

ST ANNE (Episcopal). Designed by *John Robertson* as a memorial to Anne, Duchess of Sutherland and Countess of Cromartie. The four-bay nave and N aisle were built in 1890–2, the one-bay chancel in 1898–9. Stolid Dec with fat pinnacles at the corners, except on the NW, where a conical-roofed tower rises over the entrance; steep gableted dormers on the nave roof for a picturesque village touch. In the nave's N wall, cinquefoil clearstorey windows above the aisle's almost flat roof. Inside, braced-collar roofs over the nave and chancel. Braced roof over the aisle, whose depressed arches are carried on fat columns. – On the chancel arch's S side, an expensive but routine Gothic PULPIT of Caen stone (now painted) and alabaster of *c.* 1910. – On the N, ORGAN by *William Hill & Son, Norman & Beardmore*, *c.* 1935. – Marble and alabaster Gothic ALTAR and REREDOS of 1916, the altar's front carved with reliefs of the Annunciation, Adoration of the Shepherds, and the Holy Family, the reredos with the Ascension and adoring angels. – In the chancel's S wall, an elaborate Gothic CREDENCE, again of alabaster. – STAINED GLASS. Three-light E window (the Agony, Crucifixion, and Way of the Cross) by *James Powell & Sons*, 1891. – In the nave's S wall, a scheme (Scenes from the Life of Our Lord) by *Heaton, Butler & Bayne*, 1892–*c.* 1910. – The main W window (Christ Healing the Woman with an Effusion of Blood)

*'Although the water is at first somewhat repulsive in odour and taste, it soon becomes by a little perseverance quite palatable', reported Dr Manson in the mid-C19.

‡So they were described in 1838 by the Minister of Fodderty in his report for *The New Statistical Account of Scotland*.

of 1891. – Below it, three small lancets (St John, 'Suffer little children to come unto Me', and Elijah) by *T. F. Curtis, Ward & Hughes, c.* 1900. – Also by *Curtis, Ward & Hughes,* 1899–*c.* 1901, the figures of Apostles in the N aisle.

STRATHPEFFER FREE CHURCH. Whinstone and sandstone rectangle by *William C. Joass,* 1886, making the most of a prominent site. S gable flanked by a transeptal porch on the r.; on the l., a gabled tower incongruously topped by a slate spire. In the gable's front, three widely spaced lancets below five close-set lights; trefoil opening in the apex.

PUBLIC BUILDINGS

NICOLSON MACKENZIE MEMORIAL HOSPITAL. Dated 1896. Small, with a big bay window to the S.

PUMP ROOM. Originally the Upper Pump Room. Begun *c.* 1860 and later extended S. Square porch, its steep pavilion roof with half-timbered dormers and a wooden cupola. Inside, the walls are covered with green and white tiles.

RAILWAY STATION. Now craft workshops, the old line a sunken rosebed. By *Murdoch Paterson,* 1885. Picturesque wooden building, the deep, gableted glass-and-wood awning over the platform supported by cast-iron columns.

SPA PAVILION. By *William C. Joass,* 1879. Broad gable front with carved bargeboards and a huge lunette. The lower verandah on three sides has been boarded in.

DESCRIPTION

THE SQUARE is Strathpeffer's centre. In the middle, wrought-iron railings of 1975 enclosing the MORRISON WELL, a small square basin with steps down. High on the hill to the W, the huge HIGHLAND HOTEL by *Cameron & Burnett,* 1909–11, harled, with half-timbered touches, the ends carried up as Germanic towers. In the Square's SW corner, the early C19 pedimented SPA COTTAGE, with a Regency verandah and porch; the baroque stone dormer is a late Victorian addition. Regency again at the NW corner's WHITE LODGE, its tree-trunk porch presumably a later embellishment. Behind is the single-storey HEATHERLIE by *Duncan Cameron,* 1895–7, dottily pretty with half-timbering and a ridiculous red-tiled steeple. On the Square's S side, the Pump Room and Spa Pavilion (*see* Public Buildings, above). E of the Square, a row of late C19 shops enlivened by a couple of shaped gables. Opposite is the diminutive harled and half-timbered BANK OF SCOTLAND of *c.* 1890, half-hidden by CRAIGVAR, Georgian-survival of *c.* 1860, but with bay windows. More 1860s Georgian-survival at CABERFEIDH HOUSE facing the STRATH-PEFFER HOTEL by *William C. Joass,* 1877–8, lumpish despite its iron-balconied wooden verandah. Set well back in its own grounds to the S is the BEN WYVIS HOTEL, opened in 1879 and looking like a vastly overgrown villa. It is probably by

Joass, who designed additions in 1884. Back in the main street, TIMARU by *Alexander Ross*, 1877, with a two-tier verandah, and the prettily bargeboarded TIMUKA, under a corrugated iron roof. At the village's E end, THE RED HOUSE of 1880, its jettied upper floor tile-hung. Opposite is the road down to the Railway Station (*see* Public Buildings, above).

Lane up the hill to the NE. In a field on its r., the EAGLE STONE (CLACH TIOMPAN), a fat slab whose top is partly broken and the base now set in concrete. Its front was carved in the late C7 or C8 with a determined-looking incised eagle under a decorated 'horseshoe' symbol. Higher up, EAGLESTONE HOUSE is of *c.* 1860, a *cottage orné* with bowed ends and centre porch; the roof projects over cast-iron columns to form a verandah. Further N, WINDSOR LODGE, dated 1890, and THE CRAIG (by *Joass*, 1889), both routinely gableted. Much more enjoyable is the acroterion-finialled, gabled and gableted DUNNICHEN of 1902, its glass-and-wood porch covered with red tiles. HOLLY LODGE of 1901 uses some of the same details to less effect but has an Italianate tower to compensate. Another Italian tower on the much plainer STRATHBRAN of 1882. Further W, FRANCISVILLE, a late C19 cottage with a tree-trunk porch. A more delicate wooden porch on the earlier harled cottage next door. Behind them, a small C19 GRAVEYARD. The road S past the Nicolson Mackenzie Memorial Hospital (*see* Public Buildings, above) leads down to the harled KINNETTAS HOUSE, a smart piend-roofed farmhouse villa of *c.* 1830, its first-floor casements' horizontal panes still intact. Beyond is the slightly later recessed-centred HAMILTON HOUSE, now with a single-storey wooden outshot across the front.

CASTLE LEOD. *See* p. 392.

KILVANNIE MANOR, 2.2km. NE. Prosperous early C19 farmhouse of cherrycock-pointed rough ashlar. In the centre, a later battlemented porch. The end bays' round-arched French windows and the flat-roofed dormers are C20 contributions.

FORT, Knock Farril, 2km. E. Oblong hilltop fort of the first millennium B.C., its stone rampart heavily vitrified so presumably originally laced with timber.

STROME CASTLE
6.1km. SW of Lochcarron

8030

Ruinous remains of a stronghold built on top of a promontory jutting into Loch Carron. The castle was in existence by 1472, when Alan Macildny, chief of Clan Cameron, was appointed its constable by Celestine, Lord of Lochalsh, who had acquired a charter of the surrounding lands from his brother John, Earl of Ross and Lord of the Isles, eight years before. After passing by descent to the Macdonalds of Glengarry the castle was captured and destroyed by Colin Mackenzie of Kintail in 1602. It has been a rubble-built rectangular enclosure with a door in the long N wall approached from a narrow path along the cliffside. In the W wall, a second door onto the promontory's tip. The enclosure's E end seems to have been filled by a keep overlooking the landward approach.

SUDDIE *see* EASTER SUDDIE

7080

TAIN

A market town which first grew up around the sanctuary and pilgrimage place associated with St Duthac. It seems to have been a burgh of barony by 1439 and was classed as a royal burgh by 1567, when Tain was first represented in Parliament. Redevelopment and expansion began in the late C18 and continued through the C19, accompanied by realignment of the hitherto notoriously irregular street pattern. A by-pass was built in 1979.

CHURCHES

FREE CHURCH, Scotsburn Road. Buttressed brick hall, dated 1938.

FREE PRESBYTERIAN CHURCH, King Street. Built as a United Secession chapel in 1839. Simple preaching box with ball-finialled gables. Interior remodelled and new glazing put in the round-arched windows by *William Mackintosh*, 1879.

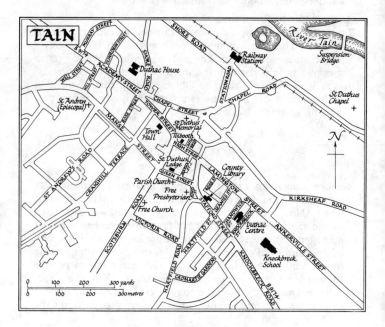

Former PARISH CHURCH, Stafford Street. Now the Duthac Centre; *see* Public Buildings, below.

PARISH CHURCH, Queen Street. Originally Tain Free Church. By *Andrew Maitland & Sons*, 1891–2. Huge Mannerist Italianate front just missing excitement. A giant Corinthian order carries the central pediment; Ionic order at the segmental-pedimented door. Campanile to the l.; at its top, a square Corinthian-pilastered belfry (without bells) carrying a round Corinthian-columned cupola. All this is a screen for the plain two-storey rectangle behind. The interior is divided into a nave and aisles by cast-iron columns (superimposed Doric and Corinthian) rising through the galleries to carry broad basket-arched arcades. Compartmented ceilings, the nave's coved and higher. – Pitch-pine GALLERY FRONTS (made by *Murdo Urquhart*), with blind Romanesque arcading. – At the s end, a shallow Corinthian-pilastered recess intended for the massive PULPIT (also by *Urquhart*), but this was pulled forward when the ORGAN by *E. H. Lawton* was introduced in 1931. – STAINED GLASS. Circular light above the organ (St Paul at Athens) of 1892. – l. of the pulpit, a colourfully modernistic window (Our Lord Healing, and the Good Samaritan) by *Douglas Hamilton*, 1950. – To the r., a characteristically expressionist window (Christ the Teacher) by *William Wilson*, 1966. – Also by Wilson, two lights (St Margaret of Scotland and St Duthac) in the E wall, 1970. – The w wall's two lights (King Solomon and St John the Divine) are by *Mary I. Wood*, 1967, sketchily drawn and brightly coloured.

ST ANDREW (Episcopal), Manse Street. By *Ross & Macbeth*, 1887. Southern English picturesque, with a steep roof and a spired wooden bellcote on the w gable. Inside, nave and one-bay chancel under a continuous wooden roof. The lancets of the side walls are grouped (pairs in the nave, triplets in the chancel) under segmental rear-arches, a detail taken from Kilmuir Wester Church's w window. – STAINED GLASS. In the E window's centre lancet, the Crucifixion, by *Ward & Hughes*, 1887. – In the w window, Our Lord with two Viking saints, after 1909. – The chancel's s window (King David and Bathsheba mourning the death of their child) is signed by *Ward & Hughes*, c. 1890. – Its N window (Miriam, David and St Cecilia) is by *William Wilson*, 1961. – In the nave's s wall, E window (the Women at the Tomb) by *Ballantine & Gardiner*, c. 1895; w window (St Andrew and St Margaret of Scotland) by *A. L. Ward*, 1910. – In the N wall, one window (Dorcas and St Margaret of Scotland) by *William Wilson*, 1955. – ORGAN by *Hamilton*.

ST DUTHUS CHAPEL, Chapel Road. Traditionally identified as the chapel dedicated to St Duthac which was burned in 1427. Ruined and roofless, it makes a shaggy presence in the prim Victorian cemetery now surrounding it. Simple rectangle, coarsely built of large sandstone blocks. Putlock holes in the gables' outer faces, their purpose unclear. A narrow roundheaded window in the centre of the s wall, another high up in the W gable, both suggestive of an early C13 date.

ST DUTHUS MEMORIAL CHURCH, Castle Brae. Two medieval churches side by side in a tidy graveyard. The roofless S church was probably built as the parish church,* c. 1300. Small rubble rectangle. In the S wall, a double lancet and door. Triple lancet in the E gable; the off-centre round-arched recess below was probably made for a later monument.

12   The N church is very much grander, built for the college of canons founded by Thomas Hay, Bishop of Ross, in 1487 at the instigation of James III, used and much altered as a parish church from the Reformation until 1814, and then heavily restored by *Robert Matheson* in 1859–70 and *Hippolyte J. Blanc* in the 1890s.

Elegantly simple tall buttressed rectangle, the C19 work's yellow sandstone contrasting with the pink C15 masonry. The W gable's four-light Y-traceried window is flanked by small canopied image niches, the l. containing the figure of a bishop (possibly St Duthac or Duthus) which was broken off from a font found inside the church c. 1790. In each of the long sides' W bays, a hoodmoulded door. That on the N has simple chamfered margins. The S is a pointed arch of two orders with plainly moulded capitals and bases; its hoodmoulds' labels, carved with the heads of a king and a bishop, are C19 replacements. In the S side's other bays, three- and four-light Y-traceried windows, the E with quatrefoils in the intersecting arcs. In the more exposed N wall, simple lancets. Geometrical tracery in the E gable's five-light window.

The interior is now one space covered by a C19 wooden roof, but a trefoil-headed PISCINA in the centre of the S wall may indicate the position of a medieval rood screen. To its E, cusp-arched SEDILIA (the E arch heavily restored). In the E gable, a blocked round-arched doorway which gave access to the (demolished) SE vestry. At the N wall's E end, two rectangular AUMBRIES, the higher one perhaps a post-Reformation insertion. Beside the NW door, a triangular-headed RECESS for a monument, now filled with a pedestal on which rests a GRAVE-SLAB carved with the relief of a priest. – FONT. A plain C13 octagon from the former St Duthus Parish Church at Suddie.

PULPIT in the centre of the S wall. It is of c. 1575 but much restored in the 1890s. Linenfold-panelled base; blind arcading above, with reticulated tracery on the back. Pinnacled and traceried 'parapet' on the sounding board. – STAINED GLASS. All the windows were filled by *James Ballantine & Son* from 1879, mostly with narrative scenes, the most ambitious in the SE (King Malcolm Canmore Conferring upon Tain the Royal Charter) and W (The Adoption of the Confession of Faith by

---

*But it is possible that the adjoining collegiate church replaced the old parish church both physically and functionally and that this is the chapel dedicated to St Duthac which was burnt in 1427 and presumably repaired by 1457, when James II endowed a chaplainry there.

the Scottish Parliament of 1560) windows. – MONUMENTS.
On the E wall, depressed-arched Gothic recesses enclosing
tablets commemorating Patrick Hamilton, protomartyr of the
Reformation, and Thomas Hog who helped persuade William
III to abolish episcopacy in 1689. They are by *J. W. Small*,
1882. – On the W wall, bronze portrait relief of Alexander Taylor
Innes by *H. S. Gamley*, 1913. – On the N wall, a bronze WAR
MEMORIAL tablet with incised figures of a schoolboy and
soldier, by *J. Wippell & Co. Ltd*, 1922. – Marble monument to
Arabella Margaret Rose †1806, with her portrait on an urn
flanked by figures of a mourning lady and a child with a dowsed
torch; it is signed by *Williams* of London. – Bronze portrait of
Alexander Wallace by *Gamley*, 1912. – Stuck high up on the N
wall is the panelled front of the old TRADES LOFT painted with 37
emblems of the crafts and the inscription

1680 GOD SAVE THE KING AND CRAFT AMEN 1776

On the outside of the church's E gable, a small and crude
classical aedicule to Hugh Munro †1701 and his first wife, Jean
Thomson. – On the former Parish Church's N wall, C17 heraldic
graveslab with emblems of mortality below and an angel of the
Resurrection above. – Inside, on the N wall, old-fashioned mid-
C18 aedicule (now missing its columns) to George Mackenzie
Ross of Aldie. On the frieze, angels' heads and a skeleton lying
to attention; on top, an armorial panel with an angel blowing
the Last Trump on its r.

ST VINCENT DE PAUL (R.C.), Cameron Road. By *Trevor Black*
of *Thoms & Nairn*, 1985–6. Drydashed and concrete-tiled, the
roof pulled sharply up at a short E gable cutting across the
corner of the square. Free-standing bell tower to the W. Neatly
angular interior. Concealed lighting over the altar; behind it, a
brick wall, in contrast to the others' white plaster.

PUBLIC BUILDINGS

COUNTY LIBRARY, Stafford Street. Small, with a baroque door.
Dated 1903.
CRAIGHILL PRIMARY SCHOOL, Craighill Terrace. By
Thomson, Taylor, Craig & Donald, 1975. Formally disposed
single-storey blockwork blocks.
DUTHAC CENTRE, Stafford Street. Built as Tain Parish Church
in 1811–14; *James Smith* was the architect. Piend-roofed box,
the ashlar front broken by insubstantial buttresses. Large
Gothick-traceried windows flanking the pulpit's position. The
slightly projecting ends are dressed up as towers with battlemented screen-walled tops. Agreeable if not very ecclesiastical,
now half-hidden by a huge monkey-puzzle tree. Less welcome
are the harled and crowstepped boxes added at each end and
the more recent W and N extensions.
DUTHAC HOUSE, Academy Street. Originally Tain Academy.
By *James Smith*, 1810–13. U-plan ashlar front, with a Roman
Doric doorpiece in the centre and three-light windows at the
ends. It must have looked less severe before a small observatory

cupola was removed in 1826. At the rear, HALL added by *Andrew Maitland & Sons*, 1896, with Diocletian windows in the pedimented gables. Converted to an old people's home, 1980.

KNOCKBRECK SCHOOL, Ankerville Street. Disused. By *Andrew Maitland & Sons*, 1877. Long and low; at each end a Gothic gable, the r. with a gableted bellcote topped by a flowery wrought-iron finial.

RAILWAY STATION, Station Road. By *Joseph Mitchell & Co.*, 1864. H-plan, with verandahs between the gables. – Lattice-girder footbridge across the tracks.

ST DUTHUS LODGE, Queen Street. Dated 1895. Small and crowstepped.

SUSPENSION BRIDGE, off Chapel Road. Designed by *David J. Reid* and made by the *Rose Street Foundry* of Inverness, 1901–2, its prettiness hidden by battleship grey paint.

TAIN ROYAL ACADEMY, Hartfield Road. By *Ross and Cromarty County Council* (project architects: *G. B. Smith* and *Hugh Crawford*), 1968–9. Curtain-walled, with baby-blue panels. Swimming pool and games hall extension by *Highland Regional Council* (project architect: *T. Forbes*).

99 TOLBOOTH AND SHERIFF COURT, High Street. The Tolbooth was built by the master mason *Alexander Stronach* in 1706–8, its defensive appearance absurdly old-fashioned. It is a square tower of rough ashlar, relieved only by the stringcourses (the lowest altered in the C19) marking each of the three stages. The small spouts draining the roof are swallowed up in the parapet added in 1733 and remodelled with a huge merlon on each face when the present clock was installed in 1877. At each corner, a bartizan, not projecting but set prudently back on the tower; tiny lucarnes on their stone spires. Within this parapet, a round steeple with the same lucarnes on its spire.

The Sheriff Court to the E was added by *Thomas Brown Jun.* in 1848–9, replacing the C18 council chamber. Unadventurous Tudorish Baronial display of bartizans and pinnacles. In the inner angle stands the MERCAT CROSS, its weathered base perhaps C16, the octagonal shaft and heraldic capital produced by *Andrew Maitland & Sons* in 1895.

TOWN HALL, Tower Street. By *Andrew Maitland & Sons*, 1874–6. 'French Renaissance', said the *Inverness Advertiser*, but in a very free version of the style. Five-light first-floor window framed in a roundheaded overarch, echoed horizontally by the bowed-balustraded balcony. Under the balcony, stilted arches, their columns' capitals carved by *D. & A. Davidson* with heavy foliage.

DESCRIPTION

KNOCKBRECK ROAD leading in from the S gives a glimpse of the gabled and bellcoted rear of Knockbreck School (*see* Public Buildings, above). In STAFFORD STREET the Duthac Centre (*see* Public Buildings, above) is set back behind its front garden and monkey-puzzle tree. Yellow sandstone Georgian-survival terraces follow. A glimpse of the Parish Church's tower (*see* Churches, above) at the end, but the route to the town centre turns down GEANIES STREET, with a view over the Dornoch Firth at its end, and then l. into LAMINGTON STREET, where the tripartite-windowed Nos. 4–8 (dated 1827) adjoin *Andrew Maitland & Sons'* small but authoritarian POST OFFICE of 1910. In ROSS STREET to the S, a Roman Doric doorpiece on the early C19 No. 1.

HIGH STREET begins with THE GROVE, a substantial but now badly altered house of *c.* 1800, standing back on the r. On the l., the ashlar-fronted Nos. 39–43 of *c.* 1830, with a blocking-course jumping up as a panelled parapet at the centre and ends. Contemporary block at Nos. 33–37 on the King Street corner, with tripartite first-floor windows. Opposite is the MONUMENT to Kenneth Murray of Geanies by *Laurence Beveridge*, 1879, a small-scale Dec Gothic version of the Scott Monument at Edinburgh; under the steeple, a white marble bust by *T. Stuart Burnett*. Then the DISTRICT COUNCIL OFFICES, built as the Commercial Bank in 1828, ineptly detailed, with the rusticated quoins of the corner and window colliding; mutuled cavetto cornice. Its W wing projects to face across Bank Street to a late Victorian gable-ended block whose canted corner is heavily corbelled out to the square. A Flemish Renaissance gesture at Nos. 18–22 High Street (by *Andrew Maitland & Sons*, 1896–7) followed by two turn-of-the-century blocks, one with harling, jettying and half-timbering, the other with oriel windows. More frivolity of *c.* 1900 on CASTLE BRAE'S E side, where half-timbering and carved bargeboards are followed by an Olde Worlde addition to the staid Georgian-survival RAILWAY HOTEL of *c.* 1875. High Street's N side ends with the mass of the Tolbooth and Sheriff Court (*see* Public Buildings, above). On the S side, demure late Georgian, into which the neo-Georgian *moderne* ROYAL BANK fails to fit. (Diversion up MARKET STREET, where the CLYDESDALE BANK, by *Andrew Maitland & Sons*, 1878, has a free Renaissance presence quite disproportionate to its size but is outdone by the late Victorian Gothic of No. 4 opposite.) After Market Street, Nos. 11–13 High Street, of *c.* 1830, its ashlar and manners both polished; entablature over its ground-floor shopfronts, another at the wallhead. Closing the street's end is the ROYAL HOTEL by *Andrew Maitland & Sons*, 1872, gabled and gableted Gothic; across the centre, a stone verandah topped by cast-ironwork. At the N end, a steeple stepping out to join the Town Hall (*see* Public Buildings, above). Beyond, on TOWER STREET'S S side, TOWER GARDENS, a big late Georgian house with widely spaced first-floor tripartite windows. Beside it, the mid-C18 No. 5 Tower Street, with a crowstepped gable; the windows which have not been enlarged have chamfered margins. On the corner of Rose Street, the PROCURATOR FISCAL'S OFFICE of *c.* 1900, half-timbered, with carved bargeboards and a red-tiled roof ridge, seems to have escaped from the seaside. More tripartite windows on No. 23 of *c.* 1840. On the street's N side, the villa-like BANK OF SCOTLAND by *George Angus*, 1845, still Georgian, with a pilastered doorpiece. For Duthac House, *see* Public Buildings, above.

Down SHORE ROAD to the N, where a large warehouse (by *Andrew Maitland & Sons*, 1884) has a pair of giant overarches in the gable. To its E, a smaller contemporary with a pedimented hoist door and a machicolated gable.

MANSE STREET to the S leads back into the centre. At its W end, St Andrew's Episcopal Church (*see* Churches, above). On the N side, MANSE HOUSE of *c.* 1800, very plain except for its Victorian wooden porch. On the S side, council housing begun by *J. Hinton Gall & Son* in 1934. Among it, at Nos. 17–19 ST ANDREWS'S ROAD, is the former manse by *James Smith*, 1822–4, with a pedimented centre and panelled angle pilasters. In QUEEN STREET is the Parish Church (*see* Churches, above), fully revealed. At the street's end, the late Victorian GLAD-STONE BUILDINGS, endearingly dumpy Renaissance.

VILLAS

HARTFIELD HOUSE, 1km. S. Shallow U-plan house of two storeys, built *c.* 1830. Pilastered doorpiece at the centre.

KNOCKBRECK HOUSE, 1km. SE. Smart double bow-fronted villa of *c.* 1820. At the straight centre, a Roman Doric columned doorpiece. Giant panelled pilasters flanking the bows. The urns on the overall blocking course were erected in the late C20.

MANSFIELD HOUSE (HOTEL), Scotsburn Road. Begun *c.* 1875 but curiously old-fashioned, looking like a late Georgian villa dressed up *c.* 1860 with battlements and bay windows. Baronial N addition, with a purposeful tower, by *Andrew Maitland & Sons*, 1902.

MORANGIE HOUSE (HOTEL), Morangie Road. Dated 1903. Low-key Baronial, with a small tower over the entrance. In the main rooms, Glasgow-type stained glass in the windows' upper panes.

DISTILLERY

GLENMORANGIE DISTILLERY, 2km. NW. By *Andrew Maitland & Sons*, 1888–9. Extensive collection of rubble buildings. Pagoda ventilators on the kilns.

TARBAT *see* PORTMAHOMACK

7070

TARBAT HOUSE
o.8km. S of Milton of Kildary

84 By *James McLeran*, 1787, an austerely classical design beautifully executed in droved ashlar. Seven-bay front, the centre three

advanced under a pediment. Restrained detail, with a band-course above the ground floor, cornices over the first-floor windows, and a dentilled main cornice. At the door, an architrave superimposed on the pilastered surround. In the harled rear's recessed centre, a three-light first-floor window and a Venetian window above. The E side incorporates some red sandstone rubble stonework from the previous house of *c.* 1690. Stable pavilion to the NW, originally of five bays, the central roundheaded opening set in a segmental overarch; it was extended E by a further bay, probably in the early C19. McLeran's plans show that a balancing NE pavilion (apparently never executed) was intended.

The interior must now (1992) be described in the past tense. From the entrance hall, its ceiling decorated with Adamish enrichment, a two-bay screen with a central Tuscan column opened into the stairhall. Another screen, with a Corinthian column, at the first floor, where the principal rooms (dining room, drawing room and parlour) were ranged along the S front.

TARBAT NESS   9080
4.5km. NE of Portmahomack

LIGHTHOUSE. Built in 1892. Tall red-and-white-striped tower with a machicolated parapet walk round the domed lantern. Utilitarian keepers' houses.

TEANINICH HOUSE   6060
0.5km. S of Alness

Small mansion house of 1784,* enlarged and reclothed in castellated garb in the early C19. The early C19 front block is of three storeys and five bays, the broader centre advanced. Battlemented, with a Tudor-arched entrance and octagonal turrets at the corners. Above, a hoodmoulded Tudor-arched first-floor window and a rose window at the second floor. Crenellated parapet with conical-roofed bartizans at the corners; the outer windows all hoodmoulded. This block is attached to the late C18 two-storey U-plan house which acquired a crenellated parapet in the early C19. Inside, entrance hall, its ceiling enriched in the post-Adam classical manner. At its rear, a Tudor-arched screen with clustered shaft columns opening to the stairhall.

---

*The date on a stone at the back.

TULLOCH CASTLE *see* DINGWALL

ULLAPOOL

Village laid out on a grid pattern by the British Fisheries Society in 1788, when a pier was built and the first lots developed for warehouses, an inn and cottages. Within six years it contained over seventy houses, nearly half of them slated, but almost immediately afterwards the herring deserted Loch Broom and the village, deprived of its main industry, was brought close to collapse. A revival of prosperity came after its purchase by Sir James Matheson in the mid-C19. Ullapool is now a tourist centre as well as a fishing port and also the mainland terminal for the ferry to Lewis.

Former PARISH CHURCH, West Argyle Street. Disused. T-plan 'Parliamentary' church (i.e. to *William Thomson*'s design) of 1829, harled except for the front, which is of rough ashlar. It is of the standard pattern, with Tudor doors and windows and a spikily pinnacled birdcage bellcote. Galleried interior.

FREE CHURCH, Quay Street. By *Andrew Maitland & Sons*, 1908–9. A broad box, the gable front dressed up with three tall lancets and a craggy gableted bellcote.

PARISH CHURCH, Mill Street. Built as Lochbroom Free Church in 1844; designed by *William Henderson* of Aberdeen. Georgian-survival box with a birdcage bellcote and roundheaded windows, their coloured glass and the roof's metal ventilator probably dating from the alterations of 1906.

HIGH SCHOOL, Quay Street. Blocky red sandstone neo-Georgian of 1929.

PIER, Shore Street. Short rubble pier of 1788, much extended in wood and concrete by *G. Woulfe Brenan*, 1912, and again in 1973.

DESCRIPTION. In the one-sided SHORE STREET and WEST SHORE STREET along the edge of Loch Broom, a preponderance of harled C19 vernacular buildings, one on the corner of West Lane poking a gable to see the view. ARGYLE STREET and WEST ARGYLE STREET on the brae behind have more of the same but with undistinguished late C20 intruders. The former Parish Church (*see* above) sulks in a small graveyard. Enjoying itself more is the CALEDONIAN HOTEL, dated 1922, white harled, with black trimmings and octagonal turrets. On the opposite corner of Quay Street is a CLOCK erected in 1899 to commemorate Sir J. Arthur Fowler. Cast-iron pillar carrying the square clock, each of its four pedimented faces' tympana decorated with a crown; on top, an urn whose leafy finial carries a weathervane. In Argyle Street to the E, the early C19 OLD BANK HOUSE, its portico's columns attempting a Roman Doric order.

BROCH, Rhiroy, 4.4km. SE. Ruin of a broch of *c.* 500 B.C.–A.D. 500, sited on the edge of a precipice, part of its wall standing to a height of *c.* 3.5m. Entrance (blocked) at the SE. Inside the court, doors to a wall cell and the stair, from which a higher door gave access to a wooden gallery supported on the scarcement ledge still visible at the N.

FORT, Dun Canna, 7.2km. NW. Heaps of stones round a promontory, the remains of two walls, the outer a broad rampart. This was a fort of the first millennium B.C. or the first millennium A.D.

FORT, Dun Lagaidh, 2.8km. SE. The site is a ridge beside the S shore of Loch Broom, its N and S sides sloping steeply. The W end has been cut off by a massive stone rampart of the first millennium B.C., now vitrified and so originally timber-laced. To the E, a second stretch of rampart with a central entrance. Traces of a thinner outer wall. On the hill's highest part, beside the second rampart, has been built a round dun of the early first millennium A.D. E entrance passage with a wall chamber opening off its N side, both now blocked. On the courtyard's W side, a doorway to a small lobby from which a stair rises within the wall. The ruins of the dun were converted to a small tower, perhaps in the C12. Traces remain of a stone wall built with lime mortar, probably also C12, which has run from the dun to the hill's N and S sides.

URQUHART   5050

Rural parish beside the Cromarty Firth, the church providing a reference point.

Former PARISH CHURCH, 0.6km. N. Ivy-clad ruin of the rectangular rubble church built in 1747–51 and abandoned in 1795. N 'aisle' rebuilt as a mausoleum in the early C19. – In the graveyard's SW corner, a BURIAL ENCLOSURE of c. 1700, the walls topped with diagonally set balusters, the entrance moulded. – Near the churchyard's N end, a wall MONUMENT dated 1741, erected by Mr Alexander Falconer, minister of Urquhart, to his wife, Elizabeth Hossack, and their children, decorated with their arms and initials and two sets of crossbones. – To its E, an enjoyable MONUMENT to James Gray † 1745, with a couple of plump angels trumpeting news of the Resurrection whilst a third attempts to prod a skeleton into life.

PARISH CHURCH. Simple box built in 1795, with roundheaded windows and a birdcage bellcote. In 1894 *Ross & Macbeth* added the long S porch and put Gothic tracery in the rectangular gable windows. Interior recast at the same time.

Former MANSE to the N built in 1777–9. Its front block was added by *William Munro*, 1854–5; corniced doorpiece and horizontal glazing.

URQUHART FERINTOSH FREE CHURCH, 1km. SW. Harled rectangle with roundheaded windows, built in 1843. The SE tower was added by *Thomas Munro*, 1907. Inside its parapet, a spired stone bellcote with thin Romanesque detail at the arched sides. – Behind the church, a three-stall cast-iron URINAL, probably late C19, made by the *Saracen Foundry*, a lion's head projecting from the cornice.

URRAY

Just the church, with its old manse nearby.

FREE CHURCH. *See* Muir of Ord.

PARISH CHURCH. Smart rubble-built rectangle whose erection was ordered by the Presbytery in 1775; work was complete by 1783. Rusticated quoins; cavetto cornice returning at the gables to hint that they have open pediments. On the W end, a birdcage bellcote with ball finials at the corners and top; another ball finial on the E gable. Roundheaded windows with projecting keyblocks and imposts. Originally the S wall had two large centre windows flanking the pulpit and two smaller end windows, each over a console-corniced door. In 1833 *John Mackenzie*, house-carpenter at Dingwall, squeezed a vestry between the two centre windows. The r. door was blocked and the window above deepened in 1890, when the interior was reorientated to the E, and the N and E galleries were removed, an alteration institutionalized by *Ian G. Lindsay*'s formation of a 'sanctuary' in 1937. – W GALLERY probably of *c.* 1780, with thin Roman Doric columns attached to the panelled front. – STAINED-GLASS E window (Suffer the Little Children to come unto Me) signed by *Alexander Strachan*, 1937.

Harled MANSE (now OLD URRAY), 0.5km. N, built in 1814, its pedimented porch added by *John Mackenzie* in 1833, the piend-roofed rear block by *William Robertson*, 1838. Ground-floor windows enlarged as bipartites in 1917.

WYVIS LODGE
14.3km. NW of Evanton

Multi-gabled shooting lodge at the W end of Loch Glass, built in 1886 for Walter Shoolbred, the owner of a firm of cabinet-makers. Two storeys, the lower floor of rubble stonework, the upper rendered and half-timbered. Deep verandah wrapped round the S end. (Interior all panelled, some of the window ingoes containing mirrors. In the back passage and gunroom, the panelling incorporates pieces of deerskin. Inglenook fireplaces in the drawing room, dining room and the first-floor's principal bedroom. Tudorish chimneypiece in the hall.)

STABLES in the same manner as the house. – Beside the loch shore, two rectangular GAME LARDERS, the larger for deer, the smaller for birds.

SHETLAND

A rugged and hilly group of islands *c.* 130km. NE of the Scottish mainland, first occupied by humans by the fourth millennium B.C. Viking invasions from *c.* A.D. 800 made Shetland part of the Norse earldom of Orkney, and like Orkney it was ceded by Denmark to the Scottish Crown in 1469.* Fishing has long been as important to the economy as farming, with oil-related activity an important source of employment and revenue in the late C20.

AITH (MAINLAND)

Small village at the head of Aith Voe, the buildings largely late C20.

CHURCH. White harled mission church of *c.* 1900, with pointed windows. – Contemporary MANSE to the E.

HARBOUR. Concrete pier and slip, probably late C19. They are overlooked by a harled C19 WAREHOUSE of two storeys and seven by four bays.

JUNIOR HIGH SCHOOL. By *Shetland Islands Council*, 1981. Low, with prominent tiled roofs.

BALIASTA (UNST)

A few scattered houses s of Loch of Cliff.

UNST FREE CHURCH. Disused and roofless. Rendered broad box of 1843, with rectangular windows. On the s gable, a pedimented ashlar bellcote. – Harled T-plan MANSE, probably contemporary, to the NW.

UNST PARISH CHURCH. Roofless rubble rectangle built in 1764. In each gable, a round-arched door under a round-arched window (the W window now without its top). The S wall's windows are rectangular. Inside, joist-holes for galleries on the N, W and E.

BALTASOUND JUNIOR HIGH SCHOOL. Part is of 1878. The rest is by *Zetland County Council*, 1967. Curtain-walled front block, saw-tooth roofs behind.

UNST LEISURE CENTRE. By *Faulkner Browns*, 1988. Drydashed

---

*It was received by James III in pledge for 8,000 crowns of the dowry owed him as a result of his marriage to Margaret of Denmark.

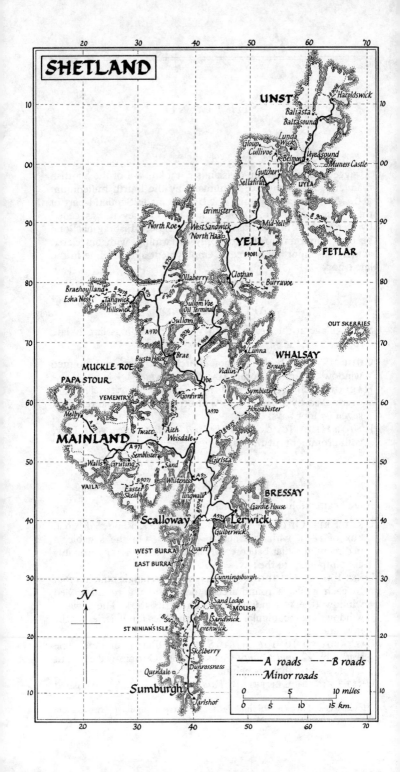

post-Modern, with round windows and low-pitched metal roofs.

BALTASOUND (UNST) 6000

Scatter of houses on the N side of a broad inlet.

ST JOHN'S CHURCH. Built in 1825–7 and much altered in 1959. Simple box, with roundheaded windows. At the SE corner, a square stone porch (the base of a tower), given a large concrete bellcote in 1959, when the W HALL was also built.

JUNIOR HIGH SCHOOL. *See* Baliasta.

HARBOUR. At the W, a rubble-built ramped JETTY, probably early C19, with contemporary STOREHOUSES on the shore behind. – To the E, a concrete PIER of *c*. 1900.

BUNESS. Built for Thomas Edmondston of Buness, *c*. 1835. Very plain two-storey harled house of six bays, crowsteps the only decoration. – To the E, contemporary GATEPIERS with spiky pyramid tops.

BELMONT (UNST) 5000
2.7km. W of Uyeasound

Mansion house of *c*. 1780 built for the Mouats of Garth, commanding the S view over the Wick of Belmont and the terminal of the Yell ferry. Sneck-harled two-storey-and-attic main block of three bays. In its S front, an open-pedimented centrepiece with a console-corniced ground-floor door, first-floor Venetian window, and a roundheaded attic window with projecting imposts and keyblock. Keyblocked outer windows at the first floor. Plain set-back addition on the E. Curved quadrants link the main block to boldly advanced pyramid-roofed pavilions. These are joined to each other by dwarf walls with rusticated gatepiers on the axis of the house.

BEORGS OF HOUSETTER *see* NORTH ROE
(MAINLAND)

BIGTON (MAINLAND) 3020

Tight-knit village of the C18 and C19.

ST NINIAN'S CHURCH. Dated 1905. Broad box with round-arched windows. Gableted S bellcote and a low porch.

BIGTON. Harled L-plan laird's house of 1788. In the inner angle, an early C19 porch with a three-light window under a segmental-arched fanlight.

BRAE (MAINLAND)

Substantial village at the isthmus between Sullom Voe and Busta Voe, the housing largely of the 1970s.

CHURCH. Built as Delting Free Church in 1846 and reduced in size in 1888. Harled box, the E gable dignified with pointed windows and a gableted bellcote.

NORTH MAINLAND SWIMMING POOL. By *Faulkner Browns*, 1988. Post-Modern octagon, drydashed in white and brown and with a blue metal roof.

BUSTA HOUSE. *See* p. 472.

CHAMBERED CAIRN, Islesburgh, 2.3km. w. Remains of a 'heel'-shaped cairn of the second or third millennium B.C., standing on a small coastal promontory. Concave façade *c.* 8.8m. across, the tips of its horns missing. Central entrance into the passage to the rectangular chamber.

CHAMBERED CAIRN, Punds Water, 4.4km. NW. Ruin of a 'heel'-shaped cairn, probably erected in the second or third millennium B.C., standing on a knoll in the middle of moorland. Except at the s corner there can be traced the external wall-face's lowest courses, which show that it rose without a batter. Concave SSE façade, unusually wide at *c.* 15m. across. In its centre, entrance to the slightly curved passage to the roofless but well-preserved trefoil-plan central chamber, its walls built of very large stones.

BRAEHOULLAND (MAINLAND)

Scatter of houses at the E end of the Esha Ness peninsula.

HALL. Built as a United Presbyterian mission church in 1871. Quite plain (and now drydashed) except for a vestigial bellcote and pointed windows in the gable. A w porch has been added. – A contemporary MANSE adjoins the church on the E.

BRESSAY

Good-sized but thinly populated island across the Bressay Sound from Lerwick.

PARISH CHURCH. Simple kirk of 1815, now drydashed. Birdcage bellcote with solid sides. Roundheaded s windows flanking the pulpit, the others rectangular. Inside, Georgian GALLERY on Roman Doric columns round three sides. – Late C19 PULPIT. – STAINED GLASS. Two s windows (St Peter and St Paul) of 1896.

ST MARY'S CHURCH. Roofless ruin of a medieval church in a graveyard beside the Voe of Cullingsburgh. The lower part of the walls of the nave, chancel and N transept survives, built of roughly coursed thin stone slabs. In the s wall, doorway to a missing s transept but not aligned with the N. Inside, three weathered GRAVESLABS. One, carved with superimposed shields under a mantled helm, commemorates Agnes Gifford † 1628. – Another, with two shields surmounted by a heart at the top and reminders of death at the bottom, was the top of a table stone, probably C18. – The third, now very worn, was a monument to Claes Jansen Bryn of the Dutch East India Company † 1636.

LIGHTHOUSE, Kirkabister. By *D. & T. Stevenson*, 1856–8. Harled round tower with a machicolated platform and cupola lantern. M-roofed keepers' houses and flat-roofed stores.

GARDIE HOUSE. Quietly assured mansion house built for William Henderson of Gardie in 1724. As first constructed it belonged to the architectural family of understated piend-roofed boxes popularized in Scotland by Sir William Bruce and James Smith. But this was no dowdy country cousin. Main block of two storeys, harled with rusticated quoins. Seven bays, the windows grouped 1/5/1. *c.* 1905 *John M. Aitken* added a shallowly pedimented attic over the five centre bays but with only three widely spaced windows. Also by Aitken is the para-peted porch, but its door's lugged architrave looks like reused work of 1724. The small single-storey wings are also additions.

WALLED GARDEN of two compartments to the w (front) and s. In its w wall and on the axis of the house, ball-finialled GATEPIERS. At the NW and SW corners of this NW com-partment, corniced BOATHOUSES, each with a round-arched entrance in the centre and niches in the slightly advanced ends. They look early C19.

At the back of the house, a little U-plan COURT OF OFFICES, probably of the later C18. In the centre of its w front, a tower whose roof is now covered with fishscale slates.

BROCH OF BURLAND *see* QUARFF (MAINLAND)

BROCH OF CULSWICK *see* EASTER SKELD (MAINLAND)

BROUGH *see* WHALSAY

BROUGH LODGE *see* FETLAR

BROUGH OF STOAL *see* MID YELL (YELL)

BURGI GEOS *see* GLOUP (YELL)

BURRAVOE (YELL)

Small village at the SW tip of Yell.

CHURCH. Now a house. Dated 1900. White-painted mission chapel with round-arched windows.

ST COLMAN'S CHURCH (Episcopal). Simple Gothic, by *R. T. N. Speir*, 1898–1900. Buttressed nave and apse built of sneck-harled granite with yellow sandstone dressings. Windows of three and four pointed lights in rectangular surrounds. Spired ventilator above the nave's E end. Lean-to W porch. Inside, a braced kingpost roof. – Wooden ALTAR, its front painted with a depiction of the Worship of Heaven.

SOUTH YELL CHURCH, 2.6km. W. Now a house. Tall rendered box built in 1841. Segmental-arched windows. Ball-finialled birdcage bellcote on the W gable, a ball finial on the E.

HARBOUR. C19 rubble pier much patched in concrete. It is watched over by a later C19 two-storey WAREHOUSE of four bays, now extended N as a shop.

SCHOOL. By *Zetland County Council*, 1967.

THE OLD HAA. Late C17 house of the Tyries, the original courtyard on its W now largely demolished for a road. Of the courtyard's walls there survive the E ends of the N and S, the N with a rectangular gateway, perhaps C19, the S with a C17 round-arched gateway surmounted by a panel (coated with cement) carved with the arms and initials of Robert Tyrie together with the date 1672.*

The house itself is a sturdy two-storey-and-attic crowstepped rectangle, now rendered. At each of the long E and W walls, a pair of stepped buttresses, presumably an early strengthening of the fabric; C20 wooden porch between the W pair. The present roof is of corrugated metal; it may have been thatched originally.

Inside, two rooms divided by the scale-and-platt wooden stair on each floor. The first floor's S room has an early C18 lugged-architraved wooden chimneypiece with a heavy corniced mantelshelf and narrow rectangular overmantel, presumably intended for a painting.

BUSTA HOUSE (MAINLAND)
1.8km. SW of Brae

Mansion house built for the Giffords of Busta and now an hotel. The harling hides a tangled building history which is not easy to unravel. It seems to have begun as a three-storey T-plan house, the S jamb placed W of centre. Scrolled skewputts on the jamb and the main block's E gable, but its original W

---

*Most of this S wall fell down in 1990 after being hit by a lorry but is to be rebuilt.

gable is crowstepped. Chamfered arrises at the windows. In the jamb's gable, a round-arched and roll-moulded door; above it, a panel with the conjoined coats of arms and initials of Thomas Gifford and his wife, Elizabeth Mitchell, together with the date 1714, which is plausible enough for the completion of this first stage. The second stage, probably later in the C18, was a short extension of the main block to the w. Then, perhaps still in the C18, came an awkwardly sited two-storey s addition, its NE corner just overlapping the jamb's sw. This range's s gable is crowstepped, as is the w half of its N. Finally there have been the hotel extensions by *Peter Watts*, 1984, a very large N addition, much too anxious to fit in, and a lean-to porch on the w side of the 1714 jamb.

Inside, the main block's first-floor E room (the Gifford Room) has early C18 finishings, with a panelled dado and china cupboard. Also early C18 is the stone chimneypiece, the ingoes panelled with shallow round-arched recesses, but it now has a C20 mantelshelf. The s range's ground floor is filled by the Long Room. Early C20 William-Adam-revival chimneypiece at the s end. At the N, an early C19 chimneypiece with fluted pilasters and frieze. It contains a late C18 cast-iron grate stamped with the arms and initials of George III. Did this come from Fort Charlotte at Lerwick?

The house sits in a rubble WALLED GARDEN. At the entrance, C18 GATEPIERS with stepped tops carrying ball finials.

STANDING STONE, 0.3km. N. Almost square granite monolith, 3.2m. high, probably erected in the second millennium B.C.

CLIBBERSWICK *see* HAROLDSWICK (UNST)

CLICKHIMIN BROCH *see* LERWICK (MAINLAND)

CLOTHAN (YELL) 4080

Place-name on the w coast of Yell.

WEST YELL CHURCH. Built in 1866 as a Free church and manse under a single roof. At the church's N gable, pointed windows and the iron framework for a bell.

CULLIVOE (YELL) 5000

A few houses and a couple of piers round the bay of the eponymous voe, with the church aloof on a hill to the s.

KIRK OF NESS, 2.5km. NW. Fragmentary and half-buried ruin

of the rubble-built medieval church of North Yell. Excavation has revealed a fair amount of the N and some of the S and W walls. It has comprised a nave, *c.* 6.3m. by 4.3m., and chancel, *c.* 4m. by 3.6m. Blocked rectangular door at the S wall's W end. In the chancel's N wall, an aumbry; recess in its S wall.

W of the church, a broken and weathered GRAVESLAB, probably early C18, its top carved with a mantled helm above a coat of arms.

ST OLAF'S CHURCH. Drydashed box built in 1832 but remodelled *c.* 1900, when its E gable was given crenellated corner buttresses and a battlemented thin tower with a projecting porch. Vestry at the W.

4020 ## CUNNINGSBURGH (MAINLAND)

Scattered housing along the A970 and to its E.

CHURCH. Dated 1910. Hall church, the pointed side windows rising into spikily pinnacled gablets.
SCHOOL. By *Baxter, Clark & Paul*, 1977.

DELTING *see* VOE (MAINLAND)

3010 ## DUNROSSNESS (MAINLAND)

Strung-out line of houses.

BAPTIST CHURCH. Built in 1912 to a design by the pastor *William Fotheringham*. Broad buttressed box with stepped gables, the roof now covered with red asbestos tiles. At the NW, a sturdy tower and vestry, both battlemented, with widely spaced merlons.
PARISH CHURCH. Harled kirk built in 1787–90. On the E gable, an ashlar birdcage bellcote with panelled sides and a ball finial. The windows are rectangular except for two tall roundheaded ones with projecting keyblocks and imposts in the centre of the S wall. The windows each side of these seem to have been converted from doors, probably in the later C19, when buttressed and gabled porches were added at the ends. On the N, a Victorian vestry and a flat-roofed C20 hall.

Inside, a GALLERY on thin fluted piers round three sides. – Against the S wall, PULPIT with a pilastered and pedimented back.
CROFT HOUSE MUSEUM, Southvoe. Mid-C19 croft buildings restored as a museum in the 1970s, when the house's front wall was largely rebuilt. Drystone walls, partly rendered; thatched roofs. The house itself is of two rooms. At its E end, a lower block containing a passage and byre. At the back and projecting E of the byre, the stable, potato store and barn, a round kiln at its NW corner. – To the SE, a NORSE MILL.

QUENDALE. *See* p. 504.

QUENDALE. *See* p. 504.

EAST BURRA

3030

Island joined by a short bridge to West Burra.

BAPTIST CHURCH. Built in 1904. Rendered, with a simplified gableted bellcote and pointed windows.

EASTER SKELD (MAINLAND)

3040

Small village, most of the housing late C20.

REAWICK CONGREGATIONAL CHURCH. White harled cruciform, dated 1863. Gableted bellcote on the long N porch;
pointed windows. Inside, a roomy PULPIT, with brass lamp
brackets. – Pretty Victorian HARMONIUM by *W. Doherty &
Co.*, of Clinton, Canada, installed here in 1966.

BROCH OF CULSWICK, 5.6km. W. Broch of *c.* 100 B.C.–A.D.
100, spectacularly sited above the cliffs at the entrance to
Gruting Voe and defended by an outer rampart. Circular as
usual, *c.* 16m. in diameter, the battered outer wall still 3m. high
in places. SE entrance, its lintel a massive triangular stone. Door
checks in the entrance passage. N of the passage is a wall cell,
which has been entered from the court; above its doorway,
rectangular openings to lighten the load on its lintel. Indications
on the inner wall-face of a projecting scarcement *c.* 3m. above
ground. There seem to have been galleries.

ESHA NESS (MAINLAND)

2070

Peninsula on the W of Mainland near its N end.

CROSS KIRK. Featureless remains of a medieval church in a
graveyard. Only the lower courses of the CHURCH's rubble
walls survive. It has been rectangular, 10.6m. by 6.1m. externally, with an entrance in the W gable. – Immediately E of the
church, a large weathered MONUMENT, probably C18, with
two coats of arms at the top and emblems of death at the
bottom. – SE of this, the plain TABLE STONE to Donald Robertson † 1848, its inscription relating that

His death was very much regretted which was caused by the stupidity
of Laurence Tulloch in Clothister who sold him nitre instead of epsom
salts by which he was killed in the space of 5 hours after taking a dose
of it.

ESHANESS LIGHTHOUSE. By *D. Alan Stevenson*, 1925–9. Short
and square tapering tower topped by an octagonal lantern.
Single-storey flat-roofed keepers' houses. All harled.

FAIR ISLE

Hilly cliff-edged island, *c.* 39km. SW of Sumburgh Head at the S tip of the Mainland of Shetland, occupied by a small crofting community famous for its knitwear. In 1954 the island was given by the ornithologist George Waterston to the National Trust for Scotland, which has since encouraged the activities of bird-watchers as well as crofters.

CHURCH OF SCOTLAND. By *Sinclair & Hardie*, 1892. White harled, with roundheaded windows and a gableted bellcote.

METHODIST CHAPEL. Rubble-walled rectangle, built in 1886. Roundheaded windows and a bellcote. Inside, two STAINED-GLASS windows of 1936.

SCHOOL. Built in 1878.

NORTH LIGHTHOUSE. By *D. Alan Stevenson*, 1889–92. Short round tower looking almost squashed by its cupola lantern. Flat-roofed stores at the base.

SOUTH LIGHTHOUSE. By *D. Alan Stevenson*, 1889–92. Round tower but taller than the North Lighthouse so the lantern less dominant, again with flat-roofed stores at the base. Two-storey block of keepers' houses.

THE HAA. Dumpy crowstep-gabled early C18 house.

FETLAR

Substantial island E of Yell. The human population is small, the birds numerous.

PARISH CHURCH, Tresta. Harled rectangle built in 1790. The gableted bellcote and roundheaded windows' wooden Y-tracery date from a Victorian remodelling which gave the interior its present character.

In the graveyard, W of the church, a mid-C18 MONUMENT signed by *John Forbes*. Aedicular, with attached Corinthianish columns. In the steep open pediment, a coat of arms flanked by trumpeting angels and surmounting the initials of James Bonar † 1752 and his wife, Jean Smith † 1737. On the pediment's ends and apex, stumpy pinnacles, probably intended for ball finials.

BROUGH LODGE. Castellated villa built for Sir Arthur Nicolson, *c.* 1830. The house is composed of three parallel oblong blocks, the central of two storeys, the flankers single-storey. On the main block, a parapet and angle bartizans, but the original roof inside the parapet has been replaced by a piended one which sits on top, and the bartizans have lost their battlements. The same treatment has been meted out to the E block, but the W still has its corbelled battlement enclosing a piend roof whose platform top runs into the main block's W wall. In the centre block's S front, a ground-floor window of three pointed lights; at the first floor, two cusped lights under a quatrefoil.

The entrance is from a small courtyard on the N, its W side formed by a rubble screen wall punctuated by basket-arched niches. In this wall, the courtyard's gateway is a round-arched pend under a large shallow pediment containing a coat of arms framed in an aedicule, now bereft of its cornice.

Further N, a slightly recessed wall, again of rubble but with brick dressings, along the W side of a service court. Entrance through a pointed arch under a 'machicolation'. At the court's NW corner, a Gothic-windowed cottage with a tower over the ogee-arched brick doorway. – Attached to the main house and extending SE, a rubble WALLED GARDEN. – On the hill to the NE, a battlemented round tower, the windows either pointed or round-arched.

GARDIE HOUSE *see* BRESSAY

GIRLSTA (MAINLAND) 4050

A few houses, a disused lime quarry with a ruined kiln and a stone pier, beside Wadbister Voe.

METHODIST CHURCH, 1.3km. W. Rubble box built in 1896.
MILL. Built in 1861, a harled rubble range of two storeys and a loft. The store and kiln are well preserved, the mill itself roofless.

GLOUP (YELL) 5000

Place-name at the N of Yell.

FISHERMEN'S MEMORIAL. Erected on the edge of a cliff in memory of the fishermen of Shetland who died in the great storm of 20 July 1881. Late Victorian stone statue of a mother holding her child and using her free arm to shield her eyes as she gazes out to sea.

FORT, Burgi Geos, 3.1km. SW. The site is a cliff-edged prom-ontory reached by a very narrow long neck of land, this danger-ous approach bordered by two rows of stones, the N laid flat, the S set on end. At the neck's end, a wall, *c.* 4m. thick, probably of the first millennium B.C.

GONFIRTH (MAINLAND) 3060

Place-name for a handful of scattered houses at the head of the eponymous firth.

METHODIST CHURCH. Dated 1900. Humble mission church built of sneck-harled granite, with a bellcote on the W gable and a chimney near the E. Pointed W windows, the others simple rectangles.

4090　　　　　　GRIMISTER (YELL)

Just a few houses s of Whale Firth.

CHURCH. Mission chapel of *c.* 1900, with a w porch and vestigial
　bellcote.

2040　　　　　　GRUTING (MAINLAND)

Scattered houses at the head of Gruting Voe.

SETTLEMENT, Gruting School, 0.7km. N. On the boulder-strewn
　hillside N of the road beside Scutta Voe, the base courses of a
　large oval house of the third millennium B.C. Entrance at the
　downhill end; at the inner end, a small cell choked with stones.
　Stone bench recess in the E wall. A second similar house has
　been bisected by the road, and a third is said to have been
　covered by the garage of the nearby school.
SETTLEMENT, Stanydale, 0.9km. N. Group of four oval houses,
　one excavated, and a larger 'temple', all probably of the third
　millennium B.C. The excavated 'temple', *c.* 19.5m. by 14.3m.,
　is like a heel-shaped cairn on plan, with a clearly defined fore-
　court at the E end. Drystone walls built of massive blocks. In
　the forecourt's centre, the entrance to the single oval room
　inside. At the room's inner (W) half, six broad wall-recesses
　separated by boulder partitions faced with upright slabs. In the
　centre of the floor, on the long E–W axis, two large post-holes
　for wooden uprights to carry the roof. The building had small
　hearths round the edge but no central fire. Was this a chieftain's
　hall or was it a temple? Nearby, the unexcavated oval houses.
　To the E, the excavated house, its walls still *c.* 0.76m. high,
　built of rough boulders enclosing a rubble and earth core. It is
　oval, *c.* 17m. by 9.7m. Jinking entrance passage making a porch
　at the SW end. Inside, a large roughly oval room with two small
　recesses on the E side, a stone bench along the W wall and a
　central hearth. Small round cell at the N end.

4030　　　　　　GULBERWICK (MAINLAND)

Extensive settlement, largely C 20.

CHURCH. Squat mission church built in 1897–8, with a bellcote
　feature on the E gable, a cross on the W. Triangular-headed side
　windows; three lancet lights in the W gable.
SCHOOL. L-plan Board school and schoolhouse of 1878–9.

5090　　　　　　GUTCHER (YELL)

Terminal for the Yell–Unst ferry.

HARBOUR. At the E, a breakwater ending in the C 20 ferry pier.
　W of this, a large C 19 rubble-built pier.

SOUTH GARTH, 0.4km. N. Harled mid-C19 laird's house of two storeys and three bays. Three-light ground-floor windows flanking the porch; the first floor's windows are two-light.

BROCH, Burra Ness, 3.4km. SE. Badly ruined broch of *c.* 100 B.C.–A.D. 100, but its wall still standing on the E to a height of 3m. It has contained galleries and an oval chamber. Scarcement in the inner wall-face towards the court. Traces of twin ramparts *c.* 28m. from the broch.

HAROLDSWICK (UNST) 6010

Settlement round a bay, the earliest houses late Georgian. R.A.F. camp at Valsgarth to the N.

CROSS KIRK, Clibberswick. Only the lowest courses of this medieval church's nave walls are visible. They are built of boulder-rubble and form a rectangle *c.* 9.8m. by 6.4m. Foundations of a chancel, *c.* 3.2m. by 4.6m., have been traced. – An outer rectangle of boulders delineates a small surrounding GRAVEYARD.

METHODIST CHURCH, Valsgarth. L-plan group of church and manse, dated 1881. At the church's S gable, a small Gothic bellcote and stone porch. – Gableted MANSE with a Victorian wood-and-glass porch.

UNITED FREE CHURCH. Disused. Harled mission chapel of 1912, with a chimney on the S gable, a porch at the N.

R.A.F. SAXA VORD, Valsgarth. Accommodation and officers' mess by the *Property Services Agency*, 1988. Drydashed, with prominent concrete skews at the steep-pitched roofs.

HILLSIDE *see* VOE (MAINLAND)

HILLSWICK (MAINLAND) 2070

Small village overlooking the Ura Firth.

NORTHMAVINE PARISH CHURCH. By *Roderick Coyne*, 1869. Harled box, with two tiers of pointed windows in the side walls and three at the S gable, whose bellcote's upper part has been replaced with a cross. Galleried interior.

ST MAGNUS BAY HOTEL. Built in 1900 by the North of Scotland & Orkney & Shetland Steam Navigation Company to accommodate package tourists. The materials were imported from Norway. It is of wood, painted black and white. U-plan, with bargeboarded gables; between them, a balconied and iron-crested verandah.

HILLSWICK HOUSE. Harled single-storey, cellar and attic main block of *c.* 1800 with a Venetian door. The bargeboarded dormers are Victorian additions. In front of the garden, contemporary GATEPIERS, one missing its ball finial. The low two-storey SE wing (THE BOOTH) looks early C18.

HOUSABISTER (MAINLAND)

Church standing by itself above the shore of South Nesting Bay.

NESTING PARISH CHURCH. Harled kirk built in 1792–4, the slates of its piended bellcast roof replaced with Redland Cambrian tiles in 1990. In each gable, a keyblocked roundheaded door with projecting imposts. Same detail at the tall windows in the centre of the N side; this wall's outer windows are smaller rectangles. S vestry; on the N, a low walled C19 BURIAL ENCLOSURE. Inside, a GALLERY round three sides. – PULPIT on the N, with a finialled circular sounding board.

JARLSHOF (MAINLAND)
1km. S of Sumburgh

Promontory occupied from c. 2000 B.C. until the C17, the buildings of almost every successive stage of occupation except the last having been abandoned and covered with wind-blown sand before the next group was put up, often on top of the buried earlier ruins. When writing *The Pirate* Sir Walter Scott used the Old House of Sumburgh, the only building then visible, as the model for 'Jarlshof', and the fictional house's name has now been applied to the site as a whole. Excavation, begun in 1897, has uncovered a bewildering complex of drystone rubble walls, now carefully preserved under turf-topped wallheads as a tidy Ancient Monument.

The first settlers probably arrived c. 2000 B.C. They enclosed at least the SE corner of the site with a wall, only two stones thick, of which a short stretch remains at the E edge. Immediately outside the wall to the N, a midden to hold the rubbish (animal bones, shells, quartz artefacts and pottery sherds) thrown over from a stone-built oval hut inside the enclosure. Remains of this hut are now very fragmentary, but excavation uncovered evidence of several layers of building, all of the second millennium B.C. The later layers were destroyed except for a large hearth, a quern and rubbing-stone, and a stone-lined cist, perhaps a water tank. Shell midden just outside the hut to the S.

This earliest settlement seems to have been abandoned and covered by sand before the next stage of occupation began in the first millennium B.C. A wall was built across the promontory from E to W, probably at least as much to protect crops from stock pasturing outside as for defence against human enemies. One stretch of this wall is uncovered at the NE and two more at the W end. The main group of five houses belonging to this later Bronze Age settlement lies S of the earlier house and immediately W of the present Museum. They form a T-shape,

probably giving a misleadingly tight-knit impression, since it is
unlikely that more than two or three were occupied and visible
at any one time. The three making up the cross-bar and the
one at the head of the tail were all originally of the same basic
type. Each was a rough oval entered from the sw; inside, in the
thickness of the stone walls, two w and two e chambers and a
larger chamber at the ne opposite the entrance. Of the ne
house, probably the earliest, little more than a part of the s wall
survives. Quite a lot more remains of the nw building. It may
have been designed primarily to house livestock. Excavation
has disclosed that its large ne chamber had a whalebone teth-
ering ring built into the wall and a saucer-like paved floor,
presumably for the accumulation of dung, from which liquid
manure drained into the central main chamber. Were the
smaller side chambers also for animals or intended for human
occupation? The building was later converted to a house, a
large kerbed hearth being built over the old sump in the central
chamber. Perhaps at the same time a stone-walled oval courtyard was added at the sw, probably to house animals, since its
e wall was pierced by a drain, later blocked when a stepped
passage was constructed to the entrance of the adjoining house.
That house, at the centre of the T's cross-bar, presumably
contemporary with the passage and so considerably later than
the nw house, is the best preserved of the group. At a late stage
in its occupation, after a period of abandonment, it was used
by a smith, perhaps from Ireland, who specialized in making
bronze swords. During his occupancy the original sw entrance
was built up and a new entrance made at the e end of the big
ne cell, the se wall cell became a rubbish dump, and the small
ne cell was altered and given a door. Probably about the same
time a single-cell potter's workshop was built sw of the old
passage to the entrance, back to back with another cell which
was apparently entered from a now lost house to the sw.

Of the two houses which form the tail of the T the n shows
three successive stages of development, each on top of the
previous one. The earliest produced a house of the standard
type, with cells in its thick walls; central hearth revealed by
excavation. After this had been abandoned and largely choked
by sand, there came a second stage of building and occupation,
the protruding top of the original wall being levelled and used
as the foundation for a new, more thinly walled house. This
house was round, again entered from the sw, its doorway's sill
stone being laid across the top of the old doorway. Inside there
was a central hearth (removed during excavation) surrounded
by posts, probably to support the roof. Side compartments were
formed by radiating upright slabs, still surviving at the nw.
Under the floor was a narrow souterrain, presumably for
storage, entered from just inside the entrance and curving round
the site of the hearth. After this house was abandoned in turn
and choked with sand, yet another was built on top of its walls,
again with a central hearth (also removed during excavation)
and with cubicle-like chambers on the n and w. In the e wall,

an opening (later blocked) to an underground passage which steps down to a low souterrain chamber E of the house, its walls formed of upright slabs carrying horizontal masonry, additional support for the flagstone roof provided by stone piers. Attached to the S of this house and at the base of the T-shape's tail are the N two-thirds of a fifth house of the late first millennium B.C. This seems to have been circular, divided by radial walls into compartments, presumably round a central hearth. W of this, remains of a detached roughly circular building, its thin stone wall a revetment holding back the surrounding soil and enclosing a space of c. 7.6m. diameter. Probably originally used as an outhouse or byre, its N arc was later contracted by the erection of an inner wall, perhaps at the same time as the building was converted to a dwelling with the erection of a central hearth. This stage of its development was accompanied by the construction of a souterrain to its NW, the passage entered from a vertical shaft inside the house leading to a roughly rectangular chamber, its roof supported on four oblong stone piers.

A new influx of settlers, probably in the C I A.D., after the earlier houses had been abandoned and covered with sand, produced a building of quite different character. This, still impressively powerful despite having lost its S half to the sea, was a round broch, c. 19.5m. in diameter, the 5.2m.-thick externally battered wall still standing to a height of c. 3m.; it may originally have been as much as 12m. high. The entrance must have been in the missing S segment. Ground-floor wall cells partly survive at the W and E, the E with an entrance from the internal court. Vertical inner wall-face to the court with a projecting scarcement to support the beams of a wooden gallery or floor 2.3m. above the ground. At the court's NW, a well at least 4m. deep, its top part built of masonry with steps down to the rock-cut shaft. From the broch's N, a contemporary wall curving out to form an enclosure on the W side. In the wall's present eroded S end, evidence of a cell.

Soon after completion of the broch the N part of its W enclosure was filled with an aisled round house, originally of c. 9.7m. internal diameter, its S segment awkwardly squashed where it abuts the broch. In the centre of this house, a hearth just visible under a later wall. Radiating from the inner wall-face, stone piers, probably replacements for wooden posts, dividing a ring of paving into compartments; doorways in the piers from one compartment to another. Scarcement c. 1.7m. above the ground, presumably for the beams of the original wooden gallery or roof.

New immigrants in the C 2 or C 3 added more houses inside the broch's enclosure and remodelled the broch itself. Their first major alteration was to build a wall across the aisled round house (largely covering its original hearth), keeping its N half as a semicircular dwelling provided with a new hearth just N of the wall. Much of the house's S half was demolished and its site partly covered by a wheel house built c. 3m. SW of the round house's new S wall and divided by alleyways from the broch itself on the E and the enclosure wall on the W. At this wheel house's NE, a rounded porch. The house itself has been *c.* 11m. in diameter, the interior originally divided by radial walls into eight paved compartments, some with aumbries, each with a stone kerb in front as a protection against sparks from the central hearth. The stone for this house was probably taken from the upper part of the broch, which may then have begun to collapse, the likely explanation for the wheel house's area being contracted by the erection of a straight partition wall *c.* 2m. W of the original side next to the broch and for the entrance being moved from the NE beside the broch to the S. The subsequent rebuilding of the compartment walls in the house's NW arc was the result of a further ill-considered development which weakened this part of the building. This was the construction of a second wheel house directly abutting (and putting pressure on) the first's NE arc and overlaying almost half the formerly habitable N semicircle of the round house, which was now abandoned. This new wheel house was smaller than the first, with an internal diameter of *c.* 7.3m. Entrance on the W through the enclosure wall against which it stood. The interior was again divided into paved compartments by masonry radial walls, their ends faced with upright slabs, their upper parts jettying out to carry roofing slabs. Perhaps a little later a third wheel house (now more fragmentary) was built inside the broch itself. In the floor of its W compartment, a stone-slabbed box. Very scanty remains of a fourth wheel house built against the E side of the broch, its floor later dug into to form a stone-lined store; another contemporary store chamber to the N (now under the S range of Old House of Sumburgh, for which *see* below).

Most of this wheel house was later replaced, perhaps about the C5, by a large round building, probably a byre. Roughly contemporary with this was the construction of a passage house immediately W of the broch's enclosure and blocking the original entrance to the second wheel house, for which a new entrance was made further N. This irregularly shaped passage house was largely underground, its walls revetments to the soil outside. Entrance on its W from a short passage originally reached by a flight of stone steps on the N but later extended W. *c.* 45m. W of the passage house, a stretch of wall running N from the beach for *c.* 20m. and then, after a gap, probably the entrance into this outer enclosure of the settlement, the wall returning E on a line just N of the surviving W stretch of late Bronze Age wall and formerly continuing at least as far as an oval cattle compound directly to the N of the broch's enclosure. This wall seems to be of the early first millennium A.D., perhaps contemporary with the wheel houses, and probably divided the settlement's arable land from the pasture beyond. Near the NW corner of this enclosure, remains of two rounded huts, the N very fragmentary (probably robbed of stone for the construction of the other), the S better preserved, its three entrances (from the NW, NE and SW) evidence of three successive stages of occupation, the last probably datable by the discovery of a stone incised with a Christian cross to the C 8.

Early in the C 9 the settlement was taken over by Vikings, and the exposed foundations of what they built during the next four centuries now give a first impression of a maze without an escape route. However, the general lines of the development and redevelopment of the site are fairly clear. The earliest Viking farm complex consisted of a hall house (orientated E–W) which lies N of the Old House of Sumburgh. It is relatively well preserved, and the original plan can still be made out. The house was oblong, c. 22m. by 12.5m., the side walls slightly bowed. A line of post-holes shows that the E gable was of wooden construction. Inside were two rooms, the W a kitchen with an oven and fireplace, the larger E room the hall, with low stone benches along the side walls and a central hearth. S of this house's W end was an outhouse of which only traces survive. W of the hall house was a small, almost square building containing a well-constructed hearth; it may have been a bath house. N of this possible bath house and abutting the late Iron Age cattle compound was an irregularly shaped stable. c. 18m. W of this was a roughly rectangular smithy and, to its NW, a now very fragmentary barn, its N side built partly over the line of the late Iron Age wall.

In the late C 9 or C 10 this complex grew with the erection of a detached barn S of the smithy and of three oblong houses N of the hall house and at right angles to it. Each of these was detached, the two E having each a narrow walled enclosure on one side. It may have been at this time that the putative bath house was abandoned.

Further development of the settlement took place in the C 11. The original hall house was extended to E and W, the E addition and the greater part of the old hall forming a byre. Of the late C 9 or C 10 houses to its N, the E was largely demolished and the site used for the erection of cattle compounds. The central house's N end was converted to a byre and a large outhouse built to the NW. A new oblong house was erected between the site of the possible bath house and the C 9 smithy, the smithy itself being replaced by a building which extended further N.

Thorough-going reconstruction of the settlement took place in the C 12 or C 13. The hall house's domestic W end was remodelled to form two rooms, each of about the same size, with a new N wall built inside the line of the C 9 wall. A large outhouse to the S (the C 9 one having been demolished), of which fragments survive, may be contemporary with this. The two remaining late C 9 or C 10 houses to the N were demolished, and a very roughly rectangular outhouse range parallel to the hall house was built across their S ends. Immediately W of this range, and at right angles to it, was built a substantial new house, its N end crossing the N foundations of the W late C 9 or C 10 house. The C 11 house W of the site of the possible bath house was rebuilt, except for its W wall, and extended N. W of this, the C11 building on the site of the smithy was enlarged to N and W. Probably at the same time, if not before, the C9 barn and byre were demolished.

Early in the C14 this complex of Viking farm buildings was abandoned and a new farmstead built E of the hall house, its SE end (now demolished in the interests of archaeological discovery) overlying the remains of the Bronze Age settlement. It consisted of two ranges separated by a narrow paved alley, the NE block, over 19m. long, being the farmhouse and the SW a large outhouse with a round kiln projecting at its NW corner. Both were much altered before being abandoned in turn, presumably in the late C16.

The final development at Jarlshof was the erection of the OLD HOUSE OF SUMBURGH immediately NE and partly on top of the C1 broch. In comparison with the earlier remains, its ruins are almost self-explanatory. It forms a quadrangle, probably begun by William Bruce of Symbister, who acquired the King's and Provost's lands of Sumburgh in 1592 and apparently built the N range and enclosed the courtyard. In August 1604, Bruce did a deal with Patrick Stewart, Earl of Orkney, by which he exchanged this estate and the 'hous of Soundburghe' for the lands of Sandwick. When this exchange was reversed in November 1605, the Earl reserved to himself 'the richt and titill of the houss laitlie bigit be the said nobill Lord upone the ground of the saidis landis of Soundburghe on the south syde of the new hall'. This house, presumably built between August 1604 and November 1605, is identifiable as the courtyard's S range, which projected a little E of the original courtyard. A later stage of C17 development was the erection of E and W ranges, both outside the courtyard, whose W wall was used as the W range's E front. The new E range overlapped the S range's NE corner, so extending the courtyard to the E. The house was ruinous by c. 1700, and its courtyard and buildings were used as a graveyard.

The walling is all of rubble. Only the lowest courses survive of the N range, whose ground floor, now divided into several rooms, may originally have been a single hall. Fireplace in the N wall. To its l., a rectangular projection containing an oval recess, possibly a close garderobe.

The W range was demolished in 1951 except for the lower courses of its E wall. Much of the S range still stands, with the remains of a forestair on its N side. The first floor has had a fireplace in each gable, so presumably it contained two rooms. The lower part of the E range survives. At its SE corner, a projecting kiln, probably an addition.

KIRK OF NESS see CULLIVOE (YELL)

LERWICK (MAINLAND)

The commercial and administrative capital of Shetland, built beside the sheltered anchorage of Bressay Sound. In 1625 it was described as 'a desert place', and by 1700 it contained only about two hundred houses. In 1753 it was reported that there were about three hundred houses in Lerwick, 'all built of Stone, and several People of good Fashion inhabit them'. By the end of the C18 the town was noted to contain merchants and shopkeepers as well as sailors and fishermen. Expansion and redevelopment began early in the C19, the town enjoying the status of a burgh of barony after 1818. In 1862 *John M. Aitken* prepared a layout plan for New Town on the higher ground W of the old burgh and substantial villas and a string of churches were built there, the development gaining impetus after a revised layout had been agreed in 1878. C20 expansion, aided by the recent growth of the off-shore oil industry, has added an outer ring of housing and a remodelling of the harbour.

CHURCHES

ADAM CLARKE METHODIST CHURCH, Hillhead. Simplified Romanesque, by *William Parslow*, 1870–2. E gable-front of hammerdressed rubble, the centre slightly advanced under a solid gabled bellcote. Parapeted porch.

BAPTIST CHURCH, Clairmont Place. By *John M. Aitken*, 1894–5. Hall church over a basement, its long sides with tall windows rising into gablets. Minimally projecting full-height porch at the SW corner.

CONGREGATIONAL CHURCH, Clairmont Place. Opened in 1820 but enlarged and recast in 1840 as a tall rubble box. On the gables, spike-topped ball finials. Pointed windows in the long sides; segmental-arched W windows. In 1893 *Alexander Campbell* added the semi-octagonal apse, its E wall rising as a crowstepped gable. At the same time he enlarged the W porch to make a crowstepped hall.

ST CLEMENT'S HALL, St Olaf Street. Broad box designed as a church hall and place of worship for Dutch fishermen; by *T. L. Bruce*, 1909–11. Crowstepped W gable-front of hammerdressed rubble, a Romanesque door under the segmental-arched four-light window. SW tower of four stages, with battered angle buttresses and a crenellated parapet.

ST COLUMBA, Greenfield Place. By *James Milne* of Edinburgh, 1826–9. Urbane two-storey piend-roofed ashlar box of three bays by four, the N front's masonry droved, the sides' and rear's stugged. First-floor belt-course. Upper windows of horizontal proportions. At the N front, delicate moulded margins to the

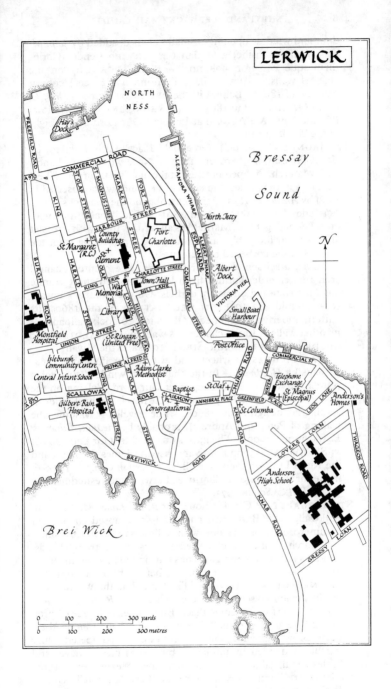

door and window openings. Small s chancel added by *John M. Aitken*, 1895. Inside, a U-plan GALLERY on slender Corin-thianesque cast-iron columns. – Blind ARCADING on the chancel walls. – At the chancel's front, a big neo-Jacobean PULPIT of 1895. – Behind it, the ORGAN by *Bryceson Bros. & Co.*, 1871; enlarged in 1895. – STAINED GLASS. Two windows ('Come Unto Me All ye that Labour'; Our Lord as the Light of the World) of 1895.

ST MAGNUS (Episcopal), Greenfield Place. Early Pointed, by *Alexander Ellis* of Aberdeen, 1863–4. Nave with a low chancel and w* porch. Stepped buttress at the nave's NE corner. Wheel windows in the gables; the chancel's N window was inserted in 1899 by *Alexander Ross*. Organ chamber on the chancel's s side. *Ellis* added the SW tower in 1891–2. Saddleback roof with crowstepped gables. Martial detail at the top, with crosslet arrowslits in the gables and stone spouts projecting from the corners of the corbelled battlement.

Inside, a scissors roof over the nave. The pointed chancel arch's inner order springs from leafy-capitalled short granite columns standing on heavy corbels. On the chancel's E wall, red-and-gold STENCILLED DECORATION of the 1860s, its pattern imperfectly matched by the late C20 flock wallpaper of its other walls. – In the chancel's s wall, two-seat SEDILIA and CREDENCE niche. – SACRAMENT HOUSE in the N wall.

STAINED GLASS. E wheel window (the Crucifixion) of 1864, perhaps by *Hardman*. – In the chancel's N window, two lights (Our Lord as the Good Shepherd; Our Lord Walking on the Water) by *Clayton & Bell*, 1899. – In the nave's w wheel window, an abstract design of the 1860s. – The N wall's w window (the Calling of Peter and Andrew), probably by *Heaton, Butler & Bayne*, is of *c.* 1900. – The nave's other lights (Our Lady on the N; SS. Margaret, John the Evangelist and James the Less, and the Risen Lord on the s) are all by *J. Ninian Comper*, 1904–6, made for the House of Charity at Lerwick and resited here by *Joseph Bell & Son* in 1973.

ST MARGARET (R.C.), Harbour Street. By *James M. Baikie* of Kirkwall, 1911. Buttressed nave and small apsed chancel, of hammerdressed grey stone with yellow sandstone dressings. NW porch. Windows of paired lancets under trefoil heads. Inside, REREDOS with figures of saints in tabernacled niches. – ALTAR front carved with a high relief of the Last Supper. – STAINED-GLASS w window ('The Church in the World', with brightly coloured scenes of Shetland life) by *C. R. Sinclair*, 1986.

ST OLAF'S HALL, Annsbrae Place. Built as Lerwick Free Church in 1848–50 and now a hall, it is by *William Henderson* of Aber-deen. Broad box with pointed windows. The parapeted ashlar s gable is divided by pinnacled buttresses into a 'nave' and 'aisles', a tall gableted bellcote on its apex. N extension of 1968.

ST RINGAN (United Free), Lower Hillhead. Originally United Presbyterian. Early Gothic, by *R. G. Sykes* of Liverpool, 1886.

*Liturgical w; really it is s.

Squat earthbound cruciform. Dumpy crossing tower with a low
pyramid roof inside its battlemented parapet. Lancet windows
at the sides, a wheel window in the N gable. Inside, a coved
hammerbeam roof. – STAINED GLASS. N wheel window
(Madonna and Child), early C20. – Five-light S window (Our
Lord administering the Sacrament) designed by *R. G. Sykes*,
1892. – ORGAN by *Harrison & Harrison*, 1897.

PUBLIC BUILDINGS

ANDERSON HIGH SCHOOL, Lovers Loan. Main block by
William Smith of Aberdeen, 1860–1. Relaxed Scots Jacobean but
with Frenchy touches provided by the pavilion-roofed entrance
tower and the large oriel to its l. – Immediately to the N, BRUCE
HOSTEL, by *W. Laidlaw Macdougall* and *W. W. Reid*, 1917–19,
pompous Wrenaissance of a sort. – S of the 1860s main block,
the JANET COURTNEY HOSTEL, tepid Art Deco by *James
Shearer* of Dunfermline, 1939. – Large ADDITIONS, with white
window units contrasting with brown aggregate panels, to
the main block, the Janet Courtney Hostel, and to the W, of
1974–8.

ANDERSON'S HOMES, Twageos Road. Built to house the
widows of fishermen and sailors, 1865. Small-scale Tudor.
Three linked blocks, the centre originally topped by a spire.
Flat-roofed additions on the W built for the conversion to flats
in 1970.

BELL'S BRAE PRIMARY SCHOOL, Gilbertson Road. By *A. A.
Foote & Son*, 1957. Additions of 1975.

BREVIK HOSPITAL, South Road. Originally the Poorhouse. By
John M. Aitken, 1886.

CENTRAL INFANT SCHOOL, King Harald Street. L-plan school
and schoolhouse, by *William Ingram* of Glasgow, 1864–5, with
a bellcote on the E gable. – Big but plain N addition, dated 1908.

CLICKIMIN LEISURE CENTRE, South Lochside. By *Faulkner
Browns*, 1985. Big and low, with drydashed walls, dominated
by shallow-pitched red metal roofs.

COUNTY BUILDINGS, King Erik Street. Originally Sheriff Court
and Prison. 1874–5, by *David Rhind* of Edinburgh. The front
block looks like a crowstepped villa. At the rear, the two-storey
PRISON, its gables again crowstepped; small segmental-arched
cell windows set high in the walls.

ELECTRICITY GENERATING STATION, Holmsgarth Road.
Diesel-powered station, by *Alexander Cattanach Jun.*, 1953.
Boxy building clad in corrugated metal, the tall chimney not
quite elegant.

GILBERT BAIN HOSPITAL, Cairnfield Road. By *Charles C.
Wright* of the *North-Eastern Regional Hospital Board*, 1958–61.

GILBERT BAIN HOSPITAL, King Harald Street. By *W. A. Baird
Laing* of Edinburgh, 1901–2. Plain single-storey Tudor with
battered chimneys.

ISLEBURGH COMMUNITY CENTRE, King Harald Street. Originally Central Public School. By *John M. Aitken*, 1901–2.

Tall and bleak Baronial, the centre hardly enlivened by its tourelles.

LIBRARY AND MUSEUM, Lower Hillhead. By *Zetland County Council*, 1966. Two storeys, the lower part an artificial stone concave, the metal-clad upper floor oversailing and with a continuous band of windows. The sides of the wooden doorpiece are carved with reliefs of a girl and boy engrossed in their books; above him, a ship, a spindle above her.

MONTFIELD HOSPITAL, Burgh Road. Crowstepped block of *c.* 1920, built as a sanatorium, now surrounded by a simple complex of 1982.

POST OFFICE, Commercial Street. By *W. T. Oldrieve* of *H. M. Office of Works*, 1908–10. Peaceful Scots Jacobean dressed in harling with sandstone dressings. Crowstepped gables and keel-shaped dormers.

SOUND PRIMARY SCHOOL, South Road. By *Baxter, Clark & Paul*, 1977, and extended by them in 1982.

TELEPHONE EXCHANGE, Greenfield Place. Fag-end neo-Georgian, by *H. M. Office of Works*, 1953; harled with cement dressings.

TOWN HALL, Hillhead. Built in 1881–3 to a design by *Alexander Ross* of Inverness, with minor amendments made by the contractor *John M. Aitken*. The general concept is reminiscent of Matthews & Lawrie's slightly earlier Town House at Inverness. Two-storey five-bay crowstep-gabled box, with tall conical-roofed angle turrets. Straight skews at the slightly advanced centre's gable, from which projects an oriel. Panels under the other first-floor windows carved with foliage and shields bearing national emblems and the coats of arms of families associated with Shetland. A rose window in the N gable, big two-light windows in the S. Behind the main block, a battlemented clock-tower with three-light pointed belfry openings; crosslet arrow slits in the small angle rounds. Inside, a passage through the ground floor to the grand stair in the tower. The whole of the main block's first floor is filled by the Hall. Straight-coved boarded ceiling with braces springing from stone corbels. A pair of heavy and elaborate canopied neo-medieval stone chimneypieces.

STAINED GLASS. In the Council Chamber (former Burgh Court Room) at the ground floor's SW corner, two lights with medallions of 1883. – One light depicting Shetland industry, by *Martin Emslie*, 1983. – Stair window (Lord Aberdour in masonic regalia), by *James Ballantine & Son*, 1883. – In the hall's S wall, two windows (King Harald Harfager and Jarl Rognvald; the consecration of King Magnus and the founding of St Magnus Cathedral), both by *Ballantine*, 1883. – All the windows in the W wall (people connected with the early history of Shetland) are by *Cox & Sons, Buckley & Co.*, 1882. – Also by them (of 1883) is the N wall's heraldic rose window and probably the four heraldic lights below.

WAR MEMORIAL, Hillhead. By *Robert S. Lorimer*, 1923–4.

Granite shaft carved with coats of arms and with a cross-finial.
Octagonal base forming the central boss of a Latin cross.

FORT CHARLOTTE
Charlotte Street and Harbour Street

C17 fort, its defences repaired and its barrack buildings erected
in the 1780s. It is now an Ancient Monument. The building of a
fort on Shetland was proposed by the Cromwellian government
in 1653, but the idea seems to have been dropped the following
year with the ending of the Dutch War. In 1665–6, during the
Second Dutch War, a fort was built at Lerwick, probably designed
by the Master Mason to the Crown *John Mylne Jun.*, who acted
as contractor. A few months after the ending of that conflict with
the signing of the Treaty of Breda in June 1667, Charles II ordered
the fort's abandonment and dismantling. Whatever damage was
then done to its defences was apparently made worse in 1673,
during the Third Dutch War, when the fort's barracks were burnt
by Dutch sailors. In 1781, at a time when France was actively
supporting the rebellious American colonies, *Captain Andrew
Frazer* directed repair of the C17 fortifications, including a rebuilding of the W wall, and the erection of new barrack blocks. On
completion of the work, the fort was rechristened Fort Charlotte
in honour of the Queen.

The site is a cliff-edge overlooking the Sound of Bressay. The
fort's walls, rubble-built and with an external batter, form an
irregular pentagon. Bastions at the corners. The zig-zag E wall
has been lowered and partly demolished. It now lacks the C18
traverse walls which extended inwards from each of its points
as a defence against enfilading fire from the high ground to the
N. C17 South Gate whose roll-moulded and roundheaded arch
has been partly built up and given a rectangular door, probably
in the 1780s. Above it, an empty panel-frame. Inside the gate,
a short segmental-vaulted passage over which climbs a flight of
steps to the now vanished wooden musketry staging to the W.
The 1780s Main Gate is at the SW, round-arched with projecting keystone and imposts on the outside. There has been an
inner passage, presumably again covered by steps to musketry
staging. The North Gate is again of the 1780s, a plain roundheaded arch.

The buildings are almost all of the 1780s. Inside the North
Gate, a latrine block which has been flushed by the overflow
from the free-standing cistern to its S, a plain block enlarged in
the C19. In the NE bastion's walled courtyard, the Powder
Magazine and Cooperage, both small. Harled North Barracks
on the N side of the enclosure, a two-storey seven-bay double-
pile with forestairs at front and back. It contained an officers'
kitchen and stores on the ground floor; on the first floor were
the commanding officer's quarters, a messroom and barrack
rooms. To its W, a small bakehouse. On the enclosure's W
side, the U-plan West Barracks. Its central range, designed to

accommodate 104 men, is a two-storey double-pile with a
block-consoled and corniced door. The taller piend-roofed
wings contained officers' rooms. Single-storey piend-roofed
South Pile to the S. In it were guardrooms, stores and accommodation for the artillery. Small Victorian store to its W.

HARBOUR

Continuous development along the shore from Commercial
Street at the S to Holmsgarth on the N edge of the town. Gillie's
Pier at the S was built for James Copland in 1817, and soon
afterwards the whole foreshore between it and Fort Charlotte was
lined with piers and lodberries (houses and stores built on piers).
Almost simultaneously the merchants Hay & Ogilvy were develop-
ing the area of Freefield to the W of North Ness with docks,
warehouses, curing yards and boat-building yards. The Victoria
Pier was built in the mid-C19 and then much extended by *W.
Dyce Cay* in 1883–6, with the Albert Wharf stretching from the
pier N to Fort Charlotte being constructed at the same time. The
next major development of the harbour came with the construction in 1904–8 of the Alexandra Wharf from Fort Charlotte
towards North Ness. A second pier, S of the Victoria Pier, was
built in 1913–15, the basin between the two now the Small Boat
Harbour. In 1957–9 the Victoria Pier was widened and extended
and the North Jetty built at the junction of the Albert and Alexandra Wharfs. Further development, some for the oil industry,
has taken place at Holmsgarth to the N.

The character is now predominantly late C19 and C20 and more
industrial than picturesque. Early C19 LODBERRIES survive in
Commercial Street at the harbour's S end. Then the SMALL
BOAT HARBOUR formed by *James Barron* in 1913–15, with a
SE concrete breakwater built on an irregular L-plan. This basin's
W side is the broad L-plan VICTORIA PIER, given its present
concrete and metal appearance by *Archibald Henderson & Partners* in 1957–9. At its SW end, a CLOCK on a tall fluted standard,
by *Bailey Pegg & Co.* of London, c. 1900. Beside the clock, a
pink granite DRINKING FOUNTAIN incised with Scriptural
texts; it was erected in 1890. ALBERT WHARF to the N is largely
of 1957–9, the date also of the NORTH JETTY. Beside the jetty,
the two-storey corrugated iron ALBERT BUILDING of 1906.
Then the concrete ALEXANDRA WHARF by *James M. Barron*,
1904–8, altered by *Henderson & Nicol* in 1927–8. On
LAURENSON'S QUAY at its N end, the utilitarian FISH-
MARKET of 1975. C19 rubble harbour wall round the point of
North Ness. To its W, the rubble-built HAY'S DOCK of *c.*
1825, with a derelict early C19 warehouse on its W side. More
early C19 warehouses and C20 sheds further W, extending to
the SKIPDOCK, which was reconstructed *c.* 1895 with a rubble
pier. C20 concrete takes over to the N at MORRISON DOCK
and the HOLMSGARTH FERRY PIER of 1975. Also of 1975, the
single-storey TERMINAL BUILDING by *Leslie D. Morrison &*

Partners, with a deep lead fascia over continuous glazing above
a rendered base.

DESCRIPTION

TWAGEOS ROAD at the SE makes a convenient starting point,
with Anderson's Homes (*see* Public Buildings, above) followed
by a garage (by *Richard Gibson, c.* 1980), its roof pretending to
be an upturned boat. Then two alternative routes, both ending
near Fort Charlotte.

The first goes up LEOG LANE to the l., where LEOG is a comfortable mid-C19 villa with a steep Jacobean centre gable and
a pedimented porch. The lane enters GREENFIELD PLACE
between St Magnus Episcopal Church (*see* Churches, above)
and the garden wall of its RECTORY, a gabled and gableted
Victorian villa by *Alexander Ellis*. At the street's end, St Columba's Church (*see* Churches, above). On the opposite corner,
the harled No. 26 CHURCH ROAD, early C19, with a tall
corniced doorpiece looking w to St Olaf's Hall (*see* Churches,
above). On the s side of ANNSBRAE PLACE, the harled No. 2
(ANNSBRAE HOUSE), 1791, is smart, with an ashlar porch and
a pair of slightly advanced pavilions. In CLAIRMONT PLACE,
two opposing but undistinguished churches, the Congregational and Baptist (*see* Churches, above). In HILLHEAD
to the N, No. 2 (GORDON COTTAGE) is early C19, with club
skewputts and a pedimented porch. After the late C19 WES-
LEYAN MANSE, with seaside half-timbering, more ecclesiastical competition between the Adam Clarke Methodist and
St Ringan's U.F. Churches (*see* Churches, above). The Town
Hall, War Memorial and County Buildings (*see* Public Buildings, above) fail to provide a strong civic presence. In KING
ERIK STREET, SHELTERED HOUSING by *Shetland Islands
Council*, 1990, and in ST OLAF STREET another spat of clerical
rivalry with St Clement's Hall and St Margaret's R.C. Church
(*see* Churches, above) in diagonally opposed corners.

The other route follows the original main thoroughfare of the
town. COMMERCIAL STREET starts with a C19 gable-ended
house on the l. On the r., Nos. 2–6, built for James Copland in
1817, of rubble and unpretentious, with storehouses and quays
jutting out into the Sound to the N. Harled and crowstepped
house at Nos. 8–10, probably early C18, with chamfered
margins at the small windows and projecting slabs above their
lintels. Then the LERWICK BOATING CLUB, by *Richard
Moira*, 1983, with a ridiculously rubbly gable. On the s side,
the harled gable-ender of *c.* 1800 at Nos. 27–29 has been
restored with a vengeance. Beyond is the three-storey three-
bay QUENDALE HOUSE of *c.* 1865, its outer windows tripartite
at the ground and first floors and bipartite at the second, the
centre first-floor window round-arched, all enjoying an open
view over the Sound. It is followed by gable-ended late Georgian houses separated by closes stepping uphill. On the r.,
another early C19 lodberry followed by a gap and the fake

lodberry which is the E wing of the plain QUEEN'S HOTEL of
c. 1860. On the corner of CHURCH ROAD, the OLD TOL-
BOOTH (now BRITISH RED CROSS SOCIETY) of 1767–70,
its rendered two-storey front dressed up with rusticated quoins
and scrolled skewputts; it had a central belfry until 1927.

W of Church Road, Commercial Street begins on the l. with No.
67, an early C19 shallow bow-front with three-light windows
overlooking the harbour. The street soon widens to form a
small square, most of its N side filled by the Post Office (see
Public Buildings, above). On the S, the ROYAL BANK OF
SCOTLAND (former Commercial Bank), a not very forceful
palazzo by *David Rhind*, 1871. The street becomes narrower
and more overtly commercial at the approach to a triangle
containing the MARKET CROSS, a squat ashlar column topped
by an interwar lamp standard.

After the Market Cross, Commercial Street is dominated by the
BANK OF SCOTLAND (former Union Bank) by *John J. Burnet*,
1904–6. Accomplished and exuberant English baroque.
Centrepiece with a big semicircular gable and a columned
porch carved with a galley in low relief. At the corners, Ionic
pilasters from whose capitals protrude grotesque heads with
strings of fruit dropping from their mouths. Another block-
buster, but of much less quality, at the Baronial GRAND
HOTEL by *W. Hamilton Beattie*, 1886–7, which tries to live up
to its name with a martial corner tower. Almost as forceful, and
rather more enjoyable, is the contemporary crowstepped and
battlemented single-storey shop opposite, with a fishscale-
slated pepperpot turret. Then relative sobriety. At the early
C19 Nos. 161–163 on the W, a central pend over BURNS
LANE, which begins well with a pair of C18 buildings facing
each over across the stone steps climbing the hill. On Commercial Street's E side, the CLYDESDALE BANK by *John
M. Aitken*, 1892, with two corner turrets, one a pepperpot,
the other aggressively battlemented. A quiet end stretch before
the street joins Esplanade below the walls of Fort Charlotte
(*see* above).

FARMHOUSES ETC.

BÖD OF GREMISTA, Gremista Road. Small harled house of two
storeys and an attic built c. 1790 to accommodate the overseer
of an adjacent fish-curing yard. Arthur Anderson, founder
of the P. & O. shipping line, was born here in 1792. Off-
centre door in the E front and another in the N gable. This
N door opens into the salt store. The E door to the kitchen
was the house's main entry. Two rooms on each of the upper
floors.

HAYFIELD, Hayfield Lane. Small piend-roofed mansion house
of c. 1840, its walls covered with render lined out as ashlar.
Three bays by three, of two storeys over an exposed basement.
Heavy classical porch on the S front.

BROCH OF CLICKHIMIN
off South Road

Tidy but impressive Ancient Monument, the surviving buildings and remains evidence of a fortified settlement which was occupied from c. 700 B.C. until c. A.D. 500. The site is a small low island in the Loch of Clickhimin, originally an arm of the sea but cut off from it in the first millennium B.C. by the formation of a storm beach which also raised the loch's level. The first phase of settlement of c. 700 B.C., probably before the damming of the loch, is represented by the remains of a small late Bronze Age farmstead. About the end of the first millennium B.C. the island was fortified by the erection of a massive drystone wall round its perimeter enclosing an area of c. 42m. by 38m. Perhaps at the same time a free-standing blockhouse or gateway was built just inside the entrance to this enclosure. The large broch itself probably followed soon after. The site seems to have been abandoned before the Viking invasions, and the water level of the loch was lowered again in 1874.

The approach is from the s across a largely artificial causeway, presumably formed in the first millennium B.C. At its N end, low remains of a drystone outer gateway, perhaps contemporary with the building of the island's perimeter wall. This gateway's threshold is formed by a stone carved with two shallow footprints, probably c. A.D. 500, but the stone may well not be *in situ*. The perimeter wall behind, running round the edge of the island before the lowering of the loch, is up to 3.6m. thick, built of roughly coursed gritstone and still standing to a height of 1.7m. Entrance passage through the wall almost aligned with the causeway. In the passage, a door-frame of upright slabs. Evidence has been found that wooden buildings, some used as byres, stood against the wall's inner face.

c. 2.75m. behind the wall is the blockhouse, its central gateway directly aligned with the entrance through the wall. It is an arc of drystone masonry, c. 13m. long and still c. 2.9m. high, both its wall-faces battered. About a third of the way along its entrance passage, the rebate for a wooden door which has been secured by a drawbar, its deep bar-hole visible on the w side. In the thickness of the wall each side of the passage, a small cell, the w reached by a stone stair in the wall, the E apparently by a ladder from above; perhaps this was a prison. On the blockhouse's inner (N) wall-face, remains of a projecting scarcement, presumably to support a wooden structure built against it. Clearly the blockhouse was intended as the fort's principal gateway, but it seems only a fragment of a fortification intended to stretch from side to side of the island. Was there a change of mind which led to the perimeter wall enclosing a larger area than originally intended?

The circular broch itself is large, c. 19.8m. in diameter, built of roughly coursed drystone masonry, the external wall-face battered and still standing to a height of c. 5.2m. The thickness of its solid base (up to 6.5m.) suggests it was a tower, perhaps

originally as much as 15m. high. Main entrance on the W,
its passage interrupted by a doorway of upright slabs. Spaces
between the passage roof's lintels enabled observation of visitors from a cell in the wall above. Over the passage's doorway
into the court, rectangular openings, probably to lessen the
weight on the lintel. Very unusually there are also two minor
entrances. The NW entrance, just above ground level, leads
through to the court; opening off its passage to the E, a lobby
and staircase inside the wall. The NE entrance, c. 1.5m. above
the ground, gives access only to a gallery inside the broch wall.
Opening off the court have been roughly oval wall cells at the
E and S, the E still with an entrance through the casing built in
the first millennium A.D. against the lower part of the original
inner wall-face, the S now entered from above. In the casing, a
small N cell, its back wall formed by the original wall-face,
which has a scarcement c. 2m. above the ground to support
the beams of wooden buildings whose post-holes have been
uncovered by excavation. The court's interior, now neat and
tidy, was converted to a wheel house in the first millennium
A.D.; its radial stone walls were still visible in the C19, when its
central hearth was excavated.

NW of the broch, the foundation of the small oval house or
farmstead of c. 700 B.C. – Between the broch and the blockhouse, foundations of a little trefoil-shaped house, probably
Pictish of the mid-first millennium A.D.

4020 ## LEVENWICK (MAINLAND)

Strung-out crofting township near the E coast of Mainland.

BROCH, 1.6km. SE. Badly damaged by a storm in 1900 but still
substantial remains of a broch, probably built at the end of the
first millennium B.C. or the beginning of the first millennium
A.D. Quite small, c. 17m. in overall diameter. Entrance at the
NE. Inside the court, N doorway to a ruinous stair, which rose
inside the wall to a gallery running round the broch's E arc to
the S, where a second stair led to a now vanished upper gallery.
A circular house has been inserted inside the courtyard, perhaps
in the C3 or C4 A.D. The broch stands on a low masonry-faced
platform surrounded by two ramparts of earth on boulder bases.

5000 ## LUNDA WICK (UNST)

Isolated graveyard containing a ruined church.

CHURCH. Substantial remains of a rubble-built rectangle, c.
4.4m. by 6.7m. It is probably C12 but the E end has been rebuilt
on the original foundations. In the W gable, a round-arched
door, its corbelled springers resting on imposts; inclined jambs.
Above, a round-arched window, its jambs inclined internally.
Built-up rectangular door, probably a later insertion, at the W

end of the s wall. Narrow rectangular windows, the s wall's w
and the blocked N window probably original, the s wall's later
E window slightly wider.

LUNNA (MAINLAND) *4060*

Little more than the church with Lunna House on a hillside to
the N.

LUNNA KIRK. White harled rectangle built in 1753 and remodelled in the early C20 with a lean-to w addition and porch-
like N doorpiece. C18 forestair at the s gable. On the E side,
buttresses; some are of the early C20, but the others are the
side walls of burial enclosures. In one of them, a squint, so
perhaps this was part of the medieval church. Inside, early C19
fittings. – GALLERY carried round three sides on Roman Doric
columns. Its short N and s fronts are panelled, the w balustraded. – On the E, two-decker PULPIT, with a circular
sounding board.
 MONUMENTS. On the E wall, a pedimented monument of *c.*
1780 to Thomas Hunter of Lunna † 1718, his wife and son, the
base carved with emblems of death. – In the N doorway,
armorial monument of *c.* 1700 to Robert Hunter of Lunna and
his wife, Margaret Leslie. – Below it, a worn stone, inscribed

ANNO MDCCXIX
PULVIS ET UMBRA SUMUS

LUNNA HOUSE. Crowstepped and harled mansion house of the
Hunters of Lunna, much enlarged by the Bruces of Sumburgh
in the early C20. The earliest part, probably late C17, is on the
E, a two-storey-and-attic block. This was made L-plan in the
early C18 by the addition of a sw jamb, its s gable bearing a
panel carved with the names of Thomas Hunter and Grisella
Bruce, who had married in 1707. The early C20 contributed a
big L-plan w extension with blocky Baronial detail and a porch
in the existing house's inner angle. Behind, a rubble-built
STEADING, probably mid-C19.
 On the old approach to the house from near Lunna Kirk to
the s, ball-finialled GATEPIERS, probably early C19. – Apparently of the same date is a small square rubble TEMPLE built
as an eyecatcher on top of the hill 0.5km. s of the house.

MELBY (MAINLAND) *1050*

Settlement with a harbour and church, beside the Sound of Papa.

SANDNESS CHURCH. Now a store. Harled box of 1792–4,
remodelled in the later C19 with a gableted bellcote and pointed
windows in the w gable. In the E gable, a reused stone inscribed
'FEAR GOD 1645 [?]'.
HARBOUR. Concrete slip, probably of *c.* 1900. On the shore, a
harled C19 house and row of stores.

MELBY HOUSE. Early C 19 laird's house of two storeys and three bays, quietly proprietorial in its oversight of the harbour.

FORT, Ness of Garth, 2.3km. NE. Remains of a fort of the late first millennium B.C., placed on a badly eroded promontory, now accessible only at low tide. It has been defended by four ramparts of earth and stones. Inside the enclosure, hollows marking the sites of oval houses.

5090   MID YELL (YELL)

Sizeable village on the s side of Mid Yell Voe.

ST JOHN'S PARISH CHURCH. Harled T-plan kirk of 1832. Rectangular windows. Flat-topped birdcage bellcote on the N jamb. Inside, W and E GALLERIES with panelled fronts. – In the centre of the S wall, PULPIT with fluted pilasters at the back; octagonal sounding board with a ball-finialled ogee top.

To the NE, HALL built in 1893, with round-arched windows. Large flat-roofed addition.

GRAVEYARD. Fragments of the W and N walls of the OLD PARISH CHURCH which seems to have been *c.* 15.2m. by 7m. Its W doorway, perhaps C 17, is round-arched. Against the N wall, two rubble-built BURIAL ENCLOSURES. In the E enclosure's S wall are two MONUMENTS, both probably C 18, one carved with an angel and a Latin inscription, the other with conjoined coats of arms under a mantled helm. – W of these enclosures, a free-standing aedicular MONUMENT with leafy capitals on the attached columns. At the top of the inscription panel, two coats of arms under a mantled helm. The entablature carries a segmental pediment carved with the initials

M
TH
PD

probably for Master Thomas Hay, minister of Yell, and his first wife, Prudence McDougal † 1730.

PIER. Mostly C 20, with a concrete superstructure on the rubble base and a long concrete extension of 1952.

SCHOOL. By *Zetland County Council*, 1966–7. Sensible and not without a hint of elegance, the flat-roofed E block contrasting with the sawtooth roofs of the W.

YELL LEISURE CENTRE. By *Faulkner Browns*, 1988. Drydashed, with huge shallow-pitch metal roofs.

FORT, Brough of Stoal, 4.6km. SE. Remains of a fort of the late first millennium B.C. on a promontory between two deep geos. Across the promontory's neck, three largely earthen ramparts, still over 2m. high, separated by deep ditches. No sign of a passage or causeway, but it may have been at one end and lost to erosion. In the enclosure, traces of building, perhaps the remains of a broch.

MOUSA

Small island, now uninhabited but with the ruin of a late c18 laird's house (THE HAA) and its broch of the c1 A.D. still standing.

BROCH. The best-preserved and tallest of all Scottish brochs, sited on a low promontory formerly defended by a rampart (only traces now visible) on the landward (E) side. The reason for the exceptional state of preservation may be that the broch itself was exceptional: its court was only *c.* 5.5m. in diameter, but the encircling wall was *c.* 5.5m. thick and thus strong enough to have survived to a height of *c.* 13.3m., having lost perhaps only 1m. from the top. Walling of coursed drystone masonry, most of the stones very small for a broch. Strong batter on the lower part of the external wall, which takes on an ogee profile as it rises to an almost vertical top, the distinctive shape perhaps accentuated by settlement. Entrance from the W side, facing the sea. About halfway along the paved passage, one door jamb formed by a flagstone set on edge and, immediately behind it, a bar-hole. Opening off the court are three doorways into large cells, each entrance surmounted by a tier of rectangular openings lightening the weight of wall over the lintel. Little aumbries in the walls of each cell. Scarcement ledge in the inner wall-face 2.1m. above the ground. At this level, a door to the stair, which rises through the five tiers of the broch's hollow-walled upper part. At a height of 3.7m., a second scarcement with another doorway to the court. Probably the scarcements supported the beams for the floor and roof of a wooden first-floor gallery. Most of the court's walling below the openings to the wall cells is masked by a later casing, perhaps of the c3 or c4 A.D., erected when a wheel house was inserted in the broch. Part of one of this wheel house's radial walls* survives in the court, as do a hearth stone and a stone-lined tank.

MUCKLE ROE

Hilly island linked to Mainland by a causeway.

CHURCH, Greentaing. Built as a United Free hall church, *c.* 1910, and very humble. Harled with rusticated cement quoins.

MUNESS CASTLE (UNST)

3.7km. E of Uyeasound

Substantial ruin of the very grand Z-plan house begun in 1598 by Laurence Bruce of Cultmalindie and apparently completed by his second son, Andrew.‡ Laurence Bruce, the Great Foud and

---

*Three of these were recorded in 1866.

‡Andrew Bruce's initials were formerly visible below the SW turret, and his name is engraved on the doorknocker from Muness Castle now at Sand Lodge (Mainland).

Admiral-Depute of Shetland, was uncle to Patrick Stewart, Earl of Orkney, whose master of works, *Andrew Crawford*, may well have provided the design.

The main block, built of local rubble (formerly harled) with imported red freestone dressings, is *c.* 22.5m. by 7.9m. externally. It has been of three storeys, but most of the top floor is now missing. Round towers at the NW and SE corners; circular turrets corbelled out at the NE and SW. In the S front, an off-centre door with a lugged and corniced architrave. It was brought here from Old Lund in 1959 on the supposition that it might originally have belonged to Muness, but it looks late C17 rather than of *c.* 1600. Above it but not in direct alignment, a worn coat of arms* with the initial L on its l. and surmounting a panel inscribed

> LIST ZE TO KNAW YIS BULDING QUHA BEGAN
> LAURENCE THE BRUCE HE WAS THAT WORTHY MAN
> QUHA ERNESTLY HIS AIRIS AND OFSPRING PRAYIS
> TO HELP AND NOT TO HURT THIS VARK ALUAYIS
> THE ZEIR OF GOD 1598

Detail is both refined and inventive. The turrets' corbelling consists of three continuous mouldings topped by two rows of chequer-set moulded corbels with dummy shotholes in the spaces between. Chamfered arrises at most windows, but those of the first-floor hall have rounded jambs. Wonderful display of gunloops and shotholes. Some at the ground floor are of the commonplace wide-splayed type, but others (e.g. those flanking the door) are inverted keyholes or prostrate figures-of-eight. At the first floor they are either quatrefoils or moulded circles. Under the main block's second-floor windows, moulded circles and saltires; at the turrets, saltires and quatrefoils.

Inside the entrance, on the r. a round-headed arch to the scale-and-platt principal stair. Immediately in front of the entrance, a low rectangular doorway into a dogleg passage which gives access to a domical-vaulted store in the SE tower and a tunnel-vaulted room at the main block's NE corner. In this room's SW corner, a winding stair to the first-floor hall, so it was probably the wine cellar. W of the main entrance, a vaulted passage along the house's S side. Two more tunnel-vaulted cellars open off it to the N. At its W end is the kitchen, occupying the full width of the house. In the kitchen's E wall, a large fireplace which seems to have been segmental-arched. Oven in the fireplace's NE corner. Another domical-vaulted store in the NW tower.

On the first floor the main block contains three rooms. The largest, in the centre, was the hall. W fireplace, the surviving fragment of its N jamb showing it had a moulded surround. Aumbry to its S. Two large windows in the S wall and one in the N. This N window is flanked by rectangular gunloop embrasures with aumbries above. Recess between the window

---

*The quartered arms of Laurence Bruce and his wife, Elizabeth Gray.

and the E embrasure. At the N end of the hall's E wall, a door to the E room and another beside it to the wine cellar's stair, both rectangular. A round-arched door from the principal stair muscles into the SE corner. W of the hall is the lord's private room, with a window as large as those in the hall and a fireplace in the W gable. In the NW tower, a closet with narrow windows and no fireplace. The first-floor E room was probably a guest-chamber; L-plan because of the stairs taking a notch out of its SW corner. Comfortably sized S window but smaller than those of the hall and private room; gable fireplace. In the SE tower's adjoining closet, generous windows and a fireplace.

The only access to the main block's second-floor W room (the lord's bedchamber) has been by a spiral stair rising in the thickness of the N wall from the private room below. Windows to the W and S; fireplace in the gable. Closets, both without fireplaces, in the NW tower and SW turret. The centre room (upper hall or withdrawing room) is reached by the principal stair. Like the hall below, it has had two windows in the S wall and one in the N, but the fireplace is on the E. Another guest-chamber to its E, with closets in the NE turret and SE tower.

NESBISTER HILL *see* WHITENESS (MAINLAND)

NESS OF BURGI *see* SUMBURGH (MAINLAND)

NESS OF GARTH *see* MELBY (MAINLAND)

NESTING *see* HOUSABISTER (MAINLAND)

NORTH HAA (YELL)
0.4km. W of West Sandwick

4080

Smart mansion house created by John Ogilvy of Quarff soon after his marriage to Barbara Grace Robertson, heiress of the estate, in 1829. Ogilvy's work was to remodel and partly rebuild what already existed. That was a haa house, possibly C17, to which had been added a front (S) block, *c.* 1770. Ogilvy rebuilt the older rear block, his new range extending E of the C18 front block. To that he gave a suavely urbane new face, rendering over the earlier stonework. Five-bay ground floor; at its centre, an urn-finialled pedimented porch with rosettes on the pilasters. Only three windows above, the outer two of three lights, the centre round-arched. Single-storey one-bay links, flush with the front wall, extend E and W to slightly advanced and pedimented pavilions, each with a Venetian window and ball finial.

Inside the porch, the present entrance door seems to have been converted from an c18 window with moulded jambs. The house's staircase has a simple wooden balustrade, probably late c18. At the attic, partly panelled sw room with a dentil cornice, looking more like *c.* 1770 than *c.* 1830.

WALLED GARDENS to front and back. The front garden, overlooking Southladie Voe, has a dwarf front wall topped by 1830s cast-iron spearhead railings. Corniced gatepiers at the entrances in the E and W walls. In the back garden, an inner segment bounded by low walls with corniced gatepiers at the N. Basket-arched entrance in the N side of the high main wall.

Rubble SLIP, perhaps c18, to the Voe to the s.

NORTHMAVINE *see* HILLSWICK (MAINLAND)

3080 # NORTH ROE (MAINLAND)

Scattered settlement around the bay of Burra Voe.

CHURCH OF SCOTLAND. Rendered box of 1870. Bellcote on the E gable, segmental-arched windows in the w. Inside, the PULPIT has two elaborate brass lamp brackets.

METHODIST CHURCH, South Haa. Built in 1878. Harled mission chapel and house, just like a double cottage except for the tall gableted bellcote.

STANDING STONES ('GIANT'S GRAVE'), Beorgs of Housetter, 4km. s. Just w of the road beside the Loch of Housetter and with the cliff-like hill of Beorgs of Housetter behind, two stones erected in the second millennium B.C., both undressed blocks of red granite, *c.* 2.7m. and 2m. high and 6m. apart. Between them, a contemporary cairn of grey stones from which pokes up a low upright slab, perhaps one side of a former cist.

3080 # OLLABERRY (MAINLAND)

Small village, mostly c20, beside the harbour, the old United Presbyterian Church on the s side of the bay.

CHURCH OF SCOTLAND. Plain mission chapel of 1865. Bellcote on the N gable, a chimney on the s.

In the small GRAVEYARD, s of the church is a tall corniced SLAB, probably early c19, its top carved with a coat of arms flanked by cherubs' heads. – N of the church, a big MONUMENT signed by *John Forbes*, 1754, and very old-fashioned for that date. Steeply pedimented Corinthianish aedicule, its ball finials carried on stalks. Two crisply carved coats of arms and an inscription beginning

INTERR'D BELOW THIS MONUMENT WE FIND
OUR VIRTUOUS CHILDREN AS THEY'RE HERE DESI[GNED?]
IN BLOOM OF YOUTH CUTT OF THIS EARTH
FREED FROM THE FORCES OF A CORRUPT AGE

Eroded emblems of death at the bottom.

UNITED PRESBYTERIAN CHURCH. Disused. Tall harled box
with a gableted bellcote; built in 1862–3. Over the N door, a
pointed window with Dec tracery. The other windows have
triangular heads. – Beside the church, its contemporary MANSE.
Georgian-survival, the l. ground- and first-floor windows each
of three lights.

HARBOUR. Small but sturdy C19 rubble pier with inset steps. It
is overlooked by the harled OLLABERRY HOUSE (HAA OF
OLLABERRY) of 1789. Club skews and a C20 parapeted porch.

OUT SKERRIES   6070

Tight-knit group of islands, the two largest (Housay and Bruray)
linked by a concrete bridge opened in 1957.

CHURCH. Built as a combined church and schoolroom in 1896
and remodelled as a church in 1967.

LIGHTHOUSE, Bound Skerry. By *D. & T. Stevenson*, 1857. Tall
round stone tower, its base of rock-faced ashlar.

PAPA STOUR   1060

Deeply indented island with crofts on its E side, the rest moorland.

CHURCH. Humble harled kirk of 1806 with a birdcage bellcote.

PETTIGARTHS FIELD *see* WHALSAY

PUNDS WATER *see* BRAE (MAINLAND)

QUARFF (MAINLAND)   4030

Scattered groups of houses (Wester and Easter Quarff) along a
narrow valley cutting through the hills of Mainland.

PARISH CHURCH. Built as a T-plan 'Parliamentary' church (i.e.
to *William Thomson*'s design) by *John Davidson* and *Thomas
Macfarlane* in 1828–9. Tudor windows of the standard type but
with wooden astragals and rectangular panes instead of the
usual lattice glazing. The tall gableted bellcote is a Victorian
replacement of the original spikily pinnacled birdcage. Inside,
the N and S ends have been partitioned off. – Tall PULPIT with
fluted pilasters on the back and an octagonal sounding board.

BROCH OF BURLAND, 1.7km. E. Well-fortified promontory crowned by the ruin of a broch of the late first millennium B.C. or early first millennium A.D. The cliff-edged headland is accessible only from the N. On this approach, first a broad and shallow ditch, followed by a stone rampart, c. 5.5m. thick, with a roughly central entrance. The path through has then crossed two further shallow ditches, each with a wall behind it, before entering the enclosure. On the enclosure's W side, remains of the broch, circular as usual, c. 20m. in diameter. Entrance passage at the SW with a guard chamber opening off its E side. Traces of galleries in the 4.6m.-thick double-skin wall.

QUENDALE (MAINLAND)
3010
2.6km. SW of Dunrossness

Early C19 harled laird's house of two storeys and three bays, now derelict. – To the N, a rubble-built MILL of 1867. Segmental-arched cart-entrances in the N front and, to their W, a double gable to which is fixed the wheel.

REAWICK see EASTER SKELD (MAINLAND)

ST NINIAN'S ISLE
3020

Small island joined to Mainland by a long sandy spit.

ST NINIAN'S CHAPEL. Remains of a cliff-top chapel uncovered by excavation in 1955–9. The chapel, probably on the site of an Iron Age dwelling, has consisted of a rubble-built rectangular nave, perhaps C12, and a slightly later and narrower chancel, its rubble walling covered by grass. – The rubble-walled ENCLOSURE to the S has been used as a burial ground probably since the Iron Age (the earliest burials found were short-cist inhumations). – ST NINIAN'S TREASURE, a hoard of Pictish silver objects probably buried under the site of the chapel during the Norse invasions of c. 800, was discovered in 1958 and is now in the Royal Museum of Scotland, Edinburgh.

SAND (MAINLAND)
3040

Small village between Seli Voe and Sand Voe.

ST MARY'S CHAPEL. Ruin of a late medieval church in a grave-yard beside the shore. The segmental-headed chancel arch still stands, as do fragments of the nave's rubble-built N and S walls. Boulders mark the lines of the side walls of the narrower chancel.

SAND HOUSE. Harled laird's house of modest but marked pre-tension, built for Sir Andrew Mitchell of Westshore in 1754.

Five-bay main block of three storeys, the second-floor windows smaller than those below. Club skewputts. Armorial panel over the corniced door. On each side of the house, a ball-finialled lean-to wing but not projecting, the r. now rebuilt as a garage. In front, a space designed as a 'flower plot' flanked by rubble WALLED GARDENS, each with a pavilion at the outer S corner. – Rusticated ball-finialled GATEPIERS on the N approach.

SAND LODGE (MAINLAND)
1.1km. N of Sandwick

4020

Mid-C19 harled laird's house. T-plan, the tail's chimneyed gable with a pediment outlined in brick. Brick eaves course. Corniced doorpiece. Extensive but plain harled additions at the back. To the E, a detached rubble-built store range. The house is set in a WALLED GARDEN. At its N, a rubble-built (formerly harled) PAVILION with a brick eaves course.

SANDNESS see MELBY (MAINLAND)

SANDWICK (MAINLAND)

4020

A few houses at the head of a promontory.

PARISH CHURCH. Harled rectangle with round-arched windows, built in 1807. It was remodelled in 1897, when the two rectangular S doors were converted to windows, a porch and gableted bellcote were added at the E end, and a porch at the W. Inside, the E gallery on utilitarian cast-iron columns is of 1807. The rest dates from 1899, when the pulpit was moved from the S to the W wall.

MANSE to the NW. A harled single-storey U-plan 'Parliamentary' manse (i.e. probably to *James Smith*'s design), built by *John Davidson* and *Thomas Macfarlane* in 1830.

JUNIOR HIGH SCHOOL. Long and low, by *Shetland Islands Council*, 1982–4. – To the N, a harled late C19 Board school.

BROCH, Burraland, 1.4km. SE. Badly ruined round broch of *c.* 100 B.C.–A.D. 100, facing over Mousa Sound. The outer wall is almost vertical except on the W, where it has a pronounced batter. There has been at least one wall gallery.

SAND LODGE. *See* above.

SCALLOWAY (MAINLAND)

4030

The main fishing port on the W coast of Mainland. Patrick Stewart, Earl of Orkney, built a castle here in 1600, and by 1602 Scalloway had replaced Tingwall as the meeting place for the 'thing' or assembly of Shetland. However, it was no more than a small village in the C18, at whose end it had only thirty-one inhabited houses. Development of the village accompanied the development of the harbour from the 1830s, and Scalloway's importance as a port increased further after 1894, when fish in Shetland came to be sold by auction rather than contract between the fishermen and curers. Expansion of the harbour since the 1950s has left the castle stranded above an expanse of concrete.

CHURCHES

CHURCH OF SCOTLAND, Main Street. Boxy kirk of 1840–1, its front rendered, the sides harled. Two tiers of rectangular windows. Piended platform roof. Ashlar birdcage bellcote on the w gable, whose small porch probably dates from the repairs of 1871–2.

CONGREGATIONAL CHURCH, off Castle Street. Dated 1838. Quite simple, with rectangular windows in the side walls. Segmental-arched windows in the front gable, which is topped by a tall and narrow ashlar bellcote. Late C19 porch in seaside-villa style.

METHODIST CHURCH, Meadowfield Place. Humble box built in 1861. Pointed windows and a craggy gableted bellcote.

PUBLIC BUILDINGS

HARBOUR. At the e end, BLACKSNESS PIER below the castle was built for the fish-curers and entrepreneurs Hay & Ogilvy in 1832 and extended by *James Barron*, 1896, to provide deep-water berths. It was extended further w in 1959 and to the e in 1981. The rest, following the curve of the bay, is still largely C19 and rubble-built but with a big C20 concrete quay at the w.

PUBLIC HALL AND LIBRARY, Berry Road. Dated 1902. Scots free style, mixing crowstepped gables with a big basket-arched window of William-Adam-revival type in the gable front. This is finished with a metal clock-cupola topped by a boat weathervane. Over the entrance, a little battlemented tower.

SCHOOL, New Road. Board school of 1876 at the N. To the w and s, very large pavilion additions by *Shetland Islands Council*, 1985–8, with white drydashed walls, tiled roofs and blue trimmings.

DESCRIPTION

CASTLE STREET on the e side of the village leads downhill to the castle (*see* below). At the head of Blacksness Pier (*see* Public Buildings, above), the FISHERMAN'S ARMS of c. 1840 with club skewputts. In NEW STREET on the e side of the bay, terraces of C19 cottages, one bearing a sandstone plaque explaining that 'THIS DIAGRAM ILLUSTRATE [*sic*] THE CAUSES OF THE SO CALLED EARTH TIDES' and with an inset piece of marble bearing the diagram and inscription:

Section at EQUATOR of EARTH. GERMAN THEORIES CON-
TROVERTED. GERMANS Are Not The Favoured of Heaven.

At the street's N end, OLD HALL, a three-storey house of five
bays, the windows grouped 1/3/1, those of the second floor
smaller than the ones below. Corniced doorpiece with a lugged
architrave. Above, a large panel carved with a deeply undercut
coat of arms under a mantled helm and with the names of James
Scott and Katharine Sinclair and the date 1750. 1750 was the
year of their marriage, but the house looks a little earlier. In
front, a heavy and extravagantly rubbly Imperial stair from the
street.

MAIN STREET on the bay's N shore is predominantly C19 two-
storey vernacular. GIBBLESTONE HOUSE, set well back, is a
simple harled villa of c. 1800 dressed up with Victorian bay
windows, dormers and porch. At the sides of the front garden,
unobtrusive housing of 1990 by *Richard Gibson*. In the garden's
front wall, gatepiers with ball finials on obelisk stalks. Further
W, the Church of Scotland (*see* Churches, above).

SCALLOWAY CASTLE
Castle Street

Large and smart tower house built for Patrick Stewart, Earl of 72
Orkney, in 1600. It was probably designed by his master of
works, *Andrew Crawford*. Four storeys and attic, built of rubble
(formerly harled) with dressings of Eday sandstone. It is L-plan,
with the square jamb's NE corner attached to the main block's
SW. Turrets at all corners, the main block's NE a stair turret
corbelled out from the first floor, the others from the third floor.
A second stair turret covered with a sloping roof rises from the
first to the second floor in the W inner angle with the jamb.
Large wallhead chimney on the main block's S front.
  Detail is sophisticated. Large windows, even those of the
ground floor comfortably sized, with chamfered margins. In
the second-floor windowsills of the main block are quatrefoil
gunloops, but the NE turret's have moulded circular gunholes,
both types just like those at Muness Castle (Unst). Another
parallel with Muness is provided by the corbelling of the main

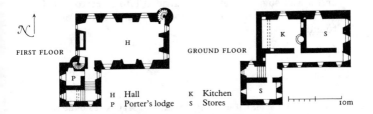

Scalloway Castle. Plans of ground and first floors.
(Redrawn by permission of the RCAHMS)

block's turrets, which have continuous mouldings topped by two tiers of chequer-set corbels with shotholes in the spaces between. The same type of corbelling but without the shotholes appears at the stair turret and SW turret of the jamb, but its other turrets are projected on continuous mouldings. In the jamb's E face, a roll-moulded round-arched door with a splayed gunloop to its l. Above the door, a horizontal panel whose inscription has worn away,* surmounted by the moulded frame for a double panel (now empty but which perhaps contained the arms of Earl Patrick and his wife) topped by a weathered coat of arms, probably those of the King.

The jamb's door opens into a tunnel-vaulted square vestibule, with the main stair straight ahead. On the vestibule's S, a segmental-arched doorway (an early C20 restoration) into a vaulted store or porter's lodge, its W part under the stair. On the vestibule's W side, a wide segmental arch into a vaulted passage running the full length of the main block. Two tunnel-vaulted rooms off this passage. The W is the kitchen. The whole of its gable wall is occupied by the fireplace. Recess in its N ingo; a second recess in the S wall just E of the fireplace. On the kitchen's E side is a well partly contained in a round-arched wall-niche (an early C20 restoration). Rectangular recess in the wall N of the well. The ground floor's E room is a large store.

The principal stair in the jamb is scale-and-platt, each flight covered by a tunnel-vault. W of the first-floor landing, an early C20 round-arched door to a porter's lodge, its floor placed at a higher level and with a N fireplace. The whole first floor of the main block is occupied by the hall. E and S fireplaces, the E's segmental arch an unconvincing restoration. Windows here and on the floors above placed in segmental-arched embrasures.

In the NE turret, a ruinous stair to the second and third floors. It is entered from a window embrasure. So too is the (restored) stair in the inner angle with the jamb, which rises in its turret only to the second floor, being carried inside the jamb to the third floor. On the second floor the jamb has contained one room with a fireplace in the N wall. In the main block, two rooms, the W with a S fireplace, the smaller E room with a fireplace in the gable; both rooms have had garderobes in the N wall. On the third floor, another room in the jamb, with a S fireplace and N garderobe. Fireplaces in the main block's gables and S wall suggest that it was divided into three rooms. It is uncertain if the turrets were roofed as closets or were open rounds.

---

*It was recorded in the C18 as reading 'PATRICIUS STEUARDUS ORCHADIÆ ET ZETLANDIÆ / COMES.I.V.R.S. / CUJUS FUNDAMEN SAXUM EST, DOM' ILLA MANEBIT / LABILIS E CONTRA SI SIT ARENA PERIT / A.D. 1600.' ('Patrick Stewart, Earl of Orkney and Shetland. James V King of Scots. That house whose foundation is on a rock shall stand but if on sand it shall fall . . . ').

SCATNESS EAST *see* SUMBURGH (MAINLAND)

SCORD OF BROUSTER *see* WALLS (MAINLAND)

SELLAFIRTH (YELL)   *5090*

A few houses on the NE side of Basta Voe.

CHURCH. Built as North Yell Free Church in 1862. Harled
Georgian-survival kirk with a ball-finialled birdcage bellcote on
the W gable, whose porch may be an addition. Rectangular
windows.

SEMBLISTER (MAINLAND)   *3050*

Place-name with the former church on the shore of The Firth
between Bixter Voe and Sandsound Voe.

SANDSTING PARISH CHURCH. Plain harled box of 1780, with
rectangular windows. The C19 porch hides a round-arched
door. Converted to a house by *Richard Gibson*, 1985.

SKELBERRY (MAINLAND)   *3010*

Handful of houses.

METHODIST CHURCH. Dated 1894. Plain box with a small
gableted bellcote and S porch. Pointed windows in the porch
and front gable.

BROCH, Clumlie, 2.1km. NE. Broch of *c.* 100 B.C.–A.D. 100
standing in a deserted croft. Circular, *c.* 20m. in diameter, the
wall still more than 2m. high. Entrance at the SE, its passage
having had door checks formed by upright slabs. Off its r. side,
a guard chamber. The inner wall to the court has been recased.
At the S, a wall cell.

SOUTHVOE *see* DUNROSSNESS (MAINLAND)

STANYDALE *see* GRUTING (MAINLAND)

SULLOM (MAINLAND)   *3070*

A few widely scattered houses on the W side of Sullom Voe.

CONGREGATIONAL CHURCH. Dated 1865. Broad harled box
with a small gableted ashlar bellcote.

3070   # SULLOM VOE OIL TERMINAL (MAINLAND)
7.8km. NE of Brae

Large, quite discreetly sited but architecturally undistinguished industrial complex built in 1973–82.

4000   # SUMBURGH (MAINLAND)

The S tip of Mainland and the site of the islands' principal airport.

SUMBURGH AIRPORT. The WILSNESS TERMINAL is by *G. R. M. Kennedy & Partners*, 1979, sensible but unexciting.

SUMBURGH HEAD LIGHTHOUSE. By *Robert Stevenson*, 1820. Short round tower with a lantern cupola; flat-roofed keepers' houses. All harled.

SUMBURGH HOUSE. By *David Rhind*, 1866–7. Gabled, gableted and bow-windowed villa enjoying the view over the West Voe but obdurately dour. Conical-roofed round tower giving a hint of pretension. Additions, attached and detached, for its present hotel use.

JARLSHOF. *See* p. 480.

FORT, Ness of Burgi, 1.9km. S. Fort made in the first millennium B.C. on a headland which projects from the S end of the Scat Ness peninsula, the present approach across a narrow natural rock arch having been less dangerous before prolonged coastal erosion. On the headland itself, a low outer rampart with an entrance at the E. Then an outer enclosure; in it, a neat rectangular mound of stones gathered during C20 excavation of the site. Inner defence of a broad (*c.* 6.4m.) rampart of earth and stone with a rock-cut ditch each side. Central passage through the rampart. Behind and at a higher level, a roughly rectangular drystone blockhouse, its SW end destroyed by erosion but still *c.* 22.5m. long and *c.* 1.2m. high. Entrance passage aligned on that through the rampart and with some roofing lintels in place. Inside the passage, door checks and bar-holes which run back into wall cells. Behind the checks, a doorway into the sizeable NE cell. The SW cell is entered from the blockhouse's inner side. To its S, a much restored small cell, probably originally entered from the blockhouse's now missing end.

FORT, Scatness East, 1.6km. S. Fragments of a fort constructed in the late first millennium B.C. It occupies a promontory, the approach defended by a rampart and ditch. Behind the ditch, ruined remains of a stone blockhouse.

SYMBISTER *see* WHALSAY

TANGWICK (MAINLAND)   *2070*

Just a few houses on the S side of the Esha Ness peninsula.

Just a few houses on the S side of the Esha Ness peninsula.

TANGWICK HAA. Unpretentious and small thick-walled and harled laird's house, perhaps C17. Straight skews. The large buttresses flanking the entrance presumably date from a repair. The E extension was left roofless in the main block's restoration by the *Peter Johnson Partnership*, 1978.

TINGWALL (MAINLAND)   *4040*

Church and manse just N of the Loch of Tingwall.

PARISH CHURCH. Harled box built in 1788–90. On the E gable, a semicircular-topped bellcote. All windows rectangular except the roundheaded ones flanking the pulpit in the centre of the S wall. Mid-C19 E porch with pointed windows. The original interior survives. Panel-fronted GALLERY on etiolated Tuscan columns round three sides. – On the S, a tall PULPIT, the back decorated with fluted pilasters; circular sounding board with a ball-finialled ogee top.

GRAVEYARD. To the church's SE, a turf-covered MAUSO-LEUM, probably part of the previous church, with a roll-moulded and round-arched E entrance which looks C17. Inside are C17 and C18 GRAVESLABS carved with heraldry and emblems of death, the one commemorating Thomas Boune † 1603 with these decorations not in relief but incised. – To the S, a small SARCOPHAGUS of *c.* 1700, the top carved with two coats of arms,* the sides with grisly reminders of mortality.

Harled late Georgian MANSE across the road to the S.

TWATT (MAINLAND)   *3050*

Small crofting township.

CHURCH. Now a store. Late Victorian mission church in a small graveyard. Steeply gabled bellcote and vestry at the N.

UYEA   *6090*

Island off the S coast of Unst.

CHAPEL. Ruin of a small church, perhaps C12. There survive the rubble-built walls of a roughly rectangular nave, *c.* 4.9m. by 3.7m. In its E wall, a narrow doorway with slightly inclined jambs to the vanished chancel. In the W gable, a blocked door, its lintel resting on roughly corbelled springers. There is now no evidence of windows. Against the W end, a late medieval

---

*The arms are of Mitchell and Umphray, so this probably commemorates John Mitchell (b. *c.* 1640), the husband of Jean Umphray.

sacristy built of larger stones. Blocked N door; one window jamb in the W wall. It has projected S of the church.

₅₀₀₀   UYEASOUND (UNST)

A few buildings round a bay.

CHAPEL, 2.6km. NE. Fragmentary remains of a roughly rectangular church, *c.* 11m. by 3.4m., with an entrance in the middle of the W gable. It may be early medieval.

CHURCH. Built as a Free church in 1843. Very broad rendered box with a shallow-pitched roof and rectangular windows. At the E gable, a ball-finialled birdcage bellcote and a round-arched door with projecting keyblock and imposts.

HARBOUR. Probably early C19. U-plan, with rubble piers. On the shore, a range of rubble-built early C19 stores.

BELMONT. *See* p. 469.

STANDING STONE, Bordastubble, 2.6km. NW. Massive irregular block, *c.* 3.6m. high, tilted towards the SW, probably set up in the second millennium B.C.

STANDING STONE, Uyea Breck, 0.6km. SE. Thinnish 3m.-high monolith overlooking Skuda Sound, erected probably in the second millennium B.C.

₂₀₄₀   VAILA

Island just off the W coast of Mainland at the mouths of Vaila Sound and Gruting Voe. Arthur Anderson, founder of the P. & O. shipping line, established a short-lived fishing station here in 1837, some of whose roofless rubble buildings survive on the W shore. In 1893 the island was acquired by a Yorkshire mill-owner, Herbert Anderton, who created the present Vaila Hall.

VAILA HALL. C17 laird's house transformed into a late Victorian castellated curiosity. The present house* was begun by Joseph Mitchell of Girlsta, a Scalloway merchant and Commissioner of Supply for Shetland, apparently in 1696 (the date above the original front door). This was a tall harled house of two storeys and three bays. In front to the N was a courtyard entered through a round-arched W gateway. By the mid-C19 the courtyard's N side had been closed by a single-storey block, probably containing the kitchen. Herbert Anderton bought Vaila in 1893 and two years later employed the Bradford architect *E. P. Peterson* to design N additions to the C17 house, which was itself dressed up with concrete crowsteps. Work was completed by 1900. In this work of the 1890s a two-storey hall was built over the courtyard, with a new two-storey block to its N. This new work is of sneck-harled local rubble with sandstone dressings. The

---

*Nothing is visible on Vaila of the 'hous and fortice' for whose erection Robert Cheyne obtained permission from James VI in 1576.

style is closer to late Georgian castellated than High Victorian Scottish Baronial. Low piend roof over the hall, almost hidden by a deep corbelled battlement with angle rounds at the ends and an armorial panel in the centre. Big but plain Romanesque entrance. The crowstepped N block is again battlemented. At its NW corner, a round tower whose parapet is carried on corbelled roundheaded arcading, with a tall bartizan projecting to the NW.

In the vestibule the two W windows which flank the front door are filled with STAINED-GLASS figures of St Magnus and Earl Rognvald, signed by *Powell Bros.* of Leeds. At the E wall, three roundheaded arches, the outer two blind, the centre filled by the door into the Great Hall. This is of two storeys. Neo-Jacobean compartmented wooden ceiling, its bosses carved with foliage. On the W side, a first-floor segmental-headed stone arcade on squat piers; it opens into a gallery above the vestibule. In the E wall opposite, four tall roundheaded windows filled with armorial stained glass (again by *Powell Bros.*). Round-arched chimneypiece with simplified Gothic columns on the N. The hall's S side is the front wall of the C17 house. In it are still exposed the roll-moulded entrance door and two first-floor windows, both with chamfered margins like those in the W gable. Below the sill of the window over the door is a worn panel carved with the Mitchell arms and the date 1696. Inside the C17 house, the W ground-floor room (now the library) has an Adam-revival chimneypiece, presumably of the 1890s. Of the same date is the heavy neo-Jacobean wooden chimneypiece, decorated with the Anderton coat of arms and motto, in the morning room to the E.

WALLED GARDEN to the S and W. The ball-finialled GATE-PIERS in its N wall look early C18.

Square two-storey TOWER on a narrow promontory 0.5km. W. Rubble-built (originally harled), with a round-arched door and window to the E. In the W front, rectangular ground-floor windows, separated by small Gothic niches from the round-arched first-floor window. All this looks early C19. The battlemented parapet and angle turret are replacements of *c.* 1900.

VALSGARTH *see* HAROLDSWICK (UNST)

VEMENTRY   2060

Hilly island off Mainland, now uninhabited but still well defended with concrete gun emplacements dating from the Second World War.

CHAMBERED CAIRN. Substantial remains on the top of Muckle Ward, the island's highest hill. The cairn was probably built in the third or second millennium B.C., apparently in two stages. The first produced a round cairn of *c.* 7.9m. diameter standing on a slightly wider masonry platform. Walling of irregular stones and with a batter suggests the cairn originally had a domed top. Entrance passage at the SSE leading to the trefoil-shaped central chamber. The second phase made the present 'heel' shape, extending the platform in front of the entrance and giving it a concave façade unbroken by any opening, built of roughly square massive blocks. This stands to a height of *c.* 1.2m. and may never have been much more. The space between this façade and the original cairn was filled with a mass of loose stones blocking the original entrance.

VOE (MAINLAND)

4060

Small village at the head of Olna Firth, with C19 houses on its S shore, 1970s housing and the two churches at Hillside on the N.

DELTING PARISH CHURCH. Built by *Bigland & Mouat*, 1953. White harled box with an angular bellcote. – Inside, built into the W wall, is the grand GRAVESLAB of Mr Alexander Dunbar †1708, its top carved with an engagingly inept coat of arms, the rest covered by a long inscription.

Former DELTING PARISH CHURCH. Roofless early C18 T-plan kirk, built of rubble and formerly harled. In the long S wall, a ground-floor rectangular window at each end. Two doors in the centre; the W has a window directly above, but a second upper-tier window misses alignment with the E door. In each gable of the main block, a round-arched door under a high-set window. At the ruinous N jamb, a forestair on the W to a first-floor door. In the gable, a big segmental-arched entrance to the burial place of the Giffords of Busta. Over this door, a large panel bearing the coats of arms and initials of Thomas Gifford and his wife, Elizabeth Mitchell, and the date 1714.

Inside the body of the church, joist-holes for lofts on the N, E and W. – On the E wall of the Gifford burial place, an C18 heraldic SLAB.

VOE HOUSE. Early C19 harled laird's house of two storeys and five bays.

WALLS (MAINLAND)

2040

Sheltered coastal village.

METHODIST CHURCH. Dated 1871. Harled box with pointed windows and a gableted bellcote. – Contemporary MANSE to the E.

ST PAUL'S PARISH CHURCH. Built in 1899–1900 to a design provided by *E. P. Peterson* of Bradford but modified for economy by *Alexander Campbell*. Drydashed, with sandstone dressings. Gableted bellcote. Round-arched windows and door with chamfered arrises, their surrounds flush with the walling.

HARBOUR. At the SW end, a concrete PIER of *c.* 1910. Rubble

SLIPS at the head of the bay. Behind them, the substantial three-storey harled BAYHALL of *c.* 1750, restored by *Shetland Islands Council* in 1978.

CHAMBERED CAIRN, Gallow Hill, 2km. NE. Shaggy ruin of a round cairn, its *c.* 25m. diameter exceptionally large for Shetland. Massive boulders round the edge. In the centre, the tops of large upright stones seem to indicate that it had a circular chamber. It probably dates from the second or third millennium B.C.

SETTLEMENT, Pinhoulland, 1.5km. E. Nucleated settlement of the third or second millennium B.C. Mounds covering seven large houses, a few traces of field-walls and many clearance cairns.

SETTLEMENT, Scord of Brouster, 2.4km. NE. Remains of four houses of the late third or early second millennium B.C., together with the walls of their fields and more than a hundred clearance cairns. At the S of the site, a roughly oval stone-walled enclosure, *c.* 60m. long. At this enclosure's N end, a large oval house (the best-preserved of the four) entered at the downhill end. Interior of 7m. by 5m. with a central hearth; round the walls, stone-built cells divided by massive boulders. Nearby, a round ring CAIRN with a kerb of large boulders.

WEISDALE (MAINLAND) 3050

Valley, its flourishing plantations unexpected in Shetland.

CHURCH. Built as a Free church in 1863, with minimal Gothic detail. At the S gable, pinnacled buttresses at the corners and slightly advanced centre, which is topped by a birdcage bellcote with a spired bellcast roof. The porch is an addition. Interior with original furnishings, including a roomy PULPIT.

KERGORD MILL. Big rubble-built cornmill of 1855, the largest in Shetland. Three storeys and five bays, the wheel now gone.

WEST BURRA 3030

Long narrow island joined by bridges to Trondra and East Burra. A village, mostly of the C 20, at Hamnavoe and smaller settlements at Bridge End and Papil.

BAPTIST CHURCH, Hamnavoe. Dated 1907. Low harled box with a gableted bellcote and Tudor-arched windows and door. A small flat-roofed addition fills the inner angle of the church and vestry.

CHURCH OF SCOTLAND, Bridge End. Built as a United Presbyterian church and manse under one roof in 1867. *Fleur-de-lis* finial on the gableted bellcote. The drydashed porch is a recent addition.

PARISH CHURCH, Papil. Disused. Built in 1804. Rubble-built box, formerly harled, with a W bellcote (its top now missing).

Rectangular windows. The interior is now derelict but has had a gallery on three sides and the pulpit in the middle of the s wall. – Rubble-built BURIAL ENCLOSURE against the E gable, probably early C19.

BRIDGE END OUTDOOR CENTRE, Bridge End. Harled late Victorian school and schoolhouse built on an islet at the head of South Voe.

_4080_ WEST SANDWICK (YELL)

Scattered settlement on the shore and to the N of Southladie Voe.

CHURCH. Sneck-harled mission chapel of 1894, with a gableted bellcote. – Contemporary MANSE attached to the w gable.

NORTH HAA. _See_ p. 501.

_5060_ WHALSAY

Comfortably sized island with agreeably low-scale hills, now occupied by crofters. Symbister at the ferry terminal is the only village.

CHURCH, Symbister. Humble sneck-harled box of _c._ 1900. Segmental-arched windows in the sides and N end; at the s gable, pointed windows and a cross.

PARISH CHURCH, Brough. T-plan kirk built in 1733 of sneck-harled rubble, the small gableted bellcote a Victorian replacement and the roof now covered with asbestos tiles. Rectangular windows and roundheaded doors (the w blocked) at the crossbar. In the s jamb's gable, a segmental-arched entrance to a tunnel-vaulted burial place occupying its ground floor. Forestair to the gallery above. Interior FURNISHINGS of the mid-C19, with a gallery round three sides and the pulpit crowned with a sounding board.

HARBOUR, Symbister. Two long drystone rubble breakwaters protect the bay. From its s shore project two concrete piers designed by _John M. Aitken, c._ 1895. – At the NE corner, the very small and shallow U-plan OLD HARBOUR with rubble-built quay and pier, perhaps C17. At the end of its s pier is a two-storey C17 böd (THE PIER HOUSE), rubble-built but with ashlar tops to the gables, of which the w is roughly triangular. On the N (harbour) side, a jettied stone canopy over the hoist for goods. The building was restored by _Richard Gibson_ in 1984. – On the Old Harbour's E side, HARBOUR VIEW, plain mid-C19 in its present rendered form but perhaps incorporating an earlier böd.

WHALSAY LEISURE CENTRE, Symbister. By _Faulkner Browns_, 1989. Big and broad, with shallow-pitched roofs, the walls drydashed in coloured patterns.

SYMBISTER HOUSE, Symbister. Now the Primary School. As built for Robert Bruce of Symbister, _c._ 1835, it was an urbane villa of two storeys over a high basement. Three bays by three, with a portico of coupled Roman Doric columns at the W front's slightly advanced centre. The ground-floor windows, originally rectangular, have been enlarged to fill their roundheaded over-arches. Awkward C20 'mansard' roof. The 1830s wings have been replaced by school additions. Built into the N extension, a large PANEL carved with the arms and initials of John Bruce Steuart and Christina Gifford and signed by *John Forbes*, 1750.

Behind the house, a contemporary courtyard STEADING. At each end of its W range, a rectangular gateway topped by big urns of simplified classical design. This range's centrepiece is a pyramid-roofed DOOCOT. Ball-finialled birdcage bellcote at the centre of the E range. The N range's W gable still has urn finials. The S has been mostly replaced by a two-storey drydashed house. – To the NE, a pair of stubbily pinnacled GATEPIERS.

FORT, Loch of Huxter. Low remains of a fort, probably of the late first millennium B.C., standing on a small island linked to the shore by a rubble causeway. On the island, just N of the causeway's end, a line of boulders may be the remains of an outer defence. Behind the boulders but not quite parallel to them, the ruin of a 12.5m.-long drystone-walled gatehouse, its central passage having door-checks and a bar-hole. Each side of the passage, a wall chamber entered from the enclosure behind. From the gatehouse's ends a drystone wall has run round the island.

HOUSES AND CAIRNS, Pettigarths Field. Two excavated HOUSES (the 'Benie Hoose' and the 'Standing Stones of Yoxie') of the third or second millennium B.C. on a hillside overlooking the sea. Both are large ovals, built of massive boulders, and contained one or two rooms and wall recesses. The entrance to each was from an oval courtyard, perhaps an enclosure for animals. Higher up on the hill to the NW, two CAIRNS, both reduced to their basecourses and tumbled stones. The earlier has been almost square, *c.* 5.2m. by 5.5m., its E front per-haps slightly concave. The chamber inside has had shallow recesses in the N, W and S walls. Immediately on its N, a round cairn in which is now exposed a rectangular slab-sided burial cist.

WHITENESS (MAINLAND)　　　3040

Area including the eponymous ness, on the W side of Mainland.

METHODIST CHURCH, Hoove. Mission chapel built in 1905, with a concrete bellcote on the N gable.

PARISH CHURCH, Loch Strom. Now a house. Harled rectangle of 1837. Rectangular windows and a birdcage bellcote.

CASTLE, Loch of Strom. On an island connected by a sandy causeway to the W shore. Ruinous remains of a rectangular tower, *c.* 5.5m. by 6.4m. externally, built of rubble and shell-lime mortar. It is perhaps late medieval.

CAIRN, Nesbister Hill, 1.2km. E. Round hill-top cairn of the second millennium B.C., *c.* 8m. in diameter. Drystone kerb. In the centre, a now uncovered cist formed of large upright slabs.

SKYE AND LOCHALSH

A district occupied by the large isle of Skye and the immediately adjoining piece of the mainland; it is predominantly hilly but has sizeable tracts of flat but not necessarily very fertile land, partly occupied by crofting settlements. For most of the Middle Ages Skye was part of the lordship of the Isles, its rulers semi-independent of the Scottish Crown and of Norse descent. After the forfeiture of that lordship in 1493, two families, the Macdonalds of Sleat and the MacLeods of MacLeod, dominated the island, the Macdonalds from the C18 attempting to establish towns and villages, Portree at last achieving a respectable size, Kyleakin becoming little more than a row of guesthouses serving some of the many tourists attracted here each summer.

ARMADALE CASTLE
2.7km. sw of Kilmore

6000

Now a ruin, the victim of neglect and dry rot, this seat of the Macdonalds was the most accomplished Georgian castellated mansion in Highland. It began as an unpretentious two-storey house in the late C18; just a three-bay centre with slightly projecting broad ends. In 1815–19 the second Lord Macdonald commissioned *James Gillespie Graham* to add a w block containing grand new public rooms.* This was a battlemented toy fort with a central tower over the vestibule and stairhall, its front corners hidden by octagonal turrets clasping the porch. Inside, the main rooms had elaborate plaster vaults and the stair's great window was filled with a STAINED-GLASS depiction of Somerled, Lord of the Isles, progenitor of the Macdonalds, by *W. R. Eginton*. In 1821 *William Smith* (under the superintendence of *John Sinclair*) added a new kitchen at the C18 house's NE corner. This original part of the house was then recased and heightened in 1855–6 by *David Bryce*, again in the castle style but with unappealing snecked rubble and mechanical detail. The low harled service court to its E is at least partly by *James Ross*, 1848. Gillespie Graham's house has been reduced to low walls except for the entrance and the first flight of the Imperial stair with its Gothick-balustered landing supported on pointed arches. The C18 block as remodelled by Bryce stands as a roofless shell.

*Gillespie Graham also designed a very much larger house than was to be built.

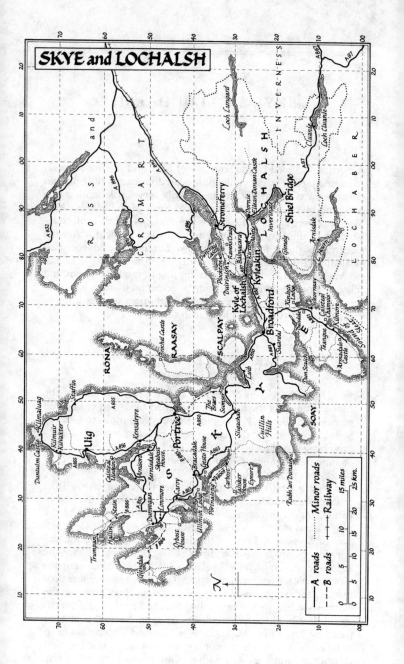

SKYE and LOCHALSH

At the entrance to the policies from the s, piend-roofed STABLES of 1820–2, built by *Macpherson & McNaughton* under the superintendence of *James Ferguson*, who may have provided the design or adapted one by *Gillespie Graham*. Broad ends with four-centred arches to the old carriage openings. Slightly set-back three-bay links, each with two tiers of Gothick windows; a central square tower crowned by a corbelled battlement. The rubble walling was harled and fussy Gothick additions were built at the back on conversion to a restaurant by *The Boys Jarvis Partnership* in 1979–84. – To their NE the drive crosses a Gothick BRIDGE built under *John Sinclair*'s superintendence in 1821–5. – W of the Castle, a roofless LAUNDRY, simple Gothick of 1820–2, built under *Ferguson*'s superintendence.

ARNISDALE
8010

Group of little-altered C19 vernacular cottages overlooking Loch Hourn.

FREE CHURCH. By *Matthews & Lawrie*, 1888. Plain harled box. Narrow lancets in the s gable, a rose window in the N.

ARNISDALE HOUSE. White harled, gabled and gableted; by *Ross & Macbeth*, 1898.

ARNISORT
3050

Hamlet near Loch Greshornish.

CHURCH. Built as a Free Church mission chapel in the late C19 and much altered in 1900, when the s gable's bellcote was replaced by a concrete croquet hoop. Round-arched windows and bracketed eaves.

BALMACARA
8020

Two hamlets (Balmacara and Balmacara Square) on the lower slopes of Sgurr Mór, the mansion house and monument beside Loch Alsh.

MONUMENT TO DONALD MURCHISON, 2.2km. W. On a rocky outcrop beside the shore. Thin grey granite obelisk with cham-fered corners; by *William Sim*, 1863 (restored 1928). The inscription records that Murchison 'SUCCESSFULLY AND FAITHFULLY PRESERVED THE LANDS OF KINTAIL AND LOCHALSH FROM 1715 TO 1722 FOR HIS CHIEF WILLIAM THE EXILED EARL OF SEAFORTH', a feat recorded also in Landseer's *Rent Day in the Highlands*.

BALMACARA HOUSE. By *Ross & Joass*, 1861, and much extended since.

BALMACARA SQUARE. On the hamlet's W side, a harled mid-C19 farm STEADING, a big Italianate tower rising in the centre of the front range.

BERNERA BARRACKS *see* GLENELG

4040 ### BERNISDALE

Strung-out village on the w side of Loch Snizort Beag.

SNIZORT FREE CHURCH. Big broad crowstepped and buttressed box by *Alexander Mackenzie*, 1843–7. Crowstepped
bellcote on the E gable; triangular-headed windows. Deep E
gallery inside. – Adjoining, the contemporary old SCHOOL.

CHURCHYARD, Skeabost Island, 1.2km. SE. Little more than
grass-covered foundations of the OLD SNIZORT PARISH
CHURCH; it may have been C16. – To the W, the ruined
TEAMPULL (ST COLUMBA'S CHURCH), a small and plain
rubble-built chapel, probably late medieval. – GRAVESLABS.
Inside the Teampull, a C16 stone carved with a knight in high
relief. It is very similar to the effigy thought to be of John
MacLeod of Minginish in St Clement's Church at Rodel
(Western Isles) and may be by the same sculptor. – Just outside
the chapel, a weathered and broken slab, perhaps C15, carved
with the relief of another knight. – To the SW, a third stone,
probably C15 or C16, also bearing the relief of a knight. In the
top r. corner, a small figure of St Michael the Archangel; in the
top l. corner, initials, thought to be those of members of the
MacSween family.

SKEABOST HOUSE. *See* p. 550.

3030 ### BRACADALE

Small village at an inlet of Loch Harport.

FREE CHURCH. Neat white harled box of 1854, still Georgian in
character.

PARISH CHURCH. Tall two-bay rectangle of sneck-harled
rubble, by *William Smith*, 1831. Big pointed-arched windows.
    In the centre of the churchyard behind, two late medieval
GRAVESLABS. One, weathered and broken, is carved with the
high-relief figure of a knight, the other with a claymore under
a foliaged cross.

BROCH (DUN BEAG), 0.7km. NW. Truncated remains of a broch
of the late first millennium B.C. or the early first millennium
A.D., built on top of a knoll. External diameter of *c.* 20m.,
the battered outer wall-face constructed of coursed blocks.
Entrance passage from the E. Inside the court, doorways to a
small wall cell, a wall gallery and, S of the entrance, a gallery
whose N end is formed by an oval cell, its S by a stairway of
about twenty steps.

GESTO HOUSE. *See* p. 534.
ULLINISH LODGE. *See* p. 553.

THE BRAES

Scattered crofts overlooking the Sound of Raasay.

CHURCH. Disused. Small Gothic mission church, by *Matthews & Lawrie*, 1879. In the *fleur-de-lis*-finialled s gable, a trefoil opening.

BROADFORD

Sizeable but undistinguished village, mostly late C19.

BROADFORD FREE CHURCH. By *G. S. Aitken*, 1873. Broad buttressed box. Blocked Gothic lights in the front gable.

BROADFORD FREE PRESBYTERIAN CHURCH. Minimal Gothic of 1958.

STRATH PARISH CHURCH. Built in 1839–41. Standard kirk with round-arched windows. On the N gable, an open-pedimented bellcote. Flat Tudor porch-doorpiece. The glazing pattern probably dates from the repairs made in 1884.

DOCTOR MACKINNON MEMORIAL HOSPITAL. Sensible complex of the 1980s including the hospital, the Community Care Centre (by *Highland Regional Council*, 1987), with big tiled roofs, and the Medical Centre (by *Magnus Gunnarson*, 1989).

PIER. L-plan rubble pier, by *James Gillespie Graham*, 1807. – Beside it, a rubble-built turf-covered SALMON HOUSE, probably early C19.

CAIRN, Achadh a' Churn. Large grass-covered round cairn, *c.* 24m. in diameter and 2.4m. high. It probably dates from the third millennium B.C.

BROCHEL CASTLE *see* RAASAY

CAISTEAL CHAMUIS / KNOCK CASTLE
0.4km. E of Teangue

Ruin of a small castle standing on a promontory on the NE side of Knock Bay. The landward approach from the N seems to have been cut by a ditch. On the promontory's E side, a rubble-built block, perhaps late C15. Small window low down in its E wall; entrance at the SW. SW wing, probably a C16 addition; it has been of two storeys. There seems also to have been a W range.

CAISTEAL GRUGAIG *see* SHIEL BRIDGE

CAISTEAL MAOL *see* KYLEAKIN

3050
CAISTEAL UISDEIN
5.2km. sw of Uig

Beside the shore at the entrance to Loch Snizort Beag, the ruin of a large rectangular tower, *c.* 15m. by 10m., traditionally said to have been built by Uistean MacGhilleaspuig (Hugh, the son of Archibald the Clerk) *c.* 1580; but the very thick walls, built of coursed basalt blocks, many set on end, and the lack of vaulting inside suggest it could be considerably earlier. At the ground floor, small loopholes at the w end of the N wall and the s wall's E end. No door, so presumably this was a store reached by a ladder from the floor above. First-floor entrance in the w wall; on its s side, a flight of steps in the wall-thickness survives of a stair to the floor or floors above. The hall's fireplace has been in the N wall.

3030
CARBOST

Undistinguished distillery village, most of the houses c 20, standing beside Loch Harport.

CHURCH OF SCOTLAND. Humble harled mission church built in the early c 20. Angular bellcote on the E gable.

FREE CHURCH. Early c 20 harled box. On the s gable, a ball-finialled crowstepped bellcote.

TALISKER DISTILLERY. By *Charles C. Doig*, 1890, and very plain.

3040
CAROY

Ruined chapel by itself on the steep wooded bank of Loch Caroy.

ST JOHN'S CHAPEL (Episcopal). Roofless ruin in a small graveyard. The chapel was built in 1836–8. Plain rubble rectangle with a tall pointed window in the E gable; the other openings are rectangular.

CAIRNS, 0.7km. NW. Two round, partly overgrown cairns in moorland above the mouth of Glen Heysdal. The s cairn has been very large, with a diameter of *c.* 35m., but is now ruinous. Some remains of a kerb formed by edge-set stones. – The N cairn is better preserved. Diameter of *c.* 27m. and *c.* 6m. high, the steep sides flattening towards the base. At the NE, a kerb of edge-set or flat stones; probably it continued all round originally. Both cairns date probably from the third millennium B.C.

CLUANIE

0010

Just an hotel beside the dam.

CLUANIE DAM. By *Sir Alexander Gibb & Partners*, 1946. Straight-forward concrete barrier across Loch Cluanie.

DORNIE

8020

Small village laid out by *D. Urquhart* in 1794 on land belonging to Colonel Francis Humberston Mackenzie of Seaforth. Short terraces of c 19 housing N and s of the bridge over Loch Long.

DORNIE CHURCH. Red sandstone mission church, by *Ross & Macbeth*, 1889. Tall slate-spired bellcote.

ST DUTHAC'S CHURCH (R.C.). Austere Gothic, by *J. A. Hansom*, 1871. Paired lancets at the buttressed nave. On its harled w gable, a gabled bellcote for two bells. Lower chancel joined by a NE vestry to the contemporary priest's house. – Inside, a scissors roof over the nave; in the chancel, a wooden pointed tunnel-vault. Chancel arch of two orders, the inner springing from heavy corbels. – STAINED GLASS. Early c 20 E window (the Baptism of Our Lord), colourful and bad. – Rather better the late c 20 abstract two-light window on the chancel's N side.

EILEAN DONAN CASTLE. *See* p. 532.

DUIRINISH

7030

Informal crofting village. On the w approach, a c 19 U-plan group of drystone walled byres and barns, originally thatched, now covered with corrugated iron. At the E end, BRIDGE of 1826, a high semicircular arch over the Allt Dhuirinish.

DUISDALE

6010

1.5km. N of Isleornsay

By *Matthews & Lawrie*, 1867. Tall twin-gabled house built of sneck-harled granite rubble with red sandstone dressings.

DUN ARDTRECK *see* PORTNALONG

DUNCRAIG CASTLE

8030

1.1km. E of Plockton

Large but uninspired Baronial mansion by *Alexander Ross*, built in 1866 for Sir Alexander Matheson, who had bought the Lochalsh estate fifteen years before. Porte cochère on the s (entrance) front; a tower on the N overlooking Loch Carron. Plain late C20 addition at the E.

DUN SCAICH
7.6km. NW of Teangue

5010

Scanty remains of a castle of enclosure, possibly of the C13, which was held by the Macdonalds of Sleat. The site, beside the mouth of Loch Eishort, is a cliff-edged rock surrounded by the sea on three sides. On the landward (E) side it has been cut off by a ditch, *c.* 6m. wide and 4.6m. deep. The ditch is spanned by two rubble-built arches, 1.8m. apart, which supported a wooden drawbridge, its pivot-holes visible on the W side immediately in front of the projecting checks of a door which has opened onto a flight of stone steps, its upper part now missing. The whole summit of the rock has been surrounded by a wall, still *c.* 4.5m. high at the SE. Remains of a garderobe at the NE corner and another at the S, where there may also have been a sea gate. At the rock's W end, grass-covered foundations of a rectangular building.

DUN TELVE *see* GLENELG

DUN TRODDAN *see* GLENELG

DUNTULM CASTLE
2.1km. W of Kilmaluag

4070

Dramatically isolated on a rocky promontory sticking into Duntulm Bay. The castle was probably built for the MacLeods of Dunvegan, who were bailies of Trotternish by the C15. The site is of great defensive strength, dropping almost sheer to the sea on the N, E and W. The S approach has been cut off by a narrow but deep ditch, presumably originally crossed by a drawbridge. Around the top of this promontory, a whinstone rubble wall, now largely non-existent on the S side and fragmentary on the N. At the NW corner the wall is corbelled out on thin slabs, the line of the lower slabs continued as a stringcourse as far as an angular projection to the E. In the main stretch of the N wall E of this, a sea gate opening onto a narrow ledge onto which men and supplies could be hoisted from a ship below. Bastion at the NE corner, its rounded lower part supporting an angular top.

The ground inside the curtain wall is far from flat, the highest point being near the SE corner. At the corner itself, a tunnel-vaulted chamber apparently contemporary with the curtain wall, which is here pierced by a S window. Aumbry in the room's

N wall. A stair against this wall leads to the remains of a detached tower on the site's summit immediately to the N. This tower, probably C 17, has been of two storeys and an attic. On its ground floor, two small rooms, the W vaulted. At the curtain's NW corner, a long two-storey building, probably also C 17.

DUNVEGAN 2040

Scrappy village at the head of Loch Dunvegan, with Dunvegan Castle in wooded policies to the N.

DUIRINISH OLD PARISH CHURCH. Roofless remains of the church built in 1689, according to the date over a door in the N wall. Simple rubble rectangle with rectangular windows and doors. On the W gable, the truncated stump of a corbelled bellcote. The ashlar-built N jamb or 'aisle' is an C 18 addition. Against the W gable, a BURIAL ENCLOSURE of 1735, its walls topped by balustrades; lugged architrave at the N door. – Inside, the church's E end and 'aisle' have been taken over as the burial place of the MacLeods of MacLeod, with arched recesses formed in the church's walls to house their memorials. – MONUMENTS. On the E wall of the 'aisle', two almost identical marble tablets with high-relief coats of arms; they commemorate John Norman MacLeod of MacLeod † 1835 (signed by *David Ness*) and his wife, Anne † 1861. – On the N wall of the body of the church, a mid-C 19 memorial to Dr Donald MacLeod, the tablet carved with a swagged sword and soldier's cap, and supported on lions' masks.

In the GRAVEYARD, SW of the church, two late medieval GRAVESLABS, each carved with a claymore. – At the graveyard's SE corner, the smart early C 18 MONUMENT to Thomas, Lord Fraser of Lovat, † 1699. Ashlar obelisk on a big corniced plinth. It was restored in the mid-C 19, when the marble inscription tablet was placed on the plinth and the marble armorial panel (much patched with cement) moved from there to the obelisk. At the same time the enclosing balustraded screen walls were demolished. – To its W, a pair of C 18 TABLE STONES with plenty of high-relief reminders of death.

DUIRINISH PARISH CHURCH. Classy white harled kirk built in 1832. It is a tall box with Y-traceried wooden mullions in the pointed windows. At the W gable, a narrow-sided tower of four stages, the first three of progressively diminishing heights, the top a big belfry; crenellated parapet with blunt pinnacles at its corners. Inside, a panelled gallery carried on Roman Doric columns round three sides. At the E end, a tall PULPIT with pinnacles at the corners of its ogee-roofed sounding board; wooden urn finial.

DUNVEGAN CASTLE
1.4km. N

Medieval stronghold of the MacLeods, dressed up as an ungainly

Georgian toy fort and now Skye's best-known tourist attraction.
In the early C 13, Leod, son of Olaf the Black, King of Man, put
together a virtual sub-kingdom. From his father and the Earl of
Ross he received Glenelg and Lewis. From his foster-father, Paul
Balkasson, the ruler of Skye, he inherited the lands of Sleat,
Trotternish, Waternish and Snizort in Skye, together with the
islands of Harris and North Uist. By his marriage to the heiress
of MacRaild Armuin he acquired Duirinish, Bracadale, Minginish
and Dunvegan. Leod's descendants, the MacLeods entitled successively as 'of Glenelg', 'of Dunvegan' and 'of MacLeod', have
held Dunvegan since then.

The name, almost certainly meaning 'Began's dun (or fort)',*
presumably commemorates some earlier Norse chieftain who had
resided here. The position near the head of Loch Dunvegan
affords a sheltered haven for galleys. The site of the castle itself is
naturally defensive, a roughly oval mass of basalt on the E side of
a small inlet of the loch, surrounded by water on the N, W and S.
On the E, a broad natural ditch has been deepened‡ and widened
to cut this side off from attack. It was probably Leod who strengthened these defences by building a stone curtain wall (perhaps
replacing an earth rampart) round the summit of the rock, its only
entrance a gate (the Sea Gate) on the W approached from the
shore by a steep and narrow flight of steps cut in the rock. More
steps inside the enclosure point towards the centre of its E side,
apparently the position of the castle's hall in the C 13.

The next stage in Dunvegan's development was the construction of a keep at the NE corner of the enclosure,§ probably
built in the C 14, the work either of Leod's son or grandson
Tormod MacLeod, 'Sheriff' of Skye, or of Tormod's son
Malcolm, who received a Crown charter of Glenelg in 1342 and
married two nieces of King Robert I in succession. It is certainly
likely that the keep had been built by 1439, when the MacLeods
are first named in an official document as 'of Dunvegan'.

A major remodelling of the castle was begun c. 1500 by Alasdair
Crotach ('Hunchbacked Alasdair') MacLeod, who built the Fairy
Tower at the enclosure's SE corner, probably as a S adjunct to the
then existing hall-range.¶ A little over a century later Alasdair
Crotach's grandson Sir Roderick (Rory Mòr) MacLeod built
a new hall-range immediately N of the Fairy Tower, the work
apparently completed by 1623, when J. Colquhowne was paid for
supplying 1,000 stones of lead, presumably for its roof. The C 14
keep must have been abandoned at about this time.‖ Work on
remodelling the castle was resumed in 1664 by Sir Roderick's

---

*The alternative derivation of the name from 'little dun' is unlikely in view of the
size of the defensible site.

‡It is less deep now than it was formerly.

§A fragment of the curtain wall visible outside the keep's NE corner shows that the
enclosure was a little bigger before the keep was built.

¶There is evidence that an earlier building, possibly a chapel, abutted the Fairy
Tower on the W.

‖It had been long abandoned when Dr Johnson and James Boswell visited Dunvegan
in 1773.

grandson Iain Breac ('Pockmarked John') MacLeod, who employed the mason *Donald Ross* to alter the early C17 hall-range. In 1684–90 Iain Breac got the master masons *John Ross* and *John Nicolson* to build a w extension to the Fairy Tower.

For most of the C18 Dunvegan remained little changed. According to Dr Johnson, Norman MacLeod (the owner from 1706 to 1772) began a repair of the keep 'but desisted in a little time, and applied his money to worse uses.' This chief's one major alteration was to make in 1748 a new E entrance (supplementing if not supplanting the Sea Gate) by forming a doorway in the short stretch of curtain wall between the hall-range and keep and providing a staircase up to it from the ditch; *John Urquhart* was the mason. Norman MacLeod's grandson and heir General Norman MacLeod began the conversion of the ragbag medieval and C17 castle into a castellated mansion. In 1790 he employed *Walter Boak*, 'architect', to carry out work costing nearly £3,950. The C14 keep, which had been used as a doocot, was given a new flat roof and battlemented parapet, its N jamb acquiring an ogee roof. NW of the keep was added a plain three-storey block, said to have been intended as a barracks, General MacLeod being then engaged in raising the Second Battalion of the Black Watch from among his tenantry. Between the keep and the hall-range he placed an entrance hall. The C13 curtain wall on the castle's W side, where it had not been incorporated in later buildings, was lowered and given a crenellated parapet. The Georgian castellation of Dunvegan was continued in 1811–14 by the General's son John Norman MacLeod, who rebuilt his father's entrance hall on a larger scale, reconstructed the top floor of the hall-range, whose lower floors acquired new windows, and added an extra floor to the sw wing. Outside the entrance he provided a martial little courtyard approached by a drawbridge. Further remodelling was made for the next chief, Norman MacLeod, by *Robert Brown Jun.* in 1840–50. The keep's N jamb was heightened and the adjoining NW wing of 1790 lowered; both gained battlements in the process. A fourth storey was added to the hall-range, which was broadened to the W, the entrance hall's portico of 1811–14 was replaced by a porch, and the drawbridge by a stone bridge. Since then the castle has been little altered, the SW wing being carefully and conservatively repaired by *Colin Sinclair* in 1938–40 after a fire.

The C13 curtain wall, largely incorporated in the castle's later harled buildings, is visible on the W side overlooking the loch, where it is now topped by crenellations of 1790. The wall is *c.* 1.8m. thick, built of local basalt rubble, the blocks roughly squared and partly coursed; the mortar, sparingly used, was of shell lime with an admixture of charcoal, apparently made from Scots pine. Almost in the middle of this W side is the Sea Gate. Originally it was 2.3m. wide, with a crude depressed arch; the surviving S jamb consists of two upended large stones only sketchily worked. Immediately inside, on the N side, a bar hole in the curtain wall revealed by the collapse of later masonry.

The gateway has been narrowed and the top of its arch blocked, perhaps as part of Sir Roderick MacLeod's early C 17 alterations, the new entrance quite peaceful-looking but containing an iron yett; an outer check shows that this used to stand behind a wooden door. Inside the curtain, a straight flight of steps in a roofless passage up to the site of a second door, its bar hole visible in the N wall. At the foot of the steps, grooves in the wall for a portcullis; it was worked from a wooden platform, two of whose joist holes survive in the N wall. From the inner doorway the main ascent into the courtyard continues straight ahead past the castle's well to the N end of the hall-range. A second and narrower flight of steps at right angles to the main path was made, probably in the C 14, for access from the inner doorway to the keep.

The main approach to the castle is now from the E. Stone bridge of 1840 across the ditch. Then the small forecourt with battlemented bastion walls made in 1811–14. The house's long E front behind looks bleak and mean, a harled Georgian barracks, the main wallhead indented with crenellations and feebly enlivened with turrets. At the l. end, the crowstepped Fairy Tower of c. 1500 is still in recognizably original form. The lower part of its outer walls is formed by the C 13 curtain. At the SE corner this is canted to fit the site, the stonework above brought to a right angle and supported on utilitarian corbels, presumably originally built to carry the curtain wall's parapet. At the top of the tower, a wall walk across the s face and returning halfway along the E gable (the return at the W gable removed when the W extension was heightened). Deep parapet with broad merlons. The projecting stone cannon gargoyles look like early C 17 additions; the original plain stone runnels draining the walk are placed at the bottom of the corbelling.

The hall-range N of the Fairy Tower completed in 1623 is of two bays, its front incorporating the curtain wall and so aligned with the tower. It was originally of three storeys, the second floor (its walling much thinner) set back behind a corbelled wall walk, its deep parapet studded with cannon spouts. In 1664 *Donald Ross* added a balustrade (probably replacing crenellation) to the wall walk's parapet; the effect of this balustraded centrepiece, flanked on the l. by the Fairy Tower's gable and on the r. by a conical-roofed turret (removed in 1811–14), was not unlike that produced by Sir William Bruce at Balcaskie (Fife) and John Mylne Jun. at Panmure (Tayside) a few years later. In the C 17 there was a huge strongly battered chimney behind the wall walk, and the range was finished with a steep slated roof. Now the walk projects in front of two plain storeys of 1840–50 topped by *Brown*'s perfunctory crenellation, a small turret on the r. marking the position of the range's N gable. N of this turret, the broad one-bay infill begun in 1790 but heightened by *Brown* to match his treatment of the hall-range. Projecting two-storey entrance hall of 1811–14 with chunky octagonal corner towers. In the centre of the parapet, a long stone, probably a fireplace lintel, rustically carved with the impaled arms of Iain Breac MacLeod † 1693 and his wife, Florence Macdonald, flanked by animals and levitating angels. The portico between the towers was replaced by a little battlemented porch in 1840.

At the castle's NE corner is the four-storey C14 keep. Under the harling its masonry is of large uncoursed stones with small pinnings. T-plan, with a short off-centre N jamb, its NE corner canted to fit the site. Originally very plain, the windows narrow slits, it acquired Georgian windows and a crenellated wallhead in *Boak*'s repairs of 1790; the main block's small corner turrets and the jamb's top floor and machicolated parapet came in *Brown*'s reconstruction of the 1840s.

To the courtyard the building's frontages are almost all those provided by *Brown*, only the Tudor hoodmoulds over the hall-range's first-floor windows providing a hint of relief from the ungainly economy of his version of the castle style.

The interior is now largely Brown's work of 1840–50. He remodelled the entrance hall with a panelled wooden ceiling of Jacobean type; central stair up to the first floor, where balconies return along the hall's side walls. On the ground floor of the hall-range to the S, three early C17 vaulted cellars linked by a corridor provided by Brown in his widening of the block to the W. On the first floor he placed a corridor on the E side, the dining room and library on the W with a view over the courtyard to Loch Dunvegan. In both rooms, thin Jacobean plaster ceilings and corniced doorcases still of Georgian character. In the Fairy Tower, a plain first-floor study (probably the bedchamber in *c.* 1500); in the wall-thickness of its NE corner, a turnpike stair to the upper floors.

The C14 entrance to the keep was from the courtyard by a door placed a little above ground level at the N end of its W wall, this entrance now enclosed by the single-storey corridor of the 1840s built along this side. From the door, a straight stair in the thickness of the N wall up to the hall (now drawing room) occupying the first floor of the main block. In this room, a Frenchy chimneypiece, presumably provided by *Brown*. At the NW corner is the entrance to a second stair in the N wall, this leading down to the keep's ground floor. In the jamb N of the hall, a small vaulted first-floor room, still with slit windows in the N and W walls (the W blocked). In the floor, a hatch into a pit-prison below whose bottom has been partly excavated out of the rock. A door placed above the original floor level has been made in the prison's N gable, perhaps a C17 insertion. The main block's ground floor, probably originally used for storage, was later made a kitchen, with a big fireplace in the S gable. A subsequent alteration inserted a vault cutting across the fireplace and blocking a window in the E wall. Probably later still was the division of the space into two rooms. In the N room are various carved stones. Among them, a SUNDIAL PEDESTAL sculpted as a lady in C17 court dress, very similar to the sundial of 1679 now at Lennoxlove (Lothian); it used to stand in the castle's courtyard. – SYMBOL STONE with a crescent and 'V-rod' design with two concentric circles. – Late C17 pedimented DORMERHEAD decorated with a thistle and the initials FM for Florence Macdonald, wife of Iain Breac MacLeod. – In the addition of 1790 w of the keep, a toplit first-floor billiard room made when *Brown* lowered this wing in the 1840s.

Beside the jetty on the other side of Castle Haven to the s, the harled and crowstepped FACTOR'S HOUSE (now two cottages), built in 1734. – The WOODLAND along the E approach to the castle was planted by John Norman MacLeod from 1811. – At the end of the drive, GATES designed by *Colin Sinclair* and executed by *Alexander Proudfoot*, 1938, wrought-iron decorated with Celtic motifs, much as would be expected at the entrance to a municipal garden. – 0.4km. N, a U-plan STEADING of 1811; in the gable of each wing, a pair of seg-mental-arched cartshed doors under a broad three-light window.

BROCH (DUN FIADHAIRT), 3.2km. NW. Low remains of a broch built in the late first millennium B.C. or the early first mil-lennium A.D. on the rocky summit of a small peninsula. Cir-cular as usual, *c.* 17m. in diameter. Main entrance on the w, its passage extended outside the broch by a pair of walls. Inside the passage, a door check and, beyond it, the entrance to a small guard chamber on each side. Unusually, there is a second entrance on the E, much narrower and with a wall gallery opening off its s side. In the inner wall-face to the court, a low doorway N of the main entrance into a pair of cells and, to its E, a doorway to the stair. The court has been divided in two by a later wall.

8020

EILEAN DONAN CASTLE
0.6km. s of Dornie

Island castle at the junction of Loch Duich, Loch Long and Loch Alsh, its photogenic appeal long exploited by the tourist industry. It was built on medieval foundations in 1912–32; the architect was *George Mackie Watson*. The site commands one of the principal E–W routes across the Highlands, and there was a castle here by 1331, when Randolph, Earl of Moray, sent a 'crowner' or royal officer to Eilean Donan to arrest 'mysdoaris', of whom fifty were executed, their heads being exposed on the castle walls. This action may have been a seizure of the castle from the Mackenzies, the 'crowner' perhaps being the Earl of Ross, who was in occu-pation by 1350, when he signed a charter there. Eilean Donan was probably again possessed by the Mackenzies before the for-feiture of the earldom of Ross in 1476, and in 1509 John Mackenzie of Kintail obtained a Crown charter of the lands of Kintail together with the castle of 'Eleandonnan'. About a century later Timothy Pont described it as 'a strong and fair dungeon upon a rock with another tower compasd with a fair Barmkin wall with orchards and trees all within ane yland of the lenth of twa pair of butts almost round ...' During the Jacobite rising of 1719 the castle was garrisoned by Spanish troops and then shelled from the loch by three Hanoverian frigates. The ruins were thereafter abandoned until 1912, when the castle was bought by Lieutenant-Colonel John MacRae-Gilstrap, who undertook its rebuilding.

The site, the summit of a small rocky island, is naturally defensive. It was enclosed by a stone wall, probably built in the C13 to replace an earlier rampart.* The enclosure is roughly 27.4m. square. From the E side projected a walled passage to a roofless hexagonal tower enclosing the well. Probably in the C14 the enclosure's NE corner was filled by a keep, its N and E walls incorporating the curtain. In the C16 an L-plan block, perhaps to house the constable of the castle, was put up at the SW corner, the N wall of its main block formed by the curtain. At about the same time a small house was built in the enclosure's SE corner. Of these buildings shown in an early C18 plan and elevation by Lewis Petit there survived by 1912 only part of the keep, the SW block's E gable, the well tower and some of the curtain wall.

Access to the island, probably originally only by boat, is now by a three-arch rubble BRIDGE of 1912–32, its triangular cutwaters topped by little bastions. The path then leads past the well tower, a plain uncrenellated projection, as shown on Petit's drawing. Its link to the main enclosure was equally plain in the C18; Watson added a machicolated bartizan. The enclosure's S side to its W is battlemented, but, except for machicolation above the gateway, the crenellation is flush with the walling below, whereas Petit showed it projected on corbelling and with a SE angle round. Watson's gateway is a martial display of pointed arches containing a portcullis; Petit showed a very simple entrance a little to the E. Of the L-plan SW block Watson rebuilt only the S range, as a severe crowstep-gabled house. The small pepperpot corner turrets and the front's crowstepped chimney-gablet which existed in the C18 were omitted. Inside the courtyard these S buildings are treated similarly, with a fussy elaboration of what was probably plain originally and an omission of decoration where it once existed. The E block was given a canted NW corner, its upper floor jettied out as a bow. To the E, a corbelled and gabled bellcote next to a bowed stairtower. The SW block is quite straightforward, with a fore-stair. On the courtyard's W side, a wall. Its N stretch is quite low. Then a pointed-arched sea gate in the position where MacGibbon and Ross‡ thought there had been one but where Petit failed to show an opening. To its N, a high wall pierced by a big segmental arch allowing views over the loch.

At the W end of the courtyard's N side a battlemented wall

*During the rebuilding, evidence was found that there had been a vitrified fort on the site.

‡David MacGibbon and Thomas Ross, *The Castellated and Domestic Architecture of Scotland*, iii (1889), pp. 82–5.

provides the backing for a verandah. Filling the NW corner is
the keep, built on the foundations of its C14 predecessor. Plain
rubble walls (the W gable harled), the N enlivened by a machicolated garderobe projection near the wallhead. At the parapet, a
NE angle round and a rectangular SE bartizan (Petit showed
round pepperpot turrets). Crowstepped NW cap-house. Inside
the parapet, a big crowstep-gabled attic. The interior is a rubbly
Edwardian stage-set for life in the Middle Ages. On the ground
floor, the tunnel-vaulted Billeting Hall, entered through a
pointed door. In its N wall, a big segmental-arched recess,
perhaps original and marking the position of a medieval fireplace. On the floor above and reached by an outside stair is the
Banqueting Hall. Over its door, the arms of MacRae and the
Crown and the date '1914–1949'. Inside the door, a medieval
iron yett found in the well in the 1880s. Oak-beamed ceiling.
Canopied stone chimneypiece of C15 derivation, with mech-
anically foliaged capitals and coats of arms on the frieze and
overmantel.

EYNORT

3020

Hamlet of C20 Forestry Commission houses with the old churchyard beside Loch Eynort to the S.

CHURCHYARD. Roofless remains of a church and a chapel.
The church, perhaps C17, is a rubble-built rectangle. In the
E gable, a large rectangular window. There seem to have
been another three windows and a door in the fragmentary
S wall.
    The chapel to the W is also of rubble. Rectangular windows
with wide internal splays. It may be late medieval. – Inside, on
its N and S walls, early C18 MONUMENTS, both carved with
coats of arms, the S commemorating Donald MacLeod of Talisker † 1732 and his wife.
    Near the centre of the graveyard, a small CROSS-
SHAFT carved in high relief with the figure of a bishop,
a subject characteristic of the C14 and C15 Iona school
of carvers, but the accompanying holly leaves and rosettes
are motifs associated with the contemporary Loch Sween
school.

GESTO HOUSE

3030
2.1km. S of Bracadale

Plain mid-Victorian mansion with a large porch. The front's
chimney gablet is an early C20 addition. Now roofless and
gutted. – U-plan STEADING of c. 1840. In it, a circular heated
henhouse with a central chimney.

GLENDALE   *1040*

Crofting hamlet beside the Hamara River near its exit into Loch
Pooltiel.

CHURCHYARD. No remains now visible of the medieval chapel. –
Propped against the S wall, a GRAVESLAB, probably C14 or
C15. At its top is carved the figure of a harper. Below is a
claymore. On its l., foliage; on the r., four panels, the top carved
with a bishop, the second with a chalice, the third now blank,
the fourth with a foliaged scroll.

FREE CHURCH. Built in the late C19 and consisting of two harled
boxes, the front piend-roofed, the back lower but the same
length.

FREE PRESBYTERIAN CHURCH. Harled rectangle of *c.* 1920
with fat pointed windows. Croquet-hoop 'bellcote' feature on
the E gable.

MILL. Water mill, perhaps mid-C18, with drystone rubble walls   124
and a reed-thatched roof. At the gable an iron wheel made by
A. & J. Main & Co. Ltd of Edinburgh, 1902, replacing an
earlier wooden wheel. It is powered by the water from a burn
channelled through a wooden lade. – To the NE, a small
thatched drystone KILN. – STORE on the hill to the E, its roof
now of corrugated iron.

GLENELG   *8020*

Small village on the shore of Glenelg Bay, a row of harled C19
and C20 houses making a short street followed by the church and
a straggle of cottages to the S.

FREE CHURCH, 1.1km. NE. Humble white-painted rubble block
of *c.* 1845.

PARISH CHURCH. Perhaps early C18 in origin but completely
recast *c.* 1830 and again in 1861–2, when the harled walls were
heightened by 0.9m. and round-arched wooden-mullioned
lights were placed in the rectangular windows of the side walls
and S gable. The N gable's roundheaded window is probably of
c. 1830; so too is the S gable's red sandstone birdcage bellcote,
its ball finial raised on a stalk.

SCHOOL. By *Inverness County Council*, 1969.

WAR MEMORIAL. A startlingly Parisian apparition in this West   59
Highland setting. It was designed by *Robert S. Lorimer*, 1920;
the sculptor was *Louis Deuchars*. Stone pedestal carrying a
colossal bronze group consisting of a scantily dressed kneeling
lady (Stricken Humanity) appealing to a similarly half-clad
figure of Peace across a mustachioed Cameron Highlander
(Victory) bemused by such goings on.

BERNERA BARRACKS. Substantial remains of an early Georgian
fort. It was put up in accordance with the Government's
decision in 1717 to replace the independent Highland companies of part-time soldiers with regular troops and to supplement the existing forts at Inverness and Fort William with

another four commanding the main routes into and across the Highlands.* The site at Bernera is adjacent to the strait of Kyle Rhea, the principal crossing for men and cattle from Skye to the mainland.‡ In 1718 *James Smith*, then Surveyor and Chief Director for Carrying on the Barracks in North Britain, inspected the proposed sites and had almost certainly produced designs for all four forts before his dismissal from office in January 1719, the same year in which *Sir Patrick Strachan* of Glenkindie contracted to build Bernera Barracks for a price of £2,444 17s. od. Rubble for the walling was quarried from the foot of Sgiath Bheinn just to the SE; limestone for mortar and harling and much of the freestone for dressings were also found locally. Work was completed in April 1723.§

The fort is a rectangular enclosure, 29.87m. by 37.19m., with projecting two-storey towers at the NW and SE corners, their outer walls angled to meet at an acute point, their inner walls pierced with musket-loops enfilading the fort's main walls. The NW tower contained a guardhouse, the SE a bakehouse. On the enclosure's E and W sides have been curtain walls, their parapet walks carried on segmental-arched vaults, each forming internally an embrasure designed for a soldier and provided with a musket-loop in the outer wall. Of the E wall, only the grass-covered base remains. The W wall still stands to the height of its parapet. In its centre, the fort's entrance, now robbed of its freestone dressings.

In the middle of each of the N and S sides stands an identical double-pile barrack block, now roofless and without floors. Rubble-built, of three storeys and cellar. The segmental-arched windows, with barely projecting keystones, are grouped 2/1/2 at both front and back. Inside each block has been a central stair giving access to four rooms on each floor. Extending from the gables are narrow chambers built against the enclosure walls. The NE (now demolished) was a latrine. Against the S barrack's E gable, remains of an outside stair to the E parapet walk. The stair to the W walk was probably at the W gable of the N barrack.

BALCRAGGIE, 1.7km. NE. Early C19 harled house with a pedimented centre. Across the road, a contemporary U-plan steading.

BROCH (DUN TELVE), 2.4km. S. The best-preserved mainland broch in Scotland, dating from the late first millennium B.C. or the early first millennium A.D. Circular as usual, *c*. 19m. in diameter, the externally battered wall still standing *c*. 10m. high. Above its base, which is of solid construction, the wall is hollow, the two faces bonded by slabs forming the ceilings and floors of narrow galleries. Entrance on the W, its passage provided

---

*The others were at Fort Augustus (Inverness), Ruthven (Badenoch and Strathspey) and Inversnaid (Strathclyde).

‡The cattle swam across the narrow strait.

§The Chief Overseers under Strachan were successively *Lieutenant John Henri Bastide* and *Major Thomas Gordon*; *Robert Mowbray* was the carpenter.

with a door check and bar-hole. On the r., beyond the door check, a guard cell. Opening off the court are doorways, one to a wall cell, the other to the surviving base of the stair which led to the wallhead. Above each of the doorways to the entrance passage and the stair, a vertical series of rectangular openings in the wall-face, presumably intended to lighten the weight on the lintel. In the court's wall-face, two scarcements, the lower 2m. above the ground, the upper at a height of *c.* 8.9m., intended to support the structural timbers of the first floor and roof of wooden buildings placed round the court. At the level of the lower scarcement, the gallery inside the wall has carefully finished sides as if it were intended to be used, perhaps for storage. Above, three complete galleries and a fragmentary one, all with very rough sides. Presumably their sole function was to reduce the weight of the wall.

Outside the broch, remains of other buildings, perhaps houses of the first millennium A.D., and what appears to be the fragment of an outer wall.

BROCH (DUN TRODDAN), 2.9km. SE. Another well-preserved circular broch of *c.* 500 B.C.–A.D. 500, about one-third of its wall still standing *c.* 7.6m. high. Entrance on the S, its passage having checks for a door and a long guard cell on the W side. Inside the court, a door on the W gives access to a cell and, to its N, the stair to the wallhead, both in the thickness of the wall. Above the doorway, a vertical series of rectangular openings to reduce the weight on the lintel. The stair's first nine steps led up to a passage, perhaps originally with a doorway onto the wooden first floor of the structure, which stood against the court's wall, the floor's beam ends supported on a scarcement in the wall. More galleries in the wall above. When the court's floor was excavated in 1920 a ring of post-holes and a central stone hearth (rebuilt several times) were discovered.

GLENSHIEL *see* SHIEL BRIDGE

HALLIN   *2050*

Strung-out crofting township in Waternish.

WATERNISH FREE CHURCH. Late C19. Very simple, with seg-mental-arched windows.

WATERNISH PARISH CHURCH. A T-plan 'Parliamentary' church (i.e. to *William Thomson*'s design), built by *John Davidson* and *Thomas Macfarlane* in 1828. Tudor-arched windows. The bellcote is now missing. Converted to a house in 1988.

Adjoining, the contemporary harled MANSE of two storeys (i.e. to *Joseph Mitchell*'s design), its porch an addition.

BROCH (DUN HALLIN), 0.7km. E. Standing on a hillside, a ruined broch of the late first millennium B.C. or the early first millennium A.D., its circular drystone wall still nearly 4m. high on the NW. The entrance has been at the SE, with an oval cell in the wall to each side. There has been a wall gallery at the SW. Traces of an outer wall enclosing the small natural terrace on which this is built.

INVERINATE

9020

Scattered settlement on the N side of Loch Duich.

CLACHAN DUICH BURIAL GROUND. Graveyard at the mouth of Strath Croe. In it, roofless remains of the medieval KINTAIL PARISH CHURCH, which was shelled by Hanoverian ships in 1719 but repaired twenty years later. It is a rubble-built single cell. Rectangular windows, robbed of their dressings, in the S wall and gables. At the S wall's W end, a door with chamfered jambs, probably C16 but perhaps dating from the repairs ordered by the Presbytery in 1649. Inside, a big bronze TABLET with a coat of arms, commemorating John MacRa [*sic*] of Conchra †1715, erected in 1915 by his successor Stuart MacRae, the long inscription relating how in 1909 the Lord King of Arms had refused to recognize Sir Colin G. MacRae as clan chief. – To its W, a granite TABLET of *c*. 1910 to the 'chiefs' of Clan MacRae put up by Sir Colin G. MacRae, 'THE PRESENT ACKNOWLEDGED CHIEF OF THE CLAN MACRAE'. – In front, the big granite GRAVESLAB of Sir Colin MacRae †1925, placed there in 1927 'BY CLANSMEN & CLANSWOMEN IN LOVING MEMORY OF THEIR CHIEF'; on it, a coat of arms.

On top of a steep little hill to the N, the Clan MacRae WAR MEMORIAL of 1927. A granite block, its front carved with the statue of a kilted soldier, his gun's muzzle resting on the ground.

KINTAIL PARISH CHURCH. By *Alexander Messer*, 1856. Tall white harled box with roundheaded windows and a Romanesque bellcote. Interior altered, but the W gallery front still has Romanesque blind arcading.

INVERINATE HOUSE. Big but plain Tudor manor built for Sir Alexander Matheson, *c*. 1850. On the front, two large gables and hoodmoulded windows.

TIGH-GEAL, 1km. E. Harled house built as Kintail Manse in 1830–1. Pediment on the projecting centre; the outer windows are two-light. – To the W, a single-storey range of OFFICES with round-arched cartshed openings.

ISLE OF RAASAY *see* RAASAY

ISLEORNSAY 6010

Church and school on the main road to the NW, inn beside the pier.

ST COLUMBA'S CHURCH. Broad-eaved mission church, by *John Robertson*, 1898–1901, built of whinstone rubble with red sandstone dressings. Curved margins at the door and windows; NW porch.

SCHOOL. Dated 1876. Prominently sited white harled school and schoolhouse forming a U-plan.

HOTEL EILEAN IARMAIN. By *John Mackenzie*, 1893–6. Small white harled and gableted inn. Rear addition with a conical-roofed tower in the inner angle, by *Robert Hurd & Partners*, 1976.

DUISDALE. *See* p. 525.

KENSALEYRE 4050

Hamlet beside Loch Eyre, an inlet of Loch Snizort Beag.

SNIZORT PARISH CHURCH. Tall harled T-plan kirk. The body is by *James Gillespie Graham*, 1800–1. Minimally pointed windows with projecting imposts; originally they had shutters. In the middle of the long S wall, a piend-roofed vestry. The piend-roofed jamb was added in 1839, squeezed between the windows of the N wall. In 1872 *Alexander Ross* added the red sandstone Gothic bellcote to the N gable. Inside, a gallery of 1801 carried on Roman Doric columns round three sides. Against the S wall, the original PULPIT with a pilastered back and sounding board.

SNIZORT UNITED FREE CHURCH. Disused. Probably by *James A. H. Mackenzie*, c. 1907. Very humble, with a corrugated-iron roof. On the S gable, a ball finial; solid 'bellcote' with no space for a bell on the N.

KENSALEYRE HOUSE. Originally Snizort Manse. By *James Gillespie Graham*, 1802–3. White harled, a small porch at the advanced and gabled centre.

CAIRN, Carn Liath, 0.4km. S. Impressive steep-sided round cairn of *c.* 24m. in diameter and 5.5m. high, constructed of quite small water-worn stones, partly covered by turf.

STONE (CLACH ARD), Tote, 2.6km. S. Pictish symbol stone, probably of the C7, its S face carved in shallow relief with a crescent and V-rod above a double disc and Z-rod. A mirror and comb symbol used to be visible near the bottom.

KILMALUAG 4070

Crofting settlement near the N tip of Skye.

CHAPEL, Cnoc a Clachain. Only the W gable still stands of the pre-Reformation chapel dedicated to St Martin. Rubble-built and windowless, a stumpy cement-covered pinnacle on top. The other walls' foundations, marked by humps in the grass, show that it has been a small rectangular building.

DUNTULM CASTLE. *See* p. 526.

See p. 526.

6000   KILMORE

Hamlet beside the parish church.

KILMORE (SLEAT PARISH) CHURCH. By *John Mackenzie*, 1876–7. A large but thrifty lanceted and buttressed box; bellcote on the N gable. Inside, a braced open roof covering the full width in a single span. – N GALLERY, its columns having angels' heads for capitals. – The Victorian FURNISHINGS are complete. Big pulpit lighted by brass lamp standards (originally for oil, now for electricity). More lamp standards of the same type at the roomy communion pew in front.

Two huge marble MONUMENTS flanking the pulpit. The l. was designed by *James Byres* and executed in Rome. Doric aedicule, the frieze's metopes carved with emblems of the arts and sciences; high-relief coat of arms in the pediment. It was erected in 1768 to commemorate Sir James Macdonald of whom the long inscription relates that

HE DIED AT ROME, WHERE NOTWITHSTANDING THE DIFFERENCE OF RELIGION SUCH EXTRAORDINARY HONOURS WERE PAID TO HIS MEMORY AS HAD NEVER GRACED THAT OF ANY OTHER BRITISH SUBJECT IN ANY FOREIGN LAND SINCE THE DEATH OF SIR PHILIP SIDNEY. THE FAME HE HAS LEFT BEHIND HIM IS THE BEST CONSOLATION TO HIS AFFLICTED FAMILY AND TO HIS COUNTRYMEN IN THIS ISLE FOR WHOSE BENEFIT HE HAD PLANNED MANY USEFUL IMPROVEMENTS, WHICH HIS FRUITFUL GENIUS SUGGESTED, AND HIS ACTIVE SPIRIT PROMOTED, UNDER THE SOBER DIRECTION OF A CLEAR AND ENLIGHTENED UNDER-STANDING. READER, BEWAIL OUR LOSS, AND THAT OF ALL BRITAIN.

– Very similar monument of 1877 to Godfrey, Lord Macdonald, on the r., but its frieze, carved with swags, urns, lyres, books and a coronet, has no triglyphs; the coat of arms' crest breaks through the pediment.

In the graveyard behind, the roofless rubble-built OLD PARISH CHURCH, dated 1687 on a stone in the W gable. Round-arched door and windows in the gables and S wall; they have had moulded margins. – Attached to its W gable, a BURIAL ENCLOSURE of 1746, its walls topped by balustrades with ball finials at the corners. – Immediately N of the old Church, an early C19 MAUSOLEUM, a toy fort in red sandstone. – N of the mausoleum, cast-iron MONUMENT to Marion Purdie † 1864, aged nine. On its top, a relief of a boy lying down with a lamb.

SLEAT OLD MANSE. Castellated Tudor eye-catcher above the road from Armadale Castle to the Parish Church. By *James Gillespie Graham*, 1811–12. L-plan main block, the S wing suggestive of a rectangular tower. In the inner angle, a battle-mented round tower.

ARMADALE CASTLE. *See* p. 519.

OSTAIG HOUSE, 1.3km. SW. This may be the house built by the Rev. John Macpherson, minister of Sleat, in the mid-C 18 and visited by Dr Johnson and James Boswell in 1773. If so it has been much altered. The first floor's three-light windows are probably early C 19, the ground floor's bay windows and porch late Victorian, the box dormer late C 20.

SABHAL MOR OSTAIG, 1.1km. SW. Steading of *c.* 1840 converted to a Gaelic college. Rubble-built, with a pavilion-roofed SE tower.

UPPER OSTAIG, 1.5km. SW. Model early C 19 piend-roofed and harled farmhouse of two storeys and three bays. The porch is a late C 19 addition.

KILMUIR 3070

Just a collection of thatched houses (the Skye Museum of Island Life) by the main road, with the parish graveyard to the E.

CHURCHYARD. The enclosing rubble WALL was built in 1832. – Near the NW corner, a very tall but plain Celtic CROSS of grey Kemnay granite erected in 1870–1* to commemorate Flora Macdonald; it was designed by *Alexander Ross*. – In the SW corner, a rubble ENCLOSURE, its entrance's moulded lintel carved with the initials of Dr John Maclean and the date 1793. Inside, a crudely lettered tablet to Dr Maclean. – A little to the W, GRAVESLAB carved with a sword, probably C 14 or C 15. – N of the enclosure, another late medieval slab, carved with the high-relief figure of a knight.

KILMUIR FREE CHURCH. *See* Kilvaxter.
KILMUIR PARISH CHURCH. *See* Kilvaxter.
SKYE MUSEUM OF ISLAND LIFE. Group of four C 19 thatched buildings (a dwelling, smithy, tailor's workshop and weaving shed), all rubble-built. Rounded corners except at the smithy, where they are rectangular.

KILVAXTER 3060

Strung-out crofting settlement.

KILMUIR PARISH CHURCH. Originally Kilmuir United Free Church. Built in 1924. Harled Gothic box. Bellcote and a lean-to porch at the N gable. SW hall added in 1938.

KILMUIR FREE CHURCH. Angular Gothic, by *Ross & Joass*, 1860, with a gableted ashlar bellcote.

SCHOOL. 1875, by *Alexander Ross*, the windows rising into gablets.

*The original cross was broken in three by a gale in 1873. The present cross is a replacement of 1880.

6010   KINLOCH LODGE
                   5.6km. N of Isleornsay

White-painted and gableted mid-C19 shooting lodge. The w
gable's bow may be part of the additions made by *John Mackenzie* in 1891. Plain E extension for the present hotel use.

                  KINTAIL *see* INVERINATE

8020   KIRTON

Just the church and a few houses beside the A82.

LOCHALSH PARISH CHURCH. White harled box of 1804–7,
designed by *Ronald Douglas*, house-carpenter at Urray. Intersecting tracery in the roundheaded windows. The bellcote has
been removed. Small ventilators on the roof dating from *R. J.
Macbeth*'s alterations of 1910. Inside, panelled semi-octagonal
gallery round three sides, the pulpit standing in the centre of
the s wall.

            KNOCK CASTLE *see* CAISTEAL CHAMUIS

7020   KYLEAKIN

Village at the SE tip of Skye; the point of entry for most visitors to
the island. *c.* 1810 *James Gillespie Graham* produced an ambitious
scheme for a formally planned town of two-storey terraced
housing above which were to rise the spires of a church and
townhouse, Caisteal Maol providing a romantic landscape feature
to the E. Very little of this was built, and Kyleakin is a sorry
introduction to Skye.

FREE CHURCH. By *J. Pond Macdonald*, 1896–7. Diminutive
pretty Gothic with bracketed eaves, fancy ridge tiles and a
wooden bellcote.

KYLEAKIN CHURCH. Built in 1875. Small lancet windows; a
stone bellcote on the W gable.

CAISTEAL MAOL, 0.7km. E. Stark remains of the castle of the
Mackinnons, who, according to tradition, had acquired lands
on Skye by the early Middle Ages. The site is a rocky outcrop
at the mouth of Loch Alsh, rising almost sheer to a height of *c.*
15m. on the N, E and s sides, and with a steep approach from
the bay on the W. The summit has been covered by a rectangular
three-storey house, the rubble walls faced inside and out with
roughly squared and coursed boulders. There survive much of
the s wall, which has a battered base, the NE corner, and the
bottom of the W wall's s two-thirds. In the s wall, a first-floor

window. w of thi: window, on the inside, a corbel showing the position of the wooden floor. A c 15 date seems likely.

KYLE HOUSE, 0.5km. w. Harled early c 19 house of two storeys and three bays, its corniced porch an addition, as is the recessed wing at the NE gable.

KYLE OF LOCHALSH

7020

Sizeable village developed since 1897, when this became the terminus of the West Highland Railway and the Kyle of Lochalsh–Kyleakin crossing became the principal ferry access to Skye.

FREE CHURCH, Plockton Road. Early c 20. Harled with red sandstone dressings. Round-arched windows and a slate-spired bellcote.

PARISH CHURCH, Church Road. By *John Robertson*, 1898–1901. Built of sneck-harled granite relieved by red sandstone, the pointed windows with Robertson's characteristic curved margins.

PRIMARY SCHOOL, Plockton Road. 1958–9, by *Robert Hurd & Partners*, and extended by them in 1968, with touches of the neo-c 17 mannerism used in their housing in Canongate, Edinburgh.

RAILWAY STATION. By *Murdoch Paterson*, 1897. Wooden block with cantilevered awnings.

DESCRIPTION. On the hillside w of the ferry pier, the LOCH-ALSH HOTEL, early c 20 in origin but so altered and extended as to be only a large white harled blob. On the N side of MAIN STREET to the N, a harled block containing the BANK OF SCOTLAND and POST OFFICE, by *Ross & Macbeth*, 1904, with four ample gablets on the front. On the r., the ROYAL BANK OF SCOTLAND, dated 1896, asymmetrical, with a canted bay window at one corner, a conical-roofed tower at the other; off-centre door in a full-height ashlar panel rising to a curvy Jacobean gablet. The KYLE HOTEL has developed into a confusingly busy assemblage of gables unified by white harl. Then a road on the l. up to THE PLOCK, a hill largely covered with sensible housing by *Robert Hurd & Partners*, 1965. Straight ahead across the railway bridge, PLOCKTON ROAD begins its exit past cottages topped by gableted dormers.

LOCHALSH see KIRTON

LONMORE

2040

Little more than a place-name for a T-junction at which stands the church.

LONEMORE FREE CHURCH. Originally Duirinish Free Church. Simple kirk of *c.* 1845. Roundheaded windows; on the N gable, a 'bellcote' finial. Inside, a gallery on Roman Doric columns round three sides.

5020   LUIB

Hamlet beside Loch Ainort.

COTTAGES. Three rubble-built thatched cottages, the roof of one
now mostly covered with corrugated iron. They probably date
from the later C19.

8020   NOSTIE

A few houses just off the A82 beside Loch Alsh.

ST DONNAN'S CHURCH (Episcopal), 0.2km. w. By *Stevenson &
Dunworth*, 1962–4. Felt-roofed drydashed shed. The E wall
inside is patterned with panels inset with stones from the Nostie
Burn. Concrete ALTAR, its pedestal carved with angels by *F. R.
Stevenson*.

2040   ORBOST HOUSE
                         4.6km. s of Dunvegan

Smart early C19 mansion of the MacLeods of Orbost. Three-bay
ashlar front. Urns on the advanced centre's pediment; wide
Roman-Doric-columned doorpiece. Giant antae at the corners
of the outer bays. The harled back wing is the house's unpretentious predecessor, probably built in 1764–5.

8030   PLOCKTON

Planned village beside Loch Carron. It was laid out in 1794 by *D.
Urquhart* for Colonel Francis Humberston Mackenzie of Seaforth,
the then proprietor of Lochalsh, and the plan was extended by
William Cumming in 1801, after the estate was sold to Sir Hugh
Innes.

FREE CHURCH, Innes Street. Disused. Twin-aisle church built
of white-painted rubble, *c.* 1845. w wall blind except for the
round-arched and hoodmoulded door. Two tiers of windows
in the E wall.

PARISH CHURCH, Innes Street. White harled T-plan 'Parliamentary' church (i.e. to *William Thomson*'s design) built by
John Davidson and *Thomas Macfarlane* in 1825–7. Tudor-arched
windows with diamond panes. The birdcage bellcote has lost
its spiky pinnacles. Inside, superimposed Doric columns
support the gallery, which runs across the N and S ends and
fills the 'aisle', at whose corners its front bows outwards. The
wooden ceiling, with a border of pierced quatrefoils, is probably
an early Victorian embellishment.

HIGH SCHOOL, Innes Street. 1964, by *Ross and Cromarty County
Council*, who enlarged it in 1969. Further extension by *Highland
Regional Council*, 1980.

PRIMARY SCHOOL, Innes Street. Parsonical Gothic by *Alexander Ross*, 1858, with a strong battered chimney on the front. Immediately to the N, a corrugated-iron extension painted black and white, perhaps part of the additions made in 1889.

RAILWAY STATION, Innes Street. By *Murdoch Paterson*, 1897. Wooden station building with scalloped bargeboards.

DESCRIPTION. The village forms a rough T-plan. After the railway station and High School, INNES STREET starts properly with the Primary School and Parish Church (for all these, *see* above). Opposite the church is the contemporary OLD MANSE, of the single-storey harled U-plan type, designed probably by *James Smith*. At the street's end, the Free Church (*see* above). In HARBOUR STREET, curving along the shore of the bay, palm trees on the E side; on the W, terraced C19 houses, mostly two-storey, with gableted first-floor windows, a cheerful mixture of harling and red sandstone, from which the PLOCKTON HOTEL's black-and-white paintwork stands out. Beside the harbour at the N end, a self-conscious thatched cottage (TULLOCH ARD).

DUNCRAIG CASTLE. *See* p. 525. See p. 525.
RAVENS' CRAIG. *See* p. 549. See p. 549.

PORTNALONG 3030

C20 crofting township at the N tip of the Minginish peninsula.

CHURCH. Early C20 harled mission church with a vestigial bellcote.

BROCH (DUN ARDTRECK). Ruin of a semi-broch of the late first millennium B.C., built on a stack of rock rising sheer from the sea. The main wall is an arc of drystone masonry, still almost 2m. high in places. In its centre, entrance passage with checks for a door and a guard chamber in the wall-thickness. The wall's inner face is battered. In it, doorways to galleries in the walls.

PORTREE 4040

A village here was projected from at least as early as 1739, but it was not until *Thomas Telford* built the harbour in 1818–20 that it began to take form, and in 1851 Portree still contained 'little more than a score of houses, the half of them slated'. It grew quickly thereafter to become the undisputed 'metropolis of Skye', although not even considerable late C20 expansion has made it more than a small town.

CHURCHES

FREE CHURCH, Bank Street. Originally United Presbyterian. By *Peddie & Kinnear*, 1858–60. Broad sneck-harled box with a rose window in the N gable; gableted bellcote.

FREE PRESBYTERIAN CHURCH, Park Road. Small-scale Gothic, by *John Mackenzie*, 1895, the broad gable-front topped by an octagonal slated bellcote.

OLD PARISH CHURCH, Bank Street. Secularized. Harled kirk of 1820, with round-arched windows. The Gothic bellcote may date from *Alexander Ross's* alterations of 1883.

PARISH CHURCH, Somerled Square. Originally Portree Free Church. By *John Hay* of Liverpool, 1850–4. Cottagey Gothic, with a w bellcote and SE porch.

ST COLUMBA (Episcopal), Park Road. By *Alexander Ross*, 1884. Nave and chancel under a continuous roof, the two-bay chancel marked off by a buttress and by having paired and triple lancet lights in the side walls. In the E gable, a stepped arrangement of three lancets. Big SW porch, the base for an unexecuted tower. The old PARSONAGE at the NE was added by *Ross* in 1891–4. – STAINED GLASS. Three-light w window (Esther), a memorial to Flora Macdonald, by *E. I. Ingram*, 1896. – On the nave's N side, one late C19 light (the Crucifixion). – On its S side, a window (emblems of St Martin) by *Patrick Ross-Smith*, 1987.

PUBLIC BUILDINGS

MASONIC HALL, Somerled Square. Blocky Wrenaissance of a sort, by *R. J. Macbeth*, 1912.

PORTREE HIGH SCHOOL, Viewfield Road. By *Inverness County Council*, 1971. A big harled block, not unlike a sensible office. – Beside it, the ELGIN HOSTEL, fag-end Baronial by *James Shearer*, 1931–3.

ROSS MEMORIAL HOSPITAL, Struan Road. Now workshops. Dated 1892.

SHERIFF COURTHOUSE, Somerled Square. Small-scale Renaissance, by *Matthews & Lawrie*, 1865, with a pedimented centre and urns on the parapet.

SKYE GATHERING HALL, off Bank Street. Built in 1879 but enlarged and completely remodelled by *James A. H. Mackenzie*, 1898, with angular Gothic windows and a wealth of crow-stepped gables and gablets.

DESCRIPTION

BRIDGE ROAD leads in from the w. The entry to SOMERLED SQUARE on the l. is marked by the CLYDESDALE BANK, designed as the North of Scotland Bank by *Matthews & Lawrie*, 1866; Georgian-survival, with consoled pediments over the ground-floor windows. The Square itself is a formal space almost bereft of formal architecture. In the centre, WAR MEMORIAL of 1922, a small version of the Edinburgh mercat cross, its shaft topped by a seated lion. On the w side, the BANK OF SCOTLAND (former Caledonian Bank), a Gothic villa of 1873 by *Matthews & Lawrie*. On the S, the Sheriff Courthouse (*see* Public Buildings, above). On the N, the Free Presbyterian and

Parish Churches (*see* Churches, above) are held apart by the Masonic Hall (*see* Public Buildings, above). The E side is largely filled by the PORTREE HOTEL, its main part on the corner with Wentworth Street large and plain by *Alexander Ross*, 1875. WENTWORTH STREET is undistinguished commercial. At its E end, BANK STREET running above the harbour, its ascent to the N focused on the early C19 THE KING'S HOUSE at the beginning of Stormyhill. At Bank Street's S end, the old Parish Church (*see* Churches, above) and the mid-Victorian ROYAL BANK OF SCOTLAND, Georgian-survival going Italianate. Then the TOURIST INFORMATION CENTRE, designed in 1800 by *James Gillespie Graham* as the Jail but quite domestic in appearance. To its E, the Skye Gathering Hall (*see* Public Buildings, above) and, behind, the Free Church (*see* Churches, above) at the foot of the path up the wooded MEALL NA H-ARCAIRSEID to the sad ruin of an octagonal tower built in 1834.

QUAY BRAE leads down from Bank Street to the harbour. On its r., an early C19 rubble-walled SALMON HOUSE built into the hillside. On the harbour's N side, BEAUMONT CRESCENT where the late Georgian austerity of Nos. 4–5's sneck-harled masonry and three-storey scale has decided presence, despite No. 5's Victorian bay windows. Along the w side of the harbour, a terrace with gableted dormer windows, the mid-C19 PIER HOTEL contributing a display of rusticated quoins and window surrounds.

MANSIONS

PORTREE HOUSE, Home Farm Road. Built in 1807–10 as the residence for the Chamberlain of the Macdonald estates; *James Gillespie Graham* was the architect. Small harled mansion house with angle pilasters framing the front; in its centre, an ashlar porch.

VIEWFIELD HOUSE, Viewfield Road. Begun *c.* 1810 as a harled two-storey house of three bays with a block-pedimented door-piece. In 1885–7 *Alexander Ross* added a gabled attic to its centre and a big cement-rendered extension to the S. On this addition's entrance (E) front, a porte cochère projecting from a battle-mented tower on one of whose corners sits a little round cap house. Bay windows to the garden to the S. The Victorian interior is wonderfully intact. Spindly drawing-room chim-neypiece; floral wallpaper of the 1880s in two bedrooms.

RAASAY   *5030*

Sizeable island off the E coast of Skye, the property of the Mac-Leods of Raasay until 1843. Thereafter, the island was developed successively for sheep-farming and as a deer forest. In 1912 it was sold to the Lanarkshire firm of William Baird & Co., who worked an iron mine NE of Inverarish linked by a railway to the concrete pier they built at Suisnish. At Inverarish they provided picturesque workers' cottages (designed by *James G. Falconer*) with bracketed eaves. The mine closed in 1919, and three years later the island was sold to the Scottish Board of Agriculture, which divided much of the workable land into crofts and introduced forestry.

KILMOLUAG CHURCHYARD. Inside the burial ground, the ruin of a CHURCH, perhaps C13, dedicated to St Moluag. It is a rubble-built rectangle. In the E gable, a narrow roundheaded window, chamfered externally and splayed inside. The W gable has contained three small lancets. Inside, joist-holes in the S wall indicate the position of a W gallery, probably post-Reformation. At this wall's E end, a late medieval arched TOMB RECESS. – To the S, a CHAPEL, also roofless, built in 1839. Ashlar walls; stone Y-tracery in the windows. Set into the E gable, a small female head, probably medieval.

RAASAY FREE CHURCH. White harled kirk of *c.* 1850. Wooden Y-tracery in the pointed windows; a birdcage bellcote on the S gable.

BROCHEL CASTLE, at the NE of the island. Craggy remains of a rubble-built stronghold of the MacLeods of Raasay, perched above the sea. The castle existed by 1549 and was probably built in the preceding century. The late C16 description still holds good: ' … ane strange little castell in this Ile, biggit on the heid of ane heich craig … ' The site is a roughly triangular rocky pinnacle, *c.* 15m. high, with almost sheer drops on the N and SW sides; a steep ridge permits an approach from the E. Below the summit's SW side is a broad V-shaped ledge on which stand the remains of a two-storey block angled to the plan of the ledge and with its NE side no more than a masonry skin against the rock-face. It has contained three rooms, with a passage leading from the approach to the centre one. On the summit itself stood a tower, shown in a sketch of 1821 by William Daniell as having been of two or three storeys with a heavy corbelled parapet. Only traces of the foundations now survive. NW of this vanished tower, at the apex of the site, stands a roughly triangular two-storey building, the upper floor jettied out above the rounded NW corner on stone 'beams'. Slit windows lighting both floors.

ISLE OF RAASAY HOTEL. Gothic villa by *Alexander Ross*, 1877, swamped by recent additions.

RAASAY HOUSE. The house of *c.* 1750, where Samuel Johnson and James Boswell stayed in 1773, is still visible as the plain rear block of the present mansion house. Its size was more than doubled *c.* 1790, when James MacLeod of Raasay added a seven-bay front block faced with local ashlar. Austere except for cornices over the ground-floor windows; a three-light first-floor window at the centre. In 1843 Raasay was bought by George Rainy, who soon after dressed up this front block with spikily finialled Jacobean gables on the advanced centre and ends, added a porch and replaced James MacLeod's single-storey wings with two-storey blocks, set slightly back from the main frontage but with bay windows for emphasis. The service range at the E end is by *Alexander Ross*, 1876–7.

To the S, a small JETTY, probably early C19. – Beside it, a mound surrounded by a battlemented dwarf wall and railings, said to have been formed as a BATTERY to defend the island against invasion during the Napoleonic Wars. Beside it, stone STATUES of mermaids, originally intended to adorn the house's mid-C19 porch.

Behind the house, a large quadrangular early C19 STEADING, its front panelled by roundheaded arches, mostly blind. In the centre, a big Italianate CLOCKTOWER added by *Alexander Ross* in 1877.

RAVENS' CRAIG   8030
2.4km. E of Plockton

Tower house built of harled breeze blocks, by *Ian Begg*, 1987–9. The site high on a hillside above Loch Carron is one unlikely to have appealed to a medieval laird, nor would he have expected to find the basement run into the slope. But the general shape would have been familiar. L-plan, the round SE jamb corbelled out to support a square cap-house; in the inner angle a stair turret carried on corbelling. Tunnel-vaulted first-floor room with idiosyncratic Gothic arches each side of the N wall's fireplace. The main hall is on the floor above, its ceiling decorated by *Norman Edgar* with small triangular panels in red and green, each bearing a motif relating to an event in the architect-owner's life. Attic studio, its S gable fully glazed.

Lower down the hill is CRAIG, also by *Ian Begg* but of 1963, and quite straightforwardly of its time.

RUBH' AN DUNAIN   3010

Uninhabited hilly peninsula jutting out between Soay Sound and Loch Brittle.

CAIRN. Round cairn of *c.* 20m. diameter and 3m. high, now mostly covered with turf and heather. On the SE, a V-shaped notch making a forecourt, some of its façade's upright slabs still standing, with drystone masonry between them. From this a still lintelled entrance passage, its inner portion higher and wider, leads to the roughly circular roofless chamber, its walls constructed of upright slabs with drystone masonry between them. It probably dates from the second or third millennium B.C.

DUN. The site is a steep-sided promontory on whose landward end has been built a curved drystone wall. Battered outer face. Entrance near the N end, now very ruinous but door checks still visible. In the wall S of the entrance and entered from the enclosure, a narrow gallery. It may have been built in the first millennium B.C.

SCONSER

Hamlet at the Skye end of the ferry to Raasay.

CHURCH. Late C19 mission church looking like a cottage, with a bellcote on the N gable.

SCONSER LODGE. By *John Mackenzie*, 1881. Plain gabled villa dressed up with a battlemented tower.

SHIEL BRIDGE

Hamlet at the NW end of Glen Shiel where it opens into Loch Duich.

GLENSHIEL FREE CHURCH, 0.3km. N. By *Ross & Joass*, 1864, the windows much enlarged later.

GLENSHIEL PARISH CHURCH, 4.4km. NW. Very simple kirk built in 1758 and enlarged and reroofed by *Murdo Macleod*, mason at Kyleakin, in 1840. *Alexander Ross* added the N gable's wooden slate-roofed bellcote in 1866.

RATAGAN HOUSE, 2.2km. NW. Small early C19 mansion house with a broad-eaved shallow-pitched roof and an awkwardly corniced doorpiece.

BROCH (CAISTEAL GRUGAIG), Totaig, 7.3km. NW. Broch of the late first millennium B.C. or early first millennium A.D., standing on a hillside overlooking the junction of Loch Alsh and Loch Duich. Entrance on the NE with a massive triangular lintel over the doorway. In the entrance passage, door checks and a bar-hole; on its E side a (blocked) guard chamber. In the court, doorways to cells in the walls and another to the stair, which rose to a passage with a doorway onto the scarcement ledge placed less than 1m. above the court's rocky and uneven surface.

SKEABOST HOUSE
1.9km. SE of Bernisdale

Free manorial style by *Alexander Ross*, 1870–1, mixing a battlemented parapet with prominent gables and Tudor hoodmoulds. Tower topped by an ogee-roofed belvedere. Additions for the present hotel use have been built at the back and sides.

SLEAT *see* KILMORE

SLIGACHAN

Just an hotel and two bridges at the meeting point of Glen Sligachan, Glen Drynoch and Glen Varragill.

BRIDGES. The old humpbacked bridge is by *Thomas Telford*, c.

1810; three roundheaded arches and triangular cutwaters. –
Immediately to the E, its C20 replacement, a single segmental
arch of concrete faced with rubble masonry.

SNIZORT

FREE CHURCH. *See* Bernisdale.
PARISH CHURCH. *See* Kensaleyre.
UNITED FREE CHURCH. *See* Kensaleyre.

STAFFIN

Scattered crofting settlement.

STAFFIN FREE CHURCH. Sturdy buttressed box built in 1875.
On the w gable's bellcote, a pipe-clay flowerpot finial.
STAFFIN FREE PRESBYTERIAN CHURCH. Built *c.* 1900, the
only adornment a quite unclassical pedimented bellcote.
STENSCHOLL PARISH CHURCH. White-painted T-plan 'Par-
liamentary' church (i.e. to *William Thomson*'s design), built by
John Davidson and *Thomas Macfarlane* in 1828–9. Lattice
glazing in the Tudor-arched windows. Spikily pinnacled
bellcote on the w gable; on the E, a cast-iron urn, the only
departure from Thomson's standard design.
  To the w, contemporary MANSE of two storeys built to *Joseph
Mitchell*'s design.
SCHOOL. Built in 1876. C20 additions on the s.

STEIN

Gap-toothed row of rendered houses along the shore of Loch
Bay. They were built in 1796 by the British Fisheries Society, but
most have acquired Victorian dormer windows.

PIER. Ramped pier built in 1796 with advice from *Thomas Telford*,
who recommended the use of Parker's cement.
WATERNISH HOUSE, 0.6km. N. The Victorian mansion house
is now a ruin. – STEADING, dated 1864 on a skewputt but
looking a good twenty years older. U-plan, with the farm buildings in the wings. These are linked by a screen wall, its central
segmental arch placed under a gable surmounted by a steep
obelisk.

STROMEFERRY

Railway halt at the s end of the disused ferry across Loch Carron.

CHURCH. Chunky in red sandstone, by *David Mackintosh*, 1888–
9. Trefoil-headed lights in the round-arched window openings.
Slate-spired bellcote.

PIER. Ramped ferry pier built in 1814.

RAILWAY STATION. By *Murdoch Paterson*, 1870. Wooden station building. – Iron lattice-girder FOOTBRIDGE.

STROMEFERRY HOTEL. Gabled purplish sandstone block on the hillside above; by *Alexander Ross*, 1882, probably incorporating an earlier building.

SUARDAL

6020

Little more than a place-name in Strath Suardal.

CILL CHRIOSD. Roofless ruin of a rubble-built single-cell church, probably C16. In the S wall, a door and rectangular windows, all checked internally, presumably for shutters. Blocked window in the E gable. – Built against this gable is the early C18 BURIAL ENCLOSURE of the Mackinnons, surmounted by a balustrade and entered through a moulded doorway. – To the SW, a late medieval GRAVESLAB carved with a foliaged cross.

TALISKER HOUSE

3030

5.4km. W of Carbost

Harled tacksman's house, the subject of much alteration over the years. The earliest part, perhaps of *c.* 1720, is the N half of the main block, originally a two-storey W-facing house of three bays. *c.* 1780 it was made T-plan by the addition of a slightly off-centre pavilion-roofed two-storey W jamb. In the later C19 the main block was doubled in length to the S and given piend-roofed dormer windows, their sides decorated with sprays of corn; a single-storey castellated bay window was added to the front of the jamb and a porch in its N inner angle. In 1925 a study was built in the S inner angle. Inside, the W jamb's ground floor contains the dining room, its segmental-arched sideboard recess late C18, the cornice and Arts and Crafts chimneypiece late C19 replacements. Late C18 stair, its ceiling's roses probably late C19. First-floor drawing room in the jamb with a straight-coved ceiling and acanthus-leaf frieze of *c.* 1780.

TEANGUE

6000

Group of houses beside Knock Bay.

SLEAT FREE CHURCH. Built in 1855. Big buttressed box, the gable front's centre slightly advanced under a tall gabled bellcote and with a porch.

CAISTEAL CHAMUIS. *See* p. 523.

TOTAIG *see* SHIEL BRIDGE

TOTE *see* KENSALEYRE

TRUMPAN

Ruined church in a solitary graveyard overlooking the Little Minch.

CHURCH. Of the medieval church there survive the E gable and N wall, and the lower parts of the S wall and W gable. Simple rectangle built of rough rubble. In the E gable, a slit window with a wide internal splay. Crudely arched door near the N wall's W end. – Inside the church, a late medieval GRAVESLAB carved with a sword set in foliage issuing from the tails of two animals; a floral cross in the upper panel. – Contemporary GRAVESLAB to the S of the church. This has the relief figure of a priest; a foliaged cross above, a chalice below.

BROCH (DUN BORRAFIACH), 2.7km. NE. Broch of the first millennium B.C. or the first millennium A.D., its battered circular wall, *c.* 13m. in diameter, still *c.* 2m.–3m. high and built of very large blocks. It has contained the usual galleries. Entrance at the NW.

UIG

Crofting village in NW Skye. To its W, pier for the ferries to Harris and North Uist.

UIG CHURCH. Humble Gothic, by *Ross & Joass*, 1860–1, with a small bellcote.

UIG FREE CHURCH. Built in 1847, white-painted minimal Gothic. The NW tower, its walls continuing those of the main building, and with a Frenchy roof topped by wrought-iron cresting, looks a late C19 addition.

TOWER. Folly of *c.* 1840, overlooking Uig Bay. Squat round tower with big crosslet loopholes and segmental-arched windows and door. Formerly used as a house, it is now roofless.

ULLINISH LODGE
2.2.km. SW of Bracadale

Built as a two-storey three-bay tacksman's house in 1757, according to the date over the blocked door and extended by one bay to the l., probably in the early C19. In the late C19 it was made L-plan by the addition of a broad-eaved wing with a verandah-portico in the inner angle.

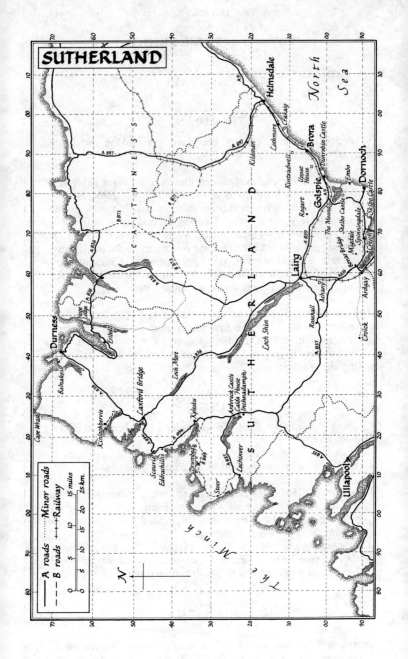

SUTHERLAND

A rugged district stretching diagonally across the N of Highland
from the prosperous farming land beside the Dornoch Firth at
the SE to the barren Cape Wrath at the NW. Until the early
C 19 the population was spread along the extensive glens which
penetrate the interior, but then the Countess of Sutherland, proprietor of most of the land, married to the immensely rich Marquess of Stafford and imbued with the principles of the
Enlightenment, undertook a radical and rational reorganization,
converting much of the land to sheep-walks, moving the inhabitants to new coastal villages and encouraging industry and fishing.
The visitor may now feel that there is only a narrow strip of
civilization along the E coast behind which rises a vast and empty
hinterland.

ACHANY
4.8km. SW of Lairg

5000

Harled laird's house of *c.* 1800, originally of three bays with a
pilastered doorpiece. It was dressed up by *Sir James Matheson*,
soon after he bought the estate in 1840, by the addition of
conical roofed round towers at the corners. These are the ends
of the new drawing room and dining room which he added to
the sides. Also of the 1840s are the pedimented stone dormerheads above the second-floor windows. Plain rear addition
of 1885 by *Andrew Maitland & Sons*.

ARDGAY

5090

Stolid village with two centres, one next to the railway station,
the other at Lower Gledfield to the NW.

Former KINCARDINE PARISH CHURCH, 1.1km. SE. Disused.
Harled rubble rectangle built by *William Macpherson*, wright in
Tain, and *Hugh Ross*, wright in Aldie, in 1799, perhaps on
medieval foundations. Symmetrically disposed openings in the
long S wall, with roundheaded windows flanking the pulpit.
The gableted bellcote probably dates from *Andrew Maitland*'s
alterations of 1862.

In the CHURCHYARD, several C 18 GRAVESLABS carved with
coats of arms and reminders of mortality. – At the W end, a late
Georgian MAUSOLEUM of V-rusticated ashlar, with a steep

pediment over the entrance and ball finials. Inside, the earliest
tablet commemorates Mrs Ann Ross †1797. – Beside the
church, a big Gothic MONUMENT to Elizabeth, wife of Sir
Charles Ross of Balnagown, by *John Henderson*, 1853–4.

On the hill to the s is the harled MANSE (now KINCARDINE
HOUSE), begun in 1769 but recast in 1827 on an irregular
T-plan.

KINCARDINE FREE CHURCH. Disused. Tall harled kirk of
1849–50. T-plan, with a minister's vestry opposite the jamb.
Round-arched windows; pyramid-roofed and ball-finialled
bellcote on the w gable. – Inside, a semi-octagonal GALLERY
on marbled cast-iron columns. – Canopied PULPIT.

KINCARDINE PARISH CHURCH. Originally Kincardine United
Free Church. Broad box, by *Andrew Maitland & Sons*, 1908.
On the sw porch's gable, a BELL moved here from the former
Parish Church. Below, a late C18 marble tablet explaining in
prose that the bell had been captured from a French ship of
war and given to the parish in 1778 by Admiral Sir John Lockhart Ross of Balnagown, and with a verse eulogy:

> When Britains Navies did a World control,
> And spread her Empire to the farthest Pole;
> High stood our Hero in the Rolls of Fame,
> And LOCKHART then became a Deathless name.
> This Bell no more shall witness Blood or Gore,
> Nor shall his Voice mix with the Cannons roar,
> But, to Kincardine by the Hero given,
> Shall call the Sinner to the peace of Heaven.

Just to the w, THE OLD SCHOOLHOUSE, designed as the
Free Church School by *Andrew Maitland*, 1852, with narrow
gabled porches to the schoolroom and master's house.

GLEDFIELD PRIMARY SCHOOL. Dumpy minimalist Gothic of
1875.

RAILWAY STATION. By *Joseph Mitchell*, c. 1865. Broad-eaved
station building with a verandah to the platform. – Lattice-
girder footbridge of characteristic Highland Railway type.

ARDVRECK CASTLE
2.1km. NW of Inchnadamph

2020

Remains of a rubble-built five-storey tower house on the neck of
a promontory jutting into Loch Assynt. It was said in 1794 to
bear the date 1591 or 1597 and is probably identifiable with the
fortalice called 'the Yle of Assint' of which Colin Mackenzie
obtained a charter in 1592 on the resignation of Torquhil
MacLeod of Lewis. It has consisted of a rectangular main block
(the s gable and ends of the E and W walls still standing) and a
SE stairtower. In the gable, four ground-floor gunloops. The
stairtower is circular for its two lower storeys and then corbelled
out on squared flagstones to a tall square cap-house. In the
w inner angle, a round turret projected on moulded corbels
contained the stair from the first-floor hall to the upper floors.

Inside, a tunnel-vaulted passage runs from the entrance in the
E inner angle across the S end of the ground floor; two vaulted
rooms N of the passage. The first-floor hall has also been
vaulted.

BALNAKEIL   *3060*

Remains of the Old Durness Parish Church beside Balnakeil
House on the shore of Balnakeil Bay.

OLD DURNESS PARISH CHURCH. Roofless rubble-built T-plan
kirk. The main block is said to have been erected by Donald
Mackay of Farr (later, first Lord Reay) in 1619, the N jamb in
1692. The gables were largely rebuilt in a reconstruction of
1727–8. The main block is a straightforward crowstepped rectangle, with a sturdy gabled bellcote on the E end. In the long
S wall, a door and two rectangular windows (all now blocked).
In each gable, a rectangular window. The W window's chamfered jambs suggest a C17 date; the E gable's window and door
have moulded jambs, probably of the 1720s. In the N aisle's E
wall, another moulded door, its worn lintel said to have borne
the inscription '16.HMK.A. . . ', the initials perhaps being those
of Hugh Mackay of Borley and his first wife, Anne, daughter
of the second Lord Reay. In the crowstepped gable, a transomed
window of two lancet lights. Documentary evidence suggests
that it is of the 1720s; if so, it is absurdly old-fashioned.

The interior is now almost featureless. Roll-moulded jambs
at the arch from the aisle into the body of the church. – In the
SE corner, a segmental-arched TOMB RECESS, early C17 but
still of medieval type. The chest's top is carved with a panel
showing a hunter pulling a bow at an up-ended stag. Beside
this panel, an inscription:

> DONALD:MAKMVRCHOV
> HIER:LYIS:LO:VAS:IL:TO:HIS
> FREIND
> VAR:TO
> HIS:FO
> TRVE:TO:HIS:MAIS
> TER:IN:VEIRD AND:VO 1623

– On top of the recess but not *in situ*, an heraldic stone (renewed
in cement) carved with the date 1619 and the initials

> D MC
> KN RM

– On the ground, the broken bowl of a stone FONT.

In the GRAVEYARD, S of the church, a big granite MONU-
MENT erected in 1827 to Robert Mackay, of Durness, the Reay
Gaelic bard. Ccorniced plinth supporting an obelisk topped by
a flaming urn. – To its W, a large ball-finialled MONUMENT
commemorating the two wives of James Anderson, Ann Innes
† 1783 and Mrs Fairly Gordon † 1790, the second eulogized in
an ineptly lettered inscription:

Though Mother and Step Mother,
When but Scarce Nineteen.
In both relations She
Did eminently Shine.
Esteem'd of every Rank,
While Maid or Wife:
Now Angel Bright
She Quaffs Immortal Life.

BALNAKEIL HOUSE. Harled mid-C18 laird's house of two storeys and attic, the main block of four bays, the wings projecting for three. Two doors in the main block's front. – To the s, a rubble-built early C19 MILL, the wheel now gone.

6090   BONAR BRIDGE

Village begun in 1820 at the E end of the bridge over the Kyle of Sutherland. Unpretentious C19 vernacular in the main street; Creich Parish Church and C20 housing on the hillside behind.

CREICH PARISH CHURCH. By *Andrew Maitland & Sons*, 1911–13; granite-built and dour. Aisled nave with transepts not projecting beyond the side walls. Sturdy buttressed tower; inside its parapet, a small octagonal stone spire with lucarnes. All the windows are lancets except the w, which has a spiral-traceried top. Inside, flat roofs over the aisles, which are divided from the nave by cast-iron columns with Gothic capitals. Braced open timber roof over the nave. The focus is a roomy PULPIT, its back now painted with a view of Bonar Bridge by *Iain Gillies*. – STAINED GLASS. Four-light w window, a memorial to Andrew Carnegie, by *Percy Bacon*, 1923, with figures of Music, Literature, Loving Kindness and Peace. – In the s wall, two more windows of 1923 (Courage and Victory; and the Resurrection and Ascension). – In the N wall, two windows (a pastoral scene, and a fishing scene) by *Roland Mitton*, 1987. – Also a window with staid figures of St Columba and the Good Shepherd, after 1933.
BRIDGE. Steel bow-string arch, by *Crouch & Hogg*, 1973.
GAIR MEMORIAL HALL. By *Andrew Maitland & Sons*, 1879, with a Flemish gablet over the door.
LIBRARY. Unassuming free Renaissance, by *J. Pond Macdonald*, 1901.
MIGDALE HOSPITAL. By *Andrew Maitland*, 1863; built as a poorhouse. Harled shallow U-plan, with a spired cupola above the central entrance, which is flanked by steep gables.
PRIMARY SCHOOL. The main block is mostly of 1878, incorporating earlier work; it was altered and extended by *Andrew Maitland & Sons* in 1892 and 1910. – E block by *D. E. A. Horne*, 1933.
WAR MEMORIAL. Bronze of a kilted soldier, erected in 1922.

BORROBOL *see* KILDONAN

BRORA   9000

Village at the mouth of the River Brora, developed in two bursts
in the C 19. Coal mining and the erection of saltpans began here
in 1598, but they seem to have been abandoned by 1630. After a
brief resumption of these industries in the third quarter of the
C 18, work began again in 1811 as one of the many schemes for
the improvement of her estates carried out by Elizabeth, Countess
(and later Duchess) of Sutherland. In that year the Welsh engineer
William Hughes was employed to direct the sinking of a 76.2m.
shaft into the coal seam. The opening of the mine 0.7km. W of
the village in 1813 was accompanied by the construction of a brick
and tile works beside it and the building of a harbour and adjacent
saltpans at the river mouth, the mine and brickworks joined to
the harbour and saltpans by a horse-drawn railway. The village
itself, described as 'Brora New Town', was laid out in 1814 on a
gridiron plan, and the first houses were put up in the next year.
Development was not rapid, even with the foundation of a distillery at Clynelish, 1.7km. NW, in 1819, and the mine, brickworks
and saltpans closed in 1828; the population was little more than
four hundred by the mid-C 19. Brora's industrial rebirth, along
strikingly similar lines, followed the arrival of the railway in 1871.
Coal mining and an associated brick industry resumed in 1872,
followed two years later by the opening of the Duke of Sutherland's Engineering Works (later converted to a woollen mill). The
mine continued to be worked until 1970, but the distillery has
been the chief source of late C 20 local employment, golf (played
here since the 1890s) of amusement.

CHRIST THE KING CHURCH (R.C.), Gower Street. By *Douglas
Reid*, 1973. Harled shed, the steep-pitched roof covered with
concrete tiles.

CLYNE FREE CHURCH, Gower Street. Big Gothic box dated
1849 on the S gable's bellcote. Porch added in 1880.

CLYNE PARISH CHURCH, Victoria Road. Originally Clyne
United Free Church. Ambitious Gothic on a small scale, by
Robert J. Macbeth, 1909. Pinnacled buttresses at the E gable and
S transept. Bow-ended vestry pretending to be a N transept.
Gabled SE porch. Bell on the W gable, but the crowning flèche
has been truncated. – STAINED-GLASS W window (St George)
of 1921.

MISSION CHURCH, Victoria Road. Now offices. Plain Gothic by
John Robertson, 1906–7. Three stepped lancets in the bellcoted S
gable.

BRIDGES. ROAD BRIDGE carrying the A9 over the River Brora,
late C 20, of concrete with an ashlar parapet. – To its E, the
narrow single-span OLD BRIDGE of squared and coursed
rubble, perhaps the one built in 1758 and repaired *c.* 1800. –
RAILWAY BRIDGE by *William Baxter*, 1870–1, of hammer-

dressed masonry. Semicircular arch over the river, a smaller arch to the s; the plate-girder span on the N is a later alteration.

HARBOUR. By *William Hughes*, 1813. Quay on the s shore of the River Brora. The basin is enclosed on the N by an artificial bank joining the shore to a small island.

RAILWAY STATION, off Victoria Road. By *William Roberts*, 1895. Severe single-storey Jacobean main block of characteristic Highland Railway type; U-plan, with an awning across the hollow centre. – Lattice-girder footbridge over the line.

WAR MEMORIAL. Baronial clocktower of *c.* 1920.

DESCRIPTION. ROSSLYN STREET brings the A9 in from the s. On the l., RACKPOOL, a little early C19 house built as a girls' school. On the r., a contemporary cottage with a pilastered doorpiece, followed by a terraced row (Nos. 8–18) with barge-boarded dormers, dated 1895. The street ends with the tri-angular FOUNTAIN SQUARE. On its N side is the SUTHERLAND ARMS HOTEL, mid-C19 in its present form, with hoodmoulds over the windows. In the middle of the square, the JUBILEE FOUNTAIN of 1897, its canopy decorated with relief busts of Queen Victoria. The main road continues downhill past the War Memorial (*see* above) to the bridge, the old bridge and railway viaduct on its r. (for these, *see* above). To the E is the Harbour (*see* above), with C19 fishertown cottages to its s. Across the River Brora to the N is VICTORIA STREET. Half-hidden on its r. is the set-back Railway Station (*see* above). On the l., a red-brick terrace of *c.* 1875 built to house workers at the DUKE OF SUTHERLAND'S ENGINEERING WORKS (now WOOLLEN MILLS), built in 1874 and later altered and extended in utilitarian fashion. Across the road, the old Mission Church (*see* above). Further out, Clyne Parish Church (*see* above) marks the exit towards Helmsdale.

BROCH, Carrol, 6.5km. NW. Sizeable remains of a broch of *c.* 500 B.C.–A.D. 500, standing on the hillside above the W shore of Loch Brora. As usual it is circular, *c.* 18m. in diameter, and built of drystone masonry. Entrance at the E with two sets of door jambs in its passage, the inner jambs provided with bar-holes. Between the pairs of jambs, a doorway on the N into an oval guard chamber in the wall-thickness. Inside the court, a doorway placed some way above the ground gives access to a wall chamber to its SE and, on the NW, to a stair. On the broch wall's inner face to the court, a scarcement ledge to support the beams of wooden structures. Outside, the broch has been defended by a wall and outer ditch.

FORT, Duchary Rock, 5.4km. W. Fort of the first millennium B.C., occupying the level summit of a rock ridge, its E and W sides virtual precipices. At the top of the steep s slope, a stone rampart, originally almost 4m. thick but much disturbed; narrow entrance near its centre. Longer rampart cutting off the comparatively easy approach from the N, returning along the fort's W side. Broad entrance near the centre of this N wall, its passage's W side lined with two huge slabs.

INVERBRORA, 1.4km. sw. Smart cottage-farmhouse by *George Alexander*, 1820–1. Single storey and attic, the outer bays with pedimented gables, the centre with the coats of arms of the Marquess of Stafford and the Countess of Sutherland over the corniced door.

CALDA HOUSE
1.7km. N of Inchnadamph

2020

Ruin of a late C17 double-pile mansion of two storeys and attic built for Kenneth, third Earl of Seaforth, or his son John Mackenzie of Assynt. The gables and some of the E and spine walls survive. Rubble-built and plain except for the segmental-arched ground- and first-floor windows.

CARN LIATH *see* GOLSPIE

CARROL *see* BRORA

CRAKAIG
1.5km. sw of Lothmore

9010

Small mansion house built in 1845, *Edward Blore* having provided a sketch design two years before. Crowstepped, with a projecting centre gable. – To the E, a large courtyard STEADING built by *Alexander Graham*, mason, and *William Munro*, wright, in 1829.

CREICH
6080

Just the remains of the old Parish Church in a graveyard beside the A9.

FREE CHURCH. *See* Migdale.

OLD PARISH CHURCH. Only the lowest courses survive of the rectangular rubble-built rectangle put up by *William Cowie* and *Alexander Ross*, house-carpenters, in 1789–91. – To its E, the square BURIAL ENCLOSURE of the Grays of Creich, its moulded door suggesting a C17 date. Beside the door, a badly weathered armorial stone. – In the field E of the churchyard, a tall CROSS SLAB (ST DENMAN'S CROSS) of the C9 or C10, one face incised with a cross.

PARISH CHURCH. *See* Bonar Bridge.

CROICK

Church and manse in isolation at the w end of Strath Carron.

PARISH CHURCH. Harled T-plan 'Parliamentary' church (i.e. to
William Thomson's design) built by *James Smith* in 1825–7.
Lattice glazing in the Tudor windows; spikily finialled bellcote
on the w gable. The stone-flagged interior is intact. – PULPIT
with fluted pilasters at the back and a sounding board. – Long
COMMUNION TABLE. – Small Victorian cast-iron STOVE. –
On the glass of the E window are scratched signatures and
messages by tenants cleared from Glencalvie in 1845.

To the w, a harled single-storey 'Parliamentary' MANSE (i.e.
designed by *James Smith*), also of 1825–7.

DORNOCH

Small town probably first established as a collection of manses
for the canons of the Cathedral founded here in the early c 13. By
1607 it was a burgh of the Bishops of Caithness, and it became a
royal burgh in 1628, but without any accompanying prosperity.
In 1810 William Young found the town 'really in a ruinous condition, I never saw any place more so.' The same year, buildings
were cleared away from near the Cathedral, a square was formed
to its s, and Castle Street and Bridge Street were laid out as a
prelude to redevelopment which replaced turf huts with stone-
walled houses. A few villas and golfers appeared in the late c 19,
followed by the railway in 1902.

CATHEDRAL

9 Much restored and partially rebuilt c 13 cathedral church of the
diocese of Caithness. Gilbert de Moravia was made Bishop of
Caithness *c.* 1223 and soon after began the erection of a new
cathedral at Dornoch.* The choir was presumably completed by
1239, when the bones of Bishop Adam were translated there from
Halkirk, and Bishop Gilbert himself was buried there in 1245.
William, Earl of Sutherland, is said to have been interred in the
s transept in 1248, but the nave was probably not roofed until
1291, when Edward I granted forty seasoned oaks from Darnaway
Forest for the fabric of the church. In 1428 a papal indulgence
was accorded to visitors contributing to the restoration (perhaps
the rebuilding or reconstruction of the nave) of the church said
to be 'collapsed in its fabric, desolate and destitute and in need
of costly repairs.' The cathedral was burned by the Master of
Caithness and Mackay of Strathnaver in 1570 and the roofless
nave's N arcade destroyed by a gale in 1605. Repair of the choir
and transepts was begun by John, Earl of Sutherland, and carried
on by his brother Sir Robert Gordon of Gordonstoun (the Tutor
of Sutherland) in 1614–22, and further repairs made in 1714,

---

*The former cathedral church was at Halkirk (Caithness).

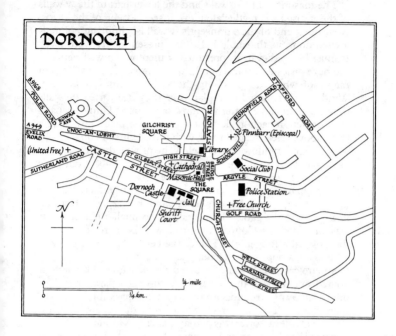

1728, 1772–5 and 1816. In 1835–7 *Elizabeth, Duchess and Countess of Sutherland*, undertook what she described as 'a plain & correct restoration', reroofing the nave's central vessel (but demolishing the remains of its side aisles) and fitting up the choir as a monument to her husband. Drawings for the scheme were produced by *William Burn*; but the Duchess, disliking his 'modern gothic in bad taste' and 'useless plans of ornaments', dismissed him before work began, and the executed designs were by *Alexander Coupar*, the Superintendent of Works on the Sutherland estates, assisted by *William Leslie*. Advice was provided by *Francis Chantrey* and sketches by the Duchess. Further work was carried out in 1924–7, when harling and plaster were stripped from the walls to expose their naked rubble to the gaze of the prurient.

Externally the cathedral is now a straightforward Latin cross. Side walls and choir gable of rubble, the other gables of ashlar. Angle buttresses added in 1835–7. The four-bay nave is entirely by *Coupar*, of the same length as its medieval predecessor but without the side aisles. In the side walls, big nook-shafted lancets, copies of the choir windows, tied together by stringcourses linking the sills and hoodmoulds. Jolly gargoyles (again copied from the choir) at the parapet. In the w gable, a Y-traceried five-light window, a near replica of the probably C15 w window but less deep so as to allow for Coupar's Tudorish porch.

The masonry of the E walls and the lower part of the W walls of the transepts is medieval; above it seems to be of the 1830s. Near the N end of the s transept's W wall is a built-up pointed-arched door, its threshold below the present churchyard level. It must be medieval, so presumably there was a wall between the nave aisles and transepts. In the N transept's E wall, a roof raggle of what was probably the sacristy removed in 1813. Windows all restored or replaced in 1835–7. In the side walls they are of the same pattern as those of the nave. Until Coupar's reconstruction each gable contained two pointed lights with a third above. He replaced these with three lights of equal height with a round window above. Below, he provided porches, each having only one of the two labels of its pointed archway's hoodmould carved with a human face.

The chancel's medieval masonry is mostly intact, but the upper part of the E gable was rebuilt and the gargoyles restored in 1835–7. In the gable, three lancets; the smaller lancet above was provided by Coupar but may well be a restoration of the original arrangement. Under the centre light, the blocked remains of a door to an E gallery inserted in 1775.

Square crossing tower of coursed rubble with small pointed-arched openings to the belfry. The corbelled parapet and its unassertive angle rounds are of 1835–7 but resemble what was there before. That may have dated from the repairs of 1714, and the medieval tower was perhaps taller.* Within the parapet, a squat slated broach spire, again of the 1830s but similar to the previous spire, put up in 1728. On each face, a gableted clock dial (the present dials are replacements of 1924). In the inner angles of the transepts and choir, small vestries with machicolated parapets and angle rounds. They were provided by *Coupar*. So too was the round stairtower in the N inner angle, built to replace an internal stair (perhaps C 17) under the crossing.

The interior's bare rubble walls present an unhappily home-spun contrast to Coupar's plaster vaults. Quadripartite vaulting over the nave; additional corbels were placed (presumably in the 1920s) below the 1830s corbels for no very obvious reason. Over the transepts and choir, pointed tunnel-vaults with applied ribs and fussy groined semi-vaults at the sides.

The medieval crossing piers (of Dornoch sandstone, their capitals and the arches of Embo stone) were restored c. 1925. Each pier is square on plan, with two faces engaged with the walls. On each of the other two faces, clustered half-engaged shafts with bell capitals and square abaci. Moulded bases (below the present floor level) with a stilted and quirked roll super-imposed on a large base roll. They carry pointed arches of two orders.

10   In the transepts' E walls and the choir the windows are moulded with a half-engaged and sunk edge-roll carried down

*As is suggested by the presence inside of corbels for an earlier floor and springers for stone ribs.

the jambs to form nook-shafts. They are smartly framed by arcading (cf. the choirs of Beauly Priory (Inverness) and Brechin Cathedral, Tayside), whose arches form hoodmoulds above. In the transepts and choir's side walls, pairs of acutely pointed narrow arches alternate with the broader arches over the windows. In the choir's E gable, just three broad arches over the closely set lancets. Sadly the attached shafts carrying the arches have been lost and not replaced. On the transepts' W walls the arcading has been reproduced (probably *c.* 1925) in a simplified form and yellow stone; it seems a misguided embellishment. In the choir's S wall, a pointed-arched PISCINA, its sill now at floor level.

The reconstruction of 1835–7 provided Chantrey's gigantic statue of the first Duke of Sutherland as the focal point at the E end of the choir. It was later moved to the nave's W end and is now in exile at Dunrobin, its place taken by the oak COMMUNION TABLE of 1911, its supporting arches carved with foliage. – At the NE crossing pier, contemporary Gothic PULPIT, again of oak with carved panels of fruit and flowers. – In the N transept, ORGAN by *Eustace Ingram,* 1893, resited in 1908 and rebuilt by *Nicolson* in 1979.

STAINED GLASS. The nave's W window (Christ and Our Lady with SS. Peter, Martha and John) is by *James Ballantine & Son,* 1891. – In the S wall, a colourful light (Our Lord with a pilgrim) by *Gordon Webster,* 1972. – Then a careful window (St Peter) of 1905 by *C. E. Kempe,* and a gaudily heraldic window (St George with small figures of SS. Andrew, Peter, Hubert and Gilbert) by *Francis H. Spear,* 1952. – In the N wall, two very routine lights by *James Ballantine II,* one (the Presentation in the Temple) of 1928, the other (Abraham) of 1916. – In the S transept's W wall, a lush post-Raphaelitish window (Madonna and Child) by *Percy Bacon & Bros.,* 1904. – Beside it, an unattributed window (Our Lord's call to those that labour and are heavy-laden) of 1925. – The S gable's central light is a memorial to Viscountess Ednam and her son Jeremy (Samuel and the Angel, their faces portraits of those commemorated) of 1931 by *Morris & Co.,* only the colouring worthy of that firm.* – To its r., a pictorial fairy tale (Charity) by *G. Maile & Son Ltd,* 1947. – In the E wall, another light by *Percy Bacon* (Suffer the Little Children) and an excruciating War Memorial window (a Warrior) by *James Ballantine II, c.* 1920. – In the N transept's gable, three darkly pictorial lights (Christ the Lover of Children, Christ the Light of the World, Christ the Good Shepherd) by *Heaton, Butler & Bayne, c.* 1910. – In the choir's S wall, a characteristically colourful memorial to Millicent, Duchess of Sutherland (Womanly Courage), by *William Wilson,* 1958. – Beside it, an heraldic memorial to the second Viscount Chaplin, with panels of his house and boat, by *C. C. Townsend & J. Howson,* 1953. – The third window in this wall (St Gilbert) is by *Crear McCartney,* 1989. – The choir's three N windows

---

***W. H. Knight* was responsible for the design.

(Literature, Christ the Peacemaker, and Music), by *Percy C. Bacon*, 1926, are a memorial to Andrew Carnegie. – The E gable's windows (Faith, Love, and Hope, with the Trinity above) are by *Christopher Whall*, after 1913. – In the S porch, two lights ('Let the fields be joyful ...', and 'Let everything that hath Breath Praise the Lord') by *Crear McCartney*, 1988.

In the nave's SW corner, a recumbent EFFIGY, said to be of Richard de Moravia † *c.* 1245, the mutilated figure of a knight dressed in chain mail with a sword across his middle, his crossed legs resting on a lion.

MONUMENTS. Now in the floor at the choir's E end but originally filling its then-blocked centre window is the large white marble tablet (by *Charles Barry*, 1849) to Elizabeth, Duchess and Countess of Sutherland. Long inscription relating how

... LEFT AN ORPHAN BY THE UNTIMELY AND ALMOST SIMULTANEOUS DEATH OF HER PARENTS SHE SUCCEEDED AT THE AGE OF THIRTEEN MONTHS TO POSSESSIONS AMONGST THE MOST EXTENSIVE AND A TITLE AMONGST THE MOST ANCIENT IN SCOTLAND ... MARRIED IN MDCCLXXXV TO GEORGE GRANVILLE LEVESON GOWER FIRST DUKE OF SUTHERLAND K. G. HER ATTACHMENT TO SUTHERLAND AND HER CLANSMEN WAS SHARED BY HER HUSBAND AND DURING A HAPPY UNION OF XLVIII YEARS WAS FOSTERED BY HIS ENCOURAGEMENT AND MADE EFFECTUAL BY HIS WEALTH.*

– At the E gable's N end, a small ogee-headed stone mentioning in rustic lettering that 'Below this is Mrs McKays Grave' and referring to her monument on the N wall, presumably the equally rustic stone to GMK and KM, with emblems of death and the date 1790. – Almost identical stone, dated 1792, on the S wall. – On the N wall, a chunkily lettered tablet to St Gilbert, by *Alexander Carrick*, 1924. – Very similar tablet to Sir Robert Gordon of Gordonstoun on the S. – Much grander is the monument in the SE corner to William, Earl of Sutherland, and his wife, Mary, † 1766: a pair of white marble Doric columns bearing coroneted urns placed against a grey marble background. It is by *John Veitch*, 1769. – On the S transept's E wall, a white marble tablet dated 1837 recording that this was the burial place of the Earls of Sutherland; crocketed finialled ogee arch enclosing a high-relief carving of the Sutherland arms. – On the transept's W wall, a pedimented tablet to Captain Kenneth Mackay † 1835, the inscription recording that:

*Less eulogistic was the Rev. Donald Sage, who described her work at Dornoch Cathedral in *Memorabilia Domestica*: 'The object of the Duchess in this restoration, was to provide a mausoleum for the remains of her late husband, and for herself; and for this purpose she spared neither her own purse, nor the feelings of her people; for in the course of the operations, she caused the very dead to be removed from their resting-place. More than fifty bodies were dug out of their graves in order to clear out a site for her own burial-vault ... The scene was revolting to humanity; but it was a fitting sequel to her treatment of her attached tenantry, whom, by hundreds, she had removed from their homes and their country.'

THERE WAS SEEN IN HIM A NOBLE REMNANT OF THAT CLASS OF
INTELLIGENT AND INDEPENDENT NATIVE GENTLEMEN WHO SO
HAPPILY UNITED THE HIGHER AND HUMBLER RANKS OF
SOCIETY, AND BY THEIR EXAMPLE AND INFLUENCE UPHELD THE
STATE OF MORAL EXCELLENCE AND SOCIAL HAPPINESS FOR
WHICH THIS COUNTRY HAS BEEN SO JUSTLY CELEBRATED.

– Below it, a stone of 1787 with ineptly carved reminders of
mortality.

CHURCHES

FREE CHURCH, Church Street. Plain box of 1843–8, recast in
1896 by *Thomas Grant*, who added a pinnacled buttressed front
to the w gable. Corbelled out from the projecting centre, a
spired bellcote. – To the s, its former SCHOOL of 1844; T-plan
with ball finials on the gables.

ST FINNBARR (Episcopal), Schoolhill. Simple but picturesque
Gothic, by *Alexander Ross*, 1912. The one-bay chancel is marked
off by buttresses and three-light side windows. Triple lancet in
the E gable. At the w end, a slate-spired wooden bellcote. The
picturesque effect was enhanced in 1966 by the addition of a
deep wooden porch. Inside, a braced-collar roof. – STAINED-
GLASS E window (Our Lord with a child, flanked by figures of
Our Lady and St Joseph) by *Percy Bacon*, *c.* 1920. – CHAMBER
ORGAN by *Bevington & Sons*.

UNITED FREE CHURCH, corner of Evelix Road and Sutherland
Road. Now a church hall. Solid late Gothic by *Robert J.
Macbeth*, 1908–9. At the gable front, flanking transeptal pro-
jections for the gallery-stairs.

PUBLIC BUILDINGS

ACADEMY, Evelix Road. Straightforward boxes clad in white
aggregate by *Eric Hall & Partners*, 1961. To their E the school
of 1911 by *William Mackintosh*, low and gabled, with a bellcote
on the centre.

JAIL, The Square. Now craft shops. Of 1842–4 and presumably
by *Thomas Brown Jun.*, the Prison Board architect. Shallow U-
plan; thin Baronial detail, with bartizans on the crowstepped
and cross-finialled wings. A stronger note is given by the screen
wall to the small courtyard on the l., whose square bartizan is
pierced by large arrowslits. At the back, small horizontal
windows to the vaulted cells. Most of the old airing yard behind
was covered by a DRILL HALL *c.* 1880; it looks like a humble
church of forty years earlier.

LIBRARY, High Street. Dated 1906. Plain with gablets.

MASONIC LODGE, Bridge Street. Now an office. By *John G.
Chisholm*, *c.* 1930.

POLICE STATION, Argyle Street. By *Highland Regional Council*
(project architect: *G. Falconer*), 1980. Of red blockwork and
very suburban.

SHERIFF COURT, The Square. By *Thomas Brown Jun.*, 1849–

50. Tudorish Baronial, with a large centre gablet; round-arched loggia on the ground floor. Small end wings, the l. with a bellcote. All very plain, but excusably so, since the plans were approved only after they 'had been divested of all external ornament, agreeably to the desire of His Grace the Duke of Sutherland.'*

SOCIAL CLUB, Schoolhill. Built as a school by *McDonald & Leslie* of Dornoch in 1845 and given its present plain L-plan appearance by *Andrew Maitland & Sons* in 1885.

DESCRIPTION

The WAR MEMORIAL at the corner of Poles Road and Evelix Road announces the beginning of the town. It is by *Alexander Carrick*, 1922, a bronze Seaforth Highlander gazing over the Dornoch Firth. Inscription on the pedestal:

ON FAME'S ETERNAL CAMPING GROUND THEIR SILENT TENTS
ARE SPREAD
AND GLORY GUARDS WITH SOLEMN ROUND THE BIVOUAC OF
THE DEAD.

At the corner with Sutherland Road, the former United Free Church (*see* Churches, above). In CASTLE STREET, a preponderance of pleasant but plain early and mid-C19 houses. CLYDESDALE BANK at the w end, by *Andrew Maitland & Sons*, 1893, Georgian-survival, with three-light windows flanking the Roman Doric doorpiece. On the N, the EAGLE HOTEL of *c.* 1840, with Tudor hoodmoulds. At the street's E end, a garden wall on the s has a stone carved with a human head. Could it have come from the Cathedral?

Cottagey mid-C19 houses in ST GILBERT STREET to the N. It leads to the undistinguished Victorian commercialism of HIGH STREET. In GILCHRIST SQUARE behind, a late Georgian L-plan terrace with a bowed N corner. On High Street's s side, beside the Cathedral churchyard, the stump of the MERCAT CROSS; it is probably early C17. E of the churchyard is TORNOVER, a smart little villa of *c.* 1840 with delicate scrolled skewputts and fancy cast-iron balusters at the steps to the door.

THE SQUARE, s of the Cathedral, is Dornoch's understated civic centre. Among the trees in the NW corner, a gaily painted FOUNTAIN, erected in 1892, of the same design as one at Portmahomack (Ross and Cromarty), i.e. with the water coming from a flagon on which sits a jolly fisherboy; crocodiles climbing down inside the domed canopy.

DORNOCH CASTLE occupies The Square's SW corner. This is the s range of the quadrangular palace of the Bishops of Caithness, built probably *c.* 1500 and certainly before 1557, when the tenth Earl of Sutherland was made its hereditary

---

*According to the Burgh Council minutes quoted in H. M. Mackay, *The Ancient Tolbooths of Dornoch* (1896), pp. 31–2.

Constable. Damaged in the attack by the Master of Caithness and Mackay of Strathnaver on the burgh in 1570, the palace was again habitable by 1615, when the twelfth Earl of Sutherland died there. It was repaired again by *Alexander Stronach* in 1720, but in 1760 was said to be ruinous. The office buildings in the E and W ranges were converted to housing but subsequently demolished, together with the screen wall and gateway on the courtyard's N side. In 1810–14 the Countess of Sutherland repaired the surviving S range, converting its NW tower into a courthouse and jail, reconstructing the main block as a 'private appartment',* and adding a parish school on old foundations in the SW inner angle. By 1850 these public uses were housed elsewhere and in 1859–60 *William Fowler* (with advice from *George Devey*) altered the building to provide a comfortable dwelling for the Sheriff of Sutherland. It was fitted up as a shooting lodge in 1881, reconstructed by *David E. A. Horne* in 1925 and is now an hotel.

The main block's harled N front, deceptively unified at first glance, bears evidence of each of the C 19 and early C 20 reconstructions. Panel carved with the arms of the Countess of Sutherland and her husband, the Marquess of Stafford, dated 1814. The heavy stepped buttress was added by *Fowler* in 1859, the conical-roofed round tower in 1881, and the crowstep-gabled and dormered top floor in 1925. Also of 1925 the setback E addition, its gable dressed up with angle rounds. The five-storey tower projecting from the NW corner is much less altered from its C 16 appearance. Ground-floor gunloops. At the top (perhaps a post-1570 reconstruction), gableted crowsteps and angle rounds prudently furnished with shotholes. In the inner angle, a comfortable stairtower decorated with stringcourses. Entrance to the garden through a pend arch of 1925 to the W. Here the 1810–14 school addition in the castle's SW corner has a big crowstepped S gable, probably an embellishment of 1881. Its Gothic door looks early C 19, but the consoled cornice above may be of 1859. At the main block's E end, a huge C 16 chimney. Quite tactful SE wing added in the 1970s. Inside the main block and NW tower, vaulted ground-floor rooms,‡ the E room's massive segmental-arched fireplace showing that it was originally the kitchen. The upper floors' character is mostly of 1925 but their C 16 arrangement seems to have been of identically planned first and second floors, each with a hall and with-drawing room in the main block and a bedchamber in the tower. One grand Gothic jamb of the first-floor hall's stone chimneypiece survives in a corridor; it seems to be of *c.* 1500.

The Sheriff Court and Jail to the E (*see* Public Buildings, above) face a Cotswoldy former POST OFFICE of *c.* 1900. At The Square's E end the Police Station (*see* Public Buildings, above) tries to be friendly where some display of authority was required. To its N, on the corner of ARGYLE STREET, SUTHERLAND

---

*'... where I propose to have my Whist Party', declared the countess in 1814.
‡The corridor's vault was removed *c.* 1977.

HOUSE of *c.* 1900, with a half-timbered and gableted first floor and ogee-topped corner turret. To the S, the mid-C19 broad-eaved DORNOCH INN, its large box dormer an unwelcome addition. Past the Free Church (*see* Churches, above) into GOLF ROAD, whose neat GRAVEYARD was laid out in 1835. To its E, LINKS HOUSE (the old Free Church Manse) of *c.* 1845, with giant angle pilasters and a vestigial overall pediment.

HOTELS AND VILLAS

BURGHFIELD HOUSE (HOTEL), Cnoc-an-Lobht. Big late Victorian villa, its unadventurous domesticity badly jolted by a very martial tower.

DORNOCH HOTEL, off Stafford Road and Argyle Street. Originally Station Hotel. By *Cameron & Burnett*, 1902–4. Large and plain, except for touches of half-timbering in contrast to the harling.

ROYAL GOLF HOTEL, Argyle Street. Originally Grange. 1896–7, by *J. R. Rhind*. Twin bows on the front, their effect spoilt by the angular two-storey porch (an afterthought of 1897).

FARMS ETC.

CIDERHALL, 4km. W. Neat farmhouse built in 1818. Steading to the W, dated 1865 and altered later.

CUTHILL, 4.8km. SW. Early C19 farmhouse with a small office range at the E end.

FILMHOR, 2.8km. SW. Admirably simple house by *Duncan Fraser*, 1970. White harled ground floor built into the hillside; dark-boarded oversailing upper storey under a very shallow butterfly roof, its two pitches of different lengths.

1030 DRUMBEG

Small village placed high above Eddrachillis Bay.

FREE CHURCH. Simple harled box of *c.* 1900, a small birdcage bellcote on the W gable. Inside, the large but boxy pulpit provides a focus.

PRIMARY SCHOOL. Plain late Victorian.

DUCHARY ROCK *see* BRORA

8000 DUNROBIN CASTLE
1.9km. NE of Golspie

91 Homespun small castle transformed into an early Victorian palace, taking full advantage of its cliff-top site to advertise its

magnificence. As part of the feudalizing and modernizing strategy of the sons of Malcolm I, extensive tracts of Sutherland were granted *c.* 1200 to Hugh de Moravia, a Morayshire knight said to have been of Flemish descent. *c.* 1235 his son William was made Earl of Sutherland. For the next six centuries the Earls of Sutherland were of local rather than national importance. Nor did they acquire great wealth: in 1766, when the infant Lady Elizabeth succeeded as Countess of Sutherland, there were rumours that the estates might have to be sold. However, in 1785 the Countess married George Granville Viscount Trentham, the heir to a huge English fortune, who succeeded his father as Marquess of Stafford in 1803.

From *c.* 1810 Lord Stafford and his wife spent much energy and money on the 'improvement' of the vast Sutherland estate, introducing large-scale sheep-farming, founding fishing villages to house the peasantry cleared from the interior, and attempting to establish industries. In 1833 Lord Stafford was created Duke of Sutherland, his wife's possession of the medieval earldom henceforth made clear by her styling herself the Duchess and Countess (more commonly the Duchess-Countess) of Sutherland. It was their son the second Duke who made of Dunrobin a fairytale concoction, some of its effect sadly lost in the remodelling after a fire in 1915.

Dunrobin's architectural development from the C13 to the 1830s was by accretion and remodelling. The site is the edge of a hill dropping almost sheer towards the shore on the s and cut off by a ditch, probably largely artificial, from the w. It was probably protected from an early date by ditches (since filled in) on the other two sides. The layout of the medieval castle, first recorded in 1401, must be conjectural, but it may have covered roughly the area of the present house, the whole being defended by a palisade or stone wall and divided laterally into an outer E court and, at the w end, an inner court containing the main living quarters. Projecting from the E side of the inner court is a keep built probably in the C13 or C14; it is now visible only from courtyards inside the house. This keep is a simple four-storey rectangular tower, *c.* 8.2m. by 7m., built of rubble, now harled on the E and N sides. In the w face, a blocked first-floor door, probably the original entrance reached by a ladder. The uncrenellated ashlar parapet and angle rounds look like C17 additions. At the NE corner, a big diagonally set Victorian buttress. On the w wall is hung a medieval iron yett; it may originally have been in the gateway to the inner court. Inside, the keep has a room on each floor, all covered by tunnel-vaults introduced in 1641. No evidence of a stair; the original access from one floor to another may have been by ladder and trapdoor.

In 1641–4 crowstepped ranges, now rendered, were built along the N and W sides of the inner court. At their NW and sw corners project round towers, both originally covered with dumpy candle-snuffer roofs, the s tower's roof heightened and given bellcast eaves above a stone frieze carved with cats' heads (the Sutherland crest) in the 1840s. In the inner angle of the N range and the keep was built a round stairtower, its rubble walling broken by stringcourses; over most of the windows, segmental pediments carved with coats of arms and the initials I^{E}S and A^{C}S for John, fourteenth Earl of Sutherland, and Anne, Countess of Sutherland, his second wife. At the top of the tower, an ogee-roofed cap-house rising above the keep.

Immediately after her marriage to Lord Trentham in 1785 the Countess of Sutherland's trustees commissioned *James McLeran* to extend and remodel Dunrobin, making it, as General James Grant of Ballindalloch informed the Countess, 'convenient Lodging for all the Company you are likely to have there without any Pomposity about an antiquated Castle ...' McLeran recast the existing w range's courtyard front with segmental and round-arched ground-floor openings, round-headed first-floor windows, and circular windows at the second. More importantly he made the existing L-plan house into a U by adding a rendered s range. This was quite unpretentious except for a battlemented parapet and round SE tower with Gothick windows and a candle-snuffer roof. McLeran's new range has been much altered. In the 1840s its courtyard elevation was overlaid by a corridor addition which partly covers the medieval well. At the same time a new roof with iron cresting was provided, the s front's battlement removed, stone dormer windows added, and the tower's candle-snuffer replaced by a much taller one. The first-floor E window was given a balcony in 1915–21.

In 1835–7 the recently widowed *Duchess-Countess of Sutherland* further extended the house, the increased accommodation intended to allow occupation of Dunrobin by herself, her elder son (the second Duke) and his family all at the same time. This extension, a NW wing containing a new kitchen and other offices, was designed by the Duchess-Countess herself in collaboration with the sculptor *Richard Westmacott*. It provided a severe castellated note with slit windows, chunkily corbelled angle rounds and machicolated chimneys.

When the second *Duke of Sutherland* inherited Dunrobin in 1841, he and his wife had eight children, all under eighteen. The marriages of their two elder daughters in 1843 and 1844 seem to have been the immediate cause for an immense enlargement of the castle, resulting* 'from a desire, by abundant accommodation for the very numerous members of the family, to induce their prolonged stay together in the north.' In 1844 the Duke commissioned designs from *Charles Barry*, whom he had previously employed at Trentham Park (Staffordshire) and Stafford (now Lancaster) House (London). Barry produced a scheme in the 'chateau-like' manner. However, it was found that this could not be fitted onto the site. The Duke himself then prepared designs in the castellated style. These were in turn abandoned in favour of a second design by the Duke,

---

*According to George Anderson and Peter Anderson, *Guide to the Highlands and Islands of Scotland* (3rd edn, 1851).

A Bedrooms
B Prince Albert's dressing room
C Queen Victoria's bedroom
D Queen Victoria's dressing room
E Boudoir
F Small drawing room
G Drawing room
H Anteroom
I Library
J Dining room

K Stairhall
L Billiard room
M Housekeeper's bedroom
N Steward's bedroom
O Office
P Closet
Q Upper half of scullery
R Upper half of kitchen

30m

Dunrobin Castle. Plan of the first floor in 1850.
(Redrawn from a plan by Sir Charles Barry)

prepared in collaboration with *William Leslie* and with much
gratuitous advice from *James Loch*, Commissioner for the Sutherland estates and Robert Adam's nephew. This design owed
a considerable debt to Barry's, especially for its treatment of the
N front, and Barry was consulted on detail during its execution.
Work began in 1845 and was completed in 1851.

This huge extension tripled the size of the castle and transformed its character from a ragbag of accretions to a display of
plutocratic grandeur, to which the earlier house became an
insignificant and barely visible appendage. At the E was placed
the main block of three storeys and an attic above a battered
basement of bullnosed granite, its colour and texture contrasting with the pale Brora ashlar of the main walling. This was
joined to the existing house by lower ranges, the S containing a
first-floor suite intended for Queen Victoria,* the N service

*The Duchess was Mistress of the Robes to the Queen.

block covering the C17 N range. The style is a mixture of Baronial-manorial and Renaissance château but with a castellated nod at the junction with the Duchess-Countess's wing of 1835–7. The composition is, or was before *Lorimer*'s alterations of 1915–21, boldly diversified. On the N (entrance) front it built up and in from the low castellated wing of 1835–7 to a tourelle on the new service block and then to a skinny clock-tower adorned with a cantilevered iron balcony and a lucarned lead spire. E of this clocktower was the main block, a deep tourelle at its NW corner. Projecting at the NE was a massive tower, its base forming a porte cochère. Tall tourelles at the angles rising well clear of the crenellated parapet, within which rose an octagonal cap-house, its top corbelled to a square to carry a high French pavilion roof. The vertical excitement was lost in *Robert S. Lorimer*'s alterations of 1915–21, when he replaced the lead-plated spires of the tourelles and clocktower with slated ogee hats and the main tower's French roof with a lower slated pyramid. The result is stodge.

The other fronts were left alone by Lorimer. On the E, an off-centre semicircular stairtower topped by a rectangular Baronial cap-house. To its l., a diagonally set stone balcony projecting from the crowstepped gable of the S range, whose walling is thickened in a V-plan to disguise the obtuse angle of its join with the E range. The long S front is fitted to the curve of the cliff-top, with obtuse angles at the junctions of the main block with the link and of the link with the C18 S range. At the main block's corners, round towers, their tall candle-snuffer spires covered with fishscale lead plates. The granite base is omitted at the lower link, whose crowstepped centre's pep-perpot turrets and big oriel window mark the position of Queen Victoria's bedroom. All these extensions of the 1840s are tied together by sill courses and machicolated parapets, their merlons sticking up between the *fleur-de-lis*-finialled dormer windows. The roofs' iron cresting of alternating strawberry leaves and thistles survives only at the SW. Carved detail emphasizing both pride of lineage and marital affection. Above the entrance tower's first-floor window, two shields resting against each other, the l. bearing the Duke's arms, the r. those of the Duchess. Over the N front's first-floor windows and the second-floor windows of its entrance tower, curly pediments broken by ducal coronets and with the entwined initials (GS and HS) of the Duke and Duchess in the tympana. Hoodmould labels of the E front's doors carved with the arms of the Earls of Suth-erland. Over the first-floor windows of the E and S elevations, coronetted strapwork pediments, again enclosing the initials GS and HS; the Sutherland motto 'Sans Peur' carved on the friezes. At the stone balconies, balustrades of crossed S's tied with carved ropes. Cats'-head gargoyles, alluding to the Suth-erland crest, on the S front.

The principal entrance is through the porte cochère, its roof a sexpartite vault, the ribs springing from attached columns whose capitals have Romanesque carving. Round-arched door into the entrance hall. Its rosetted oak ceiling is of 1919–21, the rest of the 1840s. Walls faced with Caen stone. Frieze with paired shields illustrating the family's successive matrimonial alliances. Strapworked Jacobean chimneypiece with mottoes of the Earls and Dukes of Sutherland; on the overmantel, a carved and painted display of heraldry with the Duke's arms in the centre, all this executed by *Alexander Munro, c.* 1850. To the S, a flight of steps through a semi-elliptical arch into a small vestibule, stone-vaulted, with shields at the intersection of the applied ribs. In the S wall, three round-arched niches, the centre containing a bronze statue by *Jean-Jacques Feuchère*, 1837, of Lord Stafford (later third Duke of Sutherland) in Highland dress. To the W is the stairhall, a mixture of Jacobean and Romanesque of a sort. Jacobean coved ceiling, the central compartment glazed. Two tiers of roundheaded arches springing directly from clustered shafts contain the stair, its balustrades of stone strapwork. At the house's SE corner, reached from a passage behind the stairhall is the ground-floor Cedar Room, fitted out by *Lorimer* with simple cedar panelling (by *Scott Morton & Co.*) and a shallow-compartmented plaster ceiling of generally Jacobean character, but with the addition of neo-Georgian baskets of fruit.

The first floor of the main block is filled with reception rooms. W of the stairhall is the lounge-hall. This was the billiard room in the 1840s, when it had plate-glass doors, but was recast by Lorimer with a ceiling of C 17 type, its heavy oval of fruit and foliage surrounded by vines (the Vine Room at Kellie Castle, Fife, the inspiration). N of the stairhall is the dining room, fitted up by Lorimer with oak panelling, the frieze filled with C 18 Italian *grisaille* paintings of classical scenes. Trabeated plaster ceiling, the beams encrusted with vines; plants and coats of arms in the compartments. Billiard room (originally library) to the E, remodelled in Lorimer's late C 17–early C 18 manner. It is panelled, with lugged architraves at the bookcases. On the overmantel, carvings of Grinling-Gibbonsish inspiration, with representations of books, birds and fruit together with a coat of arms at the top; more carved wood of the same sort above the S door. The ceiling is Holyrood-revival but incorporating cornucopia and flower baskets of William Adam type. Breakfast room (originally ante-room) with another Lorimer ceiling, its centrepiece an oval of fruit and foliage; rose and vine decoration in the corner panels. More Gibbonsish carving over the N and S doors.

The drawing room, occupying the whole S side of the main block, was made by Lorimer from two unequal-sized rooms (the drawing room and the small drawing room), but he retained the positions of the fireplaces, so the N one (originally of the drawing room) is off-centre. The chimneypieces are of 1919–21, with veined marble slips in surrounds of Hoptonwood stone, the friezes carved with reliefs of *putti*. Wall frieze of rose branches trailing up and down over armorial motifs. Richly crowded plaster ceiling divided into curvilinear compartments bordered with vines. Sprays of foliage in the smaller compartments. In the end compartments, reliefs of birds perched in trees. The centre compartment is filled with the huge heraldic achievement of the Dukes of Sutherland.

The first floor of the s range between the drawing room and the c 18 wing was designed as a suite for Queen Victoria, who eventually slept there, twenty years after its completion, in 1872. Along its N side, and connecting with the triangular lobby between the stairhall and drawing room, is a passage divided by transverse segmental arches into eight sexpartite-vaulted bays. s of this passage were the Queen's bedroom, flanked by her dressing room to the E, and Prince Albert's to the W. Lorimer threw the Queen's bedroom and dressing room together to form a cove-ceilinged library, sycamore-panelled in the early c 18 manner, with fluted Ionic pilasters framing the E chimneypiece. Prince Albert's dressing room (now known confusingly as Queen Victoria's Room) retains its mid-c 19 character with a simply compartmented coved ceiling above a heavy Gothic frieze.

In the c 18 s range, the two first-floor rooms (the Duke's Study and the Italian Room) are both of 1919–21, with panelling of early c 18 type. Above them are the Green and Gold Room and its dressing room, decorated in 1921 in the Louis XV style, with green stippled canvas-hung walls relieved with plenty of gilding and mirror-glass. In the Clan Room at the w range's s end, simple Lorimer panelling and a plain coved ceiling. The Cromarty Stair in this range looks late c 18.

The GARDENS to the s are of c. 1845–50. The castle sits on the top terrace, whose strongly battered and martially parapeted retaining wall breaks forward into a bastion at each corner of the s front. Second terrace below, its retaining wall topped by a procession of ball finials and enlivened by occasional buttresses and fierce machicolation. At the foot of the slope, a broad flat expanse laid out in parterres. In the s wall, ball-finialled GATEPIERS with delicate wrought and cast-iron gates, looking c 18 but apparently of 1849.

E of the main garden is the MUSEUM, its square pyramid-roofed front block built as a summerhouse by William Lord Strathnaver (later seventeenth Earl of Sutherland) in 1732. Two storeys firmly divided by a stringcourse, above a fully exposed basement. At each of the main floors, sill and lintel courses combine with the window surrounds to form regular panels of window and harled walling. Straight forestair to the corniced doorpiece. In the blind window above are panels carved with the full heraldic achievement of the Earls of Sutherland and the inscription 'William Lord Strathnaver August 1732'. Utilitarian-looking brick extension of c. 1900 at the back. Inside, amid a huge display of sporting trophies, several well-preserved CROSS-SLABS and SYMBOL STONES. – On the hillside behind, a BURIAL GROUND laid out c. 1920, its centrepiece an Italianate garden pavilion designed by *Barry*, 1840, for Trentham Park

(Staffordshire) and moved here after most of that house was demolished in 1910–12.

On the w side of the s drive leading from the castle to the shore, a second WALLED GARDEN, largely of c. 1804–8, again with ball-finialled GATEPIERS at the entrances. At the drive's s end, a pair of harled rubble bastions built in 1808, their parapets projected on two tiers of alternating corbels. Third bastion at the garden's SW corner. Its W wall, which breaks into bowed projections, was rebuilt by *William Leslie* in 1852.

Immediately N of the W garden, a square DOOCOT of harled rubble, probably mid-C18. The circular interior is lined with stone nesting boxes. – To its N, an ICEHOUSE built by *James Anderson* in 1786. It is round, with a gabled porch projecting on the E. – 0.3km. W, MEMORIAL to Harriet, Duchess of Sutherland, built in 1872–4 and designed by *John Robinson*. c. 14m.-high Eleanor Cross of white Dornoch freestone carved by *John Rhind*, enclosing a colossal bronze bust of the Duchess in bonnet and shawl by *Matthew Noble*.

The two main approaches to the castle are from the W and N. At the main W drive's far end, it enters the park through the buildings of FLAGSTAFF LODGE, built c. 1810. Two round towers, the N single-storey, the S of two storeys, both very martial, with heavily corbelled battlements and slit windows. Their gatepiers, with granite ball finials, look mid-C19. At its E end, the drive is cut through the hillside, the retaining walls dressed up with battlements and angle rounds. – At the entrance to the shore road from Golspie to the S, TOWER LODGE of 1865, an informal cottage with a conical-roofed round tower. – Between these two drives, DAIRY COTTAGE, Tudor of 1852, with mullioned windows, the upper floor's steeply gableted. At its NW corner, a fat round tower (the dairy) with machicolated eaves, this martial touch belied by the conical roof's metal-cupolaed ventilator and weathervane. To the W, a low milking parlour with a broad-eaved jerkin-head roof. – The N drive opens off the A9 between a pair of LODGES of 1851, rubble-built with rusticated quoins and crenellated parapets, each joined by a screen wall to a diminutive version of itself on the line of the road. – Behind the lodges and immediately within the park wall are the STABLES AND COACHHOUSE of 1814, two ashlar-fronted T-plan blocks, each with a cherrycock-pointed bowed tail pointing towards the drive. On their S fronts, round-headed ground-floor windows and dormers above. – N of the main road the line of the drive is continued through mid-C19 GATEPIERS with granite ball finials. – Behind them, a colossal bronze STATUE of the second Duke of Sutherland by *Matthew Noble*, 1865–6; he is dressed in Garter robes, his right hand resting on a scroll bearing the plan of Dunrobin Castle. – E of this statue, DUNROBIN CASTLE RAILWAY STATION, designed by *L. Bisset* in 1902 as the Duke of Sutherland's private halt. Picturesquely white harled with mock half-timbering and a triple-gabled tree-trunk verandah.

DURNESS

C 19 and C 20 village with crofting settlements to the E.

Former PARISH CHURCH. Now a store. Tall harled box by *Robert Brown*, 1853. Lancet windows and a gableted bellcote.
OLD PARISH CHURCH. *See* Balnakeil.
PARISH CHURCH. Originally Durness Free Church. By *William Henderson*, 1844, remodelled in 1891. A broad harled rectangle, quite plain except for the gable, which is embellished with roundheaded windows and a birdcage bellcote.

EDDRACHILLIS

Former church and manse standing together in the middle of moorland.

FREE CHURCH. *See* Scourie.
PARISH CHURCH. Now a house. Harled box built in 1728–31, its heather thatch replaced with slates later in the C 18, the spikily pinnacled bellcote put up *c.* 1839.

White harled and crowstepped L-plan MANSE (now EDDRA-CHILLIS HOTEL) built in 1835, the main block recently extended W and given a simple verandah.

EMBO

Ungentrified but not unspoilt C 19 fishing village, the rows of houses built end-on to the sea.

FISHERMEN'S HALL, Hall Street. Built in 1896 of corrugated iron with scalloped bargeboards and roundheaded windows.
PIER. By *James Barron*, 1894. Concrete, with an angled end.
SCHOOL, School Street. Disused. Very plain school and school-house of 1859–60, by *William Fowler*. E addition by *Andrew Maitland & Sons*, 1887.

81 EMBO HOUSE, 1km. SW. Ambitious but rustic laird's house of *c.* 1785, built for Robert Home Gordon, who used a West Indian fortune to buy the estate and stand for Parliament. It is crisply harled with yellow sandstone dressings. Five-bay main block of two storeys above a basement, now buried but originally exposed behind a railed area. The centre bay's walling breaks through the cornice as an attic crowned with a chimney pedi-ment. Vigorous but idiosyncratic detail. Simply moulded door-piece. Rusticated quoins up to a bandcourse joining the lintels of the ground-floor openings. At the first floor, strip quoins and almost square windows, their lintel course a frieze under the main cornice. Round-arched and keyblocked attic window in the centre. Flat stringcourse defining the base of the pediment. This main block is joined to the lower two-storey wings by slightly set-back single-storey links, each of one broad bay with a round-arched Gibbsian door (now window). At the wings,

strip quoins, almost square first-floor windows again with their lintel course a frieze for the cornice. Inside, a big ceiling rose in the entrance hall; coved ceiling at the top of the stair behind. The ground-floor dining room and drawing room flanking the hall have smart pine chimneypieces. In the w wing, a ground-floor kitchen with a big segmental-arched fireplace. Beside it, an inset stone carved with the impaled arms of Sir Robert Gordon of Embo and his wife, Jean Leslie, and the date 1657.

SKELBO CASTLE. *See* p. 591.

CAIRN. Base of a Neolithic cairn exposed by excavations in 1956–60. It has been an oval, *c.* 12.8m. long, with a short passage from the s to an antechamber and oval main chamber, its walls constructed of upright slabs with drystone masonry between. At the N end, a small polygonal second chamber, again with walls of upright slabs and drystone masonry. In the centre of the cairn between the two chambers, an inserted Bronze Age funerary cist of four edge-set slabs capped by a flagstone.

ERIBOLL

4050

Just the church all by itself on the E side of Loch Eriboll.

CHURCH. White harled Gothick mission church built in 1804. Stone spirelet on the E gable; vestry projecting from the ball-finialled w end. SE porch.

ARD NEACKIE, 3.7km. N. Simple mid-C19 harled house of two storeys and three bays. – Immediately to its s, four LIME-KILNS of the early 1870s, with semicircular and segmental draw arches. They are built into the side of the hill which formed the quarry.

GOLSPIE

8000

Planned village laid out in 1805, the sites originally held on leases from the Countess (later Duchess-Countess) of Sutherland, who thought it 'necessary in a village so near the House here [Dunrobin Castle], to have the inhabitants in some degree in our power in case of bad conduct'. Fishing was foreseen as the principal occupation of the inhabitants, most of whom were expected to have been cleared from the new sheep farms inland. In the event, many worked as labourers on the adjoining farms.

CHURCHES

FREE CHURCH, Church Street. Built in 1844–5. Rubble T-plan, with lattice glazing in the rectangular windows.

ST ANDREW, Main Street. Epitome of the Georgian parish kirk, its building history hidden under white harling. In March 1736, the Presbytery condemned the C17 church on the site* and ordered the building of a replacement. This had been completed by February 1737, when its seating was divided among the heritors. It was T-plan, the N jamb (Sutherland Aisle) looking quite domestic, with a chimney on the gable and a forestair against its E wall. Ball finial on the main block's E gable. Rectangular windows with chamfered margins; ashlar quoin strips at the corners.

In 1750 the Presbytery ordered the S wall to be repaired and the church to be made cruciform by the addition of a S 'aisle'. This work was finished by September 1751, the three windows in the new aisle's gable arranged in a triangular pattern above its door (now built up and harled over, with only the lintel exposed). In 1774 a small ogee-roofed bellcote was added to the W gable; it houses a BELL founded in 1696 and refounded in 1728 by *Robert Maxwell* of Edinburgh. The roof's 'large heavy gray Slates' were replaced with Easdale slates in 1776–8. Small porch in the SE inner angle, perhaps dating from the alterations made in 1849.

Inside, the furnishings join together happily enough despite their diversity of dates. – Box PEWS of C18 inspiration, by *George Hay*, 1953–4. – Huge PULPIT of 1738 on the W side of the entrance to the S 'aisle', its panelled octagonal base made by *Thomas Monro*, the back and sounding board by *Kenneth Sutherland*. At the back, fluted Ionic pilasters frame a keyblocked roundheaded blind arch; frieze carved with gryphons, flowers and the date. Modillion-corniced sounding board. – The simply panelled E and W GALLERIES are of 1849. – Very much grander is the SUTHERLAND LOFT in the N 'aisle', made by *Kenneth Sutherland* in 1738. Front of moulded panels with panelled pilasters at the centre and ends. Above, three Corinthian columns carrying an entablature, its frieze carved with branches and coronets, the Sutherland heraldic achievement in the centre. Inside, the loft has panelled walls and a coved ceiling. Central passage between the two rows of seats, access to the front row blocked by a wooden gate with ball finials on its fluted piers. Behind the loft, a RETIRING ROOM, its coved ceiling surviving, but the fireplace has been blocked. In a CLOSET to the NE, the N wall's panelled cupboard doors look C18. – MONUMENT to Lady Alfreda Chaplin †1881 in the S aisle, an over-prominent focus. Gothic aedicule bracketed out on corbels carved as angels holding coats of arms.

CHURCHYARD. Several C17 and C18 GRAVESLABS and TABLE STONES carved with heraldry and reminders of death. – On the N wall, a large heraldic C20 TABLET to the Gordons of Carroll.

UNITED FREE CHURCH, Fountain Road. Now a hall. By *L.*

---

*Built by Sir Robert Gordon of Gordonstoun (the Tutor of Sutherland) in 1619; it may have incorporated bits of the medieval chapel dedicated to St Andrew.

Bisset, 1905–6. Big Gothic box with plate-traceried windows in the E gable. NE tower intaken at the belfry, the pierced parapet enclosing a slated octagonal spire.

PUBLIC BUILDINGS

DRILL HALL, Old Bank Road. Disused. By *L. Bisset*, 1892. Large shed with wooden walls and a corrugated-iron roof. Wrought-iron finials to the dormer gablets; at the centre, a pagoda-roofed tower with a weathervane.

FOUNTAIN, Fountain Road. Built in 1850–1 as a memorial to Elizabeth, Duchess-Countess of Sutherland, it was designed by *Charles Barry*. Square pavilion of grey Strathfleet granite. In each front, a keyblocked roundheaded arch under a segmental pediment with a red granite ball finial. Inside, two tiers of basins, the upper of red granite with dolphin-head spouts, the lower on a cloverleaf plan.

HARBOUR. L-plan pier of wood and concrete, by *James Barron*, 1894–5; repaired and extended in 1913.

HIGH SCHOOL, off Main Street. By *Reiach & Hall*, 1963. Large loosely composed complex of two-, three- and four-storey blocks joined by single-storey links. Flat roofs, the walls clad in brick and aggregate panels. The result is sensible and humane. – To the NE, SWIMMING POOL, a rendered shed, by *Allan Ross & Allan*, 1972.

HIGH SCHOOL TECHNICAL ANNEXE, Drummuie, 1km. SW. Founded as the Sutherland Technical School by Millicent Fanny, Duchess of Sutherland, whose initials are carved on the front; it is by *J. M. Dick Peddie*, 1903–4. Scots Jacobean. U-plan, with steeply pedimented dormers on the crowstepped wings. At the lower centre block, a corbelled parapet and shaped centre gablet. – To its E, DRUMMUIE, a well-finished farm-house of *c.* 1815. Rusticated quoins and three-light ground-floor windows at the main block; the lower wings slightly set back. Rustic porch added in 1843.

LAWSON MEMORIAL HOSPITAL, Station Road. Begun in 1899 by *J. Hinton Gall*, with a broad-eaved block faced with stugged ashlar. – Big harled W addition (CAMBUSMORE WING) by *Horne & Murray*, 1936, neo-Georgian except for the centre gablet. – Detached late C20 E pavilion.

PRIMARY SCHOOL, off Back Road. Irregular complex, all single-storey and of red sandstone. The main block was built by *Alexander Coupar* in 1840–1. On top of its crowstepped centre gable, a bellcote whose cornice serves as a plate for an ogee roof topped by a ball-and-spike finial. Crowstepped wings at the SW (by *William Fowler*, 1875) and SE (of 1892). W extension of 1898. Big harled block to the W, by *E. W. Brannen*, 1938, with huge metal-framed windows and tiled fins at the entrance; it hesitates between neo-Georgian and Art Deco.

RAILWAY STATION, off Station Road. By *William Fowler*, 1868. Cottage-Tudor, with mullioned windows and bracketed eaves, the roof swept down over the platform's verandah.

Y.M.C.A. HALL, Main Street. Dated 1901. In the gable front, a
triplet of Romanesque lights. Small entrance tower, from which
projects a huge clock commemorating Queen Victoria's
Diamond Jubilee.

DESCRIPTION

STATION ROAD enters from the W with the Lawson Memorial
Hospital set behind trim lawns on the l. and the old Railway
Station below the road on the r. (for these, *see* Public Buildings,
above). On a sharp bend at the E end is the WAR MEMORIAL,
a polished granite Celtic cross, by *Donaldson & Burns*, 1922.
On its front, a bronze inscription panel bearing a relief of a
claymore; another bronze relief of the Tree of Life on the back.
Opposite, the red sandstone OLD HEAVITREE FARM of *c.*
1840, with a boldly advanced chimney-gabled centre and
unusually broad windows.

MAIN STREET's norm is the C19 vernacular terraced house or
cottage built of local red sandstone; many of these are now
rendered or harled. Standing on an open space overlooking the
sea is a domed stone column containing a BAROMETER (by
Adie & Son); a brass plate records that it was presented by the
Duke of Sutherland to the fishermen at Golspie in 1865. GLEN
COUL and GAIRLOCH, set back behind a front garden on
the N, make a mid-C19 *cottage orné* with broad eaves and tall
chimneys. No. 95 on the S, by *William Fowler*, 1867, brandishes
a crowstep-gabled cap-house above its bowed corner. For the
Y.M.C.A. Hall opposite, *see* Public Buildings, above. At the
corner of Fountain Road, a solid little block, faintly Queen
Anne, of 1906.

In FOUNTAIN ROAD, mid-Victorian villas, the first on the E
nicely Tudor, with diagonally set chimneys and mullioned
windows. At the end, the old United Free Church (*see*
Churches, above) and the eponymous Fountain (*see* Public
Buildings, above) marking the exit from the village to Ben
Bhragaidh.

Near Main Street's E end, a garden on the N fronts an L-plan
double cottage (NEWTON AND THE COTTAGE) of 1866–8,
crowstepped and with stone dormerheads. It is followed by the
mid-C19 Georgian-survival CLYDESDALE BANK. Opposite,
the rather earlier CLACH RUADH of cherrycock-pointed ashlar
and ANVIL HOUSE with a corniced doorpiece, followed by a
harled house of *c.* 1840, a Tudor chimney boldly corbelled out
from its front gable. For the self-effacing Golspie High School
on the N, *see* Public Buildings, above. Small POST OFFICE of
c. 1900 on the S with half-timbered gables, bracketed eaves,
and a little domed cupola-ventilator. On the N, the BANK OF
SCOTLAND, a harled and spikily gabled Jacobean villa built as
the British Linen Bank in 1847. Further on, THE HOLLIES,
early C19, white harled and picturesque, with broad eaves.
Opposite, single-storey blocks of sheltered housing (LOVAT
HOUSE and SEAFORTH HOUSE) of 1981. Set well away to the

SE, FORD PARK, built as the Parish Manse by *William Alexander* in 1825–7.

DUKE STREET continuing Main Street's line to the E is lined with picturesque Victorian estate cottages, interrupted by the Jacobean mass of the SUTHERLAND ESTATES OFFICE of 1894. Beyond, a small mid-C19 harled house with a Doric pilastered porch. For Tower Lodge at the entrance to Dunrobin Castle's park, *see* p. 577.

OLD BANK ROAD carries the main road N. On its l., the BEN BHRAGGIE HOTEL. Its front block is a double cottage of 1829, the l. half almost crushed by huge stone dormer windows whose sloping sides end in scrolls, the r. of two storeys. Plain block behind dated 1886. MACLEOD HOUSE SCHOOL HOSTEL was built as the Aberdeen Town & County Bank to *William Fowler*'s design in 1877. Big gabled villa with a fat-columned porch; large monkey-puzzle in the garden. On the road's E side, a wooden hut with herringbone-patterned branch walls; it may be late C19. To its N, DRILL HALL COTTAGES, with barge-boarded broad eaves and half-timbering, are dated 1896. The old Drill Hall itself (*see* Public Buildings, above) faces the SUTHERLAND ARMS HOTEL. This is now Z-plan. The main s-facing block is of 1807–9, the N and s wings, again with rusticated quoins, were added in 1826–7; in the N wing, a rusticated coach-house door. The road bends E to cross the Golspie Burn by a C20 bridge. To its N, the slightly humped OLD BRIDGE of 1808; on its parapet, a truncated obelisk carved with a coronet and Gaelic inscription. E of the burn, GOLSPIE MILLS, a large crowstepped building of 1814, the kiln contained in the jamb. Water wheel on the s gable, by *James Abernethy* of Aberdeen.

MONUMENT

SUTHERLAND MONUMENT, Ben Bhragaidh, 2km. NW. Erected 58 by his tenantry in 1836–8 as a memorial to the first Duke of Sutherland, the monument, *c.* 33m. high overall, dominates the surrounding area. Octagonal pedestal on a tall square base, both with sloped tops and built of local red sandstone. They support a colossal statue of the Duke in white Brora stone. The pedestal and base were designed by *William Burn* (with advice from Chantrey). The statue was executed by *Joseph Theakston* from a model by *Francis Chantrey*.

FARM

RHIVES HOUSE, 0.6km. NW. Built as the Dunrobin factor's house in 1840–1 by *McDonald & Leslie*, who probably provided the design. Harled and crowstepped. In the centre of the front, a big round tower corbelled out to carry a square cap-house. Shaped dormerheads carved with coroneted S's. Some ill-considered additions for its present use as an old people's home.

BROCH (CARN LIATH), 3.5km. NE. The site, a knoll overlooking

the sea, may have been artificially steepened and has had a
stone wall built round its edge. The broch itself, erected *c.* 100
B.C.–A.D. 100, is *c.* 20m. in diameter, the wall still standing to
a fair height. A protruding stone-walled low passage (formerly
roofed) leads to the entrance passage through the broch wall.
In the outer passage, checks for a door. Another pair of door
checks formed of vertical slabs, together with a bar-hole, in the
entrance passage proper. Beyond them, a doorway in the N wall
to a guard chamber (now blocked). Inside the court, opposite
the entrance passage, a door to the stair which led to the
wallhead. Traces of a scarcement at a height of *c.* 2m. in the
inner wall-face, but much of this hidden by a later casing built
when the broch was converted to a house. Some traces of wall
galleries near the entrance. In the enclosure outside the broch,
foundations of houses, some perhaps nearly contemporary with
it, others considerably later in date.

DUNROBIN CASTLE. *See* p. 570.

0010   # HELMSDALE

Large planned village laid out by the Countess of Sutherland in
1818 as a centre for the herring fishery, the mouth of the River
Helmsdale providing a natural harbour. On visiting her creation
in 1820 the Countess wrote with the pride and exaggeration of a
parent that it contained

> ... about six Herring establishments each with their Cooperages, so
> large so well built, & so full of people both men & women packing the
> casks of fish, that it looked more like a part of Liverpool than anything
> else, so handsome are the buildings & so great the bustle.

Helmsdale continued to develop through the C19, but the fishing
industry declined after the First World War and the village is now
primarily a local shopping and tourist centre.

CHAPEL-OF-EASE, Stafford Street. Disused. Built in 1838–41;
Alexander Graham was the mason, *William McLeod* the wright.
Big box, with 'Saxon' windows. On the W gable, a ball finial;
small E bellcote added by *William Fowler*, 1857. The church was
repaired and enlarged in 1896.

HELMSDALE CHURCH. Originally United Free. By *Robert J.
Macbeth*, 1908. Small and harled, with sparing Gothic detail
and a bellcote.

HELMSDALE FREE CHURCH, Dunrobin Street. Big Gothic box
by *Andrew Maitland & Sons*, 1890–2, with a transeptal stairtower each side of the pinnacle-buttressed gable front. Plate-
traceried three-light window above the gabled door; wrought-
iron finial on the bellcote.

BRIDGES. The NEW BRIDGE carrying the A9 is by *Babtie,
Shaw & Morton*, 1972. – OLD BRIDGE, a little upstream, by
Thomas Telford, 1809–11. Two semicircular arches, the pointed
cutwaters surmounted by semi-octagonal buttresses which
become pedestrian refuges at the parapet.

HARBOUR. Begun in 1818; *George Alexander* seems to have been the contractor. It then consisted of a quay on the N bank of the River Helmsdale indented with a small rectangular basin. *c.* 1820 *John Rennie* proposed the building of breakwaters to shelter the mouth of the river, but nothing appears to have been done. The harbour was extended by *Alexander* in 1823, and in 1841 *McDonald & Leslie* embanked the river's s shore. Finally in 1892 *James Barron* made a roughly triangular basin enclosed by two piers to the E, and built a breakwater (now in ruins) to the S.

PRIMARY SCHOOL, Stafford Street. Mostly of 1882, with a gableted bellcote, but incorporating earlier work.

SECONDARY SCHOOL, Old Caithness Road. Utilitarian, by the County Architect, *E. W. Brannen*, 1951–2.

RAILWAY STATION. Built for the Duke of Sutherland's Railway in 1871. Broad-eaved cottagey main building. – Footbridge over the line of characteristic Highland Railway lattice-girder type.

WAR MEMORIAL. Built in 1924, a prominently sited ogee-roofed clocktower of stugged grey ashlar above a hammer-dressed base.

DESCRIPTION. Two main streets. In the N–S STAFFORD STREET carrying the A9, RUARD was built as the Manse *c.* 1840 with a slightly recessed centre and hoodmoulded windows. Beside the Harbour (*see* above) to the E, an altered FISH-CURING HOUSE of *c.* 1817. At DUNROBIN STREET'S E end, the plain but prosperous BELGRAVE ARMS HOTEL built by *George Alexander* in 1819. At the W, the contemporary BRIDGE INN with a bowed corner. Across the Old Bridge (*see* above), a huge rubble-fronted ICE HOUSE built into the hillside; it is probably the one constructed by *William Leslie* in 1832. Above it, the War Memorial (*see* above).

BROCH, Ousdale, 5.4km. NE. *See* p. 104.

BROCH AND HUT CIRCLES, Kilphedir, 4.8km. NW. Remains of a broch of *c.* 500 B.C.–A.D. 500, standing on a hill. Now ruinous, it has been of *c.* 14.6m. diameter. Terraces to its E and W. Outer defences, now heather-grown, provided by a ditch and two ramparts; short stretch of an additional rampart protecting the enclosure's W entrance. – 0.3km. W, three HUT CIRCLES, one more substantial than the others and with a souterrain, its drystone-walled and lintelled passage *c.* 9.5m. long. More hut circles 0.2km. NW. Some have been excavated, and it was found that their roofs had been supported on wooden posts; radiocarbon testing produced a date for their occupation in the last centuries B.C.

HOPE LODGE
4060

5.7km. NE of Eriboll

Perched on the E bank of the River Hope. Cottagey shooting lodge designed by *William Fowler*, *c.* 1875, for the third Duke of Sutherland. Single-storey, with an attic in the huge roof which projects over a verandah.

INCHNADAMPH

2020

Just a church, hotel and plain shooting lodge.

ASSYNT PARISH CHURCH. By *John Robertson*, 1901–3. Cottagey, with plastered walls, the windows rising into bargeboarded dormerheads. Slate-spired bellcote on the E gable.

In the graveyard, a square rubble-built MAUSOLEUM, perhaps incorporating some of the walling of the previous parish church.

ARDVRECK CASTLE. *See* p. 556.
CALDA HOUSE. *See* p. 561.

KILDONAN

9020

Isolated church with a harled early C19 farm to its N.

PARISH CHURCH. Harled box, by *James Boag*, 1786–8. Rectangular windows. The corniced E door with chamfered margins may date from the alterations made by *William Alexander* in 1828.* Ball-finialled birdcage bellcote, an addition of 1905. The interior was reordered in the early C20, when the W and N galleries were removed and the pulpit moved from the S wall to the W end. – PULPIT, perhaps of 1768, with fluted pilasters and a heavy sounding board with a Doric entablature. – EAST GALLERY probably of 1828, with a panelled pine front; it is supported on marbled Roman Doric columns. – STAINED GLASS. Three windows in the S wall (St Donnan; the Good Shepherd; the coat of arms of Frank Sykes of Borrobol) of 1917, pictorial and bad. – E window (Saltire) of the early C20.

Built against the N wall, the BURIAL ENCLOSURE erected in 1822 to house the bodies of the Rev. Alexander Sage and his two wives.

BORROBOL, 6.9km. NW. Large and boring late C19 collection of gables, with an undemonstrative round tower.
KILDONAN HALL, 1.5km. N. Dated 1896. A big villa with two-storey canted bay windows at the gabled ends; in the centre, stepped gablets over the dormer windows.

KILPHEDIR *see* HELMSDALE

KINCARDINE *see* ARDGAY

---

*Originally the church had two doors in the S wall, one in the N, and a gallery door with a forestair in each gable.

KINLOCHBERVIE

Scattered village on Loch Inchard, the harbour dominated by
large shedlike Harbour Offices.

FREE PRESBYTERIAN CHURCH. Harled T-plan 'Parliamentary'
church (i.e. to *William Thomson*'s design), built by *William
Davidson* in 1828–9. Tudor windows (still with metal lattice-
glazing) and doors; spikily-pinnacled birdcage bellcote.
    Contemporary two-storey MANSE (designed by *Joseph
Mitchell*), now derelict.

PARISH CHURCH. Built as a Free church in 1846. Broad harled
box. Rectangular windows in the side walls, roundheaded
windows in the E gable; primitive birdcage bellcote. The E porch
was added by *Andrew Maitland & Sons*, 1882. The bargeboards
date from a reroofing of 1911, the small W hall from 1914.
Interior refurnished in 1882, with a big PULPIT and reading
desk as the focus. – In the porch, a STAINED-GLASS window
(abstract except for a cross) by *Sadie McLellan*, 1971.

KINTRADWELL
4km. N of Brora

Harled L-plan laird's house built for Captain Gordon of Carroll
in 1798. The inner angle has been filled with a single-storey
castellated and bow-windowed block, probably the addition
built in 1823.

KYLESKU

Hamlet beside the former ferry at the junction of Loch Glendhu
with Loch a'Chàirn Bhàin.

KYLESKU BRIDGE. Elegant engineering, by *Ove Arup & Part-*
ners, 1984. Curved concrete deck carried high above the water
on two pairs of V-supports joined at the top and splayed out
below.

BROCH, Loch a'Chàirn Bhàin, 1.2km. w. Ruined drystone-walled
broch of *c.* 500 B.C.–A.D. 500 standing on an islet joined to the
shore by a causeway of boulders. Circular as usual, *c.* 12m. in
diameter. The entrance has been at the SE. There seems to
have been a wall round the islet.

LAIRG

Rather nondescript village, its site fixed in 1811.

FREE CHURCH. Dated 1845. Broad box, thriftily detailed with
lancet windows and a narrow gableted bellcote. Attached to
the back, a single-storey contemporary school and schoolhouse
(now hall), their windows still with lattice glazing. The church's

interior was refurnished in 1904, when a new pulpit was installed at the W instead of the E end, a W gallery was erected, and coloured glass installed in the windows. – In the vestry, a bowed corner cupboard, presumably of 1904; it contains a urinal for the minister's use. – In the hall, the PULPIT of 1845.

MANSE of 1845 to the S, with a steep gable and gablet on the front.

PARISH CHURCH. By *William Leslie*, 1845–6. Big buttressed and lanceted granite box, dourly purposeful on its hillside site above the village. Tall gableted bellcote on the W end.

POWER STATION, 0.8km. NW. By *Shearer & Annand*, 1957. Strong mass of crazy-paved rubble beside the concrete dam.

PRIMARY SCHOOL. School and schoolhouse built in 1879 and much extended by *D. E. A. Horne*, 1936.

RAILWAY STATION. Small and plain, by *Joseph Mitchell & Co.*, 1868. – Lattice-girder footbridge of the usual Highland Railway type.

CAIRNS AND SETTLEMENT, The Ord, 1.1km. SW. Nearly on the top of this low hill, a chambered cairn of the fourth or third millennium B.C., *c.* 27m. in diameter, with remains of a concave forecourt on the S in front of the entrance passage. Surrounding it, a stone platform with a kerb of boulders (now covered in grass), added when the tomb was blocked. – To its SE, on the summit of the hill, remains of a second contemporary cairn, its mound removed, but there remain the upright slabs of its chamber, *c.* 4.2m. long, divided into three compartments. – To its S, a round cairn of the second millennium B.C., much of its kerb visible. – Scattered over the hill's lower slopes are over twenty overgrown hut circles of the first millennium B.C. and their associated clearance cairns.

LOCHINVER

Fishing village laid out *c.* 1810. The early and mid-C19 core is a one-sided street overlooking Loch Inver. The Culag Hotel stands beside the pier at the S end.

CHURCH OF SCOTLAND. Originally built as St Ninian's Church of England at Nairn in 1844–5, it was designed by *G. Fowler Jones*. It was re-erected here by *John Robertson* in 1901–3. Tall buttressed rubble cruciform. Lancet windows; a tall gableted bellcote.

FREE CHURCH. By *D. & J. R. McMillan*, 1894. Cottagey, with broad eaves and a squat pyramid-roofed tower.

FREE PRESBYTERIAN CHURCH. Dated 1897 and quite plain.

PRIMARY SCHOOL. Late C19, the windows rising into big gablets. Recent 'Fyfestone' extension.

CULAG HOTEL. By *William Fowler*, 1873. Originally designed as a shooting lodge for the third Duke of Sutherland, it was converted to an hotel in 1880 and restored in 1939 after a fire.

Very big and boring Baronial-manorial, with a conical-roofed round tower. Tawdry recent additions.

LOTHMORE

9010

A scatter of crofts N of the A9, the church to the s.

LOTH PARISH CHURCH. Built in 1821–2 and modelled on Archibald Simpson's Kintore Parish Church (Grampian) of 1819. Like the prototype, it is a big ashlar box with a full-height diagonally buttressed porch projecting from the w gable and topped by a spired bellcote. Three-light window over the door; tall two-light windows in the side walls. Unlike Kintore, the bellcote's spire and the buttresses' pinnacles are crocketed, but the window heads are uncusped. The interior was designed as a large galleried space with the pulpit at the E end flanked by windows in the gable. A floor has been inserted at gallery level. – GALLERIES carried on cast-iron clustered columns, the wooden fronts panelled with blind arcading. – More cusped arcading on the front of the PULPIT whose concave-sided sounding board, enriched with an Adamish plaster frieze and urn finial, is now hidden by the inserted floor. – Boxy PEWS, the long COMMUNION PEW filling the centre aisle. – In the SE corner, a marble MONUMENT to Major Peter Pope † 1845, with a mourning lady in high relief.

To the s, the white harled OLD MANSE, built in 1768–9 but with late C19 accretions.

CRAKAIG. See p. 561.
KILMOTE, 0.4km. SW. White harled tacksman's house with a projecting gabled centre. The door lintel carries the date 1767.

MIGDALE

6090

Small hamlet E of Bonar Bridge.

CREICH FREE CHURCH. By *Andrew Maitland & Sons*, 1880–1. Big lanceted box. Angle buttresses at the gable front, whose centre projects slightly to suggest a nave and aisles. Ball-finialled gabled bellcote.
MIGDALE HOSPITAL. See Bonar Bridge.
MIGDALE MILL. Plain mid-C19 farmhouse. To its E, a small L-plan rubble mill, probably early C19.

THE MOUND

7090

5.7km. SW of Golspie

Causeway and dam across the mouth of Loch Fleet, designed by *Thomas Telford* and built in 1813–16. The embankment itself is *c.* 910m. long. At its NE end (now by-passed), a contemporary rubble-built BRIDGE, originally of four roundheaded arches with triangular cutwaters. Two further arches were provided by *Joseph Mitchell* in 1837. The arches contain valve-gates. – Beside the bridge, an early C19 *cottage orné* with bracketed eaves and Tudor hoodmoulds.

7000   ROGART

Small village in Strath Fleet.

ROGART FREE CHURCH. Simple granite-built rectangle of 1845, still Georgian in feel, with roundheaded windows and a birdcage bellcote. The windows' coloured glass was introduced in *J. Pond Macdonald*'s alterations of 1899.

Adjoining piend-roofed MANSE of 1845, quite smart, with a console-corniced doorpiece and three-light windows.

ROGART PITFURE CHURCH. Sturdy little box built as a United Free church in 1909–10. Buttressed gable front topped by a bellcote.

ST CALLAN'S CHURCH, 2.1km. NE. Long harled kirk of 1775–7, quite plain, with rectangular windows and doors. The gableted bellcote was added by *William Fowler* in 1857. Discreet NE vestry of 1983. The internal FURNISHINGS probably belong to *George Alexander*'s repairs of 1817. Simple varnished pine PEWS, raked at the W end. – At the E end, PULPIT with attached columns and a sounding board. – Long COMMUNION PEW. – Two STAINED-GLASS windows (the Nativity, and the Penitent) by *Margaret Chilton* and *Marjorie Kemp*, 1929, characteristically brittle.

Beside the CHURCHYARD gate, a whitewashed SESSION HOUSE, probably early C19. – Just to its E, MONUMENT to Lieutenant-Colonel Alexander Sutherland †1822, a big corniced plinth bearing a ball finial.

MANSE to the S, by *William Fowler*, 1882–4. – On the hill behind, a contemporary crowstepped L-plan BARN.

PRIMARY SCHOOL. Late C19, with crowstepped gables and gablets. Unsuitable front addition of 1964–6.

RAILWAY STATION. Cottagey; built for the Sutherland Railway c. 1868.

DESCRIPTION. The mid-C19 village houses are almost pretty examples of gabled and gableted estate architecture. Beside the Railway Station (*see* above), two rubble-built MILLS of c. 1870. The W, a two-storey L-plan, was a meal mill, the broader E, of one and two storeys, a tweed mill.

4000   ROSEHALL

Small C19 and C20 village in Strath Oykel.

CHURCH OF SCOTLAND. Disused. Mission church built in 1891. Bellcote on the gable front; cheap Romanesque detail.

FREE CHURCH. Broad box of 1845. Roundheaded windows. On the E gable, the base of a bellcote; ball finial on the W.

SCOURIE   *1040*

Substantial c 19 and c 20 village beside Scourie Bay.

EDDRACHILLIS FREE CHURCH. White harled Georgian-
survival preaching box of 1846, with a rudimentary birdcage
bellcote. Roundheaded windows in the w gable, the others
rectangular. The w porch is an addition.

PRIMARY SCHOOL. Built *c*. 1875. L-plan, harled and crowstepped. Cheap mid-c 20 addition.

HARBOUR. Concrete quay and short pier built in 1902.

SCOURIE HOUSE. Late Georgian harled house of two storeys
and three bays, much extended to the w in a c 20 neo-Georgian
manner.

SKELBO CASTLE   *7090*
3.3km. NW of Embo

Medieval stronghold overlooking Loch Fleet. The lands of Skelbo
were granted by Hugo Freskyn to Archdeacon Gilbert de
Moravia (later Bishop of Caithness) *c*. 1211, and the castle was
in existence by 1290, when the English and Scottish commissioners appointed to meet the Maid of Norway gathered
there. The site is of great natural strength, a roughly triangular
hill rising abruptly from the shore of Loch Fleet to the E, its s
side sloping up from the ravine of the Skelbo Burn. At the w
there has been a ditch. The site is enclosed by a curtain wall
built of horizontal slabs interspersed with boulders. At the
enclosure's N corner a rock outcrop provides a natural motte,
now covered by a rectangular stone keep. On the evidence of
its surviving two unvaulted lower storeys, this was very simple.
Its masonry of thinner stones and long pinnings is not bonded
with that of the curtain wall, so the keep is probably later,
perhaps the replacement for a wooden structure. The curtain
may be c 13, the keep c 15. Near the sw wall's lower end is a
ruinous and altered two-storey house of *c*. 1600. Crowstepped
gables, the N skewputts carved with the portraits of a man and
woman.

To the w, a large STEADING of 1853. Nine parallel crowstepped ranges, the gables of the end blocks topped by chimneys, the centre with a birdcage bellcote. *James Loch* claimed
that the plan was 'mainly my own'.

SKIBO CASTLE   *7080*
6.2km. W of Dornoch

Huge Baronial mansion created by *Ross & Macbeth* for the multi-
millionaire philanthropist Andrew Carnegie in 1899–1903,
incorporating a not insubstantial house, also Baronial in style,
of 1880 by *Clarke & Bell* of Glasgow. That house is still visible
on the E (entrance) side but with the addition of a porte cochère.

Its main block's principal accent was a conical-roofed round tower at the SW corner. This tower lost its roof and acquired a corbelled battlement in the work of 1899–1903. To its W came a great new block, its S and W fronts an uninspired display of bay windows, turrets and crowstepped gables. The effect is that of a grand hotel, the architecture purchased by the yard.

The interior is very expensively finished but just as strongly Grand Hotel in character, Jacobean the dominant stylistic influence. Long panelled vestibule from the E entrance. Strapwork frieze and compartmented ceiling; attached Artisan Mannerist columns with spiralling foliage on their shafts framing the overmantel. Ahead is Clarke & Bell's two-storey hall, recast by Ross & Macbeth, a gallery across its S end, the main stair to the W. Each side of the stair, a Gothic arch carried on fat columns, their capitals fleshily foliaged. The l. arch contains an organ (by *Brindley & Foster*, 1904), the r. the entrance to a corridor. The Jacobean balustraded Imperial stair itself is entered through a tall stilted segmental arch. At its half-landing, a large five-light window, its roundheaded lights filled with stained glass of historical figures connected with Skibo (Bishop Gilbert of Caithness, the Marquess of Montrose and Earl Sigurd) and scenes connected with Carnegie's life (his birthplace, Skibo Castle, and the ships which took him to and brought him back from the United States); flanking smaller lights also with stained glass (a bishop, a cavalier, monks and friars). At the hall's N end, a hooded stone chimneypiece; above, two coats of arms, probably copied from a C17 original, which flank the carved date of 1663 over a panel inscribed

> CHRIST.IS.MY
> LYFE AND.RENT
> HIS PROMIS.IS
> MY.EVIDENT
> THERFOR FEAR THE
> LORD YOUR GOD

Some of this may be C17. In the E wall, a second chimneypiece; paired Artisan Mannerist piers at the overmantel. Off the hall's NE corner is the billiard room (later, Small Drawing Room). In its fireplace's ingoes, tiles painted with jolly medieval figures. SE of the hall, the Morning Room, with an Adam-revival chimneypiece. In the drawing room S of the hall, another Adam-revival marble chimneypiece. Enriched plaster ceiling, also evoking the late C18, but the pilastered overmantel and dado are suggestive of early Georgian work. W of the drawing room, the Boudoir, with a Frenchy ceiling. Above the Adam-revival chimneypiece, a wooden overmantel framing an alabaster relief of a woman with her child. Then the library, solidly Jacobean with oak bookcases and chimneypiece, its overmantel carved with a book; above the bookcases, an oak frieze decorated with the coats of arms of Scottish burghs set in strapwork. W of the library were Carnegie's study and his secretary's office. At the main block's NW corner, the dining room, Jacobean masculinity dominant, with wood-panelled walls and ceiling, the frieze carved with scrolls and cornucopia. Inglenook with a segmental arch framed by foliage-spiralled Ionic columns topped by eagles. Veined marble chimneypiece with red marble columns; above, a hooded overmantel with three niches in its front. In the basement below the dining room is the gunroom, again panelled and with a hooded Jacobean fireplace in an inglenook. On the first floor above the dining room, the Montrose Room, another essay in the Jacobean manner with an inglenook.

Terraced GARDEN to the S and W, the retaining walls balustraded or battlemented; it was laid out in 1904 by *Thomas Mawson*. – To the E, the WALLED GARDEN with a row of glasshouses along the N wall. – SW of the gardens, beside the artificial Loch Ospisdale, the SWIMMING POOL of *c*. 1900, its broad front block (containing changing rooms) single-storey with scrolls on the gables' crowsteps; small cupola ventilator. Long buttressed bath block behind, the steel structure of its glazed roof by *Mackenzie & Moncur*; originally it had a S cupola. – W of the pool, a two-storey early C20 Scots Renaissance block; crowstepped gables and gablets and two pedimented dormerheads. It was built as the electric house and private telephone exchange.

NE of the castle, the HOME FARM, its steading of 1873 plain except for crowstepped gables. – To its w, the DAIRY of *c*. 1900, a single-storey *cottage orné* fronting the dairy itself, an octagon whose red-tiled roof is extravagantly bellcast over the surrounding tree-trunk verandah. Inside, two prettily tiled rooms. – WEST LODGE, 1.5km. w of the castle, by *R. J. Macbeth*, 1907, battlemented main block with a tower in the inner angle of its crowstepped porch. Aggressively rock-faced and crenellated gatepiers.

SPINNINGDALE   6090

Randomly arranged hamlet, mostly C19. A village was founded here in 1792 and a cotton mill was built; but after being gutted by fire in 1806 the mill was abandoned.

COTTON MILL. Substantial but ruinous remains of the mill built in 1792–4. It has been of four storeys and six bays. At the S end, a stairtower with Venetian windows; semicircular heating tower at the N.

STOER   0020

Crofting village overlooking The Minch.

CHURCH. Disused and roofless T-plan 'Parliamentary' church (i.e. to *William Thomson*'s design), built by *William Davidson* in 1829. Tudor windows and doors. The birdcage bellcote has been replaced with a tall concrete cross.

STOER HEAD LIGHTHOUSE, 4.8km. NW. By *D. & T. Stevenson*, 1870. Short round tower joined to a flat-roofed block of keepers' houses.

BROCH, Clachtoll, 0.8km. SW. Broch of *c.* 500 B.C.–A.D. 500, built on the rocky shore of the Bay of Stoer. The relatively easy approach from the land on the E and S has been cut off by a stone wall, still almost 1m. high in places, running in an oblique line at a distance of *c.* 5m.-18m. from the broch. The broch itself, partly collapsed into the sea, stands *c.* 2m. high. As usual it is circular, *c.* 18m. in diameter. Over the entrance, a large triangular lintel stone to spread the weight of the wall. In the entrance passage, door-jambs and a bar-hole; behind them, low doors to small wall chambers. The internal court is choked with debris.

8000

UPPAT HOUSE
4km. NE of Golspie

Harled laird's house of two storeys and an attic. Its S block looks mid-C 18. Four unevenly spaced bays. Bow-fronted porch, probably a late C 18 addition together with the full-height back wing and the originally detached single-storey wing projecting at the SE. Big NE addition by *William Leslie*, 1846, Tudorish with a conical-roofed round corner tower. Also of 1846 the single-storey SW wing. – Just to the S, two pairs of ball-finialled late Georgian GATEPIERS. – MONUMENT to James Loch, in woodland 1.2km. SE, dated 1858. Classical, with engaged Doric granite columns and a ball-finialled pyramid roof.

WESTERN ISLES

A long string of islands, several now linked by causeways, separated by The Minch from the mainland and Skye. All except
Harris and Barra are predominantly flat. Part of the semi-independent lordship of the Isles for most of the Middle Ages, the
islands came fully under the Crown after that lordship's forfeiture
in 1493. Their populations suffered much from being cleared from
agricultural land to make way for sheep-walks in the early C19,
but later in that century and in the early C20 much of the land
was reapportioned as crofts, the crofters often doubling as weavers
of Harris Tweed.

AIGINISH see EYE (LEWIS)

AIRD CHOINNICH see ARDKENNETH (SOUTH UIST)

AMHUINNSUIDHE CASTLE (HARRIS)   *0000*

Solid castellated mansion by *David Bryce*, built in 1864–7 for the
seventh Earl of Dunmore, whose grandfather had bought Harris
thirty years before. Three-storey main block from which projects an unexciting four-storey tower. Inside, the principal
rooms are a mixture of Jacobean and Frenchy classical. – To
the W, a battlemented stone ARCH over the road, half-screening
the contemporary crowstepped STABLES.

AN TAIRBEART see TARBERT (HARRIS)

AN TAOBH TUATH see NORTHTON (HARRIS)

ARDKENNETH /AIRD CHOINNICH (SOUTH UIST)   *7040*

Little more than a place-name at the NW corner of the island.

ST MICHAEL'S CHURCH (R.C.). Long and tall harled box built
in 1829, the W part containing the church, the E a three-bay

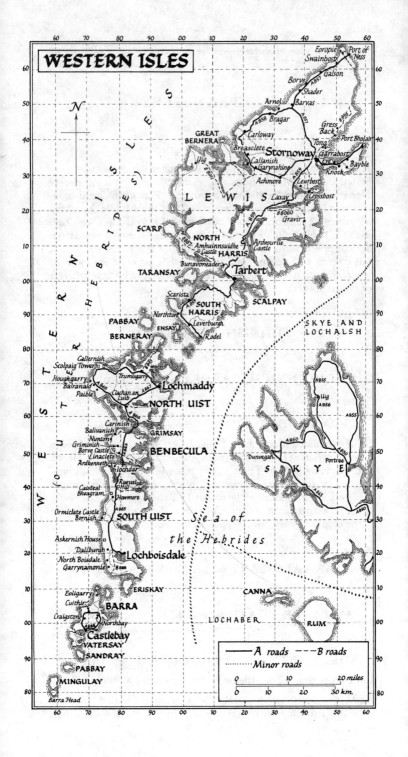

two-storey priest's house. High roundheaded windows lighting the church. Its interior is quite plain except at the E bay, whose end half is marked off as a sanctuary by a screen of three roundheaded arches carried on tapering wooden columns. Small rectangular recess for the altar. – Outside, a tall semi-realist stone STATUE of Our Lady of the Isles, by *Hew Lorimer*, 1956, a smaller version of the one on Rueval Hill.

ARDVOURLIE CASTLE (HARRIS) *1010*

Tall crowstepped and harled shooting lodge of 1863, an off-centre pitch-roofed tower over the entrance making it a picturesque presence beside Loch Seaforth.

ARNOL (LEWIS) *3040*

Small crofting township, notable for the blackhouse preserved as an Ancient Monument.

BLACKHOUSE. It was probably built in the late C19. Two parallel ranges, both with drystone walls and A-frame roofs thatched with turfs covered with straw. The longer W block's N part was the house, its S the byre, both entered by the same door. The E block was the barn, its two doors facing each other (the E now built up) providing a through-draught for winnowing.

ASKERNISH HOUSE (SOUTH UIST) *7020*
2.7km. N of Daliburgh

Piend-roofed two-storey three-bay tacksman's house of 1835. Trim in white harl with black painted dressings.

BACK/BAC (LEWIS) *4040*

Township near the E coast of Lewis.

FREE CHURCH. Big harled rectangle, dated 1891. Pointed windows; curly gableted bellcote. Galleried interior focused on the W pulpit.

SCHOOL. By *Gratton & McLean*, 1965.

BAGH A CHAISTEIL *see* CASTLEBAY (BARRA)

BAGHASDAL *see* NORTH BOISDALE (SOUTH UIST)

BAGH A TUATH *see* NORTHBAY (BARRA)

BAILE A MHANAICH *see* BALIVANICH (BENBECULA)

BAILE NA CREIGA *see* CRAIGSTON (BARRA)

BAILE NAN CAILLEACH *see* NUNTON (BENBECULA)

BAILE RAGHAILL *see* BALRANALD (NORTH UIST)

7050 BALIVANICH / BAILE A MHANAICH (BENBECULA)

Mostly an airport and barracks complex, housing soldiers working at the rocket firing and testing range on South Uist. A few thatched croft houses survive.

TEAMPULL CHALUIM CHILLE (ST MALCOLM'S CHURCH). Badly ruined remains of a medieval church, built of rubble with shell-lime mortar. It has comprised a nave and chancel, the chancel's thinner walls probably indicating that it was an addition. Small rectangular windows in the side walls; narrow door in the W gable. The E gable has fallen. – A little to the S, a WELL, enclosed by drystone walling; its waters are reputed to have cured toothache.

BARRACKS. Sizeable group, by the *Department of the Environment* (architect-in-charge: *A. R. Scott*), with detailing and supervision by *Manning Clamp & Partners* (partner-in-charge: *Anthony Dick*), 1971. Flat-roofed buildings, their walls clad in aggregate panels prefabricated on the CLASP system, but with modifications to allow for the strength of local winds. A concrete WATER TOWER like an inverted conical dish on stilts is the main feature.

NURSERY SCHOOL. Harled school and schoolhouse, by *Alexander Ross*, 1876.

PRIMARY SCHOOL. By *Inverness County Council* (County Architect: *Douglas Calder*), 1973.

7060 BALRANALD/BAILE RAGHAILL (NORTH UIST)

Isolated church on the W side of the island.

KILMUIR PARISH CHURCH. Originally North Uist Parish

Church. Cheap Gothic, by *Alexander Shairp*, 1892–4. Squat T-plan. In the s w inner angle, a two-stage tower, its battlemented parapet enclosing a slated pyramidal spire. Inside, a wealth of varnished pitch-pine, the pulpit placed in a roomy elders' enclosure.

CAIRN, Clettraval, 2.4km. NE. Badly robbed chambered cairn of the third millennium B.C. It is a long (over 29m.) wedge-shape, with some kerbstones visible on the s. At the broader E end survives the façade's s half, built of upright slabs (all now slightly out of position) diminishing in size from the 2.7m.-high stone by the entrance. Inside, a chamber of Clyde type (unique in the Western Isles), the walls constructed of overlapping slabs from whose joins project low slabs dividing the floor into five compartments. – Immediately to the w and at a lower level, remains of a round Iron Age HOUSE. Its interior has been composed of radial rooms round an open centre, presumably containing the hearth. – 0.2km. SE, a 1.4m.-high STANDING STONE. – 0.2km. to its SE, a mass of stones, the remains of a round CAIRN, which seems to have been *c.* 18m. in diameter.

BARABHAS *see* BARVAS (LEWIS)

BARPA NAN FEANNAG *see* TRUMISGARRY (NORTH UIST)

BARVAS / BARABHAS (LEWIS)   *3050*

Crofting township on the w coast.

Former PARISH CHURCH. Thrifty Gothic, by *Alexander Macdonald*, 1897–9. Buttressed rectangle with a squat SW tower. Rather altered on conversion to a house.
FREE CHURCH. Big harled C 20 T-plan kirk. Ball finials on the gables.
PARISH CHURCH. Built as a United Free church, *c.* 1910. Big piend-roofed box with tall roundheaded windows and a w bellcote.

BAYBLE / PABAIL (LEWIS)   *5030*

Crofting township on the s side of the Eye Peninsula.

POINT FREE CHURCH. Built in 1969. Hall-like, in drydash with 'Fyfestone' trimmings, the sawtooth roof providing a jazzy note.

9080   BERNERAY / EILEAN BHEARNARAIGH

Crofting island to the N of North Uist. On it, a fair number of well-preserved C 19 thatched cottages.

CHURCH. Originally a Free church. By *Thomas Binnie*, of Glasgow, 1887. Church and manse under a single roof, making a big but plain harled box. Gableted E bellcote.

Former CHURCH. Now roofless and without its bellcote. Harled T-plan 'Parliamentary' church (i.e. to *William Thomson*'s design), built in 1829. – Beside it, the contemporary two-storey 'Parliamentary' MANSE (i.e. to *Joseph Mitchell*'s design).

SCHOOL. By *Alexander Ross*, 1875.

HARBOUR. By *H. L. Waterman*, 1988. Rectangular basin enclosed by high concrete walls.

BORGH *see* BORVE (LEWIS)

7020   BORNISH / BORNAIS (SOUTH UIST)

Small and scattered crofting township.

ST MARY'S CHURCH (R.C.). Built in 1837 as a big harled box with the church (at the S) and priest's house (at the N) under the same roof. Birdcage bellcote on the S gable; tall lancet windows with wooden Y-tracery lighting the church. The building was reconstructed by *A. R. Conlon, c.* 1955, when the priest's house was converted to a chancel and given round-arched windows; at the same time were added low transepts (the W a vestry, the E a Lady Chapel), and a porch and apsidal baptistery at the S end. The interior, stripped of plaster, is now horribly rubbly.

BORNISH HOUSE. Early C 19 farmhouse, white harled and piend-roofed.

CAIRN, Reineval, 4.1km. SE. Conspicuous on a hillside. Roughly round (*c.* 21m. in diameter) cairn, probably of the third millennium B.C. Twelve of the surrounding kerb's upright slabs still stand, the largest not at the entrance on the E but at the W side facing over to the sea.

ORMICLATE CASTLE. *See* p. 621.

4050   BORVE / BORGH (LEWIS)

Crofting township in NW Lewis.

FREE CHURCH. Drydashed box of *c.* 1900, a gabled bellcote corbelled out from the S end.

BORVE CASTLE (BENBECULA)   *7050*
4.9km. s of Balivanich

Fragmentary remains of a rectangular rubble-built tower, perhaps the 'castle of Benwewyl [Benbecula]' recorded by John Fordun, *c.* 1385. The ground-floor entrance has been in the E wall; to its s, a rectangular window. In the N gable, the l. jamb of a first-floor fireplace.

BRAGAR (LEWIS)   *2040*

Crofting township, the remains of the church isolated in a grave-yard beside the sea.

TEAMPULL EOIN (ST JOHN'S CHURCH). Roofless remains of a small late medieval church built of rough rubble. Nave and narrower chancel; slit windows. Scanty remains of the stone chancel arch. Extending s of the chancel has been an L-plan bulding, its walls now reduced to their lowest courses.
SCHOOL. By *Alexander Mackenzie Sen.*, 1876.

BREASCLETE / BREASCLEIT (LEWIS)   *2030*

Township dominated by a pharmaceutical factory.

SCHOOL. By *J. Houghton Spencer*, 1876. Harled and simple, but with forceful gables and gablets.
FACTORY. Built in 1979. Elegantly corduroyed package overlooking the pier.

BUNAVONEADER / BUN ABHAINN EADARRA
(HARRIS)   *1000*

Small scattered group of houses, with the remains of a whaling station beside the shore.

WHALING STATION. The station, long abandoned, was founded by Carl Herlofson in 1904. There survive a tall and tapering square chimney of brick, and remains of the ramps up which the whale carcasses were hauled.

BUTT OF LEWIS *see* EOROPIE (LEWIS)

CAIRINIS *see* CARINISH (NORTH UIST)

7030   CAISTEAL BHEAGRAM (SOUTH UIST)

Shaggy remains of an island castle in the middle of Loch an Eileiń.
It belonged to Ronald Alansoun by 1505 and may have been
built by him. Foundations of a wall round the island's waterline.
On the highest part, the ruin of a small rectangular tower built
of lime-mortared rubble.

2030   CALLANISH / CALANAIS (LEWIS)

Small crofting township on a fat promontory sticking into Loch
Roag, the main circle of standing stones at the S giving it a more
than local fame.

6 STONES OF CALLANISH. The most impressive complex of
standing stones in Scotland, probably dating from the third or
early second millennium B.C. The stones, thin megaliths of
local gneiss, are arranged as a circle within a cross. The circle's
stones are tall, all except one over 2.7m. high, placed with their
broad faces pointing inwards. In the centre, a 4.75m.-high
pillar. c. 3m. SW, a single stone, its face towards the circle; it
may be the sole survivor of a second concentric circle. Avenues
of stones, not quite directly aligned with each other, to the
circle's N and S, the S avenue c. 3.65m. broad but with only one
E stone remaining and now 27m. long; the N avenue is 8.2m.
broad and c. 82m. long. The N stone on its W side faces the
circle instead of having its edge towards it, so probably it marks
the avenue's original end. Single lines of stones extend E and
W of the circle, each of four stones. Both are placed S of centre
and perhaps were originally parts of avenues whose N sides have
been lost.
    Inside the circle is a chambered cairn, probably an insertion,
but the circle's two E stones, which flank the cairn entrance, are
set slightly inside the circumference. From these have extended
contiguous low stones to form the partly surviving kerb of a
round cairn, 6.4m. in diameter, with the circle's central pillar
marking the kerb's W point. The cairn's unusually small size
may be a consequence of its builders feeling constrained to
respect the existing layout of standing stones, whose presence
made this a prestigious site for a burial. Now roofless, the cairn
has contained a passage leading to two small chambers, all built
of drystone masonry except for two orthostats at the entrance
to each chamber. Large oval heap of stones SW of the circle
looking like the remains of another cairn but almost certainly
those of a corn-drying kiln.
STONE CIRCLE (CALLANISH II), Cnoc Ceann a' Gharaidh,
1km. SE. Probably formed in the second millennium B.C., a
circle, c. 20m. in diameter, of standing stones, the broad faces
towards its centre. Five stones are still erect in the circle's N
and E arcs; two fallen stones on the W. In the centre, low remains
of a cairn of c. 8.5m. diameter.
STONE CIRCLE (CALLANISH III), Cnoc Fillibhir, 1.2km. SE.

Remains of two concentric circles of standing stones, the inner
c. 8.5m. in diameter, the outer 16m. Four stones in the inner
circle; in the outer circle, eight stones still erect and five which
have fallen.

STONE CIRCLE (CALLANISH IV), Ceann Hulavig, 3.2km. SE.
Five tall stones, from 2m. to 2.6m. high, three pointed and two
flat-topped, forming an oval of 13m. by 9m. In the centre, a
0.6m.-high upright stone surrounded by a small cairn.

CALLERNISH (NORTH UIST)   7070
6.3km. NE of Balranald

By *Martyn Beckett*, 1962; this is North Uist's only mansion house
but one which pretends to be a converted stables. The C18
'round square' at Gordonstoun (Grampian) was the inspiration
but this prototype's suavity is absent, perhaps not inap-
propriately, given the wildness of the site. Rendered concrete
walls; slate roof. A crowstepped gable over the pend into the
courtyard. Inside and on axis, a crowstepped porch with a big
coat of arms above the door.

CARAVAT BARP *see* CARINISH (NORTH UIST)

CARINISH / CAIRINIS (NORTH UIST)   8060

Crofting township, much of the housing C20, the harled inn mid-
C19.

CARINISH CHURCH. *See* Clachan an Luib.
CHURCH. Sneck-harled mission church of 1867, with lattice
glazing in the roundheaded windows.
TEAMPULL NA TRIONAID (CHURCH OF THE HOLY
TRINITY). Unkempt and fragmentary ruin of the church said[*]
to have been built *c.* 1200 by Bethoc, daughter of Somerled,
lord of the Isles, and first Prioress of Iona. Some confirmation
of an early date is provided by the character of the masonry,
which is of rubble brought to courses every few feet by flat
pinnings, and by the W gable's putlock holes. It has been a large
single-cell rectangle, *c.* 18.7m. by 6.5m., but most of the E gable
has gone and there are large gaps in the side walls. At the
NE, a tunnel-vaulted passage links the church to a rectangular
building constructed of cruder masonry. This is clearly an
addition, perhaps C16, but was it a chapel or a dwelling? In its
gables, rectangular windows and aumbries. There has been a
narrow door in the centre of its largely demolished N wall,
opposite the entrance to the passage. – At the church's SW
corner, a harled rubble BURIAL ENCLOSURE, probably C18.

[*]In *The Book of Clanranald.*

School. By *Alexander Ross*, 1875.

Cairn, Caravat Barp, 1.6km. E. Standing on moorland, a *c.* 50m.-
long cairn, probably of the third millennium B.C., its W end
now so covered by peat that it forms a point. Traces of a kerb
of split stones along the sides. Badly robbed E end with traces
of a SE horn. The projecting tops of upright slabs indicate the
position of a chamber.

Dun, Dun an t-Siamain, 6.5km. E. Remains of a dun of the first
millennium B.C. built on a small island approached by a curving
causeway. Wall rising directly from the water, roughly oval but
with an angle on the E side. Main entrance immediately S of
the causeway's end. Second entrance (a water gate) at the dun's
S end. Interior filled with overgrown debris.

2040　　　CARLOWAY / CARLABHAGH (LEWIS)

Large crofting township on the W side of Lewis.

Free Church. Big harled box of 1884. Pointed windows; gableted E bellcote.

Bridge. Big rubble-built segmental arch, probably mid-C19,
over the Carloway River.

Harbour. Concrete PIER of *c.* 1900. – Beside it, a late C19
rubble-built WAREHOUSE, now rather altered.

Broch (Dun Carloway), 1.9km. SW. Broch of the late first
millennium B.C. or the early first millennium A.D., prominently
sited in moorland with the ground falling steeply to the S. As
usual, it is circular, *c.* 14m. in diameter, the externally battered
wall still standing at the SE almost to the original height of over
9m. Entrance at the NW, its passage broadening at the door-
checks. On the S side, a low entrance into a roughly oval guard
chamber. Inside the court, low NE and SW doorways into wall
cells. At the SE, doorway into a lobby, from whose W end there
rises a stair in the wall-thickness. Above this entrance, a tall
vertical transomed opening, perhaps to let light into the galleries
but also to lessen the weight on the door lintel. Three galleries
above the base, the hollow wall construction clearly visible from
the N. In the wall's inner face to the court, a scarcement ledge
c. 2m. above the ground, presumably to support the first floor
of a timber structure built round the court.

6090　　CASTLEBAY / BAGH A CHAISTEIL (BARRA)

C19 and C20 village on the N shore of the eponymous bay, its
name a not over-imaginative but apt allusion to the presence of
Kisimul Castle.

Church of Our Lady Star of the Sea (R.C.). By *G.
Woulfe Brenan*, 1888. Austere Gothic, built of squared blocks
of gneiss. Nave and shorter lean-to aisles. The SE inner angle

is more than filled by a diagonally buttressed tower, its clock and belfry stages slightly intaken under the machicolated battlement surrounding the slated pyramid roof. Inside, arcades with broad depressed arches. – STAINED GLASS. Three-light N (liturgical E) window (the Crucifixion with Our Lady and St John) of *c.* 1930, brightly coloured and clearly drawn, but not very good. – Roughly contemporary S (liturgical W) window (Our Lady Star of the Sea).

Small CLERGY HOUSE to the E, contemporary with the church.

CHURCH OF SCOTLAND. Disused and derelict. Lanceted Gothic, by *Hardy & Wight*, 1892–3. Of sneck-harled gneiss rubble with Portland cement dressings. Nave with shorter four-bay aisles, their transverse roofs ending in gables. Tower of Iona Abbey derivation in the SW inner angle.

BARRA COMMUNITY SCHOOL. By *John F. Paterson* of *Western Isles Island Council*, 1983, like a well-packaged industrial shed. At the E, the former school of *c.* 1930.

STATUE, Heaval, 1.6km. NE. Carrara marble statue of Our Lady Star of the Sea, carved at Pietrafanta in 1954. *c.* 7.3m. high, but almost lost on its hillside site.

TOWER, Dùn Mhic Leòid, 2.1km. NW. Remains of a small rubble-built rectangular tower, perhaps C15, occupying most of an islet in Loch Tangusdale. It has been of three storeys, the top floor now demolished. At the ground floor, only one small window at the SE corner. Another small window in the S wall of the first floor, which has had larger openings to the E and W and a N entrance. Inside, no evidence now of fireplaces or of the stair. The floors were of wood.

KISIMUL CASTLE

Small and dour medieval castle of the MacNeils of Barra, given romantic allure by its position on an island in Castle Bay. Claims have been made* for the castle having been begun as early as the C11 or C12, but there is no mention of a castle on Barra in John Fordun's late C14 list of island fortresses or, perhaps more significantly, in the charter of 1373 by which John of Islay granted his son Reginald lands including the whole isle of Barra and which claimed to name the castles made over.‡ The first reference to Kisimul Castle was provided by Dean Monro in 1549, and it had probably been begun soon after 1427, when Gilleonan MacNeil received Barra from Alexander, Lord of the Isles.

The buildings cover almost all of their island site above high-water mark. The first part to be built was a tower house at the S, followed, probably almost without pause, by a curtain wall enclosing an irregular pentagon with a tower at its N corner and a hall and reputed 'chapel' against the wall's NW and NE stretches.

---

*Notably by The MacNeil of Barra, *Castle in the Sea* (1964), and by Stewart Cruden, *The Scottish Castle* (3rd edn, 1981).

‡The castles it did name were Castle Tioram (Lochaber) and 'Vynvawle', usually identified as Borve Castle (Western Isles).

All these were probably completed by about the mid-c 15, the combination of tower house, curtain wall and hall being paralleled at Breachacha Castle on Coll (North Strathclyde), which may even be by the same designer.* A reconstruction of *c.* 1500 heightened the parapets of the tower house, N tower and curtain wall. At about the same time the kitchen, Tanist [Heir's] House and Gokman's [Watchman's] House were built in the courtyard backing against almost all the still unencumbered stretches of the curtain. Later in the c 16 the Gokman's House was enlarged to the s, blocking the original courtyard entrance, a new entrance being opened to its w. Perhaps also c 16 was the Crew House, apparently a boathouse, built outside the enclosure on the s of the tower house. In the c 17, perhaps because the c 15 tower house was by then regarded as too uncomfortable for civilized life, the hall was extended s w and given an upper floor. The castle was abandoned in the mid-c 18, and its roofs and floors were destroyed by a fire in 1795. Further damage resulted from the mid-c 19 boom in the herring fishery, the castle being used as a quarry for ballast, so that by *c.* 1860 much of the curtain wall's N W and s W stretches, together with the Tanist House, Gokman's House and Crew House, had been almost completely destroyed. Minor repairs, apparently including reharling, were carried out *c.* 1890. In 1937 the castle was bought by the architect *Robert L. MacNeil* of Barra,‡ who began consolidation of the ruins the next year, followed by an extensive restoration which was completed in 1970.

All the buildings are of hard local gneiss, the tower house's quoins dressed, those of the other structures mostly formed of suitable boulders or edge-set slabs, and all now harled. The CURTAIN WALL, although clearly dating from a second phase of construction, since it is butt-jointed against the tower house, was almost certainly intended from the start. It runs from the s W corner of the tower house round the island to the tower house's N E corner. The main entrance, reached by steps from the water, immediately E of the tower house, is late c 16, its doorway rectangular to the outside but with a segmental arch to the courtyard. Above the entrance, a c 20 coat of arms of the MacNeils of Barra, probably in the position of a c 16 panel. At the wallhead above, a box machicolation, presumably also late c 16. The blocked c 15 entrance a little to the N E was 2.4m. wide and provided with a portcullis. It had been narrowed when the Gokman's House was built before that house's late c 16 extension led to its being built up. At the curtain's N W, a c 15 postern gate (built up in the c 17) under another c 16 machicolation. Window openings in the N W and rebuilt w stretches of the curtain to light the c 15 hall and the 1950s Tanist House. At the N W wall, two small rounded garderobe projections, their chutes discharging into the sea. The curtain's original wallhead was *c.* 1.8m. below the present one, the level

*As suggested by D. J. Turner and J. G. Dunbar, 'Breachacha Castle, Coll', *Proceedings of the Society of Antiquaries of Scotland* (1969–70).
‡Whose family had sold Barra in 1838.

of the wall-walk shown externally by a series of weep-holes along the NW stretch and a further two just W of the tower house. A blocked opening in the SE section and another under the postern gate's machicolation may be the remains of C 15 crenelles. When the parapets were heightened c. 1500, the new wall-walks behind were made of wood, their beams projecting through the wall, the putlock holes clearly visible at the E, NE and NW. Possibly the beams also supported hoardings outside the walls, but the early C 16 crenelles are too high for there to have been easy access to them. At the NE corner was a small wooden platform, presumably for a look-out post. Tower at the obtusely angled N corner with a semicircular back wall towards the courtyard, its walls heightened at the same time as those of the curtain.

The C 15 TOWER HOUSE at the S corner is a severely plain three-storey harled rectangle, c. 10m. by 9m. Above a strongly battered plinth the walls rise vertically to the top of the parapet. A few rectangular windows lighting the two upper floors. In the centre of the N wall just above the plinth, a door to the ground-floor store. It is reached by a stone forestair, probably of the late C 16 but replacing a C 15 stair in the same position, which continues across the face of the tower house up to the S curtain's wall-walk and then returns as a C 20 wooden flying bridge to a wooden platform, its beams placed in the C 15 socket-holes, outside the house's main entrance. This doorway, restored in 1961 with a semicircular head, is placed at a level between the first and second floors. Above the second floor, a line of weep-holes to drain the roof, showing the original position of the parapet walk. Like that of the curtain wall, the tower house's parapet was heightened c. 1500 and given a box machicolation above the principal entrance. In the centre of the N face, whose wall-walk behind remained at the C 15 level, one exceptionally deep crenelle. The W parapet's upper part is a C 20 restoration and now uncrenellated. On the S and E sides, unprotected by the curtain wall and so part of the castle's first line of defence, the C 16 wall-walks were of wood with beams projecting through putlock holes. On the E they seem certain to have carried an external hoarding reached through three deep crenelles (the centre one made smaller in the C 20 restoration, when the S one was blocked). There may also have been a hoarding on the now uncrenellated S face, whose wall-walk is at a higher level, only c. 1m. below the parapet's top. C 20 slated roof rising inside the parapet.

Inside the tower house the floors were all wooden. No fire-places, so presumably it was heated by peat fires in braziers. The ground floor was a store, its floor c. 1m. below the level of its entrance threshold. Internal communication, if any, to the floor above must have been by a ladder. The two upper floors are both reached from the main entrance, one by a stair going down inside the N wall, the other by a stair rising in the NE corner. In the first-floor room, windows to the W and E, the W window's embrasure narrowed, perhaps in the C 17. Garderobe

near the W end of the S wall; near its E end, an aumbry. There
has been a loft over the room's N end, presumably reached by
a ladder. The second-floor room, probably the hall, has one
window in each of the N, W and S walls and two in the E, its small
N window's almost rectangular embrasure forming a lobby at
the head of the stair from the main entrance, its larger S window's embrasure narrowed, perhaps in the early C16, after its
lintel had cracked. In the N window's W ingo an aumbry; in the
E ingo, the door to a stair up to the parapet walk. At the W
window, the N ingo contains an aumbry, the S the door into a
wall-passage to a garderobe at the house's SW corner. Small
aumbries in the ingoes of the S window.

On the roof of the tower house, clear evidence of the heightening of the parapet. Originally its walk was at the same level
all round except at the NE corner, where it stepped up to a
platform over the stairhead. At the SW corner, a door from
the walk into a garderobe in the wall. The alterations and
heightening of the parapet in c. 1500 left the C15 walk unaltered
on the N side. On the W, a narrower new walk, c. 1.2m. above
the old, was built on top with steps at each end, allowing
continued access to the garderobe. On the S and E sides the
original parapets were thickened to form narrow scarcements
providing some of the necessary support for the new walk's
wooden beams, their outer ends projecting through the new
putlock holes, their inner ends perhaps supported, as now, by
posts placed on the C15 wall-walk.

The NORTH TOWER was built as part of the curtain wall and
heightened with it in c. 1500. Its lower part is hidden from the
courtyard by the abutting hall and 'chapel', but its upper part
stands proud. The whole of this semicircular upper portion on
the S was rebuilt in the C20 restoration, which produced also
the faintly incongruous metal roof poking up above the parapet.
The floor of what is now the upper room was originally the
tower's roof, presumably reached by steps from the curtain's
wall-walk. When the curtain was heightened, the wall-walk was
raised to the level of this roof, doorways to the walk made in
the tower's parapet, which was also pierced by windows to N
and S and heightened and roofed over to form a room. At this
room's NW corner, a C15 garderobe. Trapdoor in the floor
giving access to a prison below; windowless, but with a latrine.

On the N tower's SW side is the HALL, its NE four-fifths built
in the C15, apparently at the same time as the curtain which
forms its back wall. It was given an upper storey and extended
to the SW (partly covering the castle's well) in the C17, and was
restored in 1958–60, most of its then largely missing SE wall
being rebuilt and its new slated roof provided with catslide
dormers. Strangely, the restoration gave the C17 extension's
SW gable straight skews in place of its former crowsteps and
removed the tabling of the original SW gable. On the r. of the
SW door into the hall itself, the splayed C15 ingo of a window
which seems to have been at least 1.8m. high. The two small
first-floor windows at this end of the hall and the larger window

and the door of the extension are C17, the rest conjectural. Inside, the hall is now of two-storey height, its concrete ceiling given visual support by wooden railway sleepers. At the NE gable, a fireplace of 1960 nudged by the rounded wall of the N tower. In the curtain wall at the level of the C17 upper floor, an aumbry and slop sink, suggesting there may have been a kitchen here. Almost immediately above, a narrow doorway onto the parapet walk.

End on to the hall and built against the curtain wall's NE stretch is the 'CHAPEL', apparently again C15 in origin and contemporary with the curtain. There is no evidence of its original function, the discovery inside it in 1938 of a stone basin, almost certainly a mortar, insufficient to establish an ecclesiastical origin. The lower part of its wall to the courtyard is of harled stone and contains two closely spaced doors, the SE probably original, the NW probably converted from a window when the first door's direct access to the courtyard was blocked by the erection of the Gokman's House on its S in the early C16. Small C15 window at the NW end. On top of this wall, a wooden clearstorey provided in the C20 restoration. Inside, an aumbry in the centre of the SE gable, its position hard to explain if an altar stood here. To the S, foundations of the C16 GOKMAN'S HOUSE.

Abutting the tower house's W wall and backing onto the curtain's S stretch, remains of a KITCHEN block, probably of the early C16. It has been of two storeys, with a ground-floor fireplace projecting beyond the W gable. On the first floor, another fireplace at the S and an aumbry in the W gable.

In the courtyard's NW corner, the TANIST HOUSE, built in 1957–8 on the foundations of an early C16 building. Straightforward neo-vernacular, the upper floor's windows topped by catslide dormerheads.

Outside the courtyard and S of the tower house, which it seems to have abutted, was the CREW HOUSE. Only a fragment of one wall survives but it may been have been a two-storey boathouse, with sleeping accommodation on the upper floor. It might be late C16.

CLACHAN AN LUIB (NORTH UIST) 7060

Little more than the church at the junction of the A865 and A867.

CARINISH CHURCH. Built as a Free church in 1889. Only the gableted bellcote distinguishes it from a hall. – Contemporary MANSE to the W.

CAIRN, Barpa Langass, 3.2km. NE. Probably of the third millennium B.C. Bare domed mound of stones, c. 25m. in diameter and 4m. high. Some pointed-topped kerbstones visible round the edge. On the E side has been a V-plan forecourt, the two slabs of its N side still standing. From this a passage (its outer end blocked) with slab walls supporting drystone masonry.

Central chamber, a rough oval (*c.* 4m. by 1.8m.) walled with massive slabs, the spaces between their sides and pointed or rounded tops filled with drystone masonry. Roof of three lintels.

CAIRN, Marrogh, 6km. NE. Round cairn, probably of the third millennium B.C., *c.* 24m. in diameter and 4m. high. Kerbstones round the edge. Inside, a blocked roughly circular chamber, its walls of slabs below corbelled masonry.

CAIRN, Unival, 3km. N. Low almost square cairn, *c.* 16m. by 16m., probably of the third millennium B.C. Slightly convex E façade of upright stones (some fallen or missing) joined by drystone masonry. The uprights have been tallest at the central entrance and decreased in height towards the corners. Several kerbstones on the other sides. Passage from the E into the roughly oval central chamber (now roofless). – *c.* 7m. SW, a large STANDING STONE, *c.* 3m. high, its broad face turned to the centre of the cairn.

STONE SETTING, Pobull Fhinn, 3.3km. NE. Roughly shaped pillars and boulders enclosing an oval area, *c.* 37m. by 30m., which has been partly terraced by excavation on the uphill (N) side and perhaps built up a little on the S. It may date from the second millennium B.C.

CNOC *see* KNOCK (LEWIS)

6000   CRAIGSTON / BAILE NA CREIGA (BARRA)

Settlement in a broad valley, a late Georgian farmhouse prominent.

ST BRENDAN'S CHURCH (R.C.). Opened in 1858. Harled lancet-windowed box with a small W porch. Inside, a little rectangular sanctuary formed by the side walls of flanking vestries.

CAIRN, Dun Bharpa, 1.1km. NE. Steep flat-topped mound of irregular stones, c. 335m. in overall diameter and 5.2m. high. Several unevenly spaced large kerbstones near the edge. Projecting slab tops show the line of the passage from the E and probably the position of the chamber, whose capstone may have been formed by the large broken slab on top of the cairn. It probably dates from the third millennium B.C. – To the S and well down the hillside, a rubble-walled and turf-thatched C19 COTTAGE.

3020   CROSSBOST / CROSBOST (LEWIS)

Untidy crofting township with a surprising number of surviving C19 traditional buildings, their thatch now replaced or covered with corrugated iron.

LOCHS FREE CHURCH. Big drydashed late C19 rectangle. Pointed windows and a gabletted E bellcote; galleried interior.

School. Late Victorian, large and harled.

CUITHIR / CUIDHIR (BARRA)   *6000*

Just the church and former manse standing by the roadside.

Barra Parish Church. A plan and estimate by the architect-builder *Peter Dawson* were approved in 1825, but work did not begin for another four years and was not completed until 1834. Simple harled box with a birdcage bellcote on the s gable. Roundheaded windows in the e wall and n gable. – Plain late Georgian burial enclosures against the n end and to the ne.

Harled manse (now Cuithir House), 0.3km. nw, by *John Loban*, architect in Stornoway, and *Robert Fraser*, house-carpenter in North Uist, 1814–16. Two-storey main block, its chimney-gabled centre slightly advanced, the canted dormers late c19 additions. The single-storey lateral wings are original and were intended to contain the kitchen, nursery, dairy and cellar. Stone-walled garden, also of 1814–16, at the back.

DALIBURGH / DALABROG (SOUTH UIST)   *7020*

Small crofting township.

Parish Church. Built as South Uist Free Church in 1862–3. Harled box with a cheap gableted bellcote on the s gable, a ball finial on the n; in the roundheaded windows, sashes with intersecting tracery. Interior with a deep s gallery facing the roomy pulpit.

St Peter's Church (R.C.). Big harled rectangle of 1867–8. Rusticated quoins; a simplified birdcage bellcote on the s gable. The s porch, crowned with a tall concrete bellcote of croquet hoop type, was added in the 1960s. Inside, the nave is covered with a plaster ceiling of two half-vaults meeting at a central beam. Hoodmoulds over the windows. The chancel arch to the one-bay n sanctuary was made in 1907. s gallery lit by a round window.

The Priest's House at the e was added in 1907; three flattish gablets on the front.

School. By *Inverness County Council* (County Architect: *Douglas Calder*), 1952.

Askernish House. *See* p. 597.

DUN AN T-SIAMAIN *see* CARINISH (NORTH UIST)

DUN AN STICIR see TRUMISGARRY (NORTH UIST)

EILEAN BHEARNARAIGH see BERNERAY

EIRIOSGAIGH see ERISKAY

9080   ## ENSAY

Small rugged island lying between Harris and Berneray.

CHAPEL. (Simple rubble-built chapel, probably late medieval,
restored in 1910. Quite small, c. 7.8m. by 4.4m. Slit windows,
splayed internally. Arched doorway in s wall.)

7000   ## EOLIGARRY / EOLAIGEARRAIDH (BARRA)

Scattered crofting township at the N end of Barra.

CHURCH (CILLE-BHARRA). Roofless but quite substantial
remains of the medieval parish church said to have been dedicated to St Barr.* Simple rectangle, c. 11.6m. by 4m., built of
lime-mortared rubble pinned with shells. The gables have
largely fallen but the side walls are mostly intact, the w end of
the s wall perhaps rebuilt. Near the N wall's w end, door
with a roundheaded arch set back on the jambs and later
strengthened by the insertion of two slanting lintels to make a
triangular head. One N and two s windows, all round-arched
externally and splayed to the inside with crude triangular-
headed rear-arches. A C12 date seems likely. – Inside the E
gable, remains of the seating of a stone ALTAR. – Inside the
door, a stone carved to form a BASIN, perhaps for a font.
    To the SE, fragments of a rubble-built MAUSOLEUM or
chapel. Near the N wall's E end, a small window, its lintel carved
as a roundheaded arch. It may be C15.
    To the NE, a rubble-built MAUSOLEUM, probably C16, the
walls pierced by slit windows, the roof a recent restoration.
Inside, a CAST of the C10 or early C11 Kilbar Stone,‡ its front
carved with a cross decorated with plait-work enrichment, the
back inscribed with runes stating that it commemorated Thor-
keth, daughter of Steinar. – Four late medieval GRAVESLABS,
two bearing reliefs of swords and foliage. The third is carved
with foliage. At the bottom, small relief of a stag and another
creature (? a hound); near the top, relief of a galley. The fourth
stone, perhaps C16, is more weathered. Inscription round the

*But John Fordun said, c. 1385, that the church on Barra was dedicated to the
Holy Trinity, and the name Barra itself probably means 'hilly island' and does not
refer to St Barr.
‡Now in the Royal Museum of Scotland, Edinburgh.

border. Two incised faces and a sword pommel near the top, a
rosette at the bottom.

ST VINCENT'S CHURCH (R.C.). Built in 1964. Tall roof with
swept eaves.

SCHOOL. By *Robert Robertson*, Inverness-shire County Architect,
1933.

EOROPIE / EOROPAIDH (LEWIS)   *5060*

Crofting township just S of Butt of Lewis, where stands the
lighthouse.

ST MOLUAG'S CHURCH (TEAMPULL MHOLUIDH). Medieval
kirk reroofed and restored by *James S. Richardson* in 1912.
Externally it is an unpretentious rubble-built T consisting of a
single-cell main block (quite large for the Western Isles at
13.4m. by 5.2m.), with a lean-to N sacristy and S chapel projecting at the E end. This plan can be paralleled at the Norse
cathedral of Gardar in Greenland, where similar side chapels
were added in the C13 to a C12 single-cell church. St Moluag's
may well be C13, its putlock holes suggesting a fairly early date.
Battered plinth across each gable; at the W it returns for a short
distance along the side walls, at the E it does not extend across
the sacristy or chapel. Round-arched windows in the main
block's gables and side walls, placed high up on the N, much
restored on the S, all with chamfered margins and internal
splays, the E window with a pointed rear-arch. In each side wall
there are also two square windows above the sacristy and chapel
roofs. Near the S wall's W end, a round-arched door (restored).
Slit windows lighting the sacristy and chapel.

Inside, the position of the medieval rood-beam may be
marked by recesses in the N and S walls immediately E of their
main windows. The S chapel, entered from outside through a
W door, has a big squint into the church. In the N sacristy, lamp
recesses in the W and S walls. – BELL, dated 1631, said to have
come from the medieval Stornoway Parish Church. – FONT. A
roughly worked gneiss bowl on a sandstone pedestal of 1912. –
MISCELLANEA. Collection of stone bowls, querns and mill-
stones. Among them, the worn head of a Celtic CROSS.

LIGHTHOUSE, Butt of Lewis, 1.5km. N. By *D. & T. Stevenson*,
1859–62. Tall tapering red-brick tower and a shorter foghorn
tower. Single-storey stores and two-storey keepers' houses, all
flat-roofed.

ERISKAY / EIRIOSGAIGH   *7010*

Island off South Uist, the houses C19 and C20, many harled,
several with boldly coloured tile roofs.

ST MICHAEL'S CHURCH (R.C.). Very simple Gothic of 1903,
the white rendered dressings a crisp contrast to the dark rubble

walling. Apsidal E end. Gableted bellcote on the SW porch. Inside, a three-arch wooden chancel screen. Deep W gallery with a balustered front.

SCHOOL. By *Alexander Ross*, 1876. Additions by *John Wedderspoon*, 1899, and by *Robert Robertson*, the County Surveyor, 1933.

4030 EYE / AIGINISH (LEWIS)

Small township at the w end of the Eye Peninsula.

ST COLUMBA'S CHURCH. Roofless medieval church. The main (E) part, probably C14, is a simple rubble-built rectangle. In the E gable, a big slit window with an internal splay and rectangular rear-arch. Two more slits in the S wall, the E with a pointed rear-arch. Near this wall's centre, the W jamb and part of the semicircular head of the original door, probably blocked when the obtusely arched door to its E was inserted, perhaps in the C15. At the wall's W end, a rectangular door with a nearby high-set window, both insertions, possibly C17. The church was extended *c.* 1500 by the addition of a W chapel opening into it through a round-arched chamfered doorway. In the chapel's W gable and side walls, round-arched windows. The S wall also has a round-arched door under a (blocked) rectangular window, the N wall a (blocked) square window. Inside, remains of a round-arched TOMB RECESS under the W window.

Inside the church and now fixed to the S wall, a GRAVESLAB carved in high relief with the life-size figure of a knight; it is probably late C14 or early C15. – On the N wall, the GRAVESLAB of Margaret MacLeod † 1503, carved with foliage and animals. – On the ground, a third late medieval slab, decorated with a sword.

Immediately S of the church, two late Georgian BURIAL ENCLOSURES. The E is simply corniced. The W, with rusticated quoins and a primitive battlement, is probably of 1823, the date when its two earliest tablets (commemorating Alexander Mackenzie and his family) were erected.

4050 GALSON / GABHSUNN (LEWIS)

Small settlement at the NE of Lewis.

TEAMPULL NAN CRO NAOMB (CHURCH OF THE HOLY BLOOD). Half-buried remains of a small rubble-built church, 5.8m. by 3.7m., the gables now mostly demolished. In the S wall, a W door and E window with a stepped sill. Rectangular window in the N wall. The putlock holes in the side walls suggest a C12 or C13 date.

To the S, a couple of rubble BURIAL ENCLOSURES, perhaps C18.

GARRABOST (LEWIS) 5030

Crofting township.

CHURCH. Built as a United Free church, *c.* 1910. Tall and boxy, with two tiers of roundheaded windows and a small wooden bellcote.

KNOCK FREE CHURCH. Piend-roofed rectangle of 1882. Round-headed windows and an apology for a bellcote.

GARRYNAMONIE / GEARRAIDH NA MONADH (SOUTH UIST) 7010

Church on the main road at the E end; a few crofts to the w.

CHURCH OF OUR LADY OF SORROWS (R.C.). Built in 1965. Brutalist in drydash, the monopitch roofs over the broad nave and narrower and lower chancel forming an irregular V.

GRAVIR / GRABHAIR (LEWIS) 3010

Strung-out crofting settlement.

PARK FREE CHURCH. Roughcast box of 1882. Pointed windows; gableted E bellcote.

SCHOOL. By *Inverness County Council, c.* 1970. One- and two-storey, tightly composed with monopitch roofs and a clear-storey.

GREAT BERNERA 1030

Island of low hills and lochs with some crofting settlements.

CHURCH, Breaclete. Early C20. Harled, with round-arched windows and a simplified 'bellcote' on the E gable.

BERNERA BRIDGE. Three-span metal bridge, by *Blyth & Blyth*, 1953.

BROCH (DUN BARAVAT). The site is an islet in Loch Baravat reached by a causeway. Roughly oval broch of the first millennium A.D., the N section of its wall standing to a height of *c.* 3m. Scarcement on the inner face. There have been at least two galleries in the wall.

GRESS / GRIAIS (LEWIS) 4040

Crofting township near the E coast of Lewis.

CHAPEL. Small (5.8m. by 4.3m.) rubble-built chapel, now roofless, recorded by Martin Martin *c.* 1695 as having been dedicated to St 'Aula' (?Olaf). It may be partly medieval. Slit window in the S gable. Chamfered margins at the S wall's

window and door; above this door, a weathered stone which
has been carved with the date 1681 and the initials

IB
MK

BRIDGE, S end. Superseded by the new road bridge to the E.
Early C20, of concrete, the cutwaters rising as piers above the
roadway. The metal railings are mid-C20 replacements.

GRESS LODGE. Early C19 harled farmhouse with a central
chimney gablet. – To the NE, remains of a C19 WATER MILL,
altered and extended with precast concrete in the early C20.

CAIRN, Carn a'Mharc, 2km. NW. Large cairn, now of roughly
oval shape, c. 30m. by 24m. Some large split blocks form
kerbstones on the W and S. The chamber is SE of the cairn's
centre.

GRIMINISH / GRIMINIS (BENBECULA)
7050

String of crofts along the road, the churches set back at the E and
W ends.

BENBECULA PARISH CHURCH. Originally Free Church. By
Thomas Binnie, of Glasgow, 1886. White harled box with a
gableted bellcote. – Small contemporary MANSE adjoining.

ST MARY'S CHURCH (R.C.). Plain harled rectangle with
pointed windows, built in 1884. – Contemporary sneck-harled
PRIEST'S HOUSE at right angles.

GRIMSAY / GRIOMSAIGH
8050

Island between North Uist and Benbecula, its W end joined to
these by causeways opened in 1960. At its SE tip, the ruins of St
Michael's Chapel.

ST MICHAEL'S CHAPEL. Scanty remains of a medieval chapel
which has been c. 7m. by 4m. Much of the W gable still stands.

HOUGHGARRY / HOGHA GEARRAIDH
(NORTH UIST)
7070

Nondescript crofting settlement.

NORTH UIST PARISH CHURCH. Roofless remains of the church
built in 1764. It has been a harled rubble rectangle containing
E and W galleries. Quite plain, the windows rectangular except
for two big round-arched ones which flanked the pulpit in the
centre of the S wall.

In the OLD GRAVEYARD to the E, four rubble-built BURIAL
ENCLOSURES, all probably C18, the E (that of the Macdonalds
of Clanranald) dated 1768.

HOWMORE / TOBHA MOR (SOUTH UIST)   7030

Crofting township, still with a number of C19 thatched houses.

PARISH CHURCH. Harled box built by *John McDearmid* in 1857–8. Wooden Y-tracery in the round-arched windows. Gableted bellcote on one gable, a prettily foliaged wrought-iron finial on the other. Inside, a deep E gallery.

TEAMPULL MOR, CAIBEAL DHIARMAID, and CAIBEAL NAN SAGAIRT (ST MARY'S CHURCH, ST DERMOT'S CHAPEL, and THE PRIEST'S CHAPEL). In the old parish churchyard, a collection of ruined medieval ecclesiastical buildings, all built of rubble with lime mortar. The largest, at the w, is TEAMPULL MOR, the former parish church, apparently dedicated to the Virgin Mary. Only its E gable stands higher than the foundations. It contains two segmental-headed slit windows with semicircular rear-arches. At each side and at a lower level is an aumbry. – To the s, a rectangular structure built of rougher masonry. Slit windows in the side walls and gables. The presence of an E door makes it unlikely to have been a chapel; perhaps it had a domestic use. – E of Teampull Mor, a chapel (CAIBEAL DHIARMAID), whose E gable survives. In it, a neat slit window of the same type as those of Teampull Mor. Inside, to the N of the window and just below the level of its sill, a corbel, probably to support an altar slab. s of the window, an aumbry which would have been just below the altar slab. – To the NE, the gables and remains of the side walls of another building (CAIBEAL NAN SAGAIRT). In the s wall, a slit window. Door in the E gable, so was this a mausoleum rather than a chapel? On the ground inside, a triangular-headed stone carved with the arms of Macdonald of Clanranald. – To the N, two rubble-walled BURIAL ENCLOSURES, the N containing a panel commemorating the Rev. George Munro † 1832.

IOCHDAR (SOUTH UIST)   7040

Township mostly of C20 houses but including a number of C19 thatched cottages.

CHURCH. Humble sneck-harled mission chapel, by *David Mackintosh*, 1889.
SCHOOL. By *Inverness County Council* (County Architect: *Douglas Calder*), 1963.

KISIMUL CASTLE *see* CASTLEBAY (BARRA)

KNOCK / CNOC (LEWIS)   4030

Crofting township, an eastward continuation of Eye (*see* above).

CHURCH. Late C20 but traditional harled box, with roundheaded windows and ball finials on the gables.

FREE CHURCH. *See* Garrabost.
Former MANSE. 1829; harled two-storey 'Parliamentary' manse
(i.e. to *Joseph Mitchell*'s design).

3020   LAXAY / LACASAIGH (LEWIS)

Small township N of Loch Erisort.

KINLOCH FREE CHURCH. Built in 1881 and quite plain except
for a vestigial 'bellcote'.
KINLOCH PARISH CHURCH. Built as a United Free church *c.*
1910. Segmental-arched three-light window in the E gable,
which is topped by a bellcote feature.

3020   LEURBOST / LIURBOST (LEWIS)

Crofting township overlooking Loch Leurbost.

LOCHS PARISH CHURCH. Originally United Free. By *Alexander
Macdonald*, 1913. Drydashed box with a NW 'transept', thrifty
Romanesque detail, and a gableted S bellcote.

0080   LEVERBURGH / TOB (HARRIS)

Village at the SW tip of Harris, its development begun by Lord
Leverhulme, the then proprietor of Harris, who intended it to be
a major harbour with fish-curing and kippering facilities. Work
costing £250,000 was begun in 1920 but ceased on Leverhulme's
death in 1925, after which the works were sold for £5,000 to a
demolition company.

CHURCH OF SCOTLAND. Mid-C20 small harled box with a
blocky bellcote.
FREE PRESBYTERIAN CHURCH. Late C20 space-age version of
a traditional kirk. It forms part of a complex with an OLD
PEOPLE'S HOME.

LEWS CASTLE *see* STORNOWAY (LEWIS)

7040   LINACLETE / LIONACLEIT (BENBECULA)

Small settlement overpowered by the school.

SCHOOL. By *Western Isles Islands Council*, 1988. Huge single-
storey-and-attic group, slated pitched roofs dominant.

LIURBOST *see* LEURBOST (LEWIS)

LOCH BAGHASDAIL *see* LOCHBOISDALE
(SOUTH UIST)

LOCHBOISDALE / LOCH BAGHASDAIL
(SOUTH UIST)   *7010*

Small C19 village, now the terminal for the ferry from Oban.

CHURCH. Built *c.* 1905. Sturdily buttressed mission church with
a small N apse.

SCHOOL. Dated 1909. White harled, one of the prominent gables
bearing a bellcote.

LOCHMADDY / LOCH NA MADADH (NORTH UIST) *9060*

Village on the shore beside Loch Maddy, the main ferry port from
the Uists to Skye and Harris.

CHURCH. Built as a Free Church mission *c.* 1891. Harled and
humble, with narrow round-arched windows and a cheap
bellcote.

HOSPITAL. Originally the Poorhouse. By *Kinnear & Peddie*,
1882–3, but very plain. Rubble-faced, with a centre gablet on
the E front. Harled additions by *D. Cattanach*, 1927.

OLD COURTHOUSE. The harled main block was built in 1827.
Domestic-looking but with a verandah, the openings originally
filled with bars, against the E gable. Inside, a row of vaulted
cells on the ground floor. The N jamb, added by *James Ross* in
1845, is of cherrycock-pointed ashlar, the gable topped by a
pinnacle. In the inner angles, gabled porches with round-arched
doors.

SHERIFF COURTHOUSE. An overgrown villa, by *Matthews &
Lawrie*, 1875. Broad eaves and pointed windows, the result
more Italian than Gothic.

DESCRIPTION. On the road from the ferry pier at the SE tip
of the peninsular site, the first incident is the LOCHMADDY
HOTEL, a long harled block begun in 1863 and extended by
Kinnear & Peddie in 1883–4. On the N of the road, beside an
inlet and between two ramped piers, is the OLD INN of three
storeys, harled and with a forestair; beside it, a single-storey-
and-attic rubble-built warehouse. After the Church (*see* above),
the former CALEDONIAN BANK by *Matthews & Lawrie*, 1877,
faintly Italianate, with mutuled eaves and a rope moulding over
the door. Beside the shore to its N, a rubble pier overlooked by
the harled former 'town house' of the Macleans of Boreray,
dated 1852 on a stone over the piend-roofed porch. Higher up

are the Old and Sheriff Courthouses, with the Hospital standing by itself to the NW (for these, *see* above).

MARROGH *see* CLACHAN AN LUIB (NORTH UIST)

NORTHBAY / BAGH A TUATH (BARRA)

Strung-out village, mostly C 19 and early C 20 vernacular, with some late C 20 invaders.

ST BARR'S CHURCH (R.C.). By *G. Woulfe Brenan*, 1906. Plain lancet-windowed rectangle of squared gneiss rubble, made U-plan by the projecting SE vestry and SW porch, the second topped by a croquet-hoop bellcote.

Former SCHOOL (now NORTHBAY HOUSE), 1.1km. S. By *Alexander Ross*, 1879, and quite picturesque, with a bellcote on the school's E end and a gabled schoolhouse at the S.

NORTH BOISDALE / BAGHASDAL (SOUTH UIST)

Crofting township, the graveyard lying at the SW.

GRAVEYARD. There survive three rubble-built BURIAL ENCLOSURES, all perhaps C 18. The central one has been smart, with rusticated quoins at the corners which rise up as ashlar bed-ends. Broad segmental-arched and corniced entrance in the E side. In the W wall, an empty panel frame, its triangular pediment now fragmentary.

NORTH RONA

Uninhabited island 75km. equidistant from Butt of Lewis and Cape Wrath; the name means 'Isle of Seals' (the Gaelic *ronain* = 'seals') and these are now its principal mammalian inhabitants.

CHURCH. (Roofless remains of the chapel traditionally associated with the C 8 hermit St Ronan, who came here on whaleback to escape the chattering of people on Lewis. It was built in two stages and consists of two interconnecting rooms. The E part is the earlier, possibly C 8 or C 9. It is a rough rectangle, 3.5m. by 2.4m., the E and W gables rising straight, the side walls sloping inwards up to a height of *c.* 3.5m., where they were joined by the slabs of gneiss which formed the roof. The slabs of the drystone walls are set with a slight downward slope towards the exterior so as to drain water to the outside. In the W gable, a door with a slit window above. Inside, a small niche near the S wall's E end. Stone ALTAR, the slab put back in position in 1938.

The w part is a medieval addition, its N wall continuing that of the original chapel, its s wall's inner face aligned with the outer face of the chapel's.* This wall's E part is *c.* 1.5m. thick; w of the door it thins to *c.* 0.9m. Inside, just w of the door into the original chapel, two stone piers, probably the uprights of an altar.)

NORTHTON / AN TAOBH TUATH (HARRIS)   *9080*

Crofting township.

CHAPEL, 2.8km. NW. Roofless. Small (6.4m. by 3m.) medieval rectangle built of random granite and schist rubble. In each wall, a slit window, the w placed higher than the others. Inside, a step at each end, the E still with part of the altar seating. Immediately s of the altar is a corbel, perhaps for a statue. Small aumbries beside this corbel and in the SE corner.

NUNTON / BAILE NAN CAILLEACH   *7050*
(BENBECULA)

Chapel in a graveyard, with Nunton House to the s.

CHAPEL. Roofless remains of a small (7.3m. by 4.6m.) rubble-built medieval chapel. In the w gable, a rectangular door under a rectangular niche, probably intended for a statue. Slit windows in the other walls.

NUNTON HOUSE. White harled tacksman's house, its present appearance early C19 but probably incorporating earlier work. It is L-plan and forms the w and s sides of a courtyard whose E side is enclosed by a wall, the N by a pair of pyramid-roofed pavilions. – Across the road, a mid-C19 U-plan STEADING. On the gable of its s wing, a birdcage bellcote of harled brick with a wrought-iron finial. There has been some similar feature on the N wing.

ORMICLATE CASTLE (SOUTH UIST)   *7030*
1.9km. N of Bornish

Gaunt shell of the mansion house built for the Macdonalds of Clanranald in 1701 and burned in 1715. It has been a two-storey-and-attic T-plan, built of fieldstone rubble (formerly harled). The long jamb projects to the E, its gable (containing the flues) inhospitably windowless. In each of its side walls, a blocked door and window. Five-bay w front, the openings mostly bereft of their dressings, but the centre bay's segmental-headed lintel survives. An entrance in the second bay from the l. is surmounted by a weathered armorial panel which bore the

*This medieval s wall was largely rebuilt by *F. Fraser Darling* in 1938.

arms of Macdonald of Clanranald. Lower wings project to the w, the N now represented only by its front wall, the s altered as a plain harled house but containing a big segmental-arched kitchen fireplace. Each floor of the house itself has contained three rooms in the main block and a further room in the jamb. The staircase (now missing) was presumably of wood.

To the N, a mid-C19 quadrangular STEADING of farm offices and housing.

PABAIL see BAYBLE (LEWIS)

8080   PABBAY

Island off the w coast of Harris.

TEAMPULL MHOIRE. (There survive the w gable and side walls of a rubble-built church, probably late medieval. In the gable, a rectangular door and slit window. – There has been a smaller chapel (TEAMPULL BEAG) 3.9m. to the w.)

7060   PAIBLE / PAIBEIL (NORTH UIST)

Crofting township.

FREE CHURCH. Small box of 1858. Pointed windows. Galleried interior. – To the w, contemporary MANSE with a gabled centre.
FREE PRESBYTERIAN CHURCH. Dated 1899. Very plain but quite large Gothic-windowed rectangle. Inside, the pulpit makes an impressive focus. – The adjoining MANSE with a triple-gabled front and horizontal glazing looks mid-C19.
SCHOOL. By *Inverness County Council* (County Architect: *Douglas Calder*), 1963.

5030   PORT BHOLAIR (LEWIS)

Crofting township near the tip of the Eye Peninsula.

AIRD FREE CHURCH. Simple kirk, dated 1909, the Gothic windows almost Georgian in appearance, the gableted bellcote Victorian.
LIGHTHOUSE, Rubha an Tiumpain, 2km. NE. By *D. Alan Stevenson*, 1900. Short round tower with a glazed cupola. Single-storey flat-roofed keepers' houses. All harled.

5060   PORT OF NESS / PORT NIS (LEWIS)

Harbour overlooked by C19 and C20 vernacular houses.

HARBOUR. Begun *c.* 1885 as an irregular basin enclosed by stone

walls. This soon silted up and in 1891–4 *D. & T. Stevenson*
closed the original entrance, enlarged the harbour to the E, and
added a breakwater, all executed in concrete.

REINEVAL *see* BORNISH (SOUTH UIST)

RODEL / ROGHADAL (HARRIS)   0080

Small harbour begun *c.* 1785 on Loch Rodel at the S tip of Harris.
Beside it, a plain harled hotel. The church stands on higher
ground to the NE.

ST CLEMENT'S CHURCH. Early C16 church said to have been 14
built, perhaps partly on earlier foundations, by Alasdair Crotach
('Hunchbacked Alasdair') MacLeod of Dunvegan and Harris.
The chancel at least must have been completed by 1528, when
Alasdair Crotach built his tomb there. In 1540 David John
McPersoun is named as the chaplain of St Columba's altar 'in
Rowodell'. Abandoned after the Reformation, the church was
reroofed and repaired in the 1780s and again restored by *Alexander Ross* in 1873. Harling was stripped off the walls and further
repairs* made by *W. T. Oldrieve* in 1913. It is now a piously
pointed Ancient Monument.

This, the grandest medieval building in the Western Isles,
was the ecclesiastical counterpart of the MacLeods' castle of
Dunvegan (Skye and Lochalsh) on the other side of the Little
Minch, and a visible demonstration of their lordship over
Harris. It is a rubble-built Latin cross dominated by a tall tower,
whose height is emphasized by its being built on the steeply
rising rocky ground at the church's W end. This tower is of five
stages, its N and S walls continuing the line and masonry of the
side walls of the nave, its lowest storey a partial enclosure of
the rock foundation. Above the third stage, a rope-moulded
stringcourse which jumps up in the centre of each face to frame
a sculptured stone, the W carved with the figure of a bishop
(perhaps St Clement), the N with the head of a bull, the E with
two fishermen in a boat, and the S with a sheila-na-gig. Trefoil-
headed slit windows, hoodmoulded at the top stage, whose
pointed W window is comfortably large. The deep corbelled
and crenellated parapet dates from the 1780s, when the tower's
top courses were removed; slated pyramidal spire of 1873.
Several sculptured stones from the medieval parapet have been
inserted in the main walling. In the E face, a carved horse; in
the W front, figures of two men, one kilted, the other dressed
in a tunic, trunks and hose, and a bull's head. More bulls' heads
at the E corners.

The church itself is plain. Continuous roof over the nave and
chancel. The lower transepts are not quite opposite each other,
and the N is longer and narrower than the S. In the nave,

*Notably to the tower, which had been struck by lightning in 1907.

rectangular windows of the 1780s. Of the same date are the transepts' gable windows, but the trefoil-headed slits in their E walls are original. Another slit window in the N wall of the chancel. In its s wall, a pointed window, now with an inserted lintel and the arched head infilled. Three-light E window, the cusped heads and the wheel filling the top of the arch made of schist. Above it, a hoodmould, the surviving s label carved with a human head.

Inside the church, a braced kingpost roof of 1873 over the unaisled nave and chancel. At the E end of the nave, a blocked window, its E ingo splayed, the w straight. Roundheaded arch to the N transept, pointed arch to the s, each of three orders with fillets between the bold rolls, rectangular cushion capitals and bases like inverted versions of them.

An off-centre door at the nave's w end opens onto a stone stair in the wall-thickness. This leads to the tower's first and second floors; access to the floors above must always have been by ladders. A comfortable room on each floor but no fireplaces.

At the w end of the nave, a plain stone FONT, probably late medieval. – On the sill of the nave's sw window, part of a late medieval TOMBSTONE. It is a Celtic cross, the front carved with the Crucifixion, the back with an interlaced pattern.

Placed against the N transept's w wall are five GRAVESLABS, four of them late medieval and carved with swords and foliaged borders, one including birds and beasts. The fifth bears crude reminders of death, the initials R.C. and A.M.S., and the date 1725.

The three C16 MONUMENTS commemorating chiefs of Clan MacLeod make the most impressive such collection in the Highlands and Islands. The earliest and grandest is the tomb of Alasdair (or Alexander) Crotach MacLeod in the chancel's s wall. It was erected, according to its inscription, in 1528. Round-arched tomb recess set within a broad gablet. The gablet's keystone is carved with a depiction of the Holy Trinity (a tiaraed God the Father holding a crucifix, the Dove of the Holy Spirit now missing) surrounded by emblems of the four Evangelists. On the voussoirs are pairs of Apostles alternating with angels. The Apostles on the l. side are clean-shaven and moon-faced, those on the r. have long faces and beards; probably two sculptors were responsible. The back of the tomb recess is covered with three tiers of panels. At the top, reliefs of angels swinging censers and blowing trumpets, with, in the centre, the MacLeod crest of the sun in glory. In the middle tier, the Madonna and Child are flanked by St Clement holding a skull and another bishop giving a blessing (a subject found in contemporary Irish monuments); at the ends, reliefs of a castle and a galley, emblems of the MacLeods. In the lowest tier the panels depict a hunting scene, with an armoured knight, presumably MacLeod himself, accompanied by two servants holding dogs, in pursuit of deer, the Archangel Michael battling against the Devil, and the Latin inscription. On the tomb-chest reposes the effigy of a knight, his feet resting on what looks like a crocodile. Probably all this tomb was intended to be painted with garish effect. – w of the transept arch is the tomb of William MacLeod of Dunvegan and Harris †1552. It is said to have borne the date 1539, presumably that of its erection. Round-arched tomb recess under a steep gablet, its tympanum carved with a relief of the Crucifixion with Our Lady and St John. In the recess, the effigy of a knight with hounds at his feet and head. – Now in the NW corner of the nave but formerly in the s transept, the more crudely executed effigy of a third knight, with lions at head and feet. It may commemorate John MacLeod of Minginish † c. 1557.

GRAVEYARD. S of the church, an early C18 BURIAL ENCLOS-URE, the walls topped with balustrades. On its w wall, a marble tablet carved with drapery commemorating William McLeod †1738; below it, a sandstone panel adorned with reminders of death. – w of the church, a pair of ENCLOSURES, again balustraded and probably also early C18, belonging to the MacLeods of Berneray.

RUEVAL HILL (SOUTH UIST) 7040

Statue on the w side, a meteorological station on the summit.

STATUE OF OUR LADY OF THE ISLES. Huge-scale granite depiction of the Madonna and Child, by *Hew Lorimer*, 1955–7, in characteristic semi-naturalist manner.

ST KILDA 1090

Bleak, hilly and windswept island in the Atlantic c. 66km. NW of Griminish Point on South Uist. It was owned by the MacLeods of Harris until 1871, when it was sold to MacLeod of MacLeod. Four years after the evacuation (at their own request) of the last thirty-six inhabitants in 1930, it was acquired by the fourth Marquess of Bute, from whom it passed by bequest to the National Trust for Scotland in 1957. Since then St Kilda has housed an Army missile-tracking station and a few summer visitors.

CHURCH. (By *Robert Stevenson*, 1826. Small rendered box with pointed door and windows. Inside, a roomy PULPIT of c. 1920. – Attached to the E side, a SCHOOLROOM of 1900. – At the church's s end, a single-storey MANSE (also by *Stevenson*, 1826). Originally of only three bays, it was extended to four and given a porch in the later C19. Low E addition of c. 1966.)
VILLAGE. (Laid out as a rough crescent on the relatively gently sloping ground on the N side of Village Bay and enclosed by a stone head dyke. The land inside the dyke was laid out in strips, each with a house roughly halfway along its length. At the SE beside the shore, a much restored two-storey STOREHOUSE of c. 1800. On higher ground, the Church and Manse (*see* above) and, to their w, the flat-roofed ARMY BUILDINGS of 1966

overlooking a concrete JETTY of 1901. The HOUSES, mostly ruinous, to the NW have been either turf-thatched blackhouses of the 1830s, their gables fronting the sea, their entrances at the side, or simple cottages built in 1861, bravely facing the sea, their original zinc roofs later replaced with tarred felt. Behind and sometimes in front of the houses, and also outside the dyke, oblong or oval turf-roofed buildings (*cleitean*), their drystone walls jettying inwards. A few may be houses constructed before the 1830s, but most seem to have been built as stores or byres. Roughly in the centre of the village, but behind the line of houses, a drystone-walled oval BURIAL GROUND. To its NW, a SOUTERRAIN, probably of *c.* 1000 B.C., with an almost straight passage, now 7.6m. long but originally longer, off which there is a short branch to the E.)

2090   SCALPAY

Sizeable island at the mouth of East Loch Tarbert, a string of crofts along its W coast, the lighthouse on a promontory at the SE.

LIGHTHOUSE, Eilean Glas. Complex of two lighthouses, stores and keepers' houses. It was begun in 1786–9 by *Robert Kay*, who provided a short round tower and an adjoining block of keepers' houses. This lighthouse was superseded in 1824 by a much taller tapering round tower designed by *Robert Stevenson*. Domed lantern with diamond-pane glazing; small bullseye windows under the cantilevered platform. At the same time the old lighthouse's lantern was replaced by a shallow-pitched roof. Kay's keepers' houses were converted to stores *c.* 1845, when two parallel detached ranges of single-storey houses were built, their Ægypto-Greek detail of standard *Alan Stevenson* type.

0090   SCARISTA / SGARASTA (HARRIS)

Little more than the church and its former manse on the lower slopes of a steep hillside overlooking the sea.

PARISH CHURCH. White harled two-bay box of 1838–40. Ball finials on the gables. Pointed windows, those in the long E and W walls with Y-tracery. SE vestry and N porch, both probably late Victorian. Original interior with grained PEWS; their focus is the combined READING DESK AND PULPIT, with an anta-pilastered back and sounding board.

SCARISTA HOUSE. Built as Harris Manse in 1825–7, the design being provided by *John Loban*, builder in Stornoway, and *William Mackenzie*, house-carpenter in Stornoway. White harled T-plan with a broad chimney-gablet and piend-roofed porch at the centre. Low piend-roofed wings.

SCOLPAIG TOWER (NORTH UIST)   7070
4.7km. N of Balranald

Early C19 folly on an islet in Loch Scolpaig. Two-storey battlemented octagonal tower built of harled rubble. Round-arched
door and windows.

SGARASTA *see* SCARISTA (HARRIS)

SHADER / SIADAR (LEWIS)   3050

Crofting township with a couple of small boxy churches of *c.*
1900.

SCHOOL. By *Alexander Mackenzie Sen.*, 1876.

STANDING STONE, Clach an Trushal, 1.6km. SW. Huge standing
stone, almost 6m. high, probably erected in the second or third
millennium B.C.

STORNOWAY / STEORNABHAGH (LEWIS)   4030

The only town in the Western Isles, Stornoway was made a burgh
of barony in 1607 at the time of the unsuccessful attempt by the
'Fife Adventurers' to take over Lewis from the MacLeods, whose
castle stood on an islet now covered by the ferry pier. At first built
around the point dividing the Inner and Outer Harbours, the
burgh was redeveloped and substantially expanded after 1785,
becoming a fishing port of some importance and the entrepôt for
the surrounding islands. Further development and redevelopment
took place after the Mackenzies of Seaforth sold Lewis to Sir
James Matheson in 1844. In 1920 *T. Raffles Davison* prepared a
town improvement scheme for Lord Leverhulme, the then owner
of Lewis, but this was abandoned after the gift of the parish to
the Town Council in 1923. Since then there has been some
shantytown redevelopment of the centre and extensive suburban
growth to the E and N.

CHURCHES

FREE CHURCH, Kenneth Street. Gothick-survival by *Alexander
Mackenzie*, 1851, the W gable bisected by an attached tower
stepping up to the belfry, where wrought-iron finials top the
pinnacles. Wooden Y-tracery in the pointed windows.

FREE PRESBYTERIAN CHURCH, Matheson Road. Big drydashed box of with thrifty Romanesque detail. On the E gable,
a faintly classical crown-spired bellcote.

HIGH CHURCH, Matheson Road. Built as a United Free church,
c. 1910. Roughcast box with pointed windows. The W gable-
front's centre is slightly advanced, rising into a tower topped
by a pinnacled and pyramid-spired bellcote.

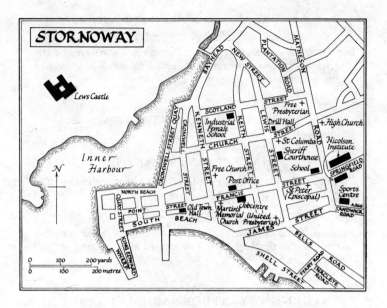

MARTIN'S MEMORIAL CHURCH, Kenneth Street and Francis
Street. Originally the English Free Church. Big Gothic box, by
R. A. Bryden, of Glasgow, 1876–8. w gable-front broken by a
recessed 'transept' containing the gallery stair on the r.; on the
l., a steeple of curiously municipal appearance, with pinnacled
angle turrets above the belfry, whose octagonal spire (intended
from the start) was added by *Alexander Macdonald* in 1910.
Inside, a nave and aisles. – At the back, an appropriately ecclesiastical HALL by *John Robertson*, 1893.

ST COLUMBA'S (OLD PARISH) CHURCH, Lewis Street. Big
plain box (now drydashed) built by *John Loban* in 1794 and
much repaired in 1831. Quite straightforward, with roundheaded and keyblocked windows in the long N and S sides.
Their stone Y-tracery looks a late C 19 insertion, probably dating
from the church's remodelling and extension in 1884–5. At that
time the w gable was made ineptly Romanesque and a sw
'transept' and porch were added, the 'transept' crowned with
a tall wood-and-lead cupola of C 17 derivation, topped with a
weathervane.

ST PETER'S CHURCH (Episcopal), Francis Street. Simple
Gothick of 1837–9. Drydashed (formerly harled) rectangle with
a narrow w tower. Pinnacles on the tower's corners; in its
w face, a Tudor-arched belfry opening. The nave's pointed
windows are original but their cusped lights look late Victorian,
probably of 1887–92, when the porch was added. Chancel by
George Macnab, 1954. Inside, a vaulted plaster ceiling with
applied ribs and big foliaged pendants. – W GALLERY, pre-

sumably of 1887, when the ORGAN (by *Bevington & Sons*; rebuilt by the *Johnson Organ Co. (Derby)*, 1985) was introduced. – STAINED GLASS. Two-light window (Faith, Hope and Charity) of 1898 in the S wall. – Round chancel window (the Adoration of the Shepherds), bright and bad, by the *Abbey Studios*, 1954. – Wooden PULPIT with statues of saints at the faces; it was formerly in the chapel of King's College, London, where it had been introduced in *G. G. Scott*'s remodelling of 1861–2. – FONT. Routine Victorian, but containing a much older stone bowl from the Flannan Isles.

UNITED PRESBYTERIAN CHURCH, James Street. Secularized. Gentle Gothic T-plan kirk of 1860. The jamb's S gable is bisected by a low pyramid-roofed and diagonally buttressed tower. Wrought-iron finials on the other gables.

PUBLIC BUILDINGS

COMHAIRLE NAN EILEAN (WESTERN ISLES COUNCIL) OFFICES, Sandwick Road. By *Dorward, Matheson & Gleave*, 1979. Blandly authoritarian three-storey cruciform. Domestic windows in the concrete aggregate walling, whose parapet partly masks the shallow-pitch roofs. A box for services over the crossing; porch in the SW inner angle.

DRILL HALL, Church Street. Late C19, with paired round-arched windows and small gableted and louvred dormers.

HARBOUR. Begun, largely as a fishing harbour, *c.* 1785, the quays and piers being built along the river at North Beach, Cromwell Street and Bayhead. In 1865 *Alan Stevenson* provided a 45.7m.-long wooden steamboat wharf at the W end of South Beach. Further development along South Beach took place in 1881 and 1890–4. There followed a major reconstruction and extension by *Henderson & Nicol* in 1926–35, Stevenson's wooden wharf being replaced by the concrete KING EDWARD WHARF. This wharf was extended in 1947–51 by *Archibald Henderson & Partners*, who also built a causeway to Goat Island at the harbour's E end and gave that island a slipway. Concrete is now the dominant material. On the King Edward Wharf, Art Deco FERRY OFFICES of 1935.

INDUSTRIAL FEMALE SCHOOL, Keith Street and Scotland Street. Now housing. Built in 1848 by Mrs (later Lady) Matheson of the Lews, who provided for instruction in Ayrshire needlework as well as more mundane academic subjects. Quiet Jacobean on an L-plan. Tall single-storey-and-attic range to Keith Street with a broad chimney gablet. Three-storey schoolhouse facing Scotland Street. The horizontal glazing is a welcome survival.

JOBCENTRE, Francis Street. Polite neo-Georgian, by *J. Wilson Paterson*, 1936–7.

LEWIS WAR MEMORIAL, 0.8km. W. Dotty Baronial tower by *J. Hinton Gall*, 1922–4. It is only 5.5m. square at the base but *c.* 26m. high, built of local gneiss with dressings of Aberdeenshire granite. Above the tall and heavily buttressed first stage, intakes before the walls rise unbroken but slightly tapered to a corbelled parapet. Open rounds at three corners; at the fourth, a circular turret with its own corbelled and battlemented parapet. Inside, a 6m.-high vaulted ground-floor room.

NICOLSON INSTITUTE, Springfield Road. The school was founded with endowments bequeathed by A. M. Nicolson † 1865 and given by Sir James Matheson of the Lews. For the surviving tower of the building opened in 1873, *see* Sports Centre, below. The present buildings line the w end of Springfield Road. On the N side, the TECHNICAL DEPARTMENT built as the Secondary School in 1898, tall two-storey three-bay free Jacobean, with broad gablets, mullioned and transomed windows and a cupola. Attached to its E end, a hall in the same manner, dated 1907. – To the E, the main HALL and classrooms, lightweight in brick and harl, by *Ross & Cromarty County Council* (County Architect: *Peter S. Leask*; architect-in-charge: *R. W. Fraser*), 1956. – On the S side of the road, a small late C19 block with shaped gables marking the centre and Romanesque windows. – To its E, harled CLASSROOM BLOCK, by *D. Matheson & Son*, 1935, neo-Georgian but with *moderne* glazing.

OLD TOWN HALL, South Beach and Cromwell Street. Big but unimpressive Flemish, the purplish Lochbroom sandstone rubble and yellow Eday freestone dressings an unappealing combination. It is by *John Robertson*, 1903–5; reconstructed to the same design after a fire by *John G. Chisholm*, 1926–9. Triple-pile plan, with a Social Institute facing South Beach, a Public Library to Cromwell Street and the Hall sandwiched between them. Thrifty display of conical-roofed towers, ogee hood-moulds and tabernacled niches on the South Beach front. Segmental-overarched three-light windows in the Hall's gables. Above the Hall, an octagonal clock-cupola with a flattened ogee roof; it makes an effect only from a distance.

POST OFFICE, Francis Street. By *W. T. Oldrieve* of *H.M. Office of Works*, 1907. Heavy-handed Queen Anne in bullnosed rubble.

SCHOOL, Francis Street. Late C19 two-storeyed cheap Jacobean with a shaped gablet at the centre. On the w, a single-storey block looking mildly ecclesiastical.

SHERIFF COURTHOUSE, Lewis Street. By *Thomas Brown Jun.*, 1843. Domestic Tudor but with a machicolated chimney and bellcote on the front gables for martial effect. Prison exercise yard to the r.; on the l., an addition by *Andrew Maitland*, 1870.

SPORTS CENTRE, Matheson Road and Sandwick Road. By *Thomson, Taylor, Craig & Donald*, 1975. Blocky composition of drydash and aggregate panels. It incorporates an Italianate tower, dated 1871, of the former Nicolson Institute, enclosed with concrete posts and railing.

DESCRIPTION

QUAY STREET runs across the tip of the Harbour (*see* Public Buildings, above). In it, the harled AMITY HOUSE (HARBOUR OFFICES), a smart villa of *c.* 1830 with three-light windows flanking a portico of etiolated Doric columns topped by a cast-iron balustrade. On the corner with NORTH BEACH, a harled early C19 warehouse. Forestair to its first-floor door; at the second floor, two gabled hoist openings breaking a line of bullseye windows. To the E, more late Georgian buildings, ending with the LEWIS HOTEL, dated 1829, with three-light windows and scrolled skewputts.

FRANCIS STREET is the town's principal E–W street. At its W end, near the harbour, nondescript late C20 buildings. On the NE corner of Bank Street, a rendered mid-C19 shop with broad gablets establishes a Georgian-survival norm confronting the bleak back of the Old Town Hall (*see* Public Buildings, above). CROMWELL STREET then cuts across. At its corner with SOUTH BEACH, the THORLEE GUEST HOUSE, late C19, with a continuous hoodmould over the segmental-arched first-floor windows; busts on the ends of the shaped gablet. In Cromwell Street's N part, CROMWELLS, early C19, with a central chimney-gablet and rusticated quoins at the upper floors' windows. Further N, the BANK OF SCOTLAND, Jacobean of 1889, its drydash an ill-judged attempt to match the colour of the red sandstone dressings. Nos. 59–61, dated 1886, are Jacobean again; kneeling children on the ends of the shaped centre gablet. N of Cromwell Street, Francis Street declines into late C20 anonymity. On the SE corner of KENNETH STREET, Martin's Memorial Church (*see* Churches, above) is powerful townscape. The blocky neo-Georgian COUNTY HOTEL (by *John G. Chisholm*, 1933) on the NE is not. Further up Kenneth Street is the Free Church (*see* Churches, above). Francis Street continues with the public presences of the Post Office and Jobcentre (*see* Public Buildings, above). Then more C20 redevelopment before simple late Georgian and Georgian-survival E of Keith Street. In LEWIS STREET to the N, Nos. 5–7 are mid-Victorian, with tall crowstepped gables, followed by the Sheriff Courthouse and St Columba's (Old Parish) Church (*see* Public Buildings and Churches, above). Francis Street ends with the pleasant No. 29 of *c.* 1840, with a heavy anta-pilastered doorpiece, and St Peter's Episcopal Church (*see* Churches, above). MATHESON ROAD to the N, prosperous and leafy, provides a *cordon sanitaire* of late C19 and early C20 villas, dividing the older town from its more recent developments.

LEWS CASTLE. Much the grandest of the very few mansions in the Western Isles, as striking for its richly wooded surroundings as its architecture. It was built in 1848 for Sir James Matheson, who had made a fortune from the opium trade. *Charles Wilson*, of Glasgow, was the architect. Large Tudor toy fort. Three-storey main block, with battlemented towers and a machicolated parapet, but quite relaxed despite these martial appendages. Porte cochère in front of the N tower. The single-storey conservatory at the SE was added by *Alexander F. Sutherland c.* 1875.

5060 SWAINBOST / SUAINEBOST (LEWIS)

Just a few houses beside the main road. To the N, the ruined church in a graveyard overlooking the sea.

TEAMPULL PHEADAIR (ST PETER'S CHURCH). Only the E gable and bottom courses of the side walls survive of the small rubble-built medieval church which was reconstructed and enlarged *c.* 1795. In the gable, a slit window with a wide internal splay.

1090 TARBERT / AN TAIRBEART (HARRIS)

The ferry port from Harris to Skye and North Uist. The site is a narrow neck of land which saves Harris from being bisected by the inlets of West and East Loch Tarbert, the village's main street a line of harled C19 vernacular houses overlooking East Loch Tarbert.

CHURCH OF SCOTLAND. Built as a Free church, *c.* 1860, and renovated in 1953. Harled T-plan, with a cement bellcote on the W gable. – Simple MANSE of 1860 adjoining.

FREE PRESBYTERIAN CHURCH. Harled box of *c.* 1900. Pointed Y-traceried window in the N gable, the other windows big rectangles. Pinnacled bellcote.

WAR MEMORIAL. Small but prominently sited castellated tower, by *John G. Chisholm*, 1922.

TOB *see* LEVERBURGH (HARRIS)

TOBHA MOR *see* HOWMORE (SOUTH UIST)

4030 TONG / TUNGA (LEWIS)

Crofting township NE of Stornoway.

TONG FARM. Two-storey-and-attic three-bay harled house built as Stornoway Parish Manse in 1808. The piend-roofed porch is an addition, perhaps dating from the repairs made by *Charles Howitt* in 1852.

8070 TRUMISGARRY / TRUMAISGE ARRAIDH (NORTH UIST)

Little more than the old church and manse beside the shore.

CHURCH. T-plan 'Parliamentary' church (i.e. to *William Thomson*'s design), built of rough ashlar in 1828–9. Now roofless and missing its bellcote.

Contemporary harled MANSE of the standard two-storey 'Parliamentary' type (i.e. by *Joseph Mitchell*). *John Davidson* and *Thomas Macfarlane* were contractors for both church and manse.

BROCH, Dun an Sticir, 4.1km. NE. The site, an islet in the tidal Loch an Sticir, is reached by causeways built of massive stone blocks. Roughly in the islet's centre is the ruined broch, *c.* 18m. in diameter, its walling much depleted. Entrance at the N, with part of a guard chamber visible to its W. There has been an oval cell in the wall's SW part and a gallery above. The broch's court is largely filled by the ruin of a rectangular building, perhaps of the C16. The broch itself probably dates from the late first millennium B.C.

CAIRN, Barpa nan Feannag, 2.8km. SW. Round cairn of *c.* 20m. diameter with a tapering down-sloping W tail *c.* 35m. long, the stones now partly covered by heather. It is probably of the third millennium B.C.

TUNGA *see* TONG (LEWIS)

UIG (LEWIS)   *0030*

Small settlement near the W coast of Lewis.

PARISH CHURCH (BAILLE-NA-CILLE). Plain T-plan kirk (now drydashed) of 1826–9. Roundheaded windows in the long S side, rectangular lights in the main gables and the side walls of the N jamb. No bellcote, just a canopy attached to the E end. The big S vestry probably dates from the alterations and additions made by *William Mackintosh* in 1878. Inside, the jamb and ends are filled by a semi-octagonal GALLERY on cast-iron columns. – The PEWS look to be of 1878. – Original PULPIT AND READING DESK with a sounding board.

SCHOOL. By *Thomson, Taylor, Craig & Donald*, 1971. Tightly composed, of one and two storeys with a clearstorey and monopitch roof.

UIG LODGE, 0.8km. S. Mid-Victorian. Harled and gabled, with a gently Italianate tower.

GLOSSARY

Particular types of an architectural element are often defined under the name of the element itself, e.g. for 'dogleg stair' see STAIR. Literal meanings, where specially relevant, are indicated by the abbreviation *lit.*

ABACUS (*lit.* tablet): flat slab forming the top of a capital, *see* Orders (fig. 16).

ABUTMENT: the meeting of an arch or vault with its solid lateral support, or the support itself.

ACANTHUS: formalized leaf ornament with thick veins and frilled edge, e.g. on a Corinthian capital.

ACHIEVEMENT OF ARMS: in heraldry, a complete display of armorial bearings.

ACROTERION (*lit.* peak): pointed ornament projecting above the apex or ends of a pediment.

ADDORSED: description of two figures placed symmetrically back to back.

AEDICULE (*lit.* little building): term used in classical architecture to describe the unit formed by a pair of orders, an entablature, and usually a pediment, placed against a wall to frame an opening.

AFFRONTED: description of two figures placed symmetrically face to face.

AGGER (*lit.* rampart): Latin term for the built-up foundations of Roman roads.

AGGREGATE: small stones added to a binding material, e.g. in harling or concrete.

AISLE (*lit.* wing): (1) passage alongside the nave, choir or transept of a church, or the main body of some other building, separated from it by col-

umns or piers; (2) (Scots) projecting wing of a church for special use, e.g. by a guild or by a landed family whose burial place it may contain.

AMBULATORY (*lit.* walkway): aisle at the E end of a chancel, usually surrounding an apse and therefore semicircular or polygonal in plan.

ANNULET (*lit.* ring): shaft-ring (q.v.).

ANSE DE PANIER (*lit.* basket handle): basket arch (*see* Arch).

ANTA: classical order of oblong section employed at the ends of a colonnade which is then called *In Antis. See* Orders (fig. 16).

ANTEFIXAE: ornaments projecting at regular intervals above a classical cornice. *See* Orders (fig. 16).

ANTHEMION (*lit.* honeysuckle): classical ornament like a honeysuckle flower (*see* fig. 1).

A   P   A   P   A

Fig. 1.   Anthemion and
Palmette Frieze

APSE: semicircular (i.e. apsidal) extension of an apartment. A term first used of the magistrate's end of a Roman basilica, and thence especially of the vaulted semicircular or polygonal end of a chancel or a chapel.

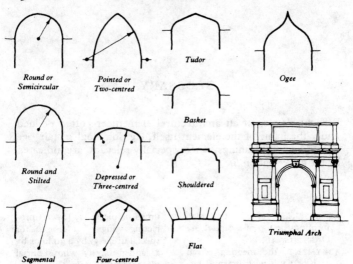

Round or Semicircular
Pointed or Two-centred
Tudor
Ogee

Round and Stilted
Depressed or Three-centred
Basket
Shouldered

Segmental
Four-centred
Flat
Triumphal Arch

Fig. 2. Arch

ARABESQUE: light and fanciful surface decoration. *See* Grotesque.

ARCADE: series of arches supported by piers or columns. *Blind Arcade:* the same applied to the surface of a wall. *Wall Arcade:* in medieval churches, a blind arcade forming a dado below windows.

ARCH: for the various forms *see* fig. 2. The term *Basket Arch* refers to a basket handle and is sometimes applied to a three-centred or depressed arch as well as the type with a flat middle. *Transverse Arch:* across the main axis of an interior space. A term used especially for the arches between the compartments of tunnel- or groin-vaulting. *Diaphragm Arch:* transverse arch with solid spandrels spanning an otherwise wooden-roofed interior. *Chancel Arch:* across the w end of a chancel. *Relieving Arch:* incorporated in a wall, to carry some of its weight, some way above an opening. *Strainer Arch:* inserted across an opening to resist any inward pressure of the side members. *Triumphal Arch:* Imperial Roman monument whose elevation supplied a motif for many later classical compositions. *Blind Arch:* framing a wall which has no opening. *Overarch:* framing a wall which has an opening, e.g. a window or door.

ARCHITRAVE: (1) formalized lintel, the lowest member of the classical entablature (*see* Orders, fig. 16); (2) moulded frame of a door or window. Also *Lugged* or *Shouldered Architrave*, whose top is prolonged into lugs (*lit.* ears).

ARCHIVOLT: continuous mouldings of an arch.

ARRIS (*lit.* stop): sharp edge at the meeting of two surfaces.

ASHLAR: masonry of large blocks wrought to even faces and square edges. *Droved Ashlar* (Scots) is finished with sharp horizontal tool-marks.

ASTRAGAL (*lit.* knuckle): moulding of round section, and hence (Scots) wooden glazing-bar between window-panes.

ASTYLAR: term used to describe an elevation that has no columns or similar vertical features.

ATLANTES: male counterparts of caryatids, often in a more demonstrative attitude of support. In sculpture, a single figure of the god Atlas may be seen supporting a globe.

ATTACHED: description of a shaft or column that is partly merged into a wall or pier.

ATTIC: (1) small top storey, especially behind a sloping roof; (2) in classical architecture, a storey above the main cornice, as in a triumphal arch.

AUMBRY: recess or cupboard to hold sacred vessels for Mass.

BAILEY: open space or court of a stone-built castle; *see also* Motte-and-Bailey.

BALDACCHINO: tent-like roof supported by columns, e.g. over some monuments of the C17–18.

BALLFLOWER: globular flower of three petals enclosing a small ball. A decoration used in the first quarter of the C14.

BALUSTER (*lit.* pomegranate): hence a pillar or pedestal of bellied form. *Balusters:* vertical supports of this or any other form, for a handrail or coping, the whole being called a *Balustrade. Blind Balustrade:* the same with a wall behind.

BARBICAN: outwork defending the entrance to a castle.

BARGEBOARDS: boards, often carved or fretted, hanging clear of the wall under sloping eaves.

BARMKIN (Scots): enclosing wall.

BARONY: *see* Burgh.

BARROW: burial mound.

BARTIZAN (*lit.* battlement): corbelled turret, square or round, at the top angle of a building.

BASE: moulded foot of a column or other order. For its use in classical architecture *see* Orders (fig. 16). *Elided Bases:* bases of a compound pier whose lower parts are run together, ignoring the arrangement of the shafts above. Capitals may be treated in the same way.

BASEMENT: lowest, subordinate storey of a building, and hence the lowest part of an elevation, below the piano nobile.

BASILICA (*lit.* royal building): a Roman public hall; hence an aisled church with a clerestorey.

BASTION: projection at the angle of a fortification.

BATTER: inward inclination of a wall.

BATTLEMENT: fortified parapet with upstanding pieces called merlons along the top. Also called Crenellation.

BAYS: divisions of an elevation or interior space as defined by any regular vertical features.

BAY WINDOW: window in a recess, with a consequent projection on the outside, named according to the form of the latter. A *Canted Bay Window* has a straight front and bevelled sides. A *Bow Window* is curved. An *Oriel Window* does not start from the ground.

BEAKER: type of pottery vessel used in the late third and early second millennia B.C.

BEAKHEAD: Norman ornamental motif consisting of a row of bird or beast heads with beaks biting usually into a roll moulding.

BEE-BOLL: wall recess designed to contain a beehive.

BELFRY (*lit.* tower): (1) bell-turret set on a roof or gable (*see also* Bellcote); (2) room or stage in a tower where bells are hung; (3) belltower in a general sense.

BELLCAST: *see* Roof.

BELLCOTE: belfry as (1) above, with the character of a small house for the bell(s), e.g. *Birdcage Bellcote:* framed structure, usually of stone.

BERM: level area separating ditch from bank on a hillfort or barrow.

BILLET (*lit.* log or block) FRIEZE: Norman ornament consisting of small blocks placed at regular intervals (*see* fig. 3).

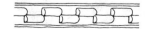

Fig. 3. Billet Frieze

BIVALLATE: of a hillfort: defended by two concentric banks and ditches.

BLIND: *see* Arcade, Arch, Balustrade, Portico.

BLOCKED: term applied to columns etc. that are interrupted by regular projecting blocks, e.g. to the sides of a Gibbs surround (*see* fig. 10).

BLOCKING COURSE: plain course of stones, or equivalent, on top of a cornice and crowning the wall.

BÖD: *see* Bü.

BOLECTION MOULDING: moulding covering the joint between two different planes and overlapping the higher as well as the lower one, especially on panelling and fireplace surrounds of the late C17 and early C18.

BOND: in brickwork, the pattern of long sides (stretchers) and short ends (headers) produced on the face of a wall by laying bricks in a particular way (*see* fig. 4).

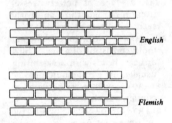

English

Flemish

Fig. 4. Bond

BOSS: knob or projection usually placed to cover the intersection of ribs in a vault.

BOW WINDOW: *see* Bay Window.

BOX PEW: pew enclosed by a high wooden back and ends, the latter having doors.

BRACE: *see* Roof (fig. 22).

BRACKET: small supporting piece of stone, etc., to carry a projecting horizontal member.

BRESSUMER (*lit.* breast-beam): big horizontal beam, usually set forward from the lower part of a building, supporting the timber superstructure.

BRETASCHE (*lit.* battlement): defensive wooden gallery on a wall.

BROCH (Scots): circular tower-like structure, open in the middle, the double wall of drystone masonry linked by slabs forming internal galleries at varying levels; found in W and N Scotland and probably dating from the earliest centuries of the Christian era.

BRONZE AGE: in Britain, the period from *c.* 2000 to 600 B.C.

BÜ or BÖD (Scots, esp. Shetland; *lit.* booth): combined house and store.

BUCRANIUM: ox skull.

BULLSEYE WINDOW: small circular window, e.g. in the tympanum of a pediment.

BURGH: formally constituted town with trading privileges. *Royal Burghs*, which still hold this courtesy title, monopolized imports and exports till the C17 and paid duty to the Crown. *Burghs of Barony* were founded by secular or ecclesiastical barons to whom they paid duty on their local trade. *Police burghs* were instituted after 1850 for the administration of new centres of population and were abolished at local government reorganization in 1975. They controlled planning, building, sewerage, lighting and cleansing.

BUT-AND-BEN (Scots, *lit.* outer and inner rooms): two-room cottage.

BUTTRESS: vertical member projecting from a wall to stabilize it or to resist the lateral thrust of an arch, roof or vault. For different types used at the corners of a building, especially a tower, *see* fig. 5. A *Flying Buttress* transmits the thrust to a heavy abutment by means of an arch or half-arch.

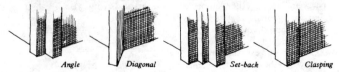

Angle   *Diagonal*   *Set-back*   *Clasping*

Fig. 5. Buttresses at a corner

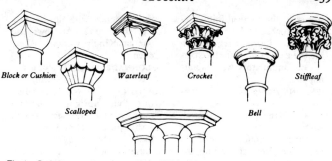

Block or Cushion *Waterleaf* *Crocket* *Stiffleaf*

Scalloped *Bell*

Fig. 6. Capitals *Elided*

CABLE MOULDING or ROPE MOULDING: originally a Norman moulding, imitating the twisted strands of a rope.

CALEFACTORY: room in a monastery where a fire burned for the comfort of the monks.

CAMBER: slight rise or upward curve in place of a horizontal line or plane.

CAMES: *see* Quarries.

CAMPANILE: free-standing bell-tower.

CANDLE-SNUFFER ROOF: conical roof of a turret.

CANOPY: projection or hood over an altar, pulpit, niche, statue, etc.

CANTED: tilted, generally on a vertical axis to produce an obtuse angle on plan, e.g. of a canted bay window.

CAP-HOUSE (Scots): (1) small chamber at the head of a turnpike stair, opening onto the parapet walk; (2) chamber rising from within the parapet walk.

CAPITAL: head or top part of a column or other order; for classical types *see* Orders (fig. 16); for medieval types *see* fig. 6. *Elided Capitals:* capitals of a compound pier whose upper parts are run together, ignoring the arrangement of the shafts below.

CARTOUCHE: tablet with ornate frame, usually of elliptical shape and bearing a coat of arms or inscription.

CARYATIDS (*lit.* daughters of the village of Caryae): female figures supporting an entablature, counterparts of Atlantes.

CASEMENT: (1) window hinged at the side; (2) in Gothic architecture, a concave moulding framing a window.

CASTELLATED: battlemented.

CAVETTO: concave moulding of quarter-round section.

CELURE or CEILURE: panelled and adorned part of a wagon roof above the rood or the altar.

CENOTAPH (*lit.* empty tomb): funerary monument which is not a burying place.

CENSER: vessel for the burning of incense, frequently of architectural form.

CENTERING: wooden support for the building of an arch or vault, removed after completion.

CHAMBERED TOMB: burial mound of the Neolithic Age having a stone-built chamber and entrance passage covered by an earthen barrow or stone cairn.

CHAMFER (*lit.* corner-break): surface formed by cutting off a square edge, usually at an angle of forty-five degrees.

CHANCEL (*lit.* enclosure): that part of the E end of a church in which the altar is placed, usually applied to the whole continuation of the nave E of the crossing.

CHANTRY CHAPEL: chapel attached to, or inside, a church, endowed for the celebration of masses for the soul of the founder or some other individual.

CHECK (Scots): rebate.

CHERRY-CAULKING or CHERRY-COCKING (Scots): masonry techniques using a line of pinstones in the vertical joints between blocks.

CHEVET (*lit*. head): French term for the E end of a church (chancel and ambulatory with radiating chapels).

CHEVRON: zigzag Norman ornament.

CHOIR: (1) the part of a church where services are sung; in monastic churches this can occupy the crossing and/or the easternmost bays of the nave, but in cathedral churches it is usually in the E arm: (2) the E arm of a cruciform church (a usage of long standing though liturgically anomalous).

CIBORIUM: canopied shrine for the reserved sacrament.

CINQUEFOIL: *see* Foil.

CIST: stone-lined or slab-built grave. First appears in Late Neolithic times. It continued to be used in the Early Christian period.

CLAPPER BRIDGE: bridge made of large slabs of stone, some built up to make rough piers and other longer ones laid on top to make the roadway.

CLASSIC: term for the moment of highest achievement of a style.

CLASSICAL: term for Greek and Roman architecture and any subsequent styles inspired by it.

CLEARSTOREY: upper storey of the walls of a church, pierced by windows.

CLOSE (Scots): courtyard or passage giving access to a number of buildings.

COADE STONE: artificial (cast) stone made in the late C18 and the early C19 by Coade and Sealy in London.

COB: walling material made of mixed clay and straw.

COFFERING: sunken panels, square or polygonal, decorating a ceiling, vault or arch.

COLLAR: *see* Roof (fig. 22).

COLLEGIATE CHURCH: a church endowed for the support of a college of priests, especially for the singing of masses for the soul of the founder. Some collegiate churches were founded in connection with universities, e.g. three at St Andrews and one at King's College, Aberdeen.

COLONNADE: range of columns.

COLONNETTE: small column.

COLUMN: in classical architecture, an upright structural member of round section with a shaft, a capital and usually a base. *See* Orders (fig. 16).

COLUMNA ROSTRATA: column decorated with carved prows of ships to celebrate a naval victory.

COMMENDATOR: one who holds the revenues of an abbey *in commendam* (medieval Latin for 'in trust' or 'in custody') for a period in which no regular abbot is appointed. During the Middle Ages most Commendators were bishops, but in Scotland during and after the Reformation they were laymen who performed no religious duties.

COMPOSITE: *see* Orders.

CONDUCTOR (Scots): down-pipe for rainwater; *see also* Rhone.

CONSERVATION: a modern term employed in two, sometimes conflicting, senses: (1) work to prolong the life of the historic fabric of a building or other work of art, without alteration; (2) work to make a building or a place more viable. Good conservation is a combination of the two.

CONSOLE: ornamental bracket of compound curved outline (*see* fig. 7). Its height is usually greater than its projection, as in (*a*).

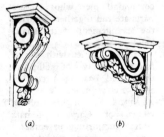

(*a*)   (*b*)

Fig. 7.   Console

COOMB CEILING or COMB CEIL-ING (Scots): ceiling whose slope corresponds to that of the roof.

COPING (*lit.* capping): course of stones, or equivalent, on top of a wall.

CORBEL: block of stone projecting from a wall, supporting some feature on its horizontal top surface. *Corbel-course*: continuous projecting course of stones fulfilling the same function. *Corbel Table*: series of corbels to carry a parapet or a wall-plate; for the latter *see* Roof (fig. 22).

CORBIE-STEPS (Scots, *lit.* crow-steps): *see* Gable (fig. 9).

CORINTHIAN: *see* Orders (fig. 16).

CORNICE: (1) moulded ledge, decorative and/or practical, projecting along the top of a building or feature, especially as the highest member of the classical entablature (*see* Orders, fig. 16); (2) decorative moulding in the angle between wall and ceiling.

CORPS-DE-LOGIS: French term for the main building(s) as distinct from the wings or pavilions.

COUNTERSCARP BANK: small bank on the down-hill or outer side of a hillfort ditch.

COURSE: continuous layer of stones etc. in a wall.

COVE: concave soffit like a hollow moulding but on a larger scale. A *Cove Ceiling* has a pronounced cove joining the walls to a flat surface in the middle.

CREDENCE: in a church or chapel, a side table, often a niche, for the sacramental elements before consecration.

CRENELLATION: *see* Battlement.

CREST, CRESTING: ornamental finish along the top of a screen, etc.

CROCKETS (*lit.* hooks), CROCK-ETING: in Gothic architecture, leafy knobs on the edges of any sloping feature. *Crocket Capital: see* Capital (fig. 6).

CROSSING: in a church, central space opening into the nave, chancel and transepts. *Crossing*

Tower: central tower supported by the piers at its corners.

CROWSTEPS (Scots): squared stones set like steps to form a skew, *see* Gable (fig. 9).

CRUCK (*lit.* crooked): piece of naturally curved timber combining the structural roles of an upright post and a sloping rafter, e.g. in the building of a cottage, where each pair of crucks is joined at the ridge.

CRYPT: underground room usually below the E end of a church.

CUPOLA (*lit.* dome): (1) small polygonal or circular domed turret crowning a roof; (2) (Scots) small dome or skylight as an internal feature, especially over a stairwell.

CURTAIN WALL: (1) connecting wall between the towers of a castle; (2) in modern building, thin wall attached to the main structure, usually outside it.

CURVILINEAR: *see* Tracery.

CUSP: projecting point formed by the foils within the divisions of Gothic tracery, also used to decorate the soffits of the Gothic arches of tomb recesses, sedilias, etc.

CYCLOPEAN MASONRY: built with large irregular polygonal stones, but smooth and finely jointed.

DADO: lower part of a wall or its decorative treatment; *see also* Pedestal (fig. 17).

DAGGER: *see* Tracery.

DAIS, or DEIS (Scots): raised platform at one end of a room.

DEC (DECORATED): historical division of English Gothic architecture covering the period from *c.* 1290 to *c.* 1350.

DEMI-COLUMNS: engaged columns, only half of whose circumference projects from the wall.

DIAPER (*lit.* figured cloth): repetitive surface decoration.

DIOCLETIAN WINDOW: semi-circular window with two mullions, so called because of its use in the Baths of Diocletian in Rome.

DISTYLE: having two columns; cf. Portico.

DOGTOOTH: typical E.E. decoration applied to a moulding. It consists of a series of squares, their centres raised like pyramids and their edges indented (*see* fig. 8).

Fig. 8. Dogtooth

DONJON: *see* Keep.

DOOCOT (Scots): dovecot. Free-standing doocots are usually of *Lectern* type, rectangular in plan with single-pitch roof, or *Beehive* type, circular in plan and growing small towards the top.

DORIC: *see* Orders (fig. 16).

DORMER WINDOW: window standing up vertically from the slope of a roof and lighting a room within it. *Dormer Head:* gable above this window, often formed as a pediment.

DORTER: dormitory, sleeping quarters of a monastery.

DOUBLE-PILE: *see* Pile.

DRESSINGS: features made of smoothly worked stones, e.g. quoins or stringcourses, projecting from the wall which may be of different material, colour or texture.

DRIPSTONE: moulded stone projecting from a wall to protect the lower parts from water; *see also* Hoodmould.

DROVED ASHLAR: *see* Ashlar.

DRUM: (1) circular or polygonal vertical wall of a dome or cupola; (2) one of the stones forming the shaft of a column.

DRY-STONE: stone construction without mortar.

DUN (Scots): a small stone-walled fort.

E. E. (EARLY ENGLISH): historical division of English Gothic architecture covering the period 1200–1250.

EASTER SEPULCHRE: recess with tomb-chest, usually in the wall of a chancel, the tomb-chest to receive the Sacrament after the Mass of Maundy Thursday.

EAVES: overhanging edge of a roof; hence *Eaves Cornice* in this position.

ECHINUS (*lit.* sea-urchin): lower part of a Greek Doric capital; *see* Orders (fig. 16).

EDGE-ROLL: moulding of semicircular or more than semicircular section at the edge of an opening.

ELEVATION: (1) any side of a building; (2) in a drawing, the same or any part of it, accurately represented in two dimensions.

ELIDED: term used to describe (1) a compound architectural feature, e.g. an entablature, in which some parts have been omitted; (2) a number of similar parts which have been combined to form a single larger one (*see* Capital, fig. 6).

EMBATTLED: furnished with battlements.

EMBRASURE (*lit.* splay): small splayed opening in the wall or battlement of a fortified building.

ENCAUSTIC TILES: glazed and decorated earthenware tiles used for paving.

EN DÉLIT: term used in Gothic architecture to describe attached stone shafts whose grain runs vertically instead of horizontally, against normal building practice.

ENGAGED: description of a column that is partly merged into a wall or pier.

ENTABLATURE: in classical architecture, collective name for the three horizontal members (architrave, frieze and cornice) above a column; *see* Orders (fig. 16).

ENTASIS: very slight convex deviation from a straight line;

used on classical columns and sometimes on spires to prevent an optical illusion of concavity.

ENTRESOL: mezzanine storey within or above the ground storey.

EPITAPH (*lit.* on a tomb): inscription in that position.

ESCUTCHEON: shield for armorial bearings.

EXEDRA: apsidal end of an apartment; *see* Apse.

FERETORY: (1) place behind the high altar where the chief shrine of a church is kept; (2) wooden or metal container for relics.

FESTOON: ornament, usually in high or low relief, in the form of a garland of flowers and/or fruit, hung up at both ends; *see also* Swag.

FEU (Scots): land granted, e.g. by sale, by the *Feudal Superior* to the *Vassal* or *Feuar*, on conditions that include the annual payment of a fixed sum of *Feu-duty*. The paramount superior of all land is the Crown. Any subsequent proprietor of the land becomes the feuar and is subject to the same obligations. Although many superiors have disposed of their feudal rights, others, both private and corporate, still make good use of the power of feudal control which has produced many well-disciplined developments in Scotland.

FIBREGLASS: *see* GRP.

FILLET: narrow flat band running down a shaft or along a roll moulding.

FINIAL: topmost feature, e.g. above a gable, spire or cupola.

FLAMBOYANT: properly the latest phase of French Gothic architecture, where the window tracery takes on undulating lines, based on the use of flowing curves.

FLATTED: divided into apartments. But flat (Scots) is also used with a special colloquial meaning. 'He stays on the first flat' means that he lives on the first floor.

FLÈCHE (*lit.* arrow): slender spire on the centre of a roof.

FLEUR-DE-LIS: in heraldry, a formalized lily as in the royal arms of France.

FLEURON: decorative carved flower or leaf.

FLOWING: *see* Tracery (Curvilinear).

FLUTING: series of concave grooves, their common edges sharp (arris) or blunt (fillet).

FOIL (*lit.* leaf): lobe formed by the cusping of a circular or other shape in tracery. *Trefoil* (three), *Quatrefoil* (four), *Cinquefoil* (five) and *Multifoil* express the number of lobes in a shape; *see* Tracery (fig. 25).

FOLIATED: decorated, especially carved, with leaves.

FORE- (*lit.* in front): *Fore-building:* structure protecting an entrance. *Forestair:* external stair, usually unenclosed.

FOSSE: ditch.

FRATER: refectory or dining hall of a monastery.

FREESTONE: stone that is cut, or can be cut, in all directions, usually fine-grained sandstone or limestone.

FRESCO: painting executed on wet plaster.

FRIEZE: horizontal band of ornament, especially the middle member of the classical entablature; *see* Orders (fig. 16). *Pulvinated Frieze* (*lit.* cushioned): frieze of bold convex profile.

FRONTAL: covering for the front of an altar.

GABLE: (1) peaked wall or other vertical surface, often triangular, at the end of a double-pitch roof; (2) (Scots) the same, very often with a chimney at the apex, but also in a wider sense: end wall, of whatever shape. *See* fig. 9. *Gablet:* small gable. *See also* Roof, Skew.

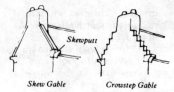

Skew Gable   *Crowstep Gable*

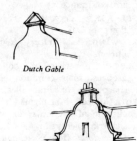

Dutch Gable

*Curvilinear or Shaped
Gable at wallhead*

Fig. 9.   Gables

GADROONING: ribbed ornament,
e.g. on the lid or base of an urn,
flowing into a lobed edge.

GAIT (Scots) or GATE: street,
usually with a prefix indicating
its use, direction or destination.

GALILEE: chapel or vestibule
usually at the w end of a church
enclosing the porch; *see also*
Narthex.

GALLERY: balcony or passage,
but with certain special meanings, e.g. (1) upper storey above
the aisle of a church, looking
through arches to the nave; also
called tribune and often erro-
neously triforium. (2) balcony
or mezzanine, often with seats,
overlooking the main interior
space of a building. (3) external
walkway projecting from a wall.

GARDEROBE (*lit.* wardrobe):
medieval privy.

GARGOYLE: water spout projecting from the parapet of a wall
or tower, often carved into
human or animal shape.

GAZEBO (jocular Latin, 'I shall
gaze'): lookout tower or raised
summer house overlooking a
garden.

GEOMETRIC: historical division of
English Gothic architecture
covering the period *c.* 1250–90.

See also Tracery. For another
meaning, *see* Staircase.

GIBBS SURROUND: C18 treatment
of door or window surround,
seen particularly in the work of
James Gibbs (1682–1754) (*see*
fig. 10).

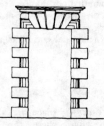

Fig. 10.   Gibbs Surround

GLACIS: long artificial slope
extending outwards and down-
wards from the parapet of a fort.

GNOMON: vane or indicator casting a shadow on to a sundial.

GRC (glass-reinforced concrete):
concrete reinforced with glass
fibre, formed in moulds, often
used for the multiple repetition
of architectural elements.

GROIN: *see* Vault (fig. 26a).

GROTESQUE (*lit.* grotto-esque):
classical wall decoration of
spindly, whimsical character
adopted from Roman examples,
particularly by Raphael, and
further developed in the C18.

GRP (glass-reinforced polyester):
synthetic resin reinforced with
glass fibre, formed in moulds,
sometimes simulating the out-
ward appearance of traditional
materials.

GUILLOCHE: running classical ornament formed by a series of
circles with linked and interlaced borders (*see* fig. 11).

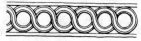

Fig. 11.   Guilloche

GUNLOOP: opening for a firearm.

GUTTAE: *see* Orders (fig. 16).

HAGIOSCOPE: *see* Squint.

HALF-TIMBERING: timber framing with the spaces filled in by plaster, stones or brickwork.

HALL CHURCH: (1) church whose nave and aisles are of equal height or approximately so. (2) (Scots C20): church convertible into a hall.

HAMMERBEAM: *see* Roof.

HARLING (Scots, *lit.* hurling): wet dash, i.e. a form of roughcasting in which the mixture of aggregate and binding material (e.g. lime) is dashed onto a rubble wall as protection against weather.

HEADER: *see* Bond.

HENGE: ritual earthwork with a surrounding bank and ditch, the bank being on the outer side.

HERITORS (Scots): proprietors of a heritable subject, especially church heritors who till 1925 were responsible for each parish church and its manse.

HERM (*lit.* the god Hermes): male head or bust on a pedestal.

HERRINGBONE WORK: masonry or brickwork in zigzag courses.

HEXASTYLE: term used to describe a portico with six columns.

HILLFORT: Iron Age earthwork enclosed by a ditch and bank system; in the later part of the period the defences multiplied in size and complexity. Hillforts vary in area and are usually built with careful regard to natural elevations or promontories.

HOODMOULD or label: projecting moulding above an arch or lintel to throw off water.

HORIZONTAL GLAZING: window panes of horizontal proportion.

HORSEMILL: circular or polygonal farm building in which a central shaft is turned by a horse to drive agricultural machinery.

HUNGRY JOINTS: *see* Pointing.

HUSK GARLAND: festoon of nutshells diminishing towards the ends (*see* fig. 12).

HYPOCAUST (*lit.* under-burning): Roman underfloor heating system. The floor is supported on pillars and the space thus formed is connected to a flue.

ICONOGRAPHY: description of the subject matter of works of the visual arts.

IMPOST (*lit.* imposition): horizontal moulding at the spring of an arch.

IN ANTIS: *see* Anta.

INDENT: (1) shape chiselled out of a stone to match and receive a brass; (2) in restoration, a secretion of new stone inserted as a patch into older work.

INGLENOOK (*lit.* fire-corner): recess for a hearth with provision for seating.

INTERCOLUMNIATION: interval between columns.

IONIC: *see* Orders (fig. 16).

JAMB (*lit.* leg): (1) one of the straight sides of an opening; (2) (Scots) wing or extension adjoining one side of a rectangular plan, making it into an L or T plan.

KEEL MOULDING: *see* fig. 13.

Fig. 13. Keel Moulding

KEEP: principal tower of a castle. Also called Donjon.

KEY PATTERN: *see* fig. 14.

Fig. 12. Husk Garland

Fig. 14. Key Pattern

KEYSTONE: middle and topmost stone in an arch or vault.

KINGPOST: *see* Roof (fig. 22).

LABEL: *see* Hoodmould. *Label Stop:* ornamental boss at the end of a hoodmould.

LADY CHAPEL: chapel dedicated to the Virgin Mary (Our Lady).

LAIGH, or LAICH (Scots): low.

LAIRD (Scots): landowner.

LANCET WINDOW: slender pointed-arched window.

LANTERN: a small circular or polygonal turret with windows all round crowning a roof (*see* Cupola) or a dome.

LAVATORIUM: in a monastery, a washing place adjacent to the refectory.

LEAN-TO: term commonly applied not only to a single-pitch roof but to the building it covers.

LESENE (*lit.* a mean thing): pilaster without base or capital. Also called pilaster strip.

LIERNE: *see* Vault (fig. 26b).

LIGHT: compartment of a window.

LINENFOLD: Tudor panelling ornamented with a conventional representation of a piece of linen laid in vertical folds. The piece is repeated in each panel.

LINTEL: horizontal beam or stone bridging an opening.

LOFT: three special senses: (1) *Organ Loft* in which the organ, or sometimes only the console (keyboard), is placed; (2) *Rood Loft*: narrow gallery over rood screen, q.v.; (3) (Scots) reserved gallery in a church, e.g. a *Laird's Loft*, or a *Trades Loft* for members of one of the incorporated trades of a burgh.

LOGGIA: sheltered space behind a colonnade.

LONG-AND-SHORT WORK: quoins consisting of stones placed with the long sides alternately upright and horizontal, especially in Saxon building.

LOUIS: convenient term used in the antique trade to describe a curvaceous chimneypiece of Louis XV character.

LOUVRE: (1) opening, often with lantern over, in the roof of a room to let the smoke from a central hearth escape; (2) one of a series of overlapping boards to allow ventilation but keep the rain out.

LOZENGE: diamond shape.

LUCARNE (*lit.* dormer): small window in a roof or spire.

LUCKENBOOTH (Scots): lock-up booth or shop.

LUGGED: *see* Architrave.

LUNETTE (*lit.* half or crescent moon): (1) semicircular window; (2) semicircular or crescent-shaped surface.

LYCHGATE (*lit.* corpse-gate): wooden gate structure with a roof and open sides placed at the entrance to a churchyard to provide space for the reception of a coffin.

LYNCHET: long terraced strip of soil accumulating on the downward side of prehistoric and medieval fields owing to soil creep from continuous ploughing along the contours.

MACHICOLATIONS (*lit.* mashing devices): on a castle, downward openings through which missiles can be dropped, under a parapet or battlement supported by deep corbels.

MAINS (Scots): home farm on an estate.

MAJOLICA: ornamented glazed earthenware.

MANSARD: *see* Roof (fig. 21).

MANSE: house of a minister of religion, especially in Scotland.

MARGINS (Scots): dressed stones at the edges of an opening. 'Back-set margins' (RCAHMS) is a misleading term because they are actually set forward from a rubble-built wall to act as a stop for the harling. Also called Rybats.

MARRIAGE LINTEL (Scots): on a house, a door or window lintel carved with the initials of the owner and his wife and the date of the work – only coincidentally of their marriage.

MAUSOLEUM: monumental tomb, so named after that of Mausolus, king of Caria, at Halicarnassus.

MEGALITHIC (*lit.* of large stones): archaeological term referring to the use of such stones, singly or together.

MERCAT (Scots): market. The *Mercat Cross* was erected in a Scottish burgh, generally in a wide street, as the focus of market activity and local ceremonial. Most examples are of post-Reformation date and have heraldic or other finials (not crosses), but the name persisted.

MERLON: *see* Battlement.

MESOLITHIC: term applied to the Middle Stone Age, dating in Britain from *c.* 5000 to *c.* 3500 B.C., and to the hunting and gathering activities of the earliest communities. *See also* Neolithic.

METOPES: spaces between the triglyphs in a Doric frieze; *see* Orders (fig. 16).

MEZZANINE: (1) low storey between two higher ones; (2) low upper storey within the height of a high one, not extending over its whole area.

MISERERE: *see* Misericord.

MISERICORD (*lit.* mercy): ledge placed on the underside of a hinged choir stall seat which, when turned up, provided the occupant with support during long periods of standing. Also called Miserere.

MODILLIONS: small consoles at regular intervals along the underside of some types of classical cornice.

MORT-SAFE (Scots): device to assure the security of a corpse or corpses: (1) iron frame over a grave; (2) building or room where bodies were kept during decomposition.

MOTTE: steep mound forming the main feature of C11 and C12 castles.

MOTTE-AND-BAILEY: post-Roman and Norman defence system consisting of an earthen mound (motte) topped with a wooden tower within a bailey, with enclosure ditch and palisade, and with the rare addition of an internal bank.

MOUCHETTE: motif in curvilinear tracery, a curved version of the dagger form, specially popular in the early C14 in England but in the early C15 in Scotland; *see* Tracery (fig. 25).

MOULDING: ornament of continuous section; *see* the various types.

MULLION: vertical member between the lights in a window opening.

MULTI-STOREY: modern term denoting five or more storeys.

MULTIVALLATE: of a hillfort: defended by three or more concentric banks and ditches.

MUNTIN: post forming part of a screen.

MUTULE: square block under the corona of a Doric cornice.

NAILHEAD MOULDING: E.E. ornamental motif, consisting of small pyramids regularly repeated (*see* fig. 15).

Fig. 15. Nailhead Moulding

NARTHEX: enclosed vestibule or covered porch at the main entrance to a church; *see also* Galilee.

NECESSARIUM: medieval euphemism for latrines in a monastery.

NEOLITHIC: term applied to the New Stone Age, dating in Britain from the appearance of the first settled farming communities from the continent *c.* 3500 B.C. until the beginning of the Bronze Age. *See also* Mesolithic.

NEWEL: central post in a circular or winding staircase, also the

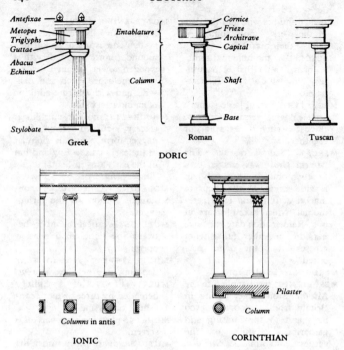

Fig. 16. Orders

principal post when a flight of stairs meets a landing.

NICHE (*lit.* shell): vertical recess in a wall, sometimes for a statue.

NIGHT STAIR: stair by which monks entered the transepts of their church from their dormitory to celebrate night services.

NOOK-SHAFT: shaft set in an angle formed by other members.

NORMAN: *see* Romanesque.

NOSING: projection of the tread of a step. A *Bottle Nosing* is half round in section.

OBELISK: lofty pillar of square section tapering at the top and ending pyramidally.

OGEE: double curve, bending first one way and then the other. *Ogee* or *Ogival Arch: see* Arch.

ORATORY: small private chapel in a house.

ORDER: (1) upright structural member formally related to others, e.g. in classical architecture a column, pilaster, or anta; (2) one of a series of recessed arches and jambs forming a splayed opening. *Giant* or *Colossal Order:* classical order whose height is that of two or more storeys of a building.

ORDERS: in classical architecture, the differently formalized versions of the basic post-and-lintel structure, each having its own rules of design and proportion. For examples of the main types *see* fig. 16. Others include the primitive Tuscan, which has a plain frieze and simple torus-moulded base, and the Composite, whose capital combines Ionic volutes with Corinthian foliage. *Superimposed Orders:* term for the use of Orders on successive levels, usually in the upward sequence of Doric, Ionic, Corinthian.

ORIEL: *see* Bay Window.

OVERARCH: *see* Arch.

OVERHANG: projection of the upper storey(s) of a building.

OVERSAILING COURSES: series of stone or brick courses, each one projecting beyond the one below it; *see also* Corbel-course.

PALIMPSEST (*lit.* erased work): re-use of a surface, e.g. a wall for another painting; also used to describe a brass plate which has been re-used by engraving on the back.

PALLADIAN: architecture following the ideas and principles of Andrea Palladio, 1508-80.

PALMETTE: classical ornament like a symmetrical palm shoot; for illustration *see* Anthemion, fig. 1.

PANTILE: roof tile of curved S-shaped section.

PARAPET: wall for protection at any sudden drop, e.g. on a bridge or at the wallhead of a castle; in the latter case it protects the *Parapet Walk* or wall walk.

PARCLOSE: *see* Screen.

PARGETING (*lit.* plastering): usually of moulded plaster panels in half-timbering.

PATERA (*lit.* plate): round or oval ornament in shallow relief, especially in classical architecture.

PEDESTAL: in classical architecture, a stand sometimes used to support the base of an order (*see* fig. 17).

Fig. 17.   Pedestal

PEDIMENT: in classical architecture, a formalized gable derived from that of a temple, also used over doors, windows, etc. For the generally accepted meanings of *Broken Pediment* and *Open Pediment see* fig. 18.

PEEL (*lit.* palisade): stone tower, e.g. near the Scottish–English border.

PEND (Scots): open-ended passage through a building on ground level.

PENDANT: hanging-down feature of a vault or ceiling, usually ending in a boss.

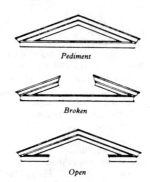

Pediment

Broken

Open

Fig. 18.   Pediments

PENDENTIVE: spandrel between adjacent arches supporting a drum or dome, formed as part of a hemisphere (*see* fig. 19).

Fig. 19.   Pendentive

PEPPERPOT TURRET: bartizan with conical or pyramidal roof.

PERISTYLE: in classical architecture, a range of columns all round a building, e.g. a temple, or an interior space, e.g. a courtyard.

PERP (PERPENDICULAR): historical division of English Gothic architecture covering the period from *c.* 1335–50 to *c.* 1530.

PERRON: *see* Stair.

PIANO NOBILE: principal floor, usually with a ground floor or basement underneath and a lesser storey overhead.

PIAZZA: open space surrounded by buildings; in the C17 and C18 sometimes employed to mean a long colonnade or loggia.

PIEND: *see* Roof.

PIER: strong, solid support, frequently square in section. *Compound Pier:* of composite section, e.g. formed of a bundle of shafts.

PIETRA DURA: ornamental or scenic inlay by means of thin slabs of stone.

PILASTER: classical order of oblong section, its elevation similar to that of a column. *Pilastrade:* series of pilasters, equivalent to a colonnade. *Pilaster Strip: see* Lesene.

PILE: a row of rooms. The important use of the term is in *Double-pile*, describing a house that is two rows thick.

PILLAR PISCINA: free-standing piscina on a pillar.

PINNACLE: tapering finial, e.g. on a buttress or the corner of a tower, sometimes decorated with crockets.

PINS (Scots): small stones pushed into the joints between large ones, a technique called cherry-caulking.

PISCINA: basin for washing the communion or mass vessels, provided with a drain; generally set in or against the wall to the s of an altar.

PIT-PRISON: sunk chamber with access above through a hatch.

PLAISANCE: summerhouse, pleasure house near a mansion.

PLATT (Scots): platform, doorstep or landing. *Scale-and-platt Stair: see* Stair.

PLEASANCE (Scots): close or walled garden.

PLINTH: projecting base beneath a wall or column, generally chamfered or moulded at the top.

POINTING: exposed mortar joints of masonry or brickwork. The finished form is of various types, e.g. *Flush Pointing, Recessed Pointing. Bag-rubbed Pointing* is flush at the edges and gently recessed in the middle of the joint. *Hungry Joints* are either without any pointing at all, or deeply recessed to show the outline of each stone. *Ribbon Pointing* is a nasty practice in the modern vernacular, the joints being formed with a trowel so that they stand out.

POPPYHEAD: carved ornament of leaves and flowers as a finial for the end of a bench or stall.

PORCH: covered projecting entrance to a building.

PORTCULLIS: gate constructed to rise and fall in vertical grooves at the entry to a castle.

PORTE COCHÈRE: porch large enough to admit wheeled vehicles.

PORTICO: in classical architecture, a porch with detached columns or other orders. *Blind Portico:* the front features of a portico attached to a wall so that it is no longer a proper porch.

POSTERN: small gateway at the back of a building.

POTENCE (Scots): rotating ladder for access to the nesting boxes of a round doocot.

PREDELLA: in an altarpiece the horizontal strip below the main representation, often used for a number of subsidiary representations in a row.

PRESBYTERY: the part of the church lying E of the choir stalls.

PRESS (Scots): cupboard.

PRINCIPAL: *see* Roof (fig. 22).

PRIORY: monastic house whose head is a prior or prioress, not an abbot or abbess.

PROSTYLE: with a row of columns in front.

PULPITUM: stone screen in a major church provided to shut off the choir from the nave and also as a backing for the return choir stalls.

PULVINATED: *see* Frieze.

PURLIN: *see* Roof (fig. 22).

PUTHOLE or PUTLOCK HOLE: putlocks are the short horizontal timbers on which during construction the boards of scaffolding rest. Putholes or put-lock holes are the holes in the wall for putlocks, and often are not filled in after construction is complete.

PUTTO: small naked boy (plural: *putti*).

QUADRANGLE: inner courtyard in a large building.

QUARRIES (*lit.* squares): (1) square (or sometimes diamond-shaped) panes of glass supported by lead strips called *Cames*; (2) square floorslabs or tiles.

QUATREFOIL: *see* Foil.

QUEENPOSTS: *see* Roof (fig. 22).

QUIRK: sharp groove to one side of a convex moulding, e.g. beside a roll moulding, which is then said to be quirked.

QUOINS: dressed stones at the angles of a building. When rusticated they may be alternately long and short.

RADIATING CHAPELS: chapels projecting radially from an ambulatory or an apse; *see* Chevet.

RAFTER: *see* Roof (fig. 22).

RAGGLE: groove cut in masonry, especially to receive the edge of glass or roof-covering.

RAKE: slope or pitch.

RAMPART: stone wall or wall of earth surrounding a castle, fortress, or fortified city. *Rampart Walk:* path along the inner face of a rampart.

RANDOM: *see* Rubble.

RATCOURSE: projecting string-course on a doocot intended to deter rats from climbing up to the flight-holes.

REBATE: rectangular section cut out of a masonry edge.

REBUS: a heraldic pun, e.g. a fiery cock as a badge for Cockburn.

REEDING: series of convex mouldings; the reverse of fluting.

REFECTORY: dining hall (or frater) of a monastery or similar establishment.

REREDORTER (*lit.* behind the dormitory): medieval euphemism for latrines in a monastery.

REREDOS: painted and/or sculp-tured screen behind and above an altar.

RESPOND: half-pier bonded into a wall and carrying one end of an arch.

RETABLE: altarpiece; a picture or piece of carving standing behind and attached to an altar.

RETROCHOIR: in a major church, an aisle between the high altar and an E chapel, like a square ambulatory.

REVEAL: the inward plane of a jamb, between the edge of an external wall and the frame of a door or window set in it.

RHONE (Scots): gutter along the eaves for rainwater; *see also* Conductor.

RIB-VAULT: *see* Vault.

RIDDEL POSTS: upright posts of the framework for hanging curtains behind and at the sides of an altar.

RINCEAU (*lit.* little branch): or antique foliage: classical ornament, usually on a frieze, of leafy scrolls branching alternately left and right (*see* fig. 20).

Fig. 20.   Rinceau

RISER: vertical face of a step.

ROCK-FACED: term used to describe masonry which is cleft to produce a natural, rugged appearance.

ROCOCO (*lit.* rocky): latest phase of the Baroque style, current in most Continental countries between *c.* 1720 and *c.* 1760, and showing itself in Britain mainly in playful, scrolled decoration, especially plasterwork.

ROLL MOULDING: moulding of semicircular or more than semicircular section.

ROMANESQUE: style in architecture which was current in the C II and C I2 and preceded the Gothic style; in England often called Norman. (Some scholars extend the use of the term Romanesque back to the C IO or C 9.)

ROOD: cross or crucifix, usually

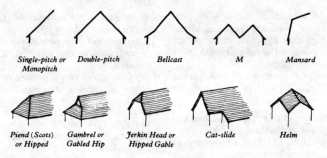

Fig. 21. Roof Forms

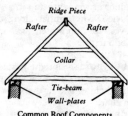

Common Roof Components

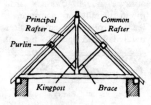

Roof with Kingpost Truss

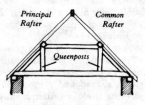

Roof with Queenpost Truss

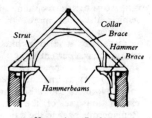

Hammerbeam Roof

Fig. 22. Roof Construction

over the entry into the chancel. The *Rood Screen* beneath it may have a *Rood Loft* along the top, reached by a *Rood Stair*.

ROOF: for external forms *see* fig. 21; for construction and components *see* fig. 22. *Wagon Roof:* lined with timber on the inside, giving the appearance of a curved or polygonal vault.

ROPE MOULDING: *see* Cable Moulding.

ROSE WINDOW: circular window with patterned tracery about the centre.

ROTUNDA: building circular in plan.

ROUND (Scots): useful term employed by the RCAHMS for a bartizan, usually roofless.

RUBBLE: masonry whose stones are wholly or partly in a rough state. *Coursed Rubble:* of coursed stones with rough faces. *Random Rubble:* of uncoursed stones in a random pattern. *Snecked Rubble* has courses frequently broken by smaller stones (snecks).

RUSTICATION: treatment of joints and/or faces of masonry to give an effect of strength. In the most usual kind the joints are recessed by V-section chamfering or square-section channelling. *Banded Rustication* has only the horizontal joints emphasized in this way. The faces may be flat but there are many other forms, e.g. *Diamond-faced*, like a shallow pyramid, *Vermiculated*, with a stylized texture like worms or worm-holes, or *Glacial*, like icicles or stalactites. *Rusticated Columns* may have their joints and drums treated in any of these ways.

RYBATS (Scots): *see* Margins.

SACRAMENT HOUSE: safe cupboard for the reserved sacrament.

SACRISTY: room in a church for sacred vessels and vestments.

SALTIRE or ST ANDREW'S CROSS: with diagonal limbs. As the flag of Scotland it is coloured white on a blue ground.

SANCTUARY: (1) area around the main altar of a church (*see* Presbytery); (2) sacred site consisting of wood or stone uprights enclosed by a circular bank and ditch. Beginning in the Neolithic, they were elaborated in the succeeding Bronze Age. The best-known examples are Stonehenge and Avebury.

SARCOPHAGUS (*lit.* flesh-consuming): coffin of stone or other durable material.

SARKING (Scots): boards laid on the rafters (*see* Roof, fig. 22) to support the covering, e.g. metal or slates.

SCAGLIOLA: composition imitating marble.

SCALE-AND-PLATT (*lit.* stair and landing): *see* Stair (fig. 24).

SCARCEMENT: extra thickness of the lower part of a wall, e.g. to carry a floor.

SCARP: artificial cutting away of the ground to form a steep slope.

SCREEN: in a church, usually at the entry to the chancel; *see* Rood Screen and Pulpitum. *Parclose Screen:* separating a chapel from the rest of the church.

SCREENS or SCREENS PASSAGE: screened-off entrance passage between the hall and the kitchen in a medieval house, adjoining the kitchen, buttery, etc.; *see also* Transe.

SCUNTION (Scots): equivalent of a reveal on the indoor side of a door or window opening.

SECTION: view of a building, moulding, etc. revealed by cutting across it.

SEDILIA: seats for the priests (usually three) on the s side of the chancel of a church; a plural word that has become a singular, collective one.

SESSION HOUSE (Scots): (1) room or separate building for meetings of the elders who form a kirk session; (2) shelter by entrance to church or churchyard for an elder receiving the collection for relief of the poor, built at expense of kirk session.

SET-OFF: *see* Weathering.

SGRAFFITO: scratched pattern, often in plaster.

SHAFT: upright member of round section, especially the main part of a classical column. *Shaftring:* motif of the C12 and C13 consisting of a ring like a belt round a circular pier or a circular shaft attached to a pier.

SHEILA-NA-GIG: female fertility figure, usually with legs wide open.

SHOULDERED: *see* Arch (fig. 2), Architrave.

SILL: horizontal projection at the bottom of a window.

SKEW (Scots): sloping or shaped stones finishing a gable which is upstanding above the roof. *Skewputt:* bracket at the bottom end of a skew.

SLATE-HANGING: covering of overlapping slates on a wall, which is then said to be *slate-hung.*

SNECKED: *see* Rubble.

SOFFIT (*lit.* ceiling): underside of an arch, lintel, etc.

SOLAR (*lit.* sun-room): upper living room or withdrawing room of a medieval house, accessible from the high table end of the hall.

SOUNDING-BOARD: horizontal board or canopy over a pulpit; also called Tester.

SOUTERRAIN: underground stone-lined passage and chamber.

SPANDRELS: surfaces left over between an arch and its containing rectangle, or between adjacent arches.

SPIRE: tall pyramidal or conical
feature built on a tower or turret. *Broach Spire:* starting from
a square base, then carried into
an octagonal section by means
of triangular faces. *Needle
Spire:* thin spire rising from the
centre of a tower roof, well inside the parapet. *Helm Spire:
see* Roof (fig. 21).

SPIRELET: *see* Flèche.

SPLAY: chamfer, usually of a reveal or scuntion.

SPRING: level at which an arch or
vault rises from its supports.
Springers: the first stones of an
arch or vaulting-rib above the
spring.

SQUINCH: arch thrown across an
angle between two walls to support a superstructure, e.g. a
dome (*see* fig. 23).

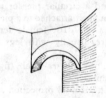

Fig. 23. Squinch

SQUINT: hole cut in a wall or
through a pier to allow a view
of the main altar of a church
from places whence it could not
otherwise be seen. Also called
Hagioscope.

STAIR: *see* fig. 24. The term *Perron* (*lit.* of stone) applies to the
external stair leading to a doorway, usually of double-curved
plan as shown. *Spiral, Turnpike*

(Scots) or *Newel Stair:* ascend-
ing round a central supporting
newel, usually in a circular
shaft. *Flying Stair:* cantilevered
from the wall of a stairwell,
without newels. *Geometric
Stair:* flying stair whose inner
edge describes a curve. *Well
Stair:* term applied to any stair
contained in an open well, but
generally to one that climbs up
three sides of a well, with
corner landings.

STALL: seat for clergy, choir, etc.,
distinctively treated in its own
right or as one of a row.

STANCHION: upright structural
member, of iron or steel or reinforced concrete.

STEADING (Scots): farm building
or buildings. A term most often
used to describe the principal
group of agricultural buildings
on a farm.

STEEPLE: a tower together with a
spire or other tall feature on top
of it.

STIFFLEAF: *see* fig. 6.

STOUP: vessel for the reception of
holy water, usually placed near
a door.

STRAINER: *see* Arch.

STRAPWORK: C16 and C17 decoration used also in the C19
Jacobean revival, resembling
interlaced bands of cut leather.

STRINGCOURSE: intermediate
stone course or moulding projecting from the surface of a
wall.

STUCCO (*lit.* plaster): (1) smooth
external rendering of a wall etc.;
(2) decorative plaster-work.

STUDS: intermediate   vertical
members of a timber-framed
wall or partition.

STUGGED (Scots): of masonry that

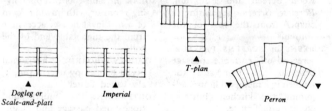

Dogleg or
Scale-and-platt

Imperial

T-plan

Perron

Fig. 24. Stair

is hacked or picked as a key for rendering; used as a type of surface finish in the C19.

STYLOBATE: solid structure on which a colonnade stands.

SWAG (*lit.* bundle): like a festoon, but also a cloth bundle in relief, hung up at both ends.

TABERNACLE (*lit.* tent): (1) canopied structure, especially on a small scale, to contain the reserved sacrament or a relic; (2) architectural frame, e.g. of a monument on a wall or free-standing, with flanking orders. Also called an Aedicule.

TAS-DE-CHARGE: coursed stone(s) forming the springers of more than one vaulting-rib.

TERMINAL FIGURE or TERM: upper part of a human figure growing out of a pier, pilaster, etc. which tapers towards the bottom.

TERRACOTTA: moulded and fired clay ornament or cladding, usually unglazed.

TERREPLEIN: level surface of a rampart behind a fort's parapet on which guns are mounted.

TESSELLATED PAVEMENT: mosaic flooring, particularly Roman, consisting of small *Tesserae* or cubes of glass, stone, or brick.

TESTER (*lit.* head): bracketed canopy, especially over a pulpit, where it is also called a sounding-board.

TETRASTYLE: term used to describe a portico with four columns.

THERMAL WINDOW (*lit.* of a Roman bath): *see* Diocletian window.

THREE-DECKER PULPIT: pulpit with clerk's stall below and reading desk below the clerk's stall.

TIE-BEAM: *see* Roof (fig. 22).

TIERCERON: *see* Vault (fig. 26b).

TILE-HANGING: *see* Slate-hanging.

TIMBER FRAMING: method of construction where walls are built of timber framework with the spaces filled in by plaster or brickwork. Sometimes the timber is covered over with plaster or boarding laid horizontally.

TOLBOOTH (Scots): tax office containing a burgh council chamber and a prison.

TOMB-CHEST: chest-shaped stone coffin, the most usual medieval form of funerary monument.

TOUCH: soft black marble quarried near Tournai.

TOURELLE: turret corbelled out from the wall.

TOWER HOUSE (Scots): compact fortified house with the main hall raised above the ground and at least one more storey above it. A medieval Scots type continuing well into the C17 in its modified forms, the L plan and so-called Z plan, the former having a jamb at one corner, the latter at each diagonally opposite corner.

TRACERY: pattern of arches and geometrical figures supporting the glass in the upper part of a window, or applied decoratively to wall surfaces or vaults. *Plate Tracery* is the most primitive form of tracery, being formed of openings cut through stone slabs or plates. In *Bar Tracery*

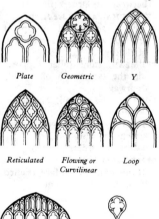

Plate Geometric Y

Reticulated Flowing or Loop
Curvilinear

Perpendicular Dagger

Quatrefoil Mouchette

Fig. 25. Tracery

the openings are separated not by flat areas of stonework but by relatively slender divisions or bars which are constructed of voussoirs like arches. Later developments of bar tracery are classified according to the character of the decorative pattern used. For generalized illustrations of the main types *see* fig. 25.

TRANSE (Scots): passage, especially screens passage.

TRANSEPTS (*lit.* cross-enclosures): transverse portions of a cross-shaped church.

TRANSOM: horizontal member between the lights in a window opening.

TREFOIL: *see* Foil.

TRIBUNE: *see* Gallery (1).

TRICIPUT, SIGNUM TRICIPUT: sign of the Trinity expressed by three faces belonging to one head.

TRIFORIUM: middle storey of a church treated as an arcaded wall passage or blind arcade, its height corresponding to that of the aisle roof.

TRIGLYPHS (*lit.* three-grooved tablets): stylized beam-ends in the Doric frieze, with metopes between; *see* Orders (fig. 16).

TRIUMPHAL ARCH: *see* Arch.

TROPHY: sculptured group of arms or armour as a memorial of victory.

TRUMEAU: stone pillar supporting the tympanum of a wide doorway.

TUMULUS (*lit.* mound): barrow.

TURNPIKE: *see* Stair.

TURRET: small tower, often attached to a building.

TUSCAN: *see* Orders (fig. 16).

TYMPANUM (*lit.* drum): as of a drum-skin, the surface framed by an arch or pediment.

UNDERCROFT: vaulted room, sometimes underground, below the main upper room.

UNIVALLATE: of a hillfort: defended by a single bank and ditch.

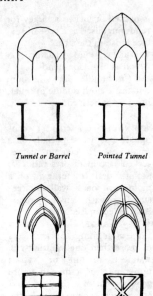

Tunnel or Barrel   *Pointed Tunnel*

Pointed Tunnels with Surface Ribs

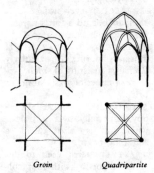

Groin   *Quadripartite*

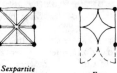

Sexpartite   *Fan*

Fig. 26. (a) Vaults

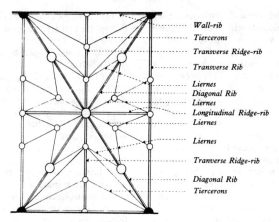

Fig. 26. (b) Ribs of a Late Gothic Vault

Labels in figure:
- Wall-rib
- Tiercerons
- Transverse Ridge-rib
- Transverse Rib
- Liernes
- Diagonal Rib
- Liernes
- Longitudinal Ridge-rib
- Liernes
- Liernes
- Tranverse Ridge-rib
- Diagonal Rib
- Tiercerons

VASSAL: *see* Feu.

VAULT: ceiling of stone formed like arches (sometimes imitated in timber or plaster); *see* fig. 26a. *Tunnel-* or *Barrel-vault*: the simplest kind of vault, in effect a continuous semicircular arch. *Pointed Tunnel-vaults* are frequent in Scottish late medieval architecture but otherwise rare. A Scottish peculiarity is the *Pointed Tunnel-vault with Surface Ribs* which are purely decorative in intention. *Groin-vaults* (usually called *Cross-vaults* in classical architecture) have four curving triangular surfaces produced by the intersection of two tunnel-vaults at right angles. The curved lines at the intersections are called groins. In *Quadripartite Rib-vaults* the four sections are divided by their arches or ribs springing from the corners of the bay. *Sexpartite Rib-vaults* are most often used over paired bays. The main types of rib are shown in fig. 26b; *transverse ribs, wall-ribs, diagonal ribs*, and *ridge-ribs. Tiercerons* are extra, decorative ribs springing from the corners of a bay. *Liernes* are decorative ribs in the crown of a vault which are not linked to any of the springing points. In a *stellar vault* the liernes are arranged in a star formation as in fig. 26b. *Fan-vaults* are peculiar to English Perpendicular architecture and differ from rib-vaults in consisting not of ribs and infilling but of halved concave cones with decorative blind tracery carved on their surfaces.

VAULTING-SHAFT: shaft leading up to the springer of a vault.

VENETIAN WINDOW: *see* fig. 27.

Fig. 27. Venetian Window

VERANDA(H): shelter or gallery against a building, its roof supported by thin vertical members.

VERMICULATION: *see* Rustication.

VESICA (*lit.* bladder): usually of a window, with curved sides and pointed at top and bottom like a rugger-ball.

VESTIBULE: ante-room or entrance hall.

VILLA: originally (1) Roman

country-house-cum-farmhouse, developed into (2) the similar C16 Venetian type with office wings, made grander by Palladio's varied application of a central portico. This became an important type in C18 Britain, often with the special meaning of (3) a country house which is not a principal residence. Gwilt (1842) defined the villa as 'a country house for the residence of opulent persons'. But devaluation had already begun, and the term implied, as now, (4) a more or less pretentious suburban house.

VITRIFIED: hardened or fused into a glass-like state.

VITRUVIAN SCROLL: running ornament of curly waves on a classical frieze. (*See* fig. 28.)

Fig. 28.　Vitruvian Scroll

VOLUTES: spiral scrolls on the front and back of a Greek Ionic capital, also on the sides of a Roman one. *Angle Volute:* pair of volutes turned outwards to meet at the corner of a capital.

VOUSSOIRS: wedge-shaped stones forming an arch.

WAINSCOT: timber lining on an internal wall.

WALLED GARDEN: C17 type whose formal layout is still seen in the combined vegetable and flower gardens of C18 and C19 Scotland. They are usually sited at a considerable distance from a house.

WALL-PLATE: *see* Roof (fig. 22).

WATERHOLDING BASE: type of Early Gothic base in which the upper and lower mouldings are separated by a hollow so deep as to be capable of retaining water.

WEATHERBOARDING: overlapping horizontal boards, covering a timber-framed wall.

WEATHERING: inclined, projecting surface to keep water away from wall and joints below.

WEEPERS: small figures placed in niches along the sides of some medieval tombs; also called mourners.

WHEEL HOUSE: round stone dwelling of the Late Iron Age with partition walls radiating from the centre like the spokes of a wheel.

WHEEL WINDOW: circular window with tracery of radiating shafts like the spokes of a wheel; *see also* Rose Window.

WYND (Scots): subsidiary street or lane, often running into a main street or gait.

YETT (Scots, *lit.* gate): hinged openwork gate at a main doorway, made of wrought-iron bars alternately penetrating and penetrated.

INDEX OF ARTISTS

INDEX OF PLACES

Principal references are in **bold** type; demolished buildings are shown in *italic*.